Second Canadian Edition

Interplay

The Process of
Interpersonal Communication

Ronald B. Adler • Lawrence B. Rosenfeld • Russell F. Proctor II • Constance Winder

OXFORD
UNIVERSITY PRESS

OXFORD
UNIVERSITY PRESS

70 Wynford Drive, Don Mills, Ontario M3C 1J9
www.oupcanada.com

Oxford University Press is a department of the University of Oxford.
It furthers the University's objective of excellence in research, scholarship,
and education by publishing worldwide in

Oxford   New York
Auckland   Cape Town   Dar es Salaam   Hong Kong   Karachi
Kuala Lumpur   Madrid   Melbourne   Mexico City   Nairobi
New Delhi   Shanghai   Taipei   Toronto

With offices in
Argentina   Austria   Brazil   Chile   Czech Republic   France   Greece
Guatemala   Hungary   Italy   Japan   Poland   Portugal   Singapore
South Korea   Switzerland   Thailand   Turkey   Ukraine   Vietnam

Oxford is a trade mark of Oxford University Press
in the UK and in certain other countries

Published in Canada
by Oxford University Press

Library and Archives Canada Cataloguing in Publication

Interplay : the process of interpersonal communication / Ronald B.
Adler ... [et al.]. — 2nd Canadian ed.

Includes bibliographical references and index.
ISBN 978-0-19-542987-9

1. Interpersonal communication—Textbooks.
I. Adler, Ronald B. (Ronald Brian), 1946–

BF637.C45 I686 2009   302.2   C2009-901088-7

Cover image: John Lau/Dreamstime.com

Oxford University Press is committed to our environment.
This book is printed on paper which contains a minimum of 10% post-consumer waste.

Printed and bound in the United States of America.

2 3 4 — 12 11 10

Contents

Part Two   Creating and Responding to Messages

Part Four   Contexts of Interpersonal Communication

From the Publisher

Good personal relationships can make life worth living, and unsatisfying ones can make us miserable. Most students recognize this fact, and they enter an interpersonal communication course ready to acquire information and skills that they can put to use in their own lives.

Despite the obvious importance of the subject, designing an academic course on interpersonal communication is no easy task. On the one hand, instructors and authors must avoid presenting the considerable amount of scholarship on the subject in so much detail that first-time students are overwhelmed. On the other hand, we have to avoid oversimplifying the material so that readers don't dismiss what we've written as 'just common sense'. The whole package must fit within an academic term and be designed in a way that facilitates teaching and learning.

This edition of *Interplay* builds on the successful approach used in the first Canadian edition that has served instructors and students well. It gives first-time students a useful, compelling, and accurate introduction to the academic study of interpersonal communication. The reader comes away with a new appreciation of how scholarship about communication in interpersonal relationships can make a difference in everyday life. To that end, this edition retains qualities that will be familiar to long-time users:

▶ An accessible writing style based on the belief that even complicated ideas can be presented in a straightforward way.

▶ A commitment to showing how scholarship offers insights about the process of interpersonal communication.

▶ The use of thought-provoking photos, sidebars, and cartoons that illustrate points in the text in a way that is more interesting and compelling than text alone.

The new edition of *Interplay* retains the best features of the previous edition:

▶ A comparison of Canadian and American Culture, describing the effects of the differences on communication (Chapter 1).

▶ A discussion of how successful relationships depend on negotiation of shared narratives (Chapter 3).

▶ Research findings on the role of communication in increasing physical attractiveness (Chapter 6).

▶ Practical material on successful communication in families and in the workplace (Chapter 12).

▶ A balanced treatment of the risks and benefits of self-disclosure and methods of maintaining privacy in personal relationships (Chapter 9).

▶ An examination of types of emotions and influences on emotional expression, including personality and gender (Chapter 4).

▶ Canada's cultural and ethnic diversity is reflected in the book's emphasis on strategies for effective intercultural communication. Issues of language and identity are explored as they pertain to First Nations people and francophones. The comparisons of the cultural aspects of communication are based on hundreds of research studies conducted in Canada, the United States, Europe, Australia, Africa, and Asia.

New to this Edition

This edition contains several improvements that reflect both progress in the field and refinements that help make the material clearer and more useful to students:

 Take Two

The Four Steps in Perception

- **Selection:** determines which information we will pay attention to and is influenced by stimuli intensity, repetition, contrast, or change and our motives and emotional state.
- **Organization:** is the process by which we arrange information in a meaningful way using perceptual schema (physical, role, interaction, and psychological constructs).
- **Interpretation:** the process of making sense of perceptions within our own minds.
- **Negotiation:** the process by which communicators influence one another's perceptions.

▶ *NEW 'Take Two' boxes* recap core concepts and terms to ensure students understand their meaning and draw linkages between them.

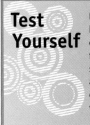 **Test Yourself**

Describe the observed differences between male and female speakers in terms of content, reasons for communicating, and conversational style. What non-sex variables have been associated with differences in the ways men and women speak?

▶ *NEW 'Test Yourself' questions* give students a great tool for study and review.

Focus on Technology

Instant Messaging and Syntax

There has been considerable speculation in the media about the potential of instant messaging (text messaging) to negatively influence people's (particularly teens') ability to use conventional grammar. The assumption is that people's use of abbreviations (e.g., *tmw* for tomorrow; *u* for you), initialization (e.g., *LOL* for laugh out loud; *TTYL* for talk to you later), and rebus (a word game that combines numbers, letters, and pictures to create words—e.g., *GR8* for great), as well as other creative adaptations of conventional language, when text-messaging will erode their ability to use normative (conventional or standard) grammar when it is required (e.g., essays, assignments, formal letters, etc.).

Intrigued by the phenomenon of texting, University of Toronto linguistics researcher Sali Tagliamonte and her undergraduate research partner Derek Denis (2008) analyzed a month's worth of unmonitored instant-messaging conversations of seventy-two young people ages fifteen to twenty years old. They also examined a quantity of speech from the same group of teenagers. What they found was that, when compared to their oral speech, their text messages were far more formal in their use of syntactic rules. The messages were not as formal as an essay but the grammar used was that of formal language. They did mix more formal grammar with other types of language; however, the use of short forms such as *LOL* comprised only a very small proportion of their messages. Tagliamonte and Denis describe the language of instant messaging as a unique new hybrid that creatively combines a variety of language features such as speech, written language, and formal and informal grammar and diction. While teachers informally report that some of the abbreviations and initializations characteristic of instant messaging are showing up in assignments and essays, Tagliamonte responds by saying that that is what school is for—to teach students what kind of language is appropriate in particular contexts (Daubs, 2008). The subjects in their study demonstrated very clearly that their grammatical skills were intact.

▶ *NEW 'Focus on Technology' boxes* draw attention to current research on interpersonal communication and new technology while showing how core material relates to topics such as text-message syntax, cell phones and forced eavesdropping, and the influence of culture on computer-mediated business negotiations.

Enhanced Pedagogy

This edition of *Interplay* builds on the pedagogical approach that has successfully helped students appreciate how scholarship leads to a better understanding of communication in the 'real world'.

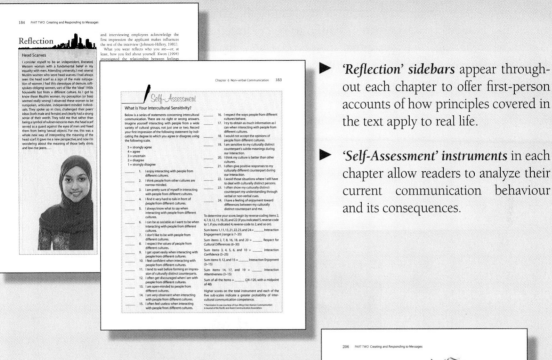

▶ *'Reflection' sidebars* appear throughout each chapter to offer first-person accounts of how principles covered in the text apply to real life.

▶ *'Self-Assessment' instruments* in each chapter allow readers to analyze their current communication behaviour and its consequences.

▶ *'Building Work Skills' exercises* in each chapter help students apply knowledge they have gained about interpersonal communication to situations they are likely to encounter in the workplace.

▶ *'Focus on Research' profiles* highlight scholarship that students will find interesting and useful on topics ranging from how women and men communicate online to how social networks differ in urban and rural Canada.

Contemporary Design

An increasingly digital, quickly changing world of communication calls for a design that evolves and adapts. We have striven for a look that is contemporary yet clean, a design that reflects the vibrancy and excitement of interpersonal communication today without sacrificing content or authoritativeness. The use of colour and novel design elements is a necessary acknowledgement to the changes wrought by new media and how readers expect information to be packaged and presented. At the same time we remain well aware that this is indeed a printed book, with both the limitations and the very real and enduring strengths that are a product of the print's long history as the pre-eminent method of codifying and transmitting knowledge.

Aids to Student Learning

While meeting instructors' expectations for accuracy, currency, and comprehensive-ness, the textbook must also speak to the needs and interests of today's students, providing them with an accessible introduction to a body of knowledge. To that end, numerous features to promote student learning are incorporated throughout the book.

▶ ***Chapter Openers*** preview the contents of each chapter, with key terms and learning objectives that provide a concise overview of the key concepts to be covered.

▶ ***Chapter Summaries*** at the end of each chapter ensure a thorough understanding of key concepts and aid in reviewing for tests and exams.

▶ ***Student Activities***, listed at the end of each chapter, reinforce concepts and ideas through practical, interactive exercises.

▶ ***Discussion Questions*** at the end of each chapter draw out key issues while encouraging readers to form their own conclusions about interpersonal communication.

Supplements

Today's textbook is no longer a volume that stands on its own—it is but the central element of a complete learning and teaching package. *Interplay: The Process of Interpersonal Communication* is no exception. The book is supported by an outstanding array of ancillary materials for both students and instructors, all available on the companion website: **www.oupcanada.com/Interplay.**

For the Instructor

- **An Instructor's Manual** includes comprehensive outlines of the text's various parts and chapters, additional questions for encouraging class discussion, and suggestions on how to use videos to enhance lectures.
- **A Test bank** offers a comprehensive set of multiple-choice, true–false, short-answer, and essay questions, with suggested answers, for every chapter.
- **PowerPoint® slides**, summarizing key points from each chapter and incorporating figures and tables from the textbook, are available to adopters of the text.

Instructors should contact their Oxford University Press sales representative for details on these supplements and for login and password information.

For the Student

The Student Study Guide offers self-testing study questions, annotated links to useful resources, and much more. Go to **www.oupcanada.com/Interplay** and follow the links!

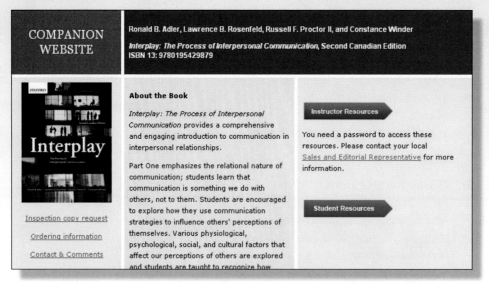

Learn more at www.oupcanada.com/Interplay

Preface

The second Canadian edition of this book was developed and shaped by many important people. First I am indebted to my reviewers, who offered sage advice, and pointed me in the right direction.

I would also like to thank my colleagues at George Brown College for their ongoing support and generosity, and my wonderful students for sharing their insights, their observations, and their infectious enthusiasm.

I am grateful to the brilliant team at Oxford University Press in Toronto—David Stover, Phyllis Wilson, Jacqueline Mason, Euan White, Kathleen McGill, and my patient, flexible, and astute developmental editor, Peter Chambers. Joe Zingrone, my superb copy editor, made this edition clearer, more accurate and better in so many ways, so we all thank you, Joe.

Finally, the motivation to communicate more effectively, to keep learning and to cherish my relationships is inspired by my family. Gerlando, Owen, and Oliver, you make me laugh, you fill my heart, and you make everything worthwhile.

Reviewers
We gratefully acknowledge the contributions of the following reviewers, whose thoughtful comments and suggestions have helped to shape this new edition:

Jean Brown, Cambrian College
Carole Courbet, Dawson College
Jack de Stefano, McGill University
Brenda Garant, Dawson College
Nycole Harding, Seneca College
Janne A. Holmgren, Mount Royal College
Karen Pappin, Huntington University at Laurentian
Wanda Pierson, Langara College

Connie Winder
George Brown College

Chapter One

Interpersonal Process

After studying the material in this chapter . . .

You Should Understand:

1. The needs that effective communication can satisfy.
2. Five insights from the communication model.
3. Five key principles of communication.
4. Four misconceptions about communication.
5. Quantitative and qualitative definitions of interpersonal communication.
6. The characteristics of competent communication.

You Should Be Able To:

1. Identify examples of the physical, identity, social, and practical needs you attempt to satisfy by communicating.
2. Demonstrate how the communication model applies to your interpersonal communication.
3. Describe the degrees to which your communication is qualitatively impersonal and interpersonal, and describe the consequences of this combination.
4. Identify situations in which you communicate competently, and those in which your competence is less than satisfactory.

Everyone communicates. Students and professors, parents and children, employers and employees, friends, strangers, and enemies—all communicate. We have been communicating with others from the moment of our birth and will keep on doing so until we die.

Why study an activity you've been doing your entire life? There are three reasons. First, studying interpersonal communication will give you a new look at a familiar topic. For instance, in a few pages, you will find that some people can go years—even a lifetime—without communicating in a truly interpersonal manner. In this sense, exploring human communication is rather like studying anatomy or botany—everyday objects and processes take on new meaning.

A second reason for studying the subject has to do with the staggering amount of time we spend communicating. For example, a study of over one thousand employees at Fortune 1000 companies revealed that workers send and receive an average of 178 messages every working day (Ginsburg, 1999). Another survey (Nellermoe et al., 1999) revealed that business professionals spend 80 percent of their business day communicating with colleagues and clients. In addition, Canadians spend a significant amount of time communicating online both at work and at home.

There is a third, more compelling reason for studying interpersonal communication. To put it bluntly, all of us could learn to communicate more effectively. Our friendships, jobs, and studies suffer because we fail to interact with others as effectively as is necessary. A group of senior executives cited lack of interpersonal skills as one of the top three skill deficits in today's workforce (Marchant, 1999). In a US survey, 'lack of effective communication' was given as the cause of relational breakups—including divorce—more often than anything else, including money, relatives or in-laws, sexual problems, previous relationships, or children (National Communication Association, 1999). If you pause now and make a mental list of communication problems you have encountered, you'll see that, no matter how successful your relationships are at home, with friends, at school, and

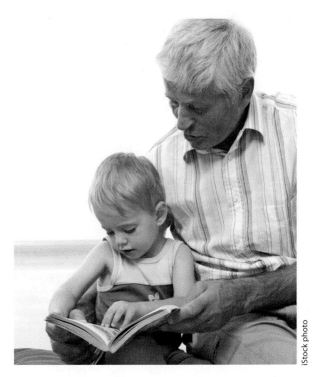

iStock photo

at work, there is plenty of room for improvement in your everyday life. The information that follows will help you improve the way you communicate with some of the people who matter most to you.

Why We Communicate

Research demonstrating the importance of communication has been around longer than you might think. Frederick II, emperor of the Holy Roman Empire from 1220 to 1250, was called *stupor mundi*—'wonder of the world'—by his admiring subjects. Along with his administrative and military talents, Frederick was a leading scientist of his time. A medieval historian described one of his dramatic, if inhumane, experiments:

> He bade foster mothers and nurses to suckle the children, to bathe and wash them, but in no way to prattle with them, for he wanted to learn whether they would speak the Hebrew language, which was the oldest, or Greek, or Latin, or Arabic, or perhaps the language of their parents, of whom they had been born. But he laboured in vain because all the children died. For they could not live without the petting and

joyful faces and loving words of their foster mothers. (Ross and McLaughlin, 1949, p. 366)

Fortunately, contemporary researchers have found less drastic ways to illustrate the importance of communication. In one study of isolation, five subjects were paid to remain alone in a locked room. One lasted for eight days. Three held out for two days, one commenting, 'Never again.' Another of the subjects lasted a mere two hours (Schachter, 1959, pp. 9–10).

The need for contact and companionship is just as strong outside the laboratory, as people who have led solitary lives by choice or necessity have discovered. W. Carl Jackson, an adventurer who sailed across the Atlantic Ocean alone in fifty-one days, summarized the feelings common to most loners:

> I found the loneliness of the second month almost excruciating. I always thought of myself as self-sufficient, but I found life without people had no meaning. I had a definite need for somebody to talk to, someone real, alive, and breathing.

You might object to stories like this, claiming that solitude would be a welcome relief from the irritations of everyday life. It's true that all of us need solitude, often more than we get. On the other hand, each of us has a point beyond which we do not *want* to be alone. Beyond this point, solitude changes from a pleasurable to a painful condition. In other words, we all need people. We all need to communicate.

Physical Needs

Communication is so important that its presence or absence affects physical health. Recent studies confirm that people who process a negative experience by talking about it report improved life satisfaction, as well as enhanced mental and physical health, compared to those who only think about it (Sousa, 2002). A study conducted with police officers found that being able to talk easily to colleagues and supervisors about work-related trauma was connected to better physical and mental health (Stephens and Long, 2000).

In extreme cases, communication can even become a matter of life or death. It is not surprising that one of the worst punishments that inmates in Western prisons are subjected to is solitary confinement. Known to North American convicts as 'the hole', segregation units have been described by both psychologists and inmates as far more damaging and harder to bear than physical punishment. The isolation from both the physical world (so that one does not know if it is day or night or what the weather is like) and the complete lack of meaningful communication with other people combine to create a situation in which most inmates would prefer to die. In his book, *Justice behind the Walls*, law professor and human-rights advocate Michael Jackson (2002) describes the effects of solitary confinement on Canadian inmates:

> My journey has taken me into segregation units— contemporary versions of Dante's *Inferno*—where prisoners scream abuse and hurl their bodily fluids and guards respond violently with fire hoses and nightsticks. I have sat with prisoners hopeless beyond tears as they contemplate suicide, and knelt at a segregation cell door, scanning through the narrow food slot the barren interior of a prisoner's world, begging a man not to use a razor blade to slash his eyeballs.

Satisfying communication isn't a necessity just for prisoners. Evidence gathered by medical researchers (e.g., Cohen et al., 1997; Hall and Havens, 2002; Maté, 2003; Ruberman, 1992) and social scientists (e.g., Duck, 1998; Zheng and Hart, 2004) shows that satisfying relationships can literally be a matter of life and death for people who lead lives in the outside world. For example,

- People who lack strong relationships run two to three times the risk of early death, regardless of whether they smoke, drink alcoholic beverages, or exercise regularly.
- Terminal cancer strikes socially isolated people more often than those who have close personal relationships.

- Divorced, separated, and widowed people are five to ten times more likely to need psychiatric hospitalization than their married counterparts.
- Perceived loneliness is one of the strongest predictors of poor health among the elderly.
- Pregnant women under stress and without supportive relationships have three times as many complications as pregnant women who suffer from the same stress but have strong social support.
- Social isolation is a major risk factor contributing to heart disease, comparable to physiological factors such as an inadequate diet, cigarette smoking, obesity, and lack of physical activity.
- Socially isolated people are four times as susceptible to the common cold as those who have active social networks.

Research like this demonstrates the importance of satisfying personal relationships, and it explains the conclusion of social scientists that communication is essential (Baumeister and Leary, 1995; Statistics Canada, 2006b). Not everyone needs the same amount of contact, and the quality of communication is almost certainly as important as the quantity. Nonetheless, the point remains: personal communication is essential for our well-being. To paraphrase a popular song, 'people who need people' aren't 'the luckiest people in the world'—they're the *only* people!

Identity Needs

Communication does more than enable us to survive. It is the way—indeed, the *major* way—we learn who we are (Fogel et al., 2002). As you'll read in Chapter 2, our sense of identity comes from the way we interact with other people. Are we smart or stupid, attractive or ugly, skilful or inept? The answers to these questions don't come from looking in the mirror. We decide who we are on the basis of how others react to us.

Deprived of communication with others, we would have no sense of identity. In his book, *Bridges Not Walls*, John Stewart (2002) dramatically

illustrates this fact by citing the case of the famous Wild Boy of Aveyron, who spent his early childhood without any apparent human contact. The boy was discovered in January 1800 while digging for vegetables in a French village garden. He showed no behaviour one would expect in a social human. He could not speak but uttered only weird cries. More significant than this absence of social skills was his lack of any identity as a human being. As author Roger Shattuck (1980, p. 37) put it, 'The boy had no human sense of being in the world. He had no sense of himself as a person related to other persons.' Only after the influence of a loving 'mother' did the boy begin to behave—and, we can imagine, think of himself—as a human.

Modern stories support the essential role that communication plays in shaping identity. In 1970, the authorities discovered a twelve-year-old girl (whom they called Genie) who had spent virtually all her life in an otherwise empty, darkened bedroom with almost no human contact. The child could not speak and had no sense of herself as a person until she was removed from her family and 'nourished' by a team of caregivers (Rymer, 1993).

Like Genie and the boy of Aveyron, each of us enters the world with little or no sense of identity. We gain an idea of who we are from the way others define us. As we explain in Chapter 2, the messages children receive in their early years are the strongest identity shapers, but the influence of others continues throughout people's lives.

Social Needs

Some social scientists have argued that besides helping define who we are, communication is the principal way relationships are created (Duck and Pittman, 1994). For example, Julie Yingling (1994) asserts that children 'talk friendships into existence.' Canadian teenagers value friendships the most, ahead of a comfortable life, recognition, and excitement (Bibby, 2001) and they spend a great deal of time developing and maintaining these relationships through communication. As we explain in Chapter 8, sometimes we deal with social needs directly by discussing our relationships with others. But more often, communication satisfies a variety of social needs without our ever addressing them overtly. Communication helps us to help and be helped by others, to feel included and worthwhile, to have fun and relax with others and to exert influence and control in social situations (Rubin, 1988). Because relationships with others are so vital, some theorists have gone so far as to argue that communication is the primary goal of human existence. Anthropologist Walter Goldschmidt (1990) calls the drive for meeting social needs 'the human career'. Positive social interaction and support appear to be the strongest determinants of quality of life (Leung and Lee, 2005).

Beyond our immediate circle of contacts, we can satisfy social needs by communicating with a larger community. There appears to be an increasing trend in North American society for people to live more socially isolated lives than their parents and grandparents did (Putnam, 2000). Since the 1950s, we eat together less, belong to fewer social clubs, and enjoy fewer visits from friends (Putnam, 2000). Large-scale social changes such as industrialization, capitalism, and the proliferation of cheap and efficient transportation have changed the communities in which we live. Many of us live farther away from our families, friends, and places of work than our ancestors did. In addition, more recent advances in technology have allowed us to do our banking, shop for groceries, visit the library, and be entertained without leaving our homes. In addition, many of us work alone. Investigations (HRDC, 1997; Statistics Canada, 2002) into the changing nature of work found a dramatic increase in the past four decades in the number of self-employed Canadians. In 2001, almost 2.3 million Canadians were self-employed—about three times the number of self-employed people in 1976. While there are numerous advantages to being self-employed, two of the more significant costs are reduced social cohesion and an increase in marital breakdowns (due, in part to the long number of hours worked). The lack of face-to-face human interaction in our lives can lead to the kinds of physical ailments and emotional problems that we described earlier.

Practical Needs

We shouldn't overlook the everyday, important functions of communication. It is the tool that lets us tell the hairstylist to take just a little off the sides, direct the doctor to where it hurts, and inform the plumber that the broken pipe needs attention *now!*

Beyond these obvious needs, a wealth of research demonstrates that communication is an essential part of effectiveness in a variety of daily situations. The abilities to speak and listen effectively have been called the most important factors in helping graduating university and college students to gain employment and advance in their careers—more important than technical competence, work experience, and academic background (Winsor et al., 1997). One survey of over four hundred employers identified 'communication skills' as the top characteristic that employers seek in job candidates (*Job Outlook '99*, 1999). Such skills were rated as more important than technical competence, work experience, and academic background. The Conference Board of Canada (2000) described communication skills and the ability to work with others as critical skills that are required for the Canadian workforce. They are skills employers want, even in the fields of science, technology, and mathematics. A survey of newspaper classified ads in the Greater Toronto Area (Statistics Canada, 2005) found that the skills looked for most often by employers were good communication skills. The Learning Partnership, a not-for-profit organization that brings together business and educators has developed several national initiatives aimed at helping young people develop work-related skills. They assert that job-specific technical skills are not enough. Employers increasingly value transferable employability skills, such as effective communication, problem solving, teamwork skills, respect for others, and active listening in their workers (Learning Partnership, 2004).

Communication is just as important outside of work. In one study, married couples who were identified as effective communicators reported happier relationships than less communicative husbands and wives (Kirchler, 1988), and another study

Test Yourself   Why do we communicate? Describe the four types of needs communication helps us to meet.

found that spouses who engaged each other verbally and didn't withdraw from each other reported greater marital satisfaction (Ridley et al., 2001). On the scholastic front, the grade point averages of US college students were related positively to their communication competence (Rubin and Graham, 1988), and school adjustment, dropout rate, and overall school achievement and academic competence were found to be highly related to students' having strong, supportive relationships (Rosenfeld and Richman, 1999; Rosenfeld et al., 1998).

In 'getting acquainted' situations, communication competence played a major role in whether a person was judged physically attractive, socially desirable, and good at the task of getting acquainted (Duran and Kelly, 1988). For example, a male who solicits his female partner's opinion, shows sensitivity to her perspective, and is generally agreeable will likely be perceived as more physically and sexually attractive than one who does not do these things. Similarly, men generally rate women who are agreeable as more attractive and desirable as mates than those who are less agreeable (Bower, 1995).

Psychologist Abraham Maslow (1968) suggests that human needs fall into five categories, each of which must be satisfied before we concern ourselves with the next one. As you read on, think about the ways in which communication is often necessary to satisfy each need. The most basic needs are *physical*: sufficient air, water, food, and rest, and the ability to reproduce as a species. The second category of Maslow's needs involves *safety*: protection from threats to our well-being. Beyond physical and safety concerns are the *social* needs we have already mentioned. After those necessities are met, Maslow suggests that each of us has the need for *self-esteem*: the desire to believe that we are worthwhile, valuable people. The final category of needs involves *self-actualization*: the desire to develop our potential to the maximum, to become the best people we can be.

The Communication Process

So far, we have talked about communication as if its meaning were perfectly clear. In fact, scholars have debated the definition of communication for years with no simple conclusions (Littlejohn, 2002). One thing is clear: human communication is a complex process with many components. In this section, we will discuss some features and principles of communication.

A Model of Communication

As the old saying goes, 'a picture is worth a thousand words.' That's what scientists had in mind when they began creating models of the communication process in the 1950s.

Over time, communication models have become increasingly sophisticated in an attempt to represent all the factors that affect human interaction. No model can completely represent the process of communication, any more than a map can capture everything about the neighbourhood where you live. Still, the model in Figure 1.1 provides a starting point for explaining the insights and principles discussed below.

Insights from the Communication Model

Figure 1.1 illustrates a number of important characteristics of communication. As you read on, note how the following insights help explain the richness of this process.

Sending and Receiving Are Usually Simultaneous In the following scenarios, ask yourself who is sending a message and who is receiving one.

- A teacher explaining a difficult concept to a student after class
- A parent lecturing a teenager about the family's curfew rules
- A salesperson giving a customer information about a product

The natural impulse is to identify the teacher, parent, and salesperson as senders, while the student, teenager, and customer are receivers. Now imagine a confused look on the student's face; the

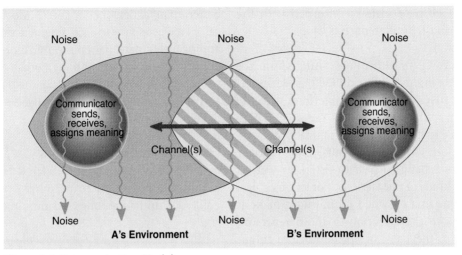

Figure 1.1 Communication Model

teenager interrupting defensively; the customer blankly staring into the distance. It's easy to see that these verbal and non-verbal responses are messages being 'sent', even while the other person is talking. Because it's often impossible to distinguish sending from receiving, our communication model replaces these roles with a more accurate word: *communicator*. This term reflects the fact people can simultaneously be senders and receivers who exchange multiple messages.

Meanings Exist in and among People Messages, whether they are verbal or non-verbal, don't have meanings in themselves; rather, meanings reside in the people who express and interpret them. Imagine that a friend says, 'I'm sorry' after showing up two hours late for a pre-arranged meeting. There are several possible 'meanings' that this expression might have: a genuine apology, an insincere attempt designed to defuse your anger, or even a sarcastic jibe. It's easy to imagine that your friend might mean one thing and you might have a different interpretation of it. The possibility of multiple interpretations means that it is often necessary to negotiate a shared meaning in order for satisfying communication to occur.

Environments Affect Communication Problems often arise because communicators occupy different environments (sometimes called *contexts*)—that

is, fields of experience that help them make sense of other people's behaviour. In communication terminology, *environment* refers not only to a physical location, but also to the personal experiences and cultural background that the participants bring to a conversation. Environments aren't always obvious. For example, one study revealed that college students who have been enrolled in debate classes tend to become more argumentative and verbally aggressive than those who have not been exposed to this sort of environment (Colbert, 1993).

Notice how the model in Figure 1.1 shows that the environments of *A* and *B* overlap. This intersecting area represents the background that the communicators have in common. If this overlap didn't exist, communication would be difficult, if not impossible.

Whereas similar environments facilitate satisfying communication, different backgrounds can make effective communication more challenging. Consider just some of the factors that might contribute to different environments and to difficulties:

- *A* might belong to one cultural group and *B* to another
- *A* might be rich and *B* poor
- *A* might be rushed and *B* have nowhere to go
- *A* might have lived a long, eventful life, and *B* might be young and inexperienced

• *A* might be passionately concerned with the subject and *B* indifferent to it

Noise Affects Communication   Another factor that makes communication difficult is what scientists call **noise**: anything that interferes with the transmission and reception of a message. Three types of noise can disrupt communication. *External noise* includes those factors outside the receiver that make it difficult to hear or listen, as well as many other kinds of distractions. For instance, too much cologne in a crowded room might make it hard for you to pay attention to another person, and sitting at the back of an auditorium might make a speaker's remarks unclear. *Physiological noise* involves biological factors in the receiver that interfere with accurate reception, such as hearing loss, illness, and so on. *Psychological noise* refers to cognitive factors that make communication less effective. For instance, a woman who hears the word *gal* or *lady* may become so irritated that she has trouble listening objectively to the rest of a speaker's message. Likewise, an insecure employee may interpret a minor suggestion the boss makes as ridicule or criticism.

Channels Make a Difference   Communication scholars use the term channel to describe the medium through which messages are exchanged. Along with face-to-face interaction, channels include telephone, email, and written messages. The communication channel being used can affect the way a receiver responds to a message (O'Sullivan, 2000). For example, a typed love letter probably won't have the same effect as a handwritten expression of affection. Likewise, ending a relationship by leaving a message on your ex-lover's voice mail makes a different statement than delivering the bad news in person.

The information in Table 1.1 can help you answer some important questions about channel selection. Is it better to say, 'I'm sorry' in person or over the phone? What channel is the best for expressing your anger? Should you approach the boss directly or write a memo when asking for a raise? Will asking a merchant for a refund by email work better than a personal request? Most communicators believe face-to-face interaction is the best approach for personal communication (Westmyer and DiCioccio, 1998), although other channels can work well in long-distance relationships (Dainton and Aylor, 2002). As Table 1.1 suggests, each channel has both pros and cons.

Communication Principles

In addition to the insights offered by the communication model, there are other principles that guide our understanding of communication.

Communication Is Transactional   One shortcoming of communication models is that they don't adequately capture a sense of the give and take in interpersonal relationships. In fact, communication is **transactional**—that is, a dynamic process created by the participants through their interaction with one another.

Perhaps the most important consequence of the transactional nature of communication is *the degree of mutual influence that occurs when we interact*. To put it simply, communication isn't something we do *to* others; rather, it is an activity we do *with* them. In this sense, communication is rather like dancing—at least the kind of dancing we do with partners.

Reflection

Choosing the Channel

I am an average person in just about every way, except that I have a speech impediment. I have good days and bad days with my speech. On the bad days, I get the idea that strangers think I'm slow and incompetent, even though people who know me don't think I'm either.

Email has become a very satisfying way for me to communicate, especially with people I don't know very well. With email, people can form opinions about me without thinking just about how I sound. I've found that my impediment isn't a problem once people know me, but at first, I think it is a real barrier; and email removes that barrier completely.

Table 1.1 Factors to Consider When Choosing a Communication Channel

	Time Required for Feedback	Amount of Information Conveyed	Sender's Control over How Message Is Composed	Control over Receiver's Attention	Effectiveness for Detailed Messages
Face-to-Face	Immediate (after contact established)	Highest (provides verbal and non verbal cues)	Moderate	Highest	Low (listeners often forget details)
Telephone	Immediate (after contact established)	High (vocal but not visual)	Moderate	Moderate (less than in face-to-face setting)	Lowest
Voice Mail	Delayed	High (vocal but not visual)	Higher (since receiver can't interrupt)	Low	Low
E-Mail	Delayed	Lowest (text only, no formatting)	High	Low	High
Instant Messaging	Potentially Quick	Lowest (text only, no formatting)	High	Moderately low	Low
Hard Copy (e.g., handwritten or typed message)	Delayed	Low (words, numbers. and images, but limited non-verbal cues)	Highest	Low	High

Adapted from Adler R. B., and Elmhorst J. (2005) *Communicating at work: Principles and practices for business and the professions*, 8th ed. New York: McGraw-Hill.

Like dancing, communication *depends on the involvement of a partner*. A great dancer who doesn't consider and adapt to the skill level of his or her partner can make both of them look bad. In communication and dancing, even two talented partners don't guarantee success. When two skilled dancers perform without coordinating their movements, the results feel bad to the dancers and look foolish to an audience.

Finally, relational communication—like dancing—is *a unique creation* that arises out of the way in which the partners interact. The way you dance probably varies from one partner to another because of the co-operative, transactional nature of dancing. Likewise, the way you communicate almost certainly varies with different partners.

Psychologist Kenneth Gergen (1991) captures the transactional nature of communication well when he points out how our success depends on interaction with others: 'One cannot be "attractive" without others who are attracted, a "leader" without others willing to follow, or a "loving

person" without others to affirm with appreciation' (p. 158).

The transactional nature of communication shows up dramatically in relationships between parents and their children. We normally think of 'good parenting' as a skill that some people possess and others lack. We judge the ability of a mother and father by how well their children turn out. The quality of interaction between parents and children is a two-way affair in that children influence parents perhaps as much as the other way around (Saohir and Chaffee, 2002). For instance, research summarized by Laura Stafford and Marianne Dainton (1994) shows that parents with low self-esteem tend to send more messages

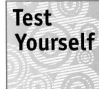
Test Yourself When developing a model for interpersonal communication, what insights regarding the nature of interpersonal communication must be considered and why?

Reflection

My Wife's Eyebrows

My wife doesn't know it, but whenever she thinks something I'm saying is foolish, she arches her eyebrows in a special way (just before she tells me something I said was 'ridiculous'). So, now, when I see her eyebrows take this funny shape, I stop and ask her what's wrong. She immediately tells me, 'I didn't say anything.' Then I tell her what she's doing with her eyebrows, and she tells me, 'You're crazy; I told you I didn't say anything.' She doesn't seem to understand that she's sending messages while she's also listening, and that her eyebrow message is loud and clear!

that weaken the self-esteem of their children, who in turn are likely to act in ways that make the parents feel even worse about themselves. Thus, a mutually reinforcing cycle arises in which parents and children shape one another's feelings and behaviour. In cases like this, it's at least difficult and probably impossible to determine who is the 'sender' of messages and who is the 'receiver'. It is more accurate to acknowledge that parents and children—just like spouses and their better halves, bosses and employees, teachers and students, or any other people who communicate with each other—act in ways that influence one another. The transactional nature of relationships is worth re-emphasizing: we do not communicate *to* others, we communicate *with* them.

Communication Can Be Intentional or Unintentional Some communication is clearly deliberate: you probably plan your words carefully before asking the boss for a raise or offering constructive criticism. Some scholars (e.g., Motley, 1990) argue that only intentional messages like these qualify as communication. However, others (e.g., Baxter and Montgomery, 1996; Buck and VanLear, 2002) suggest that even unintentional behaviour is communicative. Suppose, for instance, that a friend overhears you muttering complaints to yourself.

Even though you didn't intend her to hear your remarks, they certainly did carry a message. In addition to these slips of the tongue, we unintentionally send many non-verbal messages. You may not be aware of your sour expression, impatient shifting, or sigh of boredom, but others notice them nonetheless.

Even the seeming absence of a behaviour has communicative value. Recall the times when you sent an email or left a voice-mail message and received no reply. Like the characters in the *Cathy* cartoon on the next page, you probably assigned some meaning to the lack of a reply. Was the other person angry? Indifferent? Too busy to reply? Whether or not your hunch was correct, the point remains that all behaviour has communicative value. 'Nothing' never happens.

Scholars continue to argue about whether unintentional behaviour should be considered communication (e.g., Clevenger, 1991), and what the relationship is between language and thought (Millikan, 2001). It is unlikely that they will ever settle this issue (Griffin, 2003). In this book, we will look at the communicative value of both intentional and unintentional behaviour. We take the position that whatever you do—whether you speak or remain silent, confront or avoid a person, show emotion or keep a poker face—you provide information to others about your thoughts and feelings. In this sense, we are like transmitters that can't be shut off.

Communication Has a Content and a Relational Dimension Virtually all exchanges have a **content** dimension, which involves the information being explicitly discussed: 'Please pass the salt', 'Not now, I'm tired', 'You forgot to buy milk.' In addition to this sort of obvious content, all messages also have a **relational** component (Dillard et al., 1999; Watzlawick et al., 1967) that expresses how you feel about the other person—whether you like or dislike him or her, feel in control or subordinate, feel comfortable or anxious, and so on. For instance, consider how many different relational messages you could communicate by simply saying 'thanks a lot' in different ways.

Sometimes, the content of a message is all that matters. For example, you may not care how the directory assistance operator feels about you, as long as you get the phone number you're looking for. In a qualitative sense, however, the relational dimension of a message is often more important than the content under discussion. This explains why disputes over apparently trivial subjects become so important. In such cases, we're not really arguing over whose turn it is to take out the garbage or whether we should play tennis or swim. Instead, we're disputing the nature of the relationship. Who is in control? How important are we to each other? In Chapter 8, we will explore several key relational issues in detail.

Communication Is Irreversible We sometimes wish that we could back up in time, erasing words or acts and replacing them with better alternatives. Unfortunately, such reversal is impossible. Sometimes, further explanation can clear up the confusion or an apology can mollify another person's hurt feelings, but other times, no amount of explanation can erase the impression you have

iStock photo

Take Two

Dimensions of Every Message:
- **Content:** refers to the information explicitly being discussed.
- **Relational:** refers to how the communicators feel about each other.

created. It is no more possible to 'unreceive' a message than to 'unsqueeze' a tube of toothpaste. Words said and deeds done are irretrievable.

Communication Is Unrepeatable Because communication is an ongoing process, an event cannot be repeated. The friendly smile that worked so well when you met a stranger last week may not succeed with the person you encounter tomorrow. It may feel stale and artificial to you the second time around, or it may be wrong for the new person or occasion. Even with the same person, it is impossible to recreate an event. Why? Because both you and the other person have changed. You have both lived longer. The behaviour isn't original. Your feelings about each other may have changed. You need not constantly invent new ways to act around familiar people, but you should realize that the 'same' words and behaviour are different each time they are spoken or performed.

Communication Misconceptions

Now that we have described what communication is, we need to identify some things that it is not. Avoiding these common misconceptions (adapted from McCroskey and Richmond, 1996) can save you a great deal of trouble in your personal life.

Not All Communication Seeks Understanding Most people operate on the implicit but flawed assumption that the goal of all communication is to maximize understanding between communicators. While some understanding is necessary for us to coordinate our interaction, there are some types of communication in which understanding as we usually conceive it is not the primary goal.

Reflection

Hurtful Words Can't Be Retracted

I was adopted at the age of five. My adoptive parents were verbally abusive. On a few occasions, they said things to me in anger that I will never forget and which changed our relationship forever. 'Nobody wanted you—you should be thankful that we took you in' was one of their major hurtful messages. Even though they would apologize later, no amount of explanations ease the pain those words have caused me.

Consider, for example, the following situations:

- *The social rituals we enact every day . . .* 'How's it going?' you ask. 'Great,' the other person replies. The primary goal in exchanges like these is mutual acknowledgment: there is obviously no serious attempt to exchange information.
- *Many attempts to influence others . . .* A quick analysis of most television commercials shows that they are aimed at persuading viewers to buy products, not to understand the content of the ad. In the same way, many of our attempts to persuade others to act as we want don't involve a desire to get the other person to understand what we want—just to comply with our wishes.
- *Deliberate ambiguity and deception . . .* When you decline an unwanted invitation by saying, 'I can't make it,' you probably want to create the impression that the decision is really beyond your control. (If your goal were to be perfectly clear, you might say, 'I don't want to get together. In fact, I'd rather do almost

Test Yourself

What are the five principles that guide our understanding of interpersonal communication? Describe them and explain their significance.

Take Two

Not all communication seeks understanding. Some examples include:
- everyday social rituals
- persuasion and coercion
- deliberate ambiguity and deception

anything than accept your invitation.') In fact, we often equivocate precisely because we want to hide our true thoughts and feelings (this is explained in detail in Chapter 9).

More Communication Is Not Always Better

While failure to communicate effectively can certainly cause problems (Richmond, 1995), *too much* talking can also be a mistake. Sometimes, excessive communication is simply unproductive, as when two people 'talk a problem to death', going over the same ground again and again without making progress. There are other times when talking too much actually aggravates a problem. We've all had the experience of 'talking ourselves into a hole'—making a bad situation worse by pursuing it too far. As McCroskey and Wheeless (1976, p. 5) put it, 'More and more negative communication merely leads to more and more negative results.' In one study, college roommates revealed that thinking and talking about conflicts can actually increase relational problems (Cloven and Roloff, 1991).

There are even times when *no* interaction is the best course. When two people are angry and hurt, they may say things they don't mean and will later regret. In such cases, it is probably best to spend time cooling off, thinking about what to say and how to say it. In Chapter 4, we will help you decide when and how to share feelings.

Communication Will Not Solve All Problems

Sometimes, even the best-planned, best-timed communication won't solve a problem. For example, imagine that you ask an instructor to explain why you received a poor grade on a project you believe deserved top marks. The instructor clearly outlines the reasons why you received the low grade and sticks to that position after listening thoughtfully to your protests. Has communication solved the problem? Hardly.

Sometimes, clear communication is even the cause of problems. Suppose, for example, that a friend asks you for an honest opinion of an expensive outfit he just bought. Your clear and sincere answer, 'I think it makes you look fat,' might do more harm than good. Deciding when and how to self-disclose isn't always easy. See Chapter 9 for suggestions.

Effective Communication Is Not a Natural Ability

Most people assume that communication is an aptitude that is developed without the need for training—rather like breathing. Although nearly everyone does manage to function passably without much formal communication training, most people operate at a level of effectiveness far below their potential. In fact, communication skills are similar to athletic ability. Even the least gifted among us can improve with training and practice.

Interpersonal Communication Defined

Now that you have a better understanding of the overall process of human communication, it's time

"Let's stop this before we both say a lot of things we mean."

to look at what makes some types of communication uniquely interpersonal.

Quantitative and Qualitative Definitions

Interpersonal communication has been defined in two ways (Redmond, 1995). Most definitions take a **quantitative** approach that defines interpersonal communication as any interaction between two people. Social scientists call two persons who are interacting a **dyad,** and they often use the adjective *dyadic* to describe this type of communication. So, in a quantitative sense, the terms *dyadic communication* and *interpersonal communication* can be used interchangeably. If we use a quantitative definition, a sales clerk helping a customer or a police officer ticketing a speeding driver would be examples of interpersonal acts, whereas a teacher and class or a performer and audience would not.

Dyadic communication *is* different from the kind of interaction that occurs in larger groups (Wilmot, 1995). In a group, participants can form coalitions to get support for their positions. In a dyad, though, the partners must work matters out with each other. This difference explains why, if a task calls for competition, children prefer to play in three- or four-person groups, and if it calls for co-operation, they prefer to be in dyads (Benenson et al., 2000).

Despite the unique qualities of dyads, you might object to the quantitative definition of interpersonal communication. For example, consider a routine transaction between a sales clerk and customer, or the rushed exchange when you ask a stranger on the street for directions. Communication of this sort hardly seems the same as when you talk to a friend about a personal problem or share with family members your experiences of a year in school.

The impersonal nature of some two-person exchanges—the kind when you think, 'I might as well have been talking to a machine'—has led some scholars (e.g., Miller and Steinberg, 1975; Stewart and Logan, 1998) to argue that quality, not quantity, is what distinguishes interpersonal communication. From a **qualitative** point of view, interpersonal communication occurs when people

Reflection

Irreplaceable Loss

My dad died when I was twenty-nine years old. Ever since I was a child, I had always thought I would never reach thirty. Fortunately, I did and have made it well past, but something changed forever when I was twenty-nine. I lost a relationship that could never be replaced. After my dad died, I felt suddenly 'grown up' or as if I didn't have a 'safety net' any more. Nothing had really changed in my life to account for this feeling of being on my own except the absence of my dad and our unique ways of interacting. No one else called me by the nickname he did. It was gone. Our ways of talking, our jokes, our shared memories seemed to be evaporating. I couldn't hold on to them all by myself. I remembered sitting beside my dad at his mom's funeral. I was ten years old. I felt sad but a bit relieved that she had died because she had been sick with Alzheimer's disease for some time. It was the first funeral I had been to, and I was nervous, so I watched my dad carefully to see what to do. At one point in the service, he turned to me and with a wink said, 'Well, I'm an orphan now.' (His father had deserted the family when he was a child.) I burst out laughing. Thinking back now, I wonder if there was a little tinge of truth in his joke. I wonder if he felt the same way I did when he died—all grown up and alone without that relationship to catch him if he fell.

treat one another as unique individuals, regardless of the context in which the interaction occurs or the number of people involved. When quality of interaction is the criterion, the opposite of interpersonal communication is *impersonal* interaction, not group, public, or mass communication.

Several features distinguish qualitatively interpersonal communication from less personal exchanges. The first is *uniqueness*. Whereas impersonal exchanges are governed by the kind of social rules we learn from parents, teachers, and etiquette books, the way we communicate in a truly personal relationship is unlike our behaviour with anyone else. In one relationship, you might exchange good-natured insults, while in another, you are careful never to offend your compatriot. Likewise, you might handle conflicts with one friend or family member by expressing an opinion as soon as a disagreement arises, whereas the unwritten rule in another relationship is to withhold expressions of disagreement until resentments build up and then to clear the air periodically. Communication scholar Julia Wood (2002) coined the term *relational culture*, in which people in close relationships create their own unique ways of interacting.

A second characteristic of qualitatively interpersonal communication is *irreplaceability*. Because interpersonal relationships are unique, they cannot be replaced. This explains why we usually feel so sad when a close friendship or love affair cools down. We know that no matter how many other relationships we have in our lives, none of them will ever be quite like the one that just ended.

Interdependence is a third characteristic of qualitatively interpersonal relationships. Here, the fate of the partners is connected. You might be able to brush off the anger, affection, excitement, or depression of someone you're not involved with interpersonally, but in an interpersonal relationship, the other's life affects you. Sometimes, interdependence is a pleasure, and at other times, it is a burden. In either case, interdependence is a fact of life in qualitatively interpersonal relationships.

A fourth yardstick of interpersonal communication is *disclosure* of personal information. In impersonal relationships, we don't reveal much about ourselves, but in many interpersonal ones, communicators feel more comfortable sharing their thoughts and feelings. This does not mean that all interpersonal relationships are warm and caring, or that all self-disclosure is positive. It's possible to reveal negative, personal information: 'I'm really mad at you. . . .'

In impersonal communication, we seek payoffs that have little to do with the people involved. You listen to professors in class or talk to potential buyers of your used car in order to reach goals that have little to do with developing personal relationships. By contrast, you spend time in qualitatively

Take Two

Defining Interpersonal Communication: Quantity versus Quality

- Quantitative definitions focus on *the number of people* involved.
- Qualitative definitions focus on *the nature of the interaction* between the people involved in terms of its uniqueness, irreplaceability, amount of disclosure, and intrinsic rewards as well as the interdependence of the people involved.

interpersonal relationships with friends, lovers, and others because of the fifth characteristic of such communication: *intrinsic rewards*. It often doesn't matter what you talk about, as developing the relationship is what's important.

Because interpersonal communication is characterized by the qualities of uniqueness, irreplaceability, interdependence, disclosure, and intrinsic rewards, it forms only a small fraction of our interaction. Most of our communication is relatively impersonal. We chat pleasantly with shopkeepers or fellow passengers on the bus or plane; we discuss the weather or current events with most classmates and neighbours; we deal with co-workers and teachers in a polite way; but considering the number of people with whom we communicate, interpersonal relationships are by far the minority.

The rarity of qualitatively interpersonal communication is not necessarily unfortunate. Most of us do not have the time or energy to create personal relationships with everyone we encounter. In fact, the scarcity of interpersonal communication contributes to their value. Like precious and one-of-a-kind artwork, qualitatively interpersonal relationships are special because they are rare.

Personal and Impersonal Communication: A Matter of Balance

Now that the differences between qualitatively interpersonal and impersonal communication are clear, we need to ask some important questions. Is personal communication better than the impersonal variety? Is more personal communication the goal?

Most relationships are neither personal nor

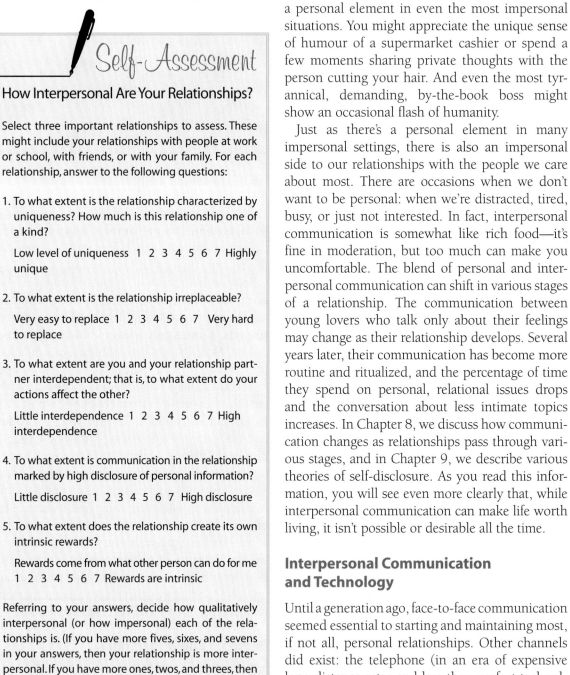

Self-Assessment

How Interpersonal Are Your Relationships?

Select three important relationships to assess. These might include your relationships with people at work or school, with friends, or with your family. For each relationship, answer to the following questions:

1. To what extent is the relationship characterized by uniqueness? How much is this relationship one of a kind?

   Low level of uniqueness 1 2 3 4 5 6 7 Highly unique

2. To what extent is the relationship irreplaceable?

   Very easy to replace 1 2 3 4 5 6 7 Very hard to replace

3. To what extent are you and your relationship partner interdependent; that is, to what extent do your actions affect the other?

   Little interdependence 1 2 3 4 5 6 7 High interdependence

4. To what extent is communication in the relationship marked by high disclosure of personal information?

   Little disclosure 1 2 3 4 5 6 7 High disclosure

5. To what extent does the relationship create its own intrinsic rewards?

   Rewards come from what other person can do for me 1 2 3 4 5 6 7 Rewards are intrinsic

Referring to your answers, decide how qualitatively interpersonal (or how impersonal) each of the relationships is. (If you have more fives, sixes, and sevens in your answers, then your relationship is more interpersonal. If you have more ones, twos, and threes, then the relationship is more impersonal.) How satisfied are you with your findings? What can you do to improve your satisfaction with these relationships?

impersonal. Rather, they fall somewhere between these two extremes. Consider your own communication and you will find that there is often a personal element in even the most impersonal situations. You might appreciate the unique sense of humour of a supermarket cashier or spend a few moments sharing private thoughts with the person cutting your hair. And even the most tyrannical, demanding, by-the-book boss might show an occasional flash of humanity.

Just as there's a personal element in many impersonal settings, there is also an impersonal side to our relationships with the people we care about most. There are occasions when we don't want to be personal: when we're distracted, tired, busy, or just not interested. In fact, interpersonal communication is somewhat like rich food—it's fine in moderation, but too much can make you uncomfortable. The blend of personal and interpersonal communication can shift in various stages of a relationship. The communication between young lovers who talk only about their feelings may change as their relationship develops. Several years later, their communication has become more routine and ritualized, and the percentage of time they spend on personal, relational issues drops and the conversation about less intimate topics increases. In Chapter 8, we discuss how communication changes as relationships pass through various stages, and in Chapter 9, we describe various theories of self-disclosure. As you read this information, you will see even more clearly that, while interpersonal communication can make life worth living, it isn't possible or desirable all the time.

Interpersonal Communication and Technology

Until a generation ago, face-to-face communication seemed essential to starting and maintaining most, if not all, personal relationships. Other channels did exist: the telephone (in an era of expensive long-distance rates and less-than-perfect technology) may have worked during temporary absences, and postal correspondence may have bridged the gap until the people involved could reconnect in person. Nonetheless, interpersonal communication seemed to require physical proximity.

Technological changes have given us new options for communicating personally. Along with affordable telephone rates, **computer-mediated communication (CMC)** provides another way to interact. Email is the most popular form of CMC, but it isn't the only one. Instant messaging and online chat are other tools that friends, family, acquaintances, and even strangers, can use for communicating.

At first glance, CMC might seem inferior to face-to-face interaction, since it lacks the rich array of non-verbal cues that are available in person. Even the telephone offers vocal cues. By contrast, CMC—at least the text-based variety—offers almost none of this richness. Some critics argue that the almost hypnotic attraction of an Internet connection discourages people from spending 'face time' with others. A small body of research supports this position. Some research has found that heavy Internet users spend less time talking in person and on the phone with friends and family members (Bower, 1998; Nie, 2001), habits which can lead to high levels of emotional loneliness (Moody, 2001). Even when people replace their face-to-face communication with online contacts, some observers claim the quality of the relationship suffers. 'Email is a way to stay in touch,' said one researcher, 'but you can't share a coffee or a beer with somebody on email or give them a hug' (Nie and Erbring, 2000, p. 19).

Other research suggests that the increased use of the Internet does not negatively affect interpersonal communication. In the 2000 General Social Survey data on individual Internet use, the overwhelming majority of Canadians (89 to 93 percent) reported that despite their increased use of the Internet, the time they spent with family, friends, and children had not decreased (Dryburgh, 2000).

Some research suggests that the Internet can actually enhance interpersonal communication. In their discussion of the effects of the Internet on social contact and community involvement, Anabel Quan-Haase and Barry Wellman (2004), from the University of Toronto, analyzed data from a variety of sources, including a sample of 20,075 North American adults (2,364 Canadians and 17,711 Americans). At the time of this survey (2000), approximately 60 percent of North American households were online. Even more

iStock photo

iStock photo

significant than the amount of communication that takes place online is its quality. Internet use was a daily activity for the majority of adults surveyed, and email appeared to support existing social contacts, not replace telephone and face-to-face communication. People who visited and called each other frequently also emailed each other frequently. Similarly, in a survey of over three thousand adults in the United States, 55 percent of Internet users said email improved communications with their family, and 66 percent reported that their contact with friends increased because of email (Horrigan et al., 2001). Among women, the rate of satisfaction was even higher: 60 percent reported better contact with their family and 71 percent with friends.

In Canada, 84 percent of Internet users have email. Relatives are most likely to email each other a couple of times a month, whereas friends email each other several times a week (Dryburgh, 2000). Foreign-born Canadian Internet users are more likely than those born in Canada to use email every day to communicate with relatives and friends. Seventy-one percent of foreign-born Canadian Internet users regularly communicate with people outside of Canada (Dryburgh, 2000). The Internet provides not only increased opportunities for communication locally but also the ability to maintain relationships over long distances.

Other research confirms that CMC can support interpersonal relationships. In a five-year survey, Internet users reported having more social contacts than non-users, as well as more community and political involvement (Katz et al., 2001). Almost 60 percent of teenagers in the United States say that their use of the Internet helps their relationships with their friends, and almost a third report that it helps them make new friends (Lenhart et al., 2001).

There are several reasons why CMC can increase both the amount and quality of interpersonal communication (Barnes, 2003). For one thing, it makes communication easier. Busy schedules and long distances can make quality time in face-to-face contact difficult or impossible. The challenge of finding time is especially difficult for people who are separated by long distances and several time zones. In relationships like this, the *asynchronous* nature of email provides a way to share information that otherwise would be impossible.

Focus on Research

Customer Service: Impersonal versus Interpersonal

It's easy to criticize cashiers and fast-food servers who seem to lack warmth or concern. On the other hand, spending too much time and energy chatting with customers brings its own set of problems. For workers whose jobs involve some measure of customer service—and research suggests that 80 percent of the US labour force fits that category—it's not always easy to balance impersonal and interpersonal communication.

Wendy Zabava Ford (2001) ran surveys and interviews with customers and employees to analyze their perceptions of appropriate customer service. She divided customer service into two types: service encounters, which are usually one-time transactions where speed and efficiency are of the essence; and service relationships, which involve multiple interactions over time and a strong social component. Not surprisingly, Ford found that customers value service relationships and seek them out from professionals such as physicians, auto mechanics, and hairdressers. On the other hand, many respondents said they prefer service by cashiers, clerks, and fast-food employees to be polite, efficient, and relatively impersonal encounters. One frustrated customer described overly social cashiers this way: 'We are not going through some big bonding process. I expect for them simply to get me through.'

One of Ford's primary conclusions is that 'there is no one best way to serve customers.' While personalized service is important in many professions, a competent communicator knows how personal to be—or not to be—in particular service situations.

Text-messaging and instant messaging are other ways to keep in touch: discovering that a friend or relative is online and starting an electronic conversation is 'like walking down the street and sometimes running into a friend,' said one computer consultant (Marriott, 1998).

Sometimes, CMC can profoundly expand the quality of interpersonal communication, taking it to a level that communication scholar Joseph Walther (1996) calls 'hyperpersonal'. Computer-mediated communication may encourage people to express opinions they might otherwise withhold. Sociolinguist Deborah Tannen (1996, p. 52) describes how email transformed the quality of two relationships:

> Email deepened my friendship with Ralph. Though his office was next to mine, we rarely had extended conversations because he is shy. Face to face he mumbled so I could barely tell he was speaking. But when we both got on email, I started receiving long, self-revealing messages; we poured our hearts out to each other. A friend discovered that email opened up that kind of communication with her father. He would never talk much on the phone (as her mother would), but they have become close since they both got online.

Experiences like these help explain why Steve Jobs, the co-founder of Apple Computer, suggested that personal computers be renamed 'interpersonal computers' (Kirkpatrick, 1992).

Interpersonal Communication and Cultural Diversity

Almost half a century ago, communication guru Marshall McLuhan (1964) coined the metaphor of the world as a 'global village' where members of all nations are connected by communication technology. Just as with members of a traditional village, McLuhan suggested, the affairs and fate of the occupants of Planet Earth are connected—for better or worse. This analysis has proved to be increasingly true in the years since McLuhan introduced it. The growth in communication technology, including international telephone service, the Internet and World Wide Web, and global television coverage brings the world into our homes. Although relatively cheap transportation has reduced the barrier of distance, making travel easier for more people than ever before, Canadians don't need to go far to be exposed to the global village.

Demographic changes have been transforming Canada into a microcosm of the global village. Canada has the second highest proportion of foreign-born citizens and the highest immigration rate in the world (Adams, 2007b). In 2006, 6.1 million, or 1 in 5, Canadians were born outside the country. Not since 1931 has the proportion of first-generation Canadians been so high (Statistics Canada, 2007). The Canadian concept of multiculturalism, where people value, celebrate, and preserve their cultural heritage rather than become assimilated into the dominant culture helps to create this microcosm of global diversity. Canada has the highest immigration rate in the world and, more than any other country, Canadians value the contributions of immigrants (Adams, 2007a).

Economic integration also creates ties that bind nations and people. National economies are increasingly connected with and affected by developments around the world. According to Industry Canada, no other major economy is as trade-oriented as Canada. The country depends on international trade to grow and prosper; and, because Canada's is a very small economy, domestic-based companies increasingly enter global markets in order to remain viable and competitive (Poloz, 2005).

Given all this information, it makes sense to examine how interpersonal communication operates between members of different cultures. Throughout this book, we will see that when people from different backgrounds interact, they face a set of challenges that are often different from when members of the same culture communicate.

Culture

Defining culture is not an easy task. One survey of scholarly literature revealed five hundred definitions, phrasings, and uses of the concept (Kroeber and Kluckholn, 1952). For our purposes, Larry Samovar and Richard Porter (2001) offer a clear and comprehensive definition of *culture*: 'the language, values, beliefs, traditions, and customs people share and learn.'

This definition shows that culture is, to a great extent, a matter of *perception* and *definition*. When you identify yourself as a member of a culture, you must not only share certain characteristics, but you must also recognize yourself and others like you as possessing these features and see others who don't possess them as members of different categories. For example, eye colour doesn't seem like a significant factor in distinguishing 'us' from 'them', whereas skin colour is more important—at least in some cases. It's not hard to imagine a society where the opposite is true. Social scientists use the term **in-groups** for groups with which we identify and **out-groups** for those that we view as different (Tajfel and Turner, 1992).

Intercultural Communication

Having defined culture, we can go on to define **intercultural communication** as the process by which members of two or more cultures exchange messages in a manner that is influenced by their different cultural perceptions and symbol systems (Samovar and Porter, 2001). Note that intercultural communication (at least as we'll use the term here) doesn't always occur when people from different cultures interact. The cultural backgrounds, perceptions, and symbol systems of the participants must have a significant influence on the exchange before we can say that culture has made a difference. Consider a few examples where culture does and doesn't play a role:

- A group of preschool children is playing together in a park. These three-year-olds don't realize that their parents may have come from different countries or even that they don't all speak the same language. At this point, we would not say that intercultural communication is taking place. Only when different norms become apparent—about diet, sharing, or parental discipline, for example—do the children begin to think of one another as different.
- Members of a school basketball team from a variety of cultural backgrounds—some East Asian, some South Asian, some Caribbean, and some European—are intent on winning the league championship. During a game, cultural distinctions aren't important. There's plenty of communication, but it is not fundamentally intercultural. Away from their games, the players are friendly when they meet, but they rarely socialize. If they did, they might notice some fundamental differences in the way members of each cultural group communicate.
- A husband and wife were raised in homes with different religious traditions. Most of the time, their religious heritage makes little difference and the partners view themselves as a unified couple. Every so often, however—perhaps during the holidays or when meeting members of each other's family—the different backgrounds are highlighted. At those times, we can imagine the partners feeling quite different from each other—thinking of themselves as members of separate cultures.

These examples show that in order to view ourselves as a member of a culture, there has to be some distinction between 'us' and 'them', between in- and out-group. We may not always be able to say precisely what the differences are. We may have only a feeling that something is different, and there are occasions when cultural influences are powerful but so subtle that they go unrecognized.

Many social scientists use the term **co-culture** to describe a subgroup that is part of an encompassing culture. For example, in North American culture it is easy to recognize categories such as age (teen culture, senior citizens), ethnicity (Asian, European), race, gender, sexual orientation, physical disabilities, and religion. Some scholars (e.g., Tannen, 1990, 1994; Mulac et al., 2001; Wood, 2002) and writers in the popular press (e.g., Gray, 1992) have even characterized men and women as belonging to different co-cultures because their communication styles are so different.

Interpersonal and Intercultural Communication

At this point, you may be wondering whether there is any communication that *is not* intercultural, or at least co-cultural. Indeed, there are many cases when communication isn't influenced by intercultural considerations. Even in an increasingly diverse world, there are still plenty of relationships in which people share a basically common background. The Irish marchers in a St Patrick's Day parade; the group of men from a small town who play poker every other Friday night; and the members of a university sorority or fraternity are likely to share fundamentally similar personal histories and, therefore, to have similar norms, customs, and values. Even when people with different cultural backgrounds communicate, shared values and experiences are often far more important than the cultural backgrounds they bring to the relationship (Singer, 1998). David may be a Jewish male whose ancestors came from Eastern Europe while Lisa is a third-generation Japanese woman whose parents are practising Christians, but they have created a life together that is usually more important than their differences and that leaves them able to deal comfortably with those differences when they do arise.

Rather than classify some exchanges as intercultural and others as free from cultural influences, it is more accurate to talk about *degrees* of cultural significance (Lustig and Koester, 1999). Encounters can fit along a spectrum of 'interculturalness'. At the 'most intercultural' end are situations where differences between the backgrounds and beliefs of communicators are high. A traveller visiting a new country for the first time with little knowledge of local society would be an obvious example. At the 'least intercultural' end of the spectrum fall exchanges where cultural differences matter little. A student from Montreal who attends a small university in the Maritimes may find life somewhat different, but the adjustment would be far less difficult than that for the international traveller. In between these extremes falls a whole range of encounters in which culture plays varying roles.

What is the relationship between intercultural communication and interpersonal relationships? William Gudykunst and Young Kim (1997) summarize an approach that helps answer this question. They suggest that interpersonal and intercultural factors combine to form a two-by-two matrix in which the importance of interpersonal communication forms one dimension and intercultural significance forms the second one (see Figure 1.2). This model shows that some interpersonal transactions (for example, a conversation between two siblings who have been raised in the same household) have virtually no intercultural elements. Other encounters (such as a traveller from Senegal trying to get directions from an Iranian-Canadian taxi driver in Vancouver) are almost exclusively intercultural, without the personal dimensions that we discuss throughout this book.

Still other exchanges—the most interesting ones for our purposes—contain elements of both intercultural and interpersonal communication. This range of encounters is broad in the global village: business people from different backgrounds try to wrap up a deal; Canadian-born and immigrant children learn to get along in school; health-care

Figure 1.2 Some Possible Interactions among Interpersonal and Intercultural Dimensions of Person-to-Person Communication

educators seek effective ways to serve patients from around the world; neighbours from different racial or ethnic backgrounds look for ways to make their streets safer and cleaner; middle-class teachers seek common ground with students from low-income neighbourhoods—the list seems almost endless. In situations like these, communicators are trying to establish some degree of relationship and understanding. When they

do find ways of connecting that account for, and even transcend, cultural differences, communicators have created what Fred Casmir (1991) calls a 'third culture': a unique relationship shared by two or more people.

Comparison of Canadian and US Culture

Since the population of the United States is roughly ten times that of Canada and five times that of the United Kingdom (World Gazetteer, 2005), it follows logically that a very large proportion of the research on interpersonal communication in Western culture has been conducted with US citizens. Canadians have a much smaller database of homegrown studies to inform them about their interpersonal communication practices. So, to what extent can we apply US findings to the Canadian context? In order to answer this question, we need to examine the similarities and differences between the two cultures, particularly in areas that are relevant to interpersonal communication.

How are Canadian values similar to US values, and how are they different? There has been considerable discussion, debate, and research

Take Two

Concepts in Intercultural Communication

Culture: the language, values, beliefs, traditions, and customs people share and learn.

In-groups: groups of people with whom we identify.

Out-groups: groups of people whom we view as different.

Co-culture: a subgroup that is part of an encompassing culture.

Intercultural communication: the process by which members of two or more cultures exchange messages in a manner that is influenced by their different cultural perceptions and symbol systems.

Canadian identity?

comparing the values and behaviour of Canadians and Americans (Adams, 2003a; Boucher, 2004; Jedwab, 2004b; Krauss, 2003). The consensus appears to be that although the two cultures are very similar when placed in the context of the many cultures in the world (Hofstede, 2001), there are some differences that are important to many Canadians—and some of those differences appear to be growing. For instance, Michael Adams, co-founder of the social research organization, Environics, has reported on three large social-values surveys conducted in Canada and the United States in 1992, 1996, and 2000. He and his Environics colleagues used those surveys in combination with over 14,000 individual interviews and previously compiled Canadian survey findings dating back to 1983 to conduct a comparative analysis of Canadian and US culture and to track shifts in social values (Adams, 2003a). In the surveys, participants were questioned about over one hundred social values. Values were defined as 'ideas that motivate people to behave the way they do, good, bad or neither' (Adams, 2003a, p. 12).

Canadians and Americans described different values, attitudes, and beliefs in many different areas. Some of the most significant in terms of their impact on interpersonal communication are attitudes toward violence, tolerance of diversity, and the relative status of men and women.

Attitudes toward Violence

Michael Adams (2003a) argues that Canadians are markedly differentiated from Americans by their attitudes toward violence. Generally, fewer Canadians perceive that they are surrounded by violence when compared with their US counterparts. Canadians are less likely to perceive violence as a normal part of everyday life or as a way of solving problems. When compared with Americans, far fewer Canadians endorsed the view that it was acceptable to use a little violence to relieve tension or frustration (Adams, 2003a, p. 53). Similarly, almost twice as many US citizens as Canadians thought it was acceptable to use violence to get what you want (23 percent compared to 13 percent). Predictions that Canadians would be more likely to endorse the use of violence and be more deferential to authority in the wake of the 11 September 2001 (9/11), attacks proved untrue. Investigations immediately following 9/11 revealed that Canadians were not ready to curtail their Charter of Rights and Freedoms without justification based on reality, not fear (Baker, 2002). Similar predictions that the events of 9/11 would contribute to less tolerance for diversity and multiculturalism in Canada also proved unfounded.

Tolerance of Diversity

Canadians consistently express the most positive attitudes towards immigration (Pew Research Centre, 2003; Adams 2007b). When the Pew Research Centre (2003) conducted an international survey of 38,000 people in 44 countries, it found Canada to be the only nation where the majority (77 percent) of respondents said immigrants have a good influence on their country. In the United States, 49 percent of the respondents felt the same way. The more significant difference was in the proportion of respondents that said immigrants were bad for their country: 18 percent of Canadians and 43 percent of US citizens surveyed. Even if respondents in both countries were not being completely truthful in order to appear more socially acceptable, Canadians appear to believe that in Canadian culture, intolerance of immigrants is not socially acceptable. The Canadians surveyed by Adams and his colleagues (2003a) were also less willing than Americans to endorse overtly racist statements such as, 'Non-whites should not be allowed to immigrate to this country.' In the 2000 survey, 13 percent of Canadians agreed with this statement, compared with 25 percent of Americans. Similarly, 14 percent of Canadians said they 'enjoyed showing foreigners how much smarter and stronger they were,' while more than twice as many (31 percent) US respondents agreed that they liked to demonstrate their superiority to foreigners. Again, these data do not imply that Canadians are not ethnocentric, or do not discriminate against immigrants and minorities, or do not engage in racist behaviour—because there is abundant evidence that Canadians

do (Canadian Council on Social Development, 2000; Henry and Tator, 2003; Jedwab, 2004a; Teelucksingh and Galabuzi, 2005). The point is that Canadians are different from Americans in the extent to which we believe these things are not acceptable in Canada.

Relative Status of Men and Women

Similarly, discrimination against women exists in Canada (Morris, Robinson, and Simpson, 1999), but Canadians are less willing than their US counterparts to endorse a view of patriarchal authority (the father must be master in his own home) or a view that men are naturally superior to women. According to the Environics 2000 survey data, 18 percent of Canadians and 49 percent of Americans said the father of a household must be the boss (Adams, 2003a). Michael Adams (2003a; 2005) argues that Canadians' more egalitarian views regarding the status of women and their unwillingness to endorse traditional family models of patriarchal authority have contributed to making us take a more relaxed view of what constitutes a family. More Canadians support the view that people living in common-law relationships and same-sex couples are proper families (Adams, 2003; Galloway and Moore, 2005). Americans appear to be much more opposed to these kinds of variations in family structure (Krauss, 2003).

At the same time that we see differences, we are also aware that in a global context, the values that are the basis for Canadian society are perceived as more similar to those of US society than to those of many other cultures. A study commissioned by the Association for Canadian Studies reported that 55 percent of Canadians believe that Canadian society has values that are similar to those of the United States (Jedwab, 2004b). Furthermore, when we look at the cultural dimensions (discussed in detail in Chapter 2) such as individualism as opposed to collectivism, uncertainty avoidance, and 'power distance' (social hierarchy), Canada and the United States have very similar rankings. Geert Hofstede (2001) used extensive statistical data to examine cultural values in fifty-three different countries around the world. One

Test Yourself — What differences have been noted between Canadian and US values and why do they matter?

value dimension he measured was the extent to which people's personal goals take priority over their allegiance to the group, 'that is, individualism as opposed to collectivism.' The United States ranks number one in promoting individualism; it is followed by Australia (ranked number two); Britain (ranked number three); and Canada and the Netherlands (tied for fourth place). Similarly, Canada and the United States rank forty-second and forty-third respectively in the degree to which each country can be classified as one that does not like uncertainty (the higher the ranking, the greater the tolerance for uncertainty in that country). Finally, power distance, which is a concept similar to that of social hierarchy, is also very similar in the United States (ranked thirty-eighth of fifty-three countries) and Canada (ranked thirty-ninth)—the higher the ranking, the more egalitarian the culture. We discuss these cultural dimensions in more detail in Chapter 2.

Given the similarities between the two cultures, at least in a global context, it seems fair to assume US interpersonal communication research findings have at least some applicability to Canadians. At the same time, it is important to be sensitive to the fact that there are real and significant differences between the two cultures and to keep a critical eye open to the possibility that these cultural differences might influence our interpretations of US research.

Communication Competence

'What does it take to communicate better?' is probably the most crucial question to ask as you read this book. Answering it has been one of the leading challenges for communication scholars. While all the answers aren't in yet, research has discovered a great deal of important and useful information about communication competence.

Communication Competence Defined and Described

Defining **communication competence** isn't as easy as it might seem. Although scholars continue to argue over a precise definition, most agree that competent communication is both *effective* and *appropriate* (Spitzberg, 2000). To understand these two dimensions, consider how you might handle everyday communication challenges, such as declining an unwanted social invitation or communicating about a friend's annoying behaviour. In cases like these, *effective* communication would get the results you want. *Appropriate* communication would do so in a way that, in most cases, enhances the relationship in which it occurs (Wiemann et al., 1997). You can appreciate the importance of both appropriateness and effectiveness by imagining approaches that would satisfy one of these criteria but not the other. Effectiveness without appropriateness might satisfy your goals, but leave others unhappy. Conversely, appropriateness without effectiveness might leave others content but you frustrated. With the goal of balancing effectiveness and appropriateness, in the following paragraphs, we outline several important characteristics of communication competence.

Motivation and Open-mindedness are Key   In order to become a more competent communicator, you must have some desire to improve your communication skills with a variety of people. You need to be open to new ways of thinking and behaving. Without an open-minded attitude, a communicator will have trouble interacting competently with people from different backgrounds. To understand open-mindedness, it is helpful to consider three traits that are incompatible with it: **Ethnocentrism** is the belief that one's own culture is superior to others. An ethnocentric person thinks—either privately or openly—that anyone who does not belong to his or her in-group is somehow strange, wrong, or even inferior.

Ethnocentrism leads to an attitude of **prejudice**—an unfairly biased and intolerant attitude toward others who belong to an out-group. (Note that the root term in *prejudice* is 'pre-judge'.) An

Take Two

Obstacles to Open-mindedness:

- **Ethnocentrism:** the belief that one's own culture is superior to others.
- **Prejudice:** an unfairly biased and intolerant attitude toward others who belong to an out-group.
- **Stereotyping:** exaggerated generalizations about a group.

important element of prejudice is **stereotyping**—exaggerated generalizations about a group. Stereotypical prejudices include the obvious exaggerations that all women are emotional, all men are sex-crazed and insensitive goons, all older people are out of touch with the modern world, and all immigrants are poorly educated. Stereotyping can even be a risk when it comes to one's knowledge of the cultural characteristics within one's own milieu, which we explore in Chapter 2. Despite general similarities within a culture, not every individual group member shares the same values and beliefs. It's encouraging to know that open-minded communicators can overcome pre-existing stereotypes and learn to appreciate people from different backgrounds as individuals.

There Is No Single Ideal or Effective Way to Communicate   Your own experience shows that a variety of communication styles can be effective. Some very successful communicators are serious, while others use humour; some are gregarious, while others are quieter; and some are more straightforward, while others hint diplomatically. Just as there are many kinds of beautiful music or art, there are many kinds of competent communication. Furthermore, a type of communication that is competent in one setting might be a colossal blunder in another. The joking insults you routinely trade with one friend might offend a sensitive family member, and last Saturday night's romantic approach would probably be out of place at work on Wednesday morning. This means that there can be no surefire list of rules or tips that will guarantee your success as a communicator.

Flexibility is especially important when members of different cultures meet. Some communication skills seem to be universal (Ruben, 1989)—for example, every culture has rules that require speakers to behave appropriately. But the definition of what kind of communication is appropriate in a given situation varies considerably from one culture to another (Chen and Sarosta, 1996; Ulrey, 2001). On an obvious level, customs like belching after a meal or appearing nude in public, which might be appropriate in some parts of the world, would be considered outrageous in others. But there are more subtle differences in competent communication. For example, qualities like self-disclosure and speaking clearly—much valued in North America—are likely to be considered overly aggressive and insensitive in many Asian cultures, where subtlety and indirectness are considered important (Kim et al., 1998).

Culture has a significant influence on how we experience our personal relationships. In a comparison of perceptions of interpersonal closeness, Turkish students reported feeling closer to others and ideally wanted greater closeness in their interpersonal relationships than did Canadian students (Uskul, Hynie, and LaLonde, 2004). Similarly, Li (2002) found that Chinese students felt closer to their family members and friends than did Canadian students.

"Wow! From down here your nostrils look huge!"

Focus on Research

Face-to-Face or Mediated Channel?

Assume for a moment that you felt a need to make a confession to your romantic partner. The confession might be about something you've done wrong, or something that would make your partner think poorly of you. How would you send your message—through a mediated channel (such as a phone call or an email) or in a face-to-face conversation?

Patrick O'Sullivan (2000) conducted research to learn about preferences for face-to-face versus mediated channels for sending messages. He surveyed 133 undergraduates in premarital romantic relationships to learn how they would offer information to their partners in four categories: *confess* (negative message about self), *boast* (positive message about self), *accuse* (negative message about partner), or *praise* (positive message about partner).

In all four categories, the students said they would favour face-to-face over mediated interactions. Nevertheless, there were differences in the degrees to which they preferred face-to-face conversations. As might be expected, the respondents said they would have little trouble sending positive messages face to face, but mediated channels appealed to them more for sending negative messages. In particular, the students rated the *confess* category as the one for which they would most likely use a mediated channel.

O'Sullivan concluded that 'individuals recognize that mediated channels can help minimize the costs for themselves or their partner associated with embarrassing or unattractive information.' This research suggests that the channels people choose for sending their messages can be an important factor in their communication.

These and other research studies—for example, a study by Johnson and colleagues (2001) of what people from different cultures perceive as competent communication behaviour in initial interactions—suggest how a knowledge of other people's cultural backgrounds might help you become a more competent intercultural communicator. If, for example, you understand that a potential friend's background is likely to make displays of respect especially important, you could adjust your communication accordingly.

Even within a single society, members of various co-cultures may have different notions of appropriate behaviour. One study revealed that ideas of how good friends should communicate varied among people with different cultural backgrounds (Collier, 1996). As a group, people from Hispanic backgrounds valued relational support most highly, while people from African backgrounds prized respect and acceptance. Those with an Asian heritage emphasized a caring, positive exchange of ideas; and people with a European heritage prized friends who recognized their needs as individuals. Findings like these mean that there can be no list of rules or tips that will guarantee your success as a communicator. They also suggest that competent communicators are able to adapt their style to suit the individual and cultural preferences of others (Chen, 1997).

Competence Is Situational Because competent behaviour varies so much from one situation and person to another, it's a mistake to think that communication competence is a trait that a person either possesses or lacks (Spitzberg, 1991). It's more accurate to talk about *degrees* or *areas* of competence.

You and the people you know are probably quite competent in some areas and less so in others. For example, you might deal quite skilfully with peers, but, at the same time, feel clumsy interacting with people much older or younger, wealthier or poorer, or more or less 'attractive' than you. In fact, your competence may vary from situation to situation. This means it's an overgeneralization to say, in a moment of distress, 'I'm a terrible communicator!' It's more accurate to say, 'I didn't handle this situation very well, but I'm better in others.'

Competence Requires Mindfulness Knowledge of how to communicate with people from different backgrounds is often 'culture-specific', to use Samovar and Porter's terminology (2001). The rules and customs that work with one group might be quite different from those that succeed with another. The ability to 'shift gears' and adapt one's style to the norms of another culture or co-culture is an essential ingredient of communication competence (Kim et al., 1996).

How can a communicator acquire the culture-specific information that leads to competence? One important element is what Stella Ting-Toomey (1999) and others call *mindfulness*—awareness of one's own behaviour and that of others. Communicators who lack this quality blunder through intercultural encounters mindlessly, oblivious of how their own behaviour may confuse or offend others, and how behaviour that they consider bizarre may simply be different from their norm.

Charles Berger (1979) suggests three strategies for moving toward a more mindful, competent style of intercultural communication: *Passive observation* involves noticing what members of a different culture do and using these insights to communicate in ways that are most effective. *Active strategies* include reading, watching films, asking experts and members of the other culture how to behave, and taking academic courses related to intercultural communication and diversity (Carrell, 1997). The third strategy, *self-disclosure*, involves volunteering personal information to people from the other culture with whom you want to communicate. One type of self-disclosure is to confess your cultural ignorance: 'This is very new to me. What's the right thing to do in this situation?' This approach is the riskiest of the three we describe here, since some cultures may not value candour and self-disclosure as much as others. Nevertheless, most people are pleased when strangers attempt to learn the practices of their culture, and they are usually more than willing to offer information and assistance.

Competence Can Be Learned To some degree, biology is destiny when it comes to communication style (Beatty and McCroskey, 1998; Hovarth, 1995). Studies of identical and fraternal twins suggest that some traits, including sociability, a short temper, and the ability to relax seem to be partially a function of our genetic makeup. In addition, a recent study by Beatty and colleagues (2001) found that social composure and wit are highly heritable. (The same study showed that articulation ability and appropriate disclosure are not.)

Fortunately, biology isn't the only factor that shapes how we communicate. Communication competence is, to a great degree, a set of skills that anyone can learn (Fortney et al., 2001). For instance, people with high communication apprehension often benefit from communication-skills training (Ayres and Hopf, 1993). Sometimes, even a modest amount of training can produce dramatic results. For example, after only thirty minutes of instruction, one group of observers became significantly more effective in detecting deception in interviews (deTurck and Miller, 1990). Even without systematic training, it is possible to develop communication skills through the processes of observation and trial and error. We learn from our own successes and failures, as well as from observing other models—both positive and negative. One study revealed that education does lead to improved communication skill: for college students, communication competence increases over the course of their undergraduate studies (Rubin et al., 1990).

Characteristics of Competent Communication

Despite the fact that competent communication varies from one situation to another, scholars have identified several common denominators that characterize effective communication in most contexts.

A Large Repertoire of Skills As we have already seen, good communicators do not use the same approach in every situation. They know that it's best sometimes to be blunt and, at other times, to be tactful—that there is a time to speak up and a time to be quiet. They understand that some situations require seriousness and others call for playfulness.

The chances of behaving competently increase with the number of options you have about how to communicate. For example, if you want to start a conversation with a stranger, your chances of success increase as you have more options available (Kelly and Watson, 1986). All it might take to get the conversational ball rolling is a self-introduction. In other cases, seeking assistance might work well: 'I've just moved here. What kind of neighbourhood is the east end?' A third strategy is to ask a question about some situational feature: 'I've never heard this band before. Do you know anything about them?' You could also offer a sincere compliment and follow it up with a question: 'Great shoes! Where did you get them?' Just as a golfer has a wide range of clubs to use for various situations, a competent communicator has a large array of behaviours from which to choose.

Adaptability Having a large repertoire of possible behaviours is one ingredient of competent communication, but you have to be able to choose the *right* one for a particular situation (Brashers and Jackson, 1999; Hample and Dallinger, 2000; Stamp, 1999). To repeat, an approach that works well in one situation might be disastrous somewhere else. Effective communication means choosing the right response for the situation.

Ability to Perform Skilfully Once you have chosen the best way to communicate, you have to do it effectively. In communication, as in other activities, practice is the key to skilful performance. Much of the information in this book will introduce you to new tools for communicating, and the Skill Builder activities at the end of each chapter will help you practise them.

Involvement Not surprisingly, effective communication takes place when the people care about one another and the topic at hand (Cegala et al., 1982). Rod Hart suggests that this involvement has several dimensions (adapted here from Knapp and Vangelisti, 2000). It includes commitment to the other person and the relationship, concern about the message being discussed, and a desire to make the relationship clearly useful. Notice that these characteristics involve two themes. The first

iStock photo

Building Work Skills

Taking the Other Person's Perspective When Sending Messages

Have you ever received a telephone or email message that left you wondering what the sender wanted you to do or why they wanted you to know this? A message may have been missing the most important information (e.g., the person's name or phone number). Or a message may have had so much detailed, irrelevant information that you couldn't wade through it all. These kinds of messages are particularly frustrating at work. We have probably all received them and sent them. Often, we leave these messages before we have really thought through our requests of others—before we have taken their perspective.

For this skill-building exercise, you need a partner from the class. First, think about a request you have needed to make or information you needed to share with someone at your workplace or at school. If you can't think of a real example, you and your partner can use one of the examples below:

- *A colleague has asked you to switch shifts because she has an appointment. You are willing to do so but must get the permission of your supervisor. Leave a message for your supervisor.*
- *You have come down with some sort of illness and will have to miss class. You have a test and an assignment due. Leave a message for your teacher.*

Jot down your message. Now, read your message from the point of view of the person you are leaving it for. Is it complete? Is it well organized? Will the recipient understand the context? Are there irrelevant details that could be omitted? Have you told them what you want or why they need to know? Once you are satisfied with your message, you can do one of the following: leave it on the voice mail of your partner from class; email it to your partner; or just read it, uninterrupted, to your partner.

Ask your partner to imagine he or she is the person you intended to send the message to. Ask your counterpart to give you some feedback about the quality of your message, particularly your ability to take the recipient's perspective.

---

is *commitment*. Good communicators care about the other person, about the subject, and about being understood. The second theme is *profitability*. The most effective communication produces good results for everyone involved.

Empathy and Perspective Taking People have the best chance of developing an effective message when they understand the other person's point of view (Ifert and Roloff, 1997). And since that person may not be good at expressing his or her thoughts and feelings clearly, the ability to imagine how an issue might look from someone else's perspective suggests why listening is such an important communication skill. Not only does it help you understand others, but it also provides information for developing strategies about how best to influence people. Empathy is such an

important element of communicative competence that researcher Mark Redmond (1989, p. 594) flatly states, 'By definition, a person cannot produce a message that is empathic that is not also communicatively competent.'

Cognitive Complexity The ability to construct a variety of different frameworks for viewing an issue is what comprises **cognitive complexity**. Imagine that a long-time friend seems to be angry with you. One possible explanation is that she is offended by something you've done. Another possibility is that something has happened in another part of her life that is upsetting. Or perhaps nothing at all is wrong and you're just being overly sensitive. Researchers have found that a large number of constructs for interpreting the behaviour of others leads to greater 'conversational sensitivity', thereby increasing the chances of acting in ways that will produce satisfying results (Burleson and Caplan, 1998; Kline and Chatani, 2001).

Self-Monitoring Psychologists use the term **self-monitoring** to describe the process of paying close attention to one's own behaviour and using these observations to shape the way one behaves. Self-monitors are able to move a part of their consciousness outside of themselves to observe their behaviour from a detached viewpoint. In doing so, they're able to think such thoughts as,

> 'I'm making a fool of myself.'

> 'I'd better speak up now.'

> 'This approach is working well. I'll keep it up.'

It's no surprise that self-monitoring generally increases one's effectiveness as a communicator (Kolb, 1998; Sypher and Sypher, 1983). The ability to ask yourself the question, 'How am I doing?' and to change your behaviour if the answer isn't positive, is a tremendous asset for communicators. People with poor self-monitoring skills often blunder through life, sometimes succeeding and sometimes failing, without the detachment to understand why.

How does your behaviour as an interpersonal communicator measure up against the standards of competence described in this chapter? Like most people, you will probably find some areas of your life that are very satisfying and others that you would like to change. As you read on in this book, realize that the information we provide in each chapter offers advice that can help your communication become more productive and rewarding.

Although the qualities described here do play an important role in communicative competence, they can be ineffective when carried to excess (Spitzberg, 1994). For example, too much self-

monitoring can make a person so self-conscious that the concern for appearance ('How do I sound?' 'How am I doing?') overshadows the need to be faithful to one's true beliefs. Likewise, an excess of empathy and cognitive complexity can lead you to see all sides of an issue so well that you become incapable of acting. In other words, both a deficiency and an excess can lead to incompetent communication.

Summary

Communication is important for a variety of reasons. Besides satisfying practical needs, meaningful communication contributes to physical health, plays a major role in defining our identity, and forms the basis for our social relationships.

Communication is a complex process that can be represented in a communication model. The model we present in this chapter depicts how communicators usually send and receive messages simultaneously. The meaning of these messages resides in the people who exchange them, not in the messages themselves. Environment and noise affect communication, as do the channels we choose for sending our messages.

A variety of principles help explain how communication operates. Communication is transactional—that is, it's a dynamic process that people create through interaction. Messages can be intentional or unintentional, and they almost always have both a content and a relational dimension. Once expressed, messages cannot be withdrawn. Also, communication is unrepeatable.

Interpersonal communication can be defined quantitatively (by the number of people involved) or qualitatively (by the nature of interaction between them). In a qualitative sense, interpersonal relationships are unique, irreplaceable, interdependent, intrinsically rewarding, and usually characterized by self-disclosure. Qualitatively interpersonal communication is relatively infrequent, even in many close relationships. While some research suggests that computer-mediated communication (CMC) is more impersonal than face-to-face communication,

Test Yourself What are the characteristics of a competent communicator?

other research shows that it can enhance interpersonal relationships.

Increasing multiculturalism in Canada and closer, globalized economic connections between Canada and other nations compel us to look at interpersonal communication in the context of cultural diversity. Intercultural communication is the process by which two or more cultures share messages in a manner that is influenced by their different cultural perceptions and symbol systems.

When reviewing interpersonal communication research, it is important to keep in mind that the majority of studies have been conducted in the United States and, although Canadians and their US counterparts are very similar in many respects, they do differ in terms of some significant social values. These include attitudes toward violence, ethnic and cultural diversity, and the relative status of men and women.

To understand the communication process, it is important to recognize and avoid several common misconceptions: Despite the value of self-expression, more communication is not always better than less. In fact, there are times when more communication can make problems worse. Even at its best, communication is not a panacea that will solve every problem. Effective communication is not a natural ability. While some people have greater aptitude at communicating, everyone can learn to interact with others more effectively.

Communication competence is the ability to be both effective and appropriate—that is, to get desired results from others in a manner that maintains the relationship on terms that are acceptable to everyone. There is no single ideal way to communicate: flexibility and adaptability are characteristics of competent communicators, as are skill at performing behaviours, involving oneself with others, empathy and perspective-taking, utilizing cognitive-complexity skills, and self-monitoring. The good news is that communication competence can be learned.

Activities

1. **Invitation to Insight**
   How much time do you spend communicating? Conduct an informal study to answer this question by keeping a two-day log of your activities. Using your findings, answer the following questions:

   a. What percentage of your waking time is spent speaking with and listening to others?

   b. Using the explanation on pages 16–17 of this chapter, describe what percentage of your entire communication is qualitatively interpersonal.

   c. How satisfied are you with your findings? How would you like to change your everyday communication?

2. **Critical Thinking Probe**
   As you have read in this chapter, communication is transactional; it is something we do *with* others and not *to* them. How does face-to-face communication differ from computer-mediated communication, such as email? Are they equally transactional?

3. **Invitation to Insight**
   How competent are you as a communicator? You can begin to answer this question by interviewing people who know you well, such as a family member, friend, or co-worker, for example. Conduct interviews with different people to determine if you are more competent in some relationships than in others.

a. Describe the characteristics of competent communicators outlined on pages 30–3 of this chapter. Be sure your interviewee understands each of them.

b. Ask your interviewee to rate you on each of the observable qualities. (It won't be possible for others to evaluate internal characteristics, such as cognitive complexity and self-monitoring.) Be sure this evaluation considers your communication in a variety of situations, because it's likely you aren't uniformly competent—or incompetent—in all of them.

c. If your rating is not high in one or more areas, discuss with your partner how you could raise it.

d. Consider whether another person might rate you differently. Why might this happen?

4. **Skill Builder**

Knowing how you want to communicate isn't the same as being able to do it competently. The technique of behaviour rehearsal provides a way to improve a particular communication skill before you use it in real life. Behaviour rehearsal consists of four steps:

a. Define your goal. Begin by deciding how you want to behave.

b. Break the goal into the kinds of behaviour it involves. Most goals are made up of several verbal and non-verbal parts. You may be able to define these parts by thinking about them yourself, by observing others, by reading about them, or by asking others for advice.

c. Practise each behaviour before using it in real life. You can practise a new behaviour by rehearsing it alone and then with others before you put it into action. Another approach is to picture yourself behaving in new ways. This mental image can increase your effectiveness.

d. Try out the behaviour in real life. You can improve your chances of success in two ways: First, work on only one subskill at a time, and start with easy situations. Don't expect yourself suddenly to behave flawlessly in the most challenging situations. Second, begin by practising your new skills in situations where you have a chance of success.

Discussion Questions

1. Why do humans communicate? Which reasons are most relevant to you?

2. Why study interpersonal communication? How might you benefit?

3. Think of someone who you believe is an effective interpersonal communicator. Give examples of the characteristics of competent communication that this person demonstrates.

4. Give an example of each of the four communication misconceptions described in Chapter 1. How have these misconceptions affected you?

5. Is it important to consider interpersonal communication in the context of cultural diversity? Why or why not?

Chapter Two

Communication and the Self

After studying the material in this chapter ...

You Should Understand:

1. The influences that shape the development of the self-concept.
2. The subjective, resistant nature of the self-concept.
3. The role of cultural values in shaping the self-concept
4. The role of self-fulfilling prophecies in shaping the self-concept and influencing communication.
5. How it is possible to change one's self-concept.
6. The nature and extent of identity management.

You Should Be Able to Identify:

1. The key elements of your self-concept.
2. The most important forces that have shaped your self-concept.
3. Cultural values that have influenced your identity.
4. Cultural values different from your own that could result in different communication patterns.
5. The influence you have on shaping the self-concept of others.
6. The elements of yourself that you may inaccurately perceive as desirable or undesirable.
7. Any self-fulfilling prophecies that you impose on yourself or on others, and that others impose on you.
8. Steps you can take to change undesirable elements of your self-concept.
9. The differences between your perceived self and various presenting selves.
10. The identity management strategies you use, and the ethical implications of those strategies.

Who are you? Before reading on, take a few minutes to try a simple experiment. First, make a list of the ten words or phrases that describe the most important features of who you are. Some of the items on your list may involve social roles: student, son or daughter, employee, and so on. Or you could define yourself by physical characteristics: fat, skinny, tall, short, beautiful, ugly. You may focus on your intellectual characteristics: smart, stupid, curious, inquisitive. Perhaps you can best define yourself in terms of moods, feelings, or attitudes: optimistic, critical, energetic. Or you could consider your social characteristics: outgoing, shy, defensive. You may see yourself in terms of belief systems: pacifist, Buddhist, vegetarian, Christian, liberal. Finally, you could focus on particular skills (or lack of them): swimmer, artist, carpenter, klutz. In any case, choose ten words or phrases that best describe you, and write them down.

Next, choose the one item from your list that is the most fundamental to who you are, and copy it onto another sheet of paper. Then pick the second-most fundamental item and record it as number two on your new list. Continue ranking the ten items until you have reorganized them all.

Now comes the most interesting part of the experience. Create a mental image of yourself. Try to paint a picture that captures not only your physical characteristics, but also the attitudes, aptitudes, feelings, and beliefs included on your list. Take plenty of time to create this image.

Now, imagine how you would be a different person if the lowest-ranked item on your list were not part of your personality or physical makeup. How would this absence affect the way you act? The way you feel? The way others behave toward you? Was it easy to give up that item? Do you like yourself more or less without it? Take a few minutes with your eyes closed to answer these questions.

Without taking back the item you've just given up, continue your fantasy by removing item number nine. What difference does its absence make for you?

Continue the process by jettisoning one item at a time until you have given them all up. Notice what happens at each step of the process. After you have gone through your entire list, reclaim the items one by one until you are back to where you started.

How do you feel after trying this exercise? Most people find the experience a powerful one. They say that it clarifies how each of the items selected is fundamental to their identity. Many people say that they gain a clear picture of the parts of themselves they value and the parts they are unhappy with.

Communication and the Self-Concept

The way you regard yourself in the exercise you just completed offers clues about your **self-concept**, that is, the relatively stable set of perceptions you hold of yourself. One way to understand the self-concept is to imagine a special mirror that not only reflects physical features, but also allows you to view other aspects of yourself—emotional states, talents, likes, dislikes, values, roles, and so on. The reflection in that mirror would be your self-concept.

Any description of your self-concept that you constructed in this exercise is only a partial one. To make it complete, you would have to keep adding items until your list ran into hundreds of words. Of course, not every dimension of your self-concept list is equally important. For example, the most significant part of one person's self-concept might consist of social roles, whereas for another, it might be physical appearance, health, friendships, accomplishments, or skills.

Self-esteem is the part of the self-concept that involves evaluations of self-worth. A

Take Two

Take Two
• **Self-concept:** the relatively stable set of perceptions you hold of yourself.
• **Self-esteem:** the part of the self-concept that involves evaluations of self-worth.

iStock photo

communicator's self-concept might include being quiet, argumentative, or serious. His or her self-esteem would be determined by how he or she felt about these qualities. High or low self-esteem has a powerful effect on communication behaviour, as Figure 2.1 shows. People who feel good about themselves have positive expectations about how they will communicate (Baldwin and Keelan, 1999). These feelings increase the chance that communication will be successful, and successes contribute to positive self-evaluations, which reinforce self-esteem. Of course, the same principle can work in a negative way with communicators who have low self-esteem.

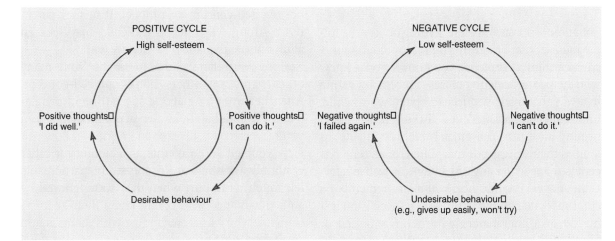

Figure 2.1 The Relationship between Self-Esteem and Communication Behaviour

Source: Adapted from H. M. Johnson (1998), *How Do I Love Me?* (3rd ed.), Salem, WI: Sheffield Publishing Co., 3, 5.

How the Self-Concept Develops

Researchers generally agree that the self-concept does not exist at birth (Rosenblith, 1992). An infant lying in a crib has no notion of self, no notion—even if verbal language were miraculously made available—of how to answer the question, 'Who am I?' At about six or seven months, the child begins to recognize 'self' as distinct from surroundings. If you have ever watched children at this age, you have probably marvelled at how they can stare with great fascination at a foot, hand, and other parts of their body that float into view, almost as if they were strange objects belonging to someone else. Then the connection is made, almost as if the child were realizing, 'The hand is me,' 'The foot is me.' These first revelations form the child's earliest concept of self. At this early stage, the self-concept is almost exclusively physical, involving the child's basic realization of existing and of possessing certain body parts over which he or she exerts some control.

As the child develops, this rudimentary sense of identity expands into a much more complete and sophisticated picture that resembles the self-concept of adults. This evolution is almost totally a product of social interaction (Wachs, 1992). Two complementary theories describe how interaction shapes the way individuals view themselves: **reflected appraisal** and **social comparison** (Burkitt, 1992; Sedikides and Skowronski, 1995).

Reflected Appraisal   Before reading on, try the following exercise. Either by yourself or aloud with a partner, think of someone you know or once knew who helped enhance your self-concept by acting in a way that made you feel accepted, worthwhile, important, appreciated, or loved. This person needn't have played a crucial role in your life, as long as the role was positive. Often, one's self-concept is shaped by many tiny nudges as well as a few giant shoves. For instance, you might remember a childhood neighbour who took a special interest in you or a grandparent who never criticized or questioned your youthful foolishness.

After thinking about this supportive person, think of someone who acted in either a big or small way to diminish your self-esteem. For instance, you may have had a coach who criticized you in front of the team, or a teacher who said or implied that you wouldn't amount to much.

After thinking about these two types of people, you should begin to see that everyone's self-concept is shaped by reflected appraisal—that is, perceptions of the judgments of those around her or him. To the extent that you have received supportive messages, you have learned to appreciate and value yourself. To the extent that you have received critical signals, you are likely to feel less valuable, lovable, and capable (Felson, 1985). Your self-concept can be seen, at least in part, as a product of the messages you've received throughout your life.

Social scientists use the term **significant other** to describe a person whose evaluations are especially influential. Messages from parents, of course, are an early and important influence on the self-concept. Supportive parents are likely to raise children with healthy self-concepts. By contrast, parents with poor, negative, or deviant self-concepts tend to have unhappy children who view themselves in primarily negative ways (Fitts, 1971), communicate less effectively (Huang, 1999), and go on to have unsatisfying relationships (Vangelisti and Crumley, 1998). Interestingly, if one parent has a good self-concept and the other a poor self-concept, the child is most likely to choose the parent with the more positive self-concept as a model. If neither parent has a strong self-concept, the child may seek an adult outside the family to identify with.

Along with family, the messages from many other significant others shape our self-concept. A teacher from long ago, a special friend or relative, or even a barely known acquaintance whom you respected can all leave an imprint on how you view yourself. Who counts as a significant other is not always obvious. In one study, participants felt much more hurt when they were ignored by an acquaintance who barely knew them than by someone who was more familiar with them (Snapp and Leary, 2001).

As we grow older, the power of messages from significant others remains (Voss et al., 1999).

Some social scientists have coined the term 'Michelangelo phenomenon' to describe the way significant others sculpt one another's self-concept (Drigotas, 2002; Drigotas et al., 1999). Romantic partners, people on the job, friends, and many others can speak and act in ways that have a profound effect on the way we view ourselves.

You might argue that not every part of your self-concept is shaped by others, that there are certain objective facts recognizable by self-observation alone. After all, nobody needs to tell you whether you are taller than others, speak with an accent, have curly hair, and so on. These facts are obvious. Indeed, some features of the self are immediately apparent. But the *significance* we attach to them—that is, the rank we assign them in the hierarchy of our list and the interpretation we give them—depends greatly on the opinions of others. After all, many of your features are readily observable, yet you don't find them important at all because nobody has regarded them as important.

Social Comparison   So far, we have looked at the way messages from other people shape the self-concept. In addition to using these messages, each of us forms our self-image by the process of social comparison. In other words, we evaluate ourselves in terms of how we compare with others.

We decide whether we are superior or inferior and similar or different by comparing ourselves to what social scientists call **reference groups**—those people we use to evaluate our own characteristics. You might feel ordinary or inferior in talent, friendships, or attractiveness if you compare yourself with an unsuitable reference group. In one study, young women's perceptions of their bodies changed for the worse after watching just thirty minutes of televised images of the 'ideal' female form (Myers and Biocca, 1992). You will probably never be as handsome or beautiful as certain Hollywood stars, as agile as a professional athlete, or as wealthy as a millionaire. When you consider the matter logically, these facts don't mean you're worthless. Nonetheless, many people judge themselves against unreasonable standards and suffer accordingly (Grodin and Lindolf, 1995). You will

Reflection

Family Comparisons

I'm the second-born son in my family. My older brother has always been a straight-A's student. In high school, he was a one of the top ten students in his graduating class. The teachers always loved him, but I have often felt jealous of his accomplishments. When I used to get mad at him, I'd call him 'Mister Perfect.' I've earned a mixture of A's and B's throughout my school career, which both my family and teachers assured me was just fine. Still, I have been convinced that nobody ever thinks of me as being especially smart, thanks to the comparisons they make with my brother.

University has been the first time that I haven't attended a school where he preceded me. I'm slowly coming to realize that I am a pretty good student. Having the chance to judge myself against other, more normal students is making a big difference in how I regard myself academically.

read more about how to avoid placing perfectionistic demands on yourself in Chapter 4.

One child's experience offers a dramatic example of how reference groups and reflected appraisal can shape identity (Padden and Humphries, 1988). Every member of Howard's immediate family—parents, brother, aunts, and uncles—was deaf. He spent his entire early childhood around deaf people and, in his preschool life, accepted that as the natural state of affairs.

Even as a young child, Howard knew about deafness. The American Sign Language sign for *deaf* was part of his everyday vocabulary. But when he began school, Howard soon discovered that the same sign had a subtle but dramatically different meaning. Among his family, *deaf* meant 'us-people who behave as expected.' But in a mostly hearing world, the same term meant 'a remarkable condition—different from normal.'

This sense of difference can shape the identity of a deaf child, especially in environments where sign language is discouraged in favour of forms of communication that are preferred in the hearing world, such as lip reading and speaking. In such an environment, it's not hard to imagine how the identity, 'I'm deaf' can come to mean 'I'm different,' and then 'I'm deficient.' Howard's physical condition didn't change when he began school, but his sense of himself changed because of the reflected appraisal of his teachers and the broader reference groups he experienced in the hearing world.

At first glance, social comparison theory seems deterministic. Besides being influenced by how others see us, we also are shaped by how we measure up to others. At second glance, however, the concept of social comparison offers a way of reshaping an unsatisfying self-concept.

To some degree, we are in control of whom we choose for comparison. It's possible to seek out people with whom we compare favourably. This technique may bring to mind a search for a community of idiots in which you would appear as a genius, but there are healthier ways of changing your standards for comparison. For instance, you might decide that it's foolish to constantly compare your athletic prowess with professionals or campus stars, your looks with movie idols, and your intelligence with members of Mensa. Once you place yourself alongside a truly representative sample, your self-concept may improve.

In addition to selecting the 'right' group with which to compare yourself, you are free to interpret the behaviour of others in a way that confirms your view of yourself (Hinde et al., 2001). For example, if you view yourself as trustworthy, you can interpret a friend's willingness to lend you money as an indication that she trusts you, thus providing confirmation of your self-concept.

Self-Concept Development in Context

Whose opinions about us matter the most? Which reference groups are available to us for comparison? When we think about how the self-concept develops, we need to consider forces that are larger than our family, friends, and immediate community members. Our identities are shaped by our age and place in history, our sex, our sexual orientation, our physical ability or disability, and our

Test Yourself Describe the processes of reflected appraisal and social comparison in the development of self-concept.

cultural background. These elements create the larger social context in which our self-concepts develop.

Language and Identity Some aspects of culture, such as language, have obvious implications for shaping the way we think and feel about ourselves. If you live in a culture where everyone speaks the same language, then language will have little noticeable impact on how you view yourself and others. But when some members of a society speak the dominant language and others speak a minority tongue, or when that second language is not prestigious, the sense of being a member of an out-group is strong. At this point, the speaker of a non-dominant language can either feel obliged to assimilate by speaking the 'better' language, or refuse to accommodate him- or herself to the majority language and maintain loyalty to the ethnic tongue (Giles et al., 1992c). In either case, the impact of language on the self-concept is powerful. On one hand, the feeling is likely to be, 'I'm not as good as speakers of the native language'; on the other, the belief is, 'There's something unique and worth preserving in my language.'

The issue of language and identity is evident in Canada's diverse multicultural society. It is strongly felt by two groups in particular: First Nations peoples and francophone Canadians. The residential school system for Natives, which was developed in the late nineteenth century and existed until the 1990s, has been implicated in the loss of First Nations languages and culture. These schools separated First Nations children from their families and communities, taught them English or French, and attempted to impart Christian values. First Nations children lost their languages and their traditions. Many Native leaders assert that the loss of indigenous languages has caused Aboriginal peoples to lose their spirits as well.

The loss of hundreds of languages that have already passed into history is an intellectual catastrophe in every way comparable in magnitude to the ecological catastrophe we face today as the earth's tropical forests are swept by fire. Each language still spoken is fundamental to the personal, social, and—a key term in the discourse of indigenous peoples—spiritual identity of its speakers. They know that without these languages they would be less than they are, and they are engaged in the most urgent struggles to protect their linguistic heritage. (Zepeda and Hill, 1991)

Although the federal government has apologized for the atrocities committed by the residential school system, the pain and loss of relationships, culture, and identity remain as a legacy. Only about one-quarter of Canada's North American Indian, Métis, or Inuit peoples know an Aboriginal language well enough to carry on a conversation (Statistics Canada, 2001b, 2006a). There are several programs aimed at helping Canadian First Nations peoples to preserve their languages (First People's Cultural Foundation) and their Aboriginal identities.

The preservation of the French language in Canada, particularly in Quebec, has created considerable controversy over the years. Perhaps the most hotly debated measure was Bill 101. Under this legislation, which was passed in 1977 by the Quebec National Assembly, the only language permitted on commercial signs was French and the right to attend an English-language elementary school was severely restricted. Many Quebeckers

iStock photo

believed that, in order for francophone culture to survive, the French language needed to be protected in an increasingly English-speaking world. Since 1977, several amendments to the legislation have helped to ease some of the tensions between French- and English-speaking Quebeckers. The fight to preserve the French language and culture in Canada continues, and although the majority of English-speaking Canadians appear to believe that French and French culture in Quebec are safe, French-speaking Canadians are less convinced (Jedwab, 2003).

Even the names a culture uses to identify its members reflect its values and shape the way its members relate to one another. When asked to identify themselves, individualistic Canadians, Americans, Australians, and Europeans would probably respond by giving their first name, surname, street, city, and country. Many Asians do it the other way around (Servaes, 1989). If you ask Hindus for their identity, they will give you their caste and village and then their name. The Sanskrit formula for identifying oneself begins with lineage and goes on to state family and house, and ends with one's personal name (Bharti, 1985). The same collectivist orientation is reflected in Chinese written language, where the pronoun *I* looks very similar to the word for *selfish* (Samovar and Porter, 2001). The Japanese language has no equivalent to the English pronoun *I*. Instead, different words are used to refer to oneself depending on the social situation, age, gender, and other social characteristics (Gudykunst, 1993).

Even within a language system, the labels that members of a co-culture use to define themselves can both reflect and help define their sense of identity. In one study, Sharon Boatswain and Richard Lalonde (2000) surveyed 101 Canadian black university students ranging in age from 18 to 50 years to find what labels they preferred and uncover the personal meanings of their preferred labels. Their work was based on a similar US study that found 'black' and 'African American' to be the preferred labels. While 'black' was the most popular first choice in the Canadian study (35 percent of respondents), it was not as strong as in the

United States. The Canadian investigation found far more diversity in preferred labels than did the US study. Respondents chose a total of thirty-five different labels across the three choice preferences (first choice, second choice, and third choice), and twenty different labels were listed as a first preference. The researchers hypothesized that this may be due to Canada's policy of multiculturalism, which encourages Canadians to retain various aspects of their heritage culture. For example, 30 percent of the respondents in the Canadian study referred to a Caribbean country or the West Indies in their primary label preference. The personal meanings respondents gave usually referred to ethnic identity or place of birth. Finally, US studies have found 'African American' to be a clear choice along with 'black', but in the Canadian study, there was little preference for the equivalent—'African Canadian'—perhaps because this term refers to a more distant cultural heritage (Boatswain and Lalonde, 2000).

Cultural Values and Norms

In addition to language, there are several other cultural values that shape our identities. Sometimes, they influence our thoughts, feelings, and perceptions of ourselves and others in ways we may not even be aware of. These include the degree to which a culture values the individual versus the group (individualism versus collectivism), the extent to which a culture accepts unequal distribution of power (power distance), the degree to which members of a culture tolerate ambiguity (uncertainty avoidance), and the extent to which a culture places high value on completion of the task at hand rather than on the process and relationships involved in getting the task done (achievement versus nurturing).

Individualism versus Collectivism

Some cultures value the individual, while others place greater emphasis on the group. Members of an **individualistic culture** view their primary responsibility as helping themselves, whereas communicators in **collectivistic cultures** feel loyalties and obligations to an in-group: a person's extended family, community, or even the organization one works for (Triandis, 1995). Individualistic cultures are also characterized by self-reliance and competition, whereas members of a collectivistic culture are more attentive to and concerned with the opinions of significant others. The consequences of a culture's individualistic-collectivistic orientation are so powerful that some scholars (e.g., Andersen, 1999) have called it the most fundamental dimension of cultural differences.

Among the world's most individualistic countries are the United States, Canada, Australia, and Britain. Latin American and Asian cultures are generally more collectivistic (Hofstede, 1984). Table 2.1 summarizes some differences between individualistic and collectivistic cultures.

Members of individualistic cultures tend to view themselves in terms of what they do, whereas people in collectivistic cultures are more likely to define themselves in terms of membership in an in-group. For instance, members of several cultures were asked to answer the question, 'Who am I?' twenty times (DeAngelis, 1992, October). North Americans were likely to answer by giving individual factors ('I am athletic'; 'I am short'). By contrast, members of more collective societies—Chinese, Filipinos, Japanese, and some South Americans, for example—responded in terms of their relationships with others ('I am a father'; 'I am an employee of _____ Corporation').

Individualistic and collectivistic cultures have very different approaches to handling disagreements. Individualistic societies are relatively tolerant of conflicts and use a direct, solution-oriented approach. By contrast, members of collectivistic cultures are less direct (Cai and Fink, 2002; Ting-Toomey, 1988). Collectivistic societies produce team players, while individualistic ones are far more likely to produce and reward superstars.

The difference between individualistic and collectivistic cultures also shows up in the level of comfort or anxiety their respective members feel when communicating. In societies where the need to conform is great, there is a higher degree of communication apprehension. For example,

Table 2.1 The Self in Individualistic and Collectivist Cultures

Individualistic Cultures	Collectivistic Cultures
Self is a separate, unique individual; should be independent, self-sufficient.	People belong to extended families or in-groups; 'we' or group orientation.
Individual should take care of himself or herself and immediate family.	Person should take care of extended family before self.
Many flexible group memberships; friends based on shared interests and activities.	Emphasis on belonging to a very few permanent in-groups, which have a strong influence over the person.
Reward for individual achievement and initiative; individual decision encouraged; individual credit and blame assigned.	Reward for contribution to group goals and well-being; co-operation with in-group members; group decisions valued; credit and blame shared.
High value on autonomy, change, youth, individual security, equality.	High value on duty, order, tradition, age, group security, status, and hierarchy.

Source: Adapted by Sandra Sudweeks from H. C. Triandis (1990), Cross-cultural studies of individualism and collectivism. In J. Berman (Ed.), *Nebraska Symposium on Motivation* (pp. 41–133). Lincoln, NB: University of Nebraska Press; and E. T. Hall (1959), *Beyond Culture*. New York: Doubleday.

as a group, residents of China, Korea, and Japan exhibit a significantly higher degree of anxiety about speaking out in public than do members of individualistic cultures such as the United States and Australia (Klopf, 1984). It's important to realize that different levels of communication apprehension do not mean that shyness is a 'problem' in some cultures. In fact, just the opposite is true: in these societies, reticence is valued. When the goal is to avoid being 'the nail that sticks out', it's logical to feel nervous when you make yourself appear different by calling attention your way. A self-concept that includes 'assertive' might make a westerner feel proud, but in much of Asia, it would more likely be cause for shame.

Power Distance

The Canadian Charter of Rights and Freedoms states that 'every individual is equal before the law and under the law and has the right to equal protection and equal benefit of the law without discrimination.' For members of democratic societies, this principle of equality is so fundamental that we accept it without question. However, not all cultures share this belief. Some operate on the assumption that certain groups of people (an aristocracy or an economic class, for example) and

some institutions (such as a church or the government) have the right to control the lives of individuals. Geert Hofstede (1984) coined the term **power distance** to describe the degree to which members of a society accept an unequal distribution of power.

Cultures with low power difference believe in minimizing the difference between various social classes. Rich and poor, educated and uneducated groups may still exist, but there is a pervasive belief that one person is as good as another regardless of his or her station in life. Low-power-difference cultures also support the notion that challenging authority is acceptable—even desirable. Citizens are not necessarily punished for raising questions about the status quo. According to Hofstede's research, Canadian and US societies have relatively low power distance, though not the lowest in the world. Austria, Denmark, Israel, and New Zealand proved to be the most egalitarian countries. At the other end of the spectrum are countries with a high degree of power distance: Philippines, Mexico, Venezuela, India, and Singapore.

The degree of power distance in a culture is reflected in key relationships (Lustig and Koester, 1999). Children who are raised in cultures with high power difference are expected to obey their

Reflection

Individuals' and Collectivists' Cultural Values

As a child growing up in a family with strong ties to the Netherlands, I learned that many of our customs and traditions were different from those of my friends at school. I lived in a very multicultural neighbourhood. My friends' cultural heritages included East Asian, South Asian, Caribbean, and southern European. Growing up, I was taught you had to work for everything. Possessions were earned by hard-working individuals. At the age of fifteen, I got my first job so I could pay for my share of the groceries. By the time I was seventeen and in my final year of high school, I was working full-time to support myself. In my family, when you reach seventeen you are considered an adult. As an adult, I was expected to leave the family home and move out on my own. My friends could not believe that my parents would ask me to leave home. They wondered if my parents really loved me. I was hurt that they would think that about my parents. Of course they loved me—they were helping me to be a strong, independent individual. This was a value we held deeply. I see now that our family's values were very much rooted in an individualistic culture. Many of my friends' families' values grew out of more collectivist traditions. Of course, our parents loved us all—their values influenced how they expressed their love to us.

parents and other authority figures to a degree that would astonish most children raised in Canada or the United States. Power automatically comes with age in many countries. For example, the Korean language has separate terms for *older brother*, *oldest brother*, *younger sister*, *youngest sister*, and so on. Parents in cultures with low power distance do not expect the same unquestioning obedience and are not surprised when children ask why when requested or told to do something.

Differences between high- and low-power-distance cultures also show up in school (Yook and Albert, 1998) and at work. In societies that accept high power differences, students and employees are expected to obey their teachers and employers without question. Students are discouraged from asking questions, because that might seem like an attack on the teacher's authority or knowledge. Similarly, employees have much less say about how they do their work. In fact, workers from these cultures are likely to feel uncomfortable when given the freedom to make their own decisions or when a more egalitarian boss asks for their opinion, because they prefer to view their bosses as benevolent decision makers. In contrast, in countries where low power distance is the norm students are more likely to be rewarded for showing initiative and for questioning their teachers and employees expect more of a say in decisions and may feel unappreciated when they are not consulted.

Uncertainty Avoidance

The desire to resolve uncertainty seems to be a trait shared by people around the world (Berger, 1988). While uncertainty may be universal, cultures have

iStock photo

different ways of coping with an unpredictable future. Hofstede (1984) uses the term **uncertainty avoidance** for the degree to which members of a culture feel threatened by ambiguous situations and how much they try to avoid them.

A culture's degree of uncertainty avoidance is reflected in the way its members communicate. In countries that avoid uncertainty, such as Portugal, Belgium, Greece, and Japan, deviant people and ideas are considered dangerous and intolerance is high (Samovar and Porter, 2001). People in these cultures are especially concerned with security, so they have a strong need for clearly defined rules and regulations. It's easy to imagine how most relationships in cultures with a high uncertainty avoidance—family, work, friendships, and romance—are likely to fit a predictable pattern. By contrast, people in a culture that is less threatened by the new and unexpected are more likely to tolerate—or even welcome—people who don't fit the norm. Residents of countries such as Singapore, Britain, Denmark, Sweden, Hong Kong, the United States, and Canada are relatively unthreatened by change. Following established rules and patterns isn't necessarily expected, and different behaviour may even be welcomed.

Achievement versus Nurturing

The term **achievement culture** describes societies that place a high value on material success and a focus on the task at hand, while **nurturing** is a descriptive term for cultures that regard the support of relationships as an especially important goal (Hofstede, 1984). Achievement or 'hard' cultures, which emphasize materialism, include Japan, Switzerland, and Germany. Nurturing or 'soft' cultures include the Scandinavian countries (Norway, Sweden, and Denmark), Spain, and France. Canada is considered a moderately achievement-oriented culture.

The portrait of an effective communicator varies from one type of culture to another. Most notably, achievement-oriented societies prescribe different roles for women and men. In these cultures, male virtues include assertiveness, independence, and individuality. Women who exhibit these traits may

be viewed unfavourably for 'acting like a man'. By contrast, in nurturing societies, there is little difference between the expected behaviour for men and women. The ideal profile for both sexes is one of co-operation, and holding the belief that personal relationships are at least as important as material achievement.

As you think about the cultural values described here, realize that cultural misunderstandings do not occur just between people from different countries. In Canada's increasingly multicultural society, people from different cultural backgrounds are likely to encounter one another 'at home', in the communities they share. Most Canadians have both a 'Canadian' culture to which they belong and one or more cultures that comprise their ethnic heritage. For some people, there is considerable harmony in the values and norms that exist in their co-cultures; for others, there is considerable discord. What we all share is the fact that our cultural values shape our perceptions of ourselves and others. Our cultural values are fundamental to the development of our self-concepts because they are central to what we believe.

Characteristics of the Self-Concept

Now that you have a better idea of how your self-concept has developed, we can take a closer look at some of its characteristics.

The Self-Concept Is Subjective   The way we view ourselves may be at odds with other people's perceptions—and often with the observable facts. For instance, people are notoriously bad judges of their own communication skills. In one study, there was no relationship between the subjects' self-evaluations as interpersonal communicators, public speakers, or listeners and their observed ability to perform well in any of these areas (Carrell and Willmington, 1996). In another study

Test Yourself   List and briefly describe each of the four cultural values that influence the development of the self-concept and interpersonal communication.

(D. Myers, 1980), a random sample of men were asked to rank themselves on their ability to get along with others. Defying mathematical laws, every subject put himself in the top half of the population. Sixty percent rated themselves in the top 10 percent of the population, and an amazing 25 percent believed they were in the top 1 percent. In the same study, 70 percent of the men ranked the quality of their leadership in the top quarter of the population, whereas only 2 percent thought they were below average. Sixty percent said they were in the top quarter in athletic ability, whereas only 6 percent viewed themselves as below average.

There are several reasons why some people have a self-concept that others would regard as unrealistically favourable. First, a self-estimation might be based on **obsolete information**. Perhaps your jokes used to be well received, or your grades were high, or your work was superior, but now the facts have changed. A self-concept might also be excessively favourable because of **distorted feedback** from others. A boss may claim to be an excellent manager because his assistants pour on false praise in order to keep their jobs. A hot-tempered professor's inflated ego may be based on the deference paid to her ideas by her colleagues in order to avoid nasty arguments.

There are also times when we view ourselves more harshly than the facts warrant. We have all experienced a temporary case of the 'uglies', convinced we look much worse than others say that we do. Research confirms what common sense suggests—people are more critical of themselves when they are experiencing these **negative moods** than when they are feeling more positive (Brown and Mankowski, 1993). Although everyone suffers occasional bouts of self-doubt that affect communication, some people suffer from long-term or even permanent states of excessive self-doubt and criticism (Gara et al., 1993). It's easy to understand how this chronic condition can influence the way these people approach and respond to others.

What are the reasons for such excessively negative self-evaluations? As with unrealistically high self-esteem, one source for an overabundance of self-criticism is obsolete information. A string of past failures in school or with social relations can linger to haunt a communicator long after they have occurred. Similarly, we have known slender students who still think of themselves as fat and clear-complexioned people who still behave as if they were acne-ridden.

Low self-esteem can also be caused by distorted feedback. Growing up in an overly critical family is one of the most common causes of a negative self-image. In other cases, the remarks of cruel friends, inconsiderate teachers, excessively demanding employers, or even memorable strangers can have a lasting effect. As we have seen, the impact of significant others and reference groups in forming a self-concept can be huge, and their effect on your self-esteem can be just as great.

iStock photo

Along with obsolete information and distorted feedback, another cause for low self-esteem is the **myth of perfection** that is common in our society. From the time most of us learn to understand language, we are exposed to models who appear to be perfect at whatever they do. This myth is clearest when we examine the stories commonly told to children. In these stories, the hero and heroine are wise, brave, talented, and victorious, whereas villains are totally evil and doomed to failure. This kind of model is easy for a child to understand, but it hardly paints a realistic picture of the world. Unfortunately, many parents perpetuate the myth of perfection by refusing to admit that they are ever mistaken or unfair. Children, of course, accept this perfectionist facade for a long time, not being in a position to dispute the wisdom of such powerful beings. From the behaviour of the adults around them comes a clear message: 'A well-adjusted, successful person has no faults.'

Thus, children learn that in order to gain acceptance they must pretend to 'have it all together', even though they know they haven't. Given this naive belief that everyone else is perfect and the knowledge that you are not, self-esteem will naturally suffer. We will have a great deal to say about perfection and other irrational ideas, both in this chapter and in Chapter 4. In the meantime, don't get the mistaken impression that it's wrong to aim at perfection as an *ideal*. We are suggesting only that you are unlikely to achieve this state, and to expect that you should will certainly lead to unnecessarily low self-esteem.

A final reason people often sell themselves short is also connected to **social expectations**. It is strange that the perfectionistic society we belong to rewards those people who downplay the strengths we demand they possess. We term these people 'modest' and find their behaviour agreeable. On the other hand, we consider some of those who honestly appreciate their own strengths to be braggarts or egotists, confusing them with the people who boast about accomplishments they do not possess (L. C. Miller et al., 1992). This convention leads most of us to talk freely about our shortcomings while downplaying our accomplishments. It's

all right to proclaim that you are miserable if you have failed to do well on a project, but it's boastful to express your pride at a job well done. It's fine to remark that you feel unattractive, but it's egocentric to say that you think you look good.

After a while, we begin to believe the types of statements we repeatedly make. The self-criticism, viewed as modesty, lowers our self-esteem, whereas the strengths and accomplishments go unmentioned and are forgotten. In the end, we see ourselves as much worse than we are.

Self-esteem may be based on inaccurate thinking, but it still has a strong effect on the way we relate to others. Table 2.2 summarizes some important differences between communicators with positive and negative self-esteem. Differences like these make sense when you realize that people who dislike themselves tend to believe that others won't like them either. Realistically or not, they imagine that others are constantly viewing them critically, and they accept these imagined or real criticisms as more proof that they are indeed unlikeable. This low self-esteem is sometimes manifested in hostility toward others, who are seen as perfect, since the communicator takes the approach that the only way to look good is to put others down.

We have been talking about self-esteem as if it were a single feeling, but in fact, you may feel better (or worse) about some parts of your self-concept than others. The Self-Assessment box, on page 51, adapted from questions on the Tennessee Self-Concept Scale (1964; Bishop et al., 1997; Fitts, 1971) provides a more detailed snapshot of your self-evaluation.

A Healthy Self-Concept Is Flexible   People change. From moment to moment, we aren't the same. We wake up in the morning in a jovial mood and have become irritated by lunchtime. We find ourselves fascinated by a conversational topic one moment, and then suddenly lose interest. You might be a relaxed conversationalist with people you know but at a loss for words with strangers. You might be patient when explaining things on the job but have no tolerance for such explanations at home.

Table 2.2 Characteristics of Communicators with Positive and Negative Self-Esteem

Persons with Positive Self-Esteem	Persons with Negative Self-Esteem
1. Are likely to think well of others.	1. Are likely to disapprove of others.
2. Expect to be accepted by others.	2. Expect to be rejected by others.
3. Evaluate their own performance more favourably.	3. Evaluate their own performance less favourably.
4. Perform well when being watched and are not afraid of the reactions of others.	4. Perform poorly when being watched and are sensitive to possible negative reactions.
5. Work harder for people who demand high standards of performance.	5. Work harder for undemanding, less critical people.
6. Are inclined to feel comfortable with others they view as superior in some way.	6. Feel threatened by people they view as superior in some way.
7. Have difficulty defending themselves against others' negative comments; are more easily influenced.	7. Are able to defend themselves against negative comments of others.

Source: Adapted from D. E. Hamachek (1982), *Encounters with Others: Interpersonal Relationships and You.* New York: Holt, Rinehart and Winston.

The self-concepts of most communicators react to these changes ('I'm patient at work;' 'I'm not patient at home'), and these changes affect self-esteem ('I'm not as good a person at home as I am in the office'). Between the ages of fourteen and twenty-three, the self-esteem of about two-thirds of the males in one study increased, while about one-third of the males felt less good about themselves (Block and Robins, 1993). The same study revealed that roughly 57 percent of women in the same age group grew to feel *less* good about themselves, while the self-esteem of the remaining 43 percent increased. After they approach the age of thirty, most people's self-concepts don't change so radically, at least not without a conscious effort, such as psychotherapy (Adler, 1992; van der Meulen, 2001; Zanobini and Usai, 2002).

As we change in these and many other ways, our self-concept must also change in order to stay realistic. An accurate self-portrait today would not be exactly the same as the one we had a year ago, a few months ago, or even yesterday. This does not mean that a person changes radically from day to day. The fundamental characteristics of your personality will stay the same for years, perhaps for a lifetime. However, it is likely that you are changing in other important ways—physically, intellectually, emotionally, and spiritually.

The Self-Concept Resists Change A realistic self-concept should recognize the way we have changed over time, but the tendency to resist revision of our self-perception is strong. Once we fasten onto a self-concept, the tendency is to seek out people who confirm it. Numerous studies (e.g., Bower, 1992; Nicotera, 1993; Swann et al., 1992) show that both university/college students and married couples with high self-esteem seek out partners who view them favourably, whereas those with low self-esteem are more inclined to seek out people who view them unfavourably. This tendency to look for information that conforms to an existing self-concept has been labelled cognitive conservatism (Greenwald, 1995; Kihlstrom and Klein, 1994). Understandably, we are reluctant to revise a favourable self-concept. If you were a thoughtful, romantic partner early in a relationship, it would be hard to admit that you might have become less considerate and attentive lately.

Self-Assessment

How Do You Feel about Yourself?

Indicate the degree to which each item is true or false for you.

If it is completely false, mark the item 1.

If it is mostly false, mark the item 2.

If it is partly false and partly true, mark the item 3.

If it is mostly true, mark the item 4.

If it is completely true, mark the item 5.

1. I am satisfied with my weight.
2. I am satisfied with my appearance.
3. I am satisfied with my height.
4. I am satisfied with my moral behaviour.
5. I am satisfied with the extent to which I am religious.
6. I am satisfied with my relationship with a supreme being.
7. I am satisfied with my family relationships.
8. I am satisfied with how well I understand my family.
9. I am satisfied with how I treat (treated) my parents.
10. I am satisfied with how sociable I am.
11. I am satisfied with the extent to which I try to please others.
12. I am satisfied with the way I treat other people.

SCORING

Add items 1, 2, and 3: This is your *physical self-esteem score*.

Add items 4, 5, and 6: This is your *moral-ethical self-esteem score*.

Add items 7, 8, and 9: This is your *family self-esteem score*.

Add items 10, 11, and 12: This is your *social self-esteem score*.

Scores in any category between 12 and 15 indicate relatively high self-esteem; scores between 3 and 6 indicate relatively low self-esteem; and scores from 7 through 11 indicate moderate self-esteem. Is your self-esteem higher in some areas than others? How are differences in your scores reflected in how you interact with other people?

Likewise, if you used to be a serious student, it isn't easy to admit that you have slacked off.

Curiously, the tendency to cling to an outmoded self-perception holds even when the new image would be more favourable. We can recall literally scores of attractive, intelligent students who would continue to view themselves as the gawky underachievers they were at the beginning of their studies. The tragedy of this sort of cognitive conservatism is obvious. People with unnecessarily negative self-esteem can become their own worst enemies, denying themselves the validation they deserve and need to enjoy satisfying relationships.

Once the self-concept is firmly rooted, only a powerful force can change it. At least four requirements must be met for an appraisal to be regarded as important (Bergner and Holmes, 2000; Gergen, 1971). First of all, the person who offers a particular appraisal must be *someone we see as competent to offer it*. Parents satisfy this requirement extremely well because as young children, we perceive that our parents know so much about us—sometimes

Reflection

Resisting a Change for the Better

Groucho Marx once said he wouldn't join any club that would have him as a member. That's how I've felt about myself most of my life. My self-esteem has been so low that I figured there must be something wrong with anybody who would be romantically interested in me.

Last summer, I met a woman who has me very confused. She's smart, beautiful, funny, and talented. What's more, last month, she told me she loves me. I spent the first week after she popped this news trying to figure out what her flaw was. Just lately, I'm starting to believe that maybe there's nothing wrong with her, and that I could be the kind of guy a woman (besides my mother) could love.

Changing my attitude isn't easy, but I really have to do it. If I keep putting myself down, I could drive this great woman away. Then I'd be left with low self-esteem instead of a once-in-a-lifetime partner.

more than we know about ourselves. Second, *the appraisal must be considered highly personal.* The more the other person seems to know about us and adapts what is being said to fit us, the more likely we are to accept judgments from this person. In addition, the appraisal must be *reasonable in light of what we believe about ourselves.* If an appraisal is similar to one we give ourselves, we will believe it; if it is somewhat dissimilar, we will probably still accept it; but if it is completely dissimilar, we will probably reject it.

Finally, appraisals that are *consistent* and *numerous* are more persuasive than those that contradict usual appraisals or those that occur only once. As long as only a *few* students yawn in class, a teacher can safely disregard them as a reflection of his or her teaching ability. In like manner, you could safely disregard the appraisal of the angry date who tells you in no uncertain terms what kind of person behaves as you did. Of course, when you get a second or third similar appraisal in a short time, the evaluation becomes harder to ignore.

The Self-Fulfilling Prophecy and Communication

The self-concept is such a powerful influence on the personality that it not only determines how you see yourself in the present but also can actually affect your future behaviour and that of others. Such occurrences come about through a phenomenon called the **self-fulfilling prophecy**.

A self-fulfilling prophecy occurs when a person's expectations of an event and her or his subsequent behaviour based on those expectations make the outcome more likely than it would otherwise be. Self-fulfilling prophecies occur all the time, although you may never have given them that label. For example, think of some experiences you may have had:

- You expected to become nervous and botch a job interview and later did so.
- You expected to have a good (or terrible) time at a social event and found your expectations being met.

Take Two

- A boss explained a new task to you, saying that you would probably find it difficult, and indeed you did.

In each of these cases, there is a good chance that the event took place as it did because you predicted that it would. You needn't have botched the interview, the party may have been boring only because you helped make it so, and you might have done better on the job if your boss hadn't spoken up. In other words, what helped make each event happen the way it did was your expectation of things going a certain way.

Types of Self-Fulfilling Prophecies There are two types of self-fulfilling prophecies. *Self-imposed prophecies* are ones that influence your behaviour. You've probably had the experience of waking up in a cross mood and saying to yourself, 'This will be a bad day.' Once you come to such a conclusion, you may act in ways that make it come true. If you avoid the company of others because you expect they have nothing to offer, your suspicions will have been confirmed—nothing exciting or new is likely to happen. On the other hand, if you approach the same day with the idea that it could be a good one, this expectation may well be met. Smile at people, and they're more likely to smile back. Enter a class determined to learn something, and you probably will. In these cases, and other similar ones, your attitude has a great

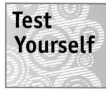

Test Yourself In order for an appraisal to change a firmly rooted self concept, it must meet four requirements. What are they?

deal to do with how you see yourself and how others see you.

Research has demonstrated the power of self-imposed prophecies. In one study, communicators who believed they were incompetent proved less likely than others to pursue rewarding relationships and more likely to sabotage their existing relationships than people who were less critical of themselves (Kolligan, 1990). On the other hand, students who considered themselves capable achieved more academically (Zimmerman, 1995). In another study, subjects who were sensitive to social rejection tended to expect rejection, see it where it may not have existed, and overreact to their exaggerated observations in ways that jeopardized the quality of their relationships (Downey and Feldman, 1996). Research also suggests that when communicators feel anxious about giving speeches, they seem to create self-fulfilling prophecies about doing poorly (MacIntyre and Thivierge, 1995).

A second category of self-fulfilling prophecy is one that governs someone else's actions (Blank, 1993). The classic example was demonstrated by Robert Rosenthal and Lenore Jacobson in a study they described in their book, *Pygmalion in the Classroom* (1968). The experimenters told teachers that 20 percent of the children in a certain elementary school showed unusual potential for intellectual growth. The names of the 20 percent were drawn by means of a table of random numbers—much as if they were drawn out of a hat. Eight months later, these unusual or 'magic' children showed significantly greater gains in IQ than the remaining children, who had not been singled out for the teachers' attention. The change in the teachers' behaviour toward these allegedly 'special' children led to changes in the intellectual performance of the randomly selected children. Among other things, the teachers gave the 'smart' students extra time to answer questions and provided more feedback to them. These children did better, not because they were any more intelligent than their classmates, but because their teachers—significant others—communicated the expectation that they could. In other words, it wasn't just what the teachers *believed* that made a difference; it was how these beliefs were conveyed by the teachers' *behaviour*.

Focus on Research

Smile: It Can Change Your Mood

Most people believe that mood determines behaviour. If you're in a good mood, you smile and laugh; if you're in a bad mood, nothing will make you grin. While there is certainly truth to this notion, researchers Chris Kleinke, Thomas Peterson, and Thomas Rutledge (1998) found the opposite can also be true. Putting a smile on your face, even if you're not in a good mood, can lead to a more positive disposition.

The researchers asked the participants in their study to fill out questionnaires that identified their pre-experiment moods. They were then randomly assigned to one of three groups. In the first group, participants were asked to mimic pictures of people with positive facial expressions. The second group mimicked pictures of people with negative facial expressions; the third group maintained neutral facial expressions while looking at the pictures. At the end of the experiment, the participants were asked to fill out the mood-assessing questionnaire once again.

As predicted, participants who mimicked pictures of smiling people reported more positive moods after engaging in the experiment. Those who mimicked scowls developed more negative moods; those who held neutral facial expressions had little or no change in disposition. This study offers a measure of support for the concept of a self-imposed self-fulfilling prophecy. Acting happy, even if you're not feeling happy, might help you become happy—because behaviour can sometimes determine mood.

To see this phenomenon in relation to the self-concept, we can say that when a teacher communicates to a child the message, 'I think you're bright,' the child accepts that evaluation and changes his or her self-concept to include it. Unfortunately, the same principle holds for students whose teachers send the message, 'I think you're stupid.'

This type of self-fulfilling prophecy has been shown to be a powerful force for shaping the self-concept and, thus, the behaviour of people in a wide range of settings. It isn't just the observer's *belief* that creates a self-fulfilling prophecy for the person who is the target of the expectations. The observer must *communicate that belief* in order for the prediction to have any effect. If parents have faith in their children but the children don't know that, they won't be affected by their parents' expectations. If a boss has doubts about an employee's ability to do a job but keeps them to him- or herself, the subordinate will not be influenced. In this sense, the self-fulfilling prophecies imposed by one person on another are as much a communication phenomenon as a psychological one.

Influence of Self-Fulfilling Prophecies The influence of self-fulfilling prophecies on communication can be strong, acting either to improve or to harm relationships. If you assume that another person is unlikeable, you will probably act in ways that communicate your feelings. In such a case, the other person's behaviour will probably match your expectations, since we usually do not go out of our way to be nice to people who aren't nice to us. If, on the other hand, you treat the other person as likeable, the results will probably be more positive.

The self-fulfilling prophecy operates in families as well. If parents tell a child enough times that she can't do anything right, her self-concept will soon incorporate this idea and she may fail at many or most of the tasks she attempts. On the other hand, if a child is often told he is a capable, lovable, or kind person, there is a much greater chance of his behaving accordingly.

The self-fulfilling prophecy is an important force in interpersonal communication, but we don't want to suggest that it explains all behaviour. There are certainly times when the expectation of an event will not bring it about. Your hope of drawing an ace in a card game will not in any way affect the chance of that card turning up in an already shuffled deck. Nor will your belief that good weather is coming stop the rain from falling. In the same way, believing you'll do well in a job interview, when you're clearly not qualified for the position, is unrealistic. Similarly, there will probably be people in life you don't like and occasions you won't enjoy, no matter what your attitude is. To connect the self-fulfilling prophecy with the 'power of positive thinking' is an oversimplification.

Nevertheless, it is important to recognize the tremendous influence that self-fulfilling prophecies have on our lives. We are what we believe we

"I don't sing because I am happy. I am happy because I sing."

Building Work Skills

The Self-Fulfilling Prophecy

Imagine yourself at work or school. Pretend you have to interact with someone (a customer, colleague, client, supervisor, parent, etc.) who has a reputation for being 'difficult'. If you can't imagine a situation, try one of the scenarios described below.

You are the assistant coach of a soccer team of eight-year-old girls and boys. The mother of a child on your team has left you a voice-mail message to call her back. The last time you saw her, she accused your colleague, the head coach, of playing other children more frequently and not giving her child enough shifts. She claimed the head coach didn't know how to put together a winning team. She didn't say what she wanted to talk to you about in her message.

You work at the returns counter of a major department store. There is a man in line whom you saw a colleague assist last week. At that time, he attempted to return a pair of pants that he had bought a month earlier and had worn and washed. He said he didn't like the style, it didn't suit him, and he wanted a full refund. He yelled at your colleague and accused him of being incompetent when he explained that the store's return policy did not allow such returns. You have to serve this man next.

List the ways in which your prior knowledge of this person might negatively affect your perception of their communication. How might your expectations influence your communication? What could you do to reduce the effects of the self-fulfilling prophecy in this situation?

are, to a great extent. In this sense, we and those around us constantly create our self-concepts and, therefore, ourselves through communication.

Changing Your Self-Concept

You have probably begun to realize that it is possible to change an unsatisfying self-concept. In the next sections, we discuss some methods for making such a change.

Have Realistic Expectations It is important to realize that some of your dissatisfaction might come from expecting too much of yourself. If you demand that you handle every act of communication perfectly, you are bound to be disappointed. Nobody is able to handle every conflict productively, to be totally relaxed and skilful in conversations, to ask perceptive questions all the time, or to be 100 percent helpful when others have problems. Expecting yourself to reach such unrealistic goals is to doom yourself to unhappiness at the start.

It is important to judge yourself in relation to your own growth and not to the accomplishments

of others. Rather than feeling miserable because you are not as talented as an expert, realize that you probably are a better, wiser, or more skilful person than you used to be and that this growth is a legitimate source of satisfaction. Perfection is fine as an ideal, but you are being unfair to yourself if you actually expect to reach it.

Have a Realistic Perception of Yourself One source of low self-esteem is inaccurate self-perception. As you've already read, such unrealistic pictures sometimes come from being overly harsh toward yourself, believing that you're worse than

 Take Two

Self-fulfilling prophecy: occurs when a person's expectations of an event and her or his subsequent behaviour based on those expectations make the outcome more likely than it would otherwise be. Such prophecies can be self-imposed (influenced by your own behaviour) or governed by the behaviour of others.

the facts suggest. Of course, it would be foolish to deny that you could be a better person than you are, but it is also important to recognize your strengths. A periodic session of bragging—acknowledging the parts of yourself that you are pleased with and the ways you've grown—is often a good way to put your strengths and shortcomings into perspective.

Unrealistically low self-esteem can also come from the inaccurate comments by others. Workers with overly critical supervisors, children with cruel 'friends', and students with unhelpful teachers are all prone to suffer from low self-esteem because of excessively negative feedback. If you fall into this category, it's important to put the unrealistic evaluations you receive into perspective and then to seek out supportive people who will acknowledge your assets as well as point out your shortcomings. Doing so is often a quick and sure boost to your self-esteem.

Have the Will to Change   Often, we say we want to change but are not willing to do the necessary work. In such cases, the responsibility for not growing rests squarely on your shoulders. At other times, we maintain an unrealistic self-concept by claiming that we *can't* be the person we'd like to be, when, in fact, we are simply not willing to do what is necessary. You can change in many ways, but only if you are willing to make the effort.

Have the Skill to Change   Trying is often not enough. You also have to know how.

First, you can seek advice—from books such as this one and a variety of other printed sources. You can also get advice from instructors, counsellors, and other experts, as well as from friends. Of course, not all the advice you receive will be useful, but if you read widely and talk to enough people, you will have a good chance of learning the things you want to know.

A second method of learning how to change is to observe models—people who handle themselves in the ways you would like to master. It has often been said that people learn more from models

than in any other way; by taking advantage of this principle, you will find that the world is full of teachers who can show you how to communicate more successfully. Become a careful observer. Watch what people you admire do and say, not so that you can copy them, but so that you can adapt their behaviour to your own personal style.

At this point, you may be overwhelmed by the difficulty of changing the way you think about yourself and the way you act. Remember, no one is saying that this process will be easy (although it sometimes is). But, even when change is difficult, it's possible if you are serious. You don't need to be perfect, but you *can* change your self-concept and raise your self-esteem, and, as a result, your communication—*if you choose to.*

Presenting the Self: Communication as Identity Management

So far, we have described how communication shapes the way communicators view themselves. In the rest of this chapter, we turn the tables and focus on the topic of **identity management**—the communication strategies that people use to influence how others view them. In the following pages, you will see that many of our messages are aimed at creating certain impressions.

Public and Private Selves

To understand why identity management exists, we have to discuss the notion of self in more detail. So far, we have referred to the self as if each of us had only one identity. In truth, however, each of us possesses several selves, some private and others public. These selves are often quite different.

The **perceived self** is the person you believe yourself to be in moments of honest self-examination. The perceived self may not be accurate in every respect. For example, you may think you are much more (or less) intelligent than an objective test would suggest. Accurate or not, the perceived self is powerful because we believe it reflects who we are. The perceived self is called 'private' because you are unlikely to reveal all of it to another person. You can verify the private nature of the perceived self by thinking of elements of your self-perception that you would not disclose. For example, you might be reluctant to share some feelings about your appearance ('I think I'm rather unattractive'), your goals ('The most important thing to me is becoming rich'), or your motives ('I care more about myself than about others').

In contrast to the perceived self, the **presenting self** is a public image—the way we want to appear to others. In most cases, the presenting self we seek to create is a socially approved image: diligent student, loving partner, conscientious worker, loyal friend, and so on. Sociologist Erving Goffman (1959, 1971) used the word **face** to describe this socially approved identity, and he coined the term **facework** to describe

Take Two

- **Perceived self:** the person you believe yourself to be in moments of honest self-examination.
- **Presenting self:** a public image, the way you want to appear to others.
- **Face:** your socially approved identity.
- **Facework:** the verbal and non-verbal ways in which you act to maintain your own presenting image and the images of others.

the verbal and non-verbal ways in which we act to maintain our own presenting image and the images of others. He argued that each of us can be viewed both as a kind of playwright who creates roles that we want others to believe and as the performer who acts out those roles. Goffman suggested that each of us maintains face by putting on a *front* when we are around others whom we want to impress. In contrast, behaviour in the *back region*—when we are alone—may be quite different. You can recognize the difference between public and backstage behaviour by remembering a time when you observed a driver, alone in his or her car, behaving in ways that would never be acceptable in public. All of us engage in backstage ways of acting that we would never exhibit in front of others. Just think about how you behave in front of the bathroom mirror when the door is locked, and you will appreciate the difference between public and private

iStock photo

iStock photo

behaviour. If you knew someone was watching, would you behave differently?

Characteristics of Identity Management

Now that you have a sense of what identity management is, we can look at some characteristics of this process.

We Strive to Construct Multiple Identities

It is an oversimplification to suggest we use identity-management strategies to create just one identity. In the course of even a single day, most people play a variety of roles: 'respectful student', 'joking friend', 'friendly neighbour', and 'helpful co-worker', to suggest just a few. We even play a variety of roles around the same person. As you grew up, you almost certainly changed characters as you interacted with your parents. In one situation, you acted as the responsible adult ('You can trust me with the car') and at another time, you were the helpless child ('I can't find my socks!'). At some times—perhaps on birthdays or holidays—you were a dedicated family member, and at other times, you may have played the role of rebel. Likewise, in romantic relationships, we switch among many ways of behaving, depending on the context: friend, lover, business partner, scolding critic, apologetic child, and so on.

The ability to construct multiple identities is one element of communication competence. For example, the style of speaking or even the language itself can reflect a choice about how to construct one's identity. Many bilingual Haitians living in Montreal understand this principle and often choose whether to use English or French, depending on the kind of identity they are seeking in a given conversation (Baker, 2001).

Identity Management Is Collaborative

As we perform like actors trying to create a front, our 'audience' is made up of other actors who are trying to create their own characters. Identity-related communication is a kind of process theatre in which we improvise scenes where our character reacts with others.

You can appreciate the collaborative nature of identity management by thinking about how you might complain to a friend or family member who has failed to pass along a phone message that arrived while you were away from home. Suppose that you decide to raise the issue tactfully in an effort to avoid seeming like a nag (desired role for yourself: 'nice person'), and also to save the other person from the embarrassment of being confronted (hoping to avoid suggesting that the other person's role is 'screw-up'). If your tactful bid is accepted, the dialogue might sound like this:

You: By the way, Beena told me she called yesterday. If you wrote a note, I guess I missed seeing it.

Other: Oh . . . sorry. I meant to write a note, but as soon as I hung up, the doorbell rang, and then I had to run off to class.

You (in friendly tone of voice): That's okay. I sure would appreciate from now on if you'd leave me a note.

Other: No problem.

In this upbeat conversation, both you and the other person accepted one another's bids for identity as basically thoughtful people. As a result, the conversation ran smoothly. Imagine, though, how differently the outcome would be if the other person didn't accept your role as 'thoughtful person':

You: By the way, Beena told me she called yesterday. If you wrote a note, I guess I missed seeing it.

Other (defensively): Okay, so I forgot. It's not that big a deal. You're not perfect yourself, you know!

Your first bid as 'nice, face-saving person' was rejected. At this point, you have the choice of persisting in trying to play the original role: 'Hey, I'm not mad at you, and I know I'm not perfect!' Or, you might switch to the new role of 'unjustly accused person', responding in an agitated manner: 'I never said I was perfect. But we're not talking about me here. . . .'

Focus on Technology

Online and On-ground Worlds, Sociability, and Identity Exploration

There has been a great deal of thinking and theorizing recently about the influence of the Internet and online communication on the concept of self, sociability, and identity development (Ellison et al., 2007; Gross, 2004; Lange, 2007; Hussain and Griffiths, 2008; Maczewski, 2002; Matsuba, 2006; Stefanone and Jang, 2007; Valkenburg et al., 2005). Some theorists suggest that computer-mediated communication, or CMC, can potentially have a negative effect on people's sociability (Kraut, et al., 1998; Nie and Hillygus, 2002); however, other researchers in both Canada and the United States suggest that the Internet, for the most part, adds to or extends personal and telephone contact (Birnie and Horvath, 2002; Pronovost, 2002; Veenhof, 2006; Wellman et al., 2002;). The majority of online communication, such as email and instant messages, takes place in private settings, among friends and family members who are part of our daily lives offline (Boase et al., 2006; Gross, 2004). Another issue regarding the Internet that is particularly relevant to the concept of self is the idea that cyberspace encompasses another 'virtual' world, in which people can create identities and initiate contact with people who are totally unrelated to their identities and relationships in the real world. The majority of research conducted to date does not fully support this idea. Social network researcher Barry Wellman (1999) and sociologist Manuel Castells (2001) document that the Internet is just one of the many tools people use to interact with others in their daily lives. The *online* world is really the 'world online'. In his philosophical exploration of the self and Internet-mediated communication, Marcelo Vieta (2004) argues that it is more useful to conceptualize the self-concept as the *interactional self*, which is 'in a constant state of interpretation of itself and its world, practically using the world online and offline as a conduit to communicate with others for self understanding' (p. 7).

Use of online communication for identity experiments designed to explore self-concept is relatively common in adolescents (Valkenburg et al., 2005). Mechthild Maczewski (2002) of the University of Victoria conducted an exploration of youth identity exploration through the Internet. Maczewski suggests that the anonymity, connectivity, and interactivity of cyberspace provide youth with unique opportunities to explore multiple identities. Because physical and local identities can be hidden in online spaces, youth could conceptualize multiple identities and interact with diverse groups of people—as well as engage in roles they might not be provided with in their 'on-ground' lives. The youth who participated in Maczewski's study described the Internet as a space of their own where they were able to connect with people they felt they could really talk to and engage in similar interests with. One participant, despite being a teenager, was given a promotion in her online job that allowed her to supervise a chat room; this experience helped her develop confidence, skills, and self-awareness that would have been difficult to attain in her on-ground life. The youth in Maczewski's study reported that their online relationships reduced their sense of isolation and expanded their consciousness.

Nicole Ellison (2007) and her colleagues at Michigan State University have been exploring the use of Facebook on students' overall mental health. She suggests that the interactions facilitated by Facebook and other social-networking websites have a positive impact on students' well-being. She argues that even if the connections people make with others on the Internet are considered 'weak ties', they can still be significant. Weak ties, contacts who are not friends or family members, can provide new perspectives and opportunities that students might not get from close relationships. For example, Patricia Lange (2007) of the University of Southern California suggests that YouTube's video-sharing and commenting features provide individuals with opportunities to project identities that match up with particular social groups.

Clearly, CMC provides people with additional opportunities to communicate with others and better explore and understand themselves.

As this example illustrates, collaboration doesn't mean the same thing as agreement (Stewart and Logan, 1998). The small issue of the phone message might mushroom into a fight where you and the other person both adopt the roles of combatants. The point here is that virtually all conversations provide an arena in which communicators construct their identities in response to the behaviour

Reflection

Multiple Me's

An assignment in my English class showed me how much I change my identity in different relationships. We had to write letters to two different people describing how we were doing in life. I wrote the first one to my grandmother, and the other to my best friend. I was amazed at the difference between the two. I was much more positive and superficial with my grandma. I talked about events—school, work, and what I was doing with other members of our family. When writing to my friend, I talked about my non-family relationships and shared a lot of information that would probably have shocked and confused my grandmother. I also used entirely different writing styles—very formal with my grandmother, lots of slang with my friend.

This assignment helped me realize that I show different sides of myself to different people. It's not that I lie to anybody. It's just that I have different identities in different relationships.

of others. As we saw in Chapter 1, communication is not made up of discrete events that can be separated from one another. Instead, what happens at one moment is influenced by what each communicator brings to the interaction and by what had happened in their relationship up to that point.

Identity Management Can Be Deliberate or Unconscious   There's no doubt that sometimes we are highly aware of managing the impressions we create. Most job interviews and first dates are clear examples of deliberate identity management. But in other cases, we unconsciously act in ways that are really small public performances. For example, experimental subjects expressed facial disgust in reaction to eating sandwiches laced with a supersaturated solution of salt water only when there was another person present; when they were alone, they made no faces upon eating the same snack (Brightman et al., 1975). Another study showed that communicators engage in facial

mimicry (such as smiling or looking sympathetic in response to another's message) only in face-to-face settings, when their expressions can be seen by the other person. When they are speaking over the phone and their reactions cannot be seen, they do not make the same expressions (Chovil, 1991). Studies like these suggest that most of our behaviour is aimed at sending messages to others—in other words, identity management. Facework is even influenced by culture: Dorothea Hamdorf (2003) found that professionals from a wide variety of countries managed their identities differently in conflicts.

You can see by now that much identity management is unconscious. The experimental subjects described by Brightman and colleagues didn't consciously think, 'Somebody is watching me eat this salty sandwich so I'll make a face' or 'Since I'm in a face-to-face conversation, I'll show I'm sympathetic by mimicking the facial expressions of my conversational partner.' Decisions like these are often made instantaneously and outside of our conscious awareness.

Despite the claims of some theorists, it seems an exaggeration to suggest that *all* behaviour is aimed at making impressions. Young children are certainly not strategic communicators. A baby spontaneously laughs when she is pleased and

Reflection

Laughing Out Loud as Self-Presentation

I've noticed lately that I often laugh at a movie or TV show as a signal to someone else in the room—as a way of saying, 'Now that's funny!' In fact, I'll sometimes laugh loudly when someone is in another room as a way of saying, 'Something really funny is going on in here.' When I'm alone in the house, I don't laugh out loud nearly as often. I guess my laughter is as much about my presenting self as it is about a humorous reaction.

If I find myself laughing out loud when no one is around, then I know what I'm laughing at is really funny!

cries when she is sad or uncomfortable, without any notion of creating an impression on others. Likewise, there are almost certainly times when we as adults act spontaneously. But when a significant other questions the presenting self that we offer up, the likelihood of our acting to 'improve' it increases. This process isn't always conscious: at an unconscious level of awareness, we monitor other people's reactions, and we swing into action when our face is threatened—especially by significant others (Leary and Kowalski, 1990).

People Differ in Their Degree of Identity Management   Some people are much more aware of their identity-management behaviour than others (Kopp, 1988; Snyder, 1979). These high self-monitors have the ability to pay attention to their own behaviour and the reactions of others, adjusting their communication to create the desired impression. By contrast, low self-monitors express what they are thinking and feeling without paying much attention to the impression they create.

There are certainly advantages to being a high self-monitor (Hamachek, 1992). People who pay attention to themselves are generally good actors who can create the impression they want, acting interested when they are bored or friendly when they really feel quite the opposite. This allows them to handle social situations smoothly, often putting others at ease. They are also good 'people readers' who can adjust their behaviour to get the desired reaction from others. Along with these advantages, there can be drawbacks to being an extremely high self-monitor. Their analytical nature may prevent them from experiencing events completely, since part of their attention will always be taken up with viewing the situation from a detached position. High self-monitors' ability to act makes it difficult to tell how they are really feeling. In fact, because high self-monitors change roles often, they may have a hard time *themselves* knowing how they really feel. People who score low on the self-monitoring scale live life quite differently from their more self-conscious counterparts. They have a simpler, more focused idea of who they are and who they want to be. Since low self-monitors are

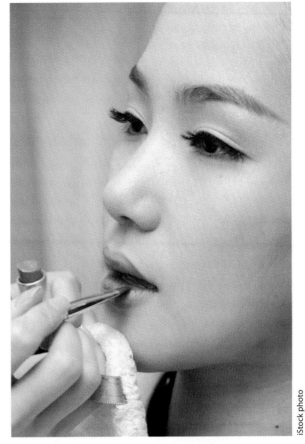

iStock photo

likely to have a narrower repertoire of behaviours, they can be expected to act in more or less the same way regardless of the situation. This means that low self-monitors are easier to read than high self-monitors. 'What you see is what you get' might be their motto. While this lack of flexibility may make their social interaction less smooth in many situations, low self-monitors can be counted on to be straightforward communicators.

By now, it should be clear that neither extremely high nor low self-monitoring is the ideal. There are some situations when paying attention to yourself and adapting your behaviour can be useful, and other times when reacting without considering the effect on others is a better approach. This need for a range of behaviour demonstrates once again the notion of communicative competence outlined in Chapter 1—flexibility is the key to successful relationships.

Why Manage Impressions?

Why bother trying to shape the opinions of others? Sometimes, we create and maintain a front to follow social rules. As children, we learn to act politely, even when we are bored. In fact, part of growing up consists of acquiring a set of manners for various occasions, such as meeting strangers, attending school, and going to church. Young children who haven't learned all the dos and don'ts of polite society often embarrass their parents with their behaviour ('Mommy, why is that man so fat?'), but by the time they enter school, behaviour that may previously have been excusable or even amusing just isn't acceptable. Good manners are often intended to make other people more comfortable. For example, able-bodied people often hide their discomfort upon encountering someone who is disabled by acting nonchalantly or stressing the similarities between themselves and the disabled person (Coleman and DePaulo, 1991).

Social rules govern our behaviour in a variety of settings. For example, it would be impossible to keep a job without meeting certain expectations. Salespeople are supposed to treat customers with courtesy. Employees need to appear reasonably respectful when talking to the boss. Some forms of clothing would be considered outrageous at work. By agreeing to take on a job, you are signing an unwritten contract that dictates you will present a certain face at work, whether or not that face reflects the way you might be feeling at a particular moment.

Even when social roles do not dictate the proper way to behave, we often manage the impression we create for personal reasons. You might, for example, dress up for a visit to traffic court in the hope that your front (responsible citizen) will persuade the judge to treat you sympathetically. You might be sociable to your neighbours so they will agree to your request that they keep their dog off your lawn.

Identity management sometimes aims at achieving relational goals. For instance, you might act in a more friendly and lively way than you feel when you meet someone new so that you will appear likeable. You could sigh and roll your eyes when

arguing politics with a classmate to gain an advantage in an argument. You might smile and preen to show the attractive stranger at a party that you would like to get better acquainted. In situations like these, you aren't being deceptive as much as 'putting your best foot forward'.

All these examples show that it is difficult—perhaps even impossible—*not* to create impressions. After all, you have to send some sort of message. If you don't appear friendly when you meet a stranger, you have to appear aloof, indifferent, hostile, or so on. If you don't act in a businesslike way, you have to act in a different way: casually or jokingly, for example. Often, the question isn't whether or not to present a face to others, but which face to present.

How Do We Manage Impressions?

How do we create a public face? In our technological age, which provides many options for communicating, the answer depends in part on the communication channel chosen.

Face-to-Face Identity Management   In face-to-face interaction, communicators can manage their front in three ways: with their manner, their appearance, and the setting. *Manner* consists of a communicator's words and non-verbal actions. Your manner plays a major role in shaping how others view you. In Chapters 5 and 6, we describe in detail how words and non-verbal behaviour create impressions. Since you *have* to speak and act, the question is not whether or not your manner sends a message; rather, it's whether or not these messages will be intentional.

Along with manner, a second dimension of identity management is *appearance*—the personal items people use to shape an image. Sometimes, appearance is part of creating a professional image. A physician's white lab coat and a police officer's uniform set the wearer apart as someone special.

A tailored suit or a rumpled outfit creates a very different impression in the business world. Off the job, clothing is just as important. We choose clothing that sends a message about ourselves: 'I'm stylish', 'I'm sexy', 'I'm athletic', and a host of other possible messages.

A final way to manage impressions is through the choice of *setting*—physical items we use to influence how others view us. In the car culture of modern Western society, the automobile is a large part of identity management. This explains why many people lust after cars that are far more expensive and powerful than they really need. A sporty convertible or fancy imported sedan doesn't just get a driver from one place to another; it also makes a statement about the kind of person he or she is. The physical setting we choose and the way we arrange it is another important way to manage impressions. What colours do you choose for the place you live? What artwork is on your walls? What music do you play? If possible, we choose a setting that we enjoy, but in many cases, we create an environment that will present the desired front to others. If you doubt this fact, just remember the last time you straightened up the house before important guests arrived. Backstage, you might be comfortable with a messy place, but your public front—at least to some people—is quite different.

Identity Management in Mediated Communication Most of the preceding examples involve face-to-face interaction, but identity management is just as pervasive and important in other types of communication. Consider the care you probably take when drafting a resumé for a potential employer, a thank-you letter in response to a gift, or a love note to a sweetheart. Besides giving careful thought to the wording of your message, you probably make strategic decisions about its appearance. Will you use plain white paper or something more distinctive? Will you type your words or write them out by hand? People think carefully about considerations like these because they instinctively know that the *way* a message is presented can say as much as the words it contains.

At first glance, the technology of computer-mediated communication (CMC) seems to limit the potential for identity management. Instant messaging and email, for example, appear to lack the 'richness' of other channels. They don't convey the tone of your voice, posture, gestures, or facial expression. Recently, though, communication scholars have begun to recognize that what is missing in CMC can actually be an *advantage* for communicators who want to manage the impressions they make.

When sending a message via email or instant messaging, people can choose their level of clarity or ambiguity, seriousness or humour, logic or emotion. Unlike face-to-face communication, electronic correspondence allows a sender to say difficult things without forcing the receiver to respond immediately, and it permits the receiver to ignore a message rather than give an unpleasant response. Options like these show that CMC can serve as a tool for identity management at least as well as face-to-face communication (Walther, 1996). In one survey, 27 percent of respondents had engaged in deceptive behaviours while online, such as lying and sex switching, and over half of US teenage Internet users say they have used more than one email address or instant-messaging screen name (Lenhart et al., 2001). A quarter of teens have pretended to be a different

"I loved your E-mail, but I thought you'd be older."

Focus on Research

Identity Management through Anonymity

In today's wired world, 'virtual group' members can communicate by computer without ever meeting in person. Along with their communicative efficiency, virtual groups give members a chance to control what personal information they reveal—or do not reveal—to one another.

A team of researchers led by Andrew Flanagin (2002) wanted to know if women guard their anonymity more carefully than men do in computer-mediated groups. The researchers monitored third- and fourth-year college students who were assigned tasks in anonymous,

computerized work groups. They found that women were, indeed, more cautious about giving out information that might identify their sex, while men were quick to offer sex-identifying clues about themselves. The women said that their contributions were accepted more readily in anonymous interaction than they would have been in face-to-face group work.

Previous research had shown that 'women in face-to-face groups are often at a disadvantage in relation to men, and are therefore less positive about communicating' (Flanagin et al., 2002). Thus, anonymous communication by computer can help women level the playing field, allowing them to manage their identities to their best advantage.

---

person online, and a third confess to having given false information about themselves while emailing and instant messaging. Statistics like these might be surprising until you consider some legitimate reasons why a teen or an adult may manage his or her online identity, such as to protect privacy and maintain physical safety.

Like email and instant messaging, personal profiles on social-networking sites, blogs, and personal websites allow their creators to manage their identities. Some observers have pointed out that the construction of these personal sites involves much more than what appears on the computer screen, and that people are also constructing their public identities (Chandler, 1998). The words, images, and sounds that people choose make a statement about who they are—or at least how they want to be regarded by others.

People who construct personal websites, enter the blogosphere, and so on create identity both by what they *include* and what they *exclude* from their homepage. Consider how featuring or withholding the following kinds of information affects how people might regard the creator of a personal profile or homepage: age, photo, educational or career accomplishments, sexual orientation, job title, interests, personal philosophy and religious beliefs, and organizations to which the page

creator belongs. You can easily think of a host of other kinds of material that could be included or excluded, and the effect that each would have on how others regard the page creator.

Communicators who want to manage impressions don't always prefer computer-mediated channels. People are generally comfortable with face-to-face interaction when they feel confident that others support the image they want to present. On the other hand, they are more likely to prefer mediated channels when their own self-presentation is threatened (O'Sullivan, 2000). See the accompanying Focus on Research box for an example of this principle in action.

Identity Management and Honesty

At first, identity management might sound like an academic label for manipulation or phoniness. And there certainly are situations where impression management is dishonest. A manipulative date who pretends to be affectionate or thoughtful in order to gain sexual favours is clearly unethical

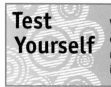

Test Yourself   What are the advantages and disadvantages of mediated communication when partaking in identity management?

and deceitful. So are job applicants who lie about their academic record to get hired or salespeople who pretend to be dedicated to customer service when their real goal is to make a quick buck. Joseph Walther (1996) reports 'the strange case of the electronic lover,' in which a man on a computer bulletin board misrepresented himself as a female therapist named Joan to women who were seeking counselling.

But not all cases of identity management are so clearly wrong. In a job interview, is it legitimate to appear more confident and reasonable than you really feel? Likewise, are you justified in being more attentive than you feel like being in a boring conversation out of courtesy to the other person? Situations like these suggest that managing impressions doesn't necessarily make you a liar. In fact, it is almost impossible to imagine how we could communicate effectively without making decisions about which front to present in one situation or another. It would be ludicrous to act the same way with strangers as you do with close friends, and nobody would show the same face to a two-year-old as he or she would to an adult. Each of us has a repertoire of faces—a cast of characters—and part of being a competent communicator is to choose the best role for a situation.

It is an oversimplification to say that there is only one honest way to behave in each circumstance and that every other response would be insincere and dishonest. Instead, identity management involves deciding which face—which part of yourself—to reveal. Which face to show to others is an important decision, but, in any case, you are sharing a real part of yourself.

Summary

The self-concept is a relatively stable set of views that people hold about themselves. It begins to develop soon after birth, being shaped by the appraisals of significant others and by social comparisons with reference groups. The self-concept develops in the context of the larger social-cultural environment. Language affects the development of our self-concepts, as do a number of fundamental values. These values include individualism versus collectivism, high or low power distance, more or less avoidance of uncertainty, and either achievement or nurturing. The self-concept is subjective and can be substantially different from the way a person is perceived by others. Although the self may evolve, the self-concept resists change.

A self-fulfilling prophecy occurs when a person's expectations of an event influence the outcome. A prophecy can consist of predictions by others, or it may be self-imposed. Self-fulfilling prophecies can be both positive and negative.

It is possible to change one's self-concept in ways that lead to more effective communication. It is necessary to have realistic expectations about how much change is possible and to begin with a realistic assessment of oneself. Willingness to make the effort to change is important, and, in some cases, change requires new information or a new skill.

Identity management consists of an individual's strategic communication designed to influence other people's perceptions of her- or himself. Identity management aims at presenting one or more faces to others, which may be different from the spontaneous behaviour that takes place in private. Some communicators are high self-monitors who are very conscious of their own behaviour, while others are less aware of how their words and actions affect others.

Identity management occurs for two reasons: In many cases, it is based on adherence to social rules and conventions. At other times, it aims at achieving a variety of content and relational goals. In either case, communicators deliberately create impressions by managing their manner and appearance, along with the settings in which they interact with others. Communicating through mediated channels can enhance a person's ability to manage impressions. Although identity management might seem manipulative, it can be an authentic form of communication. Since each person has a variety of faces that she or he can reveal, choosing which one to present is a central concern of competent communicators.

Activities

1. **Invitation to Insight: Ethical Challenge**
   Choose someone with whom you have an important interpersonal relationship, and explore how you influence each other's self-concepts.

   a. Interview your partner to discover how your words and actions influence his or her self-concept. Refer to specific incidents to illustrate these influences, and discuss which specific parts of the self-concept you have affected.
   b. Now, tell your partner how his or her behaviour has affected your self-concept. Again, be specific about the incidents and the parts of your self-concept that were affected.
   c. Once you recognize the power you have to shape another's self-concept, ask yourselves what responsibility each of you has to treat the other person in a supportive manner when you have to deliver a critical message.
   d. Using the information exchanged so far, discuss whether you are satisfied with the way you have affected each other's self-concepts. Decide how you could communicate more effectively.

2. **Invitation to Insight**
   What reference groups do you use to define your self-concept? You can recognize your social comparison groups by answering several questions:

   a. Select one area in which you compare yourself to others. In what area is the comparison made? (For example, is the comparison based on wealth, intelligence, social skill?)
   b. In the selected area, ask yourself, 'Which people am I better or worse than?'
   c. In the selected area, ask yourself, 'Which people am I the same as or different from?'

   What is the effect of using these groups as a basis for judging yourself? How might you view yourself differently if you used other reference groups as a basis for comparison?

3. **Critical Thinking Probe**
   What social forces affect the development of self-concept in childhood and beyond? To what degree do these forces contribute to healthy or unhealthy self-concepts? Use three specific messages to illustrate your answers. Then, discuss how individuals can reduce the effect of unhealthy forces in their everyday lives.

4. **Invitation to Insight**
   Describe two incidents in which self-fulfilling prophecies you have imposed on yourself have affected your communication. Explain how each of these predictions shaped your behaviour, and describe how you might have behaved differently if you had made a different prediction. Next, describe two incidents in which you imposed self-fulfilling prophecies on others. What effect did your prediction have on these people's actions?

5. **Skill Builder**
   Describe one communication-related part of your self-concept you would like to change. Use the guidelines on pages 55–6 to describe how you could make that change.
   a. Decide whether your expectations for change are realistic. Don't expect to become a new person; it should be enough to become a better one.

b. Recognize your strengths as well as your shortcomings. You may not be as bad as you think you are!

c. Decide whether you are willing to make the necessary effort to change. Good intentions are an important start, but hard work is also necessary.

d. Develop a specific plan to change the way you behave. You may want to consult books and experts as well as observe models to gain a clear idea of your new goals and how to achieve them.

6. **Ethical Challenge**

You can gain a clearer sense of the ethical implications of impression management by following these directions:

a. Make a list of the different presenting selves you try to communicate at school or work, to family members, to friends, and to various types of strangers—in either face-to-face communication or by computer-mediated communication.

b. Which of these selves are honest, and which are deceptive?

c. Are any deceptive impressions you try to create justified? What would be the consequences of being completely candid in the situations you have described?

Referring to your answers to these questions, develop a set of guidelines to distinguish ethical and unethical impression management.

7. **Role Play**

With a partner, imagine yourselves in each of the following situations, choose your respective parts in each scenario and then choose the most effective way you could act. Role-play your choices.

•   You offer to teach a friend a new skill, such as playing the guitar, using a computer program, or sharpening up a tennis backhand. Your friend is making slow progress, and you find yourself growing impatient.

•   At a party, you meet someone you find very attractive, and you are pretty sure that the feeling is mutual. On the one hand, you feel an obligation to spend most of your time with the person you came with, but the opportunity here is very appealing.

•   At work, you face a belligerent customer. You don't believe that anyone has the right to treat you this way.

•   A friend or family member makes a joke about your appearance that hurts your feelings. You aren't sure whether or not to make an issue of the remark or to pretend that it doesn't bother you.

Discussion Questions

1. What is the difference between *self-concept* and *self-esteem*? How do they affect interpersonal communication?

2. Is language important in the development of one's self-concept? Why or why not?

3. How does the federal government's policy of multiculturalism affect the development of self-concept among Canadians?

4. Given the characteristics of self-concept, how amenable is it to change? Support your position by referring both to the characteristics of the self-concept and to the guidelines for changing the self-concept.

5. Where do you draw the line between identity management as competent communication and dishonest manipulation? Support your position by referring to arguments presented in this chapter.

Chapter Three

Perceiving Others

After studying the material in this chapter ...

You Should Understand:

1. How the processes of selection, organization, interpretation, and negotiation affect a communicator's perception of others.
2. How physiological, psychological, social, and cultural factors lead communicators to perceive one another and other phenomena differently.
3. The common tendencies in perception that can sometimes lead to misperceptions.
4. The value of empathy in interpersonal communication and relationships.

You Should Be Able To:

1. Describe the factors that shape your perceptions of important people and events, and explain how these and other factors could lead another person to perceive the same people and events differently.
2. Describe an interpersonal issue from the other person's point of view, showing how and why the other person experiences the issue differently.
3. Use perception checking to clarify your understanding of another person's point of view.

'Look at it my way. . . .'
'Put yourself in my shoes. . . .'
'YOU DON'T UNDERSTAND ME!'

Statements like these reflect one of the most common communication challenges. We can talk to (or at) one another until we're hoarse and exhausted, yet we still do not really understand one another. In fact, research has found that typical dyads can interpret and explain only 25 to 50 percent of each other's behaviour accurately (Spitzberg, 1994), and that spouses consistently overestimate the degree to which they agree with their partners (Sillars et al., 1992). Some communication scholars (e.g., Eisenberg and Goodall, 2001) have suggested that complete understanding could lead to more disagreement and dissatisfaction, not smoother relationships. Nonetheless, failing to share each other's view of the world can leave us feeling isolated and frustrated, despairing that our words don't seem able to convey the depth and complexity of what we think and feel.

Just like the boxes in Figure 3.1, virtually every interpersonal situation can be seen from many points of view. Take a minute to study that figure. How many ways can you discover to view this image? If you see only one or two, keep looking. (You can see at least four ways of viewing the image by looking at Figure 3.2.) If it is hard to make quick and accurate sense of simple drawings, imagine the challenge involved in trying to understand the perspectives of other human beings, who are far more complex and multi-dimensional.

In this chapter, we provide tools for communicating in the face of perceptual differences. We begin by examining some of the many reasons why the world appears so different to each of us. After examining the perceptual factors that make understanding so difficult, we will look at tools for bridging the perceptual gap.

The Perception Process

How do we make sense of the world? How do our perceptions affect our communication with others? We will begin to answer these questions

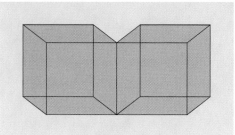

Figure 3.1 Two Cubes Touching

by taking a look at the steps by which we attach meanings to our experiences: selection, organization, interpretation, and negotiation.

Selection

Since we are exposed to more input than we can possibly manage, the first step in perception is the **selection** of which data we will attend to. There are several factors that cause us to notice some messages and ignore others.

Stimuli that are *intense* often attract our attention. Something that is louder, larger, or brighter stands out. This explains why—other things being equal—we are more likely to remember extremely tall or short people and why someone who laughs or talks loudly at a party attracts more attention (not always favourable) than quieter guests.

Repetitious stimuli, repetitious stimuli, repetitious stimuli, repetitious stimuli, repetitious stimuli, repetitious stimuli also attract attention.* Just as a quiet but steadily dripping tap can come to dominate our awareness, people who we are often exposed to will become noticeable.

Attention is also frequently related to *contrast* or *change* in stimulation. Put differently, unchanging people or things become less noticeable. This principle offers an explanation (excuse?) for why we take consistently wonderful people for granted if we see them often. It's only when they stop being so wonderful or go away that we appreciate them.

---

*The graphic demonstrations of factors influencing perception in this and the following paragraphs are borrowed from D. Coon (2001). *Psychology: Gateways to mind and behaviour* (9th ed.). Belmont, CA: Wadsworth.

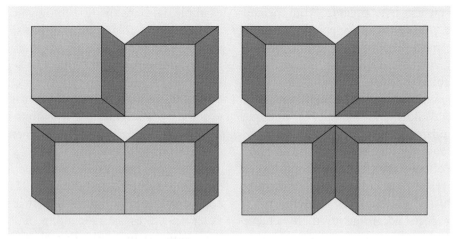

Figure 3.2 Four Sets of Two Cubes Touching

Motives also determine how we perceive people. For example, someone on the lookout for a romantic adventure will be especially aware of attractive potential partners, whereas the same person in an emergency might be oblivious to anyone but the police or medical personnel.

Our *emotional state*, as well, shapes what we select. Paula Neidenthal and her colleagues (2001) discovered that our mood affects our ability to detect other people's emotional states. They discovered that people in a happy mood were quick to notice when happy-appearing characters in a film appeared sadder, whereas unhappy subjects were quicker at noticing when sad characters appeared happier.

Organization

After selecting information from the environment, we must arrange it in some meaningful way in order to make sense of the world. We call this stage **organization**. The raw sense data we perceive can be organized in more than one way. (See Figure 3.2 for a visual example of this principle.) We do this by using *perceptual schema*, which are cognitive frameworks that allow us to give order to the information we have selected (Macrae and Bodenhausen, 2001).

Organizing Perceptions of People   We use four types of schema to classify other people (Andersen, 1999). As you read about each one, think about how you use it to organize your perceptions. *Physical constructs* classify people according to their appearance: beautiful or ugly, fat or thin, young or old, and so on. *Role constructs* use social position, such as student, lawyer, and spouse. *Interaction constructs* focus on social behaviour: friendly, helpful, aloof, and sarcastic, for example. The final organizing scheme uses *psychological constructs*: generous, nervous, insecure, and so on.

The kinds of constructs we use strongly affect the way we relate to others. For example, boys between eight and eleven years old tend to categorize their peers according to their achievements, what they like and dislike, and their personality, whereas girls in the same age range tend to perceive peers according to their background and family (Matthys and Cohen-Kettenis, 1994). What constructs do you use to classify the people you encounter in your life? Consider how your relationships might change if you used different schema.

Once we have chosen an organizing scheme to classify people, we use that scheme to make generalizations about members of the groups who fit our categories. For example, if you are especially aware of a person's sex, you might be alert to the differences between the way men and women behave or the way they are treated. If religion plays an important part in your life, you might think of members of your faith differently than you do of others. If ethnicity is important for you, you probably notice the differences between members of various ethnic groups. There's nothing wrong with making generalizations—in fact, it would be impossible to get through life without them. But they need to be made accurately. When generalizations lose touch with reality, they lead to **stereotyping**—exaggerated beliefs associated with a categorizing system. Stereotypes may be based on a kernel of truth, but they go beyond the facts at hand and make claims that usually have no valid basis.

Two characteristics distinguish stereotypes from reasonable generalizations. The first involves *categorizing others on the basis of easily recognized but not necessarily important characteristics*. For example, perhaps the first thing you notice about a person is the colour of his or her skin—but that may not be nearly as significant as the person's intelligence or achievements. The second feature that characterizes stereotypes is *ascribing a set of characteristics to most or all members of a group*. For example, you might unfairly assume that all older people are doddering or that all men are insensitive to women's concerns.

Stereotypes can plague interracial communication (B. Allen, 1995; Buttny, 1997). Surveys of college students' attitudes show that many blacks describe whites as 'demanding' and 'manipulative', while many whites describe blacks as 'loud' and 'ostentatious'. Many African-American women report having been raised with stereotypical views of whites (e.g., 'most whites cannot be trusted'). One black college professor reported a personal story revealing a surprising set of stereotypical assumptions from a white colleague. 'As the only African American at a university-sponsored party for faculty a few years ago, I was appalled when a white professor (whom I had just met) asked me to sing a Negro spiritual' (Hecht et al., 1993). Although it is possible that behaviour like this can be motivated by a desire to be friendly, it is easy to see how it can be insensitive and offensive.

By adulthood, we tend to engage in stereotyping frequently, effortlessly, and often unconsciously (Zenmore et al., 2000). Once we create and hold stereotypes, we seek out isolated incidents that support our inaccurate beliefs. For example, men and women in conflict with each other often remember only the behaviour of the opposite sex that fits their stereotypes (M. Allen, 1998). They then point to that behaviour—which might not be representative of how the other person usually behaves—as 'evidence' to support their stereotypical and inaccurate claims: 'Look! There you go criticizing me again. Typical of a woman!'

One way to avoid the kinds of communication problems that come from excessive stereotyping is to 'decategorize' others, giving yourself a chance to treat people as individuals instead of assuming that they possess the same characteristics as every other member of the group to which you assign them.

iStock photo

she complains that he is withdrawing from her. Notice that the order in which each partner punctuates this cycle affects how the dispute looks. The husband begins by blaming the wife: 'I withdraw because you nag.' The wife organizes the situation differently, starting with the husband: 'I nag because you withdraw.' Once the cycle gets rolling, it is impossible to say which accusation is accurate, as Figure 3.3 shows. The answer depends on how the sequence is punctuated.

Anyone who has seen two children argue about 'who started it' can understand that squabbling over causes and effects is not likely to solve a conflict. In fact, the kind of finger pointing that goes along with assigning blame will probably make matters worse. Rather than argue about whose punctuation of an event is correct, it's far more productive to recognize that a dispute can look different to each party and then move on to the more important question: 'What can we do to make things better?'

Interpretation

Once we have selected and organized our perceptions, we **interpret** them in a way that makes some sort of sense. Interpretation is part of almost every interpersonal act. Is the person who smiles at you across a crowded room interested in romance or simply being polite? Is a friend's kidding a sign of affection or irritation? Should you take an invitation to 'drop by any time' literally or not?

General Influences on Interpretation   There are several things that cause us to interpret a person's behaviour in one way or another. The first is our *degree of involvement* with the person. For example, research suggests that we tend to view people with whom we have or seek a relationship more favourably than those whom we observe from a detached perspective (Manusov, 1993; Neuliep and Grohskopf, 2000).

Organizing Perceptions of Events   Perceptual differences do not just involve the general categories we use to classify other people. We can also organize specific communication transactions in different ways, and these differing organizational schemes can have a powerful effect on our relationships. Communication theorists have used the term **punctuation** to describe the determination of causes and effects in a series of interactions (Watzlawick et al., 1967). You can begin to understand how punctuation operates by visualizing a running quarrel between a husband and wife. The husband accuses the wife of being a nag, while

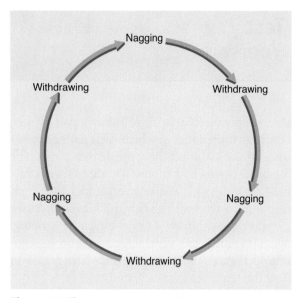

Figure 3.3 The way a communication sequence is punctuated affects its perceived meaning. Which comes first, the nagging or the withdrawing?

Relational satisfaction is a second factor that influences our interpretation. The behaviour that seems desirable when you are happy with a partner might seem completely different when the relationship isn't satisfying. For example, couples in unsatisfying relationships are more likely than satisfied partners to blame one another when things go wrong (Bradbury and Fincham, 1990; Manusov, 1993).

A third factor that influences interpretations is *past experience*. What meanings have similar events held? If, for instance, you have been cheated by landlords in the past, you might be skeptical about an apartment manager's assurances that careful housekeeping will ensure the refund of your cleaning deposit.

Assumptions about human behaviour also influence our interpretations. Do you assume people are lazy, dislike work, avoid responsibility, and

must be coerced into doing things, or do you believe people exercise self-direction and self-control, possess creativity, and seek responsibility? Imagine the differences between a boss who assumes workers fit the first description and one who assumes they fit the second (McGregor, 1960; Neuliep, 1996).

Expectations make up another factor that shapes our interpretations. For example, university students are less pessimistic about the future success of a relationship when a partner's attributes are framed in positive rather than negative terms, even though the attributes are objectively identical (Knee and Boon, 2001).

Knowledge of others affects the way we interpret their actions. For instance, if you know a friend has just been jilted by a lover or fired from a job, you'll interpret his aloofness differently than if you were unaware of what happened. If you know an instructor is rude to all students, you will be unlikely to take her remarks personally.

Cultural Influences on Interpretation The way members of a culture are taught to think and reason shapes the way they interpret other people's messages (Gudykunst and Kim, 1997). One

Reflection

Problematic Punctuation

When I was living with my parents, my father was always asking where I was going or where I had been. I interpreted his questions as too nosy, and I usually responded with hostility or silence. This made him even more concerned about what I was doing.

Now, I recognize that each of us was punctuating this situation differently. He saw me as being the problem: 'I ask you what you are doing because you never tell me.' I saw him as the cause of the problem: 'I never tell you what I'm doing because you are always pestering me.' Who started the cycle? Either way, we both lost. I have come to realize how hanging onto our different ways of punctuating the situation kept us from understanding one another.

Take Two

- **Punctuation:** the determination of causes and effects in a series of interactions.

important force that affects thinking is a culture's system of logic. Members of *individualistic cultures*, such as Canada and the United States, prize rationality and linear, logical thinking. They value the ability to be impartial—to analyze a situation from a detached perspective. They rely on facts, figures, and experts to make decisions. Members of individualistic societies tend to see the world in terms of dichotomies, such as good–bad, right–wrong, happy–sad, and so on. In contrast, members of *collectivistic cultures* are more likely to be intuitive. They prefer to get a feel for the big picture and are less impressed by precision, classification, or detachment. Collectivistic cultures are also less prone to see the world in either–or terms. They accept the fact that people, things, or ideas can be both right and wrong, good and bad at the same time.

Such categorizing doesn't mean that members of individualistic cultures are never intuitive or that collectivistic ones are never rational. The differences in ways of thinking are a matter of degree. Nonetheless, it's easy to imagine how an individualist raised in mainstream Canadian culture and someone from an extremely collectivistic Asian or First Nations culture could find their interactions perplexing. For instance, consider what might happen when a conflict arises between two romantic partners, friends, or co-workers. 'Why don't we look at this rationally,' the individualist might say. 'Let's figure out exactly what happened. Once we decide whose fault the problem is, we can fix it.' By contrast, the partner with a more collectivistic way of thinking might say, 'Let's not get caught up in a lot of details or an argument about who is right or wrong. If we can get a feel for the problem, we can make things more harmonious.' Although both partners might be speaking the same language, their modes of thinking about their relationship would be dramatically different.

Although we have talked about selection, organization, and interpretation separately, the three phases of perception can occur in different sequences. For example, a parent's or babysitter's past interpretations (such as, 'Jason is a troublemaker')

Test Yourself   Describe the general and cultural influences on the way we interpret human behaviour.

can influence future selections (his behaviour becomes especially noticeable) and the organization of events (when there's a fight, the assumption is that Jason started it). Like all communication, perception is an ongoing process in which it is hard to pin down the beginnings and endings.

Negotiation

In Chapter 1 you read that meaning is created both *in* and *among* people. So far, our discussion has focused on the inner components of perception—selection, organization, and interpretation—that take place in each individual's mind. Now, we need to examine the part of our sense-making that occurs *among* people. The process by which communicators influence one another's perceptions through communication is known as **negotiation**.

One way to explain negotiation is to view interpersonal communication as the exchange of stories. Scholars call the stories we use to describe our personal worlds **narratives** (Shaw, 1997). Just as the boxes in Figure 3.1 on page 70 can be viewed in several ways, almost every interpersonal situation can be described by more than one narrative. These narratives often differ: Some political liberals refer to conservatives as heartless, whereas conservatives call their liberal critics unrealistic. Children may say their parents are too controlling, while the parents talk about their children as irresponsible and naive. People who value cleanliness and order may label their housemates as dirty and sloppy, while those housemates would likely describe a concern for tidiness as obsessive. When our narratives clash with those of others, we can either hang onto our own point of view and refuse to consider anyone else's (usually not productive) or try to negotiate a narrative that creates at least some common ground.

Consider an example of negotiating narratives in the workplace. Patricia Sias (1996) studied the conversations of employees who talked to one another about the 'differential treatment' their colleagues had received from management about matters such as time off, pay, or work assignments. Sias's analysis revealed that these conversations were the place in which workers created and reinforced narratives about the favoured employee's behaviour and management's response. For example, workers constructing narratives about Jane Doe's habit of taking extra long lunches might decide that her late lunches aren't fair—or they might agree that late lunches aren't very important. Either way, their negotiated understanding of office events *defines* those events. Once they are defined, co-workers tend to seek reinforcement for their perceptions by keeping a mental scorecard rating their fellow employees and management. ('Did you see that Dan came in late again today?' 'Did you notice that the boss chose Midori to go on that trip to Montreal?')

Although most of us like to think we make judgments about others on our own, this research suggests that sense-making is an interactive process. In other words, reality in the workplace and elsewhere is not 'out there'; instead, we create it with others through communication.

The best chance for smooth communication is to have shared narratives. For example, romantic partners who celebrate their successful struggles against relational obstacles are happier than those who do not have this shared appreciation (Flora and Segrin, 2000). Likewise, couples that agree about the important turning points in their relationships are more satisfied than those who have different views of what incidents were most important (Baxter and Pittman, 2001).

Shared narratives do not have to be accurate to be powerful (Martz et al., 1998; Murray et al., 1996). Couples who report being happily married after fifty or more years seem to collude in a relational narrative that does not always jibe with the facts. They agree that they rarely have conflicts, although objective analysis reveals that they have had their share of disagreements. Without overtly agreeing to do so, they choose to blame outside forces or unusual circumstances for their

problems, instead of blaming each other. They offer the most charitable interpretations of each other's behaviour, believing that their spouse acts with good intentions even when things don't go well. They seem willing to forgive, or even forget transgressions. Examining this research, Judy Pearson asks,

> Should we conclude that happy couples have a poor grip on reality? Perhaps they do, but is the reality of one's marriage better known by outside onlookers than by the players themselves? The conclusion is evident. One key to a long happy marriage is to tell yourself and others that you have one and then to behave as though you do! (Pearson, 2000, p. 186)

Influences on Perception

How we select, organize, interpret, and negotiate data about others is influenced by a variety of factors. Some of our perceptual judgments are affected by physiology, others by cultural and social factors, and still others by psychological factors (Hochberg, 1998).

Physiological Influences

Sometimes, our different perspectives come from our physical environment and the ways that our bodies differ from others.

 Take Two

The Four Steps in Perception

- **Selection:** determines which information we will pay attention to and is influenced by stimuli intensity, repetition, contrast, or change and our motives and emotional state.
- **Organization:** is the process by which we arrange information in a meaningful way using perceptual schema (physical, role, interaction, and psychological constructs).
- **Interpretation:** the process of making sense of perceptions within our own minds.
- **Negotiation:** the process by which communicators influence one another's perceptions.

iStock photo

The Senses   The differences in how each of us sees, hears, tastes, touches, and smells stimuli can affect interpersonal relationships (Clark, 2000). Consider the following everyday situations:

'Turn down that radio! It's going to make me go deaf.'
'It's not too loud. If I turn it down, it'll be impossible to hear it.'

'It's freezing in here.'
'Are you kidding? We'll suffocate if you turn up the heat!'

'Why don't you pass that truck? The highway's clear for half a mile.'
'I can't see that far, and I'm not going to get us killed.'

These disputes aren't just over matters of opinion. Our reception of sensory data is different. Differences in vision and hearing are the easiest to recognize, but other gaps also exist. There is evidence that identical foods taste different to different people (Bartoshuk, 1980). Odours that please some people repel others (Montcrieff, 1966). Likewise, temperature variations that are uncomfortable to some of us are inconsequential to others. Remembering these differences won't eliminate them, but it will remind us that other people's preferences aren't crazy, just different.

Age   Older people view the world differently than younger ones because of a greater scope and number of experiences. Developmental differences also shape perceptions. Developmental psychologists (Piaget, 1952; Lourenco and Machado, 1996) describe a series of stages that children pass through on their way to adulthood. Younger children are incapable of performing mental feats that are natural to the rest of us. Until they approach the age of seven, for example, they have difficulty taking another person's point of view. This fact helps explain why youngsters often seem egocentric, selfish, and uncooperative. A parent's exasperated, 'Can't you see I'm too tired to play?' just won't make sense to a four-year-old full of energy, who imagines that everyone else feels the same as she does.

Health   Think of the last time you came down with a cold, flu, or some other ailment. Do you remember how different you felt? You probably had much less energy than usual. It's likely that you felt less sociable and that your thinking was

iStock photo

slower than usual. Such changes have a strong impact on how you relate to others. It's good to realize that someone else may be behaving differently because of illness. In the same way, it is important to let others know when you feel ill so they can give you the understanding you need.

Fatigue Just as illness can affect your relationships, so can excessive fatigue. When you have been working long hours or studying late for an exam, the world can seem quite different than when you are well rested. Again, it is important to recognize that you or anyone may behave differently when you are tired. Trying to deal with important issues at such times can get you into trouble.

Hunger   Our digestive system often rules our behaviour. One experiment demonstrated this fact (McClelland and Atkinson, 1948). Subjects were denied food for up to fourteen hours. During this time, they were asked to describe what they saw projected on a screen at very low light levels. In truth, no image at all was projected. Despite this fact, the subjects did report seeing objects. As their hunger grew, the number of food-related observations increased.

Our own experience confirms that being hungry (and becoming irritable) or having overeaten (and getting tired) affects how we interact with others. For example, a study by Katherine Alaimo and her colleagues (2001) found that teenagers who reported that their family did not get enough food to eat were almost three times as likely to have been suspended from school, almost twice as likely to have difficulty getting along with others, and four times as likely to have no friends. While the exact nature of the causes and effects in this study are hard to pin down, one thing is clear: hunger can affect our perception and communication.

Biological Cycles   Are you a 'morning person' or a 'night person'? Most of us can answer this question easily, and there's a good physiological reason why. Each of us has a daily cycle in which all sorts of changes constantly occur, including variations in body temperature, sexual drive,

alertness, tolerance to stress, and mood (Palmer, 1976; Touitou, 1998). Most of these changes are due to hormonal cycles. We often aren't conscious of these changes, but they surely affect the way we relate toward each other. For example, Jeffrey Larson and his associates (1991) discovered that couples with mismatched waking and sleeping patterns (e.g., an evening person and a morning person) reported significantly more conflict, less sexual intimacy, and less time spent conversing on important topics than couples with similar sleeping patterns. Once we are aware that our own daily cycles and those of others influence our feelings and behaviour, it becomes possible to run our lives so that we deal with important issues at the most effective times.

Have you ever had your sleep–wake pattern disrupted by your job, such as by working the night shift? Richard Adeniran and his colleagues (1996) found that night work disturbs concentration, interest, energy, sleep, and appetite. Most interesting, however, were the effects on interpersonal relationships: night work increases our sensitivity to criticism from others.

Psychological Influences

Along with physiology, our psychological state also influences the way we perceive others.

Mood   Our emotional state strongly influences how we view people and events, and, therefore, how we communicate. Sadness, for instance, impairs our ability to accurately interpret social cues (Ambady and Gray, 2002). When we are sad, we are more likely to overanalyze and misinterpret social signals given off by others. An experiment using hypnotism dramatically demonstrated how our varying moods influence our perceptions of events (Lebula and Lucas, 1945). Each subject was shown the same series of six pictures, each time having been put in a different mood. The descriptions of the pictures differed radically depending on the emotional state of the subject. The following examples are from one subject in various emotional states while describing a picture of children digging in a swampy area:

Focus on Research

Homophobia as a Perceptual Filter

What would you think if you heard two men talking and one of them said 'I love you' to the other? What if it were two women? Would you assume they are friends, or would you guess they are lovers? According to research by Kory Floyd and Mark Morman (2000), your answers would depend in part on your level of homophobia.

Floyd and Morman asked 221 heterosexual men and women to read a transcript of a hypothetical conversation between either two men or two women in which one communicator says 'I love you' to the other. The participants also completed a questionnaire measuring their levels of homophobia, which the researchers defined as 'the fear of being seen as homosexual.' As the researchers expected, those with higher levels of homophobia had more negative assessments of the affectionate statement; they also perceived the relationship of the interactants as being more romantic than platonic. Those with lower levels of homophobia were more likely to regard the affectionate statement as more platonic than romantic. In addition, the two-woman scenario was not perceived as negatively as the two-man scenario, reinforcing the notion that our culture has stronger norms against male–male affection than against female–female affection.

One implication of these findings is that affectionate verbal expressions in same-sex interactions run the risk of being misperceived—and that homophobia can contribute to those misperceptions. The words 'I love you' have no meaning until people give them meaning—and those meanings are shaped by personal attitudes as well as cultural norms and beliefs.

Happy mood: 'It looks like fun, reminds me of summer. That's what life is for, working out in the open, really living—digging in the dirt, planting, watching things grow.'

Anxious mood: 'They're going to get hurt or cut. There should be someone older there who knows what to do in case of an accident. I wonder how deep the water is.'

Critical mood: 'Pretty horrible land. There ought to be something more useful for kids of that age to do instead of digging in that stuff. It's filthy and dirty and good for nothing.'

Such evidence shows that our judgments often say more about our own attitudes than about the other people involved.

Although there's a strong relationship between mood and happiness, it is not clear which comes first—the perceptual outlook or the amount of relational satisfaction. There is some evidence that perception leads to satisfaction rather than the other way around (Fletcher et al., 1987). In other words, the attitude or expectation we bring to a situation shapes our level of happiness or

iStock photo

unhappiness. Once started, this process can create a spiral. If you are happy about your relationship, you will be more likely to interpret your partner's behaviour in a charitable way. This, in turn, can lead to greater happiness. Of course, the same process can work in the opposite direction. One remedy for serious distortions—and unnecessary conflicts—is to monitor your own moods. If you are aware of being especially critical or sensitive, you can avoid overreacting to others.

Self-Concept A second factor that influences perception is the self-concept (Hinde et al., 2001). For example, the recipient's self-concept has proved to be the greatest factor in determining whether people who are being teased interpret the teaser's motives as being friendly or hostile, and whether they respond comfortably or defensively (Alberts et al., 1996). As discussed in Chapter 2, the way we think and feel about ourselves strongly influences how we interpret others' behaviour.

Social Influences

Within a culture, our personal point of view plays a strong role in shaping perceptions.

Standpoint Theory Social scientists have developed **standpoint theory** to describe how a person's position in the world shapes his or her view of society in general and of specific individuals (Harding, 1991; Orbe, 1998). Standpoint theory is most often applied to the difference between the perspectives of privileged social groups and people who have less power, and to the perspectives of women and men (Dougherty, 2001). Unless one has been disadvantaged, it can be difficult to imagine how different the world might look to someone who has been treated badly because of race, ethnicity, gender, biological sex, sexual orientation, or socioeconomic class. After some reflection, though, it is easy to understand how being marginalized can make the world seem like a very different place.

Sex and Gender Roles Physiological differences aren't the only factors that shape the differing perceptions of men and women. Personal experiences

and social expectations are also influential. For example, one study found that women and men judge the same behaviour quite differently. Some types of behaviour that men find innocuous have been judged as being harassing by women (Dougherty, 2001). Not surprisingly, much of the difference comes from experience. That is, women who report having been harassed are more likely to find harassment in subsequent interactions (Singer et al., 1998). Experience is not the only factor, though: younger women are more likely to perceive harassment than older ones, who, presumably, have different expectations about what kinds of communication are acceptable. Also, attitudes play a role: people who disapprove of socializing and dating between co-workers are more likely to perceive harassment than those who accept this sort of relationship (Solomon and Williams, 1997).

Early theorizing by Sandra Bem (1974) suggested that stereotypical masculine and feminine ways of behaving are not opposite poles of a single continuum, but instead are two separate sets of

iStock photo

behaviour. With this view, a person—regardless of her or his biological sex—can act in a masculine manner, a feminine manner, or exhibit both types of characteristics. The masculine–feminine dichotomy, then, is replaced with four **psychological sex types**—masculine, feminine, **androgynous** (combining masculine and feminine traits), and undifferentiated (neither masculine nor feminine). The word **gender** is a shorthand term for psychological sex type. Combining the four psychological sex types with the traditional biological sex types produces four categories for men (masculine males, feminine males, androgynous males, and undifferentiated males) and four categories for women (masculine females, feminine females, androgynous females, and undifferentiated females). Although there are women and men who fit into all of the categories, in general, people see themselves as either sex-typed (masculine male or feminine female) or androgynous (Korabik and McCreary, 2000).

A person categorized in one of these eight combined psychological-biological sex types perceives interpersonal relationships differently from someone in another category. For example, masculine males probably see their interpersonal relationships as opportunities for competitive interaction, as opportunities to win something. Feminine females probably see their interpersonal relationships as opportunities to be nurturing, to express their feelings and emotions. Androgynous males and females, on the other hand, probably differ little in their perceptions of their interpersonal relationships.

Androgynous individuals tend to see their relationships as opportunities to behave in a variety of ways, depending on the nature of the relationships themselves, the context in which a particular relationship takes place, and the myriad other variables affecting what might constitute appropriate behaviour. These variables are usually ignored by the sex-typed masculine males and feminine females, who have a smaller repertoire of behaviour.

Occupational Roles   The kind of work we do also governs our view of the world. Imagine five people taking a walk through a park. One, a botanist, is fascinated by the variety of trees and plants.

Another, a zoologist is on the lookout for interesting animals. The third, a meteorologist, keeps an eye on the sky, noticing changes in the weather. The fourth, a psychologist, is totally unaware of nature, concentrating instead on the interactions among the people in the park. The fifth, a pickpocket, quickly takes advantage of the others' absorption to collect their wallets. There are two lessons in this little story. The first, of course, is to watch your wallet carefully. The second is that our occupational roles often govern our perceptions.

Perhaps the most dramatic illustration of how occupational roles shape perception occurred in the early 1970s. Stanford University psychologist Philip Zimbardo (1971) recruited a group of well-educated, middle-class young men. He randomly chose eleven to serve as 'guards' in a mock prison set up in the basement of Stanford's psychology building. He issued uniforms, handcuffs, whistles, and billy clubs to the guards. The remaining ten subjects became 'prisoners' and were put in rooms with metal bars, bucket toilets, and cots.

Zimbardo let the guards establish their own rules for the experiment. The rules were tough: no talking during meals and rest periods and after lights out. They took head counts at 2:30 A.M. Troublemakers received short rations.

Faced with these conditions, the prisoners began to resist. Some barricaded their doors with beds. Others went on hunger strikes. Several ripped off their identifying number tags. The guards reacted to the rebellion by clamping down hard on protesters. Some became sadistic, physically and verbally abusing the prisoners. The experiment was scheduled to go on for two weeks, but after six days Zimbardo realized that what had started as a simulation had become too real. It seems that *what* we are is determined largely by society's designation of *who* we are.

Cultural Influences
Cultural selection, organization, interpretation, and negotiation exert a powerful influence on the way we view communication by other people. Even beliefs about the very value of talk differ from one culture to another (Giles et al., 1992a).

Talk and Silence   Western cultures tend to view talk as desirable and use it for social purposes as well as to perform tasks. Silence has a negative value in these cultures. It is likely to be interpreted as lack of interest, unwillingness to communicate, hostility, anxiety, shyness, or a sign of interpersonal incompatibility. Westerners are uncomfortable with silence, which they find embarrassing and awkward.

On the other hand, Asian cultures tend to perceive talk quite differently. For thousands of years, Asian cultures have discouraged the expression of thoughts and feelings. Silence is valued, as Taoist sayings indicate: 'In much talk there is great weariness' or 'One who speaks does not know; one who knows does not speak.' Unlike westerners, who are uncomfortable with silence, most Asians believe that remaining quiet is the proper state when there is nothing to be said. In fact, a talkative person is often considered a show-off or a fake.

It is easy to see how these different views of speech and silence can lead to communication problems when people from various cultures meet. Both the 'talkative' westerner and the 'silent' Asian are behaving in ways they believe are proper, yet each views the other with disapproval and mistrust. Only when they recognize the different standards of behaviour can they adapt to one another, or at least understand and respect their differences.

Focus on Technology

Perceptions of Cell Phones

For most of us, it is hard to ignore a ringing telephone. Marshall McLuhan (1964) described the ringing phone as having a 'magnetic pull'. Increasingly, we hear phones ringing, buzzing, beeping or singing wherever we are. For better or worse, cell phones are a part of our world. In 2008, there were 19,910,404 cell-phone subscribers in Canada and over 3.3 billion worldwide (Canadian Broadcasting Corporation, 2008). Cell phones help us coordinate our social and work lives; they invade our social spaces; they have saved people's lives; they connect us, entertain us, and irritate us. Mobile phones have a culture and emerging etiquette of their own.

Is it rude to interrupt a restaurant conversation by answering your cell phone? Does it depend on what type of restaurant you are in? Is it okay to discuss personal information on a cell phone in a public place? People's perceptions of appropriate cell-phone etiquette vary considerably—some who have and use cell phones are generally more tolerant of their use, while others who are not cell-phone owners are less willing to abide them (Ling, 2004). But even among the growing population of cell-phone users, there doesn't appear to be a lot of agreement on what is appropriate and what is not. In her explorations of cell-phone use and culture, Sadie Plant (2001), currently at Warwick University in Britain, has observed that there are two distinctly different groups of cell-phone users: The first group is made up of those who keep their phones tucked away and try to use them as unobtrusively as possible. These people often leave the room or the table to answer a call and separate their cell-phone conversations from the real-life social situation they are in. Plant calls this group 'innies'. This group is contrasted with the second major type: 'outies'. These people display their cell phones prominently, answer and make calls in the presence of the people they are physically with, and even continue both conversations simultaneously. It is obvious that innies (and non-users) have different perceptions regarding cell-phone etiquette than outies. But where did they get these ideas?

Scott Campbell and Tracy Russo (2003) explain that our opinions about cell-phone etiquette are shaped by the way our family and friends behave with cell phones. They found that people's perceptions of when and how to use their cell phones were very similar to the perceptions of the people in their personal social networks—friends, family, and co-workers. The rules governing how and when to use new technologies evolve along with the technology. Believe it or not, people felt awkward answering their land-line phones—in their homes!—when they were first adopted. The etiquette and comfort with technology has evolved, as it will for cell phones.

Reflection

Cultural Differences in Humour

I was born and raised in Russia. One thing I find very different here [Canada] is the way people use humour. When I first arrived in this country, I noticed that my host family joked and teased me a lot. I was often offended and hurt. The problem was that neither my host family nor I understood the differences in meaning people attach to the same way of behaving. In Russia, people do not tease to express affection. In Canada, though, joking is often a way to show friendship. Once I realized this cultural difference, I became better at socializing.

Test Yourself Describe the four general areas of influence on our perceptions and provide examples within each area.

Common Tendencies in Perception

It is obvious that many factors distort the way we interpret the world. Social scientists use the term **attribution** to describe the process of attaching meaning to behaviour. We attribute meaning both to our own actions and to the actions of others, but we often use different yardsticks. Research has uncovered several perceptual tendencies that may lead to inaccurate attributions (Hamachek, 1992).

We Judge Ourselves More Charitably Than We Do Others

In an attempt to convince ourselves and others that the positive face we show to the world is true, we tend to judge ourselves in the most generous terms possible (Farah and Atoum, 2002). On the one hand, when others suffer, we often blame the problem on their personal qualities and we underestimate the impact of the situation. Social scientists have labelled this tendency the **fundamental attribution error** (Ross, 1977; 2001). On the other hand, when we experience failure, we find explanations outside ourselves but we are quick to take credit when we succeed (Ross and Nisbett, 1991). This tendency to protect our self-esteem by blaming the situation for our failures and taking personal credit for our successes is called the **self-serving bias**. Consider a few examples:

- When *they* botch a job, we think they weren't listening well or trying hard enough; when *we* make the mistake, the problem was unclear directions or not enough time.
- When *she* lashes out angrily, we say she's being moody or too sensitive; when *we* blow off steam, it is because of the pressure we've been under.

Individualism and Collectivism   People from collectivist and individualist cultures perceive interpersonal behaviour and obligations differently. For example, Au et al. (2001) gave hotel school students in China and Canada a description of how a service provider handled a complaint from a customer whose coat was stained with tea. Results showed that the students from China—collectivists—were more likely than the students from Canada—individualists—to see the service provider as the person at fault. In addition, Janoff-Bulman and Leggatt (2002), looking at motivational differences in the perception of social obligations by Hispanic (collectivist) undergraduates and Anglo-Saxon (individualist) undergraduates, found that although individuals from both cultures reported a strong sense of obligation toward close friends and family members, Hispanics felt a stronger motivation than Anglos to help more distant family and friends.

The gap between cultures often extends beyond dissimilar norms to a wide range of different experiences and feelings. The cultural values and norms (described in Chapter 2) that shape our self-concepts also lead people from different cultural backgrounds to experience the world in ways that often bear little resemblance to one another.

- When *he* gets caught speeding, we say he should have been more careful; when *we* get the ticket, we deny we were driving too fast or say, 'Everybody does it.'

Not surprisingly, these biased perceptions are especially common in troubled relationships. In one study (Schütz, 1999), couples in conflict were more likely to blame their partner for the problem than to accept responsibility for their role in the problem. The researchers point out that these results came from couples dealing with ordinary relational challenges. They observe that the fundamental attribution error and self-serving bias are likely to be even stronger in troubled relationships. Interestingly, there are a few occasions where these biases are less strong. For example, men tend to be more charitable when making judgments about women they don't know well (Kluwer et al., 1998).

We Are Influenced by Our Expectations

Suppose you took a class and were told in advance by several friends that the instructor is terrific—and that she is very funny. Would this affect the way you perceive the teacher? Probably so. There is a good chance that you would view the instructor positively and laugh at her jokes—perhaps more than you would have if you hadn't been told about her in advance. In this situation, as in others, our expectations influence our perceptions.

However, expectations do not always lead to more positive appraisals. There are times when we raise our expectations so high that we are disappointed with the events that occur. If you are told that someone you are about to meet is extremely attractive, you may create a picture in your mind of a professional model, only to be disappointed when the person doesn't live up to your unrealistic expectations. What if you had been told that the person isn't very good looking? In that case, you might have been pleasantly surprised by the person's appearance, and perhaps you would rate the person's attractiveness more positively. The point is that our expectations influence the way we see others, both positively and negatively.

It is important to know that when we are making decisions about others. Many professions require that proposals be evaluated through 'blind review'—that is, the person submitting the proposal is not allowed to offer identifying information that might influence the evaluator's appraisal. In the same way, you can probably think of times when it would be wise to avoid advance information about another person so that you will perceive the person as neutrally as possible.

We Are Influenced by the Obvious

Being influenced by what is most obvious is understandable. As you read earlier, we select stimuli from our environment that are noticeable—that is, intense, repetitive, unusual, or otherwise attention-grabbing. The problem is that the most obvious factor is not necessarily the only cause—or the most significant one—of an event. For example,

- When two children (or adults, for that matter) fight, it may be a mistake to blame the one who lashes out first. Perhaps the other one was at least equally responsible, by teasing or refusing to co-operate.
- You might complain about an acquaintance whose malicious gossiping or arguing has become a bother, forgetting that by putting up

iStock photo

iStock photo

with that kind of behaviour you have been at least partially responsible.

- You might blame an unhappy work situation on the boss, overlooking other factors beyond her control, such as a change in the economy, the policy of higher management, or demands of customers or other workers.

These examples show that it is important to take time to gather all the facts before arriving at a conclusion.

We Cling to First Impressions

Labelling people according to our first impressions is a part of the perception process that is difficult to avoid. Such labels are a way of making quick interpretations: 'She seems cheerful.' 'He seems sincere.' 'They sound awfully conceited.'

If impressions are accurate, they can be useful ways of deciding how to respond best to people in the future. However, problems arise when the labels we attach are inaccurate, for, once we form an opinion of someone, we tend to hang onto it and make any conflicting information fit that opinion.

Social scientists have coined the term **halo effect** to describe the power of a first impression to influence subsequent perceptions. The power of the halo effect has been demonstrated by research

on how employers rate job applicants (Dougherty et al., 1994). Interviewers usually form strong impressions of candidates in the first few minutes after meeting them. Once these impressions are formed, they often ask questions that confirm their image of the applicant. For example, when an interviewer forms a positive impression, she might ask leading questions aimed at supporting her positive views ('What lessons did you learn from that setback?'), interpret answers in a positive light ('Ah, taking time away from school to travel was a good idea!'), encourage the applicant ('Good point!'), and sell the company's virtues ('I think you would like working here'). Likewise, applicants who create a negative first impression are operating under a cloud that may be impossible to dispel.

Take Two

- **Fundamental attribution error:** the tendency to blame other people's problems on their personal qualities and underestimate the impact of the situation.
- **Self-serving bias:** the tendency to protect our self-esteem by blaming the situation for our failures and taking personal credit for our successes.
- **Halo effect:** the power of a first impression to influence subsequent perceptions.

Given the almost unavoidable tendency to form first impressions, the best approach is to keep an open mind and be willing to change your opinion if events prove you mistaken.

We Assume Others Are like Us

We commonly imagine that others have the same attitudes and motives that we do. The frequently mistaken assumption that other people's views are similar to our own applies in a wide range of situations. For example,

- You've heard a slightly raunchy joke that you found funny. You assume that it won't offend a friend. It does.
- You've been bothered by an instructor's tendency to get off the subject during lectures. If you were a professor, you would want to know if you were creating problems for your students; so you decide that your instructor will probably be grateful for some constructive criticism. Unfortunately, you are wrong.
- You lost your temper with a friend a week ago and said some things you regret. In fact, if someone said those things to you, you would consider the relationship finished. Imagining that your friend feels the same way, you avoid making contact. In fact, your friend feels that he was partly responsible and has avoided you because he thinks you are the one who wants to end things.

These examples show that others don't always think or feel the way we do and that assuming similarities can lead to problems. Sometimes, you can find out the other person's real position by asking directly; other times, by checking with someone else; and still other times, by making an educated guess after you have thought the matter out. All these alternatives are better than simply assuming that everyone would react the way you do.

We Favour Negative Impressions

What do you think about Harvey? He's handsome, hard-working, intelligent, and honest. He's also conceited.

Did the last quality make a difference in your evaluation? If it did, you are not alone. Research shows that when people are aware of both the positive and negative characteristics of another person, they tend to be more influenced by the undesirable traits (Baumeister et al., 2001; Kellermann, 1989). In one study, researchers found that job interviewers were likely to reject candidates who revealed negative information even when the total amount of information was highly positive (Regan and Totten, 1975).

This attitude sometimes makes sense. If the negative quality clearly outweighs any positive ones, you would be foolish to ignore it. For example, a surgeon with shaky hands and a teacher who hates children would be unsuitable for their jobs, whatever their other virtues. But much of the time, it's a bad idea to pay excessive attention to negative qualities and overlook good ones. Some people make this mistake when screening potential friends or dates. They reject some who are too outgoing or too reserved, others who aren't intelligent enough, and still others who have a strange sense of humour. Of course, it's important to find people you truly enjoy, but expecting perfection can leave you lonely.

We don't always fall into the kind of perceptual tendencies described in this section. Sometimes, for instance, people *are* responsible for their misfortunes, or our problems *are not* our fault. Likewise, the most obvious interpretation of a situation may be the correct one. Nonetheless, a large amount of research has shown again and again that our perceptions of others are often distorted in the ways we have described. The moral, then, is clear: do not assume that your negative appraisal of a person is accurate or unbiased.

Perceiving Others More Accurately

After reading this far, you can appreciate how flawed our perceptions of one another can be. It's easy to understand how these distorted perceptions can interfere with our communication. What we need, then, are tools to improve the accuracy

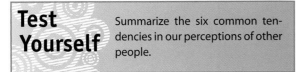

Test Yourself Summarize the six common tendencies in our perceptions of other people.

of our attributions. In the following section, we will introduce two such tools.

Perception Checking

With the likelihood for perceptual errors so great, it is easy to see how a communicator can leap to the wrong conclusion and make false assumptions. Consider the defence-arousing potential of incorrect accusations like these:

'Why are you mad at me?' (Who said I was?)
'What's the matter with you?' (Who said anything was the matter?)
'Come on now. Tell the truth.' (Who said I was lying?)

Even if your interpretations are correct, these kinds of mind-reading statements are likely to generate defensiveness. The skill of **perception checking** is a better way to share your interpretations. A complete perception check has three parts:

1. A description of the behaviour you noticed
2. Two possible interpretations of the behaviour
3. A request for clarification about how to interpret the behaviour

Perception checks for the preceding three examples would look like this:

'When you stamped out of the room and slammed the door [behaviour], I wasn't sure whether you were mad at me [first interpretation] or just in a hurry [second interpretation]. How did you feel? [request for clarification]'

'You haven't laughed much in the last couple of days [behaviour]. It makes me wonder whether something's bothering you [first interpretation] or whether you are just being quiet [second interpretation]. What's up? [request for clarification]'

'You said you really liked the job I did [behaviour], but there was something about your voice that made me think you may not like it [first interpretation]. Maybe it is just my imagination, though [second interpretation]. How do you really feel? [request for clarification]'

Perception checking is a tool to help us understand others instead of assuming that our first interpretation is correct. Because its goal is mutual understanding, perception checking is a co-operative approach to communication. Besides leading to more accurate perceptions, it signals an attitude of respect and concern for the other person, saying, in effect, 'I know I'm not qualified to judge you without some help.'

Sometimes, an effective perception check won't need all of the parts listed above to be effective:

'You haven't dropped by lately. Is anything the matter?' [single interpretation combined with request for clarification]

'I can't tell whether you are kidding me about being cheap or if you are serious [behaviour combined with interpretations]. Are you mad at me?'

'Are you sure you don't mind driving? I can use a ride if it is no trouble, but I don't want to take you out of your way.' [no need to describe behaviour]

The straightforward approach of perception checking has the best chance of working in what we identify in Chapter 5 as *low-context cultures*—ones in which members use language as clearly

iStock photo

Building Work Skills

Perception Checking

Improve your perception-checking ability by developing complete perception-checking statements for the following situations. Be sure your statements include a description of the behaviour, two equally plausible interpretations, and a request for verification.

a. You made what you thought was an excellent suggestion to your boss. He or she said, 'I'll get back to you about that right away.' It's been three weeks, and you haven't received a response yet.

b. You disagreed with a co-worker's suggestions during a meeting. When the meeting was over, you asked if anyone wanted to go for lunch and everyone agreed, with the exception of that same co-worker. The next day when you pass him in the hall, he nods but doesn't say hello or smile as he usually does.

and logically as possible. The dominant cultures of North America and Western Europe fit into this category, and members of these groups are most likely to appreciate the kind of straightforward approach that perception checking embodies. On the other hand, members of *high-context cultures* (more common in Latin America and Asia) value social harmony over clarity. High-context communicators are more likely to regard candid approaches like perception checking as potentially embarrassing, preferring instead less direct ways of understanding one another. Thus, a 'let's get this straight' perception check might work well with a Canadian manager of British or European descent who was raised to value clarity, but it could be a serious mistake with an Asian-Canadian boss who has spent most of his or her life in a high-context culture.

Building Empathy

Perception checking can help us decode messages more accurately, but it doesn't give us enough information that we can claim to fully understand another person. For example, a professor who uses perception checking might learn that a student's reluctance to ask questions is due to confusion and not lack of interest. This information would be helpful, but imagine how much more effective the professor would be if she could get a sense of how it feels to be confused, and could consider

how the material that is so familiar to her appears to the student who is seeing it for the first time. Likewise, parents whose perception checks reveal that their teenager's outlandish behaviour grows from a desire to be accepted by others do not necessarily understand (or perhaps remember) what it feels like to crave that acceptance.

Empathy Defined What we need, then, to understand others more completely is **empathy**—the ability to recreate another person's perspective, to experience the world from his or her point of view. It is impossible to achieve total empathy, but with enough effort and skill, we can come closer to this goal (Long et al., 1999).

As the term will be used here, empathy has three dimensions (Stiff et al., 1988): On one level, empathy involves *perspective taking*—the ability to take on the viewpoint of another person. This understanding requires a suspension of judgment so that for the moment you set aside your own opinions and take on those of the other person. Besides cognitive understanding, empathy also has an affective dimension—what social scientists term *emotional contagion*. In everyday language, emotional contagion means that we experience the same feelings that others have. We know their fear, joy, sadness, and so on. A third dimension of empathy is a genuine *concern* for the welfare of the other person. Not only do we think and feel as others do, but we have a sincere interest in their well-being. Full empathy requires both intellectual understanding of the other person's position and an affective understanding of his or her feelings (Kerem et al., 2001).

The linguistic roots of the word *empathy* shed light on the word's meaning. *Empathy* is derived from two Greek words that mean 'feeling (in)side', which suggests that empathy means *experiencing the other's perception*—in effect, temporarily becoming that person. This kind of understanding is very different from sympathy. The Greek roots for *sympathy* mean 'feeling with'. As this definition implies, when you feel sympathetic, you stand beside the other person. You feel compassion, but you do not share the other person's emotions. Despite your concern, sympathy involves less identification than does empathy. When you sympathize, the confusion, joy, or pain belongs to another. When you empathize, the experience becomes your own, at least for the moment.

The ability to empathize seems to exist in a rudimentary form in even the youngest children (Goleman, 1995). Virtually from birth, infants become visibly upset when they hear another baby crying, and children who are a few months old cry when they observe another child in tears. In fact, young children have trouble distinguishing someone else's distress from their own. If, for example, one child hurts its finger, another child may put its own finger in its mouth as if it were feeling pain. Researchers report cases in which children who see their parents in tears wipe their own eyes, even though they are not crying.

Although infants and toddlers may have a basic capacity to empathize, studies with twins suggest that the degree to which we have the ability to sense how others are feeling seems to vary according to genetic factors. Although some people may have an inborn edge, environmental experiences also play a role in our ability to understand others. Specifically, the way in which parents communicate with their children seems to affect their ability to understand the emotional states of others. When parents show their children how their behaviour affects other people ('Maria can't play her game now because you took her toy. She's crying because she feels sad.'), those children gain a greater appreciation that their acts have emotional consequences than when the parents simply tell them they were naughty ('That was a mean thing to do!').

The Value of Empathy   As we saw in Chapter 1, the ability to empathize is so important that it is an essential ingredient of communicative competence. Empathy can profit both the person who is doing the empathizing and the person who is being understood (Redmond, 1986).

"How would you feel if the mouse did that to you?"

Building Work Skills

Beginning to Build Empathy

When addressing the graduates at the 452nd Convocation at the University of Chicago in 1998, Jean Claude Monty, then chair, CEO, and president of BCE Inc., described empathy as one of the most important attributes of an effective leader. 'Empathy allows you to look at every situation through the customer's, employee's, shareholder's and competitor's eyes, to gain a far deeper understanding of how they're all interconnected and what your next step should be,' (Monty, 1998).

Often, the hardest time to empathize with someone is when we are involved in an argument or conflict with that person. Think about a disagreement you had recently with someone at work or school. Take a moment to jot down your perspective on the issue. Now, try honestly and accurately to imagine the other person's thoughts and feelings about the same issue. Describe the two sides of the argument to a friend or classmate. Does your friend or classmate think you have genuinely tried to perceive the issue from the other person's point of view? Has your position on this changed at all? Why or why not?

The recipient of empathy receives several benefits. The first is increased *self-esteem*. Others usually respond to your point of view with judgments such as, 'That's right . . .' or 'No, it's not that way at all. . . .' An empathic response is different. It suggests the listener is willing to accept you as you are, without any evaluations. It's flattering to find that someone is interested enough in your position to hear you out without passing judgment. The act of being understood can also be very *comforting*, whether or not the other person's reflections offer any additional help. When others empathize, a common thought is 'I'm not alone.' Finally, the target of empathy learns to *trust* the empathizer in a way that probably would not be otherwise possible.

Desirable as it is, too much empathy can lead to burnout, which has also been termed 'compassion fatigue' (Figley, 1995). Studies of workers at a psychiatric hospital showed that a high degree of responsiveness to the needs of others led to several symptoms of burnout: depersonalization of the person being helped, emotional exhaustion, reduced feelings of personal accomplishment, and, ultimately, less emotional commitment to the needy person (Le Blanc et al., 2001; Miller and Birkholt, 1995). This evidence does not mean that empathizing is a guaranteed path to burnout. Rather, it suggests that in addition to being concerned for others, it is necessary to take care of your own needs as well.

Empathy and Ethics   The golden rule of treating others as we want to be treated points to the clear relationship between the ability to empathize and the ethical principles that enable society to function in a matter that we consider civilized. In fact, research has found a link between empathy and ethical altruism (Hoffman, 1991). Bystanders who feel empathy for victims are more likely to intervene and offer help than those who are indifferent. On a larger scale, studies in Canada, the United States, and Germany have revealed a relationship between feelings of empathy and the willingness of people to follow the moral principle that resources should be allocated according to people's needs. Empathetic people have 'an

 Take Two

- **Empathy:** recreating another person's perspective and experiencing the world from his or her point of view ('feeling inside').
- **Sympathy:** feeling compassion for someone but not experiencing that person's point of view or emotions ('feeling with').

Self-Assessment

Empathy in Friendships

This questionnaire can help you determine the degree to which empathy is part of your friendships. Think of one of your close personal friendships and, with that friendship in mind, respond to each statement according to how much you agree with it.

If you agree completely, mark the statement 4.
If you agree a great deal but not completely, mark the statement 3.
If you agree somewhat, mark the statement 2.
If you agree very little, mark the statement 1.
If you do not agree, mark the statement 0.

_____   1.   I understand what my friend says.

_____   2.   I understand how my friend feels.

_____   3.   I appreciate what my friend's experiences feel like to her or him.

_____   4.   I try to see things through my friend's eyes.

_____   5.   I ask my friend questions about what his or her experiences mean to him or her.

_____   6.   I ask my friend questions about what she or he is thinking.

_____   7.   I ask my friend questions about how he or she is feeling.

_____   8.   My friend understands what I say.

_____   9.   My friend understands how I feel.

_____   10. My friend appreciates what my experiences feel like to me.

_____   11. My friend tries to see things through my eyes.

_____   12. My friend asks me questions about what my experiences mean to me.

_____   13. My friend asks me questions about what I'm thinking.

_____   14. My friend asks me questions about how I'm feeling.

Add your scores for items 1 to 7_____.
This figure represents your perception of your empathy for your friend.

Add your scores for items 8 to 14_____.
This represents your perception of your friend's empathy for you.

Each sum can range from 0 to 28—the higher the sum, the greater the empathy.

Now, have your friend respond to the items and compare your answers. The results might well contribute to greater empathy in your relationship.

interest in understanding life rather than taking sides' (Adams, 2003a).

A look at criminal behaviour also demonstrates the link between empathy and ethics. People who commit the most offensive crimes against others, such as rape and child abuse, are not inhibited by any sense of how their offences affect the victims (Goleman, 1995). Promising new treatments can possibly change offenders' behaviour and attitudes by instilling in them the ability to imagine how others are feeling. In one program, offenders read emotional descriptions of crimes similar to the ones they have committed and watch videos of victims describing what it was like to be assaulted. They also write accounts of what their offence must have felt like to the victim, read these stories to others in therapy groups, and even take part in simulated re-enactments of the crime, in which they play the role of the victim. Through strategies like these, therapists try to help offenders develop the ethical compass that makes it more difficult to be indifferent to causing suffering in others.

Requirements for Empathy   Empathy may be valuable but it is not always easy to achieve. In fact, research shows that it's hardest to empathize with people who are radically different from us in age, sex, socio-economic status, intelligence, and so forth (Cronkhite, 1976). In order to make such perceptual leaps, you need to develop several skills and attitudes.

Open-mindedness   Perhaps the most important characteristic of an empathic person is the ability and disposition to be open-minded—to set aside for the moment your own beliefs, attitudes, and values and to consider those of the other person. Open-mindedness is especially difficult when the other person's position is radically different from your own. The temptation is to think (and sometimes say), 'That's crazy!' 'How can you believe that?' or 'I'd do it this way. . . .'

Being open-minded is often difficult because people confuse *understanding* another's position with *accepting* it. These are quite different matters. To understand why a friend disagrees with you, for example, does not mean you have to give up your position and accept hers.

Imagination   Being open-minded is often not enough to make you empathetic. You also need enough imagination to be able to picture another person's background and thoughts. A happily married or single person needs imagination to empathize with the problems of a friend considering divorce. A young person needs it to empathize with a parent facing retirement. A teacher needs it to understand the problems of students, just as students can't be empathic without trying to imagine how their instructor feels.

Making the effort to put oneself in another's position can produce impressive results. In one study (Regan and Totten, 1975), college students were asked to list their impressions of people either shown in a videotaped discussion or described in a short story. Half of the students were instructed to empathize with the people as much as possible, and the other half were not given any instructions about empathizing. The results were impressive. Students who did not practise empathy were prone to attribute a person's behaviour to personality characteristics. For example, they might explain a cruel statement by saying the speaker was mean, or they might attribute a divorce to the partners' lack of understanding. The empathic students, on the other hand, were more aware of possible elements in the situation that might have contributed to the reaction. For instance, they might attribute a person's unkind behaviour to job pressures or personal difficulties instead of simply labelling that person as mean. In other words, practising empathy seems to make people more understanding.

Commitment   Because empathizing is often difficult, a third necessary quality is a sincere desire to understand another person. Listening to unfamiliar, often confusing information takes time and is not always pleasant. If you aim to be empathic, be willing to accept the challenge.

By now, you can see the tremendous difficulties we encounter when we want to understand one another. Physiological distortion, psychological interference, social and cultural conditioning all insulate us from our fellow human beings. But the news is not all bad, for with a combination of determination and skill, we can do a better job of

Test Yourself   What are the three requirements for empathy and why do people often have difficulty with the first requirement?

spanning the gap that separates us and, as a result, enjoy more satisfying interpersonal relationships.

Summary

Many communication challenges arise because of differing perceptions. The process of interpersonal perception is a complex one, and a variety of factors influence each person's view of reality.

Interpersonal perception involves four phases: selection, organization, interpretation, and negotiation. A number of influences can affect how we perceive others' behaviour. Physiological factors include our senses, age, health, fatigue, hunger, and biological cycles. Psychological factors such as mood and self-concept also have a strong influence on how we regard others. In addition, social influences, such as sex and gender roles and occupational roles, play an important part in the way we view those with whom we interact. Finally, cultural influences shape how we recognize and make sense of others' words and actions.

Our perceptions are often affected by common perceptual tendencies. We are more likely to blame others than ourselves for misfortunes. We are influenced by our expectations. We are also influenced by obvious stimuli, even if they are not the most important factors. We cling to first impressions, even if they are mistaken. We assume others are similar to us. Finally, we favour negative impressions over positive ones.

One way to verify the accuracy of our interpretations is through perception checking. Instead of jumping to conclusions, communicators who check their perceptions describe the behaviour they noticed, offer two equally plausible interpretations, and ask for clarification from their partner.

Empathy is the ability to experience the world from another person's perspective. There are three dimensions to empathy: perspective taking, emotional involvement, and concern for the other person. Empathy has benefits for both the empathizer and the recipient. Some evidence suggests that there may be hereditary influences on the ability to empathize but that this ability can be developed with practice. The requirements for empathy include open-mindedness, imagination, and commitment.

Activities

1. **Critical Thinking Probe**
   Complete the following sentences:

   a. Women _____ .

   b. Men _____ .

   c. Francophones _____ .

   d. Anglophones _____ .

   e. Muslims _____ .

   f. Older people _____ .

   Now, ask yourself the degree to which each of your responses was a stereotype and/or a generalization. Is it possible to make generalizations about the groups listed above? How could your answers to these questions change the way you perceive and respond to people in these groups?

2. **Invitation to Insight**
   You can get a better appreciation of the importance of punctuation by using the format pictured in Figure 3.3 on page 74 to diagram the following situations:

   a. A father and daughter are growing more and more distant. The daughter withdraws because she interprets her father's coolness as rejection. The father views his daughter's aloofness as a rebuff and withdraws further.

   b. The relationship between two friends is becoming strained. One makes jokes to lighten up the tension, and the other becomes more tense.

   c. A couple is on the verge of breaking up. One partner frequently asks the other to show more affection; the other withdraws physical contact.

   Explain how each of these situations could be punctuated differently by the two participants. Next, use the same procedure to explain how an event from your experience could be punctuated in at least two different ways. Describe the consequences of failing to recognize the plausibility of each of these punctuation schemes.

3. **Invitation to Insight**
   Choose one of the following situations, and describe how it could be perceived differently by each person. Be sure to include the steps of selection, organization, and interpretation. What might their narratives sound like as they negotiate their perceptions? List any relevant physiological, psychological, social, and cultural influences, and also suggest how the communicators' self-concepts may have affected their perceptions.

   a. A customer complains to a salesperson about poor service in a busy store.

   b. A parent and teenager argue about the proper time for the teen to return home after a Saturday night date.

   c. A quiet student feels pressured when called upon by an instructor to speak up in class.

   d. A woman and a man argue about whether to increase the balance in the workplace by making special efforts to hire employees from under-represented groups.

4. **Invitation to Insight**
   On pages 83–6 of this chapter, we outline several common perceptual tendencies. Describe instances in which you committed each of them, and explain the consequences of each one. Which of these perceptual tendencies are you most prone to make, and what may be the results of making it? How can you avoid these tendencies in the future?

5. **Skill Builder**
   You can develop your empathy skills by putting yourself in the shoes of someone with whom you have an interpersonal relationship. With that person's help, describe *in the first person* how the other person views an issue that is important to him or her. In other words, try as much as possible to become that person and see things from his or her perspective. Your partner will be the best judge of your ability to make this perceptual jump, so use his or her comments to modify your account. After doing the exercise, describe how your attempt changed the way you might relate to the other person.

6. **Role Play**
   With a partner, choose one of the situations described below or recall a situation in which someone displayed ambiguous non-verbal behaviour and construct a perception-checking statement. Be sure to include a description of the behaviour and two plausible but different interpretations of the behaviour as well as a request for clarification. Now, have your partner act out the ambiguous behaviour and role-play your perception-checking statement with your partner. Reverse roles.

Situation One
Your sister arrives home from school, loudly drops her books, and walks by you without a greeting. You hear her bedroom door slam shut.

Situation Two
You call a close friend to talk about your exciting plans for the weekend and he/she is quiet, answering your questions but not elaborating on the plans or asking questions or offering his/her opinion. His/her mood seems very subdued and a bit distant.

Situation Three
You arrive at work and your boss gives you a list of things to be done. She is not as talkative as usual and she quickly walks away after giving you your instructions.

Discussion Questions

1. Imagine yourself at a family meal or celebration. How might the participants' perceptions of this event differ? Consider all the influences on perception described in this chapter to gain insight into the ways in which various family members might perceive the situation differently.

2. Consider the cultural influences on perception described in this chapter and the cultural values and norms described in Chapter 2. How might the common perceptual tendency to assume that others are like us create problems in Canada's multicultural society?

3. In what types of situations can our common tendencies in perception work to our advantage, and where would these same tendencies work to our disadvantage?

4. Some communication researchers argue that empathy is perhaps the most important element of communication competence. Would you agree or disagree? Why?

Chapter Four

Emotions

After studying the material in this chapter . . .

You Should Understand:

1. The three components of emotion.
2. The factors that influence the expression of emotion in contemporary society.
3. The influence of culture, biological sex, and gender on emotional expressiveness and sensitivity.
4. The relationships among activating events, thoughts, emotions, and communication behaviour.
5. Seven fallacies leading to unnecessarily debilitative emotions that can interfere with effective communication.
6. The steps in the rational-emotive approach for coping with debilitative emotions.

You Should Be Able To:

1. Observe the physical and cognitive manifestations of some of the emotions you experience.
2. Label your own emotions accurately.
3. Identify the degree to which you express your emotions and the consequences of this level of expression.
4. Follow the guidelines in this chapter in deciding when and how to express your emotions in an important relationship.
5. Realize which of your emotions are facilitative and which are debilitative.
6. Identify the fallacious beliefs that have caused you to experience debilitative emotions in a specific situation.
7. In a specific situation, apply the rational-emotive approach to managing your debilitative emotions.

Imagine how different life would be if you lost your ability to experience emotions. An emotionless world would be free of boredom, frustration, fear, and loneliness. But the cost of such a pain-free existence would be the loss of emotions like joy, pride, and love. Few of us would be willing to make that sort of trade-off. Being aware of and experiencing emotions is fundamental to the quality of our lives. People who have suffered damage to the areas of the brain that allow them to process emotional information have serious difficulty making decisions in daily life, despite the fact that the their regular cognitive abilities are still functioning normally (Bechara, 2004). Making decisions and navigating our lives requires the combination of cognitive processes and emotional responses. Emotions help humans solve the basic problems of social living (Keltner and Haidt, 2001).

The role of emotions in human affairs is apparent to social scientists and lay people alike. The concept of emotional intelligence has become part of our everyday understanding about how effectively people get along with others. *Emotional intelligence* involves the ability to reason about emotions and use emotions to enhance thinking. People who are better at perceiving and regulating emotions (in themselves and others), who use emotions in their thinking, and who understand the meaning of emotions are said to have high emotional intelligence (Austin et al., 2004; Mayer et al., 2004). People with high emotional intelligence appear to have more meaningful friendships with others, be more skilled at motivating others, and perform better in jobs where maintenance of positive personal commitments is required (Mayer et al., 2004). In contrast, people with low emotional intelligence are more likely to engage in physical (e.g., bullying, fights) and psychological (e.g., insults, emotional torment) aggression (Swift, 2002; Trinidad and Johnson, 2002) and higher alcohol consumption (Austin et al., 2004).

Because emotions are such an important part of human communication, we will take a close look at them in the following pages. We will explore what feelings are, discuss the ways they are handled in contemporary society, and see how recognizing and expressing them can improve relationships. We'll also look at some guidelines that should give you a clearer idea of when and how to express your emotions constructively. In the final section, we'll explore a method for coping with troublesome, debilitating feelings that inhibit rather than help your communication.

What Are Emotions?

Suppose an extraterrestrial visitor asked you to explain emotions. How would you answer? You might start by saying that emotions are things that we feel. But this doesn't say much, for, in turn, you would probably describe feelings as synonymous with emotions. Social scientists generally agree that there are three components to the phenomena we label as feelings (Planalp, 1999a; Scherer, 2000).

Physiological Changes

When a person has strong emotions, many bodily changes take place. For example, the physical components of fear include an increased heartbeat, a rise in blood pressure, an increase in adrenalin secretions, a high blood sugar level, a slowing of digestion, and a dilation of the pupils. Some of these changes are recognizable to the person having them. Such physiological messages can offer a significant clue to your emotions once you become aware of them. A churning stomach or tense jaw can also be a signal that something is wrong.

iStock photo

Cognitive Interpretations

Although there may be cases in which there is a direct connection between physical behaviour and emotional states, in most situations, the mind plays an important role in determining how we feel. As we noted, some physiological components of fear are a racing heart, perspiration, tense muscles, and raised blood pressure. Interestingly enough, these symptoms are similar to the physical changes that accompany excitement, joy, and other emotions. In other words, if we were to measure the physical condition of someone having a strong emotion, we would have a hard time knowing whether that person was trembling with fear or with excitement. The recognition that the bodily components of most emotions are similar led some psychologists to conclude that the experience of fright, joy, or anger comes primarily from the labels—and the accompanying cognitive interpretations—we give to our physical symptoms (Valins, 1966). In his book, *Shyness: What It Is, What to Do about It*, psychologist Philip Zimbardo offers a good example of this principle:

> I notice I'm perspiring while lecturing. From that I infer I am nervous. If it occurs often, I might even label myself a 'nervous person'. Once I have the label, the next question I must answer is, 'Why am I nervous?' Then I start to search for an appropriate explanation. I might notice some students leaving the room, or being inattentive. I am nervous because I'm not giving a good lecture. That makes me nervous. How do I know it's not good? Because I'm boring my audience. I am nervous because I am a boring lecturer and I want to be a good lecturer. I feel inadequate. Maybe I should open a delicatessen instead. Just then a student says, 'It's hot in here, I'm perspiring and it makes it tough to concentrate on your lecture.' Instantly, I'm no longer 'nervous' or 'boring'. (Zimbardo, 1977, p. 53)

Zimbardo discusses the consequences of making inaccurate or exaggerated attributions such as these. In a survey of more than five thousand people, over 80 percent described themselves as having been shy at some time in their lives, and more than 40 percent considered themselves to be shy at present. Most significantly, those who labelled themselves 'not shy' behaved in virtually the same way as their shy counterparts. They would blush, perspire, and feel their hearts pounding in certain social situations. The biggest difference between the two groups seemed to be the label with which they described themselves. This is a significant difference. Someone who notices the symptoms we've described and thinks, 'I'm such a shy person!' will most likely feel more uncomfortable and communicate less well than another person with the same symptoms who thinks, 'Well, I'm a bit shaky (or excited) here, but that is to be expected.'

We'll take a closer look at ways to reduce unpleasant emotions through cognitive processes later in this chapter.

Non-verbal and Verbal Expression

Feelings are often apparent by observable changes. Some of these changes involve a person's appearance: blushing, sweating, and so on. Other changes involve behaviour: a distinctive facial expression, a particular posture, certain gestures, different vocal tone and rate, and so on.

Although it's reasonably easy to tell when someone is feeling a strong emotion, it's more difficult to be certain exactly what that emotion might be. A slumped posture and sigh may be a sign of sadness or fatigue. Likewise, trembling hands may indicate excitement or fear. As we shall see in Chapter 6, non-verbal behaviour is usually ambiguous, and it's dangerous to assume that it can be 'read' with much accuracy.

Although we usually think of non-verbal behaviour as the reaction to an emotional state, there may be times when the reverse is true—when non-verbal behaviour actually causes emotions. As we saw in Chapter 2 (see page 53), people can actually create emotional states by altering their facial expressions. When volunteers were coached to smile, they reported feeling better, and when they altered their expressions to look unhappy, they felt worse (Kleinke et al., 1998). Previous research by Paul Ekman and his colleagues (1983) produced similar results, with subjects feeling afraid, angry, disgusted, amused, sad,

Focus on Research

Emotions Shape Perceptions

Consider the following scenarios (Edwards et al. 2001):

- You are enjoying a conversation with an acquaint-ance. After several minutes, she or he glances at her or his watch and says, 'Well, it was nice talking with you' and ends the conversation.
- Your boss and several co-workers are leaving a meet-ing you missed. A co-worker says to you, 'I noticed you weren't at the meeting. That's okay. Sometimes, I forget to check my schedule, too.'

How would you interpret these messages? According to data collected by Renee Edwards and her colleagues, your reaction would depend in part on how lonely you are.

Loneliness is an emotion involving 'psychological dis-tress that takes the form of a painful yearning for social contact.' It seems reasonable to assume that other unpleasant emotions, such as jealousy and anxiety, have a similar effect. In a few pages, you will learn ways to minimize these sorts of debilitative emotions. But when you are feeling insecure, alone, and otherwise unhappy, recall this research and consider that other people's messages may not be as negative as you first assume. Edwards and her research team asked college students for reactions to the scenarios above; they also measured the students' levels of loneliness. As predicted, students with higher levels of loneliness perceived the messages more negatively. Lonely individuals interpreted rejec-tion in the scenario comments, even though the mes-sages have positive undertones.

The researchers concluded that loneliness affects perceptions and interpretations and, therefore, leads to 'greater difficulty with communication.'

---

surprised, and contemptuous when they created facial expressions that mimicked those feelings. As behavioural scientists like to say, it can be easier to act yourself into new ways of feeling than to feel yourself into new ways of acting.

Non-verbal behaviour is a powerful way of com-municating emotion. In fact, non-verbal actions are better at conveying attitudes than they are at expressing ideas. But sometimes, words are neces-sary to express feelings. Is your friend's uncharac-teristically short temper a sign of anger at you, or does it mean something less personal? Is a lover's unenthusiastic response a sign of boredom with you or the result of a long workday? Is a new acquaintance mistaking your friendliness for a come-on? There are times—especially in our low-context culture—when you cannot rely on percep-tiveness to make sure a message is communicated and understood accurately.

The ability to communicate clearly about feel-ings has been characterized as part of *emotional intelligence*, which we discussed earlier in this chapter. Awareness of the intensity of emotions and the vocabulary to describe them accurately is important. Although we understand many words that describe emotions in varying intensity, we tend to rely on a few basic emotional labels (happy, sad, mad) and increase or decrease their intensity with words like 'really', 'kind of', etc. Rather than using these modifiers (*I was really, really happy*) and (*I was kind of angry*) to increase or decrease the intensity of our descriptions, we can enhance others' understanding of our experi-ences by choosing more accurate descriptors such as 'ecstatic' or 'annoyed'.

Research by John Gottman and his associates (1997) has shown that the way parents talk to their children about emotions has a strong influence on the children's development. They show how the coaching approach gives children skills for com-municating about feelings in later life that lead to much more satisfying relationships. The research-ers identified two distinct parenting styles: 'emo-tion coaching' and 'emotion dismissing'. Later in this chapter, you will find some guidelines for communicating effectively about emotions.

Influences on Emotional Expression

Each of us is born with the disposition to reveal our emotions, at least non-verbally. But over time, a wide range of differences develops in emotional expression. In the next few pages, we will look at some influences that shape how people communicate their feelings.

Personality

Science has established an increasingly clear relationship between personality and the way people experience and communicate emotions (Gross et al., 1998). For example, extroverted people—those with a tendency to be cheerful and optimistic, and to enjoy social contact—report more positive emotions in everyday life than more introverted individuals (Costa and McCrae, 1980). Conversely, people with neurotic personalities—those with a tendency to worry, be anxious, and feel apprehensive—report more negative emotions than less neurotic individuals.

These personality traits are at least partially biological in origin. Psychologist Turhan Canli and his colleagues (2001) used magnetic imaging to measure the relationship between personality type and brain activity. Experimental subjects who tested high on measures of extroversion also had greater brain reactivity to positive stimuli than less extroverted people. Those who scored high on neuroticism measures had more brain reactions to negative stimuli. One member of the research team summarized the role of neurological processing:

> Depending on personality traits, people's brains seem to amplify some aspects of experience over others. All of the participants saw very positive and very negative scenes, but people's reactions were very different. One group saw the cup as being very full while the other group saw it as very empty. (Willenz, 2001)

Although personality can be a strong force, it does not have to govern your communication satisfaction. Think of shyness, which can be considered the opposite of extroversion. Introverted people can devise comfortable and effective strategies for reaching out. For example, the Internet has proved to be an effective way for reticent communicators to make contact. Chat rooms, instant messaging, email, and computer-dating services all provide a non-threatening way to approach others and get acquainted (Campbell et al., 2006; Kelly et al., 2001; Madell and Muncer, 2006; Modayil et al., 2003; Scharlott and Christ, 1995).

Culture

Over one hundred years of research confirms the fact that certain basic emotions are experienced by people around the world (Gudykunst and Kim, 1997). No matter where a person is born and regardless of his or her background, the ability to feel happiness, sadness, surprise, anger, disgust,

iStock photo

and fear seems to be universal. People from all cultures also express these emotions in similar ways, at least in their facial expressions. A smile or scowl, for example, is understood everywhere.

Of course, this does not mean that the same events generate the same emotion in all cultures. The notion of eating cod tongues might bring a smile of delight to some residents of Newfoundland, though it would cause many other Canadians to grimace in disgust. More to the point of this book, research has shown that fear of strangers and risky situations is more common among people living in North America and Europe than those living in Japan, whereas Japanese tend to be more apprehensive about relational communication than North Americans and Europeans (Ting-Toomey, 1991).

There are also differences in the degree to which people in various cultures display their feelings (Aune and Aune, 1996; Cole et al., 2002). For example, social scientists have found support for the notion that people from warmer climates are more emotionally expressive than those who live in cooler places (Pennebaker et al., 1996). Over 2,900 respondents representing 26 nationalities reported that people from the southern part of their countries were more emotionally expressive than northerners. Geert Hofstede (1980) argues that countries high in uncertainty avoidance tend to display emotions more than countries low in uncertainty avoidance. Recall from Chapter 2 that uncertainty avoidance involves the degree to which members of a culture feel threatened by ambiguous situations. Countries whose members try to avoid ambiguous situations include Greece, Portugal, Belgium, Japan, Peru, France, Spain, Argentina, and Turkey. It follows logically that displaying emotions reduces uncertainty. In contrast, cultures whose members feel comfortable with unclear situations and tolerate ambiguity are less inclined to overtly express their feelings. According to Hofstede's research, these countries include Singapore, Denmark, Sweden, Hong Kong, Ireland, Britain, India, the Philippines, the United States, and Canada.

Cultural background influences the way we interpret others' emotions as well as the way we express our own. Recognition of emotion is generally more accurate when the person expressing the emotion and the person judging the emotional display both belong to in the same cultural group (Elfenbein and Ambady, 2002a). It makes sense that it would be easier to judge another person's emotional expressions accurately if you were familiar with the subtle differences in expressive style that are part of their culture. In addition, there is evidence that in cultures where interdependence is valued, people are more skilled at reading the emotions of others. For example, Jeffrey Sanchez-Burks and his colleagues (2003) found that Koreans were better able to infer feelings and attitudes of employers than Americans were. An emphasis on relationships within a culture encourages concern about other people's feelings. A comparison of US and Japanese mothers at play with their toddlers revealed that, whereas the American mothers asked questions about objects and supplied their children with information, Japanese mothers were much more inclined to talk about feelings (Azuma, 1994; Fernald and Morikawa, 1993).

In fact, one of the most significant factors influencing emotional expression is the position of a culture on the individualism–collectivism spectrum. Members of collective cultures (such as Japan and India) prize harmony among members of their in-group and discourage the expression of any negative emotions that might upset relationships among people who belong to it. By contrast, members of highly individualistic cultures like Canada and the United States feel comfortable revealing their feelings to people they are close to (Gallois, 1993; Matsumoto, 1991). Individualists and collectivists also handle emotional expression with members of out-groups differently. Whereas collectivists are quite frank about expressing negative emotions toward outsiders, individualists are more likely to hide emotions such as dislike (Triandis, 1994). It's easy to see how differences in display rules can lead to communication problems. For example, individualistic North Americans might view collectivistic Asians as less than candid, whereas a person raised in Asia could easily regard North Americans as being overly demonstrative.

Biological Sex and Gender

Even within our culture, biological sex and gender roles often shape the ways in which men and women experience and express their emotions (Wester et al., 2002). In fact, according to Swenson and Casmir (1998), biological sex is the best predictor of the ability to detect and interpret emotional expressions—better than academic background, amount of foreign travel, cultural similarity, or ethnicity. For example, research suggests that women are more physiologically attuned to emotions than men (Canli et al., 2002). A team of psychologists tested men's and women's ability to recall emotional images and found that women were 10 to 15 percent more accurate in remembering them. Furthermore, women's reactions to these emotion-producing stimuli were significantly more intense than men's. This research provides some support for the stereotype that women are better at remembering disputes and that men are better at forgetting them. It's important to note that a person's sex is not the only factor that shapes emotional sensitivity. As you learned earlier in this chapter, personality traits also play an important role.

iStock photo

Research on emotional expression also suggests that there is some truth in the cultural stereotype of the inexpressive male and the more demonstrative female. On the whole, women are more likely than men to express a wide range of feelings verbally and non-verbally (Kunkel and Burleson, 1999). On the Internet, the same differences between male and female emotional expressiveness apply. For example, women are more likely than men to use emoticons to clarify their feelings (Witmer and Katzman, 1997).

Whether on the Internet or in face-to-face conversations, men tend to be less emotionally expressive, particularly when it comes to revealing feelings of vulnerability, including fear, sadness, loneliness, and embarrassment. On the other hand, men are less bashful about revealing their strengths and positive emotions, and both sexes feel and express anger equally (Goldsmith and Fulfs, 1999).

One's sex is not the only variable that affects emotional sensitivity. A second factor is whether or not the other person is of the same sex. For example, men are more likely to express feelings (especially positive ones) to women than to other men (Floyd, 1997a). People are generally better at recognizing emotions of members of the same sex. Of course, these sex differences are statistical averages, and many men and women do not fit these profiles.

A third factor that influences sensitivity to the emotions of others is the person or people with whom we are communicating. For example, dating and married couples are significantly better at recognizing each other's emotional cues than are strangers, just as people from the same culture seem to be better at recognizing each other's emotions (Elfenbein and Ambady, 2002b). Similarly, people are more likely to express emotions with those they know well in both face-to-face and computer-mediated communication (Derks et al., 2008).

Focus on Research

Smiles

In their review of the literature on cross-cultural differences and similarities in the functions of smiles, University of Quebec researchers Ursula Hess, Martin Beaupré, and Nicole Cheung (2002) report that smiling is highly valued in Western society.

People who smile are generally regarded more positively. They are seen as more pleasant, sincere, sociable, honest, polite, relaxed, carefree, and competent. Children draw 'nice people' and 'clever people' smiling. In addition, French Canadians as well as recent immigrants to Canada from Asian and African countries were more likely to choose a smiling expression as most appropriate for a person of their culture performing a neutral task (waiting for a computer to boot up). They chose a neutral expression for non-group members performing the same task.

Given the positive associations of smiling, it is not surprising that people smile a lot. Women smile more than men, and people of European descent smile more than Asians. Members of individualistic cultures and collectivistic cultures generally report feeling comfortable smiling to the same types of people (such as family, friends, and acquaintances), but people from Asian cultures choose a smaller or less intense smile than North Americans of European descent. Generally there are not large differences in smiling behaviour between Asian and North American cultures. People in both cultures smile frequently and evaluate smiles positively. These researchers conclude that there are not significant cross-cultural differences in smiling behaviour; however, they suggest that the slightly less frequent and less intense smiles of people from Asian cultures need to be understood by westerners in order to avoid miscommunication.

A final factor is the difference in power between the two communicators. People who are less powerful learn—probably from necessity—to read the more powerful person's signals. One experiment suggested that 'women's intuition' should be relabelled 'subordinate's intuition'. In a study of opposite-sex twosomes, the person with less control—regardless of sex—was better at interpreting the leader's non-verbal signals than vice versa (Snodgrass, 1985).

Social Conventions

Canadians have a reputation for being polite, deferential, and law-abiding people (Adams, 2003a). Mainstream North American culture generally discourages the direct expression of most emotions. Count the number of genuine emotional expressions you hear over a two- or three-day period and you will discover that such expressions are rare. People are generally comfortable making statements of fact and often delight in expressing their opinions, but they rarely disclose how they feel.

Not surprisingly, the emotions that people do share directly are usually positive (although, as

iStock photo

Duck, 1992, points out, social rules even discourage too much expression of positive feelings). Communicators are reluctant to send messages that embarrass or threaten the face of others (Shimanoff, 1988). Historians offer a detailed description of the ways contemporary society discourages expressions of anger. When compared to past centuries, North Americans today strive to suppress this 'unpleasant' emotion in almost every situation, including child-rearing, the workplace, and personal relationships (Stearns and Stearns, 1986). Research supports this analysis. One study of married couples revealed that the partners shared complimentary feelings ('I love you') or face-saving ones ('I'm sorry I yelled at you'). They also willingly disclosed both positive and negative feelings about absent third parties ('I like Fred,' 'I'm uncomfortable around Gloria'). On the other hand, they rarely verbalized face-threatening feelings ('I'm disappointed in you') or hostility ('I'm mad at you') (Shimanoff, 1985).

In computer-mediated communication, too, people are more likely to express positive emotions. Emoticons are used in CMC primarily to express emotions that strengthen the verbal part of the message and express humour (Derks et al., 2008). It is interesting that people favour the use of emoticons to convey positive emotions, as some research suggests that people receiving emails at work (where the use of emoticons is usually discouraged) are more likely to misinterpret the emoticons as being more emotionally negative or neutral than intended (Kock, 2005; Kruger, Epley, Parker, and Ng, 2005). See the Focus on Technology box on page 164 in Chapter 6 for a more detailed discussion of emotion and computer-mediated communication.

Social Roles

Expression of emotions is also limited by the requirements of many social roles. Salespeople are taught always to smile at customers, no matter how obnoxiously they are behaving. Teachers are portrayed as paragons of rationality, supposedly representing their field of expertise and instructing their students with total impartiality. Students

Reflection

Email As a Safe Channel for Emotional Expression

I've never been very close to my sister, but last year, both of us got online and started sending email messages to each other. At first, we 'e-chatted' about once a week; now, it's almost daily. What's interesting is that my sister does not show her emotions very much in person, but in her emails, she 'bares her soul' to me.

Last week, we got together in person for the first time in months. I thought we would pick right up at the same level of emotional exchange that had become the norm in our online discussions. Wrong! In face-to-face conversation, it still seemed hard for her to express her feelings. It was kind of hard for me, too.

Funny thing is, she sent me an emotional email after she got home, telling me how much she enjoyed our get-together. It was warm and touching. It was also something she would never say to me in person.

are often rewarded for asking 'acceptable' questions and otherwise being submissive creatures (Trenholm and Rose, 1980).

The result of all these restrictions is that many of us lose the ability to feel deeply. Just as a muscle withers away when it is unused, our capacity to recognize and act on certain emotions decreases without practice. It's hard to cry after spending most of one's life fulfilling the role society expects of a man, even when the tears are inside. After years of denying anger, the ability to recognize that feeling takes real effort. For someone who has never acknowledged love for one's friends, accepting that emotion can be difficult indeed.

Fear of Self-Disclosure

In a society that discourages the expression of feelings, emotional self-disclosure can seem risky to people. For a parent, boss, or teacher whose life has been built on the image of confidence and certainty, it may be frightening to say, 'I'm sorry. I was wrong.'

Moreover, someone who musters up the courage to share feelings such as these still risks unpleasant consequences. Others might misunderstand. An expression of affection might be construed as a romantic invitation, and a confession of uncertainty might appear to be a sign of weakness. Another risk is that emotional honesty might make others feel uncomfortable. Finally, there's always a chance that emotional honesty could be used against you, either out of cruelty or thoughtlessness. In Chapter 9, we discuss alternatives to complete disclosure and suggest circumstances when it can be both wise and ethical to keep your feelings to yourself.

Emotional Contagion

Along with cultural rules, social roles, and self-induced fears, our emotions are also affected by the feelings of those around us through **emotional contagion**, the process by which emotions are transferred from one person to another. As Daniel Goleman (1995, p. 115) observed, 'We catch feelings from one another as though they were some kind of social virus.'

Although people differ in the extent to which they are susceptible to emotional contagion (Doherty, 1997), most of us recognize the degree to which emotions are 'infectious'. You can probably remember times when being around a calm person made you feel more at peace, or when your previously sunny mood was spoiled by contact with someone bad-tempered. Researchers have demonstrated that this process can happen quickly, and with little or no verbal communication. In one study (Sullins, 1991), two volunteers completed a survey that described their moods. They spent two unsupervised minutes together, ostensibly waiting for the researcher to return to the room. At the end of that time, they completed another emotional survey. Time after time, the brief exposure resulted in the less expressive partner's moods coming to resemble those of the more expressive one. If an expressive communicator can shape another person's feelings with so little effort in such a short time, it's easy to understand how emotions can be even more infectious with prolonged contact.

Test Yourself — Describe seven influences on emotional expression that shape how people communicate their feelings.

Guidelines for Expressing Emotions

A wide range of research supports the value of expressing emotions appropriately. At the most basic physiological level, people who know how to share their feelings are healthier than those who do not. On the one hand, under-expression of feelings can lead to serious ailments. Inexpressive people—those who value rationality and self-control, try to keep their feelings and impulses under wraps, and deny distress—are more likely to get a host of ailments, including cancer, asthma, and heart disease (DeAngelis, 1992; Mayne, 1999). On the other hand, people who are overly expressive also suffer physiologically. When people lash out verbally, their blood pressure jumps an average of twenty points, and in some people as much as a hundred points (Mayne, 1999; Siegman and Snow, 1997). The key to health, then, is to learn how to express emotions *constructively*. In a few pages, you will find guidelines for this important communication skill.

Beyond the physiological benefits, another advantage of expressing emotions effectively is the chance of improving relationships (Kennedy-Moore and Watson, 1999). As we explain in Chapter 9, self-disclosure is one path (though not

iStock photo

the only one) to intimacy. Even on the job, many managers and organizational researchers are contradicting generations of tradition by suggesting that expressing emotions constructively can lead to career success and also help workers feel better (Nelton, 1996).

Despite its benefits, expressing emotions effectively is not a simple matter (Fussell, 2002). It's obvious that showing every feeling of boredom, fear, anger, or frustration would get you into trouble. Even the indiscriminate sharing of positive feelings—love, affection, and so on—is not always wise. On the other hand, withholding emotions can be personally frustrating and can keep relationships from growing and prospering.

The following suggestions can help you decide when and how to express your emotions. Combined with the guidelines for self-disclosure in Chapter 9, they can improve the effectiveness of your emotional expression.

iStock photo

Recognize Your Feelings

Answering the question, 'How do you feel?' is not as easy for some people as others (Peper, 2000). Communication researchers Melanie Booth-Butterfield and Steven Booth-Butterfield (1998) have found that some people (whom they term 'affectively oriented') are much more aware of their own emotional states and use information about those feelings when they make important decisions. By contrast, people with a low affective orientation are usually unaware of their emotions and tend to consider feelings to be useless and unimportant. The researchers summarize studies showing a relationship between awareness of feelings and a wide range of valuable traits, including positive relationships between parents and children, the ability to comfort others, sensitivity to non-verbal cues, and even skilful use of humour. In other words, being aware of one's feelings is an important ingredient in communication skill.

As we saw earlier in this chapter, there are a number of ways in which feelings become recognizable. Physiological changes can be a clear sign of your emotional state. Monitoring your non-verbal behaviour is another excellent way to keep in touch with your feelings. You can also recognize your emotions by observing your thoughts, as well as the verbal messages you send to others. It's not far from the verbal statement, 'I hate this!' to the realization that you are angry (or bored, nervous, or embarrassed).

Choose the Best Language

Most people suffer from impoverished emotional vocabularies. Ask them how they are feeling, and the response will almost always include the same terms: *good* or *bad*, *terrible* or *great*, and so on. Take a moment now and see how many feelings you can write down. After you have done your best, look at the Self-Assessment activity on page 109 and see which ones you have missed from this obviously incomplete list.

Many communicators think they are expressing feelings when, in fact, their statements are **emotionally counterfeit**. For example, it sounds emotionally revealing to say, 'I feel like going to a show' or 'I feel we've been seeing too much of each other.' But, in fact, neither of these statements has any emotional content. In the first sentence, the word *feel* really stands in for an intention: 'I *want* to go to a show.' In the second sentence, the 'feeling' is really a thought: 'I *think* we've been seeing too much of each other.' You can recognize the absence of emotion in each case by adding a genuine word of feeling to it—for instance, 'I'm *bored* and I want to go to a show' or 'I think we've been seeing too much of each other and I feel *confined*.'

Relying on a small vocabulary of feelings is as limiting as using only a few terms to describe colours. To say that the ocean in all its moods, the sky as it varies from day to day, and the colour of your true love's eyes are all 'blue' tells only a fraction of the story. Likewise, it's overly broad to use a term like *good* or *great* to describe how you feel in situations as different as earning a high grade, finishing a marathon, and hearing the words 'I love you' from a special person.

There are several ways to express a feeling verbally:

- Through *single words*: 'I'm angry' (or 'excited,' 'depressed', 'curious', and so on).
- By describing *what's happening to you metaphorically*: 'My stomach is tied in knots'; 'I'm on top of the world.'
- By describing *what you'd like to do*: 'I want to run away'; 'I'd like to give you a hug'; 'I feel like giving up.'

One way to clarify emotional expression is to avoid overqualifying or downplaying your emotions—'I'm a *little* unhappy' or 'I'm *pretty* excited' or 'I'm *sort of* confused.' Of course, not all emotions are strong ones. We do feel degrees of sadness and joy, for example, but some communicators have a tendency to discount almost every feeling. Do you?

Finally, you can improve emotional expression by making it clear that your feeling is centred on a specific set of circumstances, rather than the whole relationship. Instead of saying, 'I resent you', say, 'I get resentful when you do not keep your promises.' Rather than, 'I'm bored with you,' say, 'I get bored when you talk about money.'

Share Multiple Feelings

Many times, the feeling you express is not the only one you are experiencing. For example, you might often express your anger but overlook the confusion, disappointment, frustration, sadness, or embarrassment that preceded it. To understand the importance of expressing multiple emotions, consider the following examples. For each one,

Take Two

- **Emotionally counterfeit:** statements that appear to describe feelings but lack emotional content.

ask yourself two questions: How would I feel? What feelings might I express?

- An out-of-town friend has promised to arrive at your house at six o'clock. When your guest hasn't arrived by nine, you are convinced there has been a terrible accident. Just as you pick up the phone to call the police and local hospitals, your friend strolls in with an offhand remark about getting a late start.
- You and your companion have a fight just before leaving for a party. Deep inside, you know you were mostly to blame, even though you are not willing to admit it. When you arrive at the party, your companion leaves you and flirts with several other attractive guests.

In situations like these, you would probably feel several emotions. Consider the case of the overdue friend. Your first reaction to his arrival would probably be relief: 'Thank goodness, he's safe!' But you would also probably feel anger: 'Why didn't he phone to tell me he'd be late?' The second example would probably leave you with an even greater number of emotions: guilt

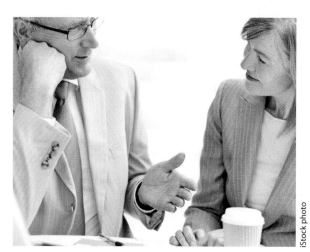

iStock photo

Self-Assessment

Identifying Your 'Favourite' Emotions

Circle the emotions that you experience often. Then put a plus sign next to those that you express effectively, and an X next to the ones that you communicate in less-than-satisfactory ways. (If one or more of your most-used or expressed emotions is not on this short list of all the possibilities, add it to the list.

____ affectionate	____ afraid	____ agitated	____ irritable	____ isolated	____ jealous
____ alienated	____ amazed	____ ambivalent	____ joyful	____ lazy	____ lively
____ angry	____ annoyed	____ anxious	____ lonely	____ lovable	____ loving
____ apathetic	____ ashamed	____ bashful	____ lovestruck	____ mad	____ mean
____ beaten	____ bewildered	____ bored	____ melancholy	____ miserable	____ misunderstood
____ bothered	____ brave	____ calm	____ mixed up	____ mortified	____ needy
____ cantankerous	____ carefree	____ caring	____ neglected	____ nervous	____ optimistic
____ cheerful	____ cocky	____ cold	____ overwhelmed	____ paranoid	____ passionate
____ comfortable	____ compassionate	____ concerned	____ peaceful	____ pessimistic	____ phony
____ confident	____ confused	____ content	____ playful	____ pleased	____ possessive
____ crazy	____ creative	____ cruel	____ preoccupied	____ prejudiced	____ pressured
____ curious	____ defeated	____ defensive	____ protective	____ puzzled	____ quiet
____ delighted	____ depressed	____ desperate	____ refreshed	____ regretful	____ relieved
____ detached	____ devastated	____ disappointed	____ rejected	____ remorseful	____ repulsed
____ disgusted	____ disturbed	____ eager	____ repulsive	____ resentful	____ restless
____ ecstatic	____ edgy	____ elated	____ restrained	____ ridiculous	____ romantic
____ embarrassed	____ empty	____ enthusiastic	____ sad	____ sadistic	____ secure
____ envious	____ evil	____ excited	____ seductive	____ self-pitying	____ self-reliant
____ exhausted	____ exhilarated	____ fearful	____ sentimental	____ sexy	____ shaky
____ fed up	____ fidgety	____ fixated	____ shocked	____ shy	____ silly
____ flattered	____ flirtatious	____ foolish	____ sincere	____ sinful	____ smug
____ forlorn	____ friendly	____ frightened	____ sorry	____ strong	____ stubborn
____ frustrated	____ furious	____ generous	____ stupid	____ subdued	____ superior
____ gentle	____ glad	____ glum	____ suicidal	____ supported	____ surprised
____ grateful	____ guilty	____ gutless	____ suspicious	____ sympathetic	____ tender
____ happy	____ harassed	____ hateful	____ tense	____ terrified	____ tired
____ helpless	____ high	____ hopeful	____ touchy	____ trapped	____ triumphant
____ hopeless	____ horrible	____ hostile	____ two-faced	____ ugly	____ uneasy
____ humiliated	____ hurried	____ hurt	____ unsure	____ useless	____ vindictive
____ hyper	____ hysterical	____ impatient	____ violent	____ vulnerable	____ warm
____ impressed	____ incompetent	____ inhibited	____ weak	____ weary	____ weepy
____ indecisive	____ inferior	____ insecure	____ wonderful	____ worried	____ wacky
____ insincere	____ interested	____ intimidated	____ youthful	____ zany	____ zonked

What lessons do your responses show? In what ways are you satisfied with your emotional expression? In what areas would you like to improve it? Keep your findings in mind as you continue reading this chapter.

at contributing to the fight, hurt and perhaps embarrassment at your friend's flirtations, and anger at this sort of vengefulness.

Despite the commonness of experiencing several emotions at the same time, we often communicate only one feeling—usually, the most negative one. In both of the preceding examples, you might show only your anger, leaving the other person with little idea of the full range of your feelings. Consider the different reaction you would get by describing *all* your emotions in these situations as well as others (see the Reflection box on page 111 for example.)

Recognize the Difference between Feeling and Acting

Just because you feel a certain way does not mean you must always act on it. In fact, there is compelling evidence that people who act out angry feelings—even by hitting a punching bag—actually feel worse than those who experience anger without lashing out (Bushman et al., 1999).

Recognizing the difference between feeling and acting can liberate you from the fear that getting in touch with certain emotions will commit you to some disastrous course of action. If, for instance, you think, 'I'm so nervous about the interview that I want to cancel it and pretend I'm sick,' it becomes possible to explore why you feel so anxious and then work to remedy the problem. Pretending that nothing is the matter, on the other hand, will do nothing to diminish your anxiety, which can then block your chances for success.

Accept Responsibility for Your Feelings

As you will soon read, people do not *make us* like or dislike them, and believing that they do denies the responsibility each of us has for our own emotions. It's important to make sure that your emotional expressions do not blame others for the way you feel. The 'I' language described in Chapter 5 makes it clear that you own your feelings. For example, instead of saying, 'You're making me angry', it is more accurate to say, 'I'm feeling angry.' Instead of uttering, 'You hurt my feelings', a more responsible statement is, 'I feel hurt when you do that.'

Choose the Best Time and Place to Express Your Feelings

Often, the first flush of a strong feeling is not the best time to speak out. If you are awakened by the racket caused by a noisy neighbour and you storm over to complain, you may say things you will later regret. In such a case, it's probably wiser to wait until you have thought out carefully how you might express your feelings in a way that would be most likely to be heard.

Even after you have waited for the first flush of feeling to subside, it's still important to choose the time that is best suited to the message. If you are rushed or tired or disturbed by some other matter, that is probably a good reason for postponing the expression of your feeling. Often, it can take a great amount of time and effort to attend to your emotions, and fatigue or distraction will make it difficult to follow through on the matter you have started. Similarly, you ought to be sure that the recipient of your message is ready to hear you out before you begin.

There are also cases where you may choose to never express your feelings. Even if you are dying to tell an instructor that her lectures leave you bored to a stupor, you might decide it's best to answer her question, 'How's class going?' with an innocuous, 'Okay.' And even though you may be irritated by the arrogance of a police officer who stops you for speeding, the smartest approach might be to keep your feelings to yourself as you're being ticketed.

Managing Difficult Emotions

Perceiving others more accurately is not the only challenge that communicators face. At times, we view *ourselves* in a distorted way. These distorted self-perceptions can generate a wide range of feelings—insecurity, anger, and guilt, to name a few—that interfere with effective communication.

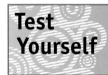

Test Yourself   What are the six guidelines to keep in mind when expressing emotions?

Reflection

Choosing the Emotion to Express First

Not long ago, our seventeen-year-old daughter spent the entire night out—without telling us about her plans to stay at a friend's. By 2:00 A.M., we were in a panic. We frantically called the police and the local hospitals, but she couldn't be found anywhere. My wife and I spent the entire sleepless night praying that she was all right and imagining all the awful things that might have happened to her.

When our daughter's car came up the driveway at 7:30 A.M., I was never so relieved in my life! But as soon as she walked in the door and I realized she was okay, I really let her have it. 'What were you thinking? How irresponsible can you be?' You can imagine how I sounded, and how defensively she reacted.

After a couple of minutes, I could see our 'conversation' headed in the wrong direction, and that it was at least partly my fault. I had shared only my anger, and not the feelings of relief, concern, and love that were even more important. 'Let's start over', I suggested. Then, I explained to her how worried we had been all night long, and what a relief it was for us to know that she was safe. What a difference! Our daughter still knew how angry we were, but she also understood that the anger came from love and concern. This experience taught me how important it is to share multiple feelings. Hearing the positive ones makes negative feelings a lot easier to accept.

To begin understanding how this process works, read on.

Facilitative and Debilitative Emotions

We need to make a distinction between **facilitative emotions**, which contribute to effective functioning, and **debilitative emotions**, which hinder or prevent effective performance. A classic example of a debilitative emotion is *communication apprehension*—feelings of anxiety that plague some people at the prospect of communicating in an unfamiliar or difficult situation such as giving a speech, meeting strangers, or being interviewed for a job.

Not surprisingly, debilitative emotions like communication apprehension can lead to a variety of problems in personal, business, educational, and even medical situations (Bourhis and Allen, 1992). When people become anxious, they generally speak less, which means their needs are not met; and when they do manage to speak up, they are less effective than their more confident counterparts (Patterson and Ritts, 1997). Research even suggests that people who express positive emotions live longer than those who focus more on negative feelings (Danner et al., 2001).

The difference between facilitative and debilitative emotions is often not one of quality as much as degree. For instance, a certain amount of anger or irritation can be constructive, since it often stimulates a person to improve the unsatisfying conditions. Rage, on the other hand, usually makes matters worse. The same is true of fear. A little bit of nervousness before a job interview may inspire you just enough to improve your performance (athletes or actors who are too relaxed usually do not do well), but a job candidate who is visibly nervous is not likely to impress potential employers (Ayres and Crosby, 1995). One big difference, then, between facilitative and debilitative emotions is their *intensity*.

A second characteristic of debilitative feelings is their extended *duration*. Feeling depressed for a while after the breakup of a relationship or the loss of a job is natural. Spending the rest of one's life grieving over the loss accomplishes nothing. In the same way, staying angry at someone for a wrong inflicted long ago can be just as punishing to the grudge holder as to the wrongdoer.

Finally, debilitative emotions are frequently based on irrational thinking that we might be unaware of. In order to minimize these emotions, we first need to examine the relationship between thinking and feeling and then explore some of the irrational beliefs people commonly hold.

Thoughts as a Cause of Feelings

The goal, then, is to find a method for getting rid of debilitative feelings while remaining sensitive to the more facilitative emotions. Fortunately, such a method—termed a **rational-emotive approach**—does exist (Ellis, 2001; Ellis and Dryden, 1997). This method is based on the idea that the key to changing feelings is to change unproductive thinking. Let's see how it works.

For most people, emotions seem to have a life of their own. They wish they could feel calm when approaching strangers, yet their voices quiver. They try to appear confident when asking for a raise, but their eyes twitch nervously. Many people would say that the strangers or the boss *makes* them feel nervous, just as they would say that a bee sting causes them to feel pain:

Activating Event	Consequence
Bee sting	Physical pain
Meeting strangers	Nervous feelings

When looking at emotions in this way, people may believe they have little control over how they feel. However, the causal relationship between activating events and emotional discomfort (or pleasure) is not as great as it seems. Cognitive psychologists and therapists argue that it is not events, such as meeting strangers or being jilted by a lover, that cause people to feel bad, but rather the *beliefs they hold* about these events.

Albert Ellis tells a story that clarifies this point. Imagine yourself walking by a friend's house and seeing your friend come to a window and call you a string of vile names. (You supply the friend and the names.) Under the circumstances, it's likely that you would feel hurt and angry. Now, imagine that instead of walking by the house, you were passing a psychiatric hospital when the same friend, who was obviously a patient there, shouted the same offensive names at you. In this case, your reaction would probably be quite different—most likely, you'd feel sadness and pity.

In this story, the activating event—being called names—was the same in both cases, and yet the emotional consequences were very different. The reason for different feelings has to do with the pattern of thinking in each case. In the first instance, you would most likely think that your friend was angry with you and that you must have done

something terrible to deserve such a response. In the second case, you would probably assume that your friend had experienced some psychological difficulty, so you would probably feel sympathetic. This example illustrates that people's *interpretations* of events determine their feelings:

Activating Event	Thought or Belief	Consequences
Being called names	'I don't deserve to be treated like this.'	Hurt, angry
Being called names	'My friend must be sick.'	Pity, sympathy

The same principle applies in more common situations. For example, the words 'I love you' can be interpreted in a variety of ways. They could be taken at face value as a genuine expression of deep affection. They might also be interpreted in a variety of other ways: for example, as an attempt at manipulation, a sincere but mistaken declaration uttered in a moment of passion, or an attempt to make the recipient feel better. One study revealed that women are more likely than men to regard expressions of love as genuine statements, instead of attributing them to some other cause (Booth-Butterfield and Trotta, 1994). It's easy to imagine how different interpretations of a statement like 'I love you' can lead to different emotional reactions:

Event		Thought		Feeling
Hearing 'I love you'	→	'This is a statement'	→	Delight genuine (perhaps)
Hearing 'I love you'	→	'S/he's just saying this to manipulate me.'	→	Anger

The key, then, to understanding and changing feelings lies in the pattern of thought, which manifests itself through **self-talk** (Vocate, 1994)—the non-vocal, internal monologue that is our process of thinking. To understand how self-talk works, pay attention to the part of you that, like a little

iStock photo

Take Two

- **Facilitative emotions:** contribute to effective functioning.
- **Debilitative emotions:** hinder and prevent effective performance; they are usually more intense and longer lasting than facilitative emotions and are frequently based on irrational thinking.
- **Rational-emotive approach:** a cognitively based therapeutic approach that involves getting rid of debilitative emotions by changing one's thinking.

voice, whispers in your ear. Take a moment now and listen to what the voice is saying.

Did you hear the voice? It was quite possibly saying, 'What little voice? I don't hear any voices!' This little voice talks to you almost constantly:

> 'Better pick up a loaf of bread on the way home.'
> 'I wonder when he's going to stop talking.'
> 'It certainly is cold today!'
> 'Are there two or four cups in a quart?'

At work or at play, while reading the paper or brushing our teeth, we all tend to think. This thinking voice rarely stops. It may fall silent for a while when you are running, riding a bike, or meditating, but most of the time, it rattles on.

Irrational Thinking and Debilitative Emotions

This process of self-talk is essential to understanding the debilitative feelings that interfere with effective communication. Many debilitative feelings come from accepting a number of irrational thoughts—we'll call them *fallacies* here—that lead to illogical conclusions and, in turn, to

debilitating feelings. We are not usually aware of these thoughts, and that makes them especially powerful (Bargh, 1988).

The Fallacy of Perfection   People who accept the **fallacy of perfection** believe that a worthwhile communicator should be able to handle any situation with complete confidence and skill. Although such a standard of perfection can serve as a goal and a source of inspiration (rather like making a hole in one for a golfer), it's totally unrealistic to expect that you can reach or maintain this level of behaviour. The truth is, people simply are not perfect. Perhaps the myth of the perfect communicator comes from people believing too strongly in novels, television, or films. In these media, perfect characters are often depicted: the perfect mate or child, the imperturbable and gregarious host, the amazingly competent professional. Although these fabrications are certainly appealing, real people will inevitably come up short compared to them.

People who believe that it's desirable and possible to be a perfect communicator come to think that they will not be appreciated if they are imperfect. Admitting mistakes, saying 'I don't know', or sharing feelings of uncertainty or discomfort thus seem to be social defects. Given the desire to be valued and appreciated, these people are tempted at least to try to *appear* perfect. They assemble a variety of social masks, hoping that if they can fool others into thinking that they are perfect, perhaps they'll find acceptance. The costs of such deception are high. If others ever detect that this veneer

Self-Assessment

Self-Talk and Resilience

There is considerable evidence that that little voice in your head is a major contributor to your ability to adapt to the challenges that life presents (Reivich and Shatte, 2002; Seligman, 1991). Research into resilience (the ability to persevere and adapt when things go awry) and optimism (looking to the future as an opportunity for achievement and happiness) suggests that flexible, accurate thinking skills are what separates people who cope well with stress from those who do not. Flexible, accurate thinking contributes to better overall physical and mental health because it mediates the negative effects of stress. Several longitudinal studies conducted at Harvard University found that flexible, accurate thinking styles in young adults predicted better physical and mental health, a more active social life, more stable long-term relationships, and greater overall life satisfaction at age eighty (Vaillant, 2002; Werner and Smith, 2001). Clearly, a resilient coping style has tremendous benefits, but how do we develop our own?

We develop our 'thinking habits' or the 'scripts' for that little voice in our heads throughout our lives, often by observing significant people in our lives (such as parents, teachers, and friends). We can learn more productive ways of thinking about and dealing with adversity at any age. One thing we can do is examine our explanatory style—our habitual ways of explaining why things happen to us. Explanatory style can be viewed in terms of three dimensions: *personalization*, *permanence*, and *pervasiveness* (Seligman, 1991). Each dimension needs to be viewed as a continuum:

When something goes wrong . . .

Who is to blame? (personalization)	Me	Not me
How long will it last? (permanence)	Always	Not always
How much of my life does it affect? (pervasiveness)	Everything	Not everything

There is no 'right' end to the continuum. The truth is usually somewhere in the middle, and a flexible, accurate thinker is able to see this. Often, however, when things go wrong, we reflexively assess these three dimensions and fall into habitual thinking traps. Some of us routinely blame ourselves and give way to despair, convinced that the difficulties confronting us will last forever and ruin our lives. Some of us are quick to blame others before giving the situation much thought, and we angrily conclude that other people have permanently ruined everything. Think about a problem your have had recently. What is your typical explanatory style, your 'explanation reflex'? Now, look at the situation more carefully. Rarely is a problem created as a result of just one person's actions; and how much of your life it affects and for how long may just depend on your point of view. Slow down and challenge your beliefs. Why not make that little voice in your head into an optimistic friend or 'life coach' rather than a harsh critic?

of confidence is false, the person hiding behind it is considered a phony. Even if the facade goes undetected, the performance consumes a great deal of psychological energy and diminishes the rewards of approval.

Not only can the myth of perfection keep others from liking you, but it also acts as a force to diminish self-esteem. How can you like yourself when you do not measure up to your own standards?

You become more liberated each time you comfortably accept the idea that you are not perfect. For example, like everyone else, you sometimes have a hard time expressing yourself. Like everyone else, you make mistakes from time to time, and there is no reason to hide it. You are honestly doing the best you can to realize your potential, to become the best person you can be.

The Fallacy of Approval Another mistaken belief is based on the idea that it is vital—not just desirable—to obtain everyone's approval. Communicators who subscribe to the **fallacy of approval** go to extreme lengths to seek acceptance from others, even to the extent of sacrificing their own principles and happiness. Adherence to this irrational myth can lead to some ludicrous situations, such as feeling nervous because people you really do not like seem to disapprove of you, or feeling apologetic when you are not at fault.

The myth of approval is irrational. It implies that some people are more respectable and more likeable because they go out of their way to please others. Often, this implication simply is not true. How respectable are people who have compromised

important values simply to gain acceptance? Are people highly regarded when they repeatedly deny their own needs as a means of buying approval? Genuine affection and respect are hardly due such characters. In addition, striving for universal acceptance is irrational because it is simply not possible.

Don't misunderstand: abandoning the fallacy of approval does not mean living a life of selfishness. It's still important to consider the needs of others. It's also pleasant—perhaps even necessary—to

Focus on Technology

Social Inclusion, the Internet, Webcams, and Text Messages

Why do we seek approval from others and why does it hurt so much when they reject us? In an extensive review of the literature regarding social and physical pain, Geoff MacDonald and Mark Leary (2005) suggest that the need to belong to a group is central to our survival as a species and that some of the same brain mechanisms that signal physical pain (e.g., stubbing your toe) are activated by social pain (e.g., not being invited to a party), too. It is interesting that we seldom ruminate about episodes of physical pain that we have experienced but we frequently relive social pain over and over again in our minds, often reconstructing the argument or incident and replacing what we said with what we wished we had said. It is also ironic that a common response to social rejection is anger. It makes sense to get angry when you have been physically hurt. Anger arouses your autonomic nervous system preparing you for a 'flight or fight' response, which can be helpful in the event of a physical threat. But physically fighting or running away seldom ingratiates you with others or helps you to be included. Nevertheless, most people persevere in their social worlds despite the scrapes and scratches of social rejection. They do this without fighting or running away because belonging is a fundamental human need.

For many people who are shy or socially anxious, venturing forth into the social world and risking social rejection can be even more challenging. Researchers have been interested in the social opportunities provided by the Internet and text-messaging (Campbell et al., 2006;

Modayil et al., 2003; Reid and Reid, 2004). They have found that the Internet provides benefits to people who have experienced social difficulties (Modayil et al., 2003). It allows them to connect with people who share the same interests and it provides opportunities to rehearse behaviour and communication skills that may help them in face-to-face social interactions (Campbell et. al., 2006). In a comparison of people using cell phones to either text or talk, Donna and Fraser Reid (2007) found that, in comparison with talkers, texters were more socially anxious and likelier to disclose information about themselves through text rather than in face-to-face or phone conversations. The Reids conclude that there is something special about texting that allows some people to translate their social anxiety into productive relationships.

While shy and socially anxious people may not necessarily use computer-mediated communication channels more than their more socially confident peers, they may experience greater benefits from the social opportunities these channels provide. Sarah Stevens and Tracy Morris (2007) found in their sample that although the university students with dating anxiety were not more likely to develop online relationships than their less-anxious peers, they were more likely to use webcams to make and maintain their relationships. These authors speculate that perhaps the blushing and trembling that socially anxious people experience when dating are less noticeable in webcam interactions compared to face-to-face encounters. Being included and feeling we have social support is paramount to our well-being and the Internet and other technologies such as mobile phones appear to provide us with more choices about how we initiate and maintain our relationships with others.

strive for the respect of certain people. The point is that the price is too high if you must abandon your own needs and principles in order to gain this acceptance.

The Fallacy of Should One huge source of unhappiness is the inability to distinguish between what *is* and what *should be*, or the **fallacy of should**. For instance, imagine a person who is full of complaints about the world:

'There should be no rain on weekends.'
'People ought to live forever.'
'Money should grow on trees.'
'We should all be able to fly.'

Beliefs such as these are obviously foolish. However pleasant such wishing may be, insisting that the unchangeable should be altered won't affect reality one bit. Yet, many people torture themselves with this sort of irrational thinking: they confuse 'is' with 'ought'. They say and think:

'That guy should drive better.'
'She shouldn't be so inconsiderate.'
'They ought to be more friendly.'
'He should work harder.'

In each of these cases, the person would *prefer* that people behaved differently. Wishing that things were better is perfectly legitimate, and trying to change them is, of course, a good idea; but it is unreasonable to insist that the world operate just as one wants it to. Parents wish that their children were always considerate and neat. Teachers wish that their students were fascinated with the subjects discussed in class and willing to study diligently. As the old saying goes, those wishes and a quarter (now more like a dollar) will get you a cup of coffee.

An obsession with what *should* be yields three bad consequences: First, it leads to unnecessary unhappiness. People who are constantly dreaming about the ideal are seldom satisfied with what they have. For instance, partners in a marriage who focus on the ways in which their spouse could be more considerate, sexy, or intelligent have a hard time appreciating the qualities of character that drew them together in the first place.

Second, the obsession keeps you from changing unsatisfying conditions. One employee, for example, constantly complains about problems on the job: there should be better training, the pay ought to be higher, the facilities should be upgraded, and so on. This person could be using the same energy to improve such conditions. Of course, not all problems have solutions; but when they do, complaining is rarely very productive. As one college manager puts it, 'Rather than complain about the cards you are dealt, play the hand well.'

Finally, this obsession tends to cause defensiveness in others. Imagine living around someone who insisted that people be more punctual, work harder, or refrain from using certain language. This kind of carping is obviously irritating. It's much easier to be around people who comment without preaching.

The Fallacy of Overgeneralization The **fallacy of overgeneralization** occurs when a person bases a belief on a *limited amount of evidence*. Consider the following statements:

'I'm so stupid! I can't understand how to do my income tax.'
'Some friend I am! I forgot my best friend's birthday.'

In these cases, people have focused on a single shortcoming as if it represented everything. Sometimes people forget that despite their difficulties, they have solved tough problems, and that although they can be forgetful, they are often caring and thoughtful.

A second, related category of overgeneralization occurs when we *exaggerate shortcomings*:

'You *never* listen to me.'
'You're *always* late.'
'I can't think of *anything*.'

Upon closer examination, such absolute statements are almost always false and they usually lead to discouragement or anger. It's better to replace overgeneralizations with more accurate messages:

'You often don't listen to me.'
'You've been late three times this week.'
'I haven't had any ideas I like today.'

The Fallacy of Causation   People who live their lives in accordance with the **fallacy of causation** believe they should do nothing that can hurt or in any way inconvenience others because it will cause undesirable feelings. For example, you might visit friends or family out of a sense of obligation rather than a genuine desire to see them, because you believe their feelings will be hurt if you don't visit them. Did you ever avoid objecting to behaviour that you found troublesome because you didn't want to cause anger? You may, on occasion, have pretended to be attentive—even though you were late for an appointment and in a rush—because you didn't want a person to feel embarrassed for 'holding you up'. Then there were the times when you substituted praise for more honest, negative responses in order to avoid hurting someone.

A reluctance to speak out in such situations often results from assuming that one person can cause another's emotions—that others, for example, are responsible for your feeling disappointed, confused, or irritated, or that you are responsible for others feeling hurt, angry, or upset. Actually, this assumption is sometimes incorrect. We may *act* in provocative ways, for which we are responsible, but each person is also responsible for the way he or she *reacts*.

To understand why each person is responsible for his or her own feelings, consider how strange it sounds to suggest that people *make* you fall in love with them. Such a statement simply doesn't make sense. It would be more correct to say that people first act in one way or another; then you may or may not fall in love as a result of these actions.

In the same way, it's not accurate to say that people *make* you angry, upset, or even happy. Behaviour that upsets or pleases one person might not bring any reaction from another. If you doubt this fact,

Reflection

Thinking about an Annoying Friend

My friend Maria talks about her personal life at length, but when I talk about myself for more than a couple of minutes, she has few comments and quickly turns the conversation back to her favourite topic: herself.

Until lately, Maria's egocentric focus was beginning to hurt my feelings. When Maria talks about herself, I think that what I have to say isn't interesting or that she doesn't care about me as a friend. I feel neglected, as if our relationship is one-sided.

Lately, I've started to think about other reasons Maria talks so much. For example, she's told me that I am a great listener and that I help her by lending an ear. Also, I've realized that Maria seldom gets to talk about herself (she spends all day talking to customers on the phone and is engaged to a very talkative guy).

So now I have started to take Maria's self-centred approach less personally. I still wish she would listen to me more, but I don't think that her egocentrism is making me resentful. It's my choice whether to accept her as she is, speak up about what I want, or see less of her.

think about people you know who respond differently to the same behaviour that you find so bothersome. (You may scream 'idiot!' when you are driving and someone switches lanes in front of you without signalling, while the person driving the car behind you may not even notice, or may notice but not care.) The contrast between their reactions and yours shows that responses are determined more by our own temperament and thinking than by the actions of others.

The Fallacy of Helplessness   The **fallacy of helplessness** suggests that forces beyond our control determine our satisfaction in life. People with this outlook continually see themselves as victims:

'There's no way a woman can get ahead in this society. It's a man's world, and the best thing I can do is to accept it.'

'I was born with a shy personality. I'd like to be more outgoing, but there's nothing I can do about that.'

'I can't tell my boss that she is putting too many demands on me. If I did, I might lose my job.'

The error in such statements becomes apparent once a person realizes that few paths are completely closed. In fact, most 'can't' statements may be more correctly restated in one of two ways.

The first is to say that you *won't* act in a certain way—that you choose not to do so. For instance, you may choose not to stand up for your rights or to follow unwanted requests, but it is usually inaccurate to claim that some outside force keeps you from doing so. The other way to rephrase a 'can't' is to say that you *don't know how* to do something. Examples of such a situation include not knowing how to complain in a way that reduces defensiveness, or not knowing how to conduct a conversation. Many difficulties a person claims can't be solved do have solutions. The task is to discover those solutions and to work diligently at applying them.

When viewed in this light, many 'can'ts' are really rationalizations to justify an unwillingness to change. Research supports the dangers of helpless thinking (Marangoni and Ickes, 1989). Lonely people tend to attribute their poor interpersonal relationships to uncontrollable causes. 'It's beyond my control,' they think. For example, lonely people are more negative than non-lonely ones about ever finding a mate. Also, they expect their relational partners to reject them. Notice the self-fulfilling prophecy in this attitude: believing that your relational prospects are dim can lead you to act in ways that make you an unattractive prospect. Once you persuade yourself that there's no hope, it's easy to give up trying. On the other hand, acknowledging that there is a way to change—even though it may be difficult—puts the responsibility for the predicament on your shoulders. Knowing that you can move closer to your goals makes it difficult to complain about the present. You *can* become a better communicator.

The Fallacy of Catastrophic Expectations   Some fearful people operate on the assumption that if something bad can happen, it probably will. This is the **fallacy of catastrophic expectations**—a position similar to Murphy's Law. These statements are typical of such an attitude:

'If I invite them to the party, they probably won't want to come.'

'If I speak up in order to try to resolve a conflict, things will probably get worse.'

'If I apply for the job I want, I probably won't be hired.'

'If I tell them how I really feel, they'll probably just laugh at me.'

Once you start imagining terrible consequences, a self-fulfilling prophecy can begin to build. One study revealed that people who believed that their romantic partners would not change for the better were likely to behave in ways that contributed to the breakup of the relationship (Metts and Cupach, 1990). Catastrophic thinking often takes the form of *rumination*—recurrent thoughts not demanded by the immediate environment. For example, jealous lovers who dwell on imagined transgressions of their partners feel more distressed than necessary and act in unhelpful ways toward their partners (Carson and Cupach, 2000).

iStock photo

Self-Assessment

Can't, Won't, or Don't Know How

Decide whether you subscribe to the fallacy of helplessness by doing an exercise: Describe two important (to you) difficulties you have in communicating with a) family members, b) people at school or at work, c) strangers, and d) friends. Use the following format for each difficulty:

I can't _____,

because _____.

Now, read the list, but with a slight difference. For each 'can't', substitute the word *won't*. Note which statements are actually 'won'ts'.

Read the list again, but this time substitute 'I do not know how to' for your original 'can't'. Rewrite any statements that are truly 'do not know hows', and decide what you could do to learn the skill that you currently lack.

On the basis of your experience, decide whether you subscribe to the fallacy of helplessness and what you could do to eliminate this sort of debilitative thinking from your life.

Minimizing Debilitative Emotions

How can you overcome irrational thinking? Social scientists have developed a simple yet effective approach (Ellis, 2001; Ellis and Dryden, 1997). When practised conscientiously, it can help you cut down on the self-defeating thinking that leads to many debilitative emotions.

Monitor Your Emotional Reactions The first step is to recognize when you are having debilitative emotions. (Of course, it's also nice to be aware of

Test Yourself List the seven fallacies or irrational types of thinking that can create debilitative emotions. Provide an example of each fallacy.

pleasant feelings when they occur!) As we suggested earlier, one way to notice feelings is through physical stimuli: butterflies in the stomach, racing heart, blushing, and so on. Although such reactions might be symptoms of food poisoning, more often they reflect a strong emotion. You also can recognize certain ways of behaving that suggest your feelings—stamping instead of walking normally, being unusually quiet, and speaking in a sarcastic tone of voice are some examples.

It may seem strange to suggest that it's necessary to look for emotions—they ought to be immediately apparent. However, the fact is that we often suffer from debilitative feelings for some time without noticing them. For example, at the end of a trying day you have probably caught yourself frowning and realized that you have been wearing that face for some time without knowing it.

Remember the two key characteristics of debilitating emotions, intensity (they are *too* intense) and duration (they last *too* long), and use them to guide your assessment.

Note the Activating Event Once you realize how you are feeling, the next step is to figure out what activating event triggered your response. Sometimes, it is obvious. If your sweetheart keeps calling you by the name of a former lover, you are likely to become upset. In other cases, however, the activating event is not so apparent.

Sometimes, there is no single activating event but instead a series of small incidents that finally trigger a debilitative feeling. This sort of thing happens when someone teases you over and over about the same thing, or when you suffer a series of small disappointments.

The best way to begin tracking activating events is to notice the circumstances in which you have debilitative feelings. Perhaps they happen when you are around *specific people*. For example, you may feel tense or angry every time you encounter a person you have struggled with in the past (Gayle and Preiss, 1999). Until those issues are dealt with, feelings about past events can trigger debilitative emotions, even in apparently innocuous situations.

In other cases, you might discover that being around certain *types of individuals* triggers debilitative emotions. For instance, you might become nervous around people who seem more intelligent or self-confident than you are. In other cases, certain *settings* can stimulate unpleasant emotions: parties, work, school. Sometimes, the *topic of conversation* is what sets you off, whether it is politics, religion, sex, or some other subject. Recognizing your activating events is an important step in minimizing debilitative emotions.

Record Your Self-Talk This is the point at which you analyze the thoughts that are the link between the activating event and your feelings. If you are serious about getting rid of debilitative emotions, it's important to actually write down your self-talk when you are learning to use this method. Putting your thoughts on paper will help you see whether or not they make any sense.

Monitoring your self-talk might be difficult at first. This is a new skill, and any new activity seems awkward. If you persevere, however, you will be able to identify the thoughts that lead to your debilitative feelings. Once you get into the habit of recognizing this internal monologue, you will be able to identify your thoughts quickly and easily.

Dispute Your Irrational Beliefs The key to success in the rational-emotive approach is to dispute your irrational beliefs. Use the discussion of irrational fallacies on pages 113–118 to find out which of your internal statements are based on mistaken thinking.

You can do this most effectively by following three steps. First, decide whether each belief you have recorded is rational or irrational. Next, explain why the belief does or does not make sense. Finally, if the belief is irrational, write down an alternative way of thinking that is more sensible and that can leave you feeling better when you are faced with the same activating event in the future.

After reading about this method for dealing with unpleasant emotions, some readers have objections:

'This rational-emotive approach sounds like nothing more than trying to talk yourself out of feeling bad.' This accusation is totally correct. After all, since we talk ourselves into feeling bad, what's wrong with talking ourselves out of bad feelings, especially when they are based on irrational thoughts? Rationalizing may be an excuse and a self-deception, but there's nothing wrong with being rational.

'The kind of disputing we just read sounds phony and unnatural. I don't talk to myself in sentences and paragraphs.' There's no need to dispute your irrational beliefs in any special literary style. You can be just as colloquial as you want. The important thing is to understand clearly what thoughts led you into your debilitative feeling so you can clearly dispute them. When the technique is new to you, it's a good idea to write or talk out your thoughts in order to make them clear. After you have had some practice, you will be able to do these steps in a quicker, less formal way.

'This approach is too cold and impersonal. It seems to aim at turning people into cold-blooded, calculating, emotionless machines.' This is simply not true. A rational thinker can still dream, hope, and love. There's nothing necessarily irrational about feelings like those. Rational people usually indulge in a bit of irrational thinking once in a while. But they usually know what they are doing. Like healthy eaters who occasionally treat themselves to a snack of junk food, rational thinkers occasionally indulge in irrational thoughts, knowing that they'll return to their healthy lifestyle soon with no real damage done.

'This technique promises too much. There's no chance I could rid myself of all unpleasant feelings, however nice that might be.' We can answer this by assuring you that rational-emotive thinking probably will not

Building Work Skills

Challenging Irrational Beliefs

Debilitative emotions at work or school can prevent you from making decisions and solving problems. Choose an important situation you faced at work or school in which you experienced debilitative emotions that interfered with your ability to communicate effectively. Use the four steps on pages 120–1 to challenge the rationality of your beliefs. How has the rational emotive approach affected your communication in this situation?

solve all your emotional problems. What it can do is reduce their number, intensity, and duration. This method is not the answer to all your problems, but it can make a significant difference—which is not a bad accomplishment.

Summary

Emotions have several dimensions. They are signalled by internal physiological changes, manifested by verbal and non-verbal reactions, and defined in most cases by cognitive interpretations. Some emotions are first-order and others are second-order. Some are primary, while others are combinations of two or more emotions. Some are intense, while others are relatively mild.

There are several reasons why people do not verbalize many of the emotions they feel. Certain personality types respond to emotions more negatively than others. Some cultures encourage and others discourage the expression of emotions. Social rules discourage the expression of some feelings, particularly negative ones. Many social roles do not allow expression of certain feelings. Some people express emotions so rarely that they lose the ability to recognize when they are feeling them. Finally, fear of the consequences of disclosing some emotions leads people to withhold expression of them.

Since total expression of feelings is not acceptable in adults, several guidelines help define when and how to share emotions. Self-awareness, clear language, and expression of multiple feelings are important. Willingness to accept responsibility for one's feelings instead of blaming them on others leads to better reactions. Choosing the proper time and place to share feelings is also important.

While some emotions are facilitative, debilitative feelings inhibit effective functioning. Many of these debilitative emotions are caused by various types of irrational thinking. It is often possible to communicate more confidently and effectively by recognizing troublesome emotions, identifying the activating event and self-talk that triggered them, and replacing any irrational thoughts with a more logical analysis of the situation.

Activities

1. **Invitation to Insight**

   The Self-Assessment exercise on page 109 explored your 'favourite' emotions without focusing on any particular personal relationship. What happens when you have a specific relationship in mind? Using the list of emotions in the Self-Assessment box, do the following exercise:

   a. Think of an important personal relationship.
   b. Identify the few emotions that are the most important for *you* in the relationship.
   c. Name the few emotions that you think are the most important for the *other person* in the relationship.
   d. Describe how you express each emotion you chose as most important for you. Think of the frequency with which you express each feeling, the circumstances in which you express it, and the ways you express it.
   e. Describe how the other person expresses each emotion you identified as most important for her or him. Think of the frequency with which the other person expresses each feeling, the circumstances in which it is expressed, and how she or he expresses it.
   f. What have you learned about yourself, the other person, and your relationship by conducting this analysis?

   If possible, invite the other person to do the same analysis and compare your results.

2. **Skill Builder**

   Choose an important emotion you experience in one of your relationships. This relationship needn't be highly personal. You might, for example, focus on an employer, an instructor, or a neighbour. Use the guidelines on pages 106–10 to determine whether and how you might express this emotion.

3. **Ethical Challenge**

   According to the rational-emotive approach, we cause our own feelings by interpreting an event in one way or another. If this is true, it is a fallacy to claim we 'make' others feel happy or sad. Do you accept this position? To what degree are you responsible for communicating in ways that 'cause' others to feel happy or sad? Use a specific incident from your life to illustrate your answer.

4. **Role Play**

   Choose a partner. Together, develop a specific scenario in which you have sent an email that your partner has interpreted much more negatively than you intended. Discuss your options to clarify this situation and then role-play your solution to the problem. Now, switch roles.

Discussion Questions

1. What are emotions? What do they contribute to the human experience of life?

2. How are first-order and second-order emotions different?

3. Seven influences on emotional expression are described in this chapter. Explain how each has influenced your ability and motivation to communicate your feelings.

4. Six guidelines for expressing emotions are described in this chapter. Do you think these guidelines are complete? Are there any guidelines you would add? Remove? Why?

5. Albert Ellis has argued that thoughts cause emotions. Would you agree or disagree? Why?

6. Several common but flawed beliefs, or fallacies, are described in this chapter. Which ones are you most susceptible to? Why do your think that is?

7. Discuss the value of self-talk in managing difficult emotions. How is the recent emergence of 'life coaches' related to this concept?

Chapter Five

Language

After studying the material in this chapter . . .

You Should Understand:

1. The symbolic nature of language.
2. That meanings are in people, not words.
3. The types of rules that govern the use of language.
4. How language affects worldview.
5. The influence of language on identity, credibility and status, affiliation, attraction, interest, power, and attitudes about sexism and racism.
6. The factors that influence precision and vagueness in language.
7. The language patterns that reveal a speaker's level of responsibility for his or her statements.
8. Three forms of disruptive language.
9. The relationship between culture and verbal styles, and the influence of language on perceptions.
10. The relationship between language use, biological sex, gender roles, and non-sex related factors.

You Should Be Able To:

1. Identify cases in which you have attributed meanings to words instead of people.
2. Analyze a real or potential misunderstanding in terms of semantic or pragmatic rules.
3. Describe how the principles presented in the section of this chapter entitled 'The Influence of Language' operate in your life.
4. Construct a message at the optimal level of specificity or vagueness for a given situation.
5. Construct statements that acknowledge your responsibility for the content of messages.
6. Rephrase disruptive statements in less inflammatory terms.
7. Explain how culture affects verbal style.
8. Identify similarities and difference between male and female language.

'I don't know what you mean by "glory",' Alice said.

Humpty Dumpty smiled contemptuously. 'Of course you do not—till I tell you. I meant "there's a nice knock-down argument for you!"'

'But "glory" does not mean "a nice knock-down argument",' Alice objected.

'When I use a word', Humpty Dumpty said, in a rather scornful tone, 'it means just what I choose it to mean—neither more nor less.'

'The question is', said Alice, 'whether you can make words mean so many different things.'

'The question is', said Humpty Dumpty, 'which is to be master—that's all.'

—Lewis Carroll, *Through the Looking Glass*

Like Alice, at one time or another everyone has felt trapped in a linguistic wonderland. Words shift meanings until we don't know what other people or even we ourselves, are saying. Although language is an imperfect vehicle with which to convey ideas, it is also a marvellous tool. On an everyday level, it allows us to carry on the normal activities that make civilized life possible. Language is a foundation for our personal relationships, and it is a tool for understanding and expressing who we are. To appreciate the tremendous importance of language, imagine how impossible life would be without it. We could survive without eyesight or hearing, and life would still be possible without a limb. But without the ability to use language, we would hardly be human—at least not in the usual sense of the word.

In this chapter, we will examine the relationship between words and ideas. We will describe some important characteristics of language and show how these characteristics affect our day-to-day communication. We will outline several types of troublesome language and show how to replace them with more effective kinds of speech. Finally, we will look at the power language has both to shape and to express our attitudes toward others.

The Nature of Language

We begin our survey by looking at some features that characterize all languages. These features explain both why language is such a useful tool and why it can be so troublesome.

Language Is Symbolic

Words are arbitrary symbols that have no meaning in themselves. For example, the word *five* is a kind of code that represents the number of fingers on your hand only because we agree that it does. As Bateson and Jackson (1964, p. 271) point out, 'There is nothing particularly five-like in the number "five".' To a speaker of French, the symbol *cinq* conveys the same meaning; to a computer, the same value is by the electronically coded symbol *00110101*.

Even sign language, as 'spoken' by most deaf people, is symbolic in nature and not the pantomime it may seem to be. Because this form of communication is symbolic and not literal, there are hundreds of different sign languages used around the world; they have evolved independently whenever significant numbers of deaf people have come together (Sacks, 1989). These distinct languages include American Sign Language, British Sign Language, French Sign Language, Danish Sign Language, Chinese Sign Language, and Australian Aboriginal and Mayan sign languages.

Language Is Governed by Rules

The only reason symbol-laden languages work at all is that people agree on how to use them. The linguistic agreements that make communication possible can be codified in rules. Languages

iStock photo

contain several types of rules. **Phonological rules** govern how sounds are combined to form words. For instance, the words *champagne*, *double*, and *occasion* have the same meaning in French and English but are pronounced differently because the languages have different phonological rules.

Syntactic rules govern the way symbols can be arranged. Notice that the following statements contain the same words, but the shift in syntax creates quite different meanings:

> Whisky makes you sick when you're well.
> Whisky, when you're sick, makes you well.

Although most of us are not able to describe the syntactic rules that govern our language, it's easy to recognize their existence by noticing how odd a statement that violates them appears. Sometimes, however, apparently ungrammatical speech is simply following a different set of syntactic rules. For example, English spoken in Newfoundland and Labrador has many non-standard features in its grammar, pronunciation, and vocabulary. If you apply the rules of Standard English syntax to the statement, 'Throw Mum down the stairs her keys', you would be confused about who or what is going down the stairs. But in parts of Newfoundland and Labrador, this construction clearly means it's Mum's keys, not Mum, that are being thrown down the stairs. There are several well-established English subsystems in the province, each with its own pronunciations and grammar.

Our use of English is also governed by **semantic rules**. Whereas syntax deals with structure, semantics governs the meaning of statements. Semantic rules reflect the ways in which speakers of a language respond to a particular symbol. Semantic rules are what make it possible for us to agree that *bikes* are for riding and *books* are for reading, and they help us know whom we will encounter when we use rooms marked MEN and WOMEN. Without semantic rules,

Focus on Technology

Instant Messaging and Syntax

There has been considerable speculation in the media about the potential of instant messaging (text messaging) to negatively influence people's (particularly teens') ability to use conventional grammar. The assumption is that people's use of abbreviations (e.g., *tmw* for tomorrow; *u* for you), initialization (e.g., *LOL* for laugh out loud; *TTYL* for talk to you later), and rebus (a word game that combines numbers, letters, and pictures to create words—e.g., *GR8* for great), as well as other creative adaptations of conventional language, when text-messaging will erode their ability to use normative (conventional or standard) grammar when it is required (e.g., essays, assignments, formal letters, etc.).

Intrigued by the phenomenon of texting, University of Toronto linguistics researcher Sali Tagliamonte and her undergraduate research partner Derek Denis (2008) analyzed a month's worth of unmonitored instant-messaging conversations of seventy-two young people ages fifteen to twenty years old. They also examined a quantity of speech from the same group of teenagers. What they found was that, when compared to their oral speech, their text messages were far more formal in their use of syntactic rules. The messages were not as formal as an essay but the grammar used was that of formal language. They did mix more formal grammar with other types of language; however, the use of short forms such as *LOL* comprised only a very small proportion of their messages. Tagliamonte and Denis describe the language of instant messaging as a unique new hybrid that creatively combines a variety of language features such as speech, written language, and formal and informal grammar and diction. While teachers informally report that some of the abbreviations and initializations characteristic of instant messaging are showing up in assignments and essays, Tagliamonte responds by saying that that is what school is for—to teach students what kind of language is appropriate in particular contexts (Daubs, 2008). The subjects in their study demonstrated very clearly that their grammatical skills were intact.

communication would be impossible, because each of us would use symbols in unique ways, unintelligible to others.

Although semantic rules help us understand the meaning of individual words, they often do not explain how language operates in everyday life. Consider the statement, 'Let's get together tomorrow.' The semantic meaning of the words in this sentence is clear enough, and yet, the statement could be taken in several ways. It could be a request ('I hope we can get together'), a polite command ('I want to see you'), or an empty cliché ('I don't really mean it'). We learn to distinguish the accurate meanings of such speech through **pragmatic rules** that tell us what uses and interpretations of a message are reasonable in a given situation. When these rules are understood by all players in the language game, smooth communication is possible. For example, one rule specifies that the relationship between communicators

plays a large role in determining the meaning of a statement. Our example, 'I want to see you', is likely to mean one thing when uttered by your boss and another entirely when it comes from your sweetheart. Likewise, the setting in which the statement is made plays a role. Saying 'I want to see you' will probably have a different meaning at the office than at a cocktail party. Of course, the non-verbal behaviour that accompanies a statement also helps us interpret its meaning.

The co-ordinated management of meaning (CMM) theory describes some types of pragmatic rules that operate in everyday conversations. It suggests that we use rules at several levels to create our own messages and interpret other people's statements (Cronen and Chetro-Szivos, 2001; Cronen et al., 1988). Table 5.1 uses a CMM framework to illustrate how two people might be confused because they are using different rules at several levels. In situations like this, it's important to make sure that

Table 5.1 Pragmatic Rules Govern the Use and Meaning of a Statement

Notice how the same message ('You look very pretty today') takes on different meaning depending on which of a variety of rules are used to formulate and interpret it.

	Boss	Employee
Content Actual words	'You look very pretty today.'	
Speech Act The intent of a statement	Compliment an employee	Unknown
Relational Contract The perceived relationship between communicators	Boss who treats employees like family members	Subordinate employee, dependent on boss's approval for advancement
Episode Situation in which the interaction occurs	Casual conversation	Possible come-on by boss?
Life Script Self-concept of each communicator	Friendly guy	Woman determined to succeed on own merits
Cultural Archetype Cultural norms that shape member's perceptions and actions	Middle-class Canadian	Working-class Canadian

Source: Adapted from W. B. Pearce and V. Cronen (1980). *Communication, Action, and Meaning.* New York: Praeger. Used by permission.

Take Two

- **Phonological rules:** govern how sounds are combined to form words.
- **Syntactic rules:** govern the way symbols can be arranged.
- **Semantic rules:** govern the meaning of statements.
- **Pragmatic rules:** tell us what interpretations of a message are reasonable in a given situation.

Figure 5.1 Ogden and Richards' Triangle of Meaning

the other person's use of language matches yours before jumping to conclusions about the meaning of his or her statements. The skill of perception checking described in Chapter 3 can be useful at times like this.

Language Is Subjective

If the rules of language were more precise and if everyone followed them, we would suffer from fewer misunderstandings. You respond to a 'while you were out' note and spend a full day trying to reach Fatima, only to find you called the wrong Fatima. You have an hour-long argument about *feminism* with a friend, only to discover that you were using the term in different ways and that you really were in basic agreement. You tease a friend in what you mean to be a playful manner, but he takes you seriously and is offended.

These problems occur because people attach different meanings to the same message. Ogden and Richards (1923) illustrated this point graphically in their well-known *triangle of meaning* (see Figure 5.1). This model shows that there is only an indirect relationship—indicated by a broken line—between a word and the thing or idea it represents. As an example of this concept, the Focus on Research box on page 131 illustrates why the question of what constitutes 'flaming' in computer-mediated communication may not be as simple as it first seems. What looks like an offensive statement to an outsider may be understood as innocuous, or even friendly, by the people involved.

The Ogden and Richards model is oversimplified in that not all words refer to physical 'things' or referents. For instance, some referents are abstract ideas (such as *love*), while others (like

angry or *exciting*) are not even nouns. Despite these shortcomings, the triangle of meaning is useful since it clearly demonstrates that meanings are in people, not words. Hence, an important task facing communicators is to establish a common understanding of the words they use to exchange messages. In this sense, communication—at least the effective kind—requires us to negotiate the meaning of our language (Duck, 1994). This brings us back to a familiar theme: meaning is both *in* and *among* people.

Language is Linked to Worldview

Does the language you speak shape the way you see and think about the world? For almost 150 years, theorists have explored issues surrounding the extent to which language influences our thoughts and perceptions of the world. For instance, bilingual speakers seem to think differently when they change languages. In one study, French Americans were asked to interpret a series of pictures. When they spoke in French, their descriptions were far more romantic and emotional than when they used English to describe the same kinds of images. Likewise, when students in Hong Kong were asked to complete a values test, they expressed more traditional Chinese values when they answered in Cantonese than when they spoke in English. In Israel, both Arab and Jewish students saw bigger distinctions between their group and 'outsiders' when using their native language than when they spoke in English, which, being a foreign language, was more neutral. Examples like these show the power of language to shape cultural identity—sometimes for better and sometimes for worse.

The **Sapir-Whorf hypothesis,** formulated by Benjamin Whorf, an amateur linguist, and anthropologist Edward Sapir (Hoijer, 1994; Whorf, 1956), proposes that people who speak different languages organize and view their world differently. Following Sapir's theoretical work, Whorf found that the language spoken by Hopi Native Americans represented a view of reality that was dramatically different from most tongues. For example, the Hopi language makes no distinction between nouns and verbs. Therefore, the people who speak it describe the entire world as being constantly in process. Whereas English speakers use nouns to characterize people or objects as being fixed or constant, the Hopi language represents them more as verbs, constantly changing. In this sense, English represents the world rather like a collection of snapshots, whereas Hopi reflects a worldview that is more like a motion picture.

In the most extreme view, proponents of **linguistic determinism** argue that language determines thought. According to this perspective, it is *impossible* for speakers of different languages to view the world identically. More recent research has cast doubt on the extreme linguistic deterministic viewpoint (see Monastersky, 2002). For example, Harry Frank and his colleagues (2000) found that although Chinese speakers have five distinct words for what North Americans would simply call 'shame', the North Americans are as capable as Chinese of experiencing distinct varieties of shame.

The more moderate notion of **linguistic relativism**—that language exerts a strong influence on perceptions—seems more valid. As one scholar put it, 'the differences between languages are not so much in what *can* be said, but in what it is *relatively easy* to say' (Hoijer in Steinfatt, 1989, p. 63). Some languages contain terms that have no English equivalents (Rheingold, 1988). For example, consider a few words in other languages that have no simple translation in English:

- *unga* (Inuit): dependent love, especially the love of a baby for its mother, wanting to be taken care of; it may also refer to the feeling of spouses or friends when they are apart and miss each other
- *nemawashi* (Japanese): the process of informally feeling out all the people involved with an issue before making a decision
- *lagniappe* (French/Creole): an extra gift given in a transaction that wasn't expected by the terms of a contract
- *lao* (Mandarin): respectful term used for older people, showing their importance in the family and in society
- *dharma* (Sanskrit): each person's unique, ideal path in life and the knowledge of how to find it

Once words like these exist and become a part of everyday life, the ideas that they represent are easier to recognize. But even without such terms, each of the concepts above is still possible to imagine. Thus, speakers of a language that includes the notion of *lao* would probably treat its older members respectfully, and those who are familiar with *lagniappe* might be more generous. However, these words don't have to be in a language for a communicator to follow these principles. While language may shape thoughts and behaviour, it doesn't dominate them absolutely.

The Influence of Language

Besides simply describing the world, language can have a strong effect on our perceptions and how we regard one another. In the following pages, we

Test Yourself Describe four features of language and how each contributes to both the usefulness of language and the potential for misunderstandings.

will examine some of the many ways language can affect our lives.

Naming and Identity

'What's in a name?' Juliet asked rhetorically. If Romeo had been a social scientist, he would have answered, 'A great deal.' Research has demonstrated that names are more than just a simple means of identification, that, in fact, they shape the way others think of us, the way we view ourselves, and the way we act (Marcus, 1976).

Different names have different connotations. In one study, psychologists asked college students to rate over a thousand names according to their likeability, how active or passive they seemed, and their masculinity or femininity. In spite of the large number of subjects, the responses were quite similar. At the time of the study, Michael, John, and Wendy were likeable and active and were rated as possessing the masculine or feminine traits of their sex. Percival, Isadore, and Alfreda were less likeable, and their sexual identity was less clear. Other research also suggests that names have strong connotative meanings. Common names are generally viewed as being more active, stronger, and better than unusual ones (Marcus, 1976).

Take Two

- **Saphir-Whorf hypothesis:** the idea that people who speak different languages organize and view their world differently.
- **Linguistic determinism:** the idea that language determines perceptions and thought.
- **Linguistic relativism:** the idea that language exerts a strong influence on perceptions and thought.

There is research to suggest that names are associated with a variety of life outcomes (Aura and Hess, 2004). Unusual names and those with unique spellings have been associated with a number of negative outcomes, such as involvement in juvenile delinquency (Kalist and Lee, 2008) and greater difficulty in obtaining job interviews (Bertrand & Mullainathan, 2004). However, mothers' level of education affects naming patterns and mothers with lower levels of education are more likely to choose unpopular names (as measured by the frequency of their use in the population). These same mothers are more likely to raise their children in disadvantaged home environments and have lower socio-economic status (Kalist and

Focus on Research

Assigning Meaning to Computerized Flaming

Imagine reading an email message typed in CAPITAL LETTERS and filled with CURSE WORDS, INSULTS, NAME CALLING, and EXCLAMATION MARKS!!! How would you interpret such a message? According to Patrick O'Sullivan and Andrew Flanagin (2003), the answer is, 'It depends'.

Considerable research has been devoted to the topic of *flaming*, usually defined as hostile and aggressive messages sent via computer. Scholars who analyze flaming look for particular markers, such as swearing, rude comments, or impolite statements. The problem is that such markers might mean something completely different to the people sending and receiving them

than they mean to third-party observers. O'Sullivan and Flanagin explain:

> The casual use of profane language between close friends can be a marker of relationship closeness. Friends have been known to address each other with hostile or vulgar terms as a form of play or friendly verbal jousting—words that they would never use casually with someone outside their social circle. . . . A similar case can be made for insults, name-calling, impolite language, and other so-called 'hostile' messages.

What makes a message a *flame* is not the words themselves; rather, it's the meanings that people assign to those words. This holds true not only in computer-mediated communication, but also in face-to-face interaction. Flaming offers further illustration that meaning is in people, not in words.

Lee, 2008). While names play a role in shaping our identities and influence the way others see us, there are significantly more substantial factors that affect our chances in life.

Names are one way parents can steep their child in a family's cultural heritage. In Canada, as in many countries around the world, cultural heritage is increasingly complex. Canadian census data (Statistics Canada, 2008) indicate that the number of mixed-race marriages continues to increase, leading to more mixed-race children. Rosalind Edwards and Chamion Caballero (2008) explored the process of choosing baby names among mixed-race couples in the United Kingdom. Edwards and Caballero found that in addition to choosing names they liked, the majority of the couples interviewed also wanted names that symbolized the child's heritages. Names our parents choose for us influence our identities and the labels we choose for ourselves and encourage others to use say a great deal about who we think we are and how we want others to view us. For many people, changes in age lead to changes in names. The diminutive that seemed to fit as a child does not fit as well in adolescence or adulthood. Thus, Vinnie may become Vince or Vincent, and Danny may insist on being called Dan or Daniel. It still may be fine for close friends to use diminutives, but not others. The shift to more formal, adult names may not be as common for women; it's not unusual to meet an adult Marcie or Susie. But when being taken seriously is the goal in a world where women are all too often treated with less respect than they deserve, having a serious-sounding name can be an asset.

Many women in Western society, aware of the power of names to influence identity, view the name they choose to identify themselves with after they marry as an important decision. They may choose to take their husband's last name, hyphenate their own name and their husband's, or keep their birth name. One study by Karen Foss and Belle Edson (1989) revealed that a woman's choice is likely to reveal a great deal about herself and her relationship with her husband. Surveys have shown that women who take their husband's names place the most importance on relationships, and that social expectations of how they should behave rate second and issues of self come last. On the other hand, women who keep their birth names put their personal concerns ahead of relationships and social expectations. Women with hyphenated names fall somewhere between the other groups—these women value self and relationships equally. Using a different approach to studying name choices, Jean Twenge (1997) found that women who wish to keep or hyphenate their names have more feminist attitudes and acknowledge a link between one's name and one's identity; on the other hand, those who want their husbands' names for themselves and their children most often cited 'tradition' as the reason, and deny that names are linked with identity.

Some research suggests that the results of either keeping or changing are not as profound as they might seem. For example, one study (Stafford and Kline, 1996) analyzed 110 well-educated married women, both name-changers and name-keepers. Contrary to what linguistic reformers may have expected, there were no significant differences between the two groups in terms of self-esteem, relationship dependency, autonomy, or feelings about the balance of control in their marriages.

"My mother is black, my father is African-American, and my grandfather is Negro. I can hardly wait to find out about me."

Credibility and Status

The words we use and the way we pronounce them have a strong influence on whether others accept or reject our ideas. In the classic musical *My Fair Lady*, Professor Henry Higgins transforms Eliza Doolittle from a lowly flower girl into a high-society woman by replacing her cockney accent with an upper-class speaking style. The power speech has to influence status is real. In 1971, British researcher Howard Giles conducted experiments demonstrating that in Britain, judgments of attractiveness and status are strongly influenced by style of speech. Other research by social psychologists in North America shows that the same principle applies on this side of the Atlantic. A significant amount of research shows that people who speak with a foreign accent are perceived as less competent, less intelligent, and less attractive than native English speakers (for a summary, see Sato, 1998).

A study of adult Canadians studying English as a second language (, L<) found that the majority of the non-native English speakers interviewed believed that people would respect them more if they pronounced English well (Derwing, 2003). Although many of the non-native speakers interviewed in his study considered native English speakers to be patient and understanding, and the majority said they did not believe they had been discriminated against because of their accent, they also believed that their accents had a negative effect on some of their social interactions with native English-speaking Canadians.

Vocabulary is just as important as accent in shaping perceptions. Scholarly speaking is a good example of this phenomenon. One illustration is the Dr Fox hypothesis (Cory, 1980): 'An apparently legitimate speaker who utters an unintelligible message will be judged competent by an audience [familiar with] the speaker's area of apparent expertise.' This hypothesis got its name from a Dr Myron L. Fox, who delivered a talk followed by a half-hour discussion on 'mathematical game theory as applied to physical education'. The audience included psychiatrists, psychologists, social workers, and

Reflection

Word Choice and Attitude

I've taken two communication classes this year and they were completely different. I just figured out a big reason why. In one class, my professor used language that made it sound as if communication had nothing to do with us. He would always refer to 'people' or 'communicators' as if they were from another planet, or at least another species. One day, he announced that his lecture topic would be 'How men and women speak when *they* are together.' If men and women are *they*, who are *we*?

My other professor talked about how *we* communicate. 'Does watching violence on television make us more aggressive?' she would ask. 'Do movies teach us how to be husbands or wives or parents?' The two different ways of using language seemed trivial at first, but now I can see that they said a lot about how each professor approached the course.

educators. Questionnaires collected after the session revealed that these educated listeners found the lecture clear and stimulating.

Despite his warm reception by this learned audience, Fox was a complete fraud. He was a professional actor who had been coached by researchers to deliver a lecture of double-talk—a patchwork of information from a *Scientific American* article mixed with jokes, non sequiturs, contradictory statements, and meaningless references to unrelated topics. When wrapped in a linguistic package of high-level professional jargon, however, the meaningless gobbledygook was judged as important information. In other words, Fox's credibility came more from his style of speaking than from the ideas he expressed.

Affiliation, Attraction, and Interest

Accent and vocabulary are not the only ways in which language reflects the status of relationships. Speech also can be a way of building and demonstrating solidarity with others. An impressive body of research has shown that communicators who want to show affiliation with one another adapt their speech in a variety of ways, including their choice of vocabulary, rate of talking, number and placement of pauses, and level of politeness (Aune and Kikuchi, 1993; Giles et al., 1992a, Giles et al., 1992b, Giles et al., 1992c). On an individual level, close friends and lovers often develop a set of special terms that serve as a way of signifying their relationship (Bell and Healey, 1992; Bell et al., 1987). Using the same vocabulary serves to set these people apart from others, reminding themselves and the rest of the world of their relationship. The same process works among members of larger groups, ranging from street gangs to soldiers. Communication researchers call the process of adapting one's speech style to that of others with whom the communicator wants to identify **convergence**.

When two or more people feel equally positive about one another, their linguistic convergence will be mutual. But when communicators want or need approval, they often adapt their speech to accommodate the other person's style, trying to say the 'right thing' or speak in a way that will help them fit in. We see this process when immigrants who want to gain the reward of material success in a new culture strive to master the host language. Likewise, employees who seek advancement tend to speak more like their superiors, supervisors adopt the speech style of managers, and managers converge toward their bosses.

The principle of speech accommodation works in reverse, too. Communicators who want to set themselves apart from others adopt the strategy of **divergence**, speaking in a way that emphasizes their differences. For example, members of an ethnic group, even though fluent in the dominant language, might use their own dialect as a way of showing solidarity with one another—a sort of 'we're proud of our heritage' strategy. Divergence also occurs in other settings. For example, a physician or lawyer who wants to establish credibility with her or his client might speak formally and use professional jargon to create a sense of distance. The implicit message here is, 'I'm different from you (and more knowledgeable).'

 Take Two

- **Convergence:** the process of adapting one's speech style to that of others with whom the communicator wants to identify.
- **Divergence:** the process of adapting one's speech in ways that emphasize differences between the speaker and others with whom the communicator wants to distance themselves from.

Power

Communication researchers have observed a number of language patterns that add to or detract from a speaker's power to influence others. Notice the difference between these two statements:

> Excuse me, sir. I hate to say this, but I . . . uh . . . I guess I won't be able to turn in the assignment on time. I had a personal emergency and . . . well . . . it was just impossible to finish it by today. I'll have it in your mailbox on Monday, okay?

> I won't be able to turn in the assignment on time. I had a personal emergency and it was impossible to finish it by today. I'll have it in your mailbox on Monday.

Whether or not the instructor finds the excuse acceptable, it's clear that the second statement sounds more confident, whereas the tone of the first is apologetic and uncertain. Table 5.2 lists several **powerless speech mannerisms** illustrated in the statements you just read. A number of studies have shown that speakers whose talk is free of these mannerisms are rated as more competent, dynamic, and attractive than speakers who sound powerless (Ng and Bradac, 1993; Reid and Ng, 1999). The effects of powerful versus powerless speech styles are also apparent in employment interview outcomes: a powerful speech style results in more positive attributions of competence and employability than a powerless one (Parton et al., 2002). Even a single type of powerless speech mannerism appears to make a person appear less authoritative or socially attractive (Hosman, 1989).

Table 5.2 Examples of Less Powerful Language

Type of Usage	Example
Hedges	'I'm kinda disappointed. . . .' 'I think we should . . .' 'I guess I'd like to. . . .'
Hesitations	'Uh, can I have a minute of your time?' 'Well, we could try this idea. . . .' 'I wish you would—er—try to be on time.'
Intensifiers	'So that's how I feel. . . .' 'I'm not very hungry.'
Polite forms	'Excuse me, sir. . . .'
Tag questions	'It's about time we got started, isn't it?' 'Don't you think we should give it another try?'
Disclaimers	'I probably shouldn't say this, but . . .'

Adapted from Adler R. B., and Elmhorst J. (2005) *Communicating at work: Principles and practices for business and the professions*, 8th ed. New York: McGraw-Hill.

However, powerful speech that gets the desired results in mainstream North American and European culture does not succeed everywhere with everyone (Samovar and Porter, 2001). In Japan, saving face for others is an important goal, so communicators there tend to speak in ambiguous terms and use hedge words and qualifiers. In most Japanese sentences, the verb comes at the end of the sentence so the action part of the statement can be postponed. Traditional Mexican culture, with its strong emphasis on co-operation, also uses hedging to smooth over interpersonal relationships. By not taking a firm stand with their speech mannerisms, Mexicans believe they will not make others feel ill at ease. Canadian First Nations and Koreans are two other cultural groups that prefer 'indirect' (for example, *perhaps*, *could be*) over 'direct' speech.

Even in North American culture, simply counting the number of powerful or powerless statements will not always reveal who has the most control in a relationship. Social rules often mask the real distribution of power. A boss who wants to be pleasant might say to a secretary, 'Would you mind retyping this letter?' In truth, both boss and secretary know this is an order and not a request, but the questioning form makes the medicine less bitter. Sociolinguist Deborah Tannen describes how politeness can be a face-saving way of delivering an order:

I hear myself giving instructions to my assistants without actually issuing orders: 'Maybe it would be a good idea to . . .'; 'It would be great if you could . . .' all the while knowing that I expect them to do what I've asked right away. . . . This rarely creates problems, though, because the people who work for me know that there is only one reason I mention tasks—because I want them done. I *like* giving instructions in this way; it appeals to my sense of what it means to be a good person . . . taking others' feelings into account. (1994, p. 101)

As this quotation suggests, high-status speakers—especially higher-status women, according to Tannen—often realize that politeness is an effective way to get their needs met while protecting the face of the less powerful person. The importance of achieving both content and relational goals helps explain why a mixture of powerful and polite

Test Yourself   Describe six powerless speech mannerisms and provide an example of each.

speech is usually most effective (Geddes, 1992). Of course, if the other person misinterprets politeness for weakness, it may be necessary to shift to a more powerful speaking style.

Sexism and Racism

Sexist language 'includes words, phrases, and expressions that unnecessarily differentiate between females and males or exclude, trivialize, or diminish' either sex (Parks and Robertson, 2000, p. 415). This type of speech can affect the self-concepts of women and men, often in subtle ways. Suzanne Romaine (1999) offers several examples of how linguistic terms can stereotype men and women. To say that a woman *mothered* her children focuses on her nurturing behaviour, but to say that a man *fathered* a child talks only about his biological role. We are familiar with terms like *working mother*, but there is no term *working father* because we assume (perhaps inaccurately) that men are the breadwinners in families.

Beyond just stereotyping women, sexist language can stigmatize them. For example, the term *unmarried mother* is common, but we do not talk about *unmarried fathers* because for many people, there is no stigma attached to this status for men. And whereas there are over two hundred English words for promiscuous women, there are only twenty for men (Stanley, 1977).

There are at least two ways to eliminate sexist language (Rakow, 1992). The first circumvents the problem altogether by eliminating sex-specific terms or substituting neutral terms. For example, using plural sentence constructions, with the word *they*, eliminates the necessity for *he, she, she and he,* or *he and she* in writing. When no sex reference is appropriate, you can substitute neutral terms. For example: *mankind* may be replaced with *humankind, humanity, human beings, human race,* and *people; man-made* may be replaced with *artificial, manufactured,* and *synthetic; manpower* may be

replaced with *labour, workers,* and *workforce;* and *manhood* may be replaced with *adulthood.* In the same way, *mailmen* are *letter carriers; firemen* are *firefighters; chairmen* are *presiding officers, leaders,* and *chairs; foremen* are *supervisors; policemen* and *policewomen* are both *police officers;* and *stewardesses* and *stewards* are both *flight attendants.* Of course, some terms refer to things that could not possibly have a sex; so, for example, a *manhole cover* could be called a *sewer lid.*

The second method for eliminating sexism is to mark sex clearly—to heighten awareness of whether the reference is to a female or a male. For example, rather than substitute *chairperson* for *chairman*, use the terms *chairman* and *chairwoman* to specify whether the person is a man or a woman. (Note also that there is nothing sacred about putting *he* before *she*; in fact, adding *she, her,* and *hers* after *he, him,* and *his,* without changing the order, continues to imply that males are the more important sex and should come first.)

Whereas sexist language usually defines the world as made up of superior men and inferior women, racist language reflects a worldview that classifies members of one racial group as superior and others as inferior (Asante, 2002). Not all language that might have racist overtones is deliberate. For example, the connotations of many words favour whites over people of colour (Person-Lynn, 1994). Words and images associated with 'white' are usually positive, whether it's the cowboy hero in white clothing or connotations of white as 'pure', 'clean', 'honourable', 'innocent', 'bright',

iStock photo

Self-Assessment

Sexist Language*

Respond to each of the following statements by indicating the extent to which you agree with it:

1 = strongly disagree; 2 = tend to disagree;
3 = undecided; 4 = tend to agree; and 5 = strongly agree.

_____ 1. Women who think that being called a 'chairman' is sexist are misinterpreting the word 'chairman'.

_____ 2. When people use the term 'man and wife', the expression is not sexist if the users do not mean it to be.

_____ 3. The elimination of sexist language is an important goal.

_____ 4. Sexist language is related to the sexist treatment of people in society.

_____ 5. When teachers talk about the history of Canada, they should change expressions, such as 'our forefathers', to expressions that include women.

_____ 6. The English language will never be changed because it is too deeply ingrained in the culture.

Add your responses to the six statements, making sure to reverse-score statements 1, 2, and 6 (if you indicated 5, change it to 1; change 4 to 2; change 2 to 4; and change 1 to 5; 3 remains 3) = _____. Scores can range from 6 to 30, and scores that are approximately 24 and higher reflect a negative attitude toward sexist language.

*This Self-Assessment box contains six of the twenty-one items on the Inventory of Attitudes Toward Sexist/Nonsexist Language-General, developed by Parks and Robertson (2000).

Reflection

Girls or Women?

I'm a member of the women's hockey team at my university—but that's not how most people on campus refer to us. They regularly call us the *girls'* hockey team, even though most of us haven't been 'girls' (at least legally) for years. It wouldn't bother me so much except they never refer to the men's hockey team as the *boys'* team. It seems to me like a case of sexist language that refuses to go away.

influence them (Giles and Franklyn-Stokes, 1989; Kirkland et al., 1987). Not only did the unwitting subjects rate the minority individual's competence lower when that person performed poorly, but they also found fault with others who associated socially with the minority person—even members of the subject's own ethnic group.

An obvious step toward eliminating racist language is to make sure your communication is free of offensive labels and slurs. Some troublesome language will be easy to identify, while other problematic speech will be more subtle. For instance, you may be unaware of using racial and ethnic modifiers when describing others, such as 'black professor' or 'Pakistani merchant' (or modifiers identifying sex, such as 'female doctor' or 'male secretary'). Modifiers like these usually are not necessary, and they can be subtle indicators of racism/sexism. If you would not use the phrases 'white professor', 'European merchant', 'male doctor', or 'female secretary', then modifiers that identify race and sex may be indicators of attitudes and language that need to be changed.

Uses (and Abuses) of Language

By now, it's apparent that language can shape the way we perceive and understand the world. Next, we will look at some specific types of usage and examine both their value and the problems they can cause.

and 'shiny'. The words and images associated with 'black' are often negative, a concept that reaches from the black hat of the villain cowboy and the black cat that causes bad luck to words and phrases like *black market*, *blackball*, and *blacklist*.

Using racist labels can have ugly consequences. Although experimental subjects who heard a derogatory label used against a member of a minority group (that the subjects did not belong to) expressed annoyance at this sort of slur, the negative terms did

Precision and Vagueness

Most people assume that the goal of language is to make our ideas clear to one another. Sometimes, however, we want to be less than perfectly clear. In the following pages, we will point out some cases where vagueness serves useful purposes as well as cases where perfect understanding is the goal.

Ambiguous Language   **Ambiguous language** consists of words and phrases that have more than one commonly accepted definition. Some ambiguous language is amusing, as the following newspaper headlines illustrate:

Police Begin Campaign to Run Down Jaywalkers
Teacher Strikes Idle Kids
20-Year Friendship Ends at the Altar

Many misunderstandings that arise from ambiguity are trivial. We remember eating dinner at a Mexican restaurant and ordering a 'tostada with beans'. Instead of being served a beef tostada with beans on the side, we were surprised to see the waiter bring us a plate containing a tostada *filled* with beans. As with most such misunderstandings, hindsight showed that the phrase *tostada with beans* has two equally correct meanings.

Other misunderstandings involving ambiguous messages can be more serious. A nurse gave one of her patients a scare when she told him that he 'would not be needing' his robe, books, and

http://www.tardsite.com

Pork.
The one you love.

Sask Pork

PATTISON

iStock photo

shaving materials any more. The patient became quiet and moody. When the nurse inquired about the odd behaviour, she discovered that the poor man had interpreted her statement to mean he was going to die soon. In fact, the nurse meant he would be going home shortly.

For another example of ambiguous language, consider the word *love*. People commonly use that term in six very different ways: *eros* (romantic love), *ludus* (game-playing love), *storge* (friendship love), *mania* (possessive, dependent love), *pragma* (logical love), and *agape* (all-giving, selfless love) (J.A. Lee, 1973; see also Hendrick et al., 1998). Imagine the conflicts that would occur between a couple who sincerely pledged their love to one another, each with a different kind of love in mind. We can imagine them asking one another, 'If you really love me, why are you acting like this?' without realizing that each of them views the relationship differently.

It's difficult to catch and clarify every instance of ambiguous language. For this reason, the responsibility for interpreting statements accurately rests in large part with the receiver. Feedback of one sort or another—for example, paraphrasing and questioning—can help clear up misunderstandings: 'You say you love me, but you want to see other people. In my book, "love" is exclusive. What about you?'

Despite its obvious problems, ambiguous language has its uses. For example, when a hospital

iStock photo

Reflection

Spilled Milk and Ambiguous Language

One of my favourite family stories happened when our son, Scott, was about three years old. He wanted to pour his own milk, and my husband, Jerry, was helping him. Little Scott carefully tilted the milk carton to the edge of the glass, and slowly the milk poured from the jug into the glass.

The glass began to fill. Jerry said, 'That's good . . . Okay, that's good . . . That's GOOD!' as the milk began to overflow the glass and spill onto the table.

Jerry asked Scott why he didn't stop pouring the milk. It was obvious to me that by saying, 'That's good,' Jerry meant, 'That's enough—you can stop now,' but what Scott heard was that he was doing a good job of pouring. You have to be very literal with three-year-olds!

system defined the nursing role of 'care coordinator' in a strategically ambiguous way, some nurses were excited and exhilarated by the challenge of crafting a new role (Miller et al., 2000). In Chapter 9, we describe how using language that is open to several interpretations can help you avoid the kind of honesty and clarity that can embarrass both the speaker and listener. For example, if a friend proudly shows you a newly completed painting and asks your opinion of it, you might answer equivocally by saying, 'Gee, it's really unusual. I've never seen anything like it,' instead of giving a less ambiguous but more hurtful response such as, 'This may be the ugliest thing I've ever seen!'

Abstraction   High-level abstractions are convenient ways of generalizing about similarities between several objects, people, ideas, or events. Figure 5.2 shows an abstraction ladder that illustrates how to describe the same phenomenon at various levels of abstraction.

We use higher-level abstractions all the time. For instance, rather than saying, 'Thanks for washing the dishes', 'Thanks for vacuuming the rug', and 'Thanks for making the bed', it's easier to say, 'Thanks for cleaning up.' In such everyday situations, abstractions are a useful kind of verbal shorthand.

Like ambiguity, high-level abstractions also can help communicators find face-saving ways to avoid confrontations and embarrassment by being deliberately unclear (Eisenberg, 1984; Eisenberg and Witten, 1987). If a friend apologizes for arriving late for a date, you can choose to brush off the incident instead of making it an issue by saying, 'Don't worry. It wasn't the end of the world'—a true statement, but less specific than saying, 'To tell you the truth, I was mad at the time, but I've cooled off now.' If your boss asks your opinion of a new idea that you think is weaker than your own approach but you don't want to disagree, you could respond with a higher-level abstraction by saying, 'It might work. . . .'

Although vagueness does have its uses, highly abstract language can cause several types of problems. The first is stereotyping. Imagine someone who has had one bad experience and, as a result, blames an entire group: 'Marriage counsellors are worthless,' 'Torontonians are all rude,' or 'Men are

Figure 5.2 Abstraction Ladder
A boss gives feedback to an employee about career advancement at various levels of specificity.

Building Work Skills

Reducing Abstract Language

A significant amount of work-related communication consisting of stating goals, making requests of others, talking about work-related problems, and complaining! No matter what type of career you have in mind, this will probably be true.

Think about using language at work in one of the following ways. Perhaps you need to make a request of a colleague or someone who reports to you, or you need to give them some negative feedback (criticism) about their work. Write down what you might say and then use Table 5.3, 'Abstract and Behavioural Descriptions,' to decide whether you have found the right balance between behavioural description and abstract description. How did you do? Could you improve your request or your criticism? How?

no good.' Overly abstract expressions like these can cause people to think in generalities, ignoring uniqueness. As we saw in Chapter 2, expecting people to act in a certain way can become a self-fulfilling prophecy. If you expect the worst of people, you have a good chance of getting it.

Besides narrowing your own options, excessively abstract language can also confuse others. Telling the hairstylist 'not too short' or 'more casual' might produce the look you want, or it might lead to an unpleasant surprise.

Overly abstract language can lead to more serious problems. For instance, accusations of sexual assault can arise because one person claims to have said 'no' when the other person insists no such refusal was ever conveyed. In response to this sort of disagreement, specific rules of sexual conduct have become more common in workplaces and educational institutions. An example of such a code of sexual conduct is the one developed at Ohio's Antioch College (1996). The policy uses low-level abstractions to minimize the chances of anyone claiming confusion about a partner's willingness. For example, the code states,

- If sexual contact and/or conduct is not mutually and simultaneously initiated, then the person who initiates sexual contact/conduct is responsible for getting verbal consent of the other individual(s) involved.

- Verbal consent [for sexual activity] should be obtained with each new level of physical and/or sexual behavior. . . . Asking 'Do you want to have sex with me?' is not enough. The request for consent must be specific to each act.

- If someone has initially consented but then stops consenting during a sexual interaction, she/he should communicate withdrawal of consent verbally (example: saying 'no' or 'stop') and/or through physical resistance (example: pushing away). The other individual(s) must stop immediately.

Reflection

'Secondary Skin Irritation'

Before radiation treatment for my stomach cancer, I was told I'd get a prescription for a salve to help heal the burns I would get. After my first treatment, I reminded the doctor about the prescription, saying, 'You haven't given me the prescription for the radiation burns.' She said, in a powerful act of trying to reduce the horror of what was happening to me with a simple shift in language, 'We no longer call them radiation burns—they're now "secondary skin irritations."' She can call them anything she wants, but all I know is that the new label didn't make them hurt any less!

Some critics have ridiculed rules like these as being unrealistically legalistic and chillingly inappropriate for romantic relationships. Whatever their weaknesses, the Antioch code illustrates how low-level abstractions can reduce the chances of a serious misunderstanding. Specific language may not be desirable or necessary in many situations, but in an era when misinterpretations can lead to accusations of physical assault, it does seem to have a useful place.

You can make your language—and your thinking—less abstract and more clear by learning to make behavioural descriptions of your problems, goals, appreciations, complaints, and requests. We use the word *behavioural* because such descriptions move down the abstraction ladder to describe the specific, observable objects and actions we're thinking about. Table 5.3 shows how behavioural descriptions are much more clear and effective than vague, abstract statements.

Euphemism **Euphemisms** (from a Greek word meaning 'to use words of good omen') are innocuous terms substituted for blunt ones. For example, young teenage girls often use euphemistic terms ('my friend', 'it') to discuss their own menstruation without feeling embarrassed (Kissling, 1996). Euphemisms can also soften the impact of information that might be unpleasant. It's easy to imagine how a relational breakup might be easier to handle with the explanation, 'I'm not ready for commitment' than with 'I want to date other people.' When choosing how to broach difficult subjects, the challenge is to be as kind as possible without sacrificing either your integrity or the clarity of your message. (The guidelines for self-disclosure that we outline in Chapter 9 will help you in this regard.)

Relative Language Relative language gains meaning by comparison. For example, do you attend a large or a small school? This depends on what you compare it to. Compared to the University of Toronto, with almost 60,000 students, your university may look small, but compared with a smaller institution, it may seem quite large.

Relative words such as *fast* and *slow*, *smart* and *stupid*, *short* and *long* are clearly defined only through comparison.

Using relative terms without explaining them can lead to communication problems. Have you ever answered someone's question about the weather by saying it was warm, only to find out the person thought it was cold? Have you followed a friend's advice and gone to a 'cheap' restaurant, only to find that it was twice as expensive as you expected? Have classes you heard were 'easy' turned out to be hard? The problem in each case resulted from failing to link the relative word to a more measurable term.

One way to avoid the pitfalls of relative language is to use numbers to define relative terms. For instance, when a friend says that she just saw a good movie, you could ask her, 'On a scale of 1 to 10, how would you rate it?' You might be surprised when she says, 'About a 6'—after all, you might have thought 'good' meant 'great', while your friend simply meant the movie was 'okay'. Using numbers can also help explain what you mean when describing how smart your brother is, how much pain you're in, or how quickly you need a report finished.

Static Evaluation 'Mohamed is a nervous guy.' 'Karen is short-tempered.' 'You can always count on Wes.' A description or evaluation that contains the word *is* can be called a static evaluation—the usually mistaken assumption that people or things are totally consistent and unchanging. Instead of labelling Mohamed as permanently and completely nervous, it would probably be more accurate to outline the situations in which he behaves nervously: 'Mohamed acts nervously until you get to know him.' The same goes for Karen, Wes, and the rest of us: we are more changeable than the way static, everyday language describes us.

Edward Sagarian (1976) writes about an unconscious language habit that imposes a static view of others. Why is it, he asks, that we say, 'He *has* a cold' but 'He *is* a convict' or a genius, a slow learner, or any other kind of behaviour that is also not necessarily permanent? Sagarian argues

Table 5.3 Abstract and Behavioural Descriptions

	Abstract Description	Behavioural Description			Remarks
		Who Is Involved	In What Circumstances	Specific Behaviour	
Problem	I'm no good at meeting strangers.'	People I'd like to date	At parties and in school	I think, 'They'd never want to date me.' Also, I don't originate conversations.	Behavioural description more clearly identifies thoughts and behaviour to change.
Goal	I'd like to be more assertive.	Telephone and door-to-door solicitors	When I don't want the product or can't afford it	Instead of apologizing, I want to keep saying, 'I'm not interested' until they go away.	Behavioural description clearly outlines how to act; abstract description does not.
Appreciation	'You've been a great boss.'	(No clarification necessary)	When I've needed to change my schedule because of school exams or assignments	'You've rearranged my hours cheerfully.'	Give both abstract and behavioural descriptions for best results.
Complaint	'I don't like some of the instructors around here.'	Professors A and B	In class, when students ask questions the professors think are stupid	They either answer in a sarcastic voice (you might demonstrate) or accuse us of not studying hard enough.	If talking to A or B, use only behavioural description. With others, use both abstract and behavioural descriptions.
Request	'Quit bothering me!'	You and your friends, X and Y	When I'm studying for exams	'Instead of asking me again and again to party with you, I wish you'd accept my comment that I need to study tonight.'	Behavioural description will reduce defensiveness and make it clear that you don't always want to be left alone.

Take Two

- **Abstraction:** convenient ways of generalizing about similarities between several objects, people, ideas, or events.
  - Advantages: provide an easy shorthand, help avoid confrontations and embarrassment.
  - Disadvantages: can lead to stereotyping, can confuse others.
- **Euphemisms:** innocuous terms substituted for blunt ones (e.g. thrifty instead of cheap).
- **Relative language:** words that gain meaning by comparison (e.g., *fast, short*).
- **Static evaluation:** the usually mistaken assumption that people or things are totally consistent and unchanging (descriptions that contain the word *is*—e.g., 'She's rude').

that such linguistic labelling leads us to typecast others and in some cases forces them to perpetuate behaviour that could be changed.

Alfred Korzybski (1933) suggested the linguistic device of dating to reduce static evaluation. He proposed adding a subscript whenever appropriate to show the transitory nature of a referent. For example, a teacher might write the following as an evaluation of a student: 'Susan [May12] had difficulty co-operating with her classmates.' Although the actual device of subscripting is awkward in writing and impractical in conversation, the idea it represents can still be used. Instead of saying, 'I'm shy,' a more accurate statement might be, 'I haven't approached any new people since I moved here.' The first statement implies that your shyness is an unchangeable trait, rather like your height, while the second one suggests that you are capable of changing.

The Language of Responsibility

Besides providing a way to make the content of a message clear or obscure, language reflects the speaker's willingness to take responsibility for her or his beliefs, feelings, and actions. This acceptance or rejection of responsibility says a great deal about the speaker, and it can shape the tone of a relationship. To see how, read on.

'It' Statements   Notice the difference between the sentences of each set:

> 'It bothers me when you're late.'
> 'I'm worried when you're late.'

> 'It's nice to see you.'
> 'I'm glad to see you.'

> 'It's a boring class.'
> 'I'm bored in the class.'

As their name implies, **'it' statements** replace the personal pronoun I with the less immediate construction *it's*. By contrast, **'I' language** clearly identifies the speaker as the source of a message. Communicators who use 'it' statements avoid responsibility for ownership of a message, instead attributing it to some unidentified body. This habit is not just imprecise; more important, it's an unconscious way to avoid taking a position. You can begin to appreciate the increased directness of 'I' language by trying to use it instead of the less direct and more evasive 'it' statements in your own conversations.

'But' Statements   Statements that take the form 'X-but-Y' can be quite confusing. A closer look at the 'but' statement explains why. *But* has the effect of cancelling the thought that precedes it:

> 'You're really a great person, but I think we ought to stop seeing each other.'

> 'You've done good work for us, but we're going to have to let you go.'

> 'This paper has some good ideas, but I'm giving it a grade of D because it's late.'

'Buts' *can* be a face-saving strategy worth using at times. When the goal is to be absolutely clear, however, the most responsible approach will deliver the central idea without the distractions that can come with 'but' statements.

'I', 'You', and 'We' Language   We've already seen that 'I' language is a way of accepting responsibility for a message. 'You' language is quite different. It expresses a judgment of the other person. Positive judgments ('You look great today!') rarely cause problems, but notice how each of the following critical 'you' statements implies that the subject of the complaint is doing something wrong:

'You left this place a mess!'
'You didn't keep your promise!'
'You're really crude sometimes!'

Despite its name, 'you' language does not have to contain the pronoun *you*, which is often implied rather than stated outright:

'That was a stupid joke!' ['Your jokes are stupid!']
'Don't be so critical!' ['You're too negative!']
'Mind your own business!' ['You're too nosy!']

Whether the judgment is stated outright or implied, it's easy to see why 'you' language can arouse defensiveness. A 'you' statement implies that the speaker is qualified to judge the target— not an idea that most listeners are willing to accept, even when the evaluation is correct.

'I' language offers a more accurate and less provocative way to express a complaint (Kubany et al., 1992; Winer and Majors, 1981). 'I' language shows that the speaker takes responsibility for the accusation by describing his or her reaction to the other's behaviour without making any judgments about its worth. A complete 'I' statement has three parts: it describes (1) the other person's behaviour, (2) your feelings, and (3) the consequences the other's behaviour has for you:

'I get embarrassed [feeling] when you talk about my bad grades in front of our friends [behaviour]. I'm afraid they'll think I'm stupid [consequence].'

'When you didn't pick me up on time this morning [behaviour], I was late for class and wound up getting chewed out by the professor [consequences]. That's why I got so angry [feeling].'

'I haven't been very affectionate [consequence] because you've hardly spent any time with me in the past few weeks [behaviour]. I'm confused [feeling] about how you feel about me.'

When the chances of being misunderstood or getting a defensive reaction are high, it's a good idea to include all three elements in your 'I' message. In some cases, however, only one or two of them will get the job done:

'I went to a lot of trouble making this dinner, and now it's cold. Of course I'm annoyed!' (The behaviour is obvious.)

'I'm worried because you haven't called me up.' ('Worried' is both a feeling and a consequence in this statement.)

Despite its obvious advantages, even the best-constructed and masterfully delivered 'I' message will not always receive a non-defensive response. As Thomas Gordon (1970, p. 145) points out, 'nobody welcomes hearing that his behaviour is causing someone a problem, no matter how the message is phrased.' Furthermore, 'I' language in large doses can start to sound egotistical (Proctor, 1989). Research shows that self-absorbed people, also known as 'conversational narcissists', can be identified by their constant use of first-person-singular pronouns (Raskin and Shaw, 1988; Vangelisti et al., 1990). For this reason, 'I' language works best in moderation.

One way to avoid overuse of 'I' language is to consider the pronoun *we*. 'We' language implies that the issue is the concern and responsibility of both the speaker and receiver of a message. Consider a few examples:

'We have a problem. We can't seem to talk about money without fighting.'

'We are not doing a very good job of keeping the apartment clean, are we?'

'We need to talk to your parents about whether we'll visit them for the holidays.'

It's easy to see how 'we' language can help build a constructive climate. Besides being immediate, it suggests a kind of 'we're in this together' orientation (Gorham, 1988). Couples who use 'we' language are more satisfied than those who rely more heavily on 'I' and 'you' pronouns (Honeycutt, 1999; Sillars et al., 1997). On the other hand, using the pronoun *we* can be presumptuous since you are speaking for the other person as well as for yourself. It's easy to imagine someone replying to the statement, 'We have a problem . . .' by saying, 'Maybe you have a problem, but don't tell me I have!'

As is summarized in the accompanying Table 5.4, all three pronouns—*I*, *you*, and *we*—have their advantages and drawbacks. Given this fact, what advice can we give about the most effective pronouns to use in interpersonal communication? A study by Russell Proctor and James Wilcox (1993) offers an answer. The researchers found that 'I'–'we' combinations (for example, 'I think that we . . .' or 'I would like to see us . . .') were strongly endorsed by college students, particularly for confrontational conversations in romantic relationships. Anita Vangelisti and her associates (1990) made a similar observation: Unlike conversational narcissists, non-narcissists combine their 'I' references with references to other persons, objects, and events. Since too much of any pronoun

sounds wrong, it is generally a good idea to combine pronouns. If your 'I' language expresses your position without being overly self-absorbed, your 'you' language shows concern for others without judging them, and your 'we' language includes others without speaking for them, you will probably come as close as possible to the ideal mix of pronouns.

Disruptive Language

Not all linguistic problems come from misunderstandings. Sometimes, people understand one another perfectly and still wind up in conflict. Of course, not all disagreements can, or should, be avoided. But eliminating three harmful linguistic habits from your communication repertoire can minimize the kind of clashes that don't need to happen, allowing you to save your energy for the unavoidable and important struggles.

Fact–Opinion Confusion Factual statements are claims that can be verified as true or false. By contrast, opinion statements are based on the speaker's beliefs. Unlike matters of fact, they can never be proved or disproved. Consider a few examples of the difference between factual and opinion statements:

Table 5.4 Pronoun Uses and Their Effects

Pronoun	Pros	Cons	Recommendations
'I' Language	• Takes responsibility for personal thoughts, feelings, and wants. • Less defence-provoking than 'you' language.	• Can be perceived as egotistical, narcissistic, and self-absorbed.	• Use descriptive 'I' messages in conflicts when the other person does not perceive a problem. • Combine 'I' with 'we' language in conversations.
'We' Language	• Signals inclusion, immediacy, cohesiveness, and commitment.	• Can speak improperly for others.	• Combine with 'I' language, particularly in personal conversations. • Use in group settings to enhance sense of unity. • Avoid when expressing personal thoughts, feelings, and wants.
'You' Language	• Signals other-orientation, particularly when the topic is positive.	• Can sound evaluative and judgmental, particularly during confrontations.	• Use 'I' language during confrontations. • Use 'You' language when praising or including others.

Fact	Opinion
It rains more in Vancouver than. in Victoria	The climate in Victoria is better than in Vancouver.
Wayne Gretzky is the all-time leading scorer in the National Hockey League.	Wayne is the greatest hockey player in the history of the game!
Canada has universal health care. The United States does not.	The quality of life in the United States is lower than in Canada when it comes to health care.

When factual and opinion statements are set side by side like this, the difference between them is clear. In everyday conversation, however, we often present our opinions as if they were facts, and in doing so we invite an unnecessary argument. For example:

- 'That was a dumb thing to say!'
- 'Spending that much on _____ is a waste of money!'
- 'You can't get a fair shake in this country unless you're a white male.'

Notice how much less antagonistic each statement would be if it were prefaced by a qualifier such as 'In my opinion . . .' or 'It seems to me. . . .'

Fact–Inference Confusion
Labelling your opinions can go a long way toward relational harmony, but this habit will not solve all linguistic problems. Difficulties also arise when we confuse factual statements with inferential statements—conclusions arrived at from an interpretation of evidence.

Arguments often result when we label our inferences as facts:

A. Why are you mad at me?
B. I'm not mad at you. Why have you been so insecure lately?
C. I'm not insecure. It's just that you've been so critical.
D. What do you mean, 'critical'? I haven't been critical. . . .

Take Two

- **'I' language:** clearly identifies the speaker as the source of the message.
- **'It' statement:** replaces pronoun 'I' with 'it' and allows speaker to avoid taking responsibility for ownership of a message.
- **'But' statement:** when 'but' is used in a statement, it has the effect of cancelling out the thought that proceeds it.
- **'You' language:** expresses judgment of the other person.

Instead of trying to read the other person's mind, a far better course is to identify the observable behaviour (facts) that has caught your attention and to describe the interpretations (inferences) that you have drawn from it. After describing this train of thought, ask the other person to comment on the accuracy of your interpretation:

'When you didn't return my phone call [fact], I got the idea that you were mad at me [inference]. Are you?' (question)

'You've been asking me lately whether I still love you [fact], and that makes me think you're feeling insecure [inference]. Is that right?' (question)

Emotive Language
Emotive language seems to describe something but really announces the speaker's attitude toward it (Hansson, 1996; Richards, 1948). If you approve of a friend's roundabout approach to a difficult subject, you might

iStock photo

call her 'tactful'; if you don't like it, you might accuse her of 'beating around the bush'. Whether the approach is good or bad is more a matter of opinion than of fact, although this difference is obscured by emotive language.

You can appreciate that emotive words are really editorial statements when you consider these examples:

If You Approve, Say	If You Disapprove, Say
cautious	cheap
eccentric	crazy
extrovert	cowardly
information	loudmouth
progressive	old-fashioned
thrifty	propaganda
traditional	radical

Not surprisingly, research shows that the relational climate suffers when communicators use emotive language. A study by Jess Alberts (1988) found that when dealing with problems, dissatisfied couples were more likely to use personal, emotive comments but that satisfied partners described the other's behaviour in neutral terms.

Culture and Language

So far, we have described attributes that characterize most languages, with a particular emphasis on English and, although there are some remarkable similarities among the world's many languages (Brown, 1991), they also differ in important respects that affect the way their speakers communicate with one another and with speakers of other tongues. In this section, we outline some of those differences.

Translation

Anyone who has tried to translate ideas from one language to another knows that the potential for misunderstanding is always present. Sometimes, the results of a bungled translation can be amusing. For example, General Motors introduced the Chevy Nova in Spanish-speaking markets without realizing that the word *nova* in Spanish means 'doesn't go'.

Test Yourself   Describe three harmful linguistic habits that contribute to conflict.

Even when choosing the right words, there's no guarantee that non-native speakers will use a foreign language correctly. For example, Japanese insurance companies warn their policyholders who are visiting the United States to avoid their cultural tendency to say 'excuse me' or 'I'm sorry' if they are involved in a traffic accident (Sugimoto, 1991). In Japan, apologizing is a traditional way to express goodwill and maintain social harmony, even if the person offering the apology is not at fault. But in the United States, an apology can be taken as an admission of guilt and result in Japanese tourists being held accountable after accidents for which they may not be responsible.

Difficult as they may be, translation and terminology constitute only one of many communication challenges facing members of different cultures and co-cultures. Now, we need to look at some more subtle challenges that can make decoding messages from members of other cultures a challenging task.

Reflection

Idioms and Translation

I hadn't realized how tricky it can be to learn a new language until I started tutoring some international students who had just arrived on campus from overseas. Most of them have an excellent textbook understanding of English, since they've been studying the language since elementary school. But knowing formal rules and vocabulary hasn't prepared them for the way everyday talk works.

Some of the idioms we take for granted as native English speakers don't make any sense. Yesterday, I counted over twenty of them in just one class lecture: 'Taking the bull by the horns', 'beating around the bush', 'shot down', 'blowing your top', 'up in the air', and so on. Until you can understand idioms like these, you miss a lot. And until you learn to use them, you sound like a textbook instead of a natural speaker.

High- versus Low-Context Cultures

Anthropologist Edward Hall (1959) identified two distinct ways that members of various cultures deliver messages. A **low-context culture** uses language primarily to express thoughts, feelings, and ideas as directly and logically as possible. To low-context communicators, the meaning of a statement lies in the words spoken. By contrast, a **high-context culture** relies heavily on subtle, often non-verbal cues to maintain social harmony (Ambady et al., 1996). Rather than upset others by speaking directly, communicators in these societies learn to discover meaning from the context in which a message is delivered, that is, the non-verbal behaviour of the speaker, the history of the relationship, and the general social rules that govern interaction between people. In Table 5.5, we summarize some key differences in how people from low- and high-context cultures use language.

Mainstream culture in Canada, the United States, and Northern Europe can be categorized near the low-context end of the scale. Inhabitants of these low-context cultures generally value straight talk and grow impatient with 'beating around the bush'. By contrast, most Asian and Middle Eastern cultures fit the high-context pattern.

In many Asian societies, for example, maintaining harmony is important, so communicators avoid speaking clearly if it helps a person to 'save face'. For this reason, communicators raised in Japanese or Korean cultures are less likely than Canadians to offer a clear 'no' to an undesirable request. Instead, they would probably use round-about expressions like 'I agree with you in principle, but . . .' or 'I sympathize with you. . . .' As T. R. Reid (1999, p. 84) explains, 'Japanese people avoid saying "no"—not because they are dishonest, but because saying a flat "no" might cause disappointment and ill-feeling. . . . So the Japanese fall back on their arsenal of euphemisms: "That would be difficult.", "We'll give your request careful thought.", "Excuse me, but . . ."'

To members of high-context cultures, communicators with a low-context style can appear overly talkative, lacking in subtlety, and redundant. On the other hand, to people from low-context backgrounds, high-context communicators often seem inexpressive or even dishonest. It is easy to see how the clash between directness and indirectness can aggravate problems between straight-talking, low-context Israelis and their Arab neighbours, whose high-context culture stresses smooth interaction. Israelis might view their Arab counterparts as evasive, while the Arabs might perceive the Israelis as insensitive and blunt.

Verbal Communication Styles

Using language is more than just a matter of choosing a particular group of words to convey an idea. Each language has its own unique character that distinguishes it from others. Matters like the amount of formality or informality, precision or vagueness, and brevity or detail are major

Table 5.5 High- and Low-Context Communication

Low Context	High Context
Majority of information carried in explicit verbal messages, with less focus on the situational context	Important information carried in contextual cues—time, place, relationship, situation; less reliance on explicit verbal messages.
Self-expression valued; communicators state opinions and desires directly and strive to persuade others to accept their own viewpoint	Relational harmony valued and maintained by indirect expression of options; communicators abstain from saying 'no' directly
Clear, eloquent speech considered praiseworthy; verbal fluency admired.	Communicators talk 'around' the point, allowing the others to fill in the missing pieces; ambiguity and use of silence admired

ingredients in speaking competently. When a communicator tries to use the verbal style from one culture in a different one, problems are likely to arise.

Consider a simple example of differing cultural rules: An elementary school teacher might encourage the class to speak up by making an incorrect statement that demands refutation: 'So, 12 divided by 4 is 6, right?' Most Canadian students of European ancestry would recognize this as a way of testing their understanding. But this style of questioning is unfamiliar to many students raised in traditional African cultures, who aren't likely to speak until they are directly questioned by the teacher (Rubin, 1986). Given this sort of difference, it's easy to imagine how some teachers might view children who were not raised in the mainstream Canadian culture as unresponsive or slow, when they are simply playing by a different set of rules.

Gudykunst and Ting-Toomey (1988) describe three important types of cultural differences in verbal style. One is *directness* or *indirectness*. We have already discussed how low-context cultures use language primarily to express thoughts, feelings, and ideas as clearly, directly, and logically as possible, while high-context cultures may speak less directly, using language to maintain social harmony.

Another way in which language styles can vary is in terms of whether they are *elaborate* or *succinct*. For instance, speakers of Arabic commonly use language that is much more rich and expressive than normally found in English. Strong assertions and exaggerations that would sound ridiculous in English are a common feature of Arabic. This contrast in linguistic style can lead to misunderstandings between people from different backgrounds:

> First, an Arab feels compelled to overexert in almost all types of communication because others expect him [or her] to. If an Arab says exactly what he [or she] means without the expected assertion, other Arabs may still think that he [or she] means the opposite. For example, a simple 'no' from a guest to the host's requests to eat more or drink more will not suffice.

To convey the meaning that he [or she] is actually full, the guest must keep repeating 'no' several times, coupling it with an oath such as 'By God' or 'I swear to God.' Second, an Arab often fails to realize that others, particularly foreigners, may mean exactly what they say even though their language is simple. To the Arabs, a simple 'no' may mean the indirectly expressed consent and encouragement of a coquettish woman. On the other hand, a simple consent may mean the rejection of a hypocritical politician. (Almaney and Alwan, 1982, p. 84)

Succinctness is most extreme in cultures where silence is valued. In many First Nations cultures in Canada, for example, the favoured way to handle ambiguous social situations is to remain quiet (Basso, 1970; Hett, 1993). When you contrast this silent style to the talkativeness that is common when people first meet in mainstream Canadian culture, it's easy to imagine how the first encounter between a Cree or Mi'kmaq and an Anglo-Canadian might be uncomfortable for both people.

A third way that languages can differ from one culture to another is in their *formality* and *informality*. The pronouns used in a language may encode politeness and formality. For example, most European languages except English have different pronouns for informal use among friends (e.g., *tu* in French and Italian) and more formal pronouns for addressing superiors and people one does not know well (e.g., *vous* in French, *lei* in Italian). In Japanese, there are even more choices depending on the rank, job, sex, and age of the person being spoken to.

The informal approach that is characteristic of North Americans is quite different from the great concern for propriety in many parts of Asia and Africa. Formality is not so much a matter of using correct grammar as of defining social relationships. For example, there are different degrees of formality for speaking to old friends, non-acquaintances whose background one knows, and complete strangers. One sign of being a learned person in Korea is the ability to use language that recognizes these relational distinctions. When you contrast these sorts of distinctions with the casual friendliness of many North Americans, even when talking to complete strangers, it's easy to see how a Korean might consider North American communicators to be boorish and how a North American might see Koreans as stiff and unfriendly.

Male and Female Use of Language

In addition to the differences among languages and cultures, there are other important differences in the way men and women use language. As well, there are many non-sex variables at play in conversation, such as a person's social philosophy, sexual orientation, occupation, gender role, and interpersonal power.

According to some theorists and researchers (e.g., Tannen, 1990; Mulac et al., 2001), there are significant differences between the way the sexes speak. Other scholars have suggested that any differences are not significant (Canary and Emmers-Sommer, 1997). What are the similarities and differences between male and female language use?

Content

Though there is certainly variation within each sex, on the average, men and women discuss a different range of topics. The first research on conversational topics was conducted over seventy years ago. Despite the changes in male and female roles since then, the results of more recent studies are remarkably similar (Bischoping, 1993; Clark, 1998; Fehr, 1996). These studies, which analyzed the communication of women and men ranging in age from seventeen to eighty, examined the topics each discussed with friends of the same sex. Certain subjects were common to both sexes: work, movies, and television proved to be frequent topics for both groups. Both men and women tended to reserve discussions of sex and sexuality for members of the same sex. Along with the similarities, there were significant differences in the conversations of men and women, especially when talking to friends. Female friends spent much more time discussing relationship problems; family, health, and reproductive matters; weight; food; clothing; and men. Women also reported discussing other women frequently. Men, on the other hand, were more likely to discuss sports, hobbies, and activities. Both men and women were equally likely to discuss personal appearance, sex, and dating in same-sex conversations.

Reasons for Communicating

Both men and women, at least in the mainstream cultures of Canada and the United States , use language to build and maintain social relationships. Regardless of the sex of the communicators, the goal of almost all ordinary conversations includes making the conversation enjoyable by being friendly, showing an interest in what the other person says, and talking about topics that interest the other person (Clark, 1998). How men and women accomplish these goals, though, is often different. Although most communicators try to make their interaction enjoyable, men are more likely than

iStock photo

women to try to make conversation fun. Their discussions involve a greater amount of joking and good-natured teasing. By contrast, women's conversations focus more often on feelings, relationships, and personal problems (Burleson et al., 1996; Samter et al., 1994). When a group of women was surveyed to find out what kinds of satisfaction they gained from talking with their friends, the most common theme mentioned was a feeling of empathy—'to know you're not alone', as some put it (Sherman and Haas, 1984). Whereas men commonly described same-sex conversations as something they liked, females characterized their woman-to-woman talks as a kind of contact they needed. The greater frequency of female conversations reflects their importance. Nearly 50 percent of the women surveyed by Sherman and Haas said they called friends at least once a week just to talk, whereas fewer than half as many men did so. In fact, 40 percent of the men surveyed reported that they never called another man just to chat.

Because they use conversation to pursue social needs, female speech often contains statements showing support for the other person, demonstrations of equality, and efforts to keep the conversation going (Clark, 1998). With these goals, it's not surprising that traditionally female speech often contains statements of sympathy and empathy: 'I've felt just like that myself,' 'The same thing happened to me!' Women are also inclined to ask questions that invite the other person to share information: 'How did you feel about that?' 'What did you do next?' The importance of nurturing a relationship also explains why stereotypically female speech is tentative. Saying, 'This is just my opinion . . .' is less likely to put off a conversational partner than a more definite, 'Here's what I think . . .'

Men's speech is often driven by quite different goals than women's. Men are more likely to use language to accomplish the job at hand than to nourish relationships. This explains why men are less likely than women to disclose their vulnerabilities, which would be a sign of weakness. When someone else is describing a problem, most language experts suggest that instead of empathizing, men are prone to offer advice: 'That's nothing to

worry about . . .' 'Here's what you need to do. . . .' Besides taking care of business, men are more likely than women to use conversations to exert control, preserve their independence, and enhance their status. This explains why men are more prone to dominate conversations and one-up their partners. Men often interrupt their conversational partners to assert their own experiences or point of view. (Women interrupt, too, but they usually do so to offer support, which is quite a different goal.)

Conversational Style

Research suggests that women speak somewhat differently in conversations than men do (for summaries, see Wood, 2002; Turner et al., 1995). For example, Mulac (1998) reports that men are more likely than women to use judgmental adjectives ('Reading can be a drag'), directives ('Think of some more'), and 'I' references ('I have a lot to do'). Women are more likely to use intensive adverbs ('He's really interested'), emotional references ('If he really cared about you . . .'), uncertainty verbs ('It seems to me . . .'), and contradictions ('It's cold, but that's okay'). Mulac summarizes style differences by claiming that men's speech is more direct, succinct (to the point), personal, and task-oriented. By contrast, female speech is more indirect, elaborate, and focused on relationships. Some theorists have argued that such differences cause women's speech to be less powerful than men's, although research does not always back up this claim (Grob et al., 1997).

Other studies have revealed that men and women behave differently in different conversational settings. For example, in mixed-sex dyads, men talk longer than women, while in same-sex situations, women talk for a longer time. Women speak more tentatively than men when they are in mixed-sex conversations, although their speech is just as confident as men's in same-sex situations. In larger groups, men talk more, whereas in smaller groups, women do more of the talking. In same-sex conversations, there are other differences: women use more questions, justifications, intensive adverbs, personal pronouns, and adverbs. Men use more directives, interruptions,

Focus on Research

Men, Women, and the Meaning of Love

'The word *love* has by no means the same sense for both sexes,' said author and philosopher Simone de Beauvoir. Researchers Beverly Fehr and Ross Broughton (2001) wanted to find out if de Beauvoir was correct—do men and women perceive love differently?

While the word *love* has dozens of definitions, research suggests that the concept of love can be reduced to two basic types: passionate love (intense arousal, attraction, and emotions) and companionate love (a bond of trust, caring, and respect). Fehr and Broughton surveyed several hundred students to learn how sex and personality type affected their perceptions of love. As predicted, the men were more prone than women to view love as passionate. Surprisingly, the women were no more prone than men to view love as companionate.

The researchers conducted further studies and found that personality type was as useful as biological sex in predicting perceptions of love. Those with dominant personalities (mostly men, but also women) tended to regard love as passionate; those with nurturing personalities (mostly females, but also males) tended to regard love as companionate.

'In light of these findings,' conclude Fehr and Boughton, 'Simone de Beauvoir's proclamation that "the word *love* has by no means the same sense for both sexes" seems rather overstated.'

and filler words to begin sentences (Mulac et al., 2001; Mulac et al., 1988).

Non-Sex Variables

Despite the differences in the way men and women speak, the link between sex and language use is not as clear-cut as it might seem. Some observers (e.g., Gray, 1992) have claimed that differences are so great that men might as well have come from Mars and women from Venus. A more sober look at the research suggests that the differences are not nearly so dramatic. For example, one analysis of over 1,200 research studies found that only 1 percent of variance in communication behaviour resulted from sex differences (Canary and Hause, 1993). There is no significant difference between male and female speech in areas such as use of profanity, use of qualifiers such as 'I guess' or 'this is just my opinion' or tag questions, and vocal fluency (Grob et al., 1997; Zahn, 1989). In light of the considerable similarities between the sexes and the relatively minor differences, communication scholars Julia Wood and Kathryn Dindia (1998) suggest that the 'men are from Mars, women from Venus' claim should be replaced by the metaphor that 'men are from North Dakota, women are from South Dakota.'

A growing body of research explains some of the apparent contradictions in similarities and differences between female and male speech by pointing out that factors other than the sex of the communicator influence language use. For example, *social philosophy* plays a role. Feminist wives talk more than their husbands do, whereas wives who do not identify themselves as feminists talk less. Orientation toward problem solving also plays a role in conversational style: whether a speaker has a co-operative or competitive orientation has greater influence on interaction than biological sex (Fisher, 1983). *Sexual orientation* may be more powerful than biological sex in determining speech mannerisms. In gay and lesbian relationships, the conversational styles of partners reflect power differences in the relationship (e.g., who is earning more money) more than the biological sex of the communicators (Steen and Schwartz, 1995).

The speaker's *occupation* also influences speaking style. For example, male early childhood educators' speech to their students resembles the language of female teachers more closely than it resembles the language of fathers at home (Gleason and Greif, 1983). Overall, doctors interrupt their patients more often than the reverse, although male patients interrupt female physicians more

Reflection

Different Roles, Different Language

As the first woman in a formerly all-male architectural firm, I feel like something of a guinea pig. Most of the partners and associates have made me feel welcome, but a small group treats me with what seems like a condescending attitude. The structural, mechanical, and electrical engineers we use as consultants are even worse. I don't think they've ever worked with a woman who wasn't a secretary. I've found that with these guys, I've changed the way I speak. I try to use more powerful language with fewer hesitations and hedges. I make more statements and ask fewer questions. In other words, I sound more like a stereotypical man.

I don't know yet whether this approach will make any difference. The point is, I sound like a different person when I'm at work more than in any other setting. It's not really an act: it's more an effort to sound professional. I guess if someone dresses differently when they go to work, there's nothing wrong with sounding different too.

often than they do male physicians (Zimmerman and West, 1975). At work, task differences exert more powerful effects on whether speakers use sex-inclusive language (such as 'he or she' instead of just 'he') than does biological sex (Rubin et al., 1994). A close study of trial transcripts showed that the speaker's experience on the witness stand and occupation had more to do with language use than did biological sex. The researcher concluded, 'So-called women's language is neither characteristic of all women nor limited only to women' (O'Barr, 1982).

Another powerful force that influences the way individual men and women speak is their *gender role*. Recall the various sex types described in Chapter 3 (page 81): masculine, feminine, and androgynous. Remember that these sex types do not necessarily line up neatly with biological sex. There are 'masculine' females as well as 'feminine' females, 'feminine' males as well as 'masculine' males, and androgynous communicators who combine traditionally masculine and feminine characteristics. Research

shows that these gender roles can influence a communicator's style more than his or her biological sex. Donald Ellis and Linda McCallister (1980) found that masculine subjects used significantly more dominant language than did either feminine or androgynous group members. Feminine members expressed slightly more submissive behaviour and more equivalence behaviour than the androgynous group members—and their submissiveness and equivalence were much greater than those of the masculine subjects.

Another factor that trumps sex differences is *power*. For instance, there are few differences between the way men and women use powerful speech (specifically, threats) when they have the same amount of bargaining strength in a negotiation (Scudder and Andrews, 1995). Findings like this suggest that characteristically feminine speech has been less a function of gender or sex than of women's historically less powerful positions in some parts of the social world.

By now, it should be clear that there are differences between the way men and women speak, but that these differences are determined by a wide variety of factors that may have little or nothing to do with biological sex. As men and women grow to have equal opportunities and more similar social experiences, we can expect that there will be fewer differences in the ways they speak.

Summary

Language is both a marvellous communication tool and the source of many interpersonal problems. Every language is a collection of symbols governed by a variety of rules. Because of its

Test Yourself Describe the observed differences between male and female speakers in terms of content, reasons for communicating, and conversational style. What non-sex variables have been associated with differences in the ways men and women speak?

symbolic nature, language is not a precise vehicle: meanings rest in people, not in words themselves. The codes that are used by members of a culture are often the most recognizable factors that shape communication between people from different cultural backgrounds. Verbal codes include language spoken and the worldview created by it as well as verbal communication style.

Besides conveying meanings about the content of a specific message, language both expresses and shapes the perceptions of its users. Terms used to name people influence the way they are regarded. The terms used to label speakers and the language they use shape other people's evaluations of the speakers' credibility and status. Language also reveals the level of affiliation, attraction, and interest of a speaker toward a subject. In addition, language patterns reflect and shape a speaker's perceived power. Finally, language reflects and influences sexist and racist attitudes.

When used carelessly, language can lead to a variety of interpersonal problems. The precision or vagueness of messages can affect a receiver's understanding of them. Both precise messages and vague, evasive messages have their uses in interpersonal relationships, and a competent communicator has the ability to choose the best level of precision for the situation at hand. Language also acknowledges or avoids the speaker's acceptance of responsibility for his or her positions, and competent communicators know how to use 'I', 'you', and 'we' statements to accept the optimal level of responsibility and relational harmony. Some language habits—confusing facts with opinions or inferences and using emotive terms—can lead to unnecessary disharmony in interpersonal relationships.

Low-context cultures (e.g., North American) rely primarily on language to express thoughts and feelings, while high-context cultures (e.g., Asian) rely heavily on subtle cues to maintain social harmony.

The relationship between the sex of the communicator and language is a complex one. There are many differences in the ways men and women speak. The content of their conversations varies, as do their reasons for communicating and their conversational style. However, not all differences in language use can be accounted for by the speaker's sex. Social philosophy, sexual orientation, occupation, and interpersonal power also influence the use of language, and psychological gender can be more of an influence than biological sex.

Activities

1. **Invitation to Insight**

   For each of the following scenes, describe one syntactic, one semantic, and one pragmatic rule:

   a. Asking an acquaintance out for a first date
   b. Declining an invitation to a party
   c. Responding to a stranger who has just said 'excuse me' after bumping into you in a crowd

2. **Invitation to Insight**

   Recall an incident in which you were misunderstood. Explain how this event illustrates the principle that 'meanings are in people, not words.'

3. **Ethical Challenge**

   The information on pages 130–7 about the influence of language shows how the words a communicator chooses can shape the perceptions of others. Create two scenarios for each type of linguistic influence listed below. The first should describe how the type of influence could be used constructively, and the second should describe an unethical application of this knowledge.

   a. Naming and identity
   b. Credibility and status
   c. Attraction and interest
   d. Power
   e. Sexism and racism

4. **Skill Builder**

   Translate the following into behavioural language:

   - An abstract goal for improving your interpersonal communication (for example, 'Be more assertive', or 'Stop being so sarcastic')
   - A complaint you have about another person (for instance, that he or she is 'selfish' or 'insensitive')

   In both cases, describe the person or people involved, the circumstances in which the communication will take place, and the precise behaviour involved. What difference will using the behavioural descriptions be likely to make in your relationships?

5. **Invitation to Insight**

   Are there ever situations in your life when it is desirable to be less clear and more vague? Use the information on pages 138–43 to answer this question and to decide whether vagueness is the most competent approach to the situation.

6. **Skill Builder**

   You can develop your skill at delivering 'I' and 'we' messages by following these steps:

   a. Visualize situations in your life when you may have sent each of the following messages:

   'You're not telling me the truth!'
   'You only think of yourself!'
   'Don't be so touchy!'
   'Quit fooling around!'
   'You don't understand a word I'm saying!'

b. Write alternatives to each statement, using 'I' language.

c. Think of three 'you' statements you could make to people in your life. Transform each of these statements into 'I' and 'we' language, and rehearse them with a classmate.

7. **Invitation to Insight**

What roles do the types of disruptive language described on pages 145–7 play in your life? Recall incidents when you have confused facts and opinions, confused facts and inferences, and used emotive language. Discuss the consequences of each type of language use, and describe how the results might have been different if you had used language more carefully.

8. **Invitation to Insight**

Some authors believe that differences between male and female communication are so great that they can be characterized as 'men are from Mars, women are from Venus.' Other researchers believe the differences are not nearly so dramatic and would describe them as 'men are from North Dakota, women are from South Dakota.' Which approach seems more accurate to you? Offer experiences from your life to support your point of view.

9. **Skill Builder**

Rewrite the following sentences to make them gender-neutral.

a. The average student is worried about his grades.

b. Ask the student to hand in his work as soon as he is finished.

c. Writers become so involved in their work that they neglect their wives and children.

10. **Role Play**

Choose a partner. Think of a real criticism (of someone else) and compose a highly abstract message to convey your complaint (e.g., 'You're so selfish'). Briefly describe the situation to your partner (who the other person is and the general situation—avoid providing specific details about the complaint) and have her or him pretend to be the person you are criticizing. Deliver your abstract criticism and have your partner respond. Now, compose a more specific behavioural description of the same complaint and deliver this criticism to your partner and have him or her respond. Discuss the differences between the two messages. What are the advantages of stating your complaints in more specific terms? Now, reverse roles and repeat the exercise.

Discussion Questions

1. What is the significance of the phrase, 'meanings are in people, not in words'?

2. Does naming something make it more or less frightening? Recall the outbreak of Severe Acute Respiratory Syndrome (SARS) in the spring of 2003. At first, doctors and public health officials did not have a name for the illness. Later, they described it as SARS—which wasn't really a name but a description of the illness. The acronym stuck. Why did the public want to name it? How does language affect our perceptions?

3. We have argued in this chapter that sexist language is a subtle form of bias. Do you agree or disagree? Why?

4. Given the subjective nature of perception, is 'we' language ever acceptable? Why or why not?

5. Do you think that news outlets use the confusion between fact and opinion, and fact and inference to their advantage? Do some news reports contain emotive language? Could these distinctions be used to distinguish between news reporting and propaganda? Why or why not?

6. Do you believe that the language a person speaks affects that person's worldview? Why or why not?

7. Given the diversity of verbal styles in different cultures, is it possible not to offend someone when you are communicating cross-culturally? Why or why not?

Chapter Six

Non-verbal Communication

After studying the material in this chapter . . .

You Should Understand:

1. The distinguishing characteristics of non-verbal communication.
2. The functions that non-verbal communication can serve.
3. The research evidence regarding detecting deception.
4. The various ways in which non-verbal messages are communicated.

You Should Be Able To:

1. Describe your non-verbal behaviour in any situation.
2. Identify non-verbal behaviour that repeats, substitutes for, complements, accents, regulates, or contradicts a verbal message.
3. Recognize and adjust the messages you send through your own non-verbal behaviour.
4. Share appropriately your interpretation of another's non-verbal behaviour.

People don't always say what they mean . . . but their body gestures and movements tell the truth!

Will he ask you out? Is she encouraging you? Know what is really happening by understanding the secret language of body signals. You can

Improve your sex life . . .
Pick up your social life . . .
Better your business life . . .

Read Body Language *so that you can penetrate the personal secrets, both of intimates and total strangers . . .*

Does her body say that she's a phony?
Does her body say that she's a manipulator?
Does her body say that she's lonely?

Unless you've been trapped in a lead mine or doing fieldwork in the Amazon Basin, claims like these are probably familiar to you. Almost every drugstore, supermarket, and airport book rack has its share of 'body language' paperbacks. They promise that, for only a few dollars and with a grade 5 reading ability, you can learn secrets that will change you from a fumbling social failure into a self-assured mind reader who can uncover a person's deepest secrets at a glance.

Claims like these are almost always exaggerations or fabrications. There *is*, of course, a scientific body of knowledge about non-verbal communication, and it *has* provided many fascinating and valuable clues to human behaviour. That's what this chapter is about. But it is unlikely the next few pages will turn you instantly into a rich, sexy, charming communication superstar; however, don't go away. Even without glamorous promises, a quick look at some facts about non-verbal communication shows that it is an important and valuable field to study.

Non-verbal Communication Defined

Since *non* means 'not' and *verbal* means 'with words', then it seems logical that *non-verbal communication* would involve 'communication without words'. This definition is an oversimplification,

however, because it fails to distinguish between *vocal* communication (by mouth) and *verbal* communication (with words). Some non-verbal messages have a vocal element. For example, the words 'I love you' have different meanings depending on the way they are spoken. Furthermore, as the accompanying cartoon suggests, a few non-spoken forms of communication are actually linguistic, and not really non-verbal in the sense most social scientists use the term. A better definition of **non-verbal communication** is 'messages expressed by non-linguistic means'.

These non-linguistic messages are important because what we *do* often conveys more meaning than what we *say*. Albert Mehrabian (1972), a psychologist working in the field of non-verbal behaviour, claimed that 93 percent of the emotional impact of a message comes from a non-verbal source, whereas only 7 percent is verbal. Anthropologist Ray Birdwhistell (1970) described a 65–35 percent split between actions and words. Although social scientists have disputed these figures (e.g., Hegstrom, 1979; Lapakko, 1997), it is a fact that non-verbal communication contributes a great deal to shaping perceptions.

You might ask how non-verbal communication can be so powerful. At first glance, it seems as if meanings come from words. To answer this question, think of a time when you watched people speaking a language you didn't understand. Although you can't understand the words being spoken, there are plenty of clues that give you

iStock photo

Take Two

> - **Non-verbal communication:** messages expressed by non-linguistic means; they can include vocal communication (e.g., voice tone) but not language (e.g., sign language).

an idea of what is going on in the exchange. By watching the speakers' facial expressions, postures, gestures, vocal tones, and other behaviour you probably can make assumptions about the way the communicators feel about one another at the moment and get some ideas about the nature of their relationship. Researchers have found that subjects who hear content-free speech—ordinary speech that has been electronically manipulated so that the words are unintelligible—can consistently recognize the emotion being expressed, as well as identify its strength (Knapp and Hall, 2002).

Characteristics of Non-verbal Communication

The many types of non-verbal communication share some characteristics. As Table 6.1 shows, these characteristics are quite different from verbal, linguistic means of communication. We will now take a look at some of the fundamental characteristics of non-verbal communication.

All Behaviour Has Communicative Value

Some theorists have suggested that *all* non-verbal behaviour conveys information. They argue that it is impossible *not* to communicate. You can understand the impossibility of non-communication by considering what you would do if someone told you not to communicate any messages at all. What would you do? Close your eyes? Withdraw into a ball? Leave the room? You can probably see that even those actions communicate messages that mean you are avoiding contact. One study (DePaulo, 1992) took just this approach. When communicators were told not to express non-verbal clues, others viewed them as dull, withdrawn, uneasy, aloof, and deceptive.

The impossibility of not communicating is significant because it means that each of us is a kind of transmitter that cannot be shut off. No matter what we do, we send out messages that say something about ourselves and our relationships with others. If, for instance, someone were observing you now, what non-verbal clues would they get about how you are feeling? Are you sitting forward or reclining back? Is your posture tense or relaxed? Are your eyes wide open, or do they keep closing? What does your facial expression communicate now? Can you make your face expressionless? Don't people with expressionless faces communicate something to you? Even uncontrollable behaviour can convey a message. You may

Table 6.1 Some Differences between Verbal and Non-verbal Communication

Verbal Communication	Non-verbal Communication
• Mostly voluntary and conscious	• Often unconscious
• Usually content-oriented	• Usually relational
• Can be clear or vague	• Inherently ambiguous
• Primarily shaped by culture	• Primarily shaped by biology
• Discontinuous or intermittent	• Continuous
• Single-channel (words only)	• Multi-channelled

Source: Adapted from p. 16 of P. Andersen (1999), *Non-verbal Communication: Forms and Functions.* Mountain View, CA: Mayfield.

not intend to show that you are embarrassed, but your blushing can still give you away. Of course, not all behaviour (intentional or not) will be interpreted correctly. Your trembling hands might be taken as a sign of nervousness when you are really just shivering from the cold. But whether or not your behaviour is intentional, and whether or not it is interpreted accurately, all non-verbal behaviour has the potential to create messages.

Although non-verbal behaviour reveals information, we are not always conscious of what we are communicating non-verbally. In one study, fewer than a quarter of experimental subjects who had been instructed to show increased or decreased liking of a partner could describe the non-verbal behaviour they used (Palmer and Simmons, 1995). Furthermore, the fact that communicators are non-verbally expressive does not mean that others will receive the abundance of unspoken messages that are available. One study comparing the richness of email to in-person communication confirmed the greater amount of information available in face-to-face conversations, but it

also showed that some communicators (primarily men) failed to recognize these messages (Dennis et al., 1999).

Non-verbal Communication Is Primarily Relational

Some non-verbal messages serve utilitarian functions. For example, a police officer directs the flow of traffic, or a team of street surveyors uses hand motions to coordinate their work. But non-verbal communication also serves a far more common (and more interesting) series of *social* functions.

Non-verbal communication plays an important role in identity management, as we discussed in Chapter 2. In many cases, the role of non-verbal communication is more important than that of verbal messages (Zuckerman et al., 1999). Similarly, the relational component of messages is most often communicated non-verbally. Non-verbal communication allows us to define the kind of relationships we want to have with others (Burgoon and Le Poire, 1999). You can appreciate this fact by thinking about the wide range of ways you could

iStock photo

© Sandra Bell-Lundy. Reprinted with permssion of King Features Syndicate.

behave when greeting another person. You could wave, shake hands, nod, smile, clap the other person on the back, give her a hug, kiss him on both cheeks, or avoid all contact. Each one of these actions sends a message about the nature of your relationship with the other person. The relational messages communicated with non-verbal communication include the degree to which people like each other, want involvement with each other and their status or power relative to each other.

Non-verbal messages perform another valuable social function: they convey emotions that we may be unwilling or unable to express or ones we may not even be aware of. In fact, non-verbal communication is much better suited to expressing attitudes and feelings than it is ideas. You can prove this for yourself by imagining how you could express each item on the following list non-verbally:

1. 'I'm tired.'
2. 'I'm in favour of universal health care.'
3. 'I'm attracted to another person in the group.'
4. 'I think prayer should be allowed in schools.'
5. 'I'm angry at someone in this room.'

This experience shows that ideas (such as statements 2 and 4) do not lend themselves to non-verbal expressions nearly as well as attitudes and feelings (statements 1, 3, and 5). This explains why it is possible to understand the attitudes or feelings of others even if you do not understand the subject of their communication.

As technology develops, an increasing number of Internet messages will include video and voice. Currently, email and instant text messages offer fewer non-verbal cues about the speaker's feelings than do face-to-face encounters or even telephone conversations. Most of us have had the experience of finding out that our email or text message has been misunderstood. The use of emoticons (keyboard characters to simulate facial expressions) or avatars (animated characters capable of a variety of facial expressions) can be used to try and capture non-verbal expressions in email and instant messages and reduce the chances for misunderstandings. Research suggests that the use of emoticons and avatars in order to capture emotional expressiveness increases the involvement and interaction between the people sharing an email or text message (Fabri and Moore, 2005; Walther and D'Addario, 2001). In the Focus on Technology box (page 164), we explore the frustrations of misunderstood email and text messages in the workplace. Clearly, the rich mixture of non-verbal and verbal messages that flow in face-to-face exchanges, or even in telephone conversations, cannot be replicated in writing.

Non-verbal Communication Is Ambiguous

In Chapter 5, we pointed out how some language can be ambiguous. (For example, the statement, 'nose piercing really makes you stand out' could be a compliment or a criticism, and the vague

Focus on Technology

Emotions, Email, and Text Messages

For Canadians, email and instant messaging are the media of choice, not just for communicating at work but for sending personal messages to friends and family. An Ipsos Reid survey conducted in 2007 found that 66 percent of Canadians preferred to communicate by email (Mossop, 2008). That same study found that Canadians receive an average of 76 legitimate email messages per week. Increasingly, people are using email to communicate with family and friends, send photos and invitations, and make important announcements such as engagements and births. People choose email because it is easy to incorporate into the way they live and work. Email and text messages don't interrupt the flow of activities in the same way telephone conversations and face-time meetings do. One of the major drawbacks with written messages, however, is that they lack non-verbal cues that communicate relational messages and emotions. According to a survey by Microsoft Corporation (2007), Canadians care about how their email and text messages are perceived by others. Those surveyed expressed concern about how the lack of emotion in written messages can cause conversations to be misinterpreted.

This is of particular concern at work, where the use of emoticons [graphic representations of facial expressions; e.g., ☺ and ;-)] and initializations (e.g., LOL means 'laugh out loud') that help to convey tone and emotion are usually discouraged by managers and supervisors (Jett, 2005). The expression of emotion in face-to-face or telephone conversations depends heavily on non-verbal cues that are absent in email and text messages. This has led some researchers to suggest that email should not or cannot convey emotion, but more recent investigations have revealed that email often communicates emotions both intentionally and unintentionally (Thompsen and Foulger, 1996; Walther and D'Addario, 2001).

Kristen Byron has explored the factors that contribute to the miscommunication of emotion in email communication in the workplace. In Byron's (2008) theoretical framework the two most common misinterpretations of emotions in workplace email are that receivers are likely to perceive emails intended to convey positive emotions as more neutral and that receivers are more likely to perceive emails as more intensely negative than was intended by the sender. There are a number of factors that influence the likelihood of miscommunication including the length of the relationship between the sender and the receiver, the gender and relative status of the sender (e.g., colleague, boss, etc.), the age and negative mood of the receiver as well as the established guidelines for the expression of emotion in the workplace. Byron argues that while more research in this area is needed, misperception of emotion in email messages can be reduced by increasing employees' awareness that emotions can be communicated, both intentionally and unintentionally, in email messages. Second, employees need to recognize that they are fallible as both email senders and receivers. A third step would be to increase the use of cues and the amount of feedback to increase the likelihood of more accurate perceptions. Senders can increase accuracy by actually verbalizing the emotion ('I am so sad happy you will be able to come to the meeting') and receivers can ask questions and state their interpretations of messages and invite the sender to respond. These strategies for perception checking (see Chapter 3) are as useful for computer-mediated communication as they are for the face-to-face variety.

statement, 'I'm almost done' could mean you have to wait a few minutes or an hour.) Most non-verbal behaviour has the potential to be even more ambiguous than verbal statements like these. To understand why, consider how you would interpret silence from your companion during an evening together. Think of all the possible meanings of this non-verbal behaviour: affection, anger, preoccupation, boredom, nervousness, thoughtfulness—the possibilities are many.

The ambiguity of non-verbal behaviour was illustrated when a supermarket chain tried to emphasize its customer-friendly approach by instructing employees to smile and make eye contact with customers. Several clerks filed grievances when some customers mistook the service-with-a-smile approach as sexual come-ons. As this story suggests, non-verbal cues are much more ambiguous than verbal statements when it comes to expressing willingness to become physically

DILBERT Reprinted by permission of United Feature Syndicate, Inc.

involved (Lim and Roloff, 1999). Romantic partners often interpret non-verbal cues as signs of sexual willingness. However, these non-verbal messages are far less likely to be misunderstood when accompanied by verbal statements. Using clearer and less ambiguous verbal messages could reduce a variety of unfortunate outcomes, ranging from a spoiled evening to lawsuits and accusations of sexual assault.

Summarizing studies on emotion recognition within and across cultures, Elfenbein and Ambady (2002a, 2002b) found that while emotions were universally recognized at better-than-chance levels, accuracy was higher when emotions were expressed and recognized by members of the same national, ethnic, or regional group, suggesting an in-group advantage. However, not all non-verbal behaviour is equally identifiable. In laboratory settings, subjects are better at identifying positive facial expressions, such as happiness, love, surprise, and interest, than negative ones, like fear, sadness, anger, and disgust (Druckmann et al., 1982). In real life, though, spontaneous non-verbal expressions are so ambiguous that observers are frequently unable to identify accurately what they mean (Elfenbein and Ambady, 2002a, 2002b; Motley, 1993).

Because non-verbal behaviour is so ambiguous, caution is wise when you are responding to non-verbal cues. Rather than jump to conclusions about the meaning of a sigh, smile, slammed door, or yawn, it is far better to use the kind of perception-checking approach described in Chapter 3. 'When you yawned, I got the idea I might be boring you. But maybe you are just tired. What's going on?' The ability to consider more than one possible interpretation for non-verbal behaviour illustrates the kind of cognitive complexity that we identified in Chapter 1 as an element of communication competence. In fact, research has demonstrated that cognitively complex people are better at decoding non-verbal behaviour than those who jump to conclusions about its meaning (Woods, 1996). Popular advice on the subject notwithstanding, it is usually not possible to read a person like a book.

Non-verbal Communication Is Influenced by Culture

Cultures have different non-verbal languages as well as verbal ones. Fiorello LaGuardia, mayor of New York from 1933 to 1945, was fluent in English, Italian, and Yiddish. Researchers who watched films of his campaign speeches with the sound turned off found that they could tell which language he was speaking by the changes in his non-verbal behaviour (Birdwhistell 1970).

The meaning of some gestures varies from one culture to another. Communicators become more tolerant of others once they understand that unusual non-verbal behaviour is the result of cultural differences. In one study, American adults were presented with videotaped scenes of speakers from Canada, France, and Germany (Warnecke et al., 1992). When the sound was cut

Focus on Research

Misinterpreting Non-verbal Behaviour: A Tragedy for Canadian First Nation Girls

In her review of the treatment of First Nations girls sentenced to Ontario Training Schools from 1933 to 1960, Joan Sangster (2002) describes the devastating effects of misinterpreting non-verbal behaviour because of cultural differences.

Sangster gives heartbreaking accounts of young First Nations girls whose emotional restraint and lack of eye contact were misinterpreted as passivity, secretiveness, and deceitfulness by the reform school staff, who were English-speaking Canadians of European descent.

Many First Nations cultures value silence and listening and do not promote overt emotional expression (either positive or negative). In contrast, the dominant Canadian culture of the 1930s to the 1960s was very much an extension of British culture in which eye contact and direct engagement were highly valued. These young girls showed their respect for and deference to the authority figures by not looking them in the eye and by keeping their feelings to themselves. The staff interpreted the girls' non-verbal behaviour as hostility and sneakiness. One school worker wrote, 'She is quiet, deep and cunning. She goes along with training ... but it is not penetrating. She has no conscience and is not progressing. ... She appears cooperative, but is deceitful' (Sangster, 2002, p. 38).

In addition, the girls had been raised in First Nations families where the parents teach their children by modelling the right behaviour and refrain from criticizing and punishing. The girls had learned to imitate adults in order to behave appropriately. This imitation was interpreted as a lack of intelligence by the school staff, who described the girls as 'dull'. The school superintendent described one girl as unable to assimilate her lessons. 'She scrapes by copying,' she wrote dismissively (Sangster, 2002, p. 36). Tragically, many girls were transferred to institutions for the mentally retarded, from which it was extremely difficult for them to be released.

There is no question that the training school staff's ethnocentrism and their racist attitudes toward First Nations peoples, which were very much a part of Canadian culture at that time, contributed to the staff's negative interpretations of the girls' behaviour. It is easy to see how an innocent lack of awareness of cultural differences in non-verbal expression can lead to tragic misunderstandings, particularly when one is dealing with children.

off, the viewers judged foreigners more negatively than they did their fellow citizens. But when the speakers' voices were added (allowing viewers to recognize that they were from a different country), the ratings of the speakers improved.

Despite differences like these, much non-verbal behaviour is universal. Certain expressions have the same meanings around the world. Smiles and laughter are a universal signal of positive emotions, for example, while the same sour expressions convey displeasure in every culture. Charles Darwin believed that expressions like these are the result of evolution, functioning as survival mechanisms that allowed early humans to convey emotional states before the development of language. The innateness of some facial expressions becomes even clearer when we examine the behaviour of children born deaf and blind (Eibl-Eibensfeldt, 1972). Despite a lack of social learning, these children display a broad range of expression. They smile, laugh, and cry in ways virtually identical to seeing and hearing infants.

While non-verbal expressions like these may be universal, the way they are used varies widely around the world. In some cultures, the overt expression of feelings like happiness or anger is discouraged. In other cultures, the same feelings are perfectly acceptable. Thus, a Japanese person might appear much more controlled and placid than an Arab, when in fact their feelings might be identical (Leathers, 1992).

The same principle operates closer to home among co-cultures. For example, observations have shown that black women in all-black groups are non-verbally more expressive and interrupt one another more than white women in all-white groups (Booth-Butterfield and Jordan, 1988). This does not mean that black women always feel more intensely than their white counterparts. A more likely explanation is that the two groups follow different cultural rules. The researchers found that in racially mixed groups both black and white women moved closer to each others' style. This non-verbal convergence shows that skilled communicators can adapt their behaviour when interacting with members of other cultures or co-cultures in order to make the exchange more smooth and effective.

Functions of Non-verbal Communication

Although we are dealing with non-verbal communication in this chapter, do not assume that people's words and actions are unrelated. Non-verbal communication interacts with verbal communication to express feelings, and relational messages, to modify a verbal message and to regulate the flow of our interactions with others. Let's take a look at the various relationships between our words and other types of expression.

iStock photo

Repeating

First, non-verbal behaviour may repeat a verbal message. If someone asked you for directions to the nearest drugstore, you could say, 'Go north about two blocks' and then repeat your instructions non-verbally by pointing north. This kind of repetition is especially useful when we're describing an idea with a visual element, such as size, shape, or direction. Repeating is so much a part of face-to-face interaction that many people regard it as a necessary part of communication (Kendon, 1994).

Substituting

We can substitute non-verbal messages for verbal ones that we communicate. For instance, the more you know someone, the easier it is to use non-verbal expressions as a kind of shorthand to substitute for words. When you see a familiar friend wearing a certain facial expression, it is not necessary to ask, 'What kind of day did you have?' In the same way, experience has probably shown you that certain kinds of looks, gestures, and other clues say, far better than words, 'I'm angry at you' or 'I feel great.'

Some kinds of non-verbal behaviour—called **emblems**—are a culturally understood substitute for verbal expressions. Nodding the head up and down is an accepted way of saying yes in most cultures. Likewise, a side-to-side head shake is a non-verbal way of saying no, and a shrug of the shoulders is commonly understood as meaning 'I do not know' or 'I'm not sure.' Remember, however,

Test Yourself Describe the four characteristics of non-verbal communication.

that some emblems—such as the thumbs-up gesture—vary from one culture to another (it means 'good job!' in Canada, the number 1 in Germany, and the number 5 in Japan). Other non-verbal signs can be ambiguous even within a single culture. For example, a wink might mean something entirely different to the person on the receiving end than it does to the person winking (Lindsey and Vigil, 1999).

Complementing and Accenting

Whereas non-verbal emblems convey meaning independently of words, **illustrators** serve the functions of complementing and accenting verbal statements. Illustrators are actions that have no meaning of their own. Snapping your fingers, running your fingers through your hair, or pounding one fist into the other can accompany a positive statement in one instance and a negative one in others. The meaning of such gestures is specific to their context.

Emblems are used consciously; you roll your eyes and circle your finger around one ear to signal 'he's crazy' in Canada (in Argentina, it means you have a phone call). Illustrators are usually unconscious (Ekman et al., 1984). We rarely plan the smiles and frowns, sighs and laughs, and all the other non-verbal behaviours that so richly complement and accent our words.

Reflection

Wishing Teachers Would Take the Hint

We students send non-verbal cues to our teachers all the time. When a class session is almost over, we start shifting in our seats, looking at the clock, and putting away our books. Sometimes it gets really loud, especially when we start zipping and unzipping our backpacks. Unfortunately, I know a few teachers who ignore us (and the clock) and just keep talking! I wish we could go back to having bells that signal the end of class. Now that's a regulator teachers can't ignore!

Regulating

Non-verbal **regulators** help control verbal interaction. The best example of such regulation is the wide array of turn-taking signals in everyday conversation (Drummond and Hopper, 1993; H. M. Rosenfeld, 1987). Research has shown that three non-verbal signals mean that a speaker has finished talking and is ready to yield to a listener: (1) changes in vocal intonation—a rising or falling in pitch at the end of a clause; (2) a drawl on the last syllable or the stressed syllable in a clause; and (3) a drop in vocal pitch or loudness when speaking a common expression such as 'you know'. You can see how these regulators work by observing almost any conversation.

Eye contact is another way of regulating verbal communication. Lack of visual contact is one way to signal turn taking or even to exclude an unwanted person from a conversation. Speakers make surprisingly little eye contact during a conversation, but they commonly focus on another person when coming to the end of their turn. Children (and some socially insensitive adults) have not learned all the subtle signals of such turn taking. Through trial and error, children learn how to 'read' other people well enough to avoid interrupting.

Contradicting

Non-verbal behaviour can often *contradict* the spoken word. If you said, 'Go north about two blocks,' and pointed south, your non-verbal message would be contradicting what you said.

Although sending such incongruous messages might sound foolish at first, there are times when we deliberately do just this. One deliberate use of *mixed messages* (as they're often called) is to send, politely but clearly, a message that might be unacceptable if it were expressed in words. For instance, think of a time when you became bored with a conversation while your companion kept rambling on. At such a time, the most straightforward statement would be, 'I'm tired of talking to you and want to go meet someone else.' Although it might feel good to be so direct, this kind of honesty is inappropriate in anyone over five years of age. Instead of being blunt in situations like this, a face-saving alternative is to express your lack of interest non-verbally. While nodding politely and murmuring 'uh-huh' and 'no kidding?' at the appropriate times to indicate your 'interest' in what's being said, you can signal a desire to leave by looking around the room, turning slightly away from the speaker, or even making a point of yawning. In most cases, such clues are enough to end the conversation without the awkwardness of expressing outright what you are thinking.

What happens when non-verbal behaviour contradicts the words we speak? In a variety of settings (including job interviews, therapy sessions, and first meetings), adults rely more on non-verbal messages than on words when interpreting the messages of others. Non-verbal cues are especially likely to carry weight when they contradict a speaker's words. In one series of experiments, friendly, neutral, and unfriendly verbal messages were paired with conflicting non-verbal behaviour (Argyle et al., 1971). Raters who judged the verbal and non-verbal messages separately found them equal in strength. But when the two messages were combined, the non-verbal statements carried as much as 12.5 times the weight of the verbal ones. This study shows that, when verbal and non-verbal messages contradict each other, we tend to believe the non-verbal.

Deception and Non-verbal Communication

Deception is an interesting facet of non-verbal communication, and one that social scientists have studied extensively. As we explain in detail in Chapter 9, people regularly send and receive messages that are not completely truthful. As you will read in Chapter 9, not all deception is self-serving or malicious: much of it is aimed at saving the face of the communicators involved. For example, you might tell a 'benevolent lie' to avoid hurting the feelings of a friend who asks about a party you attended but they were not invited to. You might say something like, 'It was okay—a bit boring,' when, in truth, you really had a great time. In a

 Take Two

The following are five functions of non-verbal communication:
- Repeating a verbal message (e.g., pointing when giving directions)
- Substituting for a verbal message (e.g., head nod); emblems are culturally understood substitutes for verbal messages
- Complementing or accenting a verbal message (e.g., snapping one's fingers); illustrators have no meaning on their own but complement a verbal message
- Regulating verbal interactions (e.g., a speaker changing vocal intonation to signal she/he is almost finished talking); regulators comprise a wide array of non-verbal turn-taking signals
- Contradicting a verbal message (e.g., sending a mixed message by nodding but also yawning)

situation like this, it is easy to see how non-verbal factors can make the face-saving deception either succeed or fail.

Hiding Deceit

Some people are better at hiding deceit than others. Most people—especially women—become more successful liars as they grow older (Buller and Burgoon, 1994). High self-monitors are usually better at hiding their deception than communicators who are less self-aware (Burgoon et al., 1994), and raters judge highly expressive liars as more honest than those who are more subdued (Burgoon et al., 1995). People who lie online are less likely to get caught compared to those who lie in face-to-face interactions (Giordano et al., 2007); however, people are much less likely to choose to lie in an email—probably because email provides a tangible record of their deceit (Hancock, Thom-Santelli, and Ritchie, 2004). People tell the most lies during telephone conversations—perhaps because, unlike in email, there is no permanent record of the untruth and, unlike in face-to-face encounters, there are fewer non-verbal cues to give them away. The least lying occurs in email; lying rates in face-to-face exchanges and text messages are about equal (Hancock, Thom-Santelli, and

Ritchie, 2004). Not surprisingly, people whose jobs require them to act differently than they feel, such as actors, lawyers, diplomats, and salespeople, are more successful at deception than the general population (Riggio and Friedman, 1983).

Detecting Deceit

Decades of research have revealed that there are no reliable non-verbal clues that indicate deception. Nonetheless, there are some clues that may reveal less than totally honest mistakes in speaking (Andersen, 1999). Liars tend to be tenser and make a more negative impression when compared to truth tellers. In addition, they are more reserved and tell less-compelling tales (DePaulo et al., 2003). For example, deceivers make more speech errors than truth tellers—stammers, stutters, hesitations, false starts, and so on. Vocal pitch often rises when people tell lies, and liars tend to hesitate more in speech (Rockwell et al., 1997). Deceivers tend to blink more often and more rapidly, fidget with their hands, and shift their posture. Inconsistency is another clue to deception because when someone acts inconsistently, he or she may be trying to hide information (Henningsen et al., 2000). Despite clues like these, it is a mistake to assume that every tongue-tied, fidgeting, eye-blinking person you encounter is a liar. Table 6.2 outlines some conditions under which liars are likely to betray themselves non-verbally. See if any of the conditions matches something from your personal experiences.

How good are people at detecting lies? People's effectiveness in uncovering deceptive messages runs a broad gamut, ranging from a 45- to 70-percent success rate (Kalbfleisch, 1992). For most of us, it appears to be quite difficult and we fare no better than chance (Vrij, 2000). In general, there are three methods for detecting lies: The first focuses on non-verbal behaviours, such as vocal qualities, facial expressions, posture, and so on. The second involves the use of equipment, such as lie detectors, to monitor physiological responses; and the third involves analyzing the content of what is said (Hancock, Curry, Goorha, and Woodworth, 2004). While each method can often distinguish between people telling the truth and those who are lying, some of the time, no method is consistently reliable. Even when people are warned that one or more subjects may be lying, they cannot consistently identify liars (George et al., 2008). Expertise in the detection of deception can be enhanced by specific training. This type of training has been conducted most often with people working in the law-enforcement system, such as police officers (Hartwig et al., 2006), but even after having been trained, few people can accurately and consistently detect lies.

Table 6.2 Circumstances in Which a Deceiver Gives Non-verbal Clues to Deception

Most Likely	Least Likely
Wants to hide emotions being experienced at the moment	Wants to hide information unrelated to emotions
Feels strongly about the information being hidden	Has no strong feelings about the information being hidden
Feels apprehensive about the deception	Feels confident about the deception
Feels guilty about being deceptive	Experiences little guilt about the deception
Gets little enjoyment from being deceptive	Enjoys the deception
Needs to construct the message carefully while delivering it	Knows the deceptive message well and has rehearsed it

Source: Based on material from: P. Ekman, P. (1981), *Mistakes When Deceiving*. In T. A. Sebeok and R. Rosenthal (Eds.), *The Clever Hans Phenomenon: Communication with Horses, Whales, Apes, and People* (pp. 269–278). New York: New York Academy of Sciences.

iStock photo

The bottom line is that non-verbal cues offer important information for detecting deception, but most lies cannot be detected through snap judgments of facial expressions or shifts in posture. Instead, people who suspect a lie tend to collect a variety of clues (including information from third parties as well as physical evidence) over a period of days, weeks, or even longer (Park et al., 2002). Jumping to conclusions based on limited information is not a wise way to react to first communications with a person, and it may lead to relational difficulties. Handle the material we present here about deception detection with care and good judgment.

Types of Non-verbal Communication

So far, we have talked about the characteristics of non-verbal communication and the ways unspoken messages relate to our use of words. Now, it is time to look at the many types of non-verbal communication.

Face and Eyes

The face and eyes are probably the most noticeable parts of the body, but the non-verbal messages from the face and eyes are not the easiest to read (Carroll and Russell, 1996). The face is a tremendously complicated channel of expression to interpret, for several reasons.

First, it is hard to describe the number and kind of expressions commonly produced by the face and eyes. For example, researchers have found that there are at least eight distinguishable positions of the eyebrows and forehead, eight more of the eyes and lids, and ten for the lower face (Ekman and Friesen, 1974a, 1975). When you multiply this complexity by the number of emotions we experience, you can see why it would be almost impossible to compile a dictionary of facial expressions and their corresponding emotions.

The eyes themselves can send several kinds of messages. Gazing and glancing are usually signals of the looker's interest. However, the *type* of interest can vary. Sometimes, as we mentioned earlier, looking is a conversational turn-taking signal that says, 'I'm finished talking. Now it's your turn.' Gazing also is a good indicator of liking (Druckmann et al., 1982). Sometimes, eye contact *reflects* liking that already exists, and at other times, it actually creates or *increases* liking—hence, the expression 'making eyes'. In other situations, eye contact indicates interest, but not attraction or approval, such as when a teacher glares at a rowdy student or a police officer 'keeps an eye on' a suspect.

iStock photo

In addition to influencing verbal responses, research by Stephen Davis and Jamie Kieffer (1998) has found at least one effect of eye contact on an important kind of non-verbal behaviour: tipping in restaurants. Davis and Kieffer discovered that customers in both small towns and large urban centres leave bigger tips when their servers (whether male or female) maintain eye contact with them. The authors speculate that good eye contact makes the atmosphere of a restaurant friendlier and allows customers to feel as if they are dining at home.

Patterns of eye contact are very much influenced by culture. In many Asian, Canadian First Nations, and some Caribbean cultures, direct eye contact between persons of different status is prohibited. If a person of lower status looks a superior in the eye, it is a sign of disrespect. Imagine how this cultural expectation can cause miscommunication in an elementary school classroom, where the teacher demands eye contact while reprimanding a child ('Look at me when I am talking to you!') but the child avoids looking the teacher in the eye in order to show respect for the authority figure.

Body Movement

Another way we communicate non-verbally is through the physical movement of our bodies—our posture, gestures, physical orientation to others, and so on. Social scientists use the term **kinesics** to describe the study of how people communicate through bodily movements.

Some social scientists claim that a language of gestures was the first form of human communication, preceding speech by tens of thousands of years (Corballis, 2002). To appreciate the communicative value of kinesic messages, stop reading for a moment and notice how you are sitting. What does your position say non-verbally about how you feel? Are there any other people near you now? What messages do you get from their present posture? By paying attention to the posture of those around you, as well as to your own, you will find another channel of non-verbal communication that reveals how people feel about themselves and others.

The English language reveals the deep links between posture and communication. English is full of expressions that tie emotional states with body postures:

'I won't take this lying down!'
'Stand on your own two feet.'
'You're all wrapped up in yourself.'
'Don't be so uptight!'

Phrases like these show an awareness of posture, even if it is often unconscious. The main reason we miss most posture messages is that they are not very obvious. In daily life, people who feel weighed down by a problem seldomly hunch over dramatically. When we're bored, we don't usually lean back or slump enough to embarrass the person with whom we're bored. In interpreting posture, then, the key is to look for small changes that might be shadows of the way people feel.

Gestures are a fundamental element of communication—so fundamental, in fact, that even people who have been blind from birth use them (Iverson, 1999; Iverson and Goldin-Meadow, 1997). Gestures are sometimes intentional—for example, a cheery wave or thumbs-up. In other cases, however, they are unconscious. Occasionally, an unconscious gesture will consist of an unambiguous emblem, such as a shrug that clearly means 'I do not know'. More often, however, there are several possible interpretations to gestures (Krauss et al., 1991). A group of ambiguous gestures consists of what we usually call *fidgeting*—movements in which one part of the body grooms, massages, rubs, holds, pinches, picks, or otherwise manipulates another part. Social scientists call these actions **manipulators**. Social rules may discourage us from performing more manipulators in public, but people still do so without noticing.

Research reveals what common sense suggests—that an increased use of manipulators is often a sign of discomfort (Ekman and Friesen, 1974b). But not *all* fidgeting signals uneasiness. People also are likely to use manipulators when relaxed; when they let their guard down (either alone or with friends), they will be more likely to fiddle with an earlobe, twirl a strand of hair, or clean their fingernails.

The amount and type of gesturing a person does can be a measure of power and status (Andersen, 1999). For example, people who gesture more are rated by observers as being in positions of control and power, whereas those who gesture less are judged by observers as being subordinate. And pointing is judged by observers as one indicator of power, since it implies at least some ability to order other people around.

Gestures can produce a wide range of reactions in receivers (Druckmann et al., 1982). In many situations, the right kinds of gestures can increase persuasiveness. Making more hand and arm movements, leaning forward, fidgeting less, and keeping one's limbs open all make a speaker more effective at influencing others (Leathers, 1992). Even more interesting is the fact that persuasiveness increases when one person mirrors another's movements. When the persuader and the audience are reasonably similar, reciprocating the other person's gestures has a positive effect, whereas acting in a contrary manner is likely to have the opposite result.

People who gesture appropriately often create impressions that differ from those of less-expressive people. They are rated as being warmer and more casual, agreeable, and energetic. They also are viewed as more enthusiastic, considerate, approachable, and likeable. On the other hand, less expressive people are viewed as more logical, cold, and analytical. Not only are they less persuasive, but they are also viewed as less likeable in general.

As with almost any non-verbal behaviour, the context in which gestures occur makes all the difference in the results they produce. Animated movements that are well received in a co-operative social setting may seem like signals of aggression or attempts at domination in a more competitive setting. Fidgeting that might suggest deviousness in a bargaining session could be appropriate when you offer a nervous apology in a personal situation. In any case, trying to manufacture insincere, artificial gestures (or any other non-verbal

Take Two

- **Kinesics:** the study of how people communicate through bodily movements.
- **Manipulators:** movements in which one part of the body grooms, massages, rubs, holds, pinches, picks, or otherwise manipulates another part.

behaviour) will probably backfire. A more useful goal is to recognize the behaviour you find yourself spontaneously delivering and to consider how it expresses the attitudes you already feel.

Touch

Contemporary research confirms the value of touch for infants (Whitman et al., 1999). Studies at the University of Miami's School of Medicine, for example, have shown that premature babies grow faster and gain more weight if they are massaged (Adler, 1993). The same institute's researchers demonstrated that massage can help premature children gain weight, make colicky children sleep better, and boost the immune function of cancer and 4 SJ patients. Massage helps newborn babies thrive, and it also helps depressed mothers of newborns feel better and smoothes the delivery process (Mwakalyelye and DeAngelis, 1995). Studies show that touch between therapists and clients can encourage a variety of beneficial changes: more self-disclosure, self-acceptance by the client, and better client–therapist relationships (Driscoll et al., 1988). In addition, patients with dementia who were administered hand massage on each hand, along with intermittent gentle touch on the arm and shoulder and calm soothing speech, became less anxious and behaved less dysfunctionally (Kim and Buschmann, 1999).

Touch also plays a large part in how we respond to others. For instance, in a laboratory task, subjects evaluated partners more positively when they were touched (appropriately, of course) by them (Burgoon et al., 1992). Besides increasing liking, touch also boosts compliance. In a study by Chris Kleinke (1977), subjects were approached by a female confederate who asked them to return a coin she had left in the phone booth they had just used. When the request was accompanied by a light touch on the subject's arm, the subject was significantly more likely to return the coin. In a similar experiment (Willis and Hamm, 1980), subjects were asked by a male or female confederate to sign a petition or complete a rating scale. Again, subjects were more likely to co-operate when they were touched lightly on the arm. In the rating-scale variation of the study, the results were especially dramatic: 70 percent of those who were touched complied, whereas only 40 percent of the untouched subjects were willing to co-operate.

Arguing that these small solicitations hardly get at the power of touch, Gueguen and Fischer-Lokou (2002) conducted an experiment in which confederates asked sidewalk passersby to look after a large and very excited dog for ten minutes so the owner could go into a pharmacy where animals were prohibited. In half of the cases, the passerby was touched during the request. The results confirmed that touch has a large effect on compliance. When touched, 55 percent agreed with the request, whereas only 35 percent of those who were not touched agreed.

An additional power of touch is its on-the-job utility. One study showed that fleeting touches on the hand and shoulder resulted in larger tips for restaurant waiters (Crusco and Wetzel, 1984). Perhaps this research is what led the Waiters Association in 1996 to advise its members to touch diners briefly when presenting the bill or returning change ('Tipping Tips', 1996). And the latest finding on touch in restaurants is that both women and men in pubs and taverns, whether in same-sex or different-sex dyads, drink more alcohol if they are touched by the server (Kaufman and Mahoney, 1999).

In contemporary society, unwanted touching is cause for concern, and even legal action. In North America, touching is generally more appropriate for women than for men (Derlega et al., 1989; Jones, 1986). Males touch their male friends less than they touch their female friends, and also less than females touch their female friends. Although women are generally more comfortable about touching than men, sex is not the only factor that shapes contact. In general, the degree of touch comfort goes along with openness to expressing intimate feelings, an active interpersonal style, and satisfactory relationships (Fromme et al., 1989). Culture also plays a role in same-sex and opposite-sex touching. For example, Saudi businessmen often hold hands as a sign of trust—a kind of touching that might easily be misinterpreted by North Americans. In contrast, Saudi women are never to be touched in public (Remland et al., 1995).

The amount of touching usually decreases with age (Knapp and Hall, 2002). Sixth-graders touch each other less than do first-graders. Parents touch their older children less often than their younger ones. As young children, most North Americans receive at least a modest amount of physical contact from their parents. The next time most people can expect to receive this level of physical caring won't come until they have chosen a partner. Even then, the nurturing seemingly brought by physical contact will most often come only from that partner—a heavy demand for one person to carry. There is considerable variation around the world in the amount of touch viewed as appropriate. Canada is regarded as a moderate touch culture. Most Asian cultures are considered non-contact cultures, and many South and Central American cultures, as well as southern European cultures, are viewed as contact cultures (Hall, 1963). In an old but interesting study, psychologist Sidney Jourard (1966) observed couples in cafés in different cities and countries and recorded the frequency of body contact between the people. The average number of touches observed in San Juan, Puerto Rico, was 180; in Paris, France, 110; in Gainesville, Florida, 2; and in London, England, 0.

Voice

Social scientists use the term **paralanguage** to describe the way a message is spoken. Vocal rate, pitch, tone, volume, and so on can give the same word or words many meanings. For example, note how many meanings come from a single sentence just by shifting the emphasis from one word to another:

This is a fantastic communication book.
(Not just any book, but *this* one in particular.)

This is a *fantastic* communication book.
(This book is superior, exciting.)

This is a fantastic *communication* book.
(The book is good as far as the study of communication goes; it may not be so great as a work of literature.)

This is a fantastic communication *book*.
(It's not a play or a CD; it's a book.)

Along with tone, speed, pitch, volume, paralanguage includes length of pauses and **disfluencies** (such as stammering and the use of 'uh', 'um', and 'er'). All these factors can do a great deal to reinforce or contradict the messages that words convey.

The effect of paralinguistic cues is strong. In fact, listeners pay more attention to paralanguage than to the content of the words when asked to determine a speaker's attitudes (Burns and Beier, 1973). Furthermore, when vocal factors contradict a verbal message (as when a speaker shouts, 'I am *not* angry!'), listeners tend to judge the speaker's intention from the paralanguage, not the words themselves (Mehrabian and Weiner, 1967). Vocal changes that contradict spoken words are not easy to conceal. If the speaker is trying to hide fear or anger, the voice will probably sound higher and louder, and the rate of talk may be faster than normal. Sadness produces the opposite vocal pattern: quieter, lower-pitched speech delivered at a slower rate (Ekman, 1985).

Paralanguage can affect behaviour in many ways, some of which are rather surprising. Studies by David Buller and Kelly Aune (1988, 1992) reveal that communicators are most likely to comply with requests delivered by speakers whose rate is similar to their own. However, speaking rate is not constant. For example, it changes when a speaker's first message does not seem to get the desired results. Charles Berger and Patrick diBattista (1993) discovered that when communicators gave directions that weren't followed, the wording of their second attempts didn't change significantly. Instead, they simply slowed down and spoke more loudly.

Sarcasm is one approach in which we use both emphasis and tone of voice to change the meaning of a statement to the opposite of its verbal message. Experience this reversal yourself with the following three statements. First say them literally, and then say them sarcastically.

'You look terrific!'
'I really had a wonderful time on my blind date.'
'There's nothing I like better than calves' brains on toast.'

Focus on Research

Mixed Messages: What Do Children Hear?

'Nice job!' These are welcome words—unless they are delivered in a sarcastic tone of voice and with a sneer. As we have noted in this chapter, when adults encounter 'mixed messages' in which words and non-verbal cues conflict, they tend to believe how people act, not what they say. Children, however, are not so adept at interpreting non-verbal cues.

Experiments by J. Bruce Morton and Sandra Trehub (2001) reveal that children interpret mixed messages in ways very different from adults. When youngsters aged four to eight were presented with positive statements (such as, 'Dad gave me a new bike for my birthday') delivered in a sad tone of voice, they gauged the speaker as happy because they paid attention to the words rather than the vocal cues. When a negative statement was read in an upbeat tone, children interpreted the message as negative—again, relying more on the content than the paralanguage. There was a direct relationship between age and sensitivity to non-verbal cues, with the youngest children relying most heavily on the words spoken.

This study helps us appreciate the often taken-for-granted importance of non-verbal cues. It also serves as a reminder that communication with children requires different approaches than those that work with adults.

As with other non-verbal messages, people often ignore or misinterpret the vocal nuances of sarcasm. Members of certain groups—children, people with weak intellectual skills, poor listeners, and people with certain forms of brain damage—are more likely to misunderstand sarcastic messages than are others (Andersen, 1992; Dennis et al., 2001; Shamay et al., 2002).

Communication through paralanguage is not always intentional. Our voices often give us away when we're trying to create an impression different from our actual feelings. You have probably had the experience of trying to sound calm and serene when you were really seething with inner nervousness. Maybe your deception succeeded for a while—just the right smile, no telltale fidgeting of the hands, posture appearing relaxed—and then, without being able to do a thing about it, right in the middle of your relaxed comments, your voice squeaked! The charade was over.

In addition to reinforcing or contradicting messages, some vocal factors influence the way a speaker is perceived by others (Castelan-Cargile and Bradac, 2001). For example, people who speak more slowly are judged as having greater conversational control than fast talkers (Tusing and Dillard, 2000), and people who judge a speaker's speech rate as similar to their own perceive the speaker as more competent and socially attractive than when the rate is different (Feldstein et al., 2001). Communicators with more attractive voices are rated higher than those whose speech sounds less attractive (Francis and Wales, 1994; Zuckerman and Driver, 1989). Just what makes a voice attractive can vary. As Figure 6.1 shows, culture can make a difference. Surveys have found that there are both similarities and differences between what Mexicans and US citizens view as the 'ideal' voice. Howard Giles and his associates (1992c) found that age combines with accent to form preferences by listeners. Older-sounding communicators whose language was accent-free were rated as most competent, while older-sounding speech by people who did not speak in a culturally standard way was judged least competent.

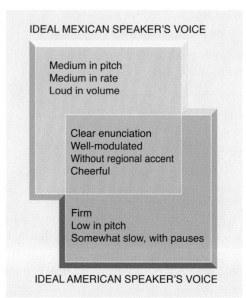

Figure 6.1 A Comparison of the Ideal Speaker's Voice Types in Mexico and the United States

Source: Reproduced from page 62 of C. A. Valentine and B. Saint Damian (1988), Communicative power: Gender and culture as determinants of the ideal voice. In C. A. Valentine and N. Hoar (Eds.), *Women and Communicative Power: Theory, Research, and Practice.* Washington, DC: National Communication Association.

Proxemics

Proxemics is the study of how people use the space around them. Each of us carries around a sort of invisible bubble of **personal space** wherever we go. We think of the area inside this bubble as our own—almost as much a part of us as our own bodies. Our personal bubbles vary in size according to the culture in which we were raised, the person we're with, and the situation. The varying size of our personal space—the distance we put between ourselves and others—gives a non-verbal clue to our feelings (Sommer, 2002).

D. Russell Crane (1987) and other researchers tested over one hundred married couples, asking partners to walk toward one another and stop

 Take Two

- **Paralanguage:** the way a message is spoken; the speaker's mode of delivery is governed by vocal rate, pitch, tone, volume, pauses, and disfluencies (e.g., stammering, use of 'um', 'er', etc.).

when they reached a 'comfortable conversational distance.' Then, they gave each partner a battery of tests to measure their marital intimacy, desire for change, and potential for divorce. The researchers discovered that there was a strong relationship between distance and marital happiness. The average space between distressed couples was about 25 percent greater than that between satisfied partners. On average, the happy couples stood 28.5 centimetres apart, while the distance between unhappy spouses averaged 37 centimetres.

In another study, Mark Snyder (1980) reported that the distance subjects unconsciously placed between themselves and others was a good indication of their prejudices. All the subjects were polled on their attitudes about homosexuality. Half the interviewers, who were confederates of the experimenter, wore GAY AND PROUD buttons and mentioned that they belonged to the Association of Gay Psychologists. The other interviewers wore no buttons and simply identified themselves as graduate students. Despite their expressions of tolerance, subjects seated themselves roughly 30 centimetres farther away from the apparently gay interviewers of the same sex.

Preferred spaces are largely a matter of cultural norms. In hyper-dense Hong Kong, people manage to live in crowded residential quarters that most North Americans would find intolerable (Chan, 1999). The distance between communicators during a conversation is very much influenced by culture. In some Middle Eastern cultures, people stand close enough to smell each other's breath—to deny another person one's breath expresses shame (Almaney and Alwan, 1982). Looking at the distances that North American communicators use in everyday interaction, Hall (1969) found four, each of which reflects a different way we feel toward others at a given time. By 'reading' which distance people select, we can get some insight into their feelings.

Intimate Distance   The first of Hall's zones begins with skin contact and ranges out to about 45 centimetres. We usually use this **intimate distance** with people who are emotionally close to us, and then

iStock photo

mostly in private situations—making love, caressing, comforting, protecting. By allowing people to move into our intimate distance, we let them enter our personal space. When we let them in voluntarily, it is usually a sign of trust: we have willingly lowered our defences. On the other hand, when someone invades this most personal area without our consent, we usually feel threatened.

Personal Distance   The second spatial zone, **personal distance**, ranges from 45 centimetres at its closest point to 1.2 metres at its farthest. Its closer end of the range is the distance at which most couples stand in public. If a third party thought to be sexually attractive stands this near one partner at a party, the other partner is likely to become alert. This 'moving in' often is taken to mean that something more than casual conversation is taking place. The far end of the personal distance range (from roughly 0.75 m to 1.2 m) is

iStock photo

the area just beyond the other person's reach. As Hall puts it, at this distance, we can keep someone 'at arm's length'. His choice of words suggests the type of communication that goes on at this range: the contacts are still reasonably close, but they're much less personal than the ones that occur 30 centimetres or so closer.

Social Distance   The third zone is **social distance**. It ranges from 1.2 metres to about 3 metres at the outside. Within this zone, the distance between communicators can have a powerful effect on how we regard and respond to others. For example, students are more satisfied with teachers who reduce (at appropriate levels, of course) the distance between themselves and their classes. They also are more satisfied with the course itself and are more likely to follow the teacher's instructions (Hackman and Walker, 1990). Likewise, medical

patients are more satisfied with doctors who use close physical proximity to convey warmth and concern (Conlee et al., 1993; Grant et al., 2000).

Public Distance   **Public distance** is Hall's term for the farthest zone, running outward from 3 metres. The closer range of public distance is the one that most teachers use in the classroom. In the farther reaches of public space—7.5 metres and beyond—two-way communication is almost impossible. Sometimes, speakers must use public distance to reach a large audience, but we can assume that anyone who chooses to use it when more closeness is possible is not interested in a dialogue.

When our spatial bubble is invaded, we usually experience stress and respond with **barrier behaviours**: strategies designed to create a barrier (or fix a broken one) between ourselves and other people (Kanaga and Flynn, 1981). Invade someone's personal space, and notice the reaction. At first, the person is most likely simply to back away, probably without realizing what is happening. Next, your partner might attempt to put an object between you, such as a desk, a chair, or some books clutched to the chest, all in an effort to get some separation. Then, the other person will probably decrease eye contact (the 'elevator syndrome', in which we can crowd in and even touch one another so long as we avoid eye contact). Furthermore, your reluctant partner might sneeze, cough, scratch, and exhibit various gestures to discourage your anti-social behaviour. In the end, if none of these actions achieves the desired goal of getting some space between the two of you, the other person might leave or 'counterattack', gently at first ('Will you move back, please?'), then more forcefully (probably with a shove).

Territoriality

While personal space is the invisible bubble we carry around, the area that serves as an extension of our physical being, **territory** remains stationary (Hidalgo and Hernandez, 2001). To lay claim to a piece of territory requires that you mark it with your ownership, such as an OCCUPIED sign on an airplane seat, a coat over the back of a chair

iStock photo

in a restaurant, or books on a desk in the library. Sometimes, people formally mark their territory with a name or some representative symbol, such as a sign in a personal parking space or a gang's emblem (Etter, 1998). As well, a fence may separate your property from your neighbour's, and a closed door clearly separates your room from the rest of the residence.

Robert Sommer (1969) watched students in a college library and found that there is a definite pattern for people who want to study alone. When the library was not crowded, students almost always chose corner seats at one of the empty rectangular tables. After each table was occupied by one reader, new readers would choose a seat on the opposite side and at the far end, thus keeping the maximum distance between themselves and the other readers. One of Sommer's associates tried

breaking these 'rules' by sitting next to and across from other female readers even though distant seats were available. She found that the women reacted defensively, signalling their discomfort

Take Two

- **Personal space:** the invisible bubble of space we consider as our own; it varies in size according to the person we're with, the culture in which we were raised, and the situation at hand.
- **Intimate distance:** skin contact to about 45 cm.
- **Personal distance:** 45 cm to 1.2 m.
- **Social distance:** 1.2 m to 3 m.
- **Public distance:** 7.5 m and beyond.
- **Barrier behaviours:** strategies to create or fix a barrier between ourselves and other people (e.g., avoiding eye contact).

through shifts in posture, by gesturing, or by moving away.

How you respond to such a manoeuvre depends on *who* enters and uses your territory (a friend is less threatening than a stranger); *why* she or he enters or uses it (for instance, a 'mistake' is less important than a 'planned attack'); *what* territory is entered or used (you may care more about a territory over which you have exclusive rights, such as your bedroom, than about a territory in a public area, such as your seat in class); and *how* it is entered or used (an invasion is more threatening than a violation). Generally, we grant people with higher status more personal territory and greater privacy. We knock before entering our supervisor's office, whereas the supervisor can usually walk into our work area without hesitating. In traditional schools, professors have offices, dining rooms, and even washrooms that are private, whereas the students, who are presumably less important, have no such sanctuaries.

Time

Social scientists use the term **chronemics** to describe the study of how humans use and structure time. The way we handle time can express both intentional and unintentional messages. Social psychologist Robert Levine (1988) describes several ways that time can communicate. For instance, in cultures like those of Canada, the United States, and northern Europe, which value time highly, waiting can be an indicator of status. 'Important' people (whose time is supposedly more valuable than others) may be seen by appointment only, while it is acceptable to intrude without notice on lesser beings. To see how this rule operates, consider how natural it is for a boss to drop into a subordinate's office unannounced, while the employee would never intrude into the boss's office without an appointment. A related rule is that low-status people must never make more important people wait. It would be a serious mistake to be late for a job interview, although the interviewer may keep you cooling your heels in the lobby. Higher-status people are often whisked to the head of a restaurant or airport line, while presumably less exalted ones are forced to wait their turn.

The use of time depends greatly on culture. In some cultures, punctuality is critically important, but in others it is barely considered (Levine and Norenzayan, 1999). Punctual Canadians often report welcoming the easygoing approach to time that is characteristic of many Caribbean countries. One psychologist discovered the difference between North and South American attitudes when he was teaching at a university in Brazil (Levine, 1988). He found that some students arrived halfway through a two-hour class and that most of them stayed and kept asking questions when the class was scheduled to end. Half an hour after the official end of the period, the professor finally closed off discussion, since there was no indication that the students intended to leave. This flexibility of time is quite different from what is common in most North American colleges and universities.

Even within a culture, rules of time vary. Consider your own experience. In school, some instructors begin and end class punctually; while with others are more casual. With some people, you feel comfortable talking for hours in person or on the phone; while with others, time seems precious and not to be 'wasted'.

Differences also may be associated with health. For example, children with attention deficit hyperactivity disorder have an impaired time perception when compared to other children (Meaux, 2002).

Physical Attractiveness

The importance of beauty has been emphasized in the arts for centuries. More recently, social scientists have begun to measure the degree to which physical attractiveness affects interaction between people. Recent findings, summarized by Knapp and Hall (2002), indicate that women who are perceived as attractive have more dates, receive higher grades in college, persuade males with greater ease, and receive lighter court sentences. Both men and women whom others view as attractive are rated as being more sensitive, kind, strong, sociable, and interesting than their less-fortunate brothers and sisters. Who is most likely to succeed in business? Place your bet on the attractive job applicant. Attractiveness is at least partly in the mind of the beholder. Some evidence suggests that, as we get to know more about people and like them, we start to regard them as better looking (Bazil, 1999). (See the accompanying Focus on Research box for further evidence of this phenomenon.)

The influence of attractiveness begins early in life. In one study, preschoolers were shown photographs of children their own age and asked to choose potential friends and enemies. The researchers found that children as young as three agreed as to who was attractive ('cute') and unattractive ('homely'). Furthermore, they valued their attractive counterparts—both of the same and the opposite sex—more highly. Also, preschool children rated by their peers as attractive were most liked, and those identified as least attractive were least liked. Children who were

Focus on Research

Communication Enhances Physical Attractiveness

How can you make yourself more physically attractive to a romantic partner? Most of us think of ways to change our appearance such as a new hairstyle or wardrobe and trips to the gym. A communication professor (Albada, Knapp, and Theune, 2002) and her associates have explored a different approach, which they have labelled Interaction Appearance Theory (IAT). IAT predicts that rewarding interactions with a partner will make him or her see you as more physically attractive.

Albada and her colleagues collected data to test IAT in three different ways: a series of interviews with people in romantic relationships, a survey of college students in newly formed dating relationships, and an analysis of diaries kept by romantic partners.

Time and again, the researchers found support for the notion that partners find one another more physically attractive as they communicate with one another in positive ways, such as offering compliments, expressing affection, and buying gifts. Here is how one man in the study recounts the shift in his appraisal of the woman he eventually married:

> Initially, I saw her as pretty average in physical attractiveness. . . . But after we dated and I fully appreciated how well we related to each other, I saw her as much more physically attractive. I actually saw her differently. Now, I can't see her as any less physically attractive.

Interaction appearance theory suggests that physical attractiveness is not a static property of an individual; instead, it is a perception that can be enhanced through good communication skills.

interviewed rated good-looking children as having positive social characteristics ('He's friendly to other children') and unattractive children negatively ('He hits other children without reason').

Teachers also are affected by students' attractiveness. Vicki Ritts and her colleagues (1992) found that physically attractive students are usually judged to be more intelligent, friendly, and popular. Even the parents of attractive students benefit from their children's good looks: they are judged by strangers as caring more about education than are parents of less attractive youngsters.

Fortunately, attractiveness is something we can control without having to call the plastic surgeon. We view others as beautiful or ugly, not just on the basis of the 'original equipment' they come with, but also on *how they use that equipment*. Posture, gestures, facial expressions, and other behaviours can increase the attractiveness of a seemingly unremarkable person. Exercise can improve the way each of us looks. Finally, our style of dress can make a significant difference in the way others perceive us.

Clothing

Besides protecting us from the elements, clothing is a tool of non-verbal communication. One writer has suggested that clothing conveys at least ten types of messages to others (Thourlby, 1978):

1. economic level
2. educational level
3. trustworthiness
4. social position
5. level of sophistication
6. economic background
7. social background
8. educational background
9. level of success
10. moral character

We do make assumptions about people on the basis of their style of clothing. For example, the way people are dressed affects judgments of their credibility. In one experiment, college students judged victims of sexual harassment differently depending on their attire. Victims dressed in black were rated as less honest and more aggressive than those dressed in light colours (Vrij and Akehurst, 1999). Not surprisingly, the perception of a woman's sexual intent increased when she wore more revealing clothes, although this effect was greater for men in the study (Koukounas and Letch, 2001). In another study, a man and a woman were stationed in a hallway so that anyone who wished to go by had to avoid them or pass between them. In one condition, the conversationalists wore 'formal daytime dress'; in the other, they wore 'casual attire'. Passersby behaved differently toward the couple, depending on the style of clothing. They responded positively to the well-dressed couple and showed more annoyance when the same people were casually dressed (Fortenberry et al., 1978).

Similar results in other situations show the influence of clothing. We are more likely to obey people dressed in high-status attire. Pedestrians are more likely to return lost coins to well-dressed people than to those dressed in low-status clothing (Bickman, 1974). People are more willing to cross the street on a red light if a well dressed person did so first (Lefkowitz et al., 1955). Communicators who wear special clothing, especially when it is appropriate to the situation, often gain persuasiveness (Burgoon et al., 2002; Lawrence and Watson, 1991; O'Neal and Lapitsky, 1991). For example, experimenters dressed in uniforms resembling police officers were more successful than those dressed in civilian clothing in requesting pedestrians to pick up litter and in persuading them to lend change to an overparked motorist (Bickman, 1974). Attire makes a difference in the classroom, too. College students' perceptions of their graduate teaching assistant's expertise decreases as his or her attire becomes more casual. On the other hand, teaching assistants who dress casually are seen as more interesting, extroverted, and sociable than those who dress more formally (Morris et al., 1996; Roach, 1997). Finally, dress is also significant in employment interviews (Kwon and Johnson-Hillery, 1999). Personnel involved in recruiting

Self-Assessment

What Is Your Intercultural Sensitivity?

Below is a series of statements concerning intercultural communication. There are no right or wrong answers. Imagine yourself interacting with people from a wide variety of cultural groups, not just one or two. Record your first impression of the following statement by indicating the degree to which you agree or disagree, using the following scale.

5 = strongly agree
4 = agree
3 = uncertain
2 = disagree
1 = strongly disagree

_____ 1. I enjoy interacting with people from different cultures.

_____ 2. I think people from other cultures are narrow-minded.

_____ 3. I am pretty sure of myself in interacting with people from different cultures.

_____ 4. I find it very hard to talk in front of people from different cultures.

_____ 5. I always know what to say when interacting with people from different cultures.

_____ 6. I can be as sociable as I want to be when interacting with people from different cultures.

_____ 7. I don't like to be with people from different cultures.

_____ 8. I respect the values of people from different cultures.

_____ 9. I get upset easily when interacting with people from different cultures.

_____ 10. I feel confident when interacting with people from different cultures.

_____ 11. I tend to wait before forming an impression of culturally distinct counterparts.

_____ 12. I often get discouraged when I am with people from different cultures.

_____ 13. I am open-minded to people from different cultures.

_____ 14. I am very observant when interacting with people from different cultures.

_____ 15. I often feel useless when interacting with people from different cultures.

_____ 16. I respect the ways people from different cultures behave.

_____ 17. I try to obtain as much information as I can when interacting with people from different cultures.

_____ 18. I would not accept the opinions of people from different cultures.

_____ 19. I am sensitive to my culturally distinct counterpart's subtle meanings during our interaction.

_____ 20. I think my culture is better than other cultures.

_____ 21. I often give positive responses to my culturally different counterpart during our interaction.

_____ 22. I avoid those situations where I will have to deal with culturally distinct persons.

_____ 23. I often show my culturally distinct counterpart my understanding through verbal or non-verbal cues.

_____ 24. I have a feeling of enjoyment toward differences between my culturally distinct counterpart and me.

To determine your score, begin by reverse-coding items 2, 4, 7, 9, 12, 15, 18, 20, and 22 (if you indicated 5, reverse-code to 1, if you indicated 4, reverse-code to 2, and so on).

Sum items 1, 11, 13, 21, 22, 23, and 24 = _____ Interaction Engagement (range is 7–35)

Sum items 2, 7, 8, 16, 18, and 20 = _____ Respect for Cultural Differences (6–30)

Sum items 3, 4, 5, 6, and 10 = _____ Interaction Confidence (5–25)

Sum items 9, 12, and 15 = _____ Interaction Enjoyment (3–15)

Sum items 14, 17, and 19 = _____ Interaction Attentiveness (3–15)

Sum of all the items = _____ (24–120, with a midpoint of 48)

Higher scores on the total instrument and each of the five sub-scales indicate a greater probability of intercultural communication competence.

* Permission to use courtesy of *Guo-Ming Chen Human Communication: A Journal of the Pacific and Asian Communication Association*.

Reflection

Head Scarves

I consider myself to be an independent, liberated, Western woman with a fundamental belief in my equality with men. Attending university, I met several Muslim women who wore head scarves. I had always seen the head scarf as a sign of the male subjugation of women. I had this stereotype of demure, soft-spoken obliging women, sort of like the 'ideal' 1950s housewife but from a different culture. As I got to know these Muslim women, my perception (or bias) seemed really wrong! I observed these women to be outspoken, articulate, independent-minded individuals. They spoke up in class, challenged their peers' ideas (both male and female) and clearly had a strong sense of their worth. They told me that rather than being a symbol of subservience to men, the head scarf served as a guard against the eyes of men and freed them from being 'sexual objects'. For me, this was a whole new way of interpreting the meaning of the head scarf. It gave me a new perspective, and now I'm wondering about the meaning of those belly shirts and low-rise jeans. . . .

and interviewing employees acknowledge the first impression the applicant makes influences the rest of the interview (Johnson-Hillery, 1981).

What you wear reflects who you are—or, at least, how you feel about yourself. Kwon (1994) investigated the relationship between feelings toward clothing and self-perceptions of college students. The findings showed that positive feelings toward one's clothing were related positively to self-perceived emotion, sociability, and work competency, and that these relationships were greater for females than for males.

Physical Environment

We conclude our look at non-verbal communication by examining how physical settings, architecture, and interior design affect communication. Begin by remembering the different homes you have visited lately. Were some of them more comfortable to be in than others? Certainly, a lot of your feelings were shaped by the people you were with, but there are some houses in which it seems impossible to relax, no matter how friendly the hosts. We've spent what seemed like endless evenings in what Knapp and Hall (2002) call 'unliving rooms', where the spotless floors, furniture coverings, and plastic lamp covers send non-verbal messages telling us not to touch anything, not to put our feet up, and not to be comfortable. People who live in such houses probably wonder why nobody ever seems to relax and enjoy themselves at their parties. They don't seem to understand that the environment they have created can communicate discomfort to their guests.

The impressions that home designs communicate can be remarkably accurate. Edward Sadalla (1987) showed ninety-nine students slides of the insides or outsides of twelve upper-middle-class homes and then asked them to infer the personality of the owners from their impressions. The students were especially accurate after glancing at interior photos. The decorating schemes conveyed accurate information about the homeowners' intellectualism, politeness, maturity, optimism, tenseness, willingness to have adventures, family orientation, and reserve. The home

iStock photo

exteriors also gave viewers accurate perceptions of the owners' artistic interests, graciousness, privacy, and quietness.

Besides communicating information about the designer, an environment can also shape the kind of interaction that takes place in it. In one experiment, subjects working in a 'beautiful' room were more positive and energetic than those working in 'average' or 'ugly' spaces (Maslow and Mintz, 1956). Inner-city adults and children who have access to landscaped public spaces interact in ways that are much more pro-social than those who have to interact in more barren environments (Taylor et al., 1998). Kuo and Sullivan (2001) found that residents of inner-city public housing who lived in relatively barren buildings reported more mental fatigue, aggression, and violence than their counterparts in buildings with nearby grass and trees.

Students see professors who have well-decorated offices as more credible than those with less attractive work areas (Teven and Comadena, 1996). Some doctors have shaped environments to improve the quality of interaction with their patients. According to environmental psychologist Robert Sommer (1969), simply removing a doctor's desk made patients feel almost five times more at ease during office visits. Sommer also found that redesigning a convalescent ward of a hospital greatly increased the interaction between patients. In the old design, seats were placed shoulder to shoulder around the edges of the ward. By grouping the chairs around small tables so that patients faced each other at a comfortable distance, the number of conversations doubled.

Reflection

Side-by-Side vs. Head-to-Head

After three years at university, I've met with plenty of professors during their office hours to discuss papers and exams. I have noticed that some of them sit behind their desks, so that we discuss my work across a barrier. Other professors set up their offices or move their chairs so that we sit next to each other while we're looking at the work.

The two layouts seem to make a difference. Having that barrier between us leaves me feeling that the conferences are more adversarial than collaborative, and I definitely feel there's a greater power difference in this setup. I don't know whether the furniture layout causes my feelings or if professors who want to exert more power choose to set up their offices in a way that reflects their attitudes. In either case, I've come to think that the significance of office design goes beyond aesthetics.

Test Yourself

List the ten types of non-verbal communication and provide an example of each.

Summary

Non-verbal communication consists of messages expressed by non-linguistic means. It is pervasive; in fact, non-verbal messages are always available as a source of information about others. Most non-verbal behaviour conveys messages about relational attitudes and feelings, in contrast to verbal statements, which are better suited to expressing ideas. Messages that are communicated non-verbally are usually more ambiguous than verbal communication.

Non-verbal communication serves many functions. It can repeat, substitute for, complement, accent, regulate, and contradict verbal messages; and it can also be used as a tool for enhancing the success of deceptive verbal messages. When people are presented with conflicting verbal and non-verbal messages, they are more likely to rely on the non-verbal ones.

Non-verbal messages can be communicated in a variety of ways—through the face and eyes, body movement, touch, voice, distance, time, physical appearance, clothing, and environment. Culture plays a significant role in determining the rules and meanings for each of these factors.

Building Work Skills

Cultural Values at Work

The Public Service Commission of Canada has published a variety of resources to help their managers promote equity in the workplace. Many of their recommendations involve strategies to deal with cultural differences in non-verbal communication (physical appearance, patterns of eye contact, speaking cadence, gestures, and so on). An important beginning strategy is being aware of your workplace values and behaviour that are influenced by your culture.

Take a moment to assess your workplace or your school environment in terms of some of the types of non-verbal communication discussed in this chapter. Pay particular attention to touch, proxemics and territoriality, time, clothing, and physical environment.

Describe your workplace in terms of these elements, and then identify the values communicated. Here are some questions to get your started.

- Who initiates touch? Who touches whom?
- Who gets the most territory? Who gets the least? Who gets the window?
- Do some people prefer greater or less social distance? Who? How do you know?
- How important is punctuality? Can some people keep others waiting with impunity?
- What do people wear? Are there differences?
- Is the physical environment clean? Are some places cleaner than others? Is the space well-designed for the work to be done? Are some places better than others?

Activities

1. **Invitation to Insight**
   Demonstrate for yourself that it is impossible to avoid communicating non-verbally by trying *not* to communicate with a friend or family member. (You be the judge of whether to tell the other person about this experiment beforehand.) See how long it takes for your partner to ask what you are doing and to report what he or she thinks you might be thinking and feeling.

2. **Critical Thinking Probe**
   Interview someone from a culture different from your own, and learn at least three ways in which non-verbal codes differ from those of the place where you were raised. Together, develop a list of ways you could break unstated but important rules about non-verbal behaviour in your partner's culture in three of the following areas:

   Eye contact
   Posture
   Gesture
   Facial expression
   Distance
   Voice
   Touch
   Time
   Clothing
   Environmental design
   Territory

   Describe how a failure to recognize different cultural codes could lead to misunderstandings, frustrations, and dissatisfaction. Discuss how an awareness of cultural rules can be developed in an increasingly multicultural world.

3. **Invitation to Insight**
   Using the video of a television program or film, find examples of the following non-verbal functions:

   Repeating
   Substituting
   Complementing
   Accenting
   Regulating
   Contradicting
   Deceiving

   If time allows, show these video examples to your classmates.

4. **Skill Builder**
   Sharpen your ability to distinguish between *observing* and *interpreting* non-verbal behaviour by following these directions:

   Sit or stand opposite a partner at a comfortable distance. For a one-minute period, report your observations of the other person's behaviour by repeatedly completing the statement, 'Now I see (*non-verbal behaviour*).' For example, you might report, 'Now I see you blinking your eyes . . . now I see you looking down at the floor . . . now I see you fidgeting with your hands. . . .' Notice that no matter what your partner does, you have an unending number of non-verbal behaviours to observe.

   For a second one-minute period, complete the sentence 'Now I see (*non-verbal behaviour*), and I think _____ ,' filling in the blank with your interpretation of the other person's non-verbal behaviour. For instance, you might say, 'Now I see you look away, and I think you are nervous about looking me in the eye . . . now I see you smiling and I think you are imagining that you agree with my interpretation. . . .' Notice that by clearly labelling your interpretation, you give the other person a chance to correct any mistaken hunches.

Repeat the first two steps, changing roles with your partner.

5. **Invitation to Insight**
How satisfied are you with the way your body looks? If you are extremely satisfied, mark **7**; if you are satisfied, mark **6**; if you are slightly satisfied, mark **5**; if you are neither satisfied nor unsatisfied, mark **4**; if you are slightly unsatisfied, mark **3**; if you are unsatisfied, mark **2**; and if you are extremely unsatisfied, mark **1**.

_____ hair   _____ eyes

_____ nose   _____ mouth

_____ back   _____ chest or breasts

_____ stomach   _____ hips

_____ sex organs   _____ teeth

_____ chin   _____ cheeks

_____ arms   _____ elbows

_____ forearms   _____ wrists

_____ hands   _____ fingers

_____ thighs   _____ knees

_____ calves   _____ buttocks

_____ height   _____ weight

_____ overall facial attractiveness

_____ overall body appearance

How does your feeling about a particular body part affect how you behave? How is your self-esteem affected by your physical appearance?

6. **Invitation to Insight**
Learn more about the non-verbal messages you send by interviewing someone who knows you well, such as a friend, family member, or co-worker. Ask your interview subject to describe how he or she knows when you are feeling each of the following emotions, even though you may not announce your feelings verbally:

Anger or irritation
Boredom or indifference
Happiness
Sadness
Worry or anxiety

Which of these non-verbal behaviours do you display intentionally, and which are not conscious? Which functions does your non-verbal behaviour perform in the situations your partner described: repeating, substituting, complementing, accenting, regulating, contradicting, and/or deceiving feelings?

7. **Invitation to Insight**
Explore your territoriality by listing the spaces you feel you 'own', such as your parking space, parts of the place you live in, and seats in a particular classroom. Describe how you feel when your territory is invaded and identify things you do to 'mark' it.

8. **Invitation to Insight**
This activity requires you to observe how people use space in a particular setting and to note reactions to violations of spatial expectations. Choose a supermarket, department store, university bookstore, or some other common setting in which people shop for things and then pay for them in a checkout line. Observe the interaction distances that seem usual between clerks and customers, between customers as they shop, and between customers in the checkout line.

a. What are the average distances between the people you observed?

b. How do people respond when one person comes too close to another or when one person touches another? How do people react to these violations of their space? How could they avoid violating each other's personal space?

c. Think back to a foreign film or a film that contains interaction between North Americans and people of another culture, as well as between people from the same culture—or try to observe people from a culture other than your own. Describe how they use spatial distance during conversations.

9. Role Play

This role play allows you to become more aware of your non-verbal behaviour and then gives you an opportunity to pay attention to all the facets of non-verbal communication by observing and copying someone else.

a. Think of an important message you need to deliver to someone significant (e.g.,

declining an invitation, asking for something the person may be unwilling to give, etc.). If you can't think of anything currently, think of a message you had to deliver in the past.

b. Deliver the message to your partner and ask her or him to copy all your non-verbal actions (except paralanguage) while you are giving the message—like you are looking into a mirror. When you are finished, discuss what you and your partner noticed about your non-verbal message.

c. Next, reverse roles. Have your partner deliver the message and you copy his or her behaviour. Be sure to pay attention to as many facets as possible (e.g., face and eyes, posture and body movement, touch, gestures, etc.). Again, discuss your observations.

Discussion Questions

1. Describe similarities and differences between verbal and non-verbal communication.
2. Why do you think non-verbal communication has so much influence on human perception? Why do we value it more than verbal communication when we are evaluating the relational content of messages? What are the limitations of non-verbal communication in this regard?
3. Describe nine types of non-verbal behaviour and rate the significance of each in your communication with others.
4. The eyes have been described as the windows to the soul. Do you agree? What channels or types of non-verbal communication are most powerful for you? Why?
5. The research evidence regarding the power of physical attractiveness over human perception is disconcerting (unless you happen to be gorgeous). What can we do to overcome our biases (both positive and negative) in this area?

Chapter Seven

Listening

After studying the material in this chapter ...

You Should Understand:

1. The importance of listening.
2. The reasons for listening to others.
3. The error of common myths, which suggest that listening is easy.
4. The habits of people who listen ineffectively.
5. The components of the listening process.
7. The differences among the listening responses introduced in this chapter.
8. The advantages and disadvantages of various listening styles.

You Should Be Able To:

1. Identify specific instances when you listen a) to understand and retain information, b) to build and maintain relationships, c) to help others, and d) to evaluate.
2. Describe the circumstances in which you listen ineffectively and the poor listening habits you use in these circumstances.
3. Identify the response styles you commonly use when listening to others.
4. Demonstrate a combination of listening styles you could use to respond effectively to another person.

The grizzled army sergeant faced a roomful of new US Signal Corps cadets, about to begin their training as radio operators.

'The equipment is a snap to operate,' he explained. 'All you have to do to send a message is to push this button on the microphone, and your voice goes out to anyone who's tuned in. Go ahead . . . give it a try.'

Each recruit picked up a microphone and began speaking. The sound of thirty amplified voices all transmitting at the same time created a loud, painful squeal.

'Okay, soldiers,' the sergeant announced. 'You just learned the first principle of radio communication. Any fool can send a message. The only way communication works is if you are willing and able to receive one too.'

The sergeant's lesson is a good one for every communicator. Speaking is important, but without listening, a message might as well never be sent. In this chapter, you will learn just how important listening is in interpersonal communication. You will learn about the many factors that make good listening difficult and you'll also find reasons for tackling those challenges. You'll see what really happens when listening takes place. Finally, you will read about a variety of listening responses that you can use to increase your own understanding, improve your relationships, and help others.

The Nature of Listening

When people think about improving their communication skills, they usually think of developing their ability to send messages. The value of listening skills is often overlooked but, as we will see, investing our time in improving those skills has innumerable benefits.

The Importance of Listening

How important is listening? If we use frequency as a measure, it ranks at the top of the list. As far back as 1927, Paul Rankin (1952) found that adults spent about 70 percent of their waking time communicating. Writing occupied 9 percent of that time, reading 17 percent, speaking 30 percent,

and listening 45 percent. One writer put Rankin's findings in perspective this way: 'We listen a book a day, speak a book a week, read a book a month, and write a book a year' (Loban, 1963). One survey, illustrated in Figure 7.1 (Barker et al., 1981), suggests that listening may have become more important since the time of Rankin's study. This is confirmed by Brown (1982), Keefe (1971), and Steil (1996), all of whom report that executives spend approximately 70 percent of their communication time listening.

Besides being the most frequent form of communication, listening may be a more highly valued skill than speaking. Andrew Wolvin, Carolyn Coakley, and Carolyn Gwynn (1999; Wolvin and Coakley, 1991) summarize numerous studies that find listening to be the most important communication skill for entry-level workers, subordinates, supervisors, and managers on several fronts: job and career success, productivity, upward mobility, communication training, and organizational effectiveness. When several hundred human resource executives were asked to identify skills of the ideal manager, the ability to listen effectively ranked at the top of the list (Winsor et al., 1997). In problem-solving groups, effective listeners are judged as having the most leadership

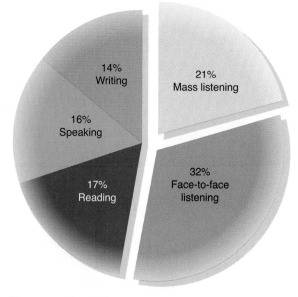

Figure 7.1 Types of Communication Activities

iStock photo

skills (Johnson and Bechler, 1998). Senior executives, students, and employers, when asked what skills were most important on the job, identified listening more often than any other skill, including technical competence, computer knowledge, creativity, and administrative talent (Gabric and McFadden, 2001; Marchant, 1999).

The business world is not the only place where listening is vital. When a group of adults was asked to rank various communication skills according to their importance, listening topped the family and social list as well as the career list (Wolvin, 1984). In committed relationships, listening to personal information in everyday conversations is considered an important ingredient of satisfaction (Prager and Buhrmester, 1998).

Unfortunately, there is no connection between how well most communicators *think* they listen and how competent they really are in their ability to understand others (Carrell and Willmington, 1996). Virtually everyone acknowledges the importance of listening—the title of an article on Native American *talking circles* puts this succinctly: 'Listen, or your tongue will make you deaf' (Wilbur et al., 2001). Unfortunately, however, people rarely

view themselves as needing to improve their own skills in receiving and understanding. A study by Judi Brownell (1990) illustrates this point vividly. A group of managers in her study were asked to rate their listening skills. Astonishingly, not one of the managers described himself or herself as a 'poor' or 'very poor' listener, and 94 percent rated themselves as 'good' or 'very good'. The favourable self-ratings contrasted sharply with the perceptions of the managers' subordinates, many of whom said their bosses' listening skills were weak. As you will soon read, some amount of poor listening is inevitable. The good news is that listening can be improved through instruction and training (Lane et al., 2000; McGee and Cegala, 1998; Spinks and Wells, 1991).

Listening Defined

So, what exactly is listening? **Listening** is the process of receiving, interpreting, and responding to spoken and non-verbal messages. Listening involves more than just hearing. **Hearing** is the process by which sound waves strike the eardrum and cause vibrations that are transmitted to the brain. Listening takes place when the brain reconstructs these electrochemical impulses into a representation of the original sound and then gives them meaning (Fernald, 2001). Barring illness, injury, or earplugs, hearing cannot be stopped. Your ears will pick up sound waves and transmit them to your brain whether you want them to or not.

Listening, however, is not so automatic. Many times, we hear but do not listen. Sometimes, we deliberately do not listen. Instead of paying attention to words or other sounds, we avoid them. Often, we block out irritating sounds, such as a neighbour's lawn mower or the roar of nearby traffic. We also stop listening when we find a subject unimportant or uninteresting. Boring stories, television commercials, and nagging complaints are common examples of messages we avoid. Other times, we think we are listening but, in fact we are simply receiving sounds and our minds are elsewhere. Listening requires not just hearing but the effort of paying attention, understanding, remembering, and responding, as we will discuss later in this chapter.

Reasons for Listening

A first step in becoming a better listener is to realize that there are several different reasons to listen and each requires a different set of attitudes and skills.

To Understand and Remember The most obvious is to *understand and retain information*. People who can do that have a chance of becoming successful, both personally and professionally (Floyd, 1985). In virtually every job, it is important to understand the instructions, advice, needs, reactions, and concerns of the people you work with.

To Evaluate A second type of listening involves *evaluating the quality of messages*. In their interesting book, *Teaching as a Subversive Activity*, Neil Postman and Charles Weingartner (1969) discuss this function of listening in their chapter called 'Crap Detecting'. They define a crap detector as someone who not only functions in a society, but also observes it, noting its obsessions, fears, strengths, and weaknesses. Critical listeners are able to hear a speaker's words and understand the ideas without necessarily accepting them or agreeing with

them. The ability to listen analytically and critically differs radically from empathic and supportive listening, but it is equally important.

To Build and Maintain Relationships A third reason for listening, which is especially relevant for interpersonal communication, is to *build and maintain relationships*. Research shows that effective listening 'builds better relationships, and poor listening weakens relationships, or prevents relationships from developing at all' (Kaufmann, 1993, p. 4). In one survey, marital counsellors identified 'failing to take the other's perspective when listening' as one of the most frequent communication problems for client couples (Vangelisti, 1994; see also Long et al., 1999).

To Help Others A fourth type of listening involves *helping others*, another important interpersonal skill. Listening is an essential tool that professionals use to help their clients. Doctors, lawyers, teachers, managers, supervisors, clergy, and therapists must listen carefully so they can offer sound assistance. Professionals are not the only people we call on for help; we also seek the counsel of friends and family. When others listen to us with understanding and concern, we can gain different and useful perspectives for solving problems.

The Challenge of Listening

Despite its importance, most people misunderstand what is required for proper listening. Many believe if they've heard another person's message, they've engaged in listening—it is as simple as

Test Yourself   Define the term *listening*. Describe four reasons for listening and provide an example of each.

that. What these people fail to realize is that good listening is not simple; in fact, it's a challenge. The challenge can be met, but only by those who do not buy into popular misconceptions about listening. Let's look at several of these misconceptions.

Listening Is Not Easy

A common myth is that listening is like breathing—a natural activity that people do without conscious effort. The fact is, there are numerous obstacles that must be overcome for people to listen effectively, and doing so sometimes involves time, concentration, and work. Researchers have identified several barriers to listening (Golen, 1990; Hulbert, 1989). A look at some of them will show why good listening is so difficult.

Information Overload   The sheer amount of speech most of us encounter every day makes it impossible to listen carefully to everything we hear. We often spend five or more hours a day listening to people talk. If you add these hours to the amount of time we devote to radio and television, you can see that it is virtually impossible for us to keep our attention totally focused for so long. Therefore, we periodically let our attention wander.

Personal Concerns   A second reason we don't always listen carefully is that we are often wrapped up in personal concerns of more immediate importance to us than the messages others are sending. It's hard to pay attention to someone else when we are anticipating an upcoming test or thinking about the wonderful time we had last night with our friends. When we still feel that we have to 'listen' politely to others, listening becomes a charade.

Rapid Thought   Listening carefully is also difficult because our minds are so active. Although we are capable of understanding speech at rates up to 600 words a minute (Drullman and Smoorenburg,

1997; Versfeld and Dreschler, 2002), the average person speaks much more slowly—between 100 and 140 words a minute. Therefore, we have a lot of 'spare time' to spend with our minds while someone is talking. The temptation is to use this time in ways that are not related to the speaker's ideas, such as thinking about personal interests, daydreaming, planning a rebuttal, and so on. The trick is to use this spare time to understand the speaker's ideas better, rather than let your attention wander.

Noise   Finally, our physical and mental worlds often present distractions that make it hard for us to pay attention to others. The sounds of other conversations, traffic, and music, as well as the kinds of psychological noise that we discussed in Chapter 1, all interfere with our ability to hear well. For example, research has supported the commonsense suspicion that background noise from a television set reduces the ability of a communicator to understand messages (Armstrong et al., 1991). Fatigue or other forms of discomfort can also distract us. For instance, consider how the efficiency of your listening decreases when you are seated in a crowded, hot, stuffy room full of moving people and other noises. In such circumstances, even the best intentions are not enough to ensure cogent understanding.

Before going any further, we want to make it clear that intensive listening is not always desirable. Given the number of messages we're exposed to, it is impractical to expect yourself to listen well 100 percent of the time. Our main concern is that you have the ability to be an accurate receiver when it really does matter.

All Listeners Do Not Receive the Same Message

When two or more people are listening to a speaker, we tend to assume that they are each hearing and understanding the same message. In fact, that is

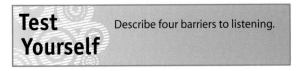

Test Yourself   Describe four barriers to listening.

not the case. Recall our discussion of perception in Chapter 3, where we pointed out the many factors that cause each of us to perceive an event in a different manner. Physiological factors, social roles, cultural background, personal interests, and needs all shape and distort the raw data we hear into very different messages. Because every person interprets data in a unique way, we have to accept the fact that we can never completely understand another person. As John Stewart (1983) and Benjamin Broome (1991) note, even the most active, empathic listener cannot actually 'lay aside' the self and truly 'walk in another's shoes'. We bring our personal perspective and experiences with us into every interaction, and they affect the way we make sense of the words and actions of others. It is no wonder that dyads typically achieve only 25 to 50 percent accuracy in interpreting or representing each other's behaviour (Spitzberg, 1994). Our listening is always coloured and limited by our unique view of the world.

Types of Non-listening

Most people have experienced the frustration of being misunderstood. Similarly, most of us have one or more bad habits that keep us from understanding the messages of others. As you read about the following types of non-listening behaviours, see which ones describe you.

Pseudo-listening is an imitation of the real thing. 'Good' pseudo-listeners give the appearance of being attentive: they look you in the eye, nod and smile at the right times, and even answer you occasionally, but their minds are elsewhere. Pseudo-listeners use a polite facade to mask their inattention.

Stage hogs are interested only in expressing their own ideas and don't care about what other people have to say. These offenders allow you to speak from time to time, but only so they can catch their breath and use your remarks as a basis for their own chatter. Research on 'conversational narcissism' (Vangelisti et al., 1990) shows that self-centred stage hogs ask questions but not other-oriented, information-seeking ones. Rather, these conversational domineers ask counterfeit questions to demonstrate their superiority and hold

Reflection

Fake Listening

I went parachuting for the first time last month. Before our first jump, we spent four hours in 'ground school'. I listened very carefully, especially during the part where they told us what to do if our chute didn't open after jumping from the plane. This was life-and-death material, and I didn't want to miss anything.

That's not the way I listen at school most of the time. I sit through most classroom lectures and it all seems like gibberish to me. I act as if I'm listening—nod at what I hope are the right times, smile when people laugh, and even scratch my head as if I'm thinking—so the teacher will assume I am listening. But I don't remember a thing afterwards. I used to think it was all the teacher's fault, but I guess part of it has to do with whether or not I bother to turn up my 'listening volume'.

the floor (we'll talk more about *counterfeit* versus *sincere* questions later in this chapter).

Selective listeners respond only to the parts of a speaker's remarks that interest them, rejecting everything else. Unless you bring up one of these pet subjects, you might as well be talking to a tree.

People who **fill in gaps** like to think that what they remember makes a whole story. These people manufacture information so that when they retell what they listened to, they can give the impression they 'got it all'. The message left is actually a distorted (not merely incomplete) version of the real message.

The habit of **insulated listening** is almost the opposite of selective listening. Instead of looking for something, these listeners avoid it. Whenever a topic arises that they would rather not deal with, insulated listeners simply fail to hear or acknowledge it.

People who engage in **defensive listening** take innocent comments as personal attacks. It's fair to assume that many defensive listeners are suffering from shaky self-images, and they avoid facing this by projecting their own insecurities onto others.

An **ambusher** will listen carefully to you, but only because the person is collecting information that he or she will use to attack what you have to say. Needless to say, using this kind of strategy will justifiably initiate defensiveness from the other person.

Components of Listening

By now, you can begin to see that there is more to listening than sitting quietly while another person speaks. In truth, *listening*—at least listening effectively—consists of five separate elements: hearing, attending, understanding, remembering, and responding.

Hearing

As we have already discussed, hearing is the physiological aspect of listening. It is the non-selective process of sound waves impinging on the ear. Hearing is the most fundamental part of listening. It can be diminished by physiological disorders, background noise, and auditory fatigue, a temporary loss of hearing caused by continuous exposure to the same tone or loudness. People who spend an evening at a rock concert or attending a fireworks display may experience auditory fatigue and, if they are exposed often enough, permanent hearing loss. Approximately three million Canadians suffer from hearing problems (Hearing Foundation of Canada, 2005).

If a person suffers from a physical impairment that prevents him or her either from hearing sounds at an adequate volume or from receiving certain auditory frequencies, then listening will obviously suffer. A study of listening effort in children (aged six to eleven) with hearing loss shows that they expend more effort in listening than children with normal hearing, resulting in fatigue (Hicks and Tharpe, 2002). Once a hearing problem has been diagnosed, it can often be treated. The real tragedy occurs when a hearing loss goes undiagnosed. Both that person and those she or he interacts with can become frustrated and annoyed at the ineffective communication that takes place. If you suspect that you or someone you know might

iStock photo

have a hearing loss, it is wise to have a physician or audiologist perform an examination.

Attending

While hearing is a physiological process, **attending** is a psychological one and is part of the process of selection that we described in Chapter 3. We would go crazy if we attended to every sound we hear, so we filter out some messages and focus on others. Needs, wants, desires, and interests determine what is attended to. Not surprisingly, research shows that we attend most carefully to messages when there is a benefit in doing so (Smeltzer and Watson, 1984). If you are planning to see a movie, you will listen to a friend's description more

 Take Two

- **Pseudo-listening:** an imitation of real listening.
- **Stage hogs:** people interested only in expressing their own ideas during conversation.
- **Selective listeners:** those who respond only to the parts of a speaker's remarks that interest them.
- **Filling in the gaps:** the practice of making up information to give the impression that one was listening and can recall the whole story.
- **Insulated listening:** the tendency to avoid or fail to hear/acknowledge certain topics.
- **Defensive listening:** the habit of interpreting innocent comments as personal attacks.
- **Ambusher:** one who listens carefully but only to gather information that can be used to attack the speaker.

iStock photo

carefully than you otherwise would. And when you want to get better acquainted with someone, you'll pay careful attention to almost anything they say, in hopes of improving the relationship. We are motivated to listen to others when we care about what they are saying.

In addition to paying attention to verbal communication, listening involves attending to the non-verbal messages people send us as well. Notice that the Chinese characters which make up the verb 'to listen' in Figure 7.2 include not just ears but eyes, too. For some people, attending to non-verbal communication poses unique challenges. People with a physiological affliction called *non-verbal learning disorder* often miss or misinterpret social cues like facial expressions, gestures, and tones of voice (Rourke, 1998). Children with this disorder often violate social conventions and can become socially isolated if they don't receive proper adult support and intervention. Understanding others requires attention to both verbal and non-verbal messages. John Carton and his colleagues (1999) found that adults' ability to attend to and accurately interpret people's facial expressions and voice tone was positively related to the well-being of their relationships with others.

Surprisingly, attending doesn't just help the listener: it also benefits the message sender. Participants in one study watched short segments of movies and then described them to listeners who varied in their degrees of attentiveness to the speaker. Later on, the researchers tested the speakers' long-term recall of details from the movie segment. Those who had recounted the segments to attentive listeners remembered more details of the movie (Pasupathi et al., 1998).

EAR

EYES

UNDIVIDED ATTENTION

HEART

Calligraphy by Angie Au.

Figure 7.2 The Chinese characters that make up the verb 'to listen' tell us something significant about this skill.

Focus on Technology

Cell Phones and Forced Eavesdropping

When asked if cell phones disturb people, the majority of Europeans and North Americans will say yes, at least some of the time (Haddon, 2000; Ling, 2004). There are lots of stories of mobile phones ringing at inopportune times (e.g., when the owner is in a public bathroom) and in inappropriate places (e.g., funerals). Another problem that westerners find disturbing is the 'forced eavesdropping' dilemma: in other words, such dilemmas are generally unwanted situations where the cell-phone user carries on loud conversations in a public space. There are times when it feels almost impossible to ignore the person beside us talking about trivial matters or, worse yet, disclosing personal information that we would rather not know. Why is it so difficult to ignore cell-phone conversations? It seems much easier to filter out the face-to-face conversations of people in our close proximity.

Perhaps, there are some features of cell-phone conversations that make them grab our attention. First, many people speak more loudly when they are talking on a cell phone compared to when they are speaking with someone sitting near them (Monk et al., 2004). This increase in volume certainly makes it easier to listen and harder to ignore. Second, we hear only one side of the cell-phone conversation, which might serve to engage us in thinking about what the other side of the conversation involves. Unlike face-to-face conversations that occur in our proximity, the cell-phone conversation may be more engaging because of what is missing and how the gaps in information can spark our curiosity and engage us in thought. Andrew Monk and his colleagues (2004) at the University of York tested this hypothesis in the United Kingdom by having actors engage in one-sided conversations on cell phones, with the other person present but inaudible in train cars. Passengers on the train rated the one-sided conversations as more noticeable and intrusive than other conversations where both people were present and audible.

In Western cultures, many cell-phone users use barrier behaviours (discussed in Chapter 6) to distance themselves from others in public spaces (Plant, 2001). These include turning away, hunching over, or lowering one's head and looking at the floor. However, in cultures where human interaction and connectivity are more highly valued than privacy and personal space, cell-phone users are less inclined to modify their behaviour. For example, in Beijing and Bangkok, people are far more tolerant of high-volume, one-sided conversations in movie theatres and other public places (Plant, 2001). Clearly, there are numerous factors that influence us in deciding what we want to listen to in public spaces.

Understanding

Paying attention—even close attention—to a message does not guarantee that you will understand what is being said. **Understanding** is composed of several elements. First, of course, you must be aware of the syntactic and grammatical rules of the language. But, beyond this basic ability, understanding a message depends on several other factors. One is your knowledge about the source of the message. That will help you decide, for example, whether a friend's insulting remark is a joke or a serious attack. The context of a message also helps you understand what is being said. A yawning response to your comments would probably have a different meaning at midnight than at noon.

Finally, understanding often depends on the listener's mental abilities. Generally speaking, the ability to make sense of messages is closely related to the listener's intelligence (Bostrom and Waldhart, 1980). As early as 1948, Ralph Nichols related successful understanding to factors that included verbal ability, intelligence, and motivation. Timothy Plax and Lawrence Rosenfeld (1979) found that the personality traits of listeners also affect their ability to understand messages. In Plax and Rosenfeld's study, people who were good at interpreting disorganized messages were especially secure, sensitive to others, and willing to understand the speaker. Listeners who were successful at understanding disorganized speech proved to be more insightful and versatile in their thinking.

Remembering

The ability to **remember** information once we've understood it, depends on several factors: the number of times the information is heard or repeated, how much information there is to store in the brain, and whether the information may be 'rehearsed' or not.

Early research on listening revealed that people remember only about half of what they hear immediately after hearing it (Barker, 1971). They forget half of what is said even if they work hard at listening. The situation would probably not be too bad if the half that people immediately remember was retained, but it is not. Within two months, half of the half is forgotten, bringing what we remember down to about 25 percent of the original message. In fact, people start forgetting immediately (within 8 hours, the 50 percent remembered drops to roughly 35 percent). Given the amount of information we are exposed to every day—from teachers, friends, radio, television, and other sources—the *residual message* (what we remember) is a small fraction of what we have heard.

This high rate of forgetfulness is not as depressing as it might seem. While most people recall very few details of their conversations, they do retain an overall impression about the speaker, especially in important relationships (Fisher and Adams, 1994). The more intensity, intimacy, trust, and commitment in the relationship, the more we pay attention to what others are saying. Thus, high recall is one characteristic of healthy interpersonal relationships.

Responding

All the steps we have discussed so far—hearing, attending, understanding, and remembering—are internal activities. A final part of the listening process involves **responding** to a message—giving observable feedback to the speaker (Bostrom, 1996; Cooper et al., 1997). One study of 195 critical incidents in banking and medical settings showed that a major difference between effective and ineffective listening was the kind of feedback offered (Lewis and Reinsch, 1988). Good listeners showed that they were attentive by displaying non-verbal behaviours, such as keeping eye contact and

iStock photo

reacting with appropriate facial expressions. Their verbal behaviour—for example, answering questions and exchanging ideas—also demonstrated their adequate attention. It's easy to imagine how other responses would signal less-effective listening. A slumped posture, bored expression, and barely stifled yawn send clear messages that you are not tuned in to the speaker.

Adding responsiveness to our listening model demonstrates the fact (discussed in Chapter 1) that communication is transactional. Listening is not just a passive activity. As listeners, we are active participants in a communication transaction. At the same time that we receive messages, we also send them.

Types of Listening Responses

Of the five components of listening described above, responding is what lets us know if others are truly tuned in to what we are saying. Think for a moment of someone you consider a good listener. Why did you choose that person? It's probably because of the way she or he behaves while you are speaking: looking you in the eye and nodding when you are talking, staying attentive while you are telling an important story, reacting with an exclamation when you say something

Test Yourself Describe the five components of listening.

Figure 7.3 Types of Listening Responses

startling, expressing empathy and support when you are suffering, and offering another perspective or advice when you ask for it (Bippus, 2001). As Figure 7.3 illustrates, listening responses like these range from reflective feedback that invites the speaker to talk without fear of being judged, to more directive responses that evaluate the speaker's messages. We'll spend the rest of the chapter looking at each of these response styles in detail.

Silent Listening

There are times when the best response is to say nothing. This is certainly true when you don't want to encourage a speaker to keep talking. For instance, there are times when a boss or instructor drones on and on when you need to leave for an appointment, or when a friend retells the story of

a love affair gone bad for what seems like the tenth time. In situations like these, a verbal response would only encourage the speaker to continue— precisely the opposite reaction you would be seeking. The best response in these cases may be **silent listening**—staying attentive and non-verbally responsive without saying anything.

Silent listening is not just an avoidance strategy. It also can be the right approach when you are open to the other person's ideas but your interjections wouldn't be appropriate. If you are part of a large audience hearing a lecture, it would probably be disruptive to ask questions and offer comments. On a more personal level, when a friend tells you a joke, butting in to ask for clarification ('There was a priest, a rabbi, and *who*?') would probably spoil your friend's rhythm.

Focus on Research

Listening to a Friend in Need: The Value of Not Intruding

Imagine that one of your friends has just had something bad happen—perhaps a breakup of a relationship or a low exam grade. The only reason you know about the bad news is because someone else told you. Would you bring up the subject to your friend and express regret? Would you offer support or advice? According to research by Ruth Anne Clark and Jesse Delia (1997), those well-meaning approaches might not be what your friend really wants or needs.

Clark and Delia asked 113 college students to imagine themselves in 6 different unpleasant situations (e.g., bad test score, brother in a car accident, dad unemployed).

The students were then asked how they would like to be approached by a friend who learned of the distressing situation from someone else. The results were somewhat surprising. Although some respondents said they would want and expect their friend to bring up the subject, the majority reported they would prefer that their friend not mention it. The researchers found that 'participants displayed a strong preference to determine for themselves whether to discuss their problem with a friend.'

The conclusions suggest there is value in being a silent listener around a troubled friend, or at most asking non-committal questions such as, 'How's it going?' If and when your friend feels like talking is the best—and perhaps the only—time to use the other listening responses discussed in this section of the text.

There are even times when silent listening can help others solve their problems. Sonia Johnson (1987) describes a powerful activity she calls 'hearing into being'. The process is simple. In brainstorming sessions, each participant has half an hour of uninterrupted floor time. 'When we are free to talk without threat of interruption, evaluation, and the pressure of time,' notes Johnson, 'we move quickly past known territory out into the frontiers of our thought' (p. 132). Johnson, who uses the technique in feminist seminars, reports that some women burst into tears when they first experience 'hearing into being' because they are not used to being listened to so seriously and completely. Ask yourself when the last time was that you talked, uninterrupted, to an attentive partner for more than a few minutes? How would you like the chance to develop your ideas without pausing for another's comments? Silent listening is a response style that many of us could profit from using—and receiving—more often.

Members of high-context and low-context cultures differ in their use of silence. Generally, in high-context cultures (i.e., many Asian and Canadian

Focus on Research

Listening to Canadian First Nations Patients

Health-care providers in Canada often work in cross-cultural situations but frequently have little or no preparation for dealing with the differing values and communication styles that these situations bring. Len Kelly and Judith Belle Brown (2002) were interested in gathering information to help doctors and other health-care professionals who serve people in First Nations communities. They conducted semi-structured one-hour interviews with ten non-Native physicians working in First Nations communities. The length of time the participants had worked in these communities ranged from 3 to 30 years, with an average of 14.4 years. The researchers found that the doctors had had to change their understanding of illness as something existing in an individual to something existing in a community, and they had to think in new ways about the elements of communication and the communication strategies they used. For the doctors, the first indicator of distinct and varied First Nations cultural values was apparent in many Native peoples' different communication styles. The doctors reported that they had had to adapt to a different pace for their discussions with patients, speak less, listen more, and become more comfortable with silence and lack of eye contact. Perhaps the most unfamiliar element of communication for non-Native physicians was the use of silence. One elder explained the importance of silent listening like this: 'We are born with two ears, two eyes, and one mouth and should use them accordingly. We should use the mouth half as much as the ears and eyes'

(Kelly and Brown, 2002, p. 1647). The doctors said they had received enormous benefits from the cross-cultural experience including changes in their understanding. One of them recalled,

The sense of humility that comes with understanding your limitations, I could illustrate with a quick story: I saw a very elderly Native lady; her daughters brought her in, she was sort of a matriarch and they called me that night and asked would I come to the house and see her and I did. Normal pulse, normal blood pressure, chest clear, everything seemed fine and I had no idea why they called me out at night, but I was pretty annoyed that they had done that . . . when one of the daughters said to me, 'Would you like a cup of tea?' and I said, 'Sure, that would be great,' and that sort of diffused my little reprimand.

I went to the kitchen and sat down to have my cup of tea and while I was having the tea, the daughters went back into the bedroom, and then one of them walked out and said, 'Well, she's gone very peacefully now,' and I said, 'What?' and ran into the bedroom. She was lying there as dead as a doornail and they said, 'Thank you very much for coming when mother died. You know we knew she was going to go and we really appreciate just you having been here.'

I thought to myself, 'Well, first of all am I ever glad that I didn't say what I had intended to say about the unnecessary visit and secondly, how the hell did they know she was dying? I honestly did not have a clue. That injected in me a great sense of humility, like whoa, they know a lot that I don't know, about their mother but also just about death and dying—and anyway, I've held onto that sense of humility and that's pretty much where I remain.' (Kelly and Brown, 2002)

Calvin and Hobbes

by Bill Watterson

First Nations cultures), silence is valued as a way to communicate respect and thoughtful consideration of others. People feel content with silence because it communicates mutual understanding (Braithwaite, 1990). In low-context cultures such as Canada and the United States, on the other hand, silence is often uncomfortable and people who don't talk are frequently evaluated negatively by others. In low-context cultures, silence somehow suggests there is a problem because people are expected to verbalize what they think.

Questioning

Regarded as 'the most popular piece of language' (Goodman and Esterly, 1990), **questioning** occurs when the listener asks the speaker for additional information. There are several reasons to ask sincere, non-directive questions:

- *To clarify meanings.* By now, you know that people who share words do not always share meanings. Good listeners don't assume they know what their partners mean; they ask for clarification with questions such as these: 'What did you mean when you said he had been "unfair" to you?' 'You said she's "religious"— how do you define that term?' 'You said you were going "fast"—could you be more specific?' Of course, be sure to use an appropriate tone of voice when asking such questions, or else they might sound like an inquisition.

- *To learn about other people's thoughts, feelings, and wants.* A caring listener and a good salesperson (Shoemaker and Johlk, 2002) may want to inquire about more than just 'the facts'. Opinions, emotions, needs, and even hopes are buried inside many messages; with sensitivity, a sincere question can draw these out. 'What do you think about the new plan?' 'How did you feel when you heard the news?' and 'Were you hoping for something different?' are examples of such probes. When inquiring about personal information, it is usually best to ask **open questions** that allow a variety of extended responses rather than **closed questions** that allow only a limited range of answers. For instance, 'How did you feel?' is an open question that allows a variety of responses, while 'Did you feel angry?' is a closed question that requires only a yes or no answer (and may direct respondents toward feelings they weren't experiencing).

- *To encourage elaboration.* People are sometimes hesitant to talk about themselves, or perhaps they aren't sure if others are interested. Remarks such as, 'Tell me more about that,' 'Try me again—I'm not sure I understand,' and 'Keep going—I'm following you' convey concern and involvement. Notice that none of these examples ends with a question mark. We can encourage elaboration simply by acknowledging that we are listening.

- *To encourage discovery.* People in the helping professions—clergy, counsellors, therapists, and so on—often ask questions to prod their clients into discovering solutions for their problems. 'Playing counsellor' can be a dangerous game, but there are times when you can use questions to encourage others to explore their thoughts and feelings. 'So, what do you see as your options?' may prompt an employee to come up with creative problem-solving alternatives. 'What would be your ideal solution?' might help a friend get in touch with various wants and needs. Most important, encouraging discovery rather than dispensing advice indicates you have faith in others' ability to think for themselves. This may be the most important message that you can communicate as an effective listener.
- *To gather more facts and details.* Just because your conversational partner tells you something, it doesn't mean you understand the whole story. As long as your questions are not intrusive (you will need to monitor the other person's non-verbal behaviour to determine this), people often appreciate listeners who want to learn more. Questions such as, 'What did you do then?' and 'What did she say after that?' can help a listener understand the big picture.

Not all questions are genuine requests for information. Whereas **sincere questions** are aimed at understanding others, **counterfeit questions** are really disguised attempts to send a message, not receive one. As such, they really fit better at the 'more directive' end of the listening response continuum shown in Figure 7.3 on page 201. It's also likely that they'll lead to a defensive communication climate, as we discuss in Chapter 10.

Counterfeit questions come in several varieties:

- *Questions that trap the speaker.* When your friend says, 'You didn't like that movie, did you?' you are being backed into a corner. It's clear that your friend disapproves, so the question leaves you with a choice to make. You can disagree and defend your position, or you can

devalue your reaction by lying or equivocating—'I guess it wasn't terrific.' Consider how much easier it would be to answer the sincere question, 'What did you think of the movie?'

Adding a tag question such as 'did you?' or 'isn't that right?' to the end of a question can be a tip-off that the asker is looking for agreement, not information. Although some listeners use these tag endings to confirm and facilitate understanding (Coates, 1986), tags can be coercive: 'You said you'd call at five o'clock, but you forgot, didn't you?' Similarly, questions that begin with 'Don't you' (such as, 'Don't you think he would make a good boss?') direct others toward a desired response. As a simple solution, changing 'Don't you?' to 'Do you?' makes the question less leading.

Leading questions not only signal what the desired answer is but also affect memory, especially in children. David Bjorklund and his colleagues (2000) showed children and adults a video of a theft and then interviewed them several days later, using both leading and free recall questions. The adults were unaffected by the type of question asked, but the children who were asked leading questions had a less accurate memory of the video than those who were asked free-recall questions.

- *Questions that make statements.* 'Are you *finally* off the phone?' is more a statement than a question—a fact unlikely to be lost on the targeted person. Emphasizing certain words can also turn a question into a statement: 'You lent money to *Tony*?' We also use questions to offer advice. The person who asks, 'Are you going to stand up to him and give him what he deserves?' has clearly stated an opinion about what should be done.
- *Questions that carry hidden agendas.* 'Are you busy Friday night?' is a dangerous question to answer. If you say no, thinking the person has something pleasant in mind, you won't like hearing, 'Good, because I need some help moving my piano.' Obviously, such questions are not designed to enhance understanding; they are setups for the proposal that follows.

Other examples include, 'Will you do me a favour?' and 'If I tell you what happened, will you promise not to get mad?' Because they are strategic rather than spontaneous, these questions are likely to provoke defensiveness (Gibb, 1961). Wise communicators answer questions that mask hidden agendas cautiously with responses such as 'It depends' or 'Let me hear what you have in mind before I answer.'

- *Questions that seek 'correct' answers.* Most of us have been victims of question askers who want to hear a particular answer. 'Which shoes do you think I should wear?' can be a sincere question—unless the asker has a predetermined preference. When this happens, the asker is not interested in listening to contrary opinions, and 'incorrect' responses get shot down. Some of these questions may venture into delicate territory. 'Honey, do you think I'm overweight?' is usually a request for a 'correct' answer—and the listener must have a fair amount of discretion and good judgment to determine a suitable response.

- *Questions based on unverified assumptions.* 'Why aren't you listening to me?' assumes the other person is not paying attention. 'What's the matter?' assumes that something is wrong. As we explained in Chapter 3, perception checking is a much better way of confirming one's assumptions. You'll recall that a perception check offers a description and interpretations, followed by a sincere request for clarification: 'When you kept looking over at the NU, I thought you weren't listening to me, but maybe I was wrong. Were you paying attention?'

No question is inherently sincere or counterfeit. As we explained in Chapter 5, the meaning and intent of any statement is shaped by its context. Moreover, a slight change in tone of voice or facial expression can turn a sincere question into a counterfeit one, and vice versa. Nonetheless, the types of questions described above are usually closer to statements than requests for information.

It's also worth noting that counterfeit questions are not always bad; in fact, they can be powerful tools for making a point. Lawyers use them to get confessions in the courtroom, and journalists ask them to uncover concealed information. Our point is that they usually get in the way of effective listening and relationship building—after all, most people don't like feeling trapped or 'grilled' in a conversation.

Paraphrasing

Paraphrasing is feedback that restates, in your own words, the message you thought the speaker sent. You may wonder, 'Why would I want to restate what is already been said?' Consider this simple exchange:

'Let's make plans to get together next weekend.'
'So you want to chat next week to make plans for Saturday?'
'No, what I meant is that we should check our calendars now to see if we're free to go to the game on Sunday.'

By paraphrasing, the listener learned that the speaker wanted to make plans now, not later—and that 'weekend' meant Sunday, not Saturday. Note that the listener rephrased rather than repeated the message. In effective paraphrasing you restate what you think the speaker has said in your own words as a way of checking the meaning you've assigned to the message. It's important that you paraphrase, not 'parrot-phrase'. If you simply repeat the speaker's comments verbatim, you will sound foolish or hard of hearing—and just as important, you still might misunderstand what is been said.

Types of Paraphrasing Statements   Restating another person's message in a way that sounds natural can sometimes be a difficult skill to master. Here are three approaches to get you started:

1. Change the speaker's wording.
   Speaker: 'Bilingual education is just another failed idea of francophones.'
   Paraphrase: 'Let me see if I've got this right. You're mad because you think bilingual education sounds good, but it doesn't work?'

Building Work Skills

Paraphrasing

Practise your ability to paraphrase in order to understand others by following these steps:

a. Choose a partner, and designate one of yourselves as person A and the other as person B. Find a subject on which you and your partner seem to disagree—a personal dispute, a philosophical or moral issue, or perhaps a matter of personal taste.

b. Person A begins by making a statement on the subject. Person B's job is to paraphrase the idea. In this step, B should feed back only what he or she heard A say, without adding any judgment or interpretation. B's job here is simply to understand A—not to agree or disagree with A.

c. Person A responds by telling B whether or not the response was accurate and by making any necessary additions or corrections to clarify the message.

d. Person B then paraphrases the revised statement. This process should continue until A is sure that B understands him or her.

e. Now, B and A reverse roles and repeat the procedure in steps a–d. Continue the conversation until both partners are satisfied that they have explained themselves fully and have been understood by the other person.

After the discussion has ended, consider how this process differed from typical conversations on controversial topics. Was there greater understanding here? Do the partners feel better about one another? Finally, ask yourself how your life might change if you used more paraphrasing in everyday conversations.

2. Offer an example of what you think the speaker is talking about.

 When the speaker makes an abstract statement, you may suggest a specific example or two to see if your understanding is accurate.

 Speaker: 'Lee is such a jerk. I can't believe the way he acted last night.'

 Paraphrase: 'You think those jokes were pretty offensive, huh?'

3. Describe the underlying theme of the speaker's remarks.

 When you want to summarize the theme that seems to have run through another person's conversation, a complete or partial perception check is useful:

 Paraphrase: 'You keep reminding me to be careful. Sounds like you're worried that something might happen to me. Am I right?'

There are several reasons why paraphrasing aids in listening. First, as the preceding examples illustrate, paraphrasing allows you to find out if the message received is the message the sender intended. Second, paraphrasing often draws out further information from the speaker, much like questioning (in fact, a good paraphrase often ends with a question, such as, 'Is that what you meant?'). Third, paraphrasing is an ideal way to take the heat out of intense discussions. When conversations become heated, it is often because the people involved believe they aren't being heard. Rather than escalate the conflict, try paraphrasing what the other person says: 'Okay, let me be sure I understand you. It sounds as if you are concerned about . . .' Paraphrasing usually stops a defensive spiral because it assures the other person of your involvement and concern. When you take the time to restate and clarify a speaker's message, your commitment to listening is hard to deny.

There are two levels at which you can paraphrase messages: the first involves feedback of factual information; the second involves describing what you believe the underlying message to be.

Paraphrasing Factual Information Summarizing facts, data, and details is important during personal or professional conversations. 'We've agreed that we'll take another few days to think about our

Focus on Research

Listening in Support
of Grieving Parents

These are the powerful and painful words of communication scholar Sally Hastings (2000):

I gave birth to a beautiful baby boy, Evan, on May 25, 1997. . . . He thrived and I lavished love upon him. I was at work when Evan was fatally injured. Evan died in my arms on October 3, 1997. Nothing in my normal existence prepared me for this change in my life. . . . Agonizing, repetitive thoughts made it hard to live with myself: Good parents do not let their children die. I was not there when my child needed me. I failed. I failed. I failed. (p. 352)

To cope with her grief, Hastings linked with face-to-face and Internet support groups. She found that other bereaved parents had similar experiences and feelings, and that participating in these groups helped her deal with her sense of loss. According to Hastings, bereaved parents become members of a supportive culture who understand each other in ways that others cannot. Those outside the bereaved community she calls 'civilians': well-meaning, concerned friends and family who can never fully understand what it is like to lose a child.

Hastings offers this advice to civilians who want to offer support to bereaved parents:

• If bereaved parents want to talk, listen. In particular, if they want to talk about their child, allow them to do so without offering advice or empty platitudes.
• When in doubt, ask. Allow the bereaved parent to clarify what is helpful and what is not.
• Don't suggest or imply that bereaved parents need to 'get over it' or 'get on with their lives'. Understand that the death of their child will forever shape their identity.

Underlying Hastings' pain is important wisdom: the best way to help others in times of great distress is to respect their feelings and provide a supportive atmosphere—and to refrain from offering evaluation and advice, which are unlikely to be appreciated—in other words, to offer the support that's needed.

choices and make a decision on Tuesday—right?' might be an effective way to conclude a business lunch. A questioning tone should be used; a listener wants to be sure that meaning has been shared. Even personal topics are sometimes best handled on a factual level: 'So, your main problem is that our friends take up all the parking spaces in front of your place. Is that it?' While this 'neutral' response may be difficult when you are under attack, it helps to clarify facts before you offer your reaction. It is also a good idea to paraphrase instructions, directions, and decisions before acting on what you *think* has been said.

Paraphrasing Personal Information While restating factual information is relatively easy, it takes a sensitive ear to listen for the other person's thoughts, feelings, and wants. The 'underlying message' is often the more important message, and effective listeners try to reflect what they hear at this level. An attentive conversationalist listens for thoughts, feelings, and wants, and is thus able to address the cognitive (rational), affective (emotional), and behavioural (desired action) domains of human experience. Read the following statement as if a married, female friend is talking to you, and listen for all three components in her message:

Jean-Pierre has hardly been home all week—he's been so busy with work. He rushes in just long enough to eat dinner, then he buries himself at his desk until bedtime. Then he tells me today that he's going fishing Saturday with his buddies. I guess men are just like that—job first, play second, family third.

What is the speaker thinking, feeling, and wanting? Paraphrasing can help you find out: 'Sounds as if you're unhappy (feeling) because you think

Test Yourself Describe the three approaches to paraphrasing another person's message and explain how paraphrasing aids listening.

Jean-Pierre's ignoring you (thought) and you want him to spend more time at home (want).' Recognize that you may not be accurate; the speaker might reply, 'No, I really don't want him to spend more time at home—I just want him to pay attention to me when he's here.' Recognize also that you could identify an entirely different think–feel–want set: 'So, you're frustrated (feeling) because you'd like Jean-Pierre to change (want), but you think it's hopeless because men have different priorities (thought).' The fact that these examples offer such different interpretations of the same message demonstrates the value of paraphrasing.

Your paraphrases don't have to be as long as the examples in the preceding paragraph. In many cases, you'll want to reflect only one or two of the think–feel–want components. The key is to give feedback that is appropriate for the situation and to offer it in a way that helps the listening process. Because paraphrasing is an unfamiliar way of responding, it may feel awkward at first. If you start by paraphrasing occasionally and then

gradually do it more often, you will begin to see the benefits of this method.

It's also a good idea to mix paraphrasing with other listening responses. If, where appropriate, you are able to combine paraphrasing, questioning, and empathizing—three response styles from the 'more reflective' end of the listening continuum—you will likely achieve gratifying results in many of your everyday conversations.

Empathizing

Empathizing is a response style that listeners use when they want to show they *identify* with a speaker. As we discussed in Chapter 3, empathy involves perspective taking, emotional contagion, and genuine concern. When listeners put the attitude of empathy into verbal and non-verbal responses, they engage in empathizing. Sometimes, these responses can be quite brief: 'Uh-huh,' 'I see,' 'Wow!' 'Ouch!' 'Whew!' 'My goodness!'. In other cases, empathizing is expressed in statements like these:

'I can see that really hurts.'
'I know how important that was to you.'
'It's no fun to feel unappreciated.'
'I can tell you're really excited about that.'
'Wow, that must be rough.'
'I think I've felt that way, too.'
'Looks like that really made your day.'
'This means a lot to you, doesn't it?'

Even statements like these may not fully capture the feeling of effective empathizing, which is not reducible to a technique or skill but is something that emerges from a relationship (Myers, 2000). Genuine empathizing requires genuine identification with another person.

Empathizing falls near the middle of the listening response continuum shown in Figure 7.3 on page 201. It is different from the more reflective responses at the left end of the spectrum, which attempt to gather information neutrally. It is also different from the more evaluative styles at the right end of the spectrum, which offer more direction than reflection. To understand how empathizing

Reflection

Letting Others Give Themselves Advice

Last week, my roommate and her boyfriend were arguing. It seemed to me that she was making a much bigger deal of the situation than she should have, but I knew it would be a mistake to tell her my opinion. Besides, I could have been wrong.

So, instead of telling her what I thought (as I usually would have done), I decided to paraphrase back what she was saying. All of a sudden, she stopped talking and smiled and said, 'Gosh, I am being really dumb. This isn't even worth wasting my time on.' I was amazed! This was exactly what I had been thinking, but she got there on her own.

This approach worked especially well with my roommate because she is the kind of person who gets defensive if you come out and tell her your opinion. I think I'll use paraphrasing more often—it certainly seems better than giving advice that people do not want to hear.

compares to other types of responses, consider these examples:

'So, your boss isn't happy with your performance and you are thinking about finding a new job.' (paraphrasing)

'Ouch—I'll bet it hurt when your boss said you weren't doing a good job.' (empathizing)

'Hey, you'll land on your feet—your boss doesn't appreciate what a winner you are.' (supporting)

Notice that empathizing identifies with the speaker's emotions and perceptions more than paraphrasing does, yet offers less evaluation and agreement than supporting responses. In fact, it is possible to empathize with others while disagreeing with them. For instance, the response 'I can tell that this issue is important to you' legitimizes a speaker's feelings without assenting to that person's point of view (note that it could be said to either a friend or a foe at a business meeting). Empathizing is therefore an important skill, not only for interacting with people you agree with, but also for responding to those who see the world differently than you.

Perhaps a better way to explain empathizing is to describe what it *does not* sound like. Many listeners believe they are empathizing when, in fact, they are offering responses that are evaluative and directive. Listeners are probably *not* empathizing when they do the following:

- *Deny others the right to their feelings.* Consider this common response to another person's problem: 'Don't worry about it.' While the remark may be intended as a reassuring comment, the underlying message is that the speaker wants the person to feel different. The irony is that the suggestion will probably not work—after all, it is unlikely that people can or will stop worrying just because you tell them to. Other examples of denying feelings are 'It's nothing to get so upset about' and 'That's a silly way to feel.' Research suggests that men are more likely than women to

offer these kinds of responses (Goldsmith and Fulfs, 1999). Research also shows that empathizing is more effective than denying the feelings and perspectives of others (Burleson and Samter, 1985, 1994).

- *Minimizing the significance of the situation.* Think about the times someone said to you, 'Hey, it's only _____.' You can probably fill in the blank a variety of ways: 'a game', 'words', 'a test', 'a party'. How did you react? You probably thought the person who said it just didn't understand. To someone who has been the victim of verbal abuse, the hurtful message wasn't 'just words'; to a child who didn't get an invitation, it wasn't 'just a party' (see Burleson, 1984); to a student who has failed an important exam, it wasn't 'just a test' (see Burleson and Samter, 1985). When you minimize the importance of someone else's experience, you are not empathizing. Instead, you are interpreting the event from your perspective and then passing judgment—rarely a helpful response.
- *Self-defending.* When your response to someone else's troubles is to defend yourself ('Don't blame me; I've done my part'), it is clear you are more concerned with yourself than with the other person. In Chapter 10, we offer detailed advice for responding non-defensively to criticism.
- *Raining on the speaker's parade.* Most of the preceding examples deal with difficult situations or messages about pain. However, empathizing involves identifying with the joys of others as well as their sorrows. Many of us can remember coming home with exciting news, only to be told, 'A 5 percent raise? That isn't so great.' 'An A-minus? Why didn't you get an A?' 'Big deal—I got one of those years ago.' Taking the wind out of someone's sails is the opposite of empathizing.

Authors Florence Wolff and Nadine Marsnik (1993) believe that empathizing requires 'fine skill and exquisite tuning to another's moods and feelings' (p. 100). Research suggests that cognitive complexity and flexibility are needed to offer these non-judgmental, other-oriented responses (Applegate, 1990). Fortunately, research also shows that the ability to offer such responses can be learned by both children and adults (Clinton and Hancock, 1991; Long et al., 1999; Wei and Li, 2001). The Activities section at the end of this chapter can offer you valuable practice in developing your skills as an empathic communicator.

Supporting

So far, we have looked at listening responses that put a premium on being reflective and non-evaluative. However, there are times when other people want to hear more than a reflection of how *they* feel—when they would like to know how *you* feel about *them*. **Supporting** responses reveal the listener's solidarity with the speaker's situation. There are several types of supportive responses:

Agreement: 'You're right—the landlord is being unfair.'
'Yes, that class was tough for me, too.'

Offers to help: 'I'm here if you need me.'
'Let me try to explain it to him.'

Praise: 'I don't care what the boss said. I think you did a great job!'
'You're a terrific person! If she doesn't recognize it, that's her problem.'

Reassurance: 'The worst part seems to be over. It will probably get easier from here.'
'I know you'll do a great job.'

Diversion: 'Let's catch a movie and get your mind off this.'
'That reminds me of the time we . . .'

There's no question about the value of receiving support when faced with personal problems. 'Comforting ability' and social support have been shown to be among the most important communication skills a friend—or a teacher, or a coach, or a parent—can have (Cunningham and Barbee, 2000; Robbins and Rosenfeld, 2001; Rosenfeld and Richman, 1999; Rosenfeld et al., 1998). The value of personal support is clear when big problems arise, but research shows that smaller, everyday distresses and upsets can actually take a bigger toll on mental health and physical well-being (Ekenrode, 1984). Social support, however, can reduce the psychological distress of people dealing with a wide range of upsets (Schwarzer, 1998). Social support has been linked to improved immune function (Baron et al., 1990), better physical health, and increased lifespan (House et. al, 1988). James Pennebaker's (1995, 1997) research suggests that just having someone to talk to about upsetting experiences can make a positive impact on your physical and mental health. Social support is one of the most important resources we have to improve our quality of life.

Men and women differ in the way they act when the opportunity to support others arises. Women are more likely than men to give supportive responses when presented with another person's problem (Hale et al., 1997; Trobst et al., 1994), and are more skilful at composing such messages (Burleson, 1982). By contrast, men tend to respond to other people's problems by offering advice or by changing the subject (Barbee et al., 1990; Derlega et al., 1994). All these responses can be helpful—it just depends on the perspective of the person seeking the support.

For social support to be effective, it must match the other person's needs (Sarason et al., 1990). This means that even though you might be doing your best to help someone, you might be wasting your effort if what you offer is not what's needed. In one study, hospice workers who received emotional support from their co-workers experienced an increase in stress, whereas those who received technical challenge support experienced a decrease (Richman and Rosenfeld, 1987). The emotional support communicated 'you are right to feel overwhelmed', while the technical challenge support communicated 'you are smart and motivated to solve the problem' and pushed the workers to find solutions.

As the accompanying comic strip illustrates, even the most sincere supportive efforts do not always help. In one survey, mourners who had recently suffered the death of a loved one said that

Reflection

Comforting a Crying Child: 'It's Okay' Is Not Okay

I have always enjoyed working with young children. Sharing their joy and excitement is such a pleasure and exploring the world with them inspires my curiosity. Another important part of my job as a caring adult in children's lives is providing comfort and support when they are upset. My first reaction when children are hurt and crying has always been to try to reassure them. When I am hugging them I find myself saying, 'It's okay. It's all right.' And things like that. I realize now that, rather than being reassuring, my words could be seen as actually denying the child's true feelings. Obviously, if you are crying and someone or something has hurt you, it really isn't okay at all in that moment! It hurts. Now, I try to say things like, 'I am here. I will try to help you feel better' when I am giving my hugs. I try to acknowledge their feelings and offer to comfort and care for them.

loss for you.' One American Red Cross grief counsellor explained to survivors of the 11 September 2001 (9/11) terrorist attacks in the United States how simply being present can be more helpful than trying to reassure grief-stricken family members who had lost loved ones in the tragedy.

> Don't say anything. Saying 'it'll be okay' or 'I know how you feel' can backfire. Right now that's not what a victim wants to hear. They want to know people are there and care about them if you need them. Be there, be present, listen. The clergy refer to it as a ministry of presence. You don't need to do anything, just be there or have them know you're available. ('Attacks on U.S. soil', 2001)

Like the other kinds of helping styles, supporting can be beneficial, but only under certain conditions (Halone and Pecchioni, 2001; Goldsmith and Fitch, 1997):

- *Make sure your expression of support is sincere.* Phony agreement or encouragement is probably worse than no support at all, since it adds the insult of your dishonesty to whatever pain the other person is already feeling.
- *Be sure the other person can accept your support.* Sometimes, people are so upset that they aren't ready or able to hear anything positive.
- *Focus on 'here and now' rather than 'then and there'.* While it is sometimes true that 'you'll feel better tomorrow,' it sometimes is not (you

80 percent of the statements made to them were unhelpful (Davidowitz and Myrick, 1984). Nearly half of these unhelpful statements were advice: 'You've got to get out more.' 'Don't question God's will.' The next most frequent response was reassurance, such as, 'She's out of her pain now.' Far more helpful were expressions that acknowledged the mourner's feelings, such as, 'I know this is a painful

© ZITS Partnership. Reprinted with Special Permission of King Features Syndicate.

can probably remember times when you felt worse the next day). More important, focusing on the future avoids supporting in the present. Even if the prediction that 'ten years from now, you will not even remember her name' proves correct, it gives little comfort to someone experiencing heartbreak today. 'Everything is going to turn out fine' and 'There are other fish in the sea—you'll land one soon' are variations on the same theme. They are promises that may not come true and that tell the person to stop feeling the way she or he feels. The intentions of people who offer these sentiments may be good, but they usually do not offer the support that's needed.

Analyzing

In **analyzing** a situation, the listener offers an interpretation of a speaker's message ('I think what's really bothering you is . . .'; 'She's doing it because . . .'; or 'Maybe the problem started when he . . .'). Interpretations are often effective in helping people who have problems to consider alternative meanings of a situation—meanings they would have never thought of without your assistance. Sometimes, an analysis helps clarify a confusing problem and provide an objective understanding of the situation. Research suggests that analytic listeners are able to listen to people who are emotionally upset without experiencing similar emotions, and this can be an advantage in solving problems (Weaver and Kirtley, 1995).

In other cases, an analysis can create more problems than it solves. There are two reasons for that: First, your interpretation may not be correct, in which case the person with the problem may become even more confused by accepting it. Second, even if your analysis is accurate, sharing it with the other person may not be useful. There is a chance that it will arouse defensiveness (analysis implies being superior and in a position to evaluate). Besides, the person with the problem may not be able to understand your view of the problem without working it out personally.

How can you know when it's helpful to offer an analysis? There are several guidelines to follow:

- *Offer your interpretation in a tentative way rather than as absolute fact.* There's a big difference between saying, 'Maybe the reason is . . .' and insisting, 'This is the truth.'
- *Your analysis ought to have a reasonable chance of being correct.* An inaccurate interpretation—especially one that sounds plausible—can leave a person more confused than before.
- *Make sure that the other person will be receptive to your analysis.* Even if you are completely accurate, your thoughts will not help if the other person is not ready to consider them. Pay attention to the other person's verbal and non-verbal cues to see how your analysis is being received.
- *Be sure that your motive for offering an analysis is truly to help the other person.* It can be tempting to offer an analysis to show how brilliant you are or even to make the other person feel bad for not having thought of the right answer in the first place. Needless to say, an analysis offered under such conditions is not helpful.

Evaluating

An **evaluating** response appraises the sender's thoughts or behaviour in some way. The evaluation may be favourable ('That's a good idea' or 'You are on the right track now') or unfavourable ('An attitude like that won't get you anywhere'). In either case, it implies that the person evaluating is in some way qualified to pass judgment on the speaker's thoughts or actions.

Sometimes, negative evaluations are purely critical. How many times have you heard responses such as, 'Well, you asked for it!' or 'I told you so!' or 'You're just feeling sorry for yourself'? Although such comments can sometimes serve as a verbal slap that 'knocks sense' into the problem holder, they usually make matters worse by arousing defensiveness in that person. After all, suggesting that someone is foolish or mistaken is an attack on the presenting image that most people would have a hard time ignoring or accepting.

Other times, negative evaluations are less critical. These involve what we usually call constructive

Self-Assessment

Your Listening Responses

Learn more about your helping style by indicating how you would most likely respond to each of the statements below. Don't try to guess the 'right' response. Choose the response that is closest to what you would probably say after hearing each statement.

1. 'I think I understand the material, but I don't know where I stand in the course. I'm not sure what the instructor expects of me, and she doesn't tell me how I'm doing. I wish I knew where I stood.'
   a) 'Has your instructor ever given you any indication of what she thinks of your work?'
   b) 'If I were you, I'd discuss it with her.'
   c) 'She's probably just trying to give everyone in the class a lot of freedom to do what they want to do.'
   d) 'It sounds as if you're worried about your grade. Is that it?'
   e) 'Don't take it so seriously. Most of the time in school, you don't know where you stand.'
   f) 'What do you think you can do to solve this situation? What have you tried?'
   g) 'I've had teachers like that, and it's a lousy situation.'

2. 'The policy in the chemistry department is supposed to be to hire lab assistants from people in the advanced chemistry classes. And now I find that this person from a beginning class is getting hired. I had my eye on that job; I've been working hard for it. I know I could be a terrific assistant if I had a chance.'
   a) 'I can tell how disappointed you are.'
   b) 'Why do you think they hired the person from the beginning class?'
   c) 'If not getting the job means not having enough money to make it through the semester, I can help out with a loan.'
   d) 'Getting ahead is very important to you, and it sounds as if you feel cheated that someone else got the job as lab assistant.'
   e) 'You should take some more chemistry classes to help you advance.'
   f) 'I told you not to get your hopes up.'
   g) 'You shouldn't complain—they probably hired the best person to be an assistant.'

3. 'I'm really tired of this. I'm taking more classes than anyone I know, and then on the same day, three of my teachers tell me that there's another assignment due on top of what's already due. I've got so many people asking me to do things that I just can't keep up, and it bothers me. I like my teachers, and my classes are interesting, but I am getting overwhelmed.'
   a) 'With so many teachers asking you to do extra assignments, it's difficult for you to accomplish all of it, and the pressure gets you down.'
   b) 'Are all these requests from your teachers required work?'
   c) 'I'm really sorry you feel so overwhelmed.'
   d) 'You seem to have too much work. Why don't you talk it over with your teachers?'
   e) 'Yikes! Sounds like things are pretty hectic for you right now.'
   f) 'You're probably overworked because you are not organized.'
   g) 'Who told you to take so many classes?'

4. 'My teacher tells the class that he would appreciate getting term projects as soon as possible to help him with grading. So I work like mad to get it completed and on his desk early. What's my reward for helping him out? Nothing! No thanks, no nothing. In fact, I think my project will sit on his desk until all the projects are handed in.'
   a) 'How often do teachers do this to you?'
   b) 'And you believed him because . . . ?'
   c) 'You ought to tell him how you feel.'
   d) 'You feel resentful because you think he's taking advantage of you?'
   e) 'I hate it when teachers do that to us!'
   f) 'I hear you! Been there, felt that—it's no fun.'
   g) 'Your reward is having finished the work early.'

5. 'He used to be one of the guys until he was made the team's coach. Now, it's like he's not my friend any more. I don't mind being told about my mistakes, but he doesn't have to do it in front of the rest of the team. Whenever I get the chance, he's going to get his!'
   a) 'Revenge is only one way of handling this.'
   b) 'I'll bet that really upset you—and I can understand why.'

---

c) 'To be told about your mistakes in front of the rest of the team is embarrassing, especially by a person you once considered a friend.'

d) 'If you didn't make so many mistakes, the coach wouldn't have to tell you about them.'

e) 'Why don't we talk it over with a few other people on the team and then go and talk to him about this situation?'

f) 'How often does he criticize you in front of the others?'

g) 'Seems like he's on a power trip.'

Listed below are the possible response types for each of the five situations. For example, if you indicated answer *a* in situation number 1, note that this is a 'questioning response'. If you indicated answer *b*, note that this is an 'advising response'. Do this for your five responses.

Questioning response: 1a, 2b, 3b, 4a, 5f

Advising response: 1b, 2e, 3d, 4c, 5e

Analyzing response: 1c, 2g, 3f, 4e, 5g

Paraphrasing response: 1d, 2d, 3a, 4d, 5c

Evaluating response: 1e, 2f, 3g, 4b, 5d

Supportive response: 1f (technical challenge support), 2c (tangible support), 3c (emotional support), 4f (listening support), 5a (emotional challenge support)

Empathizing response: 1g, 2a, 3e, 4e, 5b

Do you have a particular way of responding? What does this tell you about how you listen—that is, the kinds of information you listen for? When is your typical way of responding most and least useful? What do you think is the most useful response in each of the five situations?

---

criticism, which is intended to help the problem holder improve in the future. Friends give this sort of response about the choice of everything from clothing to jobs to friends. A common setting for constructive criticism is school, where instructors evaluate students' work in order to help them master concepts and skills. Even constructive criticism can arouse defensiveness because it may threaten the self-concept of the person at whom it is directed.

Evaluations have the best chance of being received when two conditions exist:

- *The person with the problem should have requested an evaluation from you.* Occasionally, an unsolicited judgment may bring someone to his or her senses, but more often, it will trigger a defensive response.

- *Your evaluation should be genuinely constructive and not designed as a put-down.* If you are tempted to use evaluations as a weapon, do not fool yourself into thinking that you are being helpful. Often, statements such as 'I'm telling you this for your own good' are simply not true.

Advising

When we are approached with someone's problem, the most common reaction is **to advise** (Notarius and Herrick, 1988). Giving advice involves providing the speaker with your opinion about what they should do. Advice can be offered in at least three situations. The first would be when it is requested in a straightforward manner: 'What do you think I should do?' In a second kind of situation, an ambiguous statement might sound like a request for suggestions (Goldsmith, 2000). Ambiguous statements of this sort include requests for opinions ('What do you think of Philippe?'), soliciting information ('Would that be an example of sexual harassment?'), and announcement of a problem ('I'm really confused . . .'). Finally, advice is sometimes offered even when it hasn't been solicited ('You look awful. You ought to get more sleep!').

Advice is not always as helpful as it might seem. In interviews with bereaved people who had recently lost a loved one, almost half of them received gestures of sympathy consisting of advice, yet the suggestions were rated as helpful only 3 percent of the time (Davidowitz and Myrick, 1984). Advice is most welcome under two conditions: when it has been requested, and when the adviser seems concerned with respecting the face-saving needs of the recipient (Goldsmith, 2000; Goldsmith and MacGeorge, 2000; MacGeorge et al., 2002).

Even when advice is requested and offered in a face-saving manner, there are several reasons why it often is not helpful. First, it may not offer the best suggestion about how to act. In fact, it may even be harmful. There may often be a temptation to tell others how you would behave in their place, but it is important to realize that what's right for one person may not be right for another. A related consequence of advising is that it often allows others to avoid responsibility for their decisions. A partner who follows a suggestion of yours that does not work out can always pin the blame on you. Finally, people often do not want advice. They may not be ready to accept it and instead may simply need to talk out their thoughts and feelings. Research suggests that unsolicited advice threatens the presenting self of the recipient (Goldsmith, 2000). In effect, the adviser who gives advice without being asked to do so seems to be suggesting that there is something wrong with the recipient . . . not a welcome message.

You should offer advice, then, only under the following four conditions:

- *You are sure the other person really wants to hear your suggestions.* The best indicator is a clear request for advice. If you are not sure whether the other person is seeking your opinion, it may be best to ask.
- *You have considered whether the person seeking your advice is truly ready to accept it.* This way, you can avoid the frustration of making good suggestions only to find that the person with the problem had another solution in mind all the time.
- *You are confident that your advice is correct.* Resist the temptation to act like an authority on matters you know little about or to make suggestions when you are not positive that they are the best choice. Realize that while a

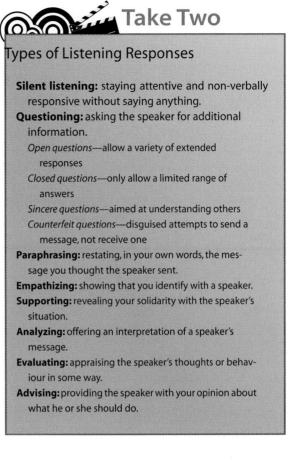

Take Two

Types of Listening Responses

Silent listening: staying attentive and non-verbally responsive without saying anything.

Questioning: asking the speaker for additional information.

Open questions—allow a variety of extended responses

Closed questions—only allow a limited range of answers

Sincere questions—aimed at understanding others

Counterfeit questions—disguised attempts to send a message, not receive one

Paraphrasing: restating, in your own words, the message you thought the speaker sent.

Empathizing: showing that you identify with a speaker.

Supporting: revealing your solidarity with the speaker's situation.

Analyzing: offering an interpretation of a speaker's message.

Evaluating: appraising the speaker's thoughts or behaviour in some way.

Advising: providing the speaker with your opinion about what he or she should do.

particular course of action worked for you, it probably will not be correct for everybody.

- *You are certain that the recipient won't blame you if the advice doesn't work out.* You may be offering the suggestions but the choice and responsibility for accepting them is up to the recipient of your advice.

Which Style to Use?

By now, it should be clear that there are many ways to respond as a listener. You also can see that each style has advantages and disadvantages. Which style is best? There is no simple answer to this question. Research shows that all response styles have the potential to help others accept their situation, feel better, and have a sense of control over their problems (Albrecht and Adelman, 1987; Burleson, 1994).

As a general rule, it is probably wise to begin with responses from the left and middle of the listening response continuum: silent listening, questioning, paraphrasing, empathizing, and supporting. Once you have gathered the facts and demonstrated your interest and concern, it's likely that the speaker will be more receptive to (and perhaps even ask for) your analyzing, evaluating, and advising responses.

You can improve the odds of choosing the best style in each situation by considering three factors. First, think about the *situation*, and match your response to the nature of the problem. People sometimes need your advice. In other cases, your encouragement and support will be most helpful, and in still other cases, your analysis or judgment may be truly useful. And, as you have seen, there are times when your questioning and paraphrasing can help others find their own answer.

Besides considering the situation, you also should think about the *other person* when deciding which approach to use. As the Focus on Research box about Sally Hastings on page 207 demonstrates, it is important to be sure that the other person is open to receiving *any* kind of help. Furthermore, you need to be confident that you will be regarded as someone whose support is valuable. The same response that would be accepted with gratitude when it comes from one communicator can be regarded as unhelpful when it is offered by the wrong person (Clark et al., 1998; Sullivan, 1996).

It is also important to match the type of response you offer with the style of the person to whom it is directed (Bippus, 2001). Some people are able to consider advice thoughtfully, while others use suggestions to avoid making their own decisions. Many communicators are extremely defensive and

are not capable of receiving analysis or judgments without lashing out. Still others are not equipped to think through problems clearly enough to profit from questioning and paraphrasing. Sophisticated listeners choose a style that fits the person.

Finally, think about *yourself* when deciding how to respond. Most of us reflexively use one or two styles (did you notice this when you completed the Self-Assessment on pages 213–14?). You may be best at listening quietly, posing a question, or paraphrasing from time to time. Or perhaps you are especially insightful and can offer a truly useful analysis of the problem. Of course, it's also possible to rely on a response style that is *unhelpful*. You may be overly judgmental or too eager to advise, even when your suggestions are not invited or productive. As you think about how to respond to another's problems, consider your weaknesses as well as your strengths.

Summary

Listening is both more frequent and less emphasized than speaking. Despite its relative invisibility, listening is at least as important as speaking. Research shows that good listening is vital to both personal and professional success. There are a variety of reasons why we listen to others. At the most basic level, we listen to understand and retain information. Perhaps more important, we listen to build and maintain our interpersonal relationships. We may listen to help others and also to evaluate their messages.

Most people's understanding of listening suffers from several misconceptions, which communicators need to correct. Listening—at least listening effectively—is quite different from merely hearing a message. Skilful listening is not easy; rather, it is a challenge that requires much effort and talent. Several barriers can hamper effective listening: hearing problems, information overload, rapid thought, and both internal and external noise. Even careful listening does not mean that all listeners will

Test Yourself   What factors should you consider before you choose how to respond as a listener?

Building Work Skills

Which Listening Style Is Best?

Explore the various types of listening responses by completing the following steps.

a. Join with two partners to form a trio. Designate members as persons A, B, and C.

b. Person A begins by sharing an actual, current work- or school-related problem with B. The problem need not be a major life crisis, but it should be a real one. Person B should respond in whatever way that seems most helpful. Person C's job is to categorize each response by B as silent listening, questioning, paraphrasing, empathizing, supporting, analyzing, evaluating, or advising.

c. After a four- to five-minute discussion, C should summarize B's response styles. Person A then describes which of the styles were most helpful and which were not helpful.

d. Repeat the same process twice more, switching roles so that each person has been in all of the positions.

e. Based on your findings, your threesome should draw conclusions about what combination of response styles can be most helpful.

receive the same message. A wide variety of factors discussed in this chapter can result in hugely varying interpretations of even simple statements.

Listening consists of several components: *hearing, paying attention to a message, understanding the statement, remembering the message after the passage of time*, and *responding to the speaker*. Listening responses are important because they let us know if others are truly tuned in to what we're saying. Listening responses can be placed on a continuum. More reflective and less directive responses include silent listening, questioning, paraphrasing, and empathizing. These put a premium on gathering information and showing interest and concern. Less reflective and more directive responses include supporting, analyzing, evaluating, and advising. These put a premium on offering input and direction. It is possible to use the 'more reflective' listening responses to help people arrive at their own decisions without offering advice or evaluation. The most effective listeners use several styles, depending on the situation, the other person, and their own personal skills and motivation.

Activities

1. **Invitation to Insight**
   You can learn to stop believing in some common myths about listening by remembering specific instances when

   a. you heard another person's message but did not pay attention to it,
   b. you attended to a message but forgot it almost immediately,
   c. you attended to and remembered a message but did not understand it accurately, or
   d. you understood a message but did not respond sufficiently to convey your understanding to the sender.

2. **Invitation to Insight**
   Keep a three-day journal of your listening behaviour, noting the time you spend listening in various situations. In addition, analyze your reasons for listening. Which goal(s) were you trying to achieve?

   a. To understand and retain information
   b. To build and maintain relationships
   c. To help
   d. To evaluate

3. **Critical Thinking Probe**
   Communication problems can arise from factors that are not easily observed. Based on your experience, decide which of the following steps in the listening process cause the greatest difficulties:

   a. hearing
   b. attending
   c. understanding
   d. remembering
   e. responding

Discuss your findings with your friends, and develop a list of remedies that can help minimize listening problems in the areas you identified.

4. **Skill Builder**
   Explore the benefits of silent listening by using a 'talking stick'. Richard Hyde (1993) developed this exercise from the Native American tradition of 'council'. Gather a group of people in a circle, and designate a particular item as the talking stick. Participants will then pass the stick around the circle. Participants may speak

   a. only when holding the stick;
   b. for as long as they hold the stick; and
   c. without interruption from anyone else in the circle.

   When a member is through speaking, the stick passes to the left and the speaker surrendering the stick must wait until it has made its way around the circle before speaking again.

   After each member of the group has had the chance to speak, discuss how this experience differs from more common approaches to listening. Decide how the desirable parts of this method could be introduced in everyday conversations.

5. **Ethical Challenge**
   What responsibility do communicators have to listen as carefully and thoughtfully as possible to other speakers? Are there ever cases where certain types of non-listening listed on pages 196–7 (e.g., pseudo-listening, stage hogging, and defensive listening) are justified? How would you feel if you knew that others were not listening to you?

6. **Role Play**

   Choose a partner.

   a. One person will provide a factual description of something they know how to do and the other person doesn't (e.g., cook a particular dish, fix something, perform a function on a particular brand of cell phone, etc.). The other person will listen and use paraphrasing to clarify and ensure he or she understands. Now, reverse roles.

   b. Next, one person will describe a personal situation (ensure you are comfortable disclosing the information) that involves thoughts and emotions. The other person will listen and paraphrase to ensure he or she understands. Now, reverse roles.

   c. Discuss the strengths and challenges of paraphrasing in both situations from the perspective of the listener and the speaker.

Discussion Questions

1. Discuss the benefits of good listening skills.
2. Describe instances in your own life when you have listened for each of the four reasons discussed in this chapter.
3. Why is listening not an easy communication task? Describe the four barriers to listening discussed in the chapter.
4. Give an example from your own experience of each of the seven types of non-listening described in this chapter.
5. Explain how things can go wrong in each of the five components of listening.
6. Describe paraphrasing and its benefits.
7. When are advising and evaluating appropriate listening responses? When should they be avoided?

Chapter Eight

Dynamics of Interpersonal Relationships

After studying the material in this chapter . . .

You Should Understand:

1. The reasons people choose others as potential relational partners.
2. The stages of relational development and the characteristics of movement between these stages.
3. The dialectical tensions that can arise as communicators attempt to satisfy conflicting needs.
4. The ways content and relational messages are communicated in interpersonal relationships.
5. The strategies that can be used to gain compliance in a relationship.

You Should Be Able To:

1. Identify the bases of interpersonal attraction in one of your relationships.
2. Describe the current stage of an important personal relationship and predict whether and how that relationship might move to a more satisfying stage.
3. Identify the dialectical tensions that influence your communication goals, the strategies you use to manage these tensions, and alternative strategies you might consider using.
4. Choose the most promising compliance-gaining strategy you could use in a given situation.

There is no question that personal relationships matter. To understand just how important they are, imagine how your life would suffer without friends, family, fellow workers, or romantic partners. Almost as bad would be to have poor relationships with these people. It's no surprise that respondents to one survey identified interpersonal relationships as more important than anything else in making their lives meaningful (Campbell et al., 1976).

What does it mean to have a relationship with another person? Communication theorist Charles Berger (1993) offers some basic conditions. For a relationship to exist, the people must be aware of each other and take each other into account. This means that the ritualistic or automated exchanges like those between customers and the person who takes orders at a fast-food restaurant wouldn't count. Another basic ingredient of a relationship is that at least one person must affect the other in some way. For example, teachers affect students (and vice versa), and family members certainly influence one another for better or worse. Berger suggests that a third ingredient of relationships is some agreement about the social form and expectations that govern the interaction. You can appreciate the importance of shared relational definitions by imagining yourself far from home, asking a stranger for directions. The way you and that person relate to each other would define the relationship. For example, is the encounter merely an exchange of information, or is it more personal? Until you and the other person work out this fundamental question, the relationship would not be defined.

Most people intuitively understand the importance of communication in the development and maintenance of interpersonal relationships. The quality of interaction helps shape the quantity of communication. For instance, Virginia Richmond (1995) found that satisfied couples talk more to each other than dissatisfied couples, especially about certain 'important' topics such as their life together at home, their sexual relationship, and their recreational time. The quality of communication is certainly as important as quantity. Besides

helping to create relational satisfaction, communication reflects the kind of relationship that exists: what kinds of feelings partners hold about each other, and where the relationship is headed.

In this chapter, we introduce some of the dynamics that characterize interpersonal relationships and the communication that occurs within them. After reading the chapter, you will see that relationships are not fixed or unchanging. Rather, they can, and often do, change over time. In other words, a relationship is less a *thing* than a *process*. You might establish a businesslike pattern with a fellow worker and later find that the relationship has changed into a friendship. Likewise, professors and students might begin interacting according to traditional roles and later find that their communication develops into some other form. The same phenomenon is true in close relationships. For example, the quality of interaction in a family usually changes when children reach late adolescence. Patterns that worked well enough between grown-ups and youngsters do not work well when

iStock photo

all the family members are adults (Preto, 1999). New definitions of power, affection, and respect may become necessary. In a sense, the relationship is reinvented. To see how, read on.

Why We Form Relationships

Why do we form relationships with some people and not with others? Sometimes, we have no choice. Children can't choose their parents, and most workers aren't able to choose their colleagues. In many other cases, however, we seek out some people and actively avoid others. Social scientists have collected an impressive body of research on interpersonal attraction (see, for example, Byrne, 1997; Poole et al., 1987). The following are some of the factors they have identified that influence our choice of relational partners.

Appearance

Most people claim that we should judge others on the basis of how they act, not how they look. However, the reality is quite the opposite (Hatfield and Sprecher, 1986). Appearance is especially important in the early stages of a relationship. In one study, a group of over seven hundred men and women were matched as blind dates, allegedly for a 'computer dance'. After the party was over, they were asked whether or not they would like to date their partners again. The result? The more physically attractive the person (as judged in advance by independent raters), the more likely he or she was seen as desirable. Other factors—social skills and intelligence, for example—did not seem to affect the decision (Walster et al., 1966).

As we discussed in Chapter 6, the influence of physical attractiveness begins early in life. Infants as young as six months prefer pictures of attractive faces to less appealing ones (Rubenstein et al., 1999). From age five on, overweight boys are viewed by peers as less attractive; tall, thin ones are judged to be introverted and nervous; and muscular and athletic youngsters are seen as outgoing, active, and popular (Aboud and Mendelson, 1998; Staffieri, 1967). The same principle continues into adult life. Handsome men and beautiful women are seen as more sensitive, kind, interesting, strong, poised, modest, sociable, outgoing, and exciting than their less attractive counterparts (Dion et al., 1972). Adults are more likely to interact with strangers they consider attractive (Mulford et al., 1998). Senior citizens also rate good-looking people as more desirable than those who are less attractive (Larose and Standing, 1998).

Although we might assume that attractive people are radically different from those who are less attractive, the truth is that we view the familiar as beautiful. Langlois and Roggman (1990) presented raters with two types of photos. Some were of people from northern European, Asian, and Latino backgrounds, while others were computer-generated images that combined the characteristics of several individuals. Surprisingly, the judges consistently preferred the composite photos of both men and women. When the features of eight or more individuals were combined into one image, viewers rated the picture as more attractive than the features of a single person or of a smaller combination of people. Thus, we seem to be drawn to people who represent the most average qualities of ourselves and those people we know. In other words, beautiful people aren't different from the rest of us. Rather, they are 'radically similar'.

Even if your appearance is not beautiful by societal standards, consider these encouraging facts. First, after initial impressions have passed, ordinary-looking people with pleasing personalities are likely to be judged as attractive (Berscheid and Walster, 1978). Second, physical factors become less important as a relationship progresses. As Don Hamachek (1982, p. 59) puts it, 'Attractive features may open doors, but apparently, it takes more than physical beauty to keep them open.'

Similarity

It's comforting to know someone who likes the same things you like, has similar values, and may even be of the same race, economic class, or educational standing. The basis for this sort of relationship, commonly known as the *similarity thesis*, is the most frequently discussed of the several bases of relationship formation (Buss, 1985). For example, friends in middle and high school reported being similar to each other in many ways, including having mutual friends, enjoying the same sports, liking the same social activities, and using (or not using) alcohol and cigarettes to the same degree (Aboud and Mendelson, 1998; Urberg et al., 1998). For adults, similarity is more important to relational happiness than even communication ability. Friends who have low levels of communication skills are just as satisfied with their relationships as are friends having high levels of skills (Burleson and Samter, 1996).

There are several reasons why similarity is a strong foundation for relationships. First, the other person serves as an external indication—a social validation—that we are not alone in our thinking, that we're not too peculiar. Someone else *did* like the same controversial book you liked. Therefore, this other person offers good support for you, reinforcing your own sense of what is right.

Second, when someone is similar to you, you can make fairly accurate predictions—whether the person will want to eat at a Thai restaurant or hear the concert you're so excited about. This ability to make confident predictions reduces uncertainty and anxiety (Duck and Barnes, 1992).

There's a third explanation for the similarity thesis. It may be that when we learn that other people are similar to us, we assume they will probably like us, so we in turn like them. The self-fulfilling prophecy creeps into the picture again.

iStock photo

Similarity turns from attraction to dislike when we encounter people who are like us in many ways but who behave in a strange or socially offensive manner (Cooper and Jones, 1969; Taylor and Mette, 1971). For instance, you have probably disliked people others have said were 'just like you' but who talked too much, were complainers, or had some other unappealing characteristic. In fact, there is a tendency to have stronger dislike for similar but offensive people than for those who are offensive but different. One likely reason is that such people threaten our self-esteem, causing us to fear that we may be as unappealing as they are. In such circumstances, the reaction is often to put as much distance as possible between ourselves and this threat to our ideal self-image.

Complementarity

The old saying 'opposites attract' seems to contradict the principle of similarity we just described. In truth, though, both are valid. Differences strengthen a relationship when they are *complementary*—when each partner's characteristics satisfy the other's needs. For instance, couples are more likely to be attracted to each other when one partner is dominant and the other passive (Nowicki and Manheim, 1991; Winch, 1958). Relationships also work well when the partners agree that one will exercise control in certain areas ('You make the final decisions about money') and the other will take the lead in different ones ('I'll decide how we ought to decorate the place'). Strains occur when control issues are disputed.

Studies that have examined successful and unsuccessful couples over a twenty-year period show the interaction between similarities and differences. When partners are radically different, the dissimilar qualities that at first appear intriguing later become cause for relational breakups (Felmlee, 1998). Partners in successful marriages were similar enough to satisfy each other physically and mentally, but were different enough to meet each other's needs and keep the relationship interesting. The successful couples found ways to keep a balance between their similarities and differences while adjusting to the changes that occurred over the years.

Rewards

Some relationships are based on an economic model called **social exchange theory** (Homans, 1961; Thibaut and Kelley, 1959). This approach suggests that we often seek out people who can give us rewards that are greater than or equal to the costs we encounter in dealing with them. Social exchange theorists define rewards as any outcomes we desire. They may be tangible (a nice place to live, a high-paying job) or intangible (prestige, emotional support, companionship). Costs are undesirable outcomes, such as unpleasant work, emotional pain, and so on. A simple formula captures the social exchange explanation for why we form and maintain relationships:

Rewards – Costs = Outcome

According to social exchange theorists, we use this formula (often unconsciously) to calculate whether a relationship is a 'good deal' or 'not worth the effort', that is, whether the outcome is positive or negative.

At its most blatant level, an exchange approach seems cold and calculating; but it seems quite appropriate in some types of relationships. A healthy business relationship is based on how well the parties help one another, and some friendships are based on an informal kind of barter: 'I don't mind listening to the ups and downs of your love life because you rescue me when the house needs repairs.' Even close relationships have an element of exchange. Friends and lovers often tolerate each other's quirks because the comfort and enjoyment they get make the less-than-pleasant times worth accepting.

Costs and rewards do not exist in isolation. We define them by comparing a certain situation with alternatives. For example, consider a hypothetical woman, Gloria, who is struggling to decide whether to remain in a relationship with Raymond, her long-time boyfriend. Raymond does love Gloria, but he has a hair-trigger temper and he has become verbally abusive from time to time. Also, Gloria knows that Raymond was unfaithful to her at least once. In deciding whether or not to stay with Raymond, Gloria will use two standards.

The first is her **comparison level** (CL)—her minimum standard of what behaviour is acceptable. If Gloria believes that relational partners have an obligation to be faithful and treat one another respectfully at all times, then Raymond's behaviour will fall below her comparison level. On the other hand, if Gloria adopts a 'nobody's perfect' standard, she is more likely to view Raymond's behaviour as meeting or exceeding her comparison level.

Gloria will also rate Raymond according to her **comparison level of alternatives** (CL^{alt}). This standard refers to a comparison between the rewards she is receiving in her present situation and those she could expect to receive in others. If, for example, Gloria doesn't want to be alone, her CL^{alt} would be lower than her present situation; but if she is confident that she could find a kinder partner, her CL^{alt} would be higher than the status quo.

Social exchange theorists suggest that communicators unconsciously use this calculation to decide whether to form and stay in relationships. At first, this information seems to offer little comfort to communicators who are in unsatisfying relationships such as those where $CL > CL^{alt}$. But there are alternatives to being stuck in situations where the costs outweigh the rewards. First, you might make sure that you are judging your present relationship against a realistic comparison level. Expecting a situation to be perfect can be a recipe for unhappiness. (Recall the discussion of the 'fallacy of should' in Chapter 4.) If you decide that your present situation truly falls below your comparison level, you might look for alternatives you have not considered. And finally, the skills introduced

Take Two

- **Social exchange theory:** the practice of seeking out people who can give us rewards greater than the costs of dealing with them.
- **Comparison level** (CL): a minimum standard of behaviour that is acceptable.
- **Comparison level of alternatives** (CL^{alt}): a comparison between rewards in present situation and those one could expect to receive from others.

throughout this book may help you negotiate a better relationship with the other person.

Competence

We like to be around talented people, probably because we hope their skills and abilities will rub off on us. On the other hand, we are uncomfortable around those who are too competent—probably because we look bad by comparison. Elliot Aronson and his associates (1966) demonstrated how competence and imperfection combine to affect attraction by having subjects evaluate tape recordings of candidates for a quiz program. One was a 'perfect' candidate who answered almost all the questions correctly and modestly admitted that he was an honours student, athlete, and college yearbook editor. The 'average' candidate answered fewer questions correctly, had average grades, was a less-successful athlete, and was a low-level member of the yearbook staff. Toward the end of half the tapes, the candidates committed a blunder, spilling coffee all over themselves. The remaining half of the tapes contained no such blunder. These, then, were the four experimental conditions: (1) a person with superior ability who blundered; (2) a person with superior ability who did not blunder; (3) an average person who blundered; and (4) an average person who did not blunder. The students who rated the attractiveness of these four types of people revealed an interesting and important principle of interpersonal attraction. The most attractive person was the superior candidate who blundered. Next was the superior person who did not blunder. Third was the average person who did not blunder. The least attractive person was the average person who committed the blunder.

Aronson's conclusion was that we tend to like people who are somewhat flawed because they remind us of ourselves. However, there are some qualifications to this principle. People with especially positive or negative self-esteem find 'perfect' people more attractive than those who are competent but flawed (Helmreich et al., 1970). Furthermore, women tend to be more impressed by uniformly superior people, whereas men find desirable but 'human' subjects especially attractive (Deaux, 1972). On the whole, though, the best

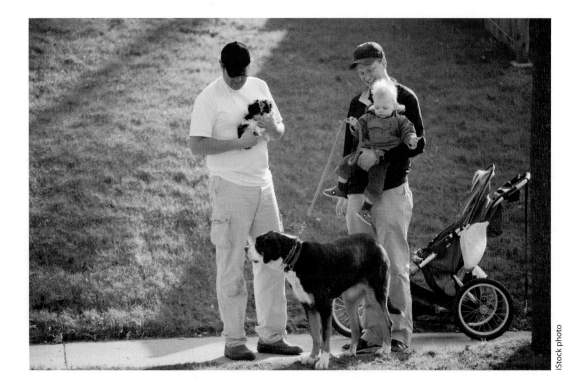

iStock photo

way to gain the liking of others is to be good at what you do but also to admit your mistakes.

Proximity

As common sense suggests, we are likely to develop relationships with people whom we often interact with. In many cases, proximity leads to liking. For instance, we're more likely to develop friendships with close neighbours than with distant ones, and the chances are good that we will choose as a mate a person we cross paths with often. Facts like these are understandable when we consider that proximity allows us to get more information about other people and benefit from a relationship with them. Also, people in close proximity may be more similar to us than those not close—for example, if we live in the same neighbourhood, the odds are we have the same socio-economic status.

Familiarity, on the other hand, can breed contempt. Evidence to support this fact comes from police blotters as well as university laboratories. Thieves frequently prey on nearby victims, even though the risk of being recognized is greater. Most aggravated assaults occur within the family or among close neighbours. Similarly, you are likely to develop strong personal feelings, either positive or negative, toward others you encounter frequently.

Disclosure

Telling others important information about yourself can help build liking (Derlega et al., 1993; Dindia, 2002). Sometimes, the basis of this attraction comes from learning about ways we are similar, either in experiences ('I broke off an engagement myself') or in attitudes ('I feel nervous with strangers, too'). Self-disclosure also increases liking because it is a sign of regard. Sharing private information is a form of respect and trust—a kind of liking that we have already seen increases attractiveness.

Not all disclosure, however, leads to liking. Research shows that the key to satisfying self-disclosure is *reciprocity*, that is, getting back an amount and kind of information equivalent to that which you reveal (Altman, 1973; Derlega et al., 1976; Dindia, 2000a). A second important ingredient in successful self-disclosure is *timing*.

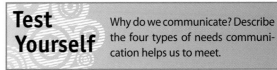

Test Yourself   Why do we communicate? Describe the four types of needs communication helps us to meet.

It's probably unwise to talk about your sexual insecurities with a new acquaintance or express your pet peeves to a friend at your birthday party. The information you reveal ought to be appropriate for the setting and stage of the relationship (Archer and Berg, 1978; Wortman et al., 1976). Chapter 9 contains more information on the subject of self-disclosure.

Communication and Relational Dynamics

Even the most stable relationships vary from day to day and over longer periods of time. Communication scholars have tried to describe and explain how communication creates and reflects the changing dynamics of relational interaction. In the following sections, we describe two very different characterizations of relational development and interaction.

Developmental Models of Interpersonal Relationships

One of the best-known models of relational stages was developed by Mark Knapp (Knapp and Vangelisti, 2000; see also Avtgis et al., 1998; Welch and Rubin, 2002), who broke the waxing and waning of relationships into ten steps. Other researchers have suggested that in addition to explaining how people come together and come apart, any model of relational communication ought to contain a third area, **relational maintenance**—communication aimed at keeping relationships operating smoothly and satisfactorily. Relational maintenance includes behaving in a positive way, being open, and assuring your partner that you are committed to the relationship (Dainton, 2000). Figure 8.1 shows how Knapp's ten stages fit into this three-part view of relational communication. This model seems most useful

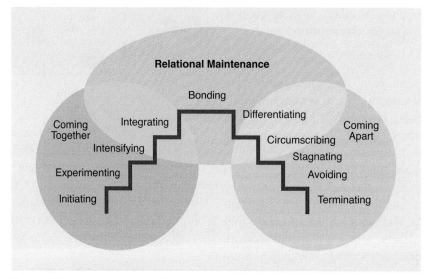

Figure 8.1 Stages of Relational Development

Source: From Mark L. Knapp and Anita L. Vangelisti, *Interpersonal Communication and Human Relationships* (4th Ed.). Published by Allyn and Bacon, Boston, MA. Copyright © 2000 by Pearson Education. Reprinted by permission of the publisher.

for describing communication between romantic partners, but in many respects, it works well for other types of close relationships. As you read the following section, consider how the stages could describe a long-term friendship, a couple in love, or even business partners.

Initiating   The goals in the initiating stage are to show that you are interested in making contact and to demonstrate that you are a person worth talking to. Communication during this stage is usually brief, and it generally follows conventional formulas, such as handshakes, comments about innocuous subjects such as the weather, and friendly remarks. Such behaviour may seem superficial and meaningless, but it is a way of signalling that you are interested in building some kind of relationship with the other person. It allows us to say, without saying, 'I'm a friendly person, and I'd like to get to know you.'

Beginning a relationship requires a fair measure of skill. One study revealed several strategies that are both efficient and socially acceptable ways to learn about others (Douglas, 1987). The first is *networking*—getting information about the other person from a third party who helps the

first moments of contact go well. Another strategy is *offering*—putting yourself in a favourable position to be approached by the desired partner. Offering strategies might include picking a seat in class near the person you would like to meet, or hanging around the hors d'oeuvre at a party until the attractive person drops by for a snack. A third technique is *approaching*—signalling your desire for contact, either verbally or non-verbally. Typical approaches include smiles and self-introductions. (Incredibly, there are people who never even try such seemingly obvious strategies, instead waiting for interesting people to approach them.) A final initiating strategy is *sustaining*—behaving in ways to keep the conversation going. Asking questions is a typical sustaining technique.

Other approaches tested in the study proved less effective, either because they didn't work or because they were socially inappropriate. Expressing feelings ('Do you like me?') was too forward for most initial contacts. Remaining silent (either to be coy or from an inability to know what to say) didn't work. Seeking favours that were inconvenient to the other person was rarely successful. Finally, diminishing oneself ('I'm such a dope!') seldom worked well.

Beginning a relationship—especially a romantic one—can be particularly difficult for people who are shy. As we noted in Chapter 4, computer-mediated communication can make it easier for reticent people to strike up a relationship. One study of an online dating service found that participants who described themselves as shy expressed a greater appreciation for the system's anonymous, non-threatening environment than did non-shy users (Scharlott and Christ, 1995). Similarly, people who become anxious in social situations often prefer using text messages to attempt intimate contact with other people rather than talking to them on the phone (Reid and Reid, 2007). Communicating by way of written messages (email, text) has the advantage of allowing the sender to carefully compose the message and present him- or herself in a particular way (identity management)—as a result, many people are often more candid in their text messages (Reid and Reid, 2005). Text-messaging and online dating certainly have benefits for shy people; however, contrary to the stereotype, socially isolated and lonely people are not the primary users of these methods for initiating interaction with others. Text-messaging has become the communication technology of choice among young people and is expected to surpass voice calls (Harley et al., 2007; Reid and Reid, 2007). Robert Brym of the University of Toronto and Rhonda Lenton of York University, who surveyed users of Canada's largest online dating service, found online daters to be sociable and self-confident. Online daters belonged to more clubs and sports organizations than the Canadian population in general, and they reported regular social contact and leisure activities with friends and family. Why, then, do these busy, sociable people use online dating services? Brym and Lenton's data (2003) suggest that online dating is a convenient and efficient way to form relationships with people they would otherwise never meet.

Experimenting   After meeting someone new, we generally begin the search for common ground. This search usually begins with the basics: 'Where are

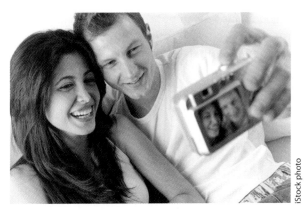

iStock photo

you from? What program are you in?' From there, we look for other similarities: 'You're a runner, too? How many kilometres do you run a week?'

It usually doesn't take long for communicators who are interested in one another to move from initiating to **experimenting**. The shift seems to occur even more rapidly in cyberspace than in person (Pratt et al. 1999; Tidwell and Walther, 2002). People who develop relationships by email begin asking questions about attitudes, opinions, and preferences more quickly than those in face-to-face contact. It probably helps that people using email can't see each other's non-verbal reactions—they don't have to worry about blushing, stammering, or looking away if they realize that they asked for too much information too quickly.

The hallmark of experimenting is small talk. We tolerate the ordeal of small talk because it serves several functions. First, it is a useful way to find out what interests we share with the other person. It is also a way to 'audition' the other person—to help us decide whether a relationship is worth pursuing. In addition, small talk is a safe way to ease into a relationship. You have not risked much as you decide whether to proceed further. Finally, small talk does provide some kind of link to others. It's often better than being alone.

The kind of information we look for during the experimentation stage depends on the nature of the relationship we are seeking (Miller, 1998; Stewart et al., 2000). For example, both men and women who are seeking short-term relationships look for someone with an exciting personality and a good sense of humour. Being trustworthy and romantic becomes more important when people seek long-term relationships.

Intensifying   At the next stage, the kind of qualitatively personal relationship that we defined in Chapter 1 begins to develop. Dating couples use a wide range of communication strategies to express their feelings of attraction (Tolhuizen, 1989). In this intensifying stage, about a quarter of the time, they express their feelings directly to discuss the state of the relationship. More often, they use less-direct methods of communication—spending an increasing amount of time together, asking for support from one another, doing favours for the partner, giving tokens of affection, hinting and flirting, expressing feelings non-verbally, getting to know

the partner's friends and family, and trying to look more physically attractive (Richmond et al., 1987).

Although commitment grows as a relationship intensifies, communication between partners shows that doubts can still remain. Romantic partners use a variety of strategies to test each other's commitment (Baxter and Wilmot, 1985; Bell and Buerkel-Rothfuss, 1990). These approaches include asking direct questions, testing the partner by presenting challenges that require proof of commitment, hinting in order to gain expressions of commitment, and asking third parties for information. While that kind of behaviour is frequent in the early stages of a relationship, it usually declines as the partners spend more time together.

The intensifying stage is usually a time of relational excitement and even euphoria. For romantic

Focus on Research

Caught between Two Worlds: Canadian Children with Collectivist Cultural Backgrounds

Parents from more collectivist cultural backgrounds and those from more individualistic cultures often have very different views of love, dating, and marriage. Individualistic societies, like Canada, which emphasize self-reliance and independence, allow children far greater freedom in choosing their friends and potential spouses than would be permitted in more collectivist societies, such as India or other South Asian countries. In many collectivist cultures, dating is not practised or it leads quickly to marriage, and marriages are often arranged by parents or matchmakers. In these cultures, a marriage is not between two individuals but between two families. Individualistic North Americans, led by conceptions of romantic love, are often uncomfortable with these ideas.

How then, do Canadian-born children of immigrant parents manage the differences in expectations between their two worlds? The issue that is the strongest source of conflict between parents and children is dating (Hynie, 1998). But there is hope of some potential resolutions to these differences. Immigrant parents do appear willing

to concede some control over their children's marriages, and immigrant children tend to offer some endorsement of their parents values regarding marriage (Wakil et al., 1981). For example, some research suggests that South Asian immigrant children believe that both children and parents should have some say in marital decisions. Often, children will agree to some form of arranged marriage provided that they have final say about the choice of a spouse (Wakil et al., 1981). This practice is not so different from using a dating service. The big advantage is that the people looking for your potential partner (often your parents) probably know you well, love you, and have your best interests at heart. The big disadvantages include not being able to be yourself when meeting the 'candidates' because of family involvement, having only a small pool of candidates to choose from because of restrictive parental criteria (e.g., culture, religion, status or caste, education level, and wealth), and having a limited period of time to find the right person. Ali Kazimi and Geeta Sondhi made a thought-provoking film about young Canadians trying to balance the demands of their collectivistic cultural heritage and the individualistic values of Canadian society. The film, available through the National Film Board of Canada, is called *Some Kind of Arrangement*.

Focus on Technology

Only Initiating and Experimenting? Text-Messaging, Instant-Messaging, and Relationship Development

Socially interactive technologies such as instant messaging and text-messaging have been criticized for developing mostly superficial relationships. Text-messaging is becoming an increasingly popular communication technology, especially among people under thirty years of age (Shiu and Lenhart, 2004). There is a fear that these technologies create a series of 'weak ties'; people engage in the initiating and experimenting stages of relationship development but seldom move on to deeper stages of the process. Stacey Young (2004) found some support for this idea in the early stages of computer-mediated relationship development. It makes sense that many relationships brought along via texting and online communication would have less depth than those that

also involve face-to-face communication. However, it appears that more people use instant messaging and text messages to keep in touch with, and improve their relationships with, previously established friends rather than to develop new relationships (Lenhart et al., 2001). In addition, these technologies allow people to communicate with 'friends of friends', and although these relationships may never develop into deep and meaningful relationships, they can still provide social support and expand social interaction. These networks of weak ties have an impact on our health and well-being. For instance, Peter Bearman and James Moody (2004) found a substantial social-network effect on girls' thoughts of suicide. Specifically, adolescent girls whose friends were not also friends of one another experienced more suicidal thoughts than girls whose friends were interconnected. Given what we know about the power of social support (see Chapters 1 and 7), having interconnected social networks is probably a benefit.

partners, it is often filled with starstruck gazes, goosebumps, and daydreaming. As a result, it's a stage that is regularly depicted in movies and romance novels—after all, we love to watch lovers in love. The problem, of course, is that the stage doesn't last forever. Sometimes, romantic partners who stop feeling goosebumps begin to question whether they are still in love. While it is possible that they are not, it also could be that they've simply moved on to a different stage in their relationship—such as integrating.

Integrating   As the relationship strengthens, the individuals enter an integrating stage. They begin to take on an identity as a social unit. Invitations begin to come addressed to a couple. Social circles merge. The partners share each other's commitments: 'Sure, we'll spend Thanksgiving with your family.' Common property may begin to be designated—our apartment, our car, our song (Baxter, 1987). Partners develop their own personal idioms (Bell and Healey, 1992) and forms of play (Baxter, 1992). They develop routines and rituals

that reinforce their identity as a couple—jogging together, eating at a favourite restaurant, expressing affection with a goodnight kiss, and worshipping together (Afifi and Johnson, 1999). As these examples illustrate, the stage of integrating is a time when we give up some characteristics of our former selves and become different people.

As we become more integrated with another person, our sense of obligation to him or her grows (Roloff et al., 1988). We feel obliged to provide a variety of resources, such as class notes and money, whether or not the other person asks for them. When intimates do make requests of one another, they are relatively straightforward. Gone are the elaborate explanations, inducements, and apologies. In short, partners in an integrated relationship expect more from each other than they do in less intimate associations.

As integration increases and as we become more intimate, uncertainty about our relationship decreases: we become clearer about relationship norms and about what behaviour is appropriate and inappropriate. In addition, our ability to influence each other's daily activities increases, such as the amount of time spent with friends and studying (Solomon and Knobloch, 2001). Reducing uncertainty about our partner and the relationship enhances attraction and feelings of closeness (Knobloch and Solomon, 2002).

Bonding   During the bonding stage, the partners make symbolic public gestures to show the world that their relationship exists. These gestures can take the form of a contract between business partners or a licence to be married. Bonding usually generates social support for the relationship. Custom and law impose certain obligations on partners who have officially bonded.

Bonding usually marks an important turning point in relationships. Up to now, the relationship may have developed at a steady pace. Experimenting gradually moved into intensifying and then into integrating. Now, however, there is a spurt of commitment. The public display and declaration of exclusivity make this a critical period in the relationship. Although most people would agree that there are turning points, research shows that couples do not always agree about what specific events marked those points in their relationships. About 45 percent of the time, the partners do not identify the same events as turning points (Baxter and Bullis, 1986). Baxter and Pittman (2001) found that the more turning points on which members of a couple agreed, the greater their satisfaction as a couple.

iStock photo

Differentiating   Now that the two people have formed this commonality, they need to re-establish individual identities. How are we different? How am I unique? Former identifications as 'we' now emphasize 'I'. Differentiating often takes place when a relationship begins to experience the first, inevitable feelings of stress. Whereas happy employees might refer to 'our company', the description might change to 'this company' when a raise or some other request isn't forthcoming. We see this kind of differentiation when parents argue over the misbehaviour of a child: 'Did you see what *your* daughter just did?'

Differentiation can also be positive—people need to be individuals as well as part of a relationship. The key to successful differentiation is to maintain commitment to a relationship while creating the space for being individuals as well (we will describe this later in the chapter as the *connection–autonomy dialectic*).

Circumscribing   So far, we have been looking at the growth of relationships. Although some reach a plateau of development, going on successfully for as long as a lifetime, others pass through several stages of decline and dissolution. In the circumscribing stage, communication between members decreases in quantity and quality (Duck, 1987). Subtle hints of dissatisfaction grow more evident. When one or both partners start working later at the office, seeking less and less romance, and arguing more and more, there begins to form a pattern that is hard to ignore (Kellermann et al., 1991). Ironically, both partners in a circumscribed relationship still cooperate in one way, namely by suppressing the true state of the relationship. They hide its decline from others and even from themselves (Vaughn, 1987). Restrictions and restraints characterize this stage, and dynamic communication becomes static. Rather than discuss a disagreement (which requires some degree of energy on both parts), members opt for withdrawal, either mental (through silence or daydreaming and fantasizing) or physical (by spending less time together). Circumscribing doesn't involve total avoidance, which comes later. Rather, it entails a shrinking of interest and commitment.

iStock photo

Stagnating   If circumscribing continues, the relationship begins to stagnate. Members behave toward each other in old, familiar ways without much feeling. No growth occurs. The stagnating relationship is a hollow shell of its former self. We see stagnation in many workers who have lost enthusiasm for their job yet continue to go through the motions for years. The same sad event occurs for some couples who unenthusiastically have the same conversations, see the same people, and follow the same routines without any sense of joy or novelty.

Avoiding   When stagnation becomes too unpleasant, people in a relationship begin to create distance between each other by avoiding. Sometimes, they do it under the guise of excuses ('I've been sick lately and can't see you'); at other times, directly ('Please don't call me; I don't want to see you now'). In either case, by this point, the writing is on the wall about the future of the relationship.

Research by Jon Hess (2000) reveals that there are several ways we gain distance. One way is *expressing detachment*, such as avoiding the other person altogether, or 'tuning them out'. A second way is *avoiding involvement*, such as leaving the room, ignoring the person's questions, steering clear of touching, and being superficially polite. *Showing antagonism* is a third technique, which includes behaving in a hostile way and treating the other person as a lesser person. A fourth strategy is to *dissociate mentally* from the other person, such as by thinking about the other person as less capable

or as unimportant. A vicious circle is started when one person avoids the other: the more one person avoids the other, the greater the odds the other will reciprocate. And the more topics for discussion that are avoided, the less satisfactory the relationship will be (Sargent, 2002).

Terminating   Termination has its own distinguishable pattern (Battaglia et al., 1998). Characteristics of this stage include summary dialogues of where the relationship has gone and the desire to dissociate. The relationship may end with a cordial dinner, a note left on the kitchen table, a phone call, or a legal document stating the dissolution. Depending on each person's feelings, this terminating stage can be quite short or it may be drawn out over time, with bitter jabs made at each other. In either case, termination doesn't have to be totally negative. Understanding each other's investments in the relationship and needs for personal growth may dilute the hard feelings.

Baxter (1982) and Cody (1982) found that the strategy partners use to disengage depends on the degree of intimacy their relationship had reached. In the least intimate relationships, one partner simply withdraws (physically or emotionally) from the other. In slightly more intimate relationships, one partner is likely to request they see less of each other. When intimacy has been greater, the

Reflection

Culture and Relational Stages

I think Knapp's model does a good job of describing relational stages in Western culture, but it doesn't work everywhere in the world. My parents were born in India, and their families arranged their marriage when my mother and dad were children. They hardly knew one another when they were married, so most of the experimenting, integrating, and intensifying actually came after their official bonding (i.e., marriage), not before. I'm happy to say that they do love one another, but it happened in a very different way than it usually does in this part of the world.

disengaging partner makes an effort to explain the reason for leaving in a way that takes the other's feelings into account. In the most intimate relationships, the initiator expresses grief over the disengagement. In fact, Cody found that the more intimate the relationship, the greater the feeling of obligation to justify terminating it.

How do the individuals deal with each other after a romantic relationship has ended? The best predictor of whether the individuals will become friends is whether they were friends before their romantic involvement (Metts et al., 1989). The way the couple splits up also makes a difference. It is no surprise to find that friendships are most possible when communication during the breakup was positive, such as expressions that there were no regrets for time spent together and other attempts to minimize hard feelings. When communication during the breakup is negative (manipulative, complaining to third parties), friendships are less likely.

Survivors of broken relationships offer a number of reasons why their relationships do not last (Cupach and Metts, 1986). These reasons are summarized in Table 8.1. The tendency is to blame the breakup on the other person more than on oneself, although divorced women are more likely to blame themselves. Men are more likely to pin the responsibility on their ex-wives or on outside forces.

Is it possible for ex-romantic partners to have a platonic friendship? Schneider and Kenny (2000)

Take Two

Stages of Relational Development

Coming Together
- Initiating: make contact; demonstrate that you are worth talking to
- Experimenting: search for common ground; engage in small talk
- Intensifying: begin to develop a personal relationship; spend more time together and experience excitement

Relational Maintenance
- Integrating: take on identity as social unit; routines, rituals, and obligations grow
- Bonding: make symbolic gesture to announce relationship publicly (e.g., marriage, business partnership)
- Differentiating: re-establish individual identities; can be both stressful and/or positive
- Circumscribing: decrease the quantity and quality of communication; avoid talking about problems in relationship

Coming Apart
- Stagnating: go through hollow routines; no growth in relationship; little joy or novelty
- Avoiding: create distance—express detachment, avoid involvement, show antagonism, dissociate mentally
- Terminating: end relationship; can be negative, positive, or both

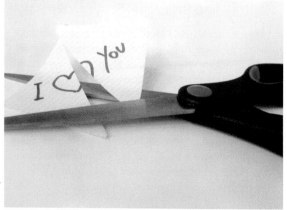
iStock photo

surveyed heterosexual men and women (average age nineteen) who reported having a friend who was once a romantic partner and another friend with whom there was never any romantic involvement. Results indicated more positive qualities associated with the platonic friend and more negative qualities (in addition to more romantic desires) associated with the ex-romantic partner. The relationships also had different rules; the platonic, not romantic, friend was the one to ask for personal advice, share news and successes with, and volunteer to help in time of need. The relationship with the platonic friend also had more benefits—having fun and receiving help—while the relationship with the ex-romantic had more costs—feeling irritated and feeling that you are

Table 8.1 Reasons Offered for Termination of Relationship

I. **Characteristics of the individuals themselves**
'I began to feel lonely.'
'She said she felt trapped.'
'He was too conservative.'

II. **Lack of fulfilment of relational roles**
'He found no joy in being a father.'
'There were no sexual relations.'
'He tried to tell me what I had to do to be his wife.'
'She went back to school.'

III. **Unsatisfactory relational cohesiveness and intimacy**
'We no longer wanted the same things in life.'
'We did nothing together as a couple.'
'We had different needs.'

IV. **Poor regulation of interaction**
'He wouldn't listen.'
'All our discussions ended in arguments.'
'He threatened me.'

V. **Third-party involvements**
'I had an affair with an exciting older man.'
'When I found out she'd been seeing other guys, I was very hurt.'
'The unexpected pregnancy was more than we could handle.'
'I lost my job.'

Source: Adapted from W. R. Cupach and S. Metts (1986), Accounts of relational dissolution: A comparison of marital and non-marital relationships. *Communication Monographs, 53,* 311–354.

wasting your time when you are with the person. So the answer to the question is, probably not.

Dialectical Perspectives on Relational Dynamics

Stage-related views like the one described in the preceding pages characterize communication as differing in important ways at various points in the life of a relationship. According to the stage approach, what happens during initiating, experimenting, or intensifying is different from the kind of communication that occurs during differentiating, circumscribing, or avoiding.

Not all theorists agree that relational stages are the best way to explain interaction in relationships. Some suggest that communicators grapple with the same kinds of challenges whether a relationship is brand new or has lasted decades.

Their focus, then, is on the ongoing maintenance of relationships (Lee, 1998). They argue that communicators seek important but apparently incompatible goals. The struggle to achieve these goals creates **dialectical tensions**, conflicts that arise when two opposing or incompatible forces exist simultaneously.

In recent years, communication scholars such as Leslie Baxter and Barbara Montgomery (1996), William Rawlins (1992), and Brian Spitzberg (1994) have identified several dialectical forces that make successful communication challenging. They suggest that the struggle to manage these tensions creates the most powerful dynamics in relational communication. In the following pages, we will discuss three influential dialectical tensions, which are summarized in Table 8.2. As the table shows, we experience dialectical challenges both *internally*, vis-à-vis our partners, and *externally* as we and our relational partners encounter other people whose desires clash with our own.

Integration versus Separation   No one is an island. Recognizing this fact, we seek out involvement with others. But, at the same time, we are unwilling to sacrifice our entire identity to even the most satisfying relationship. The conflicting desires for connection and independence are embodied in the **integration–separation dialectic**. This set of apparently contradictory needs creates communication challenges that can show up both within a relationship and between the partners and the world.

Internally, the struggle shows up in the **connection–autonomy dialectic**. We want to be close to others, but at the same time, we seek independence. Sociolinguist Deborah Tannen (1986, p. 31) captures the insoluble integration–separation dialectic nicely by evoking the image of two porcupines trying to get through a cold winter:

They huddle together for warmth, but their sharp quills prick each other, so they pull away. But then they get cold. They have to keep adjusting their closeness and distance to keep from freezing and from getting pricked by their fellow porcupines—the source of both comfort and pain.

Table 8.2 Dialectical Tensions

	Dialectic of Integration–Separation	Dialectic of Stability–Change	Dialectic of Expression–Privacy
Internal Manifestations	Connection–Autonomy	Predictability–Novelty	Openness–Closedness
External Manifestations	Inclusion–Seclusion	Conventionality–Uniqueness	Revelation–Concealment

Source: From L. A. Baxter (1994), A dialogic approach to relationship maintenance. In D. J. Canary and L. Stafford (Eds.), *Communication and Relational Maintenance* (p. 240). San Diego, CA: Academic Press.

We need to get close to each other to have a sense of community, to feel we're not alone in the world. But we need to keep our distance from each other to preserve our independence, so others do not impose on or engulf us. This duality reflects the human condition. We are individual and social creatures. We need other people to survive, but we want to survive as individuals.

Baxter (1994) describes the consequences for relational partners who cannot manage the conflicting needs for connection and autonomy. Some of the most common reasons that relationships break up involve the failure of partners to satisfy one another's needs for connection: 'We barely spent any time together'; 'My partner wasn't committed to the relationship'; 'We had different needs.' But other complaints involve excessive demands for connection: 'I was feeling trapped'; 'I needed freedom.'

In accounts of relational turning points, both men and women in heterosexual romantic pairs cited the connection–autonomy dialectic as one of the most significant factors affecting their relationship (Baxter and Erbert, 1999). This dialectical tension was crucial when they were negotiating turning points related to commitment, conflict, disengagement, and reconciliation. Research also shows that managing the dialectical tension between connection and autonomy is as important during divorce as it is at the beginning of a marriage, as partners seek ways to salvage and reconcile the unbreakable bonds of their personal history (including finances, children, and friends) with their new independence (Pam and Pearson, 1998). Even at the end of life, the connection–autonomy dialectic comes

into play. When a loved one is in an extended period of declining health, the partner often feels torn between the desire to stay close and the need to let go. This tension is especially poignant when one partner suffers from Alzheimer's disease and becomes mentally absent while physically present (Baxter et al., 2002).

Parents and children must deal constantly with the conflicting tugs of connection and autonomy, as we describe in Chapter 9 in some detail. These struggles do not end when children grow up and leave home. Parents experience the mixed feelings of relief at their new freedom and a longing to stay connected to their adult children. Likewise, grown children feel excitement at being on their own, and yet miss the bonds they had likely taken for granted since the beginning of their lives (Blacker, 1999; Fulmer, 1999).

The tension between integration and separation also operates externally, when people in a relationship struggle to meet the competing needs of the **inclusion–seclusion dialectic**. They struggle to

iStock photo

reconcile a desire for involvement with the 'outside world' with the desire to live their own lives, free of what can feel like interference from others. For example, when the end of a busy week comes, does a couple accept the invitation to a party (and sacrifice the chance to spend quality time with each other), or do they decline the invitation (and risk losing contact with valued friends)? Does a close-knit nuclear family choose to take a much-anticipated vacation together (disappointing their relatives), or do they attend a family reunion (losing precious time to enjoy one another without any distractions)?

Stability versus Change   Stability is an important need in relationships, but too much of it can lead to feelings of staleness. The **stability–change dialectic** operates both between partners and between the couple and others outside the relationship. Within a relationship, the **predictability–novelty dialectic** captures another set of tensions. Although nobody wants a completely unpredictable relational partner ('you are not the person I married!'), humorist Dave Barry exaggerates only slightly when he talks about the boredom that can come from spouses knowing each other too well:

> After a decade or so of marriage, you know *everything* about your spouse, every habit and opinion and twitch and tic and minor skin growth. You could write a seventeen-pound book solely about the way your spouse eats. This kind of intimate knowledge can be very handy in certain situations—such as when you are on a TV quiz show where the object is to identify your spouse from the sound of his or her chewing—but it tends to lower the passion level of a relationship. (Barry, 1990, p. 47)

At an external level, the **conventionality–uniqueness dialectic** captures the challenges that people in a relationship face when trying to meet other people's expectations as well as their own. On one hand, stable patterns of behaviour do emerge that enable others to make useful judgments like 'happy family' or 'dependable organization'. But

Reflection

One Plus One Makes Three

I've been to a lot of weddings in the last few years, and several couples have included a ceremony that got me thinking about dialectical challenges in a marriage. There are usually three candles in a holder—two that are lit on the outsides and a centre one that is not. The bride and groom each take an outside candle and light the centre one, symbolizing that they've created a new union together.

The part that comes next is most interesting to me. Some couples blow out their own individual candles, leaving only the centre one burning. Others leave their own individual candles burning.

I like the symbolism of leaving all three candles burning. It reminds me of the connection–autonomy dialectic that we talked about in class. If only the centre one is burning, there's connection without autonomy. If only the outside ones are burning, it is autonomy without connection. Leaving all three lit says to me that being a couple is important, but so is being an individual.

those blanket characterizations can stifle people in relationships, who may sometimes want to break away from the expectations others hold of them. For example, it can be a burden to play the conventional role of 'happy family' or 'perfect couple' during a time of conflict when the couple feels the need to behave in less stereotypical ways.

iStock photo

Expression versus Privacy Disclosure is one characteristic of interpersonal relationships. Yet, along with the drive for intimacy, we have an equally important need to maintain some space between ourselves and others. These sometimes-conflicting drives create the **expression–privacy dialectic**.

The internal struggle between expression and privacy shows up in the **openness–closedness dialectic**. What do you do in an intimate relationship when a person you care about asks an important question that you don't want to answer? 'Do you think I'm attractive?' 'Are you having a good time?' Because of your commitment to the relationship, you may wish to be honest, but your concern for the other person's feelings and a desire for privacy may lead you to be less than completely honest. Partners use a variety of strategies to gain

privacy from each other (Burgoon et al., 1989; Petronio, 2000). For example, they may confront the other person directly and explain that they do not want to continue a discussion, or they may be less direct and offer non-verbal cues, change the topic, or leave the room. Because this dialectic raises so many communication challenges, we will explore it in depth in Chapter 9.

The same conflicts between openness and privacy operate externally in the **revelation–concealment dialectic**. If you and a long-time fellow worker have not been getting along, do you answer the boss's question, 'How's it going?' honestly, or do you keep your disagreement to yourselves?

Although all of the dialectical tensions play an important role in managing relationships, some occur more often than others. In one study (Pawlowski, 1998), young married couples reported that autonomy–connection was the most frequent tension (30.8 percent of all reported contradictions). Predictability–novelty was second (occurring 21.7 percent of the time), and inclusion-seclusion was third (21.4 percent). Less common were tensions between openness–closedness (12.7 percent), conventionality–uniqueness (7.5 percent), and revelation–concealment (6 percent). Of all the dialectical tensions, the most important ones to manage, at least in romantic relationships, seem to be autonomy–connection and openness–closedness (Baxter and Erbert 1999; Erbert, 2000).

Strategies for Managing Dialectical Tensions Managing the dialectical tensions outlined in these pages presents communication challenges. There are at least eight ways these challenges can be managed (Griffin, 2003):

- *Denial* In the strategy of denial, communicators respond to one end of the dialectical spectrum and ignore the other. For example, a couple caught between the conflicting desires for stability and novelty might find their struggle for change too difficult to manage. So they choose to follow predictable, if unexciting, patterns of relating to one another.

Take Two

- **Dialectical tensions**: conflicts that arise when two opposing forces exist simultaneously; they exist within personal relationships and also between individuals/couples and the external world.
- **Integration–separation**: conflicting desires for connection and independence within a relationship.
- **Connection–autonomy**: conflicting desires for connection and independence within an individual.
- **Inclusion–seclusion**: conflicting desires for connection and separation between people in a relationship and the external world.
- **Stability–change**: conflicting needs for constancy and variation within a relationship.
- **Predictability–novelty**: conflicting needs for constancy and variation within an individual.
- **Conventionality–uniqueness**: conflicting needs for conformity and distinctiveness between people in a relationship and the expectations of the external world.
- **Expression–privacy**: conflicting needs to share information but also to keep things confidential within a relationship.
- **Openness–closedness**: conflicting needs to disclose information but also to keep things confidential within an individual.
- **Revelation–concealment**: conflicting needs to disclose information about a relationship but also to hide that information from the external world.

Focus on Research

Going Public or Staying Private: Dialectical Tensions of Battered Women

For many couples, the expression–privacy dialectic centres on decisions to reveal or conceal good news about their relationship. 'Should we tell our friends that we're dating?' or 'Is it time for you to meet my family?' are questions they might ask about sharing positive relational information with others. For some couples, however, the concealed news is not so pleasant. Lara Dieckmann (2000) looked into the world of battered women and found that most of them wrestle with the dialectic of staying private or going public about the abuse in their relationships.

Dieckmann conducted in-depth interviews at an agency for battered women in Chicago. She also talked to shelter volunteers and drew upon her experience as a legal advocate for battered women. Her goal was to interpret 'abused women's experience in relation to their social and political context and with reference to their own words.' A word that Dieckmann used to describe the women's experience is *balance*—that is, their need to constantly balance the competing demands of privacy and publicity, secrecy and disclosure, safety and danger. Telling other people that she is being abused by her partner can be the first step in disengaging from a violent relationship, but it can also threaten a woman's self-esteem, her security, and her very life. Consider, for example, the dilemma of a battered woman who wants to ask her friends and family for help, but fears that her mate will find out and react violently. Or imagine the spouse whose shame at confessing to being victimized conflicts with the desire to reveal her problem.

From the outside, it can be hard to understand why victims of abuse keep quiet about their awful situations. But understanding the dialectical tension between openness and privacy can help us appreciate the dilemmas often faced by partners in abusive relationships.

- *Disorientation* In this mode, communicators feel so overwhelmed and helpless, they are unable to confront their problems. They might fight, freeze, or even leave the relationship. Partners who discover soon after the honeymoon that living a 'happily-ever-after', conflict-free life is impossible might become so terrified that they decide their marriage is a mistake.
- *Alternation* Communicators who use this strategy choose one end of the dialectical spectrum at some times, and the other end on different occasions. Friends, for example, might manage the autonomy–connection dialectic by alternating between times when they spend a large amount of time together and other periods when they live independent lives.
- *Segmentation* Partners who use this tactic compartmentalize different areas of their relationship. For example, a couple might manage the openness–closedness dialectic by sharing almost all their feelings about mutual friends with one another, but keeping certain parts of their past romantic histories private.

- *Balance* Communicators who try to balance dialectical tensions recognize that both forces are legitimate and try to manage them through compromise. As we point out in Chapter 11, compromise is inherently a situation in which everybody loses at least a little of what he or she wants. A couple caught between the conflicting desires for predictability and novelty might seek balance by compromising with a lifestyle that is neither as predictable as one wants nor as surprise-filled as the other seeks—not an ideal outcome.
- *Integration* With this approach, communicators simultaneously accept opposing forces without trying to diminish them. Barbara Montgomery (1993) describes a couple who accept the need both for predictability and for novelty by devising a 'predictably novel' approach. Once a week, they would do something together that they had never done before. Similarly, Dawn Braithwaite and her colleagues (1998) found that step-families often manage the tension between the 'old

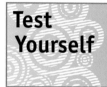

Test Yourself   Describe eight ways to manage the inevitable dialectical tensions that exist in relationships. Provide an example of each.

family' and the 'new family' by adapting and blending their family rituals.

- *Recalibration* Communicators can respond to dialectical challenges by reframing them so that the apparent contradiction disappears. Consider how a couple who felt hurt by each other's unwillingness to share parts of their past might redefine the secrets as creating an attractive aura of mystery instead of being a problem to be solved. The desire for privacy would still remain, but it would no longer compete with a need for openness about every aspect of the past.

- *Reaffirmation* This approach acknowledges that dialectical tensions will never disappear. Instead of trying to make them go away, reaffirming communicators accept—or even embrace—the challenges they present. The metaphorical view of relational life as a kind of roller coaster reflects this orientation, and communicators who use reaffirmation view dialectical tensions as part of the ride.

Characteristics of Relational Development

Whether you analyze a relationship in terms of stages or dialectical dynamics, two characteristics are true of every interpersonal relationship.

Relationships Are Constantly Changing Relationships are rarely stable for long periods of time. In fairy tales, a couple may live happily ever after, but in real life this sort of equilibrium is less common. Consider a husband and wife who have been married for some time. Although they have formally bonded, their relationship will probably shift forward and backward along the spectrum of stages, and different dialectical tensions will become more or less important at different times.

Richard Conville (1991) captures this constant change by describing relational cycles in which the partners continually move through a series of stages before returning to ones they previously encountered, although at a new level. He pictures this movement as a kind of helix, as shown in Figure 8.2. According to Conville, we move from security (*integration* in Knapp's terminology) to disintegration (*differentiating*) to alienation (*circumscribing*) to resynthesis (*intensifying*, *integrating*) to a new level of security. This cycle repeats itself again and again. This back-and-forth movement reflects the dialectical tensions identified by Baxter and others.

Movement Is Always to a New Place Even though a relationship may move back to a stage it has experienced before, it will never be the same as before. For example, most healthy long-term relationships will go through several phases of experimenting, as the partners try out new ways of behaving with each other. Although each phase has the same general features, the specifics will feel different each time. Similarly, how partners manage the openness–closedness dialectic at one time will affect how they experience and manage it at

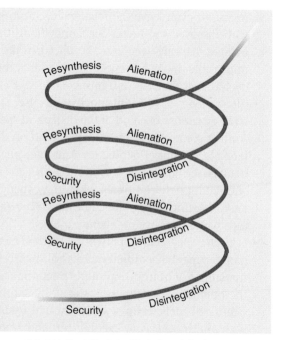

Figure 8.2 A Helical Model of Relational Cycles

another time with the same or different relational issues. As you learned in Chapter 1, communication is irreversible. Partners can never go back to 'the way things were'. Sometimes, this fact may lead to regrets, but it can also make relationships exciting since it lessens the chance for boredom and can lead to novelty and growth (Montgomery, 1993).

Communicating about Relationships

By now, it is clear that relationships are complex, dynamic, and important. How do communicators address relational issues with one another?

Content and Relational Messages

In Chapter 1, we saw that every message has a **content** and a **relational dimension**. The most obvious component of most messages is their content—the subject being discussed. The content of statements like 'It's your turn to do the dishes' or 'I'm busy Saturday night' is obvious.

But content messages are not the only information being exchanged when two people communicate. In addition, every message—both verbal and non-verbal—also has a second, relational dimension, which makes statements about how the communicators feel toward one another (Dillard et al., 1999; Watzlawick et al., 1967). These relational messages deal with one or more of the social needs: for intimacy, affinity, respect, and control. Consider the two examples we just mentioned:

- Imagine two ways of saying, 'It's your turn to do the dishes'—one that is demanding and another that is matter of fact. Notice how the different non-verbal messages make statements about how the sender views control in this part of the relationship. The demanding tone says, in effect, 'I have a right to tell you what to do around the house,' whereas the matter-of-fact one suggests, 'I'm just reminding you of something you might have overlooked.'
- You can easily imagine two ways to deliver the statement, 'I'm busy Saturday night'—one with some affection and the other without.

Reflection

Sending the Wrong Relational Message

I work thirty hours a week and have a full course load at school, so I am very busy. Sometimes, when my little brother wants to hang out and talk, I give him the brush-off. While he's telling me about his day, I keep typing on the computer or reading a book. After a while, I sigh and start replying automatically, 'yeah, yeah.' Last night, he asked, 'Why don't you like me any more?' I realized that, in my obsession with staying on top of my work, I've been giving him the wrong impression. Next time, I'll either give him my attention or let him know explicitly that I can't.

Like these messages, every statement we make goes beyond discussing the subject at hand and says something about the way the speaker feels about the recipient. You can prove this fact by listening for the relational messages implicit in your own statements to others and theirs to you.

Most of the time, we are unaware of the relational messages that bombard us every day. Sometimes, these messages don't capture our awareness because they match our belief about the amount of control, liking, or intimacy that is appropriate in a relationship. For example, you will probably not be offended if your boss tells you to drop everything and tackle a certain job, because you agree that supervisors have the right to direct employees. However, if your boss delivered the order in a condescending, sarcastic, or abusive tone of voice, you would probably be offended. Your complaint wouldn't be with the order itself, but with the way it was delivered. 'I may work for this company,' you might think, 'but I'm not a slave or an idiot. I deserve to be treated like a human being.'

Expression of Relational Messages

Exactly how are relational messages communicated? As the boss–employee example suggests, they are usually expressed non-verbally. To test this fact for yourself, imagine how you could act while saying,

'Can you help me for a minute?' in a way that communicates each of the following messages:

superiority
helplessness
friendliness
aloofness
sexual desire
irritation

Although non-verbal behaviour is a good source of relational messages, remember that it is ambiguous. The sharp tone you take as a personal insult might be due to fatigue, and the interruption you take as an attempt to ignore your ideas might be a sign of pressure that has nothing to do with you. Before you jump to conclusions about relational clues, it is a good idea to verify the accuracy of your interpretation with the other person: 'When you cut me off, I got the idea you are angry at me. Is that right?'

Not all relational messages are non-verbal. Social scientists use the term **metacommunication** to describe messages that refer to other messages. In other words, metacommunication is communication about communication. Whenever we discuss a relationship with others, we are metacommunicating: 'I wish we could stop arguing so much,' or 'I appreciate how honest you've been with me.' Verbal metacommunication is an essential ingredient in successful relationships. Sooner or later, there are times when it becomes necessary to talk about what is taking place between you and the other person. The ability to focus on the kinds of issues described in this chapter can be the tool for keeping your relationship on track.

Despite its importance, overt metacommunication is not a common feature of most relationships (Fogel and Branco, 1997; Wilmot, 1987). In fact, there seems to be an aversion to it, even among many intimates. When ninety people were asked to identify the taboo subjects in their personal relationships, the most frequent topics involved metacommunication (Baxter and Wilmot, 1985). For example, people were reluctant to discuss the state of their current relationships and the norms

Take Two

- **Content dimension of a message:** the subject being discussed.
- **Relational dimension of a message:** a statement describing how the speaker feels about the listener (can be non-verbal or verbal).
- **Metacommunication:** messages that refer to other messages.

('rules') that governed their lives together. Other studies suggest that when metacommunication does occur, it sometimes threatens the recipient and provokes conflict (Hocker and Wilmot, 1997).

Gaining Compliance in Interpersonal Relationships

Whether the goal is to gain control, affection, or respect, we use communication to get what we want. Social scientists use the term **compliance-gaining strategies** to define the tactics we use to persuade others to think or act in the way we want. Researchers have identified over sixty such strategies (Kellerman and Cole, 1994). Sometimes, the choice of approaches is conscious. If you are trying to impress a potential boss or romantic partner, you will probably think carefully about what to say or do. Once relationships develop, we still do our share of strategizing. A teenager who wants to borrow the family car, a spouse who wants to propose a vacation that his or her mate might not like, and a friend who needs to explain why he or she forgot to show up for a date are all likely to weigh their words carefully before speaking. In other cases, we do not consciously strategize, but even then it's likely that as competent communicators we consider a number of ways to get what we want before choosing what we hope will be the best approach.

The Self-Assessment box on page 245 lets you consider which strategies you use to ensure that your relational partners comply with your requests. The strategies in the Self-Assessment are from research by Kellerman and Cole (1994).

Skill at compliance-gaining develops early in childhood (Dillard, 1990; Monastersky, 2000). By the age of one, most infants understand that they can influence the actions of others through their behaviour. Their tears and tantrums, laughter and cuddles, gestures, and other movements are conscious attempts to express their needs. They form rough but often effective requests, or perhaps commands: 'Feed me!' 'Pick me up!' 'I want it now!' By age three, children develop primitive strategies to get what they want. They are able to adapt their messages in terms of simplicity, politeness, and topic. For example, one child might find that politeness pays dividends, so 'please' and 'thank you' become means to an end. Another might find that saying 'I love you' puts grown-ups in a better mood. These decisions are not conscious, of course. Rather, they are *scripts* that develop from a process of trial and error.

By the time a child reaches kindergarten, age-specific personalized strategies and scripts replace generalized ones. A child realizes that the approach that works with Dad may fail miserably with Mom and that what may be regarded as cute at home is

a misdemeanour at school. As children grow up, they become even more skilful at creating messages that gain co-operation or agreement from others. They are able to consider a variety of approaches and choose the one that appears most likely to succeed.

Types of Compliance-Gaining Strategies

Over the past quarter century, researchers have devised a variety of ways to describe compliance-gaining strategies (Gass and Seiter, 1999; Goss and O'Hair, 1988). The particular strategies we use to get what we seek from others can vary from one type of relationship to another. For example, dating couples who want to intensify their relationship use the strategies listed in Table 8.3. When the goal is to increase the level of physical intimacy, a wide range of approaches can be used, including logic, pleading, bargaining, flattery, and physical impositions (Christopher and Frandsen, 1990). During a conflict in which there is swearing, threats of violence, and other types of

Table 8.3 Compliance Strategies Used to Intensify Dating Relationships (Listed in Order of Frequency)

Frequency of Use	
39.2%	Increased contact: Interact with partner more often and for longer periods of time.
29.1%	Relationship negotiation: Initiate or engage in direct give-and-take discussion of relationship.
26.1%	Social support and assistance: Ask for advice, assistance, or support.
17.6%	Increase rewards: Compliment, do favours, perform tasks to increase rewards.
16.6%	Direct relational bid: Request directly, without discussion, a more serious exclusive relationship.
16.1%	Token of affection: Give gifts, cards, flowers, sentimental items to partner.
15.1%	Personalized communication: Self-disclosure or use of language that reflects uniqueness of relationship (e.g., pet names).
14.1%	Verbal expressions of affection: Directly express feeling of affection to partner.
13.1%	Suggestive actions: Hint, flirt, play hard-to-get, and other deceptive or non-open methods to communicate feelings.
12.1%	Non-verbal expressions of affection: Touching, sustained eye contact, and so on.
11.6%	Social enmeshment: Get to know friends and family of the partner or get the partner to know one's own friends and family.
9.5%	Accept definitional bid: Agree to a direct request for a more serious/exclusive relationship.
9.5%	Personal appearance: Attempt to look physically attractive for one's partner.

Source: Adapted from J. H. Tolhuizen (1989). Communication strategies for intensifying dating relationships: Identification, use and structure. *Journal of Social and Personal Relationships, 6*, 413–434. Reprinted by permission of Sage Publications, Ltd.

aggression, common strategies are to restrain the other person and make him or her feel like a bad person (Olson, 2002b). Whatever the approach, skill in compliance-gaining communication can help people get what they seek in ways that do not compromise the other person's feelings of self-worth (Ifert and Roloff, 1997).

In what follows, we describe approaches that combine most of the elements discussed in previous classification systems. As you read each category, think of times when you have used a particular approach, or when it has been used by someone to gain your compliance.

Direct Requests   The most straightforward way to gain compliance is to ask for it, or make a **direct request** (item 12 in the Self-Assessment box on page 245 is an example). We usually preface a request with a reason: 'I have to work late tonight . . .' and then make a polite request: 'So, could you pick up a few things downtown for me?' (Tracy, 1984). Along with its simplicity and honesty, this approach is a surprisingly effective way to get what you want. College students have reported that the best way to get social support is to ask for it (Conn and Peterson, 1989). This approach even works well with strangers. One famous study illustrates its power (Langer, 1978). Experimenters waiting in line to use a copying machine were able to move ahead of others by asking, 'May I use the Xerox machine because I'm in a rush?' Over 90 percent of the customers let the requester go ahead. People were almost as willing to comply when the reason was a weak one: 'May I use the Xerox machine because I have to make some copies?' Even without a reason for letting the requester cut in, over 60 percent of the people complied.

Indirect Appeals   When it is awkward or ineffective to make a direct request, we often use **indirect appeals**, hoping that the other person will infer or assume our real intent (Goss and O'Hair, 1988). (Item 21 in the Self-Assessment box is the most obvious example, but item 1 also can be construed as an indirect appeal.) Indirect appeals usually take the form of hints: 'You're driving downtown?

What a coincidence—I was just going to catch a bus myself!' 'You're tired of that sweater? I think it's great!'

While hints are strategic by definition, they are often a sensible and ethical way to seek compliance. Asking others directly may make them uncomfortable or put them on the spot. For example, it's usually impolite to invite yourself to a party, but hinting that you're free gives the host a chance to include you—or pretend not to have noticed the unspoken request. The risk of hints is that the other person may not recognize them. Nonetheless, they are a useful part of a repertoire for getting what you want from others.

Indirect approaches are especially useful when a direct approach might result in physical harm. Researchers who have studied abusive relationships have found that battered wives are more likely to use indirect approaches with their husbands than are spouses in non-violent marriages (Rudd and Burant, 1995).

Reciprocity   Even if others are not inclined to do what we want just because we ask them, they will often comply because of the powerful social norm of reciprocity. This is the convention that obligates us to return favours, even when we dislike the other person (Cialdini, 1988; Garko, 1990) (items 6, 11, and 26 in the Self-Assessment box are examples). If I have given you a ride or helped you study, you are likely to do me a favour when I ask, even though you might prefer not to.

When used in a manipulative manner, the norm of reciprocity is a tool for tricking people into doing things they otherwise wouldn't do. For instance, a devious person might offer to lend you some money, knowing you don't need it, so that you will feel obliged to give him a loan the next time he asks. But in many cases, reciprocity is a kind of social lubricant that keeps relationships running. By helping others, we feel altruistic and, thus, help ourselves. In this sense, reciprocity can be a win-win approach, in which both people profit.

Reward and Punishment   Sometimes, we comply because there is a reward for doing so: 'If you make

Self-Assessment

Assessing Your Compliance-Gaining Strategies

With one of your friendships in mind, check which of the following strategies you use to get your relational partner to comply with your requests.

_____ 1. I indicate my willingness to work on the request myself; that is, I offer to do it myself as a means of getting her or him to do it.

_____ 2. I ask my partner to help me out of the goodness of his or her heart—to be altruistic and just do it for me.

_____ 3. I point out that only a bad person would not comply with my request.

_____ 4. I point out that a good person would do what I want.

_____ 5. I behave in ways to bother my partner until she or he does what I want.

_____ 6. I try to strike a deal: I'll do what my partner wants if my partner does what I want.

_____ 7. I tell my partner how doing what I want will benefit her or him personally.

_____ 8. I tell my partner how doing what I want will benefit me personally.

_____ 9. I compliment my partner on his or her abilities.

_____ 10. I criticize my partner on a personal level.

_____ 11. I remind my partner of things I have done for her or him.

_____ 12. I simply state what I want without giving any reasons to comply.

_____ 13. I point out that other people cannot help me or do what is needed.

_____ 14. I point out that I have no choice but to make the request, and that I do so reluctantly.

_____ 15. I downplay what I want and try to get my partner to see my request as easy for him or her to comply with.

_____ 16. I point out that it would be unfair for my partner to refuse my request.

_____ 17. I point out that other people will view my partner negatively if she or he does not comply.

_____ 18. I point out that I will view my partner negatively if he or she does not comply.

_____ 19. I point out that other people will view my partner positively if she or he complies.

_____ 20. I point out that I will view my partner positively if he or she complies.

_____ 21. I hint at what I want and hope my partner will figure it out.

_____ 22. I give my partner logical reasons why she or he should comply.

_____ 23. I keep repeating my request until my partner complies.

_____ 24. I try to charm my partner into complying with my request by being very friendly and expressing positive emotions.

_____ 25. I do nice things for my partner in advance of making my request.

_____ 26. I promise to do something my partner wants if he or she complies with my request.

_____ 27. I try to get my partner to see that by not complying, she or he will feel bad about herself or himself.

_____ 28. I try to get my partner to see that by complying, he or she will feel good about himself or herself.

_____ 29. I get someone else to intervene and make my request for me.

_____ 30. I try to get my partner to think my request is really her or his own idea.

_____ 31. I tell my partner I will punish him or her if he or she does not comply.

_____ 32. Other: _____
_____.

Look over the strategies you checked and see if they have anything in common. Also, determine if the strategies you rejected have anything in common, and think about why you rejected them. Finally, consider what your compliance-gaining strategies tell you about the kind of relationship you have with the other person.

dinner tonight, I'll wash the dishes and pay for a movie later.' The flip side of rewards, of course, is punishments: 'If you try anything like that again, we're through!' (Many of the items in the Self-Assessment box are examples of these strategies; 7, 24, and 25, are reward strategies, and 5, 23, and 31 are punishment strategies.)

Not all threats and promises have immediate outcomes. Sometimes, they lay out more general consequences. A dentist might advise a patient to floss daily in order to avoid losing his teeth later in life. Likewise, an English teacher might tell her students that people who can't read or write are headed for dead-end jobs.

Rewards or punishments may be blatant: 'I'll give you five dollars for washing my dirty clothes,' or 'If you don't pay the rent on time, I'm moving out.' Sometimes, the positive or negative consequences we project are more subtle, such as being friendlier when another person co-operates or becoming less talkative when things do not go our way.

Not surprisingly, communication in a relationship is more satisfying when positive compliance-gaining strategies prevail over negative ones (Grant et al., 1994). Still, some relationships are better suited than others to the use of power-based appeals of reward and punishment. For example, a boss might reasonably persuade an employee to work harder by suggesting that promotions go to workers who make an extra effort on the job. But even in relationships where power is distributed unevenly, rewards and punishments are not used as often as we might think. One study compared the compliance-gaining methods of parents in prime-time family television programs with the methods used by real-life parents. Television parents used commands 39 percent of the time—much more often than in real families (Haefner and Comstock, 1990).

Face-Maintenance   Rewards aren't always obvious. Sometimes, we appeal to others by flattering their egos, inducing them to comply because it makes them feel better about themselves. **Face-maintenance strategies** lead others to act in ways that reinforce their presenting self and at the same time give us what we want (Goss and O'Hair, 1988) (items 4, 19, and 20 in the Self-Assessment box are examples). For example, you might get a friend to help you work on a difficult assignment by saying, 'You're so smart and so good at explaining things. I know I could do better if you gave me a hand.' Since the desire to maintain a presenting self is strong, others may provide what you are seeking for their sake, because it enhances their image. Your friend might not feel like helping you study, but lending a hand lets her think, 'I really am pretty smart, and I'm helpful, too. I'm a good person!'

Face-maintenance strategies are not always cynical attempts to manipulate others. They are often ways to shape others in a socially desirable manner. Research has found, for example, that when a person feels guilty, soliciting compliance with a positive self-feeling message—'You'll feel really good about yourself if you help out'—is a more effective strategy than a direct request (Boster et al., 1999). A parent might urge a child to perform a task by using this approach: 'Now that you are six years old, I know you can clean up your room without my having to nag you.' Likewise, a boss might give an employee an important assignment by saying, 'I know I can count on you to do a good job.' In cases like these, face-maintenance can

"The old persuasive approach is out. From now on, they put out their campfires or you <u>bite</u> them."

create a self-fulfilling prophecy. By creating idealized images of other people, we can induce them to become the person they want to be.

Relational Appeals Sometimes, we comply with others out of respect or affection (items 2 and 8 in the Self-Assessment box are examples). **Relational appeals** fall into this category. They consist of strategies that rely on the target's relationship with the person making the request. Some relational appeals are straightforward requests for help: 'I know you think those jokes are funny, but I'm embarrassed when you tell them. Would you stop telling them, for me?'

Other relational appeals may be just as sincere, but more calculating: 'If you really care about me, you won't drink and drive.' In every case, a relational appeal offers no other reason for complying beyond honouring the wishes of someone whose feelings are important to you. These appeals are most effective in intimate relationships, where the partners already feel a strong obligation to one another (Roloff et al., 1988). This explains why the requests of intimate partners are less elaborate than those of mere acquaintances. They contain fewer apologies, explanations, and inducements. Simply making the request seems to include this implied reasoning: 'You owe it to me to do what I ask.'

Which Strategy to Choose?

There is no single best compliance-gaining strategy. As we saw in Chapter 1, competent communicators have a wide repertoire of strategies and are skilful at choosing the best one for the circumstances. Sometimes, the best strategy varies by culture. In cultures that place a high value on relational connectedness and personal duty, such as many Asian cultures and First Nations cultures, invoking obligations is a powerful compliance-gaining strategy. But in more individualistic cultures, such as Canada and the United States, a

preferred strategy is to give reasons or explanations (Fitch, 1994; Ma and Chuang, 2001).

Once we have developed the skill to consider various ways to gain compliance, we weigh a number of factors in choosing the most promising approach. Some factors to weigh are the level of intimacy (spouse versus neighbour), dominance (employee versus boss), resistance (agreeable versus reluctant target), rights (reasonable versus unreasonable request), personal benefits of the persuader (high or low reward), and the consequence of rejection (Cody and McLaughlin, 1980; Cody et al., 1983). Of course, the personality of both the compliance seekers and their targets play into the selection of a compliance-gaining strategy. For example, Richard Falvo (2002) found that people who are verbally aggressive are more inclined to select anti-social compliance-gaining tactics and to view them as successful.

There are several possible obstacles to compliance that need to be taken into account when you are selecting a strategy. Danette Ifert and Michael Roloff (1998) described six of them. First, the person of whom you are making a request may not have what you are asking for: 'I don't have any'. Second, your request may be seen as an imposition: 'I'm too busy'; 'I have other plans.' Third, your request could be interpreted as inappropriate: 'It's none of my business'—perhaps because it's viewed as your own responsibility: 'Do it yourself.' Fourth, there may be no incentive to comply: 'Why should I do what you ask?' Fifth, the person may simply balk at complying, 'I don't want to', without giving a reason. And sixth, you may get a request to postpone your own request: 'I can't do it now, but maybe later'; 'Can you wait a week?'

Although there is no single 'best' strategy for gaining compliance, three principles can help you choose the best approach for a given situation (Cody et al., 1981).

Which Strategy Has the Best Chance of Immediate Success? Since your goal is to gain the other person's co-operation, you need to choose the approach that promises to have the best chance of success. This means you must tailor your approach to the characteristics of the person involved. The approach that might work with a friend might fail with a professor or even another friend. Unlike public speakers, who often have to persuade a diverse audience, you can tailor your approach to the characteristics of the single person you want to reach. For example, Vincent Waldron and James Applegate (1998) found that using person-centred tactics during verbal disagreements—that is, adapting to the other person's feelings, motivations, and understandings—increased persuasiveness.

As you analyze the other person, consider all the appeals listed on pages 243–7 and in the Self-Assessment on page 245, and then select the one that seems most promising. Is the other person likely to prefer a straightforward request, or would an indirect approach work better? Are you better off using logic to support your bid, or should you ask for compliance as a personal favour? Do your respective social roles make the promise of reward or punishment appropriate, or should you try a different tack?

How Will the Strategy Affect the Long-Term Well-Being of the Relationship?

As you consider which approach to use, do not focus exclusively on short-term gains. Be sure to communicate in a way that keeps the long-term quality of the relationship comfortable. For example, you might be able to persuade a reluctant partner to give up studying to join you for an evening on the town by using a combination of relational and face-maintaining appeals ('I really was looking forward to spending the evening with you') and threats ('If you don't go tonight, don't expect me to party next time you ask'). Even if you succeed in this short-term goal, pestering the other person to do something that really isn't appealing is probably not worth the cost.

Does the Strategy Conform to Your Values and Personal Style?

Some approaches are clearly unethical. For example, Scott Christopher and Michael Frandsen (1990) point out the unfortunate fact that some dating partners rely on ridicule, guilt, alcohol, and persistence to gain sexual favours. Most people would agree that telling outright lies is not justified, although you may feel justified using the kinds of equivocation and 'benevolent lies' that we describe in Chapter 9. In any case, you should feel comfortable with whatever approaches you take. One test is whether you would be embarrassed to confess your strategy to the other person involved if he or she confronted you, or if you would feel uncomfortable if the other person used the strategy with you.

In addition to ethical considerations, the strategies you use should fit your personal style of communicating. You probably feel more comfortable with some of the strategies listed above than with others. Your preferred style might be to make straightforward requests, perhaps backing them up with evidence. Or you might be more inclined to demonstrate the desirability of co-operating by emphasizing the face-maintaining benefits and other rewards.

Don't rule out a particular strategy just because you are not used to using it. You may feel a bit awkward trying it, but it still may be the best strategy for a particular situation. Compliance-gaining, like any skill, takes time to develop. Whatever strategy you use, short- and long-term success probably depends on your sincerity. If you are going to compliment the other person, be sure your praise is sincere. If you ask the other person to comply because the request is personally important, be sure you mean what you say. If you seem to be deceiving or manipulating the other person, your chances of success will shrink, as will your ability to be persuasive in the future.

 Take Two

When choosing which compliance-gaining strategy to use, consider the following:
- The chances of immediate success—tailor it to the recipient;
- the effects on the long-term well-being of the relationship—what are the costs?; and
- your values and style—gauge your ethical and personal comfort level, but don't rule out a strategy because you have never used it before.

Building Work Skills

Gaining Compliance

Our work often requires us to make requests of others—co-workers, supervisors, clients or customers, or students. Think of a situation at work or at school in which you have had to make an important request of another person who was your superior. Describe the approach you used. Were you successful?

Now, describe a request you made of an equal or subordinate. What type of strategy did you use in this situation? Were you successful? Compare the situations. Did you use different strategies? Why or why not?

Review the types of compliance-gaining strategies described in this chapter. Would another approach have been more or less effective in each of the two situations you described above? Why?

Summary

Several conditions must be satisfied for a personal relationship to exist. The people must be aware of each other and take each other into account, there must be mutual influence, and there must be some agreement about the social form and expectations that govern the interaction. The last condition suggests that relationships change over time—that they are continually in flux.

There are several explanations for why we form relationships with some people and not with others. These explanations include appearance (physical attractiveness), similarity, complementarity, rewards, competence, proximity, and disclosure. The explanation for which there is the most evidence is similarity—in general, people are attracted to others who are like them.

Some theorists argue that interpersonal relationships may go through as many as ten stages of growth and deterioration. They suggest that communication may reflect more than one stage at a given time, although one stage will be dominant. Other models describe the dynamics of interpersonal communication in terms of dialectical tensions, that is, mutually opposing, incompatible desires that can never be completely resolved. Both models characterize relationships as constantly changing, so that communication is more of a process than a static thing.

Messages have both content and relational dimensions. While the content aspect of a message may be obvious, the relational aspect is less clear. Relational messages are sometimes expressed overtly by verbal metacommunication; however, they are conveyed non-verbally more frequently.

Communicators use a variety of compliance-gaining strategies to achieve their relational goals. These strategies include direct requests, indirect appeals, reciprocity, promises or delivery of rewards and punishments, acts that maintain the other's face, and relational appeals. The choice of a particular compliance-gaining strategy depends on several short- and long-term considerations.

Activities

1. **Critical Thinking Probe**

   Some critics claim that Knapp's model of relational stages is better at describing romantic relationships than other types. Use a variety of romantic and non-romantic interpersonal relationships from your experience to evaluate the breadth of his model. If the model does not describe the developmental path of all types of interpersonal relationships, can you suggest alternative models?

2. **Invitation to Insight**

   How do you manage the dialectical tensions in your important relationships? Is there a pattern to what you and the other person do, or does it depend on the type of relationship you have? Identify at least two dialectical tensions in two different relationships—one relationship, perhaps, with a person with whom you work closely, and the other with a romantic partner. How is each tension managed? Which approach do you and your partner tend to use (denial, disorientation, alternation, segmentation, balance, integration, recalibration, or reaffirmation)? What seem to be the conditions that determine which method you and your partner use?

3. **Ethical Challenge**

   As you read on pages 235–40, consider that we often face conflicting goals when we communicate in an attempt to meet our own needs and those of others. Use the information on these pages to identify a situation in which your personal goals conflict with those of another person. What obligation do you have to communicate in a way that helps the other person reach his or her goals? Is it possible to honour this obligation and still try to satisfy your own needs?

4. **Skill Builder**

   Describe three unexpressed relational messages in one or more of your interpersonal relationships.

   a. Explain how you could have used meta-communication to express each one. Consider skills you learned in other chapters, such as perception checking, 'I' language, and paraphrasing.

   b. Discuss the possible benefits and drawbacks of this kind of metacommunication in each of the situations you identified. On the basis of your discussion here, what principles do you believe should guide your decisions about whether and when to focus explicitly on relational issues?

5. **Ethical Challenge**

   Which of the compliance-gaining strategies described on pages 243–7 and in the Self-Assessment box on page 245 do you use most often? Describe specific instances in which you used each one. Discuss whether these strategies are ethical. In answering this question, consider how willing you would be to disclose your strategies to the people they are directed to. Also, consider how you would feel if others used these strategies with you.

6. **Role Play**

   Choose a partner. Think of a request you need to make of someone you have a personal relationship with (e.g., family member, friend, supervisor, etc.). Briefly describe this person to your partner so he or she can get into character for the role-play scenario. Review the compliance-gaining strategies on pages 243–7 and the considerations when choosing a strategy on pages 247–8. Now, choose a compliance-gaining strategy and try it out with your partner. Discuss the strengths

and challenges of this strategy from the perspective of the sender and the receiver. Now, switch roles and repeat the exercise.

Discussion Questions

1. Why do we form relationships with other people?
2. Do you think Knapp's model of the stages of relational development can be adapted to more collectivist cultures? Why or why not?
3. Describe the dialectical tensions that exist in one of your relationships (e.g., with your parents, a friend, or a romantic partner). How do you manage these tensions in that relationship?
4. Lara Dieckman describes how dialectical tensions between disclosure and privacy influence women who are abused by their partners. Use the six reasons for forming relationships described in this chapter to explain why a person might enter into an abusive relationship and seek to maintain it.
5. Despite its importance, metacommunication is not a common feature of most relationships. Why do you think this is?
6. Are compliance-gaining strategies other than direct requests dishonest? Why or why not?
7. Which compliance-gaining strategies conform to your values and personal style? Why?

Chapter Nine

Intimacy and Distance in Relationships

After studying the material in this chapter ...

You Should Understand:

1. The dimensions of intimacy and distance in interpersonal relationships.
2. The dialectical forces that encourage both intimacy and privacy.
3. How notions of intimacy are shaped by gender and cultural influences.
4. The characteristics of and reasons for self-disclosure.
5. The risks and benefits of self-disclosure.
6. The types, functions, and extent of benevolent lies, equivocation, and hints.

You Should Be Able To:

1. Identify the optimal blend of intimacy and distance in your personal relationships.
2. Identify the degree to which you engage in self-disclosure with people in your life and the circumstances in which you do so.
3. Use the Johari Window model to represent the level of self-disclosure in one of your relationships.
4. Express the reasons you self-disclose in a selected relationship.
5. Compose responses to a situation that reflect varying degrees of candour and equivocation.
6. Name the potential risks and benefits of disclosing in a selected situation.
7. Use the guidelines in this chapter to decide whether or not to disclose important information in one of your relationships.

Intimacy and Distance: Striking a Balance

The 1970s musical group Three Dog Night said it well: one *can* be the loneliest number. For most of us, the desire to connect with others is a powerful force. As we explained in Chapter 1, strong attachments with others not only make us happier, they can also make us healthier and help us live longer.

In their book *Intimacy: Strategies for Successful Relationships*, C. Edward Crowther and Gayle Stone (1986) offer a reminder of just how important close relationships can be. As part of a study of people who were dying in hospices and hospitals in the United States and England, Crowther and Stone asked each person what mattered most in his or her life. Fully 90 percent of these terminally ill patients put intimate relationships at the top of the list. As a fifty-year-old mother of three children who was dying of cancer put it, 'You need not wait until you are in my condition to know nothing in life is as important as loving relationships' (p. 13).

Dimensions of Intimacy

What does it mean to be intimate? Does intimacy mean spending time together? Sharing feelings? Having sex? Going through thick and thin? Are intimacy and love identical?

Webster's New Collegiate Dictionary defines **intimacy** as arising from 'close union, contact, association, or acquaintance'. This closeness can occur in a variety of relationships (Berscheid et al., 1989).

When researchers asked several hundred college students to identify their 'closest, deepest, most involved, and most intimate relationship,' the answers were varied. Roughly half (47 percent) identified a romantic partner. About a third (36 percent) chose a friendship. Most of the rest (14 percent) cited a family member.

Intimacy comes in many forms (Lippert and Prager, 2001). One type is *emotional*: sharing important information and feelings. In the second half of this chapter, we have a great deal to say about these kinds of self-disclosures.

Another form of intimacy is *physical*. Even before birth, the developing fetus experiences a kind of physical closeness with its mother that will never happen again, 'floating in a warm fluid, curling inside a total embrace, swaying to the undulations of the moving body and hearing the beat of the pulsing heart' (Morris, 1973, p. 7). As they grow up, fortunate children are continually nourished by physical intimacy by being rocked, fed, hugged, and held. As we grow older, the opportunities for physical intimacy are less regular but still possible and important. Some physical intimacy is sexual, but this category also can include affectionate hugs, kisses, and even struggles. Companions who have endured physical challenges together —for example, in sports or during emergencies— form a bond that can last a lifetime.

iStock photo

Reflection

Intimacy through Grief

I have grown closer to many people through shared activities. My soccer teammates and I definitely bonded over the past season, and my best friend and I moved to a new level after backpacking through South America. But the 'shared activity' that stands out for me as an intimacy builder is death. Last year, I experienced the tragedy of losing a friend who died in a car accident. Grieving with our surviving group was the saddest thing I've ever experienced, and I wouldn't wish the experience on anyone. But I must say that our shared loss has created a special bond among the four of us.

In other cases, intimacy comes from *intellectual* sharing. Not every exchange of ideas counts as intimacy, of course. Talking about next week's mid-term with your professor or classmates isn't likely to forge strong relational bonds. But when you engage another person in an exchange of important ideas, a kind of closeness develops that can be powerful and exciting.

Shared activities can provide a fourth way to emotional closeness (Wood and Inman, 1993). Not all shared activities lead to intimacy. You might work with a colleague for years without feeling any sort of emotional connection. But some shared experiences—struggling together against obstacles or living together as housemates are good examples—can create strong bonds. Play is one valuable form of shared activity. Leslie Baxter (1992) found that both same-sex friendships and opposite-sex romantic relationships were characterized by several forms of play. Partners invented private codes, fooled around by acting like other people, teased one another, and played games—everything from having punning contests to arm wrestling.

The amount and type of intimacy can vary from one relationship to another (Speicher, 1999). Some intimate relationships exhibit all four qualities of emotional disclosure, physical intimacy, intellectual exchanges, and shared activities. Other intimate relationships exhibit only one or two. Of course, some relationships aren't close ones in any way. Acquaintances, roommates, and co-workers may never become intimate. In some cases, even family members develop smooth but relatively impersonal relationships.

Not even the closest relationships always operate at the highest level of intimacy. At some times, you may share all of your thoughts or feelings with a friend, family member, or lover; at other times, you may withdraw. You may freely share your feelings about one topic and stay more distant regarding another one. The same principle holds for physical intimacy, which waxes and wanes in most relationships.

Despite the fact that no relationship is *always* intimate, it is hardly desirable to live without *any* sort of intimacy. For example, one study revealed that subjects who fear intimacy while dating

Take Two

Forms of Intimacy

- **Emotional:** the exchange of important information and feelings.
- **Physical:** physical closeness both sexual and non-sexual.
- **Intellectual:** the exchange of important and profound ideas.
- **Shared activities:** mutual experiences such as struggling together or playing.

expect less satisfaction in a long-term relationship and report feeling more distant from even long-time dating partners (Sherman and Thelen, 1996; Thelen et al., 2000).

Dimensions of Distance

Intimacy in a relationship is important, but so is distance. Sometimes, we create physical and emotional space between ourselves and others whose behaviour we find bothersome, such as an intrusive relative or annoying co-worker. There are also times when we feel the need to distance ourselves, at least temporarily, from people we genuinely care for (Hess, 2000).

Just as there are a variety of ways to be intimate, there are different ways to gain distance in a relationship. Jon Hess (2002) identified fifteen strategies for gaining and maintaining distance in a relationship (you read about some of them in Chapter 8). The most common strategy for creating distance, at least among students, is *avoidance*. We can avoid unwanted contact physically, or by other means. For example, if your phone service includes call display, you can screen your incoming messages and ignore ones from unwanted callers.

Other common avoidance tactics include being *reserved*—saying little when you're with the other person; by *shortening interaction*, perhaps by not asking questions or engaging in non-verbal behaviour that encourages the other person to talk; by *restricting topics*, especially those that might be personal or intimate; and by using *restraint*—for instance, avoiding joking or other attention-getting

Take Two

Forms of Distance

- **Avoidance:** evading contact with others.
- **Being reserved:** holding back expression of thoughts and feelings.
- **Shortening interactions:** not asking questions and/or providing non-verbal cues to encourage conversation.
- **Restricting topics:** limiting what is discussed.
- **Restraint:** not joking or encouraging contact.
- **Deception:** lying.

behaviours that often encourage unwanted contact. *Deception* is a sixth way to distance yourself. We will have more to say about lies—benevolent and otherwise—later in this chapter.

The Dialectics of Intimacy and Distance

Intimacy and distance are both important. It is impossible to have a close relationship with everyone because there simply isn't enough time and energy. Even if we could become intimate with everyone we encounter, few of us would want that much closeness. Consider the range of everyday contacts that do not require any sort of intimacy. Some are based on economic exchange (with the people at work or the shopkeeper you visit several times a week); some are based on group membership (in a place of worship or school); some are based on physical proximity (to neighbours or through carpooling); and some grow out of third-party connections (mutual friends, child care). Simply engaging in conversational give-and-take with both strangers and acquaintances can be enjoyable.

These examples suggest that intimacy isn't essential, even with people we encounter often. It's possible to have a very satisfying relationship with some friends, neighbours, co-workers, or even some family members without a high degree of closeness (Weiss, 1998). You can probably think of several satisfying relationships that include moderate or even low amounts of intimacy. This doesn't mean that intimacy is unimportant—just that it isn't the *only* measure of relational satisfaction.

Some scholars have pointed out that an obsession with intimacy can lead to *less* satisfying relationships (Bellah et al., 1985; Parks, 1982). People who consider intimate communication to be the only kind worth pursuing place little value on relationships that do not meet this standard. This can lead them to regard interaction with strangers and casual acquaintances as superficial, or at best as the groundwork for deeper relationships. When you consider the pleasure that can come from polite but distant communication, the limitations of this view become clear. Intimacy is definitely rewarding, but it is not the only way of relating to others.

Another look at two of the dialectical tensions introduced in Chapter 8 reminds us that all relationships—even the closest ones—require some distance. We value privacy as well as disclosure, and autonomy is just as important as connection. On a short-term basis, the desire for intimacy waxes and wanes, regardless of the stage of the relationship. C. Arthur VanLear (1991) found that lovers and married couples often go through periods of much sharing, alternating with times of relative withdrawal. Likewise, they experience periods of passion and then times of little physical contact. Friends, too, have times of high disclosure, when they share almost every feeling and idea, and then disengage for days, months, or even longer.

The dialectical tension between intimacy and distance seems to make sense. Intimacy is rather like chocolate. We may enjoy or even crave it, but too much of a good thing can extinguish the desire for more. Despite this fact, the tension between the opposing drives of openness and closedness can be a dilemma for many friends, co-workers, family members, and lovers. For example, many former couples report that the breakup of their relationships was caused in great part by their inability to manage the contradictions between the desires for intimacy and distance (Baxter, 1994; Kramer, 1997).

The need for autonomy can manifest itself in a number of ways, such as the desire to make separate friends, to engage in activities that do not include the spouse, or to make a career move that might disrupt the relationship. As we explained in the Chapter 8 discussion of relational stages, this movement from closeness to autonomy may lead to the breakup of relationships; however, it also can be part of a maintenance cycle that continuously redefines the relationship in new forms that recapture or even surpass the intimacy that existed in the past.

Given the equally important needs for intimacy and distance, the challenge is to communicate in a manner that provides the best possible mix of intimate and non-intimate relationships (Petronio, 1991). The material in the rest of this chapter can help you find the optimal level of intimacy in your relationships.

Influences on Intimacy and Distance

What is the ideal amount of intimacy? The answer varies according to who is giving the answer. You know from personal experience that different people seek different levels of intimacy. What factors lead to these differences? Two of the most powerful influences are gender and culture.

Male and Female Intimacy Styles

Until recently, most social scientists believed that women were better than men at developing and maintaining intimate relationships. This view grew from the assumption that the disclosure of personal information is the most important ingredient of intimacy. Most research *does* show that women (taken as a group, of course) are somewhat more willing than men to share their most personal thoughts and feelings (Dindia and Allen, 1992), although the differences aren't as dramatic as most people believe (Dindia, 2000b, 2002). In some situations, such as between therapist and patient, there appear to be no differences at all (Roe, 2001).

Many social scientists who explored the relationship between biological sex, gender, and communication interpreted the relatively lower rate of male self-disclosure as a sign that men were unwilling or unable to develop close relationships.

iStock photo

Some (e.g., Weiss and Lowenthal, 1975) argued that the female trait of revealing information and feelings made them more 'emotionally mature' and 'interpersonally competent' than men. The title of one book captured this attitude of female superiority and male deficiency: *The Inexpressive Male: A Tragedy of American Society* (Balswick, 1988). Personal-growth programs and self-help books urged men to achieve closeness by learning to open up and share their feelings.

But more recent scholarship has begun to show that emotional expression is not the *only* way to develop close relationships (Floyd, 1996; Inman, 1996; Johnson, 1996). Whereas women place a somewhat higher value on talking about personal matters as a measure of closeness, men are more likely to create and express closeness by doing things together. In one study, more than 75 percent of the men surveyed said that their most meaningful experiences with friends came from

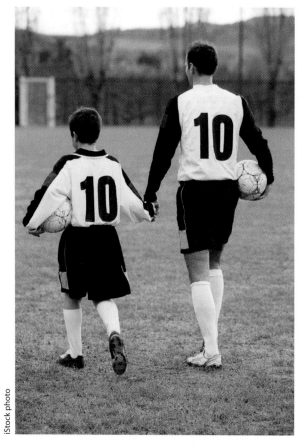

iStock photo

arise between the sexes. For example, a woman who looks for emotional disclosure as a measure of affection may overlook an 'inexpressive' man's efforts to show he cares by doing favours or spending time with her. Fixing a leaky tap or taking a hike may look like ways to avoid getting close, but to the man who proposes them, they may be measures of affection and bids for intimacy. Likewise, differing ideas about the timing and meaning of sex can lead to misunderstandings. Whereas many women think of sex as a way to *express* an intimacy that has already developed, men are more likely to see it as a way to *create* that intimacy (Reissman, 1990). In this sense, the man who encourages sex early in a relationship or after a fight may not just be a testosterone-crazed lecher. Rather, he may view the shared activity as a way to build closeness. By contrast, the woman who views personal talk as the pathway to intimacy may resist the idea of physical closeness before the emotional side of the relationship has been discussed.

As with all research looking at women's and men's communication, it is important to realize that no generalization applies to every person. Furthermore,

shared activities (Swain, 1989). They reported that through shared activities they 'grew on one another', developed feelings of interdependence, showed appreciation for one another, and demonstrated mutual liking. Likewise, men regarded practical help as a measure of caring. Findings like these show that, for many men, closeness grows from activities that do not always depend heavily on disclosure. A friend is a person who does things *for* you and *with* you. Of course, it's important not to assume that all men who value shared activities are reluctant to share feelings, or that doing things together isn't important to women. Recent scholarship offers convincing evidence that, in many respects, the meaning of intimacy is more similar than different for men and women (Goldsmith and Fulfs, 1999).

Whatever differences do exist between male and female styles of intimacy help explain some of the stresses and misunderstandings that can

iStock photo

stereotypes are changing. For example, an analysis of prime-time television sitcoms showed that male characters who reveal personal information generally receive favourable responses from other characters (Good et al., 2002). In addition, researchers Mark Morman and Kory Floyd (2002) note that a cultural shift is taking place in North America, in that fathers are becoming more affectionate with their sons than they were in previous generations—although some of that affection is still expressed through shared activities.

Cultural Influences on Intimacy

Historically, the notions of public and private behaviour have changed dramatically (Adamopoulos, 1991; Gadlin, 1977). What would be considered intimate behaviour today was quite public at times in the past. For example, in sixteenth-century Germany, newlyweds were often expected to consummate their union in a bed carried by witnesses who would validate the marriage! (See Adamopoulos and Bontempo, 1986.) Conversely, in England as well as in colonial North America, the customary level of communication between spouses was once quite formal—not much different from the way acquaintances or neighbours spoke to one another.

Today, the notion of intimacy varies from one culture to another. In one study, researchers asked residents of Britain, Japan, Hong Kong, and Italy which of thirty-three rules that regulated interaction in social relationships they followed (Argyle and Henderson, 1985). The rules governed a wide range of communication behaviour: everything from the use of humour, to shaking hands, to the management of money. The results showed that the greatest differences between Asian and European cultures involved the rules for dealing with intimacy, including showing emotions, expressing affection in public, sexual activity, and respecting privacy. In addition to differences in notions of intimacy, the amount of intimacy individuals desire also varies from one culture to another. In a comparison of members of collectivistic and individualistic cultures (Turkish and mainstream Canadian), researchers from Toronto's

York University studied the participants' ratings of ideal closeness in a variety of relationships (i.e., with friends, family, and acquaintances) (Uskul et al., 2004). Both the Turkish and the Canadian participants ideally wanted to be closest to their romantic partner; however, the Turkish participants wanted to have greater intimacy than the Canadians in all types of relationships. The Turks also said they did feel closer to friends, family, and acquaintances than the Canadians did.

Disclosure is especially high in mainstream North American society. In fact, United States citizens do more disclosing than members of any other culture studied (Gudykunst, 1986). They are likely to reveal more about themselves to acquaintances and even to strangers. By contrast, Germans and Japanese tend to reveal little about themselves, except in personal relationships with a select few (Seki et al., 2002). In some collectivist cultures, such as those of Taiwan and Japan, there is an especially great difference in the way people communicate with members of their in-groups (such as family and close friends) and with those they view as outsiders (Seki et al., 2002; Triandis, 1994). They generally do not reach out to strangers, often waiting until they are properly introduced before entering into a conversation. Once introduced, they address outsiders with formality and go to extremes to hide unfavourable information about in-group members from them. By contrast, members of more individualistic cultures, such as those of Canada, the United States, and Australia, make less distinction between personal and casual relationships. They are more familiar with strangers and reveal more personal information, making them excellent 'cocktail party conversationalists'. Social psychologist Kurt Lewin (1936) captured the difference nicely when he noted that Americans were easy to meet but difficult to get to know, while Germans were difficult to meet but then easy to know well.

Differences like these mean that the level of self-disclosure that is appropriate in one culture may seem completely inappropriate in another one. If you were raised in Canada or the United States, you may view people from other cultures

Focus on Research

Do Rural and Small-Town Canadians Really Have an Advantage When It Comes to Social Relationships?

There has long been a popular idea that people living in rural areas and small towns enjoy greater intimacy with their friends and neighbours when compared to people living in large urban centres like Toronto, Montreal, Vancouver, and Ottawa. Big cities are characterized as cold and uncaring, whereas people living on farms and in small towns are often portrayed as warm, friendly, and eager to help each other out, especially when it comes to battling the 'elements' or inclement Canadian weather. But is there any truth to these stereotypes? Statistics Canada (2005) explored some of these ideas in the 2003 General Social Survey on Social Engagement, and here is what they discovered:

• Depending on how you define *rural* (Statistics Canada offers six different definitions) between 6 and 11 million Canadians, or between 22 and 38 percent of the population, live in rural areas.
• Rural people are more likely than city dwellers to know most or all of their neighbours and more likely to trust them.
• Between 52 and 61 percent of rural Canadians said they knew all their neighbours. That's three times

higher than people from the four largest urban centres (Toronto, Montreal, Vancouver, and Ottawa), where only 16 percent said they knew all their neighbours. In addition, rural Canadians were more likely than urban Canadians to have a strong sense of belonging to their community.
• About one-third of rural residents (32 percent) expressed a strong sense of belonging to the local community compared to only 19 percent of those living in cities with a population over one million.
• Although rural Canadians were more likely than their city cousins to say their neighbours could be trusted a lot, the percentage of people who had helped or been helped by their neighbours was not significantly different in urban and rural areas. Nor did that neighbourly trust generalize into greater trust of people in general. Fifty-two percent of people living in large urban areas and 59 percent of rural dwellers said that most people could be trusted. The proportion of people living in medium-sized cities who said most people could be trusted was the same as rural dwellers.

So, it appears that there is evidence to support the idea that rural Canadians know and trust their neighbours to a greater degree than urban Canadians, but if you get your car stuck in the snow, country people and city people are equally likely to help dig you out.

as reserved and perhaps standoffish. The converse is also true. To members of other cultures, North Americans probably appear like exhibitionists who spew out personal information to anyone within earshot.

A principle to keep in mind when communicating with people from different cultures is that it is important to consider their norms for appropriate intimacy. On one hand, do not mistakenly judge them according to your own standards. Likewise, be sensitive about honouring their standards when talking about yourself. In this sense, choosing the proper level of intimacy is not too different from choosing the appropriate way of dressing or eating when encountering members of a different culture: what seems familiar and correct at home may not be suitable with strangers.

Self-Disclosure in Relationships

One way we judge the strength of relationships is by the amount of information we share with others. 'We don't have any secrets,' some people proudly claim. As we explained in Chapter 1, one ingredient in qualitatively interpersonal relationships is disclosure. In Chapter 8, we described how people find others more attractive when they share certain private information with them. Given the obvious importance of self-disclosure, we need to take a closer look at the subject. Just what is it? When is it desirable? How can it best be done?

A Definition of Self-Disclosure

You might argue that aside from secrets, it is impossible *not* to make yourself known to others. After

Reflection

Intimacy Varies by Culture, Generation, and Individual Personality

When I was growing up, Friday night dinners at my grandparents' house seemed like formal occasions. There were really no big differences between these mealtimes and ordinary mealtimes at our house, but Friday night dinners felt different. The conversations seemed to lack emotion. It was very polite and rather stiff. Conversations with my grandparents always had that distant feeling. At first, I thought it was because my grandparents were older, but when I visited a friend's Italian grandparents, I realized some older people express their emotions a lot. So then I wondered if it was a cultural thing. My grandparents were born in Switzerland and moved to Canada as young adults. Then I visited my relatives in Switzerland, and they seemed relaxed and open about revealing their feelings. So it didn't seem to be a purely cultural phenomenon either. Maybe there are a lot of things—including our individual personalities—that influence how easily we reveal our feelings.

all, every time you open your mouth to speak, you're revealing your tastes, interests, desires, opinions, beliefs, or some other bit of information about yourself. Even when the subject is not a personal one, your choice of what to talk about tells the listener something about who you are. In Chapter 6, we discussed the fact that each of us communicates non-verbally even when we're not speaking. For instance, a yawn may mean that you're tired or bored, a shrug of your shoulders may indicate uncertainty or indifference, and how close or how far you choose to stand from your listener may be taken as a measure of your friendliness or comfort.

Test Yourself   Describe the influences of gender and culture on intimacy and distance.

If every verbal and non-verbal behaviour in which you engage is self-revealing, how can self-disclosure be distinguished from any other act of communication? Psychologist Paul Cozby (1973) offers an answer. He suggests that in order for a communication act to be considered self-disclosing, it must meet the following criteria: (1) It must contain personal information about the sender, (2) the sender must communicate this information verbally, and (3) another person must be the target. Put differently, the subject of self-disclosing communication is the *self*, and information about the self is *purposefully communicated to another person*.

Although this definition is a start, it ignores the fact that some messages intentionally directed toward others are not especially revealing. For example, telling an acquaintance, 'I don't like clams' is quite different from announcing, 'I don't like you.' Let us take a look at several factors that further distinguish self-disclosure from other types of communication.

Honesty   It almost goes without saying that true self-disclosure has to be honest. It's not revealing to say, 'I've never felt this way about anyone before' to every Saturday night date, or to preface every lie with the statement 'Let me be honest . . .'

As long as you are honest and accurate to the best of your knowledge, communication can qualify as an act of self-disclosure. On the other hand, painting an incomplete picture of yourself (telling only part of what is true) is not genuine disclosure. We will talk more about the relationship between honesty and disclosure later in this chapter.

Depth   A self-disclosing statement is generally regarded as being personal—containing relatively 'deep' rather than 'surface' information. Of course, what is personal and intimate for one person may not be for another. You may feel comfortable admitting your spotty academic record, short temper, or fear of spiders to anyone who asks, whereas others would be embarrassed to do so. Even basic demographic information, such as age, can be extremely personal for some people.

iStock photo

Availability of Information Self-disclosing messages must contain information that the other person is not likely to know at the time or be able to obtain from another source without a great deal of effort. For example, describing your conviction for a drunk-driving accident might feel like an act of serious disclosure because the information concerns you, is offered intentionally, is honest and accurate, and is considered personal. However, if the other person could obtain that information elsewhere without much trouble—from a glance at the morning newspaper or from various gossips, for example—your communication would not disclose very much.

Context of Sharing Sometimes, the self-disclosing nature of a statement comes from the setting in which it is uttered. For instance, relatively innocuous information about family life seems more personal when a student shares it with the class (Myers, 1998), or when an athlete tells it to her coach (Officer and Rosenfeld, 1985). This sort of sharing creates a more personal atmosphere because it changes the relationship from a purely 'business' level to a more personal one.

We can summarize our definitional tour by saying that **self-disclosure** (1) has the self as subject, (2) is intentional, (3) is directed at another person, (4) is honest, (5) is revealing, (6) contains information generally unavailable from other sources, and (7) gains much of its intimate nature from the context and culture in which it is expressed.

Although many acts of communication may be self-revealing, this definition makes it clear that few of our statements may be classified as self-disclosure. Pearce and Sharp (1973) estimate that as little as 2 percent of our communication qualifies as self-disclosure. Other research confirms this. For example, most conversations—even among friends—focus on everyday mundane topics and disclose little or no personal information (Dindia et al., 1997; Duck and Miell, 1986). Even partners in intimate relationships don't talk about personal matters very often (Duck, 1991).

Degrees of Self-Disclosure

Although our definition of self-disclosure is helpful, it doesn't include the important fact that not all self-disclosure is equally revealing—that some disclosing messages tell more about us than others.

Social psychologists Irwin Altman and Dalmas Taylor (1973; Taylor and Altman, 1987) describe two ways in which communication can be more or less disclosing. Their **social penetration model** is pictured in Figure 9.1. The first dimension of self-disclosure in this model involves the **breadth** of information volunteered—the range of subjects being discussed. For example, the breadth of disclosure in your relationship with a fellow worker will expand as you begin revealing information about your life away from the job, as well as on-the-job details. The second dimension of disclosure is the **depth** of the information being volunteered—the shift from relatively unrevealing messages to more personal ones.

Depending on the breadth and depth of information shared, a relationship can be defined as casual or intimate. In a casual relationship, the breadth may be great, but not the depth. A more intimate relationship is likely to have high depth in at least one area. The most intimate relationships are those in which disclosure is great in

Test Yourself Describe all the qualities of self-disclosure.

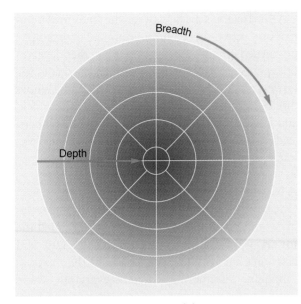

Figure 9.1 Social Penetration Model

both breadth and depth. Altman and Taylor see the development of a relationship as a progression from the periphery of their model to its centre, a process that usually takes place gradually. Each of your personal relationships probably has

a different combination of breadth of subjects and depth of revelation. Figure 9.2 pictures a student's self-disclosure in one relationship.

What makes the disclosure in some messages deeper than others? One way to measure depth is by how far it goes on two of the dimensions that define self-disclosure. Some revelations are certainly more *significant* than others. Consider the difference between saying, 'I love my family' and 'I love you.' Other statements qualify as deep disclosure because they are *private*. Sharing a secret that you have told to only a few close friends is certainly an act of self-disclosure, but it's even more revealing to divulge information that you have never told anyone.

Another way to classify the depth of disclosure is to look at the types of information that can be revealed. *Clichés* are ritualized, stock responses to social situations—virtually the opposite of self-disclosure: 'How are you doing?' 'Fine.' Although hardly revealing, clichés can serve as a valuable kind of shorthand that makes it easy to keep the social wheels greased and can indicate the potential for further, possibly more profound conversation.

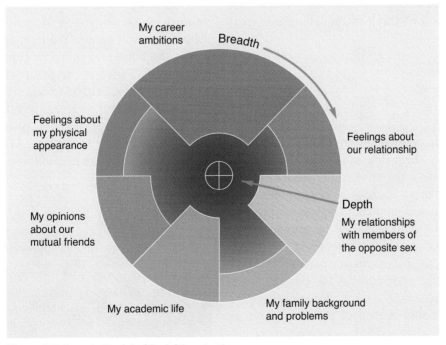

Figure 9.2 Sample Model of Social Penetration

Another kind of message involves communicating *facts*. Not all factual statements qualify as self-disclosure. To qualify, they must fit the criteria of being intentional, significant, and not otherwise known: 'This isn't my first try at college. I dropped out a year ago with terrible grades.' Facts like these can be meaningful in themselves, but they also have a greater significance in a relationship. Disclosing important information suggests a level of trust and commitment that signals a desire to move the relationship to a new level of intimacy.

Opinions can be a revealing kind of self-disclosure since they often reveal more about a person than facts alone do. If you know where the speaker stands on a subject, you can get a clearer picture of how your relationship might develop. Likewise, every time you offer a personal opinion, you are giving others valuable information about yourself.

The fourth level of self-disclosure—and usually the most revealing one—involves the expression of *feelings*. At first glance, feelings might appear to be the same as opinions, but there's a big difference. 'I don't think you're telling me about what's on your mind' is an opinion. Notice how much more we learn about the speaker by looking at three different feelings that could accompany this statement: 'I don't think you're telling me what's on your mind . . .

> *and I'm suspicious.'*
> *and I'm angry.'*
> *and I'm hurt.'*

What is the optimal amount of self-disclosure? Several factors help determine the 'best' level of openness. One is the amount of *perceived* disclosure. This is a better measure of happiness than the *actual* amount, and couples in satisfying relationships tend to overestimate the amount of personal information their partners reveal.

Another factor that shapes satisfaction is how well the level of disclosure matches the expectations of the communicators. If we get what we believe is a reasonable amount of candour from others, we are happy. If they tell us too little—or even too much—we become less satisfied (Rubin et al., 1980).

A third factor is the fit between the amount of information offered by communicators. For example, unmarried couples are happiest when their levels of openness are roughly equal. Some married couples, however, are most satisfied when one spouse enjoys disclosing and the other is a good listener (Rosenfeld and Bowen, 1991). These factors, as well as others, lead to the guidelines for when to self-disclose, found on pages 279–82 of this chapter.

A Model of Self-Disclosure

One way to illustrate how self-disclosure operates in communication is to look at a model called the **Johari Window**, developed by Joseph Luft and Harry Ingham (Luft, 1969; Janas, 2001).

Imagine a frame that contains everything there is to know about you: your likes and dislikes, your goals, your secrets, your needs—everything. This frame could be divided into information you know about yourself and things you don't know. It could also be split into things others know about you and things they don't know. Figure 9.3 represent these divisions.

Part 1 represents the information that both you and the other person already have. This part is your *open area*. Part 2 represents the *blind area*: information of which you are unaware but that the other person knows. You learn about information in the blind area primarily through feedback from others. Part 3 of the Johari Window represents your *hidden area*: information that you know but are not willing to reveal to others. Items in this hidden area become public primarily through self-disclosure. Part 4 of the Johari Window represents information that is *unknown* to both you

Take Two

- **Social penetration model:** two ways, measured by breadth and depth, that communication can be more or less disclosing.
- **Breadth:** the range of subjects discussed.
- **Depth:** the personal nature of information (significant and private self-disclosures, clichés, facts, opinions, and feelings).

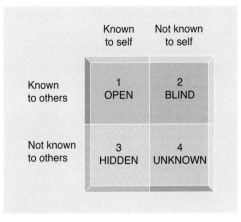

Figure 9.3 Johari Window

Source: .Figures 9.3 through 9.5 are from J. Luft, *Group Process: An Introduction to Group Dynamics.* Copyright © 1963, 1970 by Joseph Luft. Used with the permission of Mayfield Publishing Company.

and to others. At first, the unknown area seems impossible to verify. After all, if neither you nor others know what it contains, how can you be sure it exists at all? We can deduce its existence because we are constantly discovering new things about ourselves. For example, it is not unusual to discover that you have an unrecognized talent, strength, or weakness. Items move from the unknown area into the open area when you share your insight, or into the hidden area, where it becomes a secret.

The relative size of each area in our personal Johari Windows changes from time to time according to our moods, the subject we are discussing, and our relationship with the other person. Despite these changes, a single Johari Window could represent most people's overall style of disclosure. Figure 9.4 pictures windows representing four extreme styles of interaction.

Style I depicts a person who is neither receptive to feedback nor willing to self-disclose. This person takes few risks and may appear aloof and uncommunicative. The largest quadrant is the unknown area: such people have a lot to learn about themselves, as do others.

Style II depicts a person who is open to feedback from others but does not voluntarily self-disclose. This person may fear exposure, possibly because of a distrust of others. People who fit this pattern may appear highly supportive at first. After all, they want to hear *your* story, and they appear willing to deny themselves by remaining quiet. Then, this first impression fades, and, eventually, you may see them as distrustful and detached. A Johari Window describing such people has a large hidden area.

Style III in Figure 9.4 describes people who discourage feedback from others but disclose freely. Like the people pictured in Style I, they may distrust the opinions of others. They certainly seem self-centred. Their largest quadrant is the blind area. They do not encourage feedback and thus fail to learn much about how others view them.

Style IV depicts people who are both willing to disclose information about themselves and be open to other people's ideas. They are trusting enough to seek the opinions of others and to express their own. If taken to extremes, this communication style can be intimidating and overwhelming

Figure 9.4 Four Styles of Disclosure

because it violates the usual expectations of how non-intimates ought to behave. In moderation, however, this open style provides the best chance for developing highly interpersonal relationships.

Interpersonal communication of any significance is virtually impossible if the individuals involved have small open areas. Going a step further, you can see that a relationship is limited by the individual who is less willing to disclose. Figure 9.5 illustrates this situation with Johari Windows. A's window is set up in reverse so that A's and B's open areas are adjacent. Notice that the amount of communication (represented by the arrows connecting the two open areas) is dictated by the size of the smaller open area of A. The arrows originating from B's open area and being turned aside by A's hidden and blind areas represent unsuccessful attempts to communicate.

You have probably found yourself in situations that resemble Figure 9.5. Perhaps you have experienced the frustration of not being able to get to know someone who was too reserved. Perhaps you have blocked another person's attempts to build a relationship with you in this way. Whether you picture yourself more like Person A or more like Person B, the fact is that self-disclosure on both sides is an important ingredient in the development of most interpersonal relationships.

Risks and Benefits of Self-Disclosure

By now, it should be clear that neither all-out disclosure nor complete privacy is desirable. In the following pages we will outline both the risks and benefits of opening yourself to others.

Benefits of Self-Disclosure Although the amount of self-disclosure varies from one person and relationship to another, all of us share important information about ourselves at one time or another. What leads us to open up? Derlega and Grzelak (1979), Kelly (1999), and Agne et al. (2000) present a variety of reasons for disclosing in any particular situation. We can build upon their work by showing how these reasons have at least potential benefits.

Catharsis Sometimes, you might disclose information in an effort to 'get it off your chest'. Catharsis can indeed relieve the burden of pent-up emotions, but when it is the *only* goal of disclosure, the results of opening up may not be good. This is especially true when the person disclosing does not take the relationship with the recipient into account (Kelly et al., 2001). Consider, for example, the likely effects of confessing to a friend your unflattering opinion of him or her: 'To tell you the truth, I've always thought your jokes are stupid

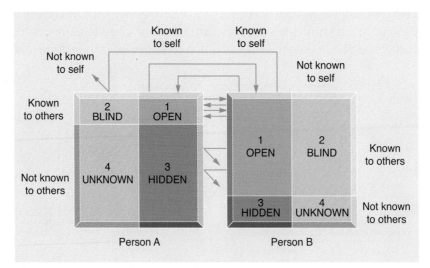

Figure 9.5 How Limited Disclosure Blocks Communication

Test Yourself   Describe the four quadrants of the Johari Window and their relationship to receptivity to feedback.

and that you're egotistical.' You might feel better for getting this secret off your chest, but your friend may not feel better about you after this confession. Later in this chapter, you will read guidelines for disclosing that improve your chance of achieving catharsis in a way that helps, instead of harming relationships.

Self-clarification   It is often possible to clarify your beliefs, opinions, thoughts, attitudes, and feelings by talking about them with another person. This gaining of insight by 'talking the problem out' occurs in many psychotherapies, but it also goes on in other relationships, ranging all the way from close friendships to conversations with bartenders or hairdressers. When the purpose for disclosing is to gain new insights, people who self-disclose tend to feel more positive about their secrets and come to terms with them (Kelly et al., 2001).

Self-validation   If you disclose information with the hope of seeking the listener's agreement ('I think I did the right thing'), you are seeking validation of your behaviour—confirmation of a belief you hold about yourself. On a deeper level, this sort of self-validating disclosure seeks confirmation of important parts of your self-concept. Self-validation through self-disclosure is an important part of the 'coming out' process through which gay people recognize their sexual orientation and choose to integrate this knowledge into their personal, familial, and social lives (Han, 2001; Savin-Williams, 2001).

Reciprocity   A well-documented conclusion from research is that one person's act of self-disclosure makes it more likely that the other person will reveal personal information (Derlega et al., 1993; Dindia, 2000b, 2002). There is no guarantee that revealing personal information about yourself will trigger self-disclosures by others, but your own honesty can create a climate that makes the other person feel safer, and perhaps even obligated to match your level of candour. Sometimes, revealing personal information will cause the other person to do so within the same conversation. It's easy to imagine how telling a partner how you feel about the relationship ('I've been feeling bored lately') would generate the same degree of candour ('You know, I've felt the same way!'). Reciprocity does not always occur at the same time. Telling a friend today about your job-related problems might help her feel comfortable telling you about her family history later, when the time is right for this sort of disclosure.

Impression formation   Sometimes, we reveal personal information to make ourselves more attractive, and research shows that this strategy seems to work. One study revealed that both men's and women's attractiveness was associated with the amount of self-disclosure in conversations (Stiles

iStock photo

Self-Assessment

Analyzing Your Self-Disclosure Choices

Part 1: Why you disclose

Use the following scale to indicate your reasons for self-disclosing. These reasons are likely to vary for each relationship you analyze, so you may choose to repeat this self-assessment more than once. Keep one relationship in mind as you complete the self-assessment.

1 = This is definitely not a reason I self-disclose.
2 = This is probably not a reason I self-disclose.
3 = I am unsure whether this is a reason I self-disclose.
4 = This is probably a reason I self-disclose.
5 = This is definitely a reason I self-disclose.

_____ 1. I disclose as a means to get something off my chest—to vent my feelings.

_____ 2. I disclose as a way to clarify what my beliefs, feelings, opinions, thoughts, and so on are—to use the other person as a 'sounding board'.

_____ 3. I disclose to get the other person to agree with me about how I see the situation.

_____ 4. I disclose as a way to encourage the other person to talk to me.

_____ 5. I disclose certain pieces of information so as to create a particular impression of myself.

_____ 6. I disclose to keep the other person current with what is happening to me, so that our relationship 'doesn't fall behind'.

_____ 7. I disclose to be able to achieve some particular goal—for example, to increase my control over the other person, the situation, or our relationship.

_____ 8. I disclose so I can get advice, support, or assistance from this person.

_____ 9. I disclose because I 'owe it' to this person, or feel obligated, because this person has the right to know.

_____ 10. I disclose to the other person because we care for each other, trust one another, and support one another.

Part 2: Reasons for not disclosing

Use the scale below to identify your reasons for not disclosing personal information. As before, you may choose to repeat this self-assessment for each of your important relationships, but keep one relationship in mind for each evaluation.

1 = This is definitely not a reason I avoid self-disclosing.
2 = This is probably not a reason I avoid self-disclosing.
3 = I am unsure whether this is a reason I avoid self-disclosing.
4 = This is probably a reason I avoid self-disclosing.
5 = This is definitely a reason I avoid self-disclosing.

_____ 1. I can't find the opportunity to self-disclose.

_____ 2. I don't want to upset or hurt the person—perhaps put the person's life in an uproar.

_____ 3. I can't think of a way to self-disclose.

_____ 4. The information I disclose might be used against me in some way.

_____ 5. I might be treated differently after I self-disclose.

_____ 6. I might be treated as if I were 'crazy' after I self-disclose.

_____ 7. I don't think I'll get support if I self-disclose.

_____ 8. I might not be understood.

_____ 9. My self-disclosure might hurt our relationship.

_____ 10. What I self-disclose might be told to people I would prefer not know.

_____ 11. I don't self-disclose because our relationship isn't close enough.

_____ 12. What I self-disclose might be told to people I would prefer to tell myself.

_____ 13. I don't know how to put what I want to say into words.

What are your most important or usual reasons for disclosing? What are your most important or usual reasons for not disclosing? What does this information reveal to you about how you use self-disclosure in your relationships, and the kinds of relationships you have?

et al., 1996). Consider a couple on their first date. It's not hard to imagine how one or both partners might share personal information to appear more sincere, interesting, sensitive, or curious about the other person. The same principle applies in other situations. A salesperson might say, 'I'll be honest with you . . .' primarily to show that she is on your side, and a new acquaintance might talk about the details of his past in order to seem more friendly and likeable. Whether or not you try to create a good impression depends on whether you expect to have future dealings with this person (Tidwell, 1998).

Maintenance and enhancement of relationships
Research demonstrates that we like people who disclose personal information to us. In fact, the relationship between self-disclosure and liking works in several directions. We like people who disclose personal information to us, we reveal more about ourselves to people we like, and we tend to like others more after we have disclosed to them (Dindia, 2000b).

Beyond fostering liking, disclosure (if it is appropriate, of course) can keep relationships healthy (Fitzpatrick and Sollie, 1999; Lippert and Prager, 2001; Vittengl and Holt, 2000). Not surprisingly, partners who reveal personal information to each other often avoid the sorts of misunderstandings that lead to unhappiness. For example, the bond between grandparents and grandchildren grows stronger when the honesty and depth of sharing between them are high (Downs, 1988). Stepchildren who self-disclose to their step-parents feel as if the step-parents understand them better (Martin et al., 1999). Even relative strangers who work together in groups are more productive, cohesive, and committed to their job when they are encouraged to share their feelings about the task at hand (Elias et al., 1989).

Appropriate self-disclosure is positively related to marital satisfaction (Rosenfeld and Bowen, 1991; Waring and Chelune, 1983). One study revealed that distressed couples who sought counselling disclosed less information to each other and communicated more ambiguously than couples who were not distressed (Chelune et al., 1985). Couples recognize the value of disclosure. Disclosing spouses give their relationships higher evaluations and have more positive expectations than partners who disclose less. In one sample of fifty couples, the amount of overall disclosure in their relationships was a good predictor of whether the partners remained together over the four years in which they were studied (Sprecher, 1987).

Whether lack of self-disclosure is a cause or a symptom of troubled marriages is not clear. However, couples who learn to change their communication styles are likely to find their relationships growing stronger. A number of studies have demonstrated that increased self-disclosure can improve troubled marriages (Vito, 1999; Waring, 1981). With the guidance of a skilled counsellor or therapist, partners can learn constructive ways to open up.

Moral obligation Sometimes, we disclose personal information out of a sense of moral obligation. People who are HIV-positive, for example, are often faced with the choice of whether or not they should tell their health-care providers and their partner. Robert Agne and his colleagues (2000) found that patients usually did disclose their HIV status to their health-care provider because they felt it was the responsible thing to do for themselves (to help fight their illness) and to protect the provider—even if they risked their pride, dignity, and being stigmatized. Val Derlega and his colleagues (2000), who looked at the reasons for telling one's partner about a positive HIV diagnosis, found that they saw disclosing 'as a duty' and as a way to educate the partner.

Social influence As we saw in Chapter 8, self-disclosure can be an effective compliance-gaining strategy. Revealing personal information may increase your control over the other person and, sometimes, over the situation in which you and the other person find yourselves. For example, a valued employee who tells the boss that another firm has made overtures to her will probably have a better chance of getting raises and improvements in her working conditions.

In addition to disclosing to help ourselves, people sometimes reveal personal information to help others. This practice is common in self-help groups such as Alcoholics Anonymous (Hegelson and Gottlieb, 2000). On a larger scale, one study revealed that guests who chose to self-disclose on a particular television talk show said their primary motive was 'evangelical'. They felt a calling to address injustices and to remedy stereotypes (Priest and Dominick, 1994).

Self-defence   Sometimes, you may choose to disclose something before someone else discloses it for you. A review of the social influence literature by Williams and Dolnik (2001) suggests that disclosing negative or damaging information about oneself is frequently used as an adaptive social influence strategy.

Lawrence Rosenfeld and Leslie Kendrick (1984) found that college students' most important reasons for disclosing depend on whether the other person is a stranger or a friend. When the target was a friend, the students disclosed to maintain and enhance the relationship, to clarify their own feelings, and to both reciprocate their partner's revelations and encourage their partner to reciprocate their own disclosures. When the target was a stranger, the primary reasons for disclosing were to encourage the other person to disclose and reciprocate the other's revelations. This makes sense, because reciprocity of information provides a basis for deciding whether to continue the relationship and how personal it is likely to be. Another reason for disclosing to strangers was to make a good impression.

The Risks of Self-Disclosure While the benefits of disclosing are certainly important, opening up can also involve risks that make the decision to disclose a difficult and sometimes painful one (Cline and McKenzie, 2000; Niederhoffer and Pennebaker, 2002). The risks of self-disclosure fall into several categories (Derlega et al., 2000; Rosenfeld, 1979, 2000).

Take Two

Benefits of Self-Disclosure

- **Catharsis:** revealing thoughts, feelings, and emotions to release emotional burden.
- **Self-clarification:** talking about beliefs, thoughts, opinions, and attitudes to gain insight.
- **Reciprocity:** disclosing information to increase the likelihood that the other person will do the same.
- **Impression formation:** revealing personal information in order to make ourselves more attractive.
- **Maintenance and enhancement of relationships:** foster liking and maintain healthy relationships through disclosure.
- **Social influence:** disclosing information to exert control over others.
- **Self-defence:** disclosing something before someone else does.

Rejection   John Powell (1969) summed up the risks of disclosing in answering the question that forms the title of his book, *Why Am I Afraid to Tell You Who I Am?* 'I am afraid to tell you who I am, because, if I tell you who I am, you may not like who I am, and that's all I have.' The fear of disapproval is powerful. Sometimes, it is exaggerated and illogical, but there are real dangers in revealing personal information:

> A: I'm starting to think of you as more than a friend. To tell the truth, I think I love you.
> B: I think we should stop seeing one another.

Negative impression   Even if disclosure does not lead to total rejection, it can create a negative impression.

> A: You know, I've never had a relationship with a woman that lasted more than a month.
> B: Really? I wonder what that says about you.

Decrease in relational satisfaction   Besides affecting others people's opinions of you, disclosure can lead to a decrease in the satisfaction that comes from a relationship. Consider a scenario like this, where the incompatible wants and needs of both people become clear through disclosure:

A: Let's get together with Pierre and Michelle on Saturday night.

B: To tell you the truth, I'm tired of seeing Pierre and Michelle. I don't have much fun with them, and I think Pierre is kind of a jerk.

A: But they're my best friends!

Loss of influence   Another risk of disclosure is a possible loss of influence in the relationship. Once you confess a secret weakness, your control over how the other person views you can be diminished.

A: I'm sorry I was so sarcastic. Sometimes, I build myself up by putting you down.

B: Is that it? I'll never let you get away with that again!

Loss of control   Revealing something personal about yourself means losing control of the information. What might happen if the person tells someone else what you disclosed—people you prefer not to know, or whom you would like to tell yourself?

A: I never really liked Leslie. I agreed to go out because it meant a good meal in a nice restaurant.

B: Really? Leslie would certainly like to know that!

Hurt the other person   Even if revealing hidden information leaves you feeling better, it might hurt others—cause them to be upset, for example. It's probably easy to imagine yourself in a situation like this:

A: Well, since you asked, I have felt less attracted to you lately. I know you can't help it when your skin breaks out, but it is kind of a turnoff.

B: I know! I don't see how you can stand me at all!

Increased awareness   Paradoxical as it sounds, a final risk of self-disclosure is that it often leads to increased awareness. As you reveal yourself to others, you often learn more about yourself. This awareness can expose a need for you to change, and this might be difficult or painful. If ignorance is bliss, self-awareness can sometimes be quite the opposite—at least temporarily.

A: Talking to you about my smoking—and listening to myself!—makes it clear to me that I need to quit . . . and I'm not sure I'm ready to do that.

Alternatives to Self-Disclosure

Though self-disclosure plays an important role in interpersonal relationships, it's not the only type of communication available. To understand why complete honesty is not always easy or ideal, consider some familiar situations:

Your friend, who is headed out the door for an important job interview, says, 'I know I'll never get this job! I'm really not qualified, and besides, I look terrible.' You agree with your friend's assessment.

A romantic partner asks why you haven't been affectionate lately. 'Are you getting bored with me?' your partner asks. If you were to be completely honest, you would reply, 'Yes.'

You have just been given a large, extremely ugly lamp as a gift by a relative who visits your home often. How would you answer the question, 'Where will you put it?'

Situations like these highlight some of the issues that surround deceptive communication. On one hand, our moral education and common sense lead us to abhor anything less than the truth. James Jaksa and Michael Pritchard (1994) point out that the very existence of a society seems based on a foundation of truthfulness. While isolated cultures do exist where deceit is a norm (Turnbull, 1988), they are dysfunctional and constantly on the verge of breakdown.

Although honesty is desirable in principle, it often has risky, unpleasant consequences. It's tempting to sidestep situations where self-disclosure would

Focus on Technology

Does the Future Belong to the Uninhibited?

In her *New York* magazine article about the tendency of younger people to disclose personal information on the Internet (through social-networking sites, personal pages, blogs, etc.), Emily Nussbaum (2007) explores older people's and younger people's differing views on privacy. She observes that people under 30 years of age are much more willing than older people to put their personal information out in public. Nussbaum describes the phenomenon of archiving adolescence through blogs, pictures, and videos and suggests that, while older people may balk at the amount of disclosure young people are willing to engage in, their notions of privacy may be outdated. After all, many public places are surveyed with video cameras; debit, credit cards, and cell phones can be used to monitor our whereabouts; and even the videos we watch on YouTube can be identified (Hartley, 2008).

Although they are a relatively recent phenomenon (e.g., Facebook and MySpace were both created in 2004), most university and college students use social-networking sites regularly. Canada is second only to the United States in having the largest number of Facebook users in the world, with Toronto being the largest geographic Facebook community globally (Geist, 2007). In their exploration of what information students at a large university in the American Midwest included in their profiles, Joy Peluchette and Katherine Karl (2008) found that 80 percent of the students used at least one social-networking site (e.g., Facebook, MySpace, Friendster) and over 50 percent of them logged in every day. They found that men were more likely than women to post risqué pictures of themselves and 20 percent of the students reported that they would not want future employers to see some of the information they had included in their profiles. Peluchette and Karl recommend that colleges and universities warn students about the potential implications of what they post on the Internet since the intended audiences (friends and family) are not always the actual recipients of the information posted. Sometimes, it is difficult to judge the long-term risks of such public and possibly permanent types of disclosure; however, keeping in mind the risks and guidelines for disclosure outlined in this chapter can't hurt.

---

be difficult, but examples like the ones you just read show that avoidance is not always possible.

Take Two

Risks of Self Disclosure

- **Rejection:** fear of disapproval.
- **Negative impression:** if not outright rejection, it can make you look bad.
- **Decrease in relational satisfaction:** relationships can suffer from disclosure.
- **Loss of influence:** reveal your weakness and you may have less influence over others.
- **Loss of control:** people can tell others and, thus, control information that you want to manage.
- **Hurt the other person:** might cause the other person to be upset.
- **Increased awareness:** self-discovery can be difficult or painful.

Research and personal experience show that communicators—even those with the best intentions—are not always completely honest when they find themselves in situations when honesty would be uncomfortable (O'Hair and Cody, 1993). Five common alternatives to self-disclosure are remaining silent or secretive, lying, equivocating, hinting, and avoiding. We will take a closer look at the first four of these alternatives in the following pages. *Avoiding* is discussed in Chapter 11.

Silence and Secrecy

When confronted directly by your spouse about your lack of affection you don't really have the luxury of the 'No comment' (the non-verbal speak to the hand) response favoured by many politicians, lawyers, and movie stars. There are situations, however, when you can keep information to yourself. Keeping silent is one way to avoid disclosing information you would rather keep private, particularly in situations when you are not asked directly. In their exploration of the dark and light sides of avoidance and secrets, Tamara Afifi, John Caughlin, and Waid Afifi (2007) discuss what characterizes secrecy. They suggest that secrets involve intentionally concealing private information that the individual considers too risky to reveal. Not all silence is secretive, however, when you choose silence over disclosure you have made a choice to conceal information, at least in that particular situation. As we have discussed throughout this text, talk–silence patterns vary by culture, and many Canadians find prolonged silences uncomfortable. However, this is not the case in many Asian and Canadian First Nations cultures. Within a culture, some people are more inclined to keep their emotions and thoughts to themselves (Vrij et al., 2003). Investigations into the advantages and disadvantages of secrecy have revealed that most people think that there are definitely some drawbacks about secrecy. Specifically, keeping secrets appears to have negative effects on intimacy as well as health and well-being (Pennebaker, 1997)—but there are definitely disadvantages to speaking up, too. The willingness of people to voice their opinions is very much related to their perceptions of support of their point of view (Hayes et al., 2001). People keep secrets to avoid feeling upset, ashamed, and embarrassed (Vrij, et. al., 2003). In addition, they may choose silence in order to avoid receiving unwanted advice or upsetting others. Determining whether or not information is just private (others have no claim to it) or whether it is a secret (we are keeping it from people who have a right to know) involves considering the ethics of evasion which we will discuss a little later in this chapter.

Lying

A **lie** is a deliberate attempt to hide or misrepresent the truth. To most of us, lying seems to be a breach of ethics. In fact, extensive lying is usually a sign of relational distress (Cole, 2001).

Lying to gain unfair advantage over an unknowing victim seems clearly wrong, but another kind

iStock photo

of untruth—the 'benevolent lie'—is not so easy to condemn as completely unethical. **Benevolent lies** are defined (at least by the people who tell them) as not being malicious—and perhaps they are even helpful to the person they are told to. Though most people favour honesty in close relationships, they do admit that there are cases when benevolent lying is not only necessary but also the right thing to do. The most obvious reason for benevolent lying is to protect the other person's feelings. You can almost certainly recall times when you have been less than truthful in order to avoid hurting someone you care for.

Whether or not they are innocent, benevolent lies are certainly common. In one study, 130 subjects were asked to keep track of the truthfulness of their everyday conversational statements (Turner et al., 1975). Only 38.5 percent of these statements—slightly more than one-third—proved to be totally honest. In another study, both students and community members reported lying regularly, at least once a day (DePaulo et al., 1996). The majority of these lies were reported to be not very serious and caused little regret (Kashy and DePaulo, 1998).

Reasons for Lying What reasons do people give for being deceitful? When subjects in DePaulo and colleagues' study (1996) were asked to give a lie-by-lie account of their motives for concealing or distorting the truth, five major reasons emerged.

To save face Over half of the lies in the study were justified as a way to prevent embarrassment. Sometimes a lie saves face for the recipient, as when you pretend to remember someone at a party in order to save the person from the embarrassment of being forgotten. Married couples are especially likely to lie in order to protect the feelings of their spouse (Metts, 1989). In other cases, a self-serving lie protects the speaker from humiliation. For instance, you might cover up your mistakes by blaming them on outside forces: 'You didn't receive the cheque? It must have been delayed in the mail.' Manipulative people, less highly socialized people, and people with less gratifying same-sex relationships tell more self-serving lies, whereas people with higher-quality same-sex relationships tell relatively more lies aimed at preserving the face of others (Kashy and DePaulo, 1998).

To avoid tension or conflict Sometimes, it seems worthwhile to tell a small lie to prevent a large conflict. For example, you might say you're not upset at a friend's teasing to prevent the argument that would result if you showed your annoyance. It's often easier to explain your behaviour in dishonest terms than to make matters worse. You might explain your apparent irritation by saying, 'I'm not mad at you; it's just been a tough day.'

To guide social interaction Sometimes, we lie to make everyday relationships run smoothly. You might pretend to be glad to see someone you actually dislike or fake interest in a dinner companion's boring stories to make a social event pass quickly. Children who are not skilled at or interested in these social lies are often a source of embarrassment to their parents.

To expand or reduce relationships Some lies are designed to make a relationship grow: 'You're going downtown? I'm headed that way. Can I give you a ride?' 'I like science fiction, too. What have you read lately?' One study (Rowatt et al., 1999) illustrated the pervasiveness of lying to further relationships.

Reflection

Withholding the Truth from My Parents

I've been going out with a guy for several months. He's white and I'm black, which is no problem for us or our friends. I haven't told my parents about his race, though, because it would make them very uncomfortable.

Even though I'm not lying to my family, I feel uneasy not telling them an important part of the truth. Still, I have decided to tell them only once I'm sure this relationship will become more serious. There's just no point in getting them upset over nothing.

A majority of college students (both men and women) willingly lied to improve their chances of getting a date with an attractive partner. Exaggerations and untruths covered a wide range of topics, including their attitudes about love, personality traits, income, past relationships, career skills, and intelligence—all in the direction of making themselves more similar to the attractive prospects.

Romance is not the only area where people lie to enhance their relationships. You might try to impress a potential employer by calling yourself a management student when you have only taken a course or two in business. Sometimes, we tell untruths to reduce interaction with others. Lies in this category often allow the teller of the lie to escape unpleasant situations: 'I really have to go. I should be studying for a test tomorrow.' In other cases, people lie to end a relationship entirely: 'You're really great, but I'm just not ready to settle down yet.'

To gain power We sometimes tell lies to show that we are in control of a situation. Turning down a last minute request for a date by claiming you're busy can be one way to put yourself in a one-up position, saying, in effect, 'Don't expect me to sit around waiting for you to call.' Lying to get confidential information—even for a good cause—also falls into the category of achieving power.

These five reasons are not the only way to categorize lies. Exaggerations, for example, are not covered in this list. Table 9.1 lists several other reasons for distorting the truth.

Most people think benevolent lies are told for the benefit of the recipient. For example, the majority of subjects in the DePaulo et al. study (1996) claimed such lying was 'the right thing to do'. Other research paints a less flattering picture of who benefits most from lying. One study found that two out of every three lies are told for 'selfish reasons' (Hample, 1980). Other research by Paula Lippard (1988) suggests that this figure is too low. Of 322 lies recorded, 75.8 percent were for the benefit of the liar. Fewer than 22 percent were for the benefit of the person hearing the lie, and a mere 2.5 percent were intended to aid a third person.

One measure of the acceptability of lying is the fact that most people are willing to accept obvious lies without challenging them. In fact, there are some circumstances when lies are considered preferable to the undiluted truth (Hubbell, 1999; McCornack,

1992). Peter Andersen (1999) outlines the conditions when we are most likely to let statements that we know are untruthful go unchallenged:

1. *When we expect others to lie.* (You listen with amusement to a friend or relative's tall tales, even though you know they are exaggerations.)
2. *When the lie is mutually advantageous.* (A fellow employee's self-serving account of a job mix-up might get you off the hook, too.)
3. *When a lie helps us avoid embarrassment.* (A dinner guest assures you that your meal was delicious, even though you know it tasted awful.)
4. *When the lie helps us avoid confronting an unpleasant truth.* (One spouse might not threaten the tenuous stability of the marriage by referring to a partner's suspected infidelity.)
5. *When we have asked the other person to lie.* (A patient might tell the doctor, 'Don't let me know if it's malignant.')

Table 9.1 Some Reasons for Lying

Reason	Example
Acquire resources	'Oh, please let me add this class. If I don't get in, I'll never graduate on time!'
Protect resources	'I'd like to lend you the money, but I'm short myself.'
Initiate and continue interaction	'Excuse me, I'm lost. Do you live around here?'
Avoid conflict	'It's not a big deal. We can do it your way. Really.'
Avoid interaction	'That sounds like fun, but I'm busy Saturday night.'
Leave taking	'Oh, look what time it is! I've got to run!'
Present a competent image	'Sure I understand. No problem.'
Increase social desirability	'Yes, I've done a fair amount of skiing.'
Exaggeration	'You think this is cold? Let me tell you about how cold it was on that trip. . . .'

Source: Adapted from categories originally presented in C. Camden, M. T. Motley, and A. Wilson (1984), White lies in interpersonal communication: A taxonomy and preliminary investigation of social motivations, *Western Journal of Speech Communication, 48*, 315.

Effects of Lies   Lies can elicit different responses. Feelings like dismay and betrayal are greatest when the relationship is most intense, the subject is very important, and when there was previous suspicion that the other person wasn't being completely honest. Of these three factors, the importance of the information lied about proved to be the key factor in provoking a relational crisis. For example, survey respondents whose parents did not communicate about problems before announcing an impending divorce reported lower self-esteem and less satisfaction with their deceptive mothers (Thomas et al., 1995).

An occasional benevolent lie in an otherwise honest relationship does not pose much threat. Major deception, though—especially when it is part of a pattern of deceit—is likely to provoke a relational crisis. In fact, the discovery of major deception can lead to the end of a relationship. More than two-thirds of the subjects in a study by McCornack and Levine (1990a) reported that their relationship had ended since they discovered a lie. Furthermore, they attributed the breakup directly to the deception.

The lesson here is clear: lying about major parts of your relationship can have the gravest of consequences. If preserving a relationship is important to you, then honesty—at least about important matters—really does appear to be the best policy.

Focus on Research

What Is a Lie, and When Is It a Good Thing? Cross-Cultural Comparisons

In a fascinating study, investigators from Canada and the People's Republic of China explored adults' concepts about lying and the truth (Fu et al., 2001). Their purpose was to examine further the findings of a previous study (Lee et al., 1997), in which Chinese and Canadian children had been told stories about characters who did pro-social or anti-social deeds. The characters were then questioned by their teachers about what they had done. The Chinese children evaluated the characters who lied about their pro-social deeds more favourably than the characters who told the truth about their pro-social deeds. In contrast, the Canadian children evaluated the children who told the truth about their pro-social deeds more favourably than the children who lied. Lee and colleagues (1997) suggested the children were influenced by the emphasis in Chinese culture on modesty and self-effacement. The Chinese children believed that lying for reasons of modesty was a good thing and that telling the truth about good deeds was morally undesirable. The older the Chinese children were, the more likely they were to evaluate lying to hide one's good deeds as positive and telling the truth about one's good deed as undesirable.

Fu and colleagues (2001) wondered whether these same differences between Asian and Western children in evaluating the morality of lying would hold up for Asian and Western adults. They conducted a very similar experiment with seventy-nine Canadian adults and ninety-seven Chinese adults. Like the Chinese children, the Chinese adults evaluated the character who lied about doing a pro-social act more favourably than the character who told the truth. However, unlike the children, the Chinese adults considered the untruthful statements made to conceal the person's own good deeds not to be lies. Almost all the Canadian adults considered these untruthful statements to be lies, as did almost all the Canadian and Chinese children in the previous study.

This study was the first to find evidence that concepts of lying may not be universal and may be determined by social-cultural conventions. In this instance, the untruthful statement may not be considered a lie because it serves a highly valued virtue in Chinese collectivist culture—modesty. Modesty is an important virtue for maintaining group cohesiveness and harmony. The fact that the older Chinese children in the first study evaluated the untruthful statements made to conceal one's good deeds more favourably than the younger Chinese children did and that the Chinese adults then moved these untruthful statements out of the category of 'lies' supports the notion that conceptualizations and evaluations of lying are not universal and continue to develop well into adulthood.

Test Yourself What reasons do people give for lying and what are the effects of lies?

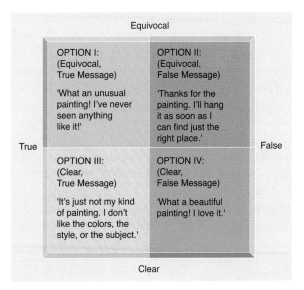

Figure 9.6 Dimensions of Truthfulness and Equivocation

Equivocation

Lying is not the only alternative to self-disclosure. When faced with the choice between lying and telling an unpleasant truth, communicators can—and often do—equivocate. As we explained in Chapter 5, **equivocal language** has two or more equally plausible meanings.

Sometimes, we send equivocal messages without meaning to, resulting in confusion. 'I'll meet you at the apartment' could refer to more than one place. But other times we are deliberately vague. When a friend asks what you think of an awful outfit, you could say, 'It's really unusual—one of a kind!' Likewise, if you are too angry to accept a friend's apology but don't want to appear petty, you might say, 'Don't mention it.'

The value of equivocation becomes clear when you consider the alternatives. Consider the dilemma of what to say when you have been given an unwanted present—an ugly painting, for example—and the giver asks what you think of it. How can you respond? On the one hand, you need to choose between telling the truth and lying. At the same time, you have a choice of whether to make your response clear or vague. Figure 9.6 displays these choices.

After considering the alternatives, it is clear that the first option—an equivocal, true response—is far preferable to the other choices in several respects. First, it spares the receiver embarrassment. Rather than flatly saying no to an unappealing invitation, it may be kinder saying, 'I have other plans'—even if those plans are to stay home and watch television.

A study by Sandra Metts and her colleagues (1992) shows how equivocation can save face in difficult situations. Several hundred college students were asked how they would turn down unwanted sexual overtures from a person whose feelings were important to them: a close friend, a

prospective date, or a dating partner. The majority of students chose a diplomatic reaction ('I just don't think I'm ready for this right now') as being more face-saving and comfortable than a direct statement like 'I just don't feel sexually attracted to you.' The diplomatic reaction seemed sufficiently clear to get the message across, but not so blunt as to embarrass or humiliate the other person. (Interestingly, men said they would be better able to handle a direct rejection than women did. The researchers suggest that one reason for the difference is that traditionally men make the sexual overtures and, thus, are more likely to expect rejection.)

Besides saving face for the recipient, honest equivocation can be less stressful for the sender than either telling the truth bluntly or lying. Because equivocation is often easier to take than the cold, hard truth, it spares the teller from feeling guilty. It's less taxing on the conscience to say, 'I've never tasted anything like this' than to say, 'This meal tastes terrible,' even though the latter comment is more precise. Few people *want* to lie, and equivocation provides an alternative to deceit.

Equivocal language may also save the speaker from being caught lying. If a potential employer asks about your grades during a job interview, you would be safe saying, 'I had a B average last semester,' even though your overall grade average is closer to C. The statement isn't a complete answer, but it is honest as far as it goes. As Bavelas and colleagues (1990, p. 171) put it, 'Equivocation is neither a false message nor a clear truth, but rather an alternative used precisely when both of these are to be avoided.'

In addition to preventing dishonesty, saving face, and minimizing stress, equivocation can be quite effective at making a point. Renee Edwards and Richard Bello (2001) explored how receivers interpreted equivocal statements, such as telling a friend that his or her speech was 'interesting' instead of saying, 'You messed up.'

DILBERT reprinted by permission of United Feature Syndicate, Inc.

Besides regarding the equivocal statements as more polite, they had no trouble discerning the intended meaning—that the speech was poor, to use our example.

Given these advantages, it is not surprising that most people will usually choose to equivocate rather than tell a lie. In a series of experiments, subjects chose between telling a face-saving lie, the truth, and equivocating (Bavelas et al., 1990). Only 6 percent chose the lie, and between 3 and 4 percent chose the hurtful truth. By contrast, over 90 percent chose the equivocal response. People may say they prefer telling the truth to equivocating, but given the choice, they prefer to finesse the truth (Robinson et al., 1998).

Hinting

Hints are more direct than equivocal statements. Whereas an equivocal message is not necessarily aimed at changing another's behaviour, a hint seeks to get the desired response from the other person. As Michael Motley (1992) suggests, some hints are designed to save the receiver from embarrassment:

Direct Statement	Face-Saving Hint
You're too overweight to be ordering dessert.	These desserts are terribly overpriced.
I'm too busy to continue with this conversation. I wish you would let me go.	I know you're busy; I'd better let you go.

Other hints are less concerned with protecting the receiver than with saving the sender from embarrassment:

Direct Statement	Face-Saving Hint
Please don't smoke here; it bothers me.	I'm pretty sure that smoking isn't permitted here.
I'd like to invite you out for lunch, but I don't want to risk a 'no' answer to my invitation.	Gee, it's almost lunch time. Have you ever eaten at that new Italian restaurant around the corner?

Take Two

Alternatives to Self-Disclosure

- **Silence or secrecy:** say nothing.
- **Lying:** deliberately attempt to hide or misrepresent the truth.
- **Equivocation:** give a response that has two or more equally plausible meanings.
- **Hinting:** a face-saving response designed to get a desired response.

The success of a hint depends on the other person's ability to pick up the unexpressed message. Your subtle remarks may go right over the head of an insensitive receiver, or one who chooses not to respond to them. If this happens, you still have the choice to be more direct. If the costs of a straightforward message seem too high, you can withdraw without risk.

The Ethics of Evasion

It is easy to see why people often choose hints, equivocations, and benevolent lies instead of complete self-disclosure. These strategies are a way to manage difficult situations that is easier than the alternatives for both the speaker and the receiver of the message. In this sense, successful liars, equivocators, and hinters can be said to possess a certain kind of communicative competence. On the other hand, there *are* times when honesty is the right approach, even if it is painful. At times like these, evaders could be viewed as lacking either the competence or the integrity to handle a situation effectively.

Are hints, benevolent lies, and equivocations ethical alternatives to self-disclosure? Some of the examples in these pages suggest the answer is a qualified yes. Many social scientists and philosophers agree. For example, researchers David Buller and Judee Burgoon (1994) argue that the morality of a speaker's motives for lying, not the deceptive act itself, ought to be judged. Another approach is to consider whether the effects of a lie will be worth the deception. Ethicist Sissela Bok (1978) says deception may be justified if it does good, prevents harm, or protects a larger truth. Perhaps the right questions to ask, then, are whether an indirect message is truly in the interests of the receiver and whether this sort of evasion is the only effective way to behave. Bok suggests another way to check the justifiability of a lie. Imagine how others would respond if they knew what you were really thinking or feeling. Would they accept your reasons for not telling the truth?

Guidelines for Self-Disclosure

Self-disclosure is a special kind of sharing that is not desirable in every situation. Let us look at some guidelines that can help you recognize how to express yourself in a way that's rewarding for you and for the others involved.

Building Work Skills

Disclosure at Work

Imagine a situation at work where you have made a mistake. Imagine that part of the reason for your error is related something personal (for example, conflict in a relationship, a disability you have, a bias you have). In order for the problem to be corrected, you need to tell either your co-worker or your boss or supervisor. Whom would you tell? What would you tell them? How much information would you reveal? Describe the risks and benefits of the choices you made. Share your approach and list of the risks and benefits with a classmate. Do they agree with your analysis? Why or why not?

Is the Other Person Important to You?

There are several ways in which someone might be important. Perhaps you have an ongoing relationship deep enough that sharing significant parts of yourself justifies keeping your present level of togetherness intact. Or perhaps the other person is someone you know but not intimately. Now you see a chance to grow closer, and disclosure may be the path toward developing that personal relationship.

Is the Risk of Disclosing Reasonable?

Most people intuitively calculate the potential benefits of disclosing against the risks of doing so (Fisher, 1986; Vangelisti et al., 2001). This approach makes sense. Even if the probable benefits are great, opening yourself up to almost certain rejection may be asking for trouble. For instance, it might be foolhardy to share your important feelings with someone who is likely to betray your confidences or ridicule them. On the other hand, knowing that your partner will respect the information makes the prospect of speaking out more reasonable.

Revealing personal thoughts and feelings can be especially risky on the job (Eisenberg, 1990; Eisenberg and Witten, 1987). The politics of the workplace sometimes require communicators to keep their feelings to themselves in order to accomplish both personal and organizational goals. You may find the opinions of a boss or customer personally offensive but decide to bite your tongue rather than risk your job or lose goodwill for the company.

In calculating the risks of disclosing, be sure that you are realistic. It is sometimes easy to imagine disastrous consequences that in fact are quite unlikely.

Is the Self-Disclosure Appropriate?

Self-disclosure is not an all-or-nothing proposition. It's possible to reveal information in some situations and keep it to yourself in others. One important variable is the relational stage (VanLear, 1987; Won-Doornick, 1979). Research shows that sharing personal information is appropriate during the integrating stage of a relationship, where

Reflection

Equivocation Provides Comfort

My mother made her share of mistakes in raising my sisters and me. Now, her health is failing and I am aware that every conversation we have may be our last one.

My mom is understandably scared of death and in need of comfort. Last week, I told her, 'You have taught me a lot about being a mother.' I didn't tell her that many of the lessons I learned from her taught me what not to do when I have daughters of my own.

My vagueness wasn't a lie, but it wasn't the entire truth either. I'm comfortable with my equivocation here. This is no time for complete, brutal honesty.

partners grow closer by disclosing. But, once the same relationship has reached a maintenance stage, the frequency of personal disclosures drops (Sillars et al., 1987). This makes sense, for by now the partners have already revealed much of their private selves. Even the closest long-term relationships are a mixture of much everyday, non-intimate information and less frequent but more personal messages. Finally, realize that even intimate partners need to be sensitive to the timing of a message. If the other person is tired, preoccupied, or in a bad mood, it may be a good idea to postpone an important conversation.

Is the Disclosure Relevant to the Situation at Hand?

The kind of disclosure that is often a characteristic of highly personal relationships usually is not appropriate in less personal situations. For instance, a study of classroom communication revealed that sharing all feelings—both positive and negative—and being completely honest resulted in less cohesiveness than a 'relatively' honest climate in which pleasant but superficial relationships were the norm (Rosenfeld and Gilbert, 1989).

iStock photo

Even during a phase of high disclosure, sharing *everything* about yourself isn't necessarily constructive. Usually, the subject of appropriate self-disclosure involves the relationship rather than personal information (Sillars et al., 1987). Furthermore, it is usually most constructive to focus your disclosure about the relationship on the 'here and now' as opposed to 'there and then'. 'How am I feeling now?' 'How are we doing now?' These are suitable topics in the sharing of personal thoughts and feelings. There are certainly times when it is relevant to bring up the past, but only as it relates to what's going on in the present.

Is the Disclosure Reciprocated?

There is nothing quite as disconcerting as talking your heart out to someone, only to discover that the other person has yet to say anything to you that is half as revealing. You think to yourself, 'What am I doing?' Unequal self-disclosure creates an unbalanced relationship, one with potential problems.

The reciprocal nature of effective disclosure doesn't mean that you are obliged to match every one of another person's revelations. You might reveal personal information at one time, while the other person could open up at a later date. There are even times when reciprocal self-disclosure can be taken as stage hogging. For instance, if a close friend is talking about his opinion of your relationship, it is probably better to hear him out and bring up your perspective later, after he has made his point.

There are only a few times when one-way disclosure is acceptable. Most of them involve formal, therapeutic relationships in which a client or patient approaches a trained professional with the goal of resolving a problem. For instance, you

Test Yourself Describe the seven factors you need to consider before disclosing information about yourself to others.

would not necessarily expect your physician to tell you about her or his own ailments during an office visit.

Will the Effect Be Constructive?

Self-disclosure can be a vicious tool if it is not used carefully. Every person has a psychological boundary beyond which are subjects about which the person is extremely sensitive. Jabbing in that area is a sure way to disable another person, usually at great cost to the relationship. It's important to consider the effects of your candour before opening up to others. Comments such as 'I've always thought you were pretty unintelligent' or 'Last year, I made love to your best friend' may sometimes resolve old business and thus be constructive, but they can also be devastating—to the listener, to the relationship, and to your self-esteem.

Is the Self-Disclosure Clear and Understandable?

When expressing yourself to others, it is important to be intelligible. This means describing the sources of your message clearly. For instance, it's far better to describe another person's behaviour by saying, 'When you don't answer my phone calls or drop by to visit any more . . .' than to complain vaguely, 'When you avoid me . . .'

It is also vital to express your *thoughts* and *feelings* explicitly. 'I feel worried because I'm afraid you don't care about me' is more understandable than 'I don't like it . . .'

Summary

Intimacy—a sense of closeness with others—comes in several forms: emotional, physical, and intellectual, and that found in shared activities. As important as intimacy is to relationships, so is distance. We can create distance from others through a variety of means such as avoidance, restricting communication, or deception. Intimacy is not essential to all relationships, and even in relationships where it is important, it is not important all the time. Intimacy and distance exist together in a dialectical tension—as opposing forces in a constant battle for balance. Whether in a growing relationship, a stable one, or a deteriorating one, intimacy and distance form a cyclical pattern where first one and then the other is more important.

Gender and culture exert a strong influence on both the amount of intimacy in a relationship and how that intimacy is communicated. A female intimacy style is usually characterized by self-disclosure, and a male intimacy style by shared activities. These differences exist within larger cultural differences. Each culture has rules that govern intimate communication, from touching in public to the disclosure of personal information. Also, each culture defines the extent to which any relationship should be formal and distant or close and intimate.

An important determinant of intimacy, although not the only determinant, is self-disclosure. Self-disclosure consists of honest, revealing messages about the self that are intentionally directed towards others. Disclosing communication contains information that is generally unavailable from other sources. Revealing personal information does not guarantee that this communication will be perceived by others as disclosing. The percentage of messages that are truly self-disclosing is relatively low. A number of factors govern whether a communicator will be judged as being a high- or low-level discloser.

The social penetration model describes two dimensions of self-disclosure: breadth and depth. Disclosure of feelings is usually more revealing than disclosure of opinions, and disclosure of opinions is usually more revealing than disclosure of facts. Clichés are the least revealing.

The Johari Window model is a useful way to illustrate self-disclosure. A window representing one person can illustrate the amount of information that an individual reveals to others, hides, is blind to, and is unaware of. Windows representing two communicators reveal how differing levels of disclosure can affect the level of intimacy in a relationship.

Communicators disclose personal information for a variety of reasons: catharsis, self-clarification, self-validation, reciprocity, impression formation, relationship maintenance and enhancement, moral obligation, social control, and self-defence. There also are several reasons to choose not to self-disclose: the possibility of rejection or of leaving a negative impression, a decrease in relational satisfaction, a loss of influence, a loss of control, the potential to hurt others, and the possibility of pain associated with increased self-awareness.

Four alternatives to revealing self-disclosures are silence, lies, equivocations, and hints. Non-malicious, 'benevolent lies' serve a variety of functions: saving face for the sender or receiver, avoiding tension or conflict, guiding social interaction, managing relationships,

and gaining power. When discovered by the recipient, lies may provoke a relational crisis, especially if the content of the information lied about is important. In some cases, however, communicators make the choice to let lies go unchallenged. Equivocation can allow a communicator to be honest without being blunt and causing an undesirable reaction. Hints, more direct than equivocation, are used primarily to avoid embarrassment. Hints are risky in that they depend on the other person's ability to pick up unexpressed messages.

Lies, equivocations, and hints may be ethical alternatives to self-disclosure; however, whether they are or not depends on the speaker's motives and the effects of the deception. When deciding whether or not to disclose, communicators should consider a variety of factors, such as the importance of the other person; the risk involved; the appropriateness, relevance, and constructiveness of the disclosure; whether the disclosure will be reciprocated; and whether the disclosure is clear and understandable.

Activities

1. **Invitation to Insight**

   What kinds of intimacy characterize your relationships? Answer the questions below as you think about your relationship with an important person in your life:

   a. What is the level of physical intimacy in your relationship?
   b. What intellectual intimacy do you share?
   c. How emotionally intimate are you? Is your emotional intimacy deeper in some ways than in others?
   d. What shared activities are important in this relationship?
   e. Has your intimacy level changed? If so, in what ways?

   After answering these questions, ask yourself how satisfied you are with the amount of intimacy in this relationship. Identify any changes you would like to occur, and describe the steps you could take to make them happen.

2. **Invitation to Insight**

   You can get a sense of how your desires for both intimacy and distance operate by following these directions:

   a. Choose an important interpersonal relationship with someone you encounter on a frequent, regular basis. You might choose a friend, family member, or romantic partner.
   b. For at least a one-week period, chart how your communication with this relational partner reflects your desire for either intimacy or distance. Use a 7-point scale in which behaviour seeking high intimacy receives a 7 and behaviour designed to avoid physical, intellectual, and/or emotional contact receives a 1. Use ratings from 2 to 6 to represent intermediate stages. Record at least one rating per day, making more-detailed entries if your desire for intimacy or distance changes during that period.
   c. What tactics did you use to establish or maintain distance?
   d. After charting your communication, reflect on what the results tell you about your personal desire for intimacy and distance. Consider the following questions:

   i. Was there a pattern of alternating phases of intimacy and distance during the time you observed?
   ii. Was this pattern typical of your communication in this relationship over a longer period of time?
   iii. Does your communication in other relationships contain a similar mixture of intimacy and distance?
   iv. Most important, are you satisfied with what results you discovered in this exercise? If not, how would you like to change your communication behaviour?

3. **Critical Thinking Probe**

   Using the definition of self-disclosure on page 260, identify five times when you have received self-disclosing messages from others. How did these acts affect you as the recipient, how did they affect the sender, and how did they affect any other people? Combine your findings with those of your classmates. On the basis of the information you have collected, to what degree would you say that self-disclosure is a positive form of communication?

4. **Ethical Challenge**

   Recall three recent situations in which you used each of the following evasive approaches: silence, benevolent lying, equivocating, and hinting. Write an anonymous description of each situation on a separate sheet of paper. Submit the cases to a panel of 'judges' (most likely fellow students), who will use the criteria of justifiable motives and desirable effects to evaluate the morality of this deception. Invite the 'judges' to consider how they would feel if they knew someone used these evasive approaches with them.

5. **Skill Builder**

   Use the guidelines on pages 279–82 to develop one scenario in which you *might* reveal a self-disclosing message. Create a message of this type, and use the information in this chapter to discuss the risks and benefits of sharing the message.

6. **Skill Builder**

   a. Make a list of some personal information you have not shared with a family member. Then, make a second list of information you haven't disclosed to a friend.

   b. For each item on your lists, consider:
      • the worst consequences if you were to reveal this information, and
      • the best possible consequences from disclosing this information.

   c. Evaluate the most likely outcome if you were to disclose, and then conduct a risk-benefit analysis to decide whether or not to keep the information private or share it.

7. **Role Play**

   Think of a question that you might be asked by someone significant in your life that you would prefer not to answer. Consider which alternative to disclosure you might use in this situation and prepare your response. Ask a partner to take the role of the significant other and pose the question and you will then act out your response. Discuss the strengths and challenges of your approach. Now, reverse roles.

Discussion Questions

1. Describe the four different types of intimacy presented in the chapter and give an example of each from your own relationships. Do you think an ideal intimate relationship would include all four? Why or why not?

2. Describe the six strategies for creating distance in relationships described in the chapter and give examples of each. Why is it necessary to create distance at times?

3. Describe the different ways men and women develop and maintain intimacy in relationships? Is one style better than the other? Why or why not?

4. The level of self-disclosure viewed as appropriate varies between cultures. Describe some of the differences. What is your experience?

5. Distinguish self-disclosure from other types of communication. Give an example.

6. What are the risks and benefits of lying?

7. How are lying, hinting, and equivocation different? Are they morally different?

8. Natives of the United States are more disclosing than members of any other culture studied. Germans and Japanese people tend to disclose the least. Given Canada's multiculturalism, where do you think we fall on the self-disclosure continuum?

Chapter Ten

Key Terms
aggressiveness
ambiguous response
argumentativeness
certainty
communication climate
complaining
confirming message
controlling communication
defensiveness
description
disagreeing message
disconfirming message
empathy
equality
evaluation
face
face-threatening acts
impersonal response
impervious response
incongruous response
interrupting response
irrelevant response
neutrality
presenting self
problem orientation
provisionalism
spiral
spontaneity
strategy
superiority
tangential response

Communication Climate

After studying the material in this chapter ...

You Should Understand:

1. The definition of communication climate.
2. The importance of being valued and confirmed.
3. The characteristics of confirming, disagreeing, and disconfirming messages.
4. The nature of positive and negative communication spirals.
5. The relationship between the presenting self (face) and defensiveness.
6. The types of messages that are likely to create positive communication climates.
7. The various ways to transform negative communication climates.

You Should Be Able To:

1. Identify confirming, disagreeing, and disconfirming messages and patterns in your own relationships.
2. Identify the parts of your presenting self (face) that you defend, and the consequences of doing so.
3. Create messages that are likely to build supportive rather than defensive communication climates.
4. Create appropriate non-defensive responses to real or hypothetical criticisms.

How would you describe your most important relationships? Fair and warm? Stormy? Hot? Cold? Just as physical locations have characteristic weather patterns, interpersonal relationships have unique climates, too. You can't measure the interpersonal climate by looking at a thermometer or glancing at the sky, but it's there nonetheless. Every relationship has a feeling, a pervasive mood that colours the actions of the participants.

What Is Communication Climate?

The term **communication climate** refers to the social tone of a relationship. A climate doesn't involve specific activities as much as the way people feel about each other as they carry out those activities. Consider two interpersonal communication classes. Both meet for the same length of time and follow the same syllabus. It's easy to imagine how one of these classes might be a friendly, comfortable place to learn, whereas the other could be cold and tense—even hostile. It is not the course content that differs—it is the way the people in the classroom feel about and treat each other.

Just as every classroom has a unique climate, so does every relationship. Romances, friendships, and families—just like neighbourhoods, cities, and countries—can be defined by their social tone. Another obvious place for observing the effect of a climate impact is the workplace, which may explain why the topic is so widely studied (Scarpero, 2000; Shadur et al., 1999). Have you ever held a job where backbiting, criticism, and suspicion were the norm? Or have you been lucky enough to work where the atmosphere was positive, encouraging, and supportive? If you have experienced both, you know what a difference climate makes. Other studies (e.g., Guzley, 1992; Odden and Sias, 1997) reinforce the fact that employees are more committed at jobs in which they experience a positive communication climate. David Pincus (1986) arrived at a similar conclusion: communication climate is strongly related to job satisfaction and performance. Whether it is the workplace, classroom, or home, people look for and stay in communication climates that affirm and support them.

Like their meteorological counterparts, communication climates are shared by everyone involved. It's rare to find one person describing a relationship as open and positive while another characterizes it as cold and hostile. And, just like the weather, communication climates can change over time. A relationship can be overcast at one time and sunny at another. Carrying the analogy to its conclusion, we should say that communication climate forecasting is not a perfect science. Unlike the weather, however, people can change their communication climates—and that's why it is important to understand them. We'll look at several climate issues in this chapter: how communication climates develop, how and why we respond defensively in certain climates, and what can be done to create positive climates and transform negative ones.

How Communication Climates Develop

Why does some communication create a positive climate while other communication has the opposite effect? A short but accurate answer is that communication climates are determined by the degree to which people see themselves as *valued*. Communicators who perceive others as liking, appreciating, and respecting them react positively, whereas those who feel unimportant or abused react negatively. Social scientists use the term **confirming** communication to describe messages that convey valuing. In one form or another, confirming messages say, 'you exist', 'you matter', 'you're important'. By contrast, **disconfirming** communication signals a lack of regard. In one form or another, disconfirming messages say, 'I don't care about you', 'I don't like you', 'you're not important to me'.

As we have stressed throughout this book, every message has a relational dimension along with its content. This means that we send and receive confirming and disconfirming messages virtually whenever we communicate. Serious conversations about our relationships may not be common (Goldsmith and Baxter, 1996), but we convey our attitudes about one another even when we talk about everyday matters. In other words, it isn't what we communicate about that shapes a relational climate as much as *how* we speak and act toward one another.

It is hard to overstate the importance of confirming messages and the impact of disconfirming ones. Children who lack confirmation suffer more intense feelings of anxiety, depression, grief, jealousy, and loneliness, higher incidences of mental and physical illness, and a broad range of behavioural problems, such as criminality and suicide (Osterman, 2001). In school, a sense of belonging is associated with a positive attitude toward school, class work, and teachers, and greater participation, school engagement, and achievement. Victims of hateful speech can experience the same long-term consequences that follow other traumas: feeling dazed, shocked, ill, and angry (Leets, 2002). A confirming climate is also important in marriage, where it is the best predictor of marital satisfaction (Clarke, 1973; Veroff et al., 1998). Satisfied couples have a 5:1 ratio of positive to negative statements, while the ratio for dissatisfied partners is 1:1 (Gottman, 2003; see also Canary and Emmers-Sommer, 1997).

Like beauty, the decision about whether a message is confirming or disconfirming is in the eyes of the beholder (Vangelisti and Crumley, 1998). Consider, for example, times when you took a comment that might have sounded unsupportive to an outsider ('You turkey!') as a sign of affection within the context of your personal relationship. Likewise, a comment that the sender might have meant to be helpful ('I'm telling you this for your own good . . .') could easily be regarded as a disconfirming attack.

Levels of Message Confirmation

Figure 10.1 shows that the range of confirming and disconfirming communication includes several categories of messages, which we describe in the following pages.

Confirming Messages   There is no guarantee that others will regard even your best attempts at confirming messages the way you intend them, but research shows that three increasingly positive types of messages have the best chance of being perceived as confirming (Cissna and Sieberg, 1999):

Recognition   The most fundamental act of confirmation is to recognize the other person. Recognition seems easy and obvious, yet there are many times when we do not respond to others on this basic level. Failure to write to or visit a friend is a common example. So is failure to return a phone message. Likewise, avoiding eye contact and not approaching someone you know can send a negative message. Of course, this lack of recognition may simply be an oversight. You may not notice your friend, or the pressures of work and school may prevent you from staying in touch. Nonetheless, if the other person *thinks* you avoided contact, the message has the effect of being disconfirming.

Acknowledgment   Acknowledging the ideas and feelings of others is a stronger form of confirmation than simple recognition. Listening is probably the most common form of acknowledgment. Silently and attentively paying attention to another person's words is one measure of your interest. Not surprisingly, employees give high marks to

Confirming	Disagreeing	Disconfirming
Endorsement		Impervious
Acknowledgement		Interrupting
Recognition		Irrelevant
	Argumentativeness	Tangential
	Complaining	Impersonal
	Aggressiveness	Ambiguous
		Incongruous
VALUING		**NON-VALUING**

Figure 10.1 Confirmation–Disconfirmation Continuum

iStock photo

managers who solicit their opinions—even when the managers don't accept every suggestion (Allen, 1995). As we saw in Chapter 7, reflecting the speaker's thoughts and feelings can be a powerful way to offer support when others have problems.

Endorsement   Whereas acknowledgment says you are interested in another person, endorsement means that you agree with her or him or otherwise find that person important. It's easy to see why endorsement is the strongest type of confirming message, since it communicates the highest form of valuing. The most obvious form of endorsement is agreeing, but it isn't necessary to agree completely with other people in order to endorse their message. You can probably find something in the message that you endorse. 'I can see why you were so angry', you might reply to a friend, even if you don't approve of his or her outburst. Of course, outright praise is a strong form of endorsement, one you can use surprisingly often once you look for opportunities to do so. Non-verbal endorsement also can enhance the quality of a relational climate. For example, simple acts like maintaining eye contact and nodding while someone speaks can confirm the value of a speaker's idea. On a more intimate level, embraces can sometimes communicate endorsement in ways that words cannot.

Disagreeing Messages   Between confirming and disconfirming lies a type of message that isn't always easy to categorize. A disagreeing message essentially says, 'You're wrong'. In its most

constructive form, disagreement includes two confirming components: recognition and acknowledgment. At its worst, a brutal disagreeing message can so devastate another person that the benefits of recognition and acknowledgment are lost. Because there are better and worse ways to disagree with others, disagreeing messages need to be put on a positive-to-negative scale. We will do just that in this section as we discuss three types of disagreement: *argumentativeness*, *complaining*, and *aggressiveness*.

Argumentativeness   Normally when we call a person argumentative, we're making an unfavourable evaluation. However, the ability to create and deliver a sound argument is something we admire in lawyers, talk-show participants, letters to the editor, and political debates. Taking a positive approach to the term, communication researchers define argumentativeness as presenting and defending positions on issues while attacking positions taken by others (Infante and Rancer, 1982). Rather than being a negative trait, argumentativeness is associated with a number of positive attributes, such as enhanced self-concept (Rancer et al., 1992), communicative competence (Onyekwere et al., 1991), and positive climate in the workplace (Infante and Gorden, 1987).

The key to maintaining a positive climate while arguing a point is the *way* you present your ideas. It is crucial to attack issues, not people. In addition, a sound argument is received better when it's delivered in a supportive, affirming manner (Infante and Gorden, 1989). The supportive kinds of messages outlined on pages 298–304 show how it is possible to argue in a respectful, constructive way.

Complaining   When communicators aren't prepared to argue, but still want to register dissatisfaction, they often complain. Like all disagreeing messages, some ways of complaining are better than others. Jess Alberts (1988, 1990) found that satisfied couples tend to offer behavioural complaints ('You always throw your socks on the floor'), while dissatisfied couples make more complaints aimed at personal characteristics ('You're a slob'). Personal complaints are more likely to result in an escalated conflict episode (Alberts and Driscoll, 1992). The reason should be obvious—complaints about personal characteristics attack a more fundamental part of the presenting self. Talking about socks deals with a habit that can be changed; calling someone a slob is a character assault that is unlikely to be forgotten when the conflict is over. Marriage researcher John Gottman (2000) has found that complaining is not a sign of a troubled relationship—in fact, it's usually healthy for spouses to get their concerns out in the open. However, when a couple's communication is filled with personal and disrespectful criticism, it is often a symptom of a marriage headed for divorce.

Aggressiveness   The most destructive way to disagree with another person is through aggressiveness. Dominic Infante and his associates (1992, p. 116) define verbal aggressiveness as the tendency to 'attack the self-concepts of other people in order to inflict psychological pain'. Unlike argumentativeness, aggressiveness demeans the worth of others. Name calling, put-downs, sarcasm, taunting, yelling, badgering—all are methods of 'winning' disagreements at someone else's expense.

It should come as no surprise that aggressiveness has been found to have a variety of serious consequences. Aggressive behaviour is especially hurtful when it comes from people who are close to us (Martin et al., 1996). Research shows it is associated with physical violence in marriages (Infante et al., 1989), juvenile delinquency (Atkin et al., 2002; Straus et al., 1989), depression (Segrin and Fitzpatrick, 1992), and a negative climate in both the workplace (Infante and Gorden, 1985, 1987, 1989) and the classroom (Myers and Rocca, 2001). Myers and Rocca compared argumentativeness and verbal aggressiveness and found that 'when instructors are perceived to engage in argumentativeness, they promote student . . . motivation; when instructors are perceived to engage in verbal aggressiveness, they contribute negatively to student perceptions of classroom climate and diminish student . . . motivation' (p. 131). In Chapter 11, we describe how 'win–win' approaches to

conflict are healthier and more productive than the 'win–lose' tactics of aggressiveness.

Disconfirming Messages   Disconfirming messages are subtler than confirming ones, but potentially more damaging. Disconfirming communication implicitly says, 'You don't exist; you are not valued.'

Disconfirming messages, unfortunately, are part of everyday life. Though an occasional disconfirming message may not injure a relationship, a pattern of them usually indicates a negative communication climate. Sieberg and Larson (1971) found it was easiest to recognize disconfirming communication by observing responses to the messages of others. They noted seven types of disconfirming responses:

Impervious response   An impervious response fails to acknowledge the other person's communicative attempt, either verbally or non-verbally. Failing to return a phone call or answer a letter or email is an impervious response. Impervious responses also happen in face-to-face settings. They are especially common when adults and children communicate. Parents often become enraged when they are ignored by their children; likewise, children feel diminished when adults pay no attention to their questions, comments, or requests. Most experts agree that being ignored by significant others is psychologically damaging (Holte and Wichstrom, 1990; Laing, 1961). This explains why the 'silent treatment' can be so disturbing, and why the cruellest punishment children can bestow on others is to ignore them.

Interrupting response   As its name implies, an interrupting response is made when one person begins to speak before the other is through making a point.

Customer: I'm looking for an outfit I can wear on a trip I'm . . .
Salesperson: I've got just the thing. It is part wool and part polyester, so it won't wrinkle a all.
C: Actually, wrinkling isn't that important. I want something that will work as a business outfit and
. . .

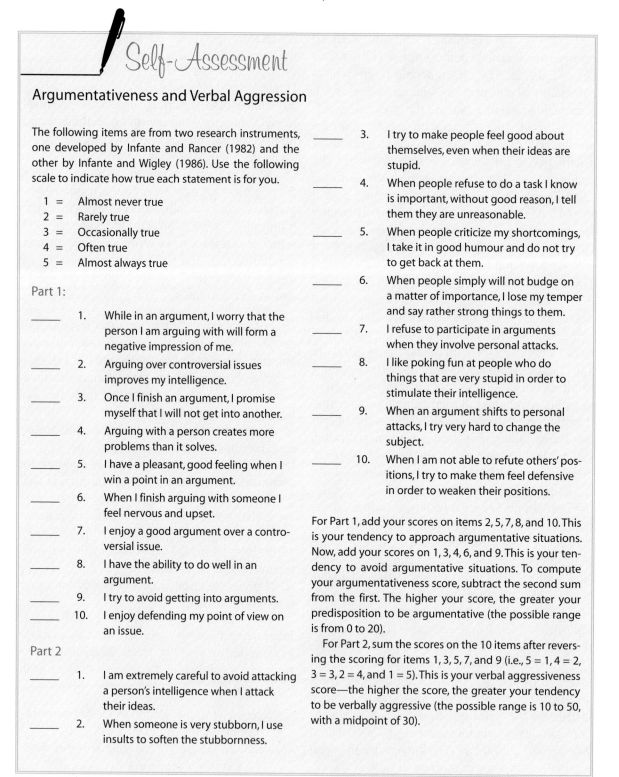

Self-Assessment

Argumentativeness and Verbal Aggression

The following items are from two research instruments, one developed by Infante and Rancer (1982) and the other by Infante and Wigley (1986). Use the following scale to indicate how true each statement is for you.

1 = Almost never true
2 = Rarely true
3 = Occasionally true
4 = Often true
5 = Almost always true

Part 1:

_____ 1. While in an argument, I worry that the person I am arguing with will form a negative impression of me.

_____ 2. Arguing over controversial issues improves my intelligence.

_____ 3. Once I finish an argument, I promise myself that I will not get into another.

_____ 4. Arguing with a person creates more problems than it solves.

_____ 5. I have a pleasant, good feeling when I win a point in an argument.

_____ 6. When I finish arguing with someone I feel nervous and upset.

_____ 7. I enjoy a good argument over a controversial issue.

_____ 8. I have the ability to do well in an argument.

_____ 9. I try to avoid getting into arguments.

_____ 10. I enjoy defending my point of view on an issue.

Part 2

_____ 1. I am extremely careful to avoid attacking a person's intelligence when I attack their ideas.

_____ 2. When someone is very stubborn, I use insults to soften the stubbornness.

_____ 3. I try to make people feel good about themselves, even when their ideas are stupid.

_____ 4. When people refuse to do a task I know is important, without good reason, I tell them they are unreasonable.

_____ 5. When people criticize my shortcomings, I take it in good humour and do not try to get back at them.

_____ 6. When people simply will not budge on a matter of importance, I lose my temper and say rather strong things to them.

_____ 7. I refuse to participate in arguments when they involve personal attacks.

_____ 8. I like poking fun at people who do things that are very stupid in order to stimulate their intelligence.

_____ 9. When an argument shifts to personal attacks, I try very hard to change the subject.

_____ 10. When I am not able to refute others' positions, I try to make them feel defensive in order to weaken their positions.

For Part 1, add your scores on items 2, 5, 7, 8, and 10. This is your tendency to approach argumentative situations. Now, add your scores on 1, 3, 4, 6, and 9. This is your tendency to avoid argumentative situations. To compute your argumentativeness score, subtract the second sum from the first. The higher your score, the greater your predisposition to be argumentative (the possible range is from 0 to 20).

For Part 2, sum the scores on the 10 items after reversing the scoring for items 1, 3, 5, 7, and 9 (i.e., 5 = 1, 4 = 2, 3 = 3, 2 = 4, and 1 = 5). This is your verbal aggressiveness score—the higher the score, the greater your tendency to be verbally aggressive (the possible range is 10 to 50, with a midpoint of 30).

S: We have a terrific blazer that you can dress up or down, depending on the accessories you choose.

C: That's not what I was going to say. I want something that I can wear as a business outfit, but it ought to be on the informal side. I'm going to . . .

S: Say no more. I know just what you want.

C: Never mind. I think I'll look in some other stores.

Irrelevant response   It is disconfirming to give an irrelevant response, making comments totally unrelated to what the other person was just saying.

Focus on Research

Organizational Climate: Bullying in the Workplace

On 6 April 1999, a former employee of OC Transpo in Ottawa went on a shooting rampage at his former workplace, killing four employees. He then took his own life. The investigation that followed revealed that the killer had been the victim of workplace harassment. Though most provinces in Canada require employers to have policies on sexual harassment and racial discrimination, only Quebec has legislation in place to outlaw workplace bullying (Canada Safety Council, 2005). The amendment to the Quebec Labour Standards Act outlaws behaviours such as repeated insults, vulgar remarks, or gestures that are offensive, demeaning, or undermine a person's self-esteem. A similar amendment was proposed to the Canada Labour Code but was never passed into law. Among the recommendations at the coroner's inquest into the OC Transpo killings was that employers develop policies to prevent violence and harassment on the job (Canada Safety Council, 2004).

According to the International Labour Organization (1996), Canada ranks fourth in the world in the prevalence of workplace aggression, significantly ahead of the United States. In its survey, the ILO defined violence as assaults and sexual assaults. Though some analysts question the methodology of this study, it is still alarming that data from a variety of sources—the Canadian Human Rights Commission, Statistics Canada, the Canadian Union of Public Employees, and the Association of Workers' Compensation Boards of Canada—all suggest that violence and hostility at work are increasing (Hynes, 2001).

Who bullies others at work? The overwhelming majority of bullies are bosses, some are co-workers, and a minority are people who bully employees in more senior positions. A bully is equally likely to be a woman or a man. Who gets bullied? Contrary to the popular stereotype of the victim being an oddball or loner, the majority of victims of workplace bullying are competent and capable employees who are generally well-liked by their co-workers. Workplace bullies are most likely to pick on someone who is co-operative and non-confrontational (Canada Safety Council, 2004).

Violence in the workplace has enormous costs for the individuals involved and also for the organizational climate as a whole. Victims of workplace bullying have increased anxiety, health problems, and domestic difficulties (because of the stress at work), and declining productivity and are more likely to be absent from work and eventually leave the organization (Hershcovis et al., 2007; Hynes, 2001). Given that they are capable and competent employees, this is a loss to the organizations they work for. Bullying lowers morale for all employees and contributes to an atmosphere of fear, anger, and depression. The employer pays for bullying with lost productivity, absenteeism, high staff turnover, and severance packages and lawsuits (Canada Safety Council, 2004; Hynes 2001).

Among Canadian corporations, the most frequent response to bullying seems to be to ignore it. The Conference Board of Canada reports that although 69 percent of their member companies surveyed view workplace violence as significant in their organization, only 42 percent have policies to deal with it (Hynes, 2001). Developing a policy or corporate strategy on workplace violence is the first step in dealing with it. At an individual level, it is important for victims of workplace bullying to assert their right to a healthy, respectful workplace environment.

A: What a day! I thought it would never end. First, the car overheated and I had to call a tow truck, and then the computer broke down at work.

B: Listen, we have to talk about a present for Ann's birthday. The party is on Saturday, and I have only tomorrow to shop for it.

A: I'm really beat. You won't believe what the boss did. Like I said, the computer was down, and in the middle of that mess, he decided he absolutely had to have the sales figures for the last six months.

B: I just can't figure what would suit Ann. She's been so generous to us, and I can't think of anything she needs.

A: Why don't you listen to me? I beat my brains out all day and you don't give a damn!

B: And you don't care about me!

Tangential response Unlike the three kinds of behaviour just discussed, a tangential response does acknowledge the other person's communication. However, the acknowledgment is used to steer the conversation in a new direction. Tangents can come in two forms: One is the 'tangential shift', which is an abrupt change in conversation. For example, a little boy runs into the house excited, showing his mother the rock he found. She says, 'Wash your hands; that rock is dirty.' In a 'tangential drift', the speaker makes a token connection with what the other person is saying and then moves the conversation in another direction entirely. In the same scenario, the mother might look at the rock, say, 'Hmmm, nice rock,' and then immediately add, 'Go and wash your hands before dinner.'

Impersonal response In an impersonal response, the speaker conducts a monologue filled with impersonal, intellectualized, and generalized statements. The speaker never really interacts with the other on a personal level.

Employee: I've been having some personal problems lately, and I'd like to take off early a couple of afternoons to clear them up.

Boss: Ah, yes. We all have personal problems. It seems to be a sign of the times.

Reflection

Driving My Father Crazy

My brother had a very bad habit. Whenever our father would call him, Leo would simply not answer—I mean, he would just sit there and act as if he hadn't heard my dad. Most of the time, our father just figured Leo wasn't at home, but those times he knew he was home and was *purposefully* ignoring him, he'd get a bit crazy.

Now that I have children of my own, I can understand how my father was feeling. There's nothing quite as disconfirming as being ignored—being told 'You don't exist!'—by your own child.

Ambiguous response An ambiguous response contains a message with more than one meaning. The words are highly abstract or have private meanings for the speaker alone.

A: I'd like to get together with you soon. How about Tuesday?

B: Uh, maybe so. Anyhow, see you later.

A: How can I be sure you mean it?

B: Who knows what anybody means?

Incongruous response An incongruous response contains two messages that seem to deny or contradict each other, one at the verbal level and the other at the non-verbal level.

He: Darling, I love you!

She: I love you, too. [*giggles*])

Teacher: Did you enjoy the class?

Student: Yes. [*yawns*]

It is important to note again that disconfirming messages, like virtually every other type of communication, are a matter of perception. A message that might not be intended to devalue the other person can be interpreted as disconfirming. For example, your failure to return a phone call or respond to the email of an out-of-town friend might simply be the result of a busy schedule, but

Take Two

- **Communication climate:** the social tone of a relationship.
- **Confirming communication:** messages that convey valuing (levels: recognition, acknowledgment, endorsement).
- **Disagreeing messages:** messages that say, 'You're wrong' but can include confirming components (types: argumentativeness, complaining, aggressiveness).
- **Disconfirming communication:** messages that signal a lack of regard (types: impervious, interrupting, irrelevant, tangential, impersonal, ambiguous, incongruous).

if the other person views the lack of contact as a sign that you don't value the relationship, the effect will be just as strong as if you had deliberately intended to convey a slight.

Defensiveness

It is no surprise that disconfirming and disagreeing messages can pollute a communication climate. Perhaps the most predictable reaction to a hostile or indifferent message is defensiveness.

The word *defensiveness* suggests protecting yourself from attack, but what kind of attack? Seldom when you become defensive is a physical threat involved. If you are not threatened by bodily injury, what *are* you guarding against? To answer this question, we need to talk more about notions of **presenting self** and **face**, both of which were introduced in Chapter 2. Recall that the presenting self consists of the physical traits, personality characteristics, attitudes, aptitudes, and all the other parts of the image you want to present to the world. Actually, it is a mistake to talk about a single face, as we try to project different selves to different people. You might try to impress a potential employer with your seriousness but also want your friends to see you as a joker. Of course, not all parts of your presenting self are equally significant. Letting others know that you are left-handed or a Gemini is probably less important to you than convincing them you are good-looking or loyal.

When others are willing to accept and acknowledge important parts of our presenting image, there is no need to feel defensive. On the other hand, when others confront us with **face-threatening acts**—messages that seem to challenge the image we want to project—we are likely to resist

iStock photo

what they say. **Defensiveness**, then, is the process of protecting our presenting self, our face.

You can understand how defensiveness operates by imagining what might happen if an important part of your presenting self were attacked. Suppose an instructor criticized you for making a stupid mistake. Or consider how you would feel if a friend called you self-centred or your boss labelled you as lazy. You would probably feel threatened if these attacks were untrue. But your own experience will probably show that you sometimes respond defensively even when you know that the criticism is justified. For instance, you have probably responded defensively at times when you *did* make a mistake, act selfishly, or cut corners in your work. In fact, we often feel most defensive when criticism is right on target (Stamp et al., 1992).

Some people are more prone to defensiveness than others. Individualistic people are more likely to interpret other people's messages as neutral or critical, whereas people with a communal orientation are likely to interpret ambiguous messages as supportive (Edwards, 1998).

The topics that trigger defensiveness also vary. Sometimes, sensitive topics are personal. You may feel a strong need to protect your image of athletic skill or intelligence, while another person may be more concerned with appearing fashionable or funny. Some research suggests that defence-provoking topics can vary by sex. In one study, men interpreted messages about mental or physical errors (such as misfiling a document or tripping on a carpet) more defensively than women did. Males and females were equally defensive about messages regarding their clothes and hair, but women were more defensive about messages that focused on weight (Futch and Edwards, 1999).

Who offers the potentially defence-arousing remark or criticism also matters. Matthew Hornsey and his colleagues (2002) conducted three experiments examining group members' responses to criticism from in-group (other Australians) and out-group (people from another country) members. They found that in-group criticisms were tolerated surprisingly well, whereas out-group criticisms were met with defensiveness—probably because in-group criticisms are seen as more legitimate and constructive.

Snapp and Leary (2001) found parallel results. When participants in their study were ignored by a person they hardly knew, they were significantly more hurt than when ignored by someone who knew them better. The researchers offer several reasons for this result, one of which is that familiar relationships provide a buffer against hurt feelings. Defensive responses to being ignored by a stranger may include 'He's such a social idiot' and 'What's wrong with *me*?' But if the other person is a friend, you are more likely to make an excuse: 'She didn't see me' or 'He must be preoccupied.'

So far, we have talked about defensiveness as if it is only the responsibility of the person who feels threatened. If this were the case, the prescription would be simply to grow a thick skin, admit your flaws, and stop trying to manage impressions. This approach isn't just unrealistic—it also ignores the role played by those who send face-threatening messages. In fact, competent communicators protect the face needs of others as well as their own. For example, the people whom college students judge as close friends are those who provide 'positive face support' by endorsing the presenting image of others (Cupach and Messman, 1999). Findings like this make it clear that defensiveness is *interactive*: all communicators contribute to the climate of a relationship.

At this point, you might be wondering how you can send a face-honouring message when you have a genuine complaint against someone. The answer lies in the two-dimensional nature

Take Two

- **Presenting self:** physical traits, personality characteristics, attitudes and aptitudes, and all other parts of the image you want to present to the world.
- **Face:** different selves we present to different people.
- **Face-threatening acts:** messages that seem to challenge the image we want to project.
- **Defensiveness:** process of protecting our presenting self (face).

iStock photo

of communication. On a content level, you can express dissatisfaction with the other person, but on a relational level you can be saying—explicitly or non-verbally—that you value him or her. In the second half of this chapter, we make specific suggestions for creating messages that are both honest and supportive.

Climate Patterns

Once a communication climate is formed, it can take on a life of its own. The pattern can be either positive or negative. In one study of married couples, each spouse's response in conflict situations was found to be similar to the other's statement (Burggraf and Sillars, 1987). Conciliatory statements (for example, support, accepting responsibility, agreeing) were likely to be followed by conciliatory responses. Confrontive acts (for example, criticism, hostile questions, fault finding) were likely to trigger an aggressive response. The same pattern held for other kinds of messages. Avoidance led to avoidance, analysis evoked analysis, and so on. This was also found in a study on disagreements of married couples (Newton and Burgoon, 1990). Videotaped interactions revealed that accusations from one partner triggered accusations in response, and that communication

satisfaction was highest when both partners used supportive rather than accusatory tactics.

This reciprocal pattern can be represented as a **spiral** (Wilmot, 1987). Some spirals are negative. In poorly adjusted and abusive couples, for example, one spouse's complaint is likely to produce a countercomplaint or denial by the other (Sabourin and Stamp, 1995; Sutter and Martin, 1999). The cartoon on the next page provides an amusing but sad image of how tit-for-tat spirals can take on lives of their own.

Dudley Cahn (1992) summarizes studies showing that even among well-adjusted couples, negative communication is more likely to be reciprocated than positive—and that once hostility is expressed, it usually escalates. You can probably recall this sort of negative spiral from your own experience: one attack leads to another, until a skirmish escalates into a full-fledged battle:

A: [*mildly irritated*] Where were you? I thought we agreed to meet here half an hour ago.

B: [*defensively*] I'm sorry. I got hung up at the library. I don't have as much free time as you do, you know.

A: I wasn't *blaming* you, so don't get so touchy. I do resent what you just said, though. I'm busy enough. And I've got lots of better things to do than wait around for you!

B: Who's getting touchy? I just made a simple comment. You've been really defensive lately. What's the matter with you?

Fortunately, spirals can also work in a positive direction. One confirming behaviour leads to a similar response from the other person, which in turn leads to further confirmation by the first person (Le Poire and Yoshimura, 1999).

Spirals—whether positive or negative—rarely go on indefinitely. When a negative spiral gets out of hand, the partners may agree to back off from their disconfirming behaviour. 'Hold on,' one may say, 'this is getting us nowhere.' At this point, there may be a cooling-off period, or the partners may work together more constructively to solve their

	1	2	3	4	5	6	7	8	9	10	11	12	13	14	15	16	17	18	19	20	21	22	23	24	25	26	27	28	29	30	31	R	H	E
TAT	3	0	0	1	0	0	0	0	0	0	0	6	0	0	0	1	0	0	0	0	0	0	8	0	0	3	9	7	1	1	2	6	48	63	6
TIT	3	0	0	1	0	0	0	0	0	0	0	6	0	0	0	1	0	0	0	0	0	0	8	0	0	3	9	7	1	1	2	6	48	63	6

Game called on account of infinity

problem. If the partners pass 'the point of no return', the relationship may end. As we saw in Chapter 1, it is impossible to take back a message once it has been sent, and some exchanges are so lethal that the relationship can't survive them. Positive spirals also have their limit. Even the best relationships go through rocky periods in which the climate suffers. However, the accumulated goodwill and communication ability of the partners can make these times less frequent and intense.

Creating Positive Climates

Even the 'best' message is not guaranteed to create a positive climate. A complimentary comment can be interpreted as sarcasm; an innocent smile can be perceived as a sneer; an offer to help can be seen as condescension. Because human communication is so complex, there are no foolproof words, phrases, or formulas for creating positive climates.

However, there is a helpful study that has stood the test of time: Jack Gibb's (1961) categorization of supportive and defensive behaviour (see Table 10.1). After observing groups for several years, Gibb was able to isolate six types of defence-arousing communication and six contrasting kinds of behaviour that seem to reduce the level of threat and defensiveness. His findings have common-sense appeal and multiple applications. As a result, they've played an important part in communication textbooks, training seminars, journals, and research studies (Moss, 1999; Proctor and Wilcox,

1993). We will use them here to discuss how positive climates can be created by sending supportive rather than defence-provoking messages.

Evaluation versus Description

The first type of defence-arousing message Gibb identified is **evaluation**. An evaluative message judges the other person, usually in a negative way. Consider this message: 'You don't care about me!' Evaluative messages like this have several characteristics that make them so face-threatening. They judge what the other person is feeling rather than describing the speaker's thoughts, feelings, and wants. They don't explain how the speaker arrived at his or her conclusion, and they lack specifics. Furthermore, they are often phrased in the kind of defence-arousing 'you' language that we described in Chapter 5. It's easy to understand why evaluative statements often trigger a defensive spiral.

Do the climate-threatening properties of evaluative messages mean that it's impossible to tell others how some of the things that they do bother you? No. It simply means that you must be alert to more constructive ways to do so. **Description** is a way to offer your thoughts, feelings, and wants without judging the listener. Descriptive messages make documented observations that are specific and concrete. As we mentioned earlier when discussing complaining, description focuses on behaviour that can be changed rather than on personal characteristics that cannot be changed. In addition, descriptive messages often use 'I' language, which tends to provoke less defensiveness than 'you' language (Proctor and Wilcox, 1993; Winer and Majors, 1981). Contrast the evaluative 'You don't care about me' with this more descriptive message: 'I'm sorry that we don't spend as much time together as we

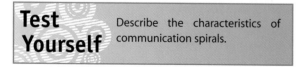

Test Yourself Describe the characteristics of communication spirals.

Focus on Technology

Does the Channel Affect the Climate?

Does the channel you choose to send your message influence the receiver's interpretation? Are text messages and emails perceived differently from voice messages? It appears that the channel you choose influences some relational aspects of the message for both the receiver and the sender.

Joseph Walther (1996) argues that computer-mediated communication (CMC) technologies, particularly text-based CMC such as email that are asynchronous and devoid of many non-verbal cues, can facilitate socially desirable communication. The act of sending an email message, instead of a voice-mail or face-to-face one, eliminates the need to monitor and control non-verbal behaviours and allows the sender more time to create a carefully composed message. Kirk Duthler (2006) explored Walther's proposition in his exploration of the relative politeness of voice-mail requests versus email requests. He found that email requests were typically more polite than their voice-mail counterparts.

In her study of evaluative feedback, Stephanie Watts (2007) compared feedback delivered by voice mail to feedback delivered by email. Students attending a large university in the American Midwest were required to compose and deliver positive and negative feedback messages about a group project to a receiver who had participated in the project. The participants were randomly assigned to the voice-mail or the email condition and both senders and receivers completed a questionnaire about the experience of delivering or receiving the feedback. Watts found that there were no differences in the effectiveness of the email and the voice-mail messages. She did find differences in the perceptions of the messages between the senders and the receivers. Senders of negative email feedback perceived it as more negative than did the recipients of the negative email feedback, but this was not true for voice-mail messages. Also, senders of negative voice-mail feedback felt more uncomfortable delivering their messages than recipients felt receiving the negative comments.

In addition to the channel and the main message content, little things seem to count, too. In her case study of email correspondence in employment settings, Joan Waldvogel (2005; 2007) found that people used cordial greetings and closings significantly more in the workplace that valued harmony and interpersonal relationships, and where co-operation and solidarity were highly valued. In contrast, in the organization Waldvogel studied that had low morale and high mistrust of management, emails were indirect and socially distant. Senders were much less likely to use a greeting such as the recipient's name or a word (e.g., 'Hello', 'Good morning all') or a farewell statement (e.g., 'Cheers', 'Have a good day').

Relational aspects of messages between individuals and within larger organizations involve a complex mix of factors, not the least of which is the channel selected to send a message.

did during the summer. When we don't talk during the week, I sometimes feel unimportant. Maybe we could set up a phone call time on Wednesdays—that would mean a lot to me.'

Note several things about this descriptive message. First, the focus is on the speaker's thoughts, feelings, and wants, with little or no judgment. Second, the message addresses something specifically (a desire to talk more often) and refrains from making sweeping character generalizations (for example, 'You don't care!'). The message also provides information about how the speaker arrived at this conclusion and offers a possible solution. Although it may seem ideal, even this sort of

Table 10.1 The Gibb Categories of Defensive and Supportive Behaviour

Defensive Behaviour	Supportive Behaviour
1. Evaluation	1. Description
2. Control	2. Problem Orientation
3. Strategy	3. Spontaneity
4. Neutrality	4. Empathy
5. Superiority	5. Equality
6. Certainty	6. Provisionalism

message may not get a non-defensive response. Its effectiveness will be determined by when, where, and how it is communicated (you can imagine how it would be received if it were said in front of a roomful of relatives or in a whining tone of voice). The point is, by contrasting evaluative and descriptive messages, you can see how and why some messages are more likely to create positive climates than others.

Let's look at more examples:

Evaluation	Description
You're not making any sense.	I don't understand the point you're trying to make.
You're inconsiderate.	I would appreciate it if you'd let me know when you're running late—I was worried.
That's an ugly tablecloth.	I'm not crazy about big blue stripes: I like something subtler.

Control versus Problem Orientation

A second defence-provoking message involves some attempt to control another. **Controlling communication** occurs when a sender seems to be imposing a solution on the receiver with little regard for the receiver's needs or interests. The object of control can involve almost anything: where to eat dinner, what television program to watch, whether to remain in a relationship, or how to spend a large sum of money. Whatever the situation, people who act in controlling ways create a defensive climate. None of us likes to feel that our ideas are worthless and that nothing we say will change other people's determination to have their way. Yet, this is precisely the attitude a controller communicates. Whether with words, gestures, tone of voice, or through some other channel, whether control is accomplished through status, insistence on obscure or irrelevant rules, or physical power, the controller generates hostility wherever he or she goes. The unspoken message is 'I know what's best for you, and if you do as I say, we will get along.'

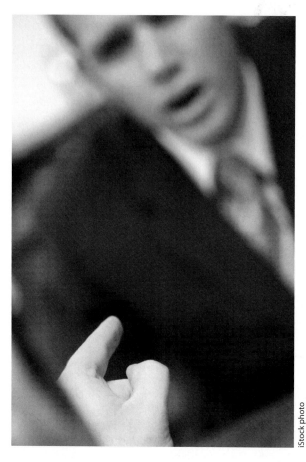

iStock photo

In **problem orientation,** however, communicators focus on finding a solution that satisfies both their own needs and those of the others involved. The goal here is not to 'win' at the expense of your partner but to work out some arrangement in which everybody feels like a winner. (In Chapter 11, we have a great deal to say about 'win–win' problem solving as a way to find problem-oriented solutions.) Problem orientation is often typified by 'we' language (see Chapter 5), which suggests the speaker is making decisions *with* rather than *for* other people.

Here are some examples of how some controlling and problem-orientation messages might sound:

Controlling	Problem Orientation
Get off the phone—now!	I need to make an important call. If you can give me five minutes, I'll let you know when I'm off.

iStock photo

There's only one way to handle this problem . . .

Looks like we have a problem. Let's work out a solution we can both live with.

Either you start working harder, or you're fired!

The production in your department hasn't been as high as I'd hoped. Any ideas on what we could do?

Strategy versus Spontaneity

Gibb uses the word **strategy** for defence-arousing messages in which speakers hide their ulterior motives. The terms *dishonesty* and *manipulation* reflect the nature of strategy. Even if the intentions that motivate strategic communication are honourable, the victim of deception who discovers the attempt to deceive is likely to feel offended at having been tricked.

As we discussed in Chapter 7, counterfeit questions are a form of strategic communication because they try to trap others into desired responses. Indirect and double messages also can be strategic ploys that lead to defensive reactions. In addition, many sales techniques are strategic, as they give customers limited information and then make it difficult to say no. This is not to say that all sales techniques are wrong or unethical, but most strategic ones are not well-suited to interpersonal relationships. If you have ever become defensive when you thought a friend was doing a 'sales job' on you, you understand the concept.

Spontaneity is the behaviour that contrasts with strategy. Spontaneity simply means being honest with others instead of trying to manipulate them. What it does not mean is blurting out what you're thinking as soon as an idea comes to you. As we discussed in Chapter 9, there are appropriate (and inappropriate) times for self-disclosure. You would undoubtedly threaten other people's presenting selves if you were 'spontaneous' about every opinion that crossed your mind. That's not what Gibb intended in using the term *spontaneity*. What he was after was to set aside hidden agendas that others both sense and resist. You can probably remember times when someone asked you a question and you answered suspiciously with 'Hmmm . . . why do you want to know?' Your defensive antennae were up because you detected an underlying strategy. If the person had told you honestly why he or she was asking the question, then your defences probably would have been lowered. That's what we mean by spontaneity.

Here are some examples:

Strategy	Spontaneity
What are you doing Friday after work?	I have a piano I need to move Friday after work. Can you give me a hand?
Have you ever considered another line of work?	I'm concerned about your job performance over the last year; let's set up a time to talk about it.
Tom and Judy go out to dinner every week.	I'd like to go out for dinner more often.

This is a good place to pause and talk about larger issues regarding the Gibb model. First, Gibb's emphasis on being direct is better suited for low-context cultures like Canada and the United States, which value a straightforward approach, than for high-context cultures. Second, there are ways in which each of the communication approaches Gibb labels as 'supportive' can be used to exploit others and, therefore, violate the spirit of positive climate building. For instance, consider spontaneity. Although it sounds paradoxical at first, spontaneity can be a strategy, too. Sometimes, you'll see people using honesty in a calculating way, being just frank enough to win someone's trust or sympathy. This 'levelling' is probably the most defence-arousing strategy of all because once we've learned someone is using frankness as a manipulation, there is almost no chance we will ever trust that person again.

On a broader level, Ray (1993) observes that supportive communication can actually be used to restrict and control others. By creating a warm climate, we increase someone's dependence on us, thereby giving ourselves significant power over them. Before going any further, we want to say loudly and clearly that this violates the intent of climate building. If you act supportively for ulterior reasons, you have misunderstood the idea behind this chapter, and you are liable to cause even more defensiveness than before. None of the ideas we present in this book can go into a 'bag of tricks' that can be used to control others. If you ever find yourself using them in this way, it may be time to take stock of your motives and ethical standards.

Neutrality versus Empathy

Gibb used the term **neutrality** to describe a fourth behaviour that arouses defensiveness. Probably a better word would be *indifference*. For example, 911 emergency telephone dispatchers are taught to be neutral in order to calm down the caller, but they should not communicate indifference (Shuler, 1998). In Gibb's terminology, a neutral attitude is disconfirming because it communicates a lack of concern for the welfare of another and implies that the other person is not very important to you. This apparent indifference is likely to promote defensiveness because people do not like to think of themselves as worthless, and they will protect a self-concept that sees them as worthwhile.

The poor effects of neutrality become apparent when you consider the hostility that most people have for the large, impersonal organizations they have to interact with: 'They think of me as a number instead of a person'; 'I felt as if I were being handled by computers and not human beings.' These common statements reflect reactions to being handled in an indifferent, neutral way.

The behaviour that contrasts with neutrality is **empathy**. Gibb found that empathy helps rid communication of the quality of indifference. When people show that they care for the feelings of another, there's little chance that the person's self-concept will be threatened. Empathy means accepting another's feelings, putting yourself in another's place. This does not mean you need to agree with that person. By simply letting someone know about your care and respect, you will be acting in a supportive way. Gibb noted the importance of non-verbal messages in communicating empathy. He found that facial and bodily expressions of concern are often more important to the recipient than the words used.

We have addressed the concept of empathy in Chapter 3 and the skill of empathizing in Chapter 7; let's see what empathic messages look like when contrasted with neutral ones:

Neutrality	Empathy
This is what happens when you don't plan properly.	Ouch—looks like this didn't turn out the way you expected.
Sometimes, things just don't work out. That's the way it goes.	I know you put a lot of time and effort into this project.
Don't get too excited—everybody gets promoted sooner or later.	I'll bet you're pretty excited about the promotion.

Superiority versus Equality

A fifth behaviour creating a defensive climate involves **superiority**. Jake Harwood, Howard Giles, and their associates (Harwood et al., 1997; Harwood and Giles, 1996) summarize a body of research that describes how patronizing messages irritate recipients ranging from young students to senior citizens. Any message that suggests, 'I'm better than you' is likely to arouse feelings of defensiveness in the recipients.

Many times in our lives, we communicate with people who possess less talent or knowledge than we do, but it is not necessary to convey an attitude of superiority in these situations. Gibb found ample evidence that many who have superior skills and talents are capable of projecting feelings of equality rather than superiority. Such people communicate that, although they may have greater talent in certain areas, they see other human beings as having just as much worth as themselves.

Charles Beck and Elizabeth Beck (1996) observe that **equality** is put to the test when a person *does not* have superior skills, yet is in a position of authority. Supervisors sometimes have less expertise in certain areas than their subordinates but believe it would be beneath them to admit it. You have probably been in situations where you knew more about the subject than the person in charge—be it a boss, a teacher, a parent, or a salesperson—yet this person acted as if he or she knew more. Did you feel defensive? No doubt. Did that person feel defensive? No doubt, as well. Both of you were challenging each other's presenting self, so the climate probably became hostile. A truly secure person can treat others with equality even when there are obvious differences in knowledge,

talent, and status. Doing so creates a positive climate in which ideas are evaluated not on the basis of who contributed them, but rather on the merit of the ideas themselves.

What does equality sound like? Here are some examples:

Superiority	Equality
When you get to be in my position someday, then you'll understand.	I'd like to hear how the issue looks to you. Then I can tell you how it looks to me.
You don't know what you're talking about.	I'm not sure I agree.
No, that's not the right way to do it!	I'd be happy to help if you'd like—just let me know.

Certainty versus Provisionalism

Have you ever run into people who are positive they are right? Who know that theirs is the only or proper way of doing something? Who insist that they have all the facts and need no additional information? If you have, you have met individuals who project the defence-arousing behaviour that Gibb calls **certainty**.

How do you react when you are the target of such certainty? Do you suddenly find your energy directed to proving the dogmatic individual wrong? If you do, you're reacting normally—if not very constructively.

Reflection

Be Careful How You Give the Boss a Suggestion

My brother is a pretty smart guy, especially when it comes to running a business, but he got into trouble when he tried to give his boss advice. As my brother tells it, he went to the head of the company and gave a short speech about how things were not run well and what could be done to make the business more efficient. When my brother was through, the boss said, 'You're right, Raj—everything you said is true—but nobody talks to me that way. You're fired.' My brother came off as superior to the owner of the company. He essentially told him, 'I'm smarter than you are'—not a smart move on his part.

iStock photo

Communicators who regard their own opinions with certainty while disregarding the ideas of others demonstrate a lack of respect for others. It's likely the recipient will take the certainty as a personal affront and react defensively.

In contrast to dogmatic certainty is **provisionalism**, in which people may have strong opinions but are willing to acknowledge that they don't have a monopoly on the truth and will change their stand if another position seems more reasonable. Provisionalism often surfaces in a person's choice of words. While certainty regularly uses the terms *can't*, *never*, *always*, *must*, and *have to*, provisionalism uses *perhaps*, *maybe*, *possibly*, *might*, and *may*. It's not that provisional people are spineless—they simply recognize that discussion is aided by open-minded messages. Winer and Majors (1981) found that provisional word choice does indeed enhance communication climate.

Let's look at some examples:

Certainty	Provisionalism
That will *never* work!	My guess is that you'll run into problems with that approach.
You'll hate that class! Stay away from it!	I didn't like that class very much; I'm not sure you would, either.
You won't get anywhere without a university education. Mark my words.	I think it's important to get that degree. I found it was hard to land an interview until I had one.

You have probably noticed a great deal of overlap between the various Gibb components. For instance, look at the final example under 'Provisionalism'. The statement is likely to create a positive climate, not only because it is provisional rather than certain, but also because it is descriptive rather than evaluative, problem-oriented rather than controlling, and equal rather than superior. You may also have noticed a tone underlying all of the supportive examples: *respect*. By valuing and confirming others—even if you disagree with them—you create a respectful climate that helps enhance a positive

communication climate, both now and in future interactions. Communication scholars Sonja Foss and Cindy Griffin (1995) use the term *invitational rhetoric* to describe this sort of respectful approach that strives to understand others and invite them to see your point of view, rather than dominating them in defence-provoking ways.

There are no guarantees that you will achieve positive responses or outcomes, but if you send supportive messages, your odds for interpersonal success should improve.

Transforming Negative Climates

The world would be a happier place if everyone communicated supportively. But how can you respond non-defensively when others use evaluation, control, superiority, and all the other attacking behaviours Gibb identified? Despite your best intentions, it is difficult to be reasonable when you are faced with a torrent of criticism. Being attacked is hard enough when the critic is clearly being unfair, but it's often even more threatening when the judgments are accurate. Despite the accuracy of your critic, the tendency is either to counterattack aggressively with a barrage of verbal aggression or to withdraw non-assertively.

Since neither of these responses is likely to resolve a dispute, we need other ways of behaving. There are two such methods. Despite their apparent simplicity, they have proved to be among the most valuable skills communicators can learn.

Seek More Information
The response of seeking more information makes good sense when you realize that it's foolish to respond to a critical attack until you understand what the other person has said. Even comments

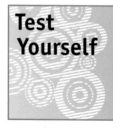

Test Yourself Describe the Gibb categories of defensive and supportive behaviours and how they can contribute to creating a more defensive-arousing or a less defensive-arousing response.

Building Work Skills

Criticism That Arouses Less Defensiveness

Using the Gibb categories of defensive and supportive behaviour, analyze the components of the following message.

> This project coordinator job seems to be too challenging for you! You're constantly wasting my time. *You* need to take minutes of the team meetings and send them to me if I am unable to attend. *You're* the coordinator, after all. These things happen when you don't plan properly. When you have been here as long as I have, you'll know better.

What defensive-arousing elements does it include? Now, rewrite the criticism using more supportive statements.

that at first appear to be totally unjustified or foolish often prove to contain at least a grain of truth and, sometimes, much more.

Many readers object to the idea of asking for details when they are criticized. Their resistance grows from confusing the act of *listening open-mindedly* to a speaker's comments with *accepting* them. Once you realize that you can listen to, understand, and even acknowledge the most hostile comments without necessarily accepting them, it becomes much easier to hear another person out. If you disagree with a speaker's objections, you will be in a much better position to explain yourself once you understand the criticism. On the other hand, after carefully listening to the other person's remarks, you may just see that they are valid, in which case you have learned some valuable information about yourself. In either case, you have everything to gain and nothing to lose by paying attention to the critic.

Focus on Research

Emotional Regulation: The Key to Reducing Defensiveness

In the research conducted for the completion of a master's degree in psychology at the University of British Columbia, Edward Peck (1998) described how effective group counsellors reduce defensive communication and create group climates which foster trust. In these climates people are more productive, content, and resourceful.

Using Gibb's categories, Peck documented actual techniques that effective counsellors used to reduce defensiveness in their group therapy sessions. Peck then analyzed this interview data in relationship to the literature on effective group leadership, using Gibb's theory as a theoretical framework. The leaders described challenging incidents, their internal and external responses, and the outcomes of these incidents.

The most critical feature identified by the counsellors was how they used their own emotional reactions to recognize when incidents were arousing defensiveness within the group. They needed to start with themselves and regulate their own internal emotions before they could apply any of the strategies to reduce defensiveness in the group.

Peck's research has implications for all of us. Before we can use Gibb's categories to create a more positive communication climate, we must find resources to regulate our own emotions. The therapists in Peck's study used self-talk to help them gain control of their feelings in defence-arousing situations. Once again that little voice in our heads can help us to create more constructive communications.

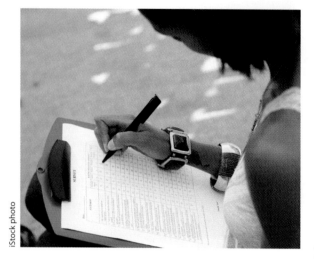

Of course, after one has spent years of instinctively resisting criticism, learning to listen to the other person will take some practice. To make matters clearer, here are several ways in which you can seek additional information from your critics.

Ask for Specifics   Often, the vague attack of a critic is virtually useless even if you sincerely want to change. Abstract accusations such as 'You're being unfair' or 'You never help out' can be difficult to understand. In such cases, it is a good idea to request more specific information from the sender. 'What do I *do* that's unfair?' is an important question to ask before you can judge whether the accusation is correct. 'When haven't I helped out?' you might ask before agreeing with or disputing the accusation.

If you already solicit specifics by using questions and are still accused of reacting defensively, the problem may be in the *way* you ask. Your tone of voice and facial expression, posture, or other non-verbal clues can give the same words radically different connotations. For example, think of how you could use the question, 'Exactly what are you talking about?' to communicate either a genuine desire to know or your belief that the speaker is crazy. It is important to ask for specific information only when you genuinely want to learn more from the speaker, as asking under any other circumstances will merely make matters worse.

Guess about Specifics   Sometimes, even your sincere and well-phrased requests for specific details won't meet with success. There may be instances when your critics won't be able to define precisely the behaviour they find offensive. If such is the case, you will hear comments like 'I can't tell you exactly what's wrong with your sense of humour—all I can say is that I don't like it.' In other cases, your critics may know exactly what they don't like, but for some reason they seem to get a perverse satisfaction out of making you struggle to figure them out. In instances like these, you can often learn more clearly what is bothering your critic by *guessing* at the specifics of a complaint. In a sense, you become both detective and suspect, the goal being to figure out exactly what 'crime' you have committed. Like the technique of asking for specifics, guessing must be done with goodwill if it is to produce satisfying results. You need to convey to the critic that for both of your sakes, you are truly interested in finding out what is the matter. Once you have communicated this intention, the emotional climate generally becomes more comfortable because, in effect, both you and the critic are seeking the same goal.

Here are some typical questions you might hear from someone guessing about the details of another person's criticism:

'So, you object to the language I used in writing the paper. Was my language too formal?'

'Okay, I understand that you think the outfit looks funny. What is it that's so bad? Is it the colour? Does it have something to do with the fit? The fabric?'

'When you say that I'm not doing my share around the house, do you mean that I haven't been helping enough with the cleaning?'

Paraphrase the Speaker's Ideas   Another strategy is to draw out confused or reluctant speakers by paraphrasing their thoughts and feelings, using the reflective listening skills that we described in Chapter 7. Paraphrasing is especially good in helping others solve their problems—and since people generally criticize you because your behaviour creates some problem for them, the method is especially suitable at such times.

One advantage of paraphrasing is that you don't have to guess about the specifics of your behaviour that might be offensive. By clarifying or amplifying what you understand critics to be saying, you will learn more about their objections. A brief dialogue between a disgruntled customer and a store manager who is an exceptional listener might sound like this:

Customer: The way you people run this store is disgusting! I just want to tell you that I'll never shop here again.

Manager [*reflecting the customer's feeling*]: It seems that you're quite upset. Can you tell me your problem?

Customer: It isn't *my* problem; it is the problem your salespeople have. They seem to think it's a great inconvenience to help a customer find anything around here.

Manager: So, you didn't get enough help finding the items you were looking for, is that it?

Customer: Help? I spent twenty minutes looking around in here before I even talked to a staffer. All I can say is that it's a hell of a way to run a store.

Manager: So, what you're saying is that the salespeople seemed to be ignoring the customers?

Customer: No. They were all busy with other people. It just seems to me that you ought to have enough help around to handle the crowds that come in at this hour.

Manager: I understand now. What frustrated you the most was the fact that we didn't have enough staff to serve you promptly.

Customer: That's right. I have no complaint with the service I get once I'm waited on, and I've always thought you had a good selection here. It's just that I'm too busy to wait so long for help.

Manager: Well, I'm glad you brought this to my attention. We certainly don't want loyal customers going away mad. I'll try to see that it doesn't happen again.

This conversation illustrates two advantages of paraphrasing. First, the critic often reduces the intensity of the attack once he or she realizes that the complaint is being heard. Criticism often grows

from the frustration of unmet needs—which, in this case, was partly a lack of attention. As soon as the manager genuinely demonstrated interest in the customer's plight, the customer began to feel better and was able to leave the store relatively calmly. Of course, paraphrasing won't always mollify your critic, but even when it does not, there is still another benefit that makes the technique worthwhile. In the sample conversation, the manager learned some valuable information by taking time to understand the customer. As you read earlier, even apparently outlandish criticism often contains at least a grain of truth, and, thus, a person who is genuinely interested in improving would be wise to hear it out.

Ask What the Critic Wants   Sometimes, your critic's demand will be obvious:

'Turn down that music!'

'I wish you'd remember to tell me about phone messages.'

'Would you clean up your dirty dishes now!'

In other cases, however, you will need to do some investigating to find out what the critic wants from you:

A: I can't believe you invited all those people over without asking me first!

B: Are you saying you want me to cancel the party?

A: No, I just wish you'd ask me before you make plans.

C: You are so critical! It sounds as if you don't like *anything* about this paper.

D: But you asked for my opinion. What do you expect me to do when you ask?

C: I want to know what's wrong, but I don't just want to hear criticisms. If you think there's anything good about my work, I wish you'd tell me that, too.

This last example illustrates the importance of accompanying your questions with the right nonverbal behaviour. It's easy to imagine two ways D could have said, 'What do you expect me to do when you ask?' One would show a genuine desire to clarify what C wanted, whereas the other would have been clearly hostile and defensive. As with all of the styles in this section, your responses to criticism have to be sincere in order to work.

Ask about the Consequences of Your Behaviour

As a rule, people complain about your actions only when some need of theirs is not being met. One way to respond to this kind of criticism is to find out exactly what troublesome consequences your behaviour has for them. You will often find that actions which seem perfectly legitimate to you cause some difficulty for your critic. Once you have understood this, comments that previously sounded foolish take on a new meaning:

> Neighbour A: You say that I ought to have my cat neutered. Why is that important to you?
>
> Neighbour B: Because at night, he picks fights with my cat, and I'm tired of paying the vet's bills.
>
> Worker A: Why do you care whether I'm late for work?
>
> Worker B: Because when the boss asks, I feel obliged to make up some story so you won't get into trouble, and I don't like to lie.
>
> Husband: Why does it bother you when I lose money at poker? You know I never gamble more than I can afford.
>
> Wife: It's not the cash itself. It's that when you lose, you're in a grumpy mood for two or three days, and that's no fun for me.

Ask What Else Is Wrong

It might seem crazy to invite more criticism, but sometimes asking about other complaints can uncover the real problem:

> A: Are you mad at me?
>
> B: No, why are you asking?
>
> A: Because the whole time we were at the picnic you hardly spent any time talking to me. In fact, it seemed as if whenever I came over to where you were, you went off somewhere else.
>
> B: Is anything else wrong?
>
> A: Well, to be honest, I've been wondering lately if you are tired of me.

This example shows that asking if anything else bothers your critic is not just an exercise in masochism. If you can keep your defensiveness in check, probing further can lead the conversation to issues that are the source of the critic's real dissatisfaction.

But sometimes, it is not enough to solicit more information from a critic. For instance, what do you do when you fully understand the other person's objections and still feel a defensive response on the tip of your tongue? You know that if you try to protect yourself, you'll wind up in an argument; on the other hand, you simply cannot accept what the other person is saying about you. The solution to such a dilemma is outrageously simple and is discussed in the following section.

Agree with the Critic

But, you protest, how can I honestly agree with comments I don't believe are true? In the following pages, we will answer this question by showing that there is virtually no situation in which you can't honestly accept the other person's point of view and still maintain your position. To see how this can be so, you need to realize that there are several different types of agreement, one of which you can use in almost any situation.

Agree with the Truth

Agreeing with the truth is easy to understand, though not always easy to practise. You agree with the truth when another person's criticism is factually correct:

> 'You're right; I am angry.'
>
> 'I suppose I was just being defensive.'
>
> 'Now that you mention it, I did get pretty sarcastic.'

Agreeing with the facts seems quite sensible when you realize that certain matters are indisputable. If

Test Yourself Describe the ways you can seek more information from your critic and how these strategies can contribute to a more positive communication climate.

Reflection

Agreeing with a Critic Can Be Liberating

I've always been a very thrifty person. Sometimes, I wish I were more of a free-and-easy spender, but I'm just not. When my apartment mates and I shop for food, I'm always looking for bargains.

Just after we covered the part of our textbook that talked about agreeing with a critic, we were in the market and I was doing my usual 'we can't afford that' routine. One of my housemates said, 'You are really a tightwad!' Instead of arguing, I agreed with the truth of his accusation and said, 'You're right, I am!' This surprised us both, and we both started to laugh. It felt great to acknowledge the reality of his claim without getting defensive.

you agree to be somewhere at 4:00 and don't show up until 5:00, you are late, no matter how good your excuse is. If you have broken something you borrowed, run out of gas, or failed to finish a job you started, there's no point in denying the fact. In the same way, if you are honest you will have to agree with many interpretations of your behaviour, even when they are not flattering. You do get angry, act foolishly, fail to listen, and behave inconsiderately. Once you rid yourself of the myth of perfection, it's much easier to acknowledge these truths.

If it is so obvious that the descriptions others give of your behaviour are often accurate, why is it so difficult to accept them without being defensive? The answer lies in a confusion between agreeing with the *facts* and accepting the *judgment* that so often accompanies them. Most critics don't merely describe the action that offends them; they also evaluate it, and it is the evaluation that we resist:

'It's silly to be angry.'

'You have no reason for being defensive.'

'You were wrong to be so sarcastic.'

It is such judgments that we resent. By realizing that you can agree with—even learn from—the

descriptive part of many criticisms and still not accept the accompanying evaluations, you will often have a response that is both honest and non-defensive. A conversation between a teacher and a student illustrates this point:

Teacher: Look at this paper! It's only two pages long and it contains twelve misspelled words. I'm afraid you have a real problem with your writing.

Student: You're right. I know I don't spell well at all.

T: I don't know what's happening in the lower grades. They just don't seem to be turning out people who can write a simple, declarative sentence.

S: You're not the first person I've heard say that.

T: I should think you'd be upset by the fact that after so much time in English composition classes, you haven't mastered the basics of spelling.

S: You're right. It does bother me.

Reflection

Coping with Criticism as a Martial Art

I've been taking self-defence lessons for a year, and I think there are a lot of similarities between judo and agreeing with your critic. In both techniques, you don't resist your attacker. Instead you use the other person's energy to your advantage. You let your opponent defeat himself.

Last week, I used 'verbal judo' on a very judgmental friend who called me a hypocrite because I'm a vegetarian but still wear leather shoes. I knew that nothing I could say would change his mind, so I just agreed with his perception by saying, 'I can see why you think I'm not consistent.' (I really *could* see how my lifestyle looks hypocritical to him, although I don't agree.) No matter what he said, I replied (in different ways), 'I understand why it looks that way to you.' And each time, I *meant* it. I won't always agree with my critics this way, any more than I'll always use judo. But it certainly is a useful approach to have at my disposal.

Notice that in agreeing with the teacher's comments, the student did not in any way demean herself. Even though there may have been extenuating circumstances to account for her lack of skill, the student didn't find it necessary to justify her errors—because she wasn't saddled with the burden of pretending to be perfect. By simply agreeing with the facts, she was able to maintain her dignity and avoid an unproductive argument.

Of course, in order to reduce defensiveness it is important that your agreement with the facts be honest and admitted without malice. It's humiliating to accept inaccurate descriptions, and maliciously pretending to agree with these only leads to trouble. You can imagine how unproductive the above conversation would have been if the student had spoken the same words in a sarcastic tone. Agree with the facts only when you can do so sincerely. Although it will not always be possible, you'll be surprised at how often you can use this simple response.

Agreeing with criticism is fine, but by itself, it isn't an adequate response to your critic. For instance, once you have admitted to someone that you are defensive, habitually late, or sarcastic, you can expect that person to ask what you intend to do about this behaviour. Such questions are fair. In most cases, it would be a mistake simply to understand another's criticism, to agree with the accusations, and then to go on behaving as before. Such behaviour makes it clear that you have no concern for the speaker. The message that comes through can sound like this: 'Sure, I now understand what I've done to bother you. You're right, I have been doing it and I'll probably keep on doing it. If you don't like the way I've been behaving, that's tough!' Such a response might be appropriate for dealing with people you genuinely don't care about—someone who is manipulative or abusive, for example—but it is clearly not suitable for people who matter to you.

Before reading on, then, understand that responding non-defensively to criticism is just the *first* step in resolving the conflicts that usually prompt an attack. In order to resolve your conflicts fully, you will need to learn the skills that we describe in Chapter 11.

Agree with the Odds Sometimes, a critic will point out possible unpleasant consequences of your behaviour:

'If you don't talk to more people, they'll think you're a snob.'

'If you don't exercise more, you'll wind up having a heart attack one of these days.'

'If you run around with that crowd, you'll probably be sorry.'

Often, such comments are genuinely helpful suggestions that others make for your own good. In other cases, however, they are really devices for manipulating you into behaving the way your critic wants you to. For instance, 'If we go to the football game, you might catch cold' could mean 'I don't want to go to the football game.' 'You'll probably be exhausted tomorrow if you stay up late' could be translated as 'I want you to go to bed early.' In Chapter 11, we will have more to say about such methods of indirect aggression, but for now, it is sufficient to state that such warnings often generate defensiveness. A mother–son argument shows this outcome:

Mother: I don't see why you want to ride that motorcycle. You could wind up in an accident so easily. (*states the odds of having an accident*)

Son: Oh, don't be silly. I'm a careful driver, and besides you know that I never take my bike on the highway. (*denies the odds*)

M: Yes, but every time I pick up the paper I read about someone being hurt or killed. There's always a danger that some crazy driver will miss seeing you and run you off the road. (*states the odds of incurring an injury*)

S: Oh, you worry too much. I always look out for the other driver. And besides, you have a lot better manoeuvrability on a motorcycle than in a car. (*denies the odds of incurring an injury*)

M: I know you're careful, but all it takes is one mistake and you could be killed. (*states the odds of being killed*)

S: Somebody is killed shaving or taking a shower every day, but you don't want me to stop doing those things, do you? You're just exaggerating the whole thing. (*denies the odds of being killed*)

From this example, you can see that it is usually self-defeating to deny another person's predictions. You don't convince the critic, and your opinions stay unchanged as well. Notice the difference when you agree with the odds (though not the demands) of the critic:

M: I don't see why you want to drive that motorcycle. You could wind up in an accident so easily. (*states the odds of having an accident*)

S: I suppose there is a chance of that. (*agrees with the odds*)

M: You're darned right. Every time I pick up the newspaper, I read about someone being hurt or killed. There's always a danger that some crazy driver will miss seeing you and run you off the road. (*states the odds of incurring an injury*)

S: You're right; that could happen [*agrees with the odds*], but I don't think the risk is great enough to keep me off the bike.

M: That's easy for you to say now. Someday, you could be sorry you didn't listen to me. (*states the odds of having regrets*)

S: That's true. I really might regret driving the bike someday—but I'm willing to take that chance. (*agrees with the odds*)

Notice how the son simply considers his mother's predictions and realistically acknowledges the chance that they might come true. While such responses may at first seem indifferent and callous, they can help the son avoid the pitfall of indirect manipulation. Suppose the conversation were a straightforward one, in which the mother was simply pointing out to her son the dangers of motorcycle riding. He acknowledges that he understands her concern and even agrees with the possibility that her prediction could come true. If, however, her prediction were really an indirect way of saying, 'I don't want you to ride any more,' then the son's response would force her to clarify her demand so that he could deal with it openly. At this point, they might be able to figure out a solution that would let the son satisfy his need for transportation and excitement and, at the same time, allow his mother to alleviate her concern.

In addition to bringing hidden agendas into the open for resolution, agreeing with the odds also helps you become aware of some possible previously unconsidered consequences of your actions. Instead of blindly denying the chance that your behaviour is undesirable, agreeing with the odds will help you look objectively at whether your course of action is in fact the best one. You may agree with your critic that you really should change your behaviour.

Agree in Principle Criticism often comes in the form of abstract ideals against which you are unfavourably compared:

'I wish you wouldn't spend so much time on your work. Relaxation is important, too, you know.'

'You shouldn't expect so much from your kids. Nobody's perfect.'

'What do you mean, you're not voting? The government is going to get better only when people like you take more of an interest in it.'

'You mean you're still upset by that remark? You ought to learn how to take a joke better.'

In cases like these, you can accept the principle that the criticism is based on and still behave as before. After all, some rules do allow occasional exceptions, and people are often inconsistent. Consider how you might sincerely agree with the criticisms above without necessarily changing your behaviour:

'You're right. I am working hard right now. It probably is unhealthy, but finishing the job is worth the extra strain to me.'

'I guess my expectations for the kids are awfully high, and I don't want to drive them crazy. I hope I'm not making a mistake.'

'You're right: if everybody stopped voting, the system would fall apart.'

'Maybe I *would* be happier if I could take a joke in stride. I'm not ready to do that, though, at least not for jokes like that one.'

Agree with the Critic's Perception What about times when there seems to be no basis whatsoever for agreeing with your critics? You've listened carefully and asked questions to make sure you understand the objections, but the more you listen, the more positive you are that they are totally wrong. There is no truth to the criticisms, you can't agree with the odds, and you can't even accept the principle the critics are putting forward. Even here, there's a way of agreeing—this time, not with the critics' conclusions, but with their right to perceive things their way:

A: I don't believe you have been to all the places you were just describing. You're probably just making all this up so that we will think you are hot stuff.

B: Well, I can see how you might think that. I've known people who lie to get approval.

C: I want to let you know right from the start that I was against hiring you for the job. I think the reason you got it was because you're a woman.

D: I can understand why you'd believe that with all the anti-discrimination laws on the books. I hope that after I've been here for a while, you'll change your mind.

E: I don't think you're being totally honest about your reasons for wanting to stay home. You say it's because you have a headache, but I think you're avoiding Li Ping and Owen.

F: I can see why that would make sense to you since Li Ping and I got into an argument the last time we were together. All I can say is that I do have a headache.

Such responses tell your critics that you are acknowledging the reasonableness of their perceptions, even though you don't agree or wish to change your behaviour. This coping style is valuable, as it lets you avoid debates over who is right and who is wrong, which can turn an exchange of ideas into an argument. Notice the difference in the following scenes.

Dispute the Perception

A: I don't see how you can stand to be around Josh. The guy is so crude—he gives me the creeps.

B: What do you mean, crude? He's a really nice guy. I think you're just touchy.

A: Touchy! If it's touchy to be offended by disgusting behaviour, then I'm guilty.

B: You're not guilty about anything. It's just that you are too sensitive when people kid around.

A: Too sensitive, huh? I don't know what's happened to you. You used to have such good judgment about people. . . .

Agree with the Perception

A: I don't see how you can stand to be around Josh. The guy is so crude—he gives me the creeps.

B: Well, I enjoy being around him, but I guess I can see how his jokes would be offensive to some people.

A: You're darned right. I don't see how you can put up with him.

B: Yeah. I guess if you didn't appreciate his humour, you wouldn't want to have much to do with him.

Notice how in the second exchange, person B was able to maintain his own position without attacking A's in the least. Such acceptance is the key ingredient for successfully agreeing with your critic's perceptions. Using acceptance, you clarify that you are in no way disputing his or her views. Because you have no intention of attacking your critic's views, your critic is less likely to be defensive.

All these responses to criticism may appear to buy peace at the cost of denying your feelings. However, as you can see by now, counterattacking usually makes matters worse. The non-defensive responses you have just learned will not solve problems or settle disputes by themselves. Nevertheless, they *will* make a constructive dialogue possible, setting the stage for a productive solution. How to achieve productive solutions is the topic of Chapter 11.

Test Yourself   Explain the ways you can agree with your critic and how this approach contributes to a more positive communication climate.

Summary

Communication climate refers to the social tone of a relationship. The most influential factor in shaping a communication climate is the degree to which the people involved see themselves as being valued and confirmed. Messages have differing levels of confirmation. We can categorize them as confirming, disagreeing, or disconfirming.

Confirming messages, which communicate that 'you exist and are valued', involve recognition, acknowledgment, or endorsement of the other party. Disagreeing messages, which communicate 'you are wrong', use argumentativeness, complaining, or aggressiveness. Disconfirming messages, which communicate 'you do not exist and are not valued', include responses that are impervious, interrupting, irrelevant, tangential, impersonal, ambiguous, or incongruous. Over time, these messages form climate patterns that often take the shape of positive or negative spirals.

Defensiveness is at the core of most negative spirals. Defensiveness occurs when individuals perceive that their presenting self is being attacked by face-threatening acts. We become particularly defensive about flaws that we don't want to admit and those that touch on sensitive areas. Both the attacker and the person attacked are responsible for creating defensiveness, since competent communicators protect other people's face needs as well as their own.

Jack Gibb suggested a variety of ways to create a positive and non-defensive communication climate. These include being descriptive rather than evaluative, problem-oriented rather than controlling, spontaneous rather than strategic, empathic rather than neutral, equal rather than superior, and provisional rather than certain.

When you are faced with criticism by others, there are two alternatives to responding defensively: seeking additional information from the critic and agreeing with some aspect of the criticism. When performed sincerely, these approaches can transform an actual or potentially negative climate into a more positive one.

Building Work Skills

Responding Non-defensively to Criticism

As a student (in a co-op work placement, field practicum, or work-placement setting) or as a new employee, we often get a lot of evaluative feedback or 'constructive criticism'. Think of a time when your job-related skills were criticized and you reacted defensively. If you are having trouble getting started, imagine yourself receiving one of the following comments:

'You are not taking enough initiative.'
'You are not very receptive to feedback.'
'You are not acting like a team player.'

Now, use the strategies described in the 'Transforming Negative Climates' section of this chapter to seek more information from your critic and or agree with that person. What might you say? Role-play your response with a classmate. Make sure your non-verbal communication agrees with your sincere intent to gather more information. Does your partner think you are genuine?

Activities

1. **Invitation to Insight**
    Identify three personal relationships that matter to you. For each relationship,
    a. Come up with a weather phrase that describes the current climate of the relationship.
    b. Come up with a weather phrase that forecasts the climate of the relationship over the next year.
    c. Consider why you chose the phrases you did. In particular, describe how feeling valued and confirmed played a part in the climates you perceived and predicted.

2. **Critical Thinking Probe**
    Mental health experts generally believe it is better to have others disagree with you than ignore you. Express your opinion on this matter, using specific examples from personal experiences to support your position. Next, discuss whether (and how) it is possible to disagree without being disconfirming.

3. **Skill Builder**
    Develop your ability to communicate supportively instead of triggering defensive reactions in others. Restate each of the following 'you' statements as an 'I' message. Use details from your own personal relationships to create messages that are specific and personally relevant.

    a. 'You're thinking only of yourself.'
    b. 'Don't be so touchy.'
    c. 'Quit fooling around!'
    d. 'Stop beating around the bush and tell me the truth.'
    e. 'You're a slob!'

4. **Ethical Challenge**
    Gibb argues that spontaneous rather than strategic communication reduces defensiveness. However, in some situations a strategic approach may hold the promise of a better climate than a completely honest message. Consider situations such as these:

    a. You don't find your partner very attractive. He or she asks, 'What's the matter?'
    b. You intend to quit your job because you hate your boss, but you don't want to offend him or her. How do you explain the reason(s) for your departure?
    c. You are tutoring a high school student in reading or math. The student is sincere and a hard worker but is perhaps the most dull-witted person you have ever met. What do you say when the teenager asks, 'How am I doing?'

    Describe at least one situation from your experience where complete honesty increased another person's defensiveness. Discuss whether candour or some use of a strategy might have been the best approach in this situation. How can you reconcile your approach with Gibb's arguments in favour of spontaneity?

5. **Invitation to Insight**
    Review the Gibb behaviours discussed on pages 298–304, and then answer the following questions:

    a. Which defence-provoking behaviour do you find most annoying?
    b. Who in your life uses that behaviour most often?

c. What part of your presenting self is threatened by that behaviour?

d. How do you normally respond to that behaviour?

e. What behaviour do you wish that person would do instead?

6. **Role Play**

Practise responding non-defensively to critical attacks by following these steps:

a. Describe five criticisms you are likely to encounter from others in your day-to-day communication. If you have trouble thinking of criticisms, invite one or more people who know you well to supply some real, sincere grievances.

b. For each criticism, write one or more non-defensive responses using the categories on pages 304–12. Be sure your responses are sincere and that you can offer them without counterattacking your critic.

c. Practise your responses, either by inviting a friend or classmate to play the role of your critics or by approaching your critics directly and inviting them to share their complaints with you.

Discussion Questions

1. Describe the three levels of confirming messages and give examples of each. Can you endorse another person without recognizing and acknowledging him or her? Why or why not?

2. The authors argue that argumentativeness is a more positive approach to disagreeing than complaining or aggressiveness. Do you agree? Why or why not?

3. What elements do all types of disconfirming messages have in common? Explain.

4. Explain how defensiveness is the process of protecting your presenting self. Give an example to illustrate.

5. It has been said that we often feel most defensive when the criticism we receive is accurate. Would you agree or disagree? Why?

6. How can Jack Gibb's categories of supportive behaviour help you to reduce defensiveness in others?

7. What are the advantages and disadvantages of seeking more information when you are criticized?

Chapter Eleven

Managing Conflict

After studying the material in this chapter . . .

You Should Understand:

1. The five elements of conflict.
2. That conflict is natural and inevitable.
3. The characteristics of functional and dysfunctional conflicts.
4. The differences among non-assertiveness, indirect communication, passive aggression, direct aggression, and assertiveness.
5. The ways individuals interact to create relational conflict systems.
6. The characteristics of win–lose, lose–lose, and win–win problem solving.

You Should Be Able To:

1. Recognize and accept the inevitability of conflicts in your life.
2. Identify the behaviours that characterize your dysfunctional conflicts and suggest more functional alternatives.
3. Identify the conflict styles you use most commonly and evaluate their appropriateness.
4. Use the assertive message format.
5. Describe the relational conflict system in one of your important relationships.
6. Use the win–win problem-solving approach to resolve an interpersonal conflict.

Once upon a time, there was a world without conflicts. The leaders of each nation recognized the need for co-operation and met regularly to solve any potential problems before they could grow. They never disagreed on matters needing attention or on ways to handle these matters, and so there were never any international tensions, and of course there was no war.

Within each nation, things ran just as smoothly. The citizens always agreed on who their leaders should be, so elections were always unanimous. There was no social friction among various groups. Age, race, and educational differences did exist, but each group respected the others, and all got along harmoniously.

Human relationships were always perfect. Strangers were always kind and friendly to each other. Neighbours were considerate of each other's needs. Friendships were always mutual, and no disagreements ever spoiled people's enjoyment of one other. Once people fell in love—and everyone did—they stayed happy. Partners liked everything about each other and were able to fully satisfy each other's needs. Children and parents agreed on every aspect of family life and were never critical or hostile toward each other. Each day was better than the one before.

Of course, everybody lived happily ever after.

This story is obviously a fairy tale. Regardless of what we may wish for or dream about, a conflict-free world just doesn't exist. Even the best communicators, the luckiest people, are bound to wind up in situations when their needs don't match the needs of others. Money, time, power, sex, humour, aesthetic taste, and a thousand other

iStock photo

issues arise and keep us from living in a state of perpetual agreement.

For many people, the inevitability of conflict is a depressing fact. They think that the existence of ongoing conflict means that there is little chance for happy relationships with others. Effective communicators know differently. They realize that although it's impossible to *eliminate* conflict, there are ways to *manage* it effectively. The skilful management of conflict can open the door to healthier, stronger, and more satisfying relationships.

What Is Conflict?

Stop reading for a moment and make a list of as many different conflicts as you can think of. Include conflicts you have experienced personally and those that involved other people only. The list will probably show you that conflict takes many forms. Sometimes, there is angry shouting, as when parents yell at their children. In other cases, conflicts involve restrained discussion, as in labour-management negotiations or court trials. Sometimes, conflicts are carried on through hostile silence, as in the unspoken feuds of angry couples. Finally, conflicts may wind up with physical fighting between friends, enemies, or even total strangers.

Whatever forms they may take, all interpersonal conflicts share certain similarities. William Wilmot and Joyce Hocker (2001) provide a thorough definition of conflict. They state that **conflict** is an expressed struggle that inevitably occurs between at least two interdependent parties who perceive incompatible goals, scarce rewards, and interference from the other party in achieving their goals. The various parts of this definition can help you gain a better understanding of how conflict operates in everyday life.

Expressed Struggle

In order for conflict to exist, all the people involved must know that there is some disagreement. You may be upset for months because a neighbour's loud music keeps you awake at night, but no conflict exists until the neighbour learns about your problem. An expressed struggle does not have to be verbal. You can show your displeasure with someone without saying a word. A dirty look, the silent treatment, and avoiding the other person are all ways of expressing yourself. One way or another, both people must know that a problem exists before it fits our definition of conflict.

Perceived Incompatible Goals

All conflicts look as if one person's gain would be another's loss. For instance, consider the neighbour whose music keeps you awake at night. It appears that someone has to lose. If the neighbour turns down the noise, then she loses the enjoyment of hearing the music at full volume; but if she keeps the volume up, then you're still awake and unhappy.

The goals in this situation really aren't completely incompatible—solutions do exist that allow both people to get what they want. For instance, you could achieve peace and quiet by closing your windows or getting the neighbour to close hers. You might use earplugs, or perhaps the neighbour could get a set of earphones, which would allow the music to play at full volume without bothering anyone. If any of these solutions prove workable, the conflict disappears.

Unfortunately, people often fail to see mutually satisfying answers to their problems. As long as they *perceive* their goals to be mutually exclusive, the conflict is real, albeit unnecessary.

Perceived Scarce Rewards

Conflicts also exist when people believe there is not enough of something to go around: affection, money, space, and so on. Time is often a scarce commodity. As authors, teachers, and people who value their families, the writers of this textbook are constantly in the middle of struggles about how to use the limited time we have at home. Should we work on this book? Spend time with our families? Enjoy the luxury of being alone? With only twenty-four hours in a day, we're bound to wind up in conflicts with our families, editors, students, colleagues, and friends—all of whom want more of our time than we have available to give.

Interdependence

However antagonistic they may feel, the people in a conflict are dependent upon each other. The welfare and satisfaction of one depends on the actions of another. If this were not true, there would be no need for conflict, even in the face of scarce resources and incompatible goals. In fact, many conflicts remain unresolved because the people fail to understand their interdependence. One of the first steps toward resolving a conflict is to take the attitude that 'we're all in this together'.

Inevitability

Conflicts are bound to happen, even in the best relationships. College students who have kept diaries of their relationships report that they take part in about seven arguments a week (Benoit and Benoit, 1987). In another survey (Samter and Cupach, 1998), 81 percent of the respondents acknowledged that they had conflicts with friends. Even the 19 percent who claimed their friendships were conflict-free used terms like 'push and pull' or 'little disagreements' to describe the tensions that inevitably occurred. Among families, conflict can be even more frequent. Researchers who recorded dinner conversations for 52 families found an average of 3.3 'conflict episodes' per meal (Vuchinich, 1987). The frequency of conflicts does vary over the life of a relationship. For example, partners married forty years or more report having fewer conflicts than earlier in their relationship, since many contested issues (such as children, in-laws, and money) are no longer present (Dickson et al., 2002). But for most of us, most of the time, conflict is an inescapable fact of life.

Since it is impossible to *avoid* conflicts, the challenge is to handle them effectively when they do arise. More than twenty years of research shows that both happy and unhappy relationships have conflicts, but that they perceive them and manage them in very different ways (Wilmot and Hocker, 2001). Unhappy couples argue in ways categorized in this book as destructive. They are more concerned with defending themselves than solving problems; they fail to listen carefully to each another, have little or no empathy for their partners, use evaluative 'you' language, and ignore each other's relational messages.

Many satisfied couples handle their conflicts more effectively. They recognize that disagreements are healthy and know that conflicts need to be faced (Crohan, 1992; Ridley et al., 2001). While they may argue vigorously, they use skills like perception checking to find out what the other person is thinking, and they let the other person know that they understand the other side of the dispute (Canary et al., 1991). These people are willing to admit their mistakes, a habit that contributes to a harmonious relationship and also helps solve the problem at hand.

Despite the fact that relationships can survive and even prosper from constructive disagreements, most people view conflict as something to be avoided whenever possible. Some common metaphors reflect this attitude (Wilmot and Hocker, 2001). It's common to talk about conflict as a kind of war: 'He shot down my arguments'; 'Okay, fire away'; 'Don't try to defend yourself!' Another metaphor suggests that conflict is explosive: 'Don't blow up!'; 'I needed to let off steam'; 'You've got a short fuse.' Sometimes conflict seems like a kind of trial, in which one person accuses another: 'Come on, admit you're guilty'; 'Stop accusing me!'; 'Just listen to my case.' Also common is language that suggests conflict is a mess: 'Let's not open this can of worms'; 'That's a sticky situation'; 'Don't make such a stink!' Even the metaphor of a game implies that one side has to defeat the other: 'That was out of bounds'; 'You're not playing fair'; 'Okay, you win!'

Conflicts may not always be easy, but they *can* be constructive. A more positive analogy is to view conflict as a kind of dance in which partners work together to create something that would be impossible without their co-operation. You may have to persuade the other person to become your partner, and you may be clumsy together at first; but with enough practice and goodwill, you can work together instead of at cross-purposes.

The attitude partners bring to their conflicts can make the difference between success and failure. One study by Sandra Metts and William Cupach

(1990) revealed that college students in romantic relationships who believed that conflicts are destructive were most likely to neglect or leave the relationship and less likely to seek a solution than couples who had less negative attitudes. Similarly, Ann Ruvolo and her colleagues (2001) found that women who avoid conflict feel less secure in their dating relationships than those who don't.

As you will read later in this chapter, both gender and culture shape the way people view and communicate in conflicts. For now, the important point is that differences do exist and must be dealt with in one way or another. Simply wishing they would go away rarely works.

Functional and Dysfunctional Conflicts

Some bacteria are 'good', aiding digestion and cleaning up waste, whereas others are 'bad', causing infection. There are helpful forest fires, which clean out dangerous accumulations of underbrush, and harmful ones, which threaten lives and property. In the same way, some conflicts can be beneficial. They provide a way for relationships to grow by solving the problem at hand and often improving other areas of interaction. Other conflicts can be harmful, causing pain and weakening a relationship. Communication scholars usually describe harmful conflicts as *dysfunctional* and beneficial ones as *functional* (Canary and Messman, 2000).

What makes some conflicts functional and others dysfunctional? Usually, the difference does not rest in the subject of the conflict, as it is possible to have good or poor results on almost any issue. Certain individual styles of communication can be more productive than others. In other cases, the success or failure of a conflict will depend

 Take Two

- **Conflict:** an expressed struggle between at least two interdependent parties who perceive incompatible goals, scarce rewards, and interference from the other party in achieving goals; conflict is inevitable.

iStock photo

on the method of resolution the communicators choose (Alberts and Driscoll, 1992). We will talk more about types of conflict resolution later in this chapter. Now, though, we will describe some characteristics that distinguish functional from dysfunctional conflicts.

Integration versus Polarization

In a **dysfunctional conflict**, the outcomes fall short of what is possible and have a damaging effect on the relationship. Biases are rampant. Participants see themselves as 'good' and the other person as 'bad', their actions as 'protective' and the other's as 'aggressive', their behaviour as 'open and trustworthy' and the other's as 'sneaky and deceitful'. Alan Sillars and his colleagues (2000) found that in severe conflicts and dissatisfied relationships, married people saw their spouses as more blameworthy than themselves. Researchers Robert Blake and Jane Mouton (1964) found that people engaged in this kind of polarization underestimate the commonalities shared with the other person and miss areas of agreement and goodwill.

By contrast, participants in a **functional conflict** achieve the best possible outcome, even strengthening the relationship. They realize that the other person's needs may be legitimate, too. A person who is allergic to cigarette smoke recognizes that smokers are not necessarily evil people who delight in inflicting torment, while the smoker sympathizes with the other person's need for cleaner air. In such issues, functional conflict is marked by mutual respect (Foss and Griffin, 1995).

Co-operation versus Opposition

Participants in a dysfunctional conflict see each other as opponents and view the other's gain as their loss: 'If you win, I lose' is the attitude. This belief keeps partners from looking for ways to agree or finding solutions that can satisfy them both. People rarely try to redefine the situation in more constructive ways, and they seldom give in, even on non-critical issues.

A more functional approach recognizes that co-operation may bring about an answer that leaves everyone happy. Even nations basically hostile to each other often recognize the functional benefits of cooperating. For example, although many member countries of the United Nations have clear-cut differences in certain areas, they work together to alleviate world hunger and to encourage peaceful solutions to world conflict. Such co-operation is also possible in interpersonal conflicts. We have a great deal to say about co-operative problem solving later in this chapter.

Confirmation versus Disconfirmation

In functional conflicts, the people involved may disagree but they are not disagreeable. By using the kinds of supportive behaviour described on pages 298–304 in Chapter 10 (description instead of evaluation, provisionalism instead of certainty, etc.), it is possible to tackle the problem at hand without attacking the person with whom you share it. When partners treat one another with affection and without behaving dominantly, relational satisfaction increases—even in the face of conflict (Hubbard, 2001).

Agreement versus Coercion

In destructive conflicts, the participants rely heavily on power to get what they want. 'Do it my way, or else' is a threat commonly stated or implied in dysfunctional conflicts. Money, favours, friendliness, sex, and sometimes even physical coercion become tools for forcing the other person to give in. Needless to say, victories won with such power plays do not do much for a relationship.

More enlightened communicators realize that power plays are usually a bad idea, not only on ethical grounds but also because they can often backfire. Rarely is a person in a relationship totally powerless; it is often possible to win a battle only to lose the war. One classic case of the dysfunctional consequences of using power to resolve conflicts occurs in families where authoritarian parents turn their children's requests into 'unreasonable demands'. It's easy enough to send five-year-olds out of the room for some real or imagined misbehaviour, but when they grow into teenagers they acquire many ways of striking back.

De-escalation versus Escalation

In destructive conflicts, the problems seem to grow larger instead of smaller. As we saw in Chapter 10, defensiveness is reciprocal: the person you attack is likely to strike back even harder. We all have seen a small incident get out of hand and cause damage out of proportion to its importance.

One clear sign of functional conflict is that in the long run, the behaviour of the participants solves more problems than it creates. We say 'long run' because facing up to an issue instead of avoiding it will usually make life more difficult for a while. In this respect, handling conflicts functionally is rather like going to the dentist: you may find it painful for a short time, but you are only making matters worse if you don't face the problem.

Focusing versus Drifting

In dysfunctional conflicts, the partners often bring in issues having little or nothing to do with the original problem. Take, for example, a wife and husband having trouble deciding whether to spend the holidays at his or her parents' home. As they begin to grow frustrated at their inability to solve the disagreement, their interaction sounds like this:

A: Your mother is always trying to latch onto us!
B: If you want to talk about latching on, what about your folks? Ever since they loaned us that money, they've been asking about every dime we spend.
A: Well, if you could ever finish with school and hold down a decent job, we wouldn't have to worry about

Test Yourself Describe the characteristics that distinguish functional conflict from dysfunctional conflict.

money so much. You're always talking about wanting to be an equal partner, but I'm the one paying all the bills around here.

You can imagine how the conversation would go from here. Notice how the original issue became lost as the conflict expanded. Such open-ended hostility is unlikely to solve any of the problems it brings up, not to mention its potential for creating problems that didn't even exist before.

One characteristic of communicators who handle conflict well is their ability to keep focused on one subject at a time. Unlike those dysfunctional battlers that George Bach and Peter Wyden (1968) call 'kitchen sink fighters', skilful communicators might say, 'I'm willing to talk about how my parents have been acting since they made us that loan, but first let's settle the business of where to spend the holidays.' In other words, for functional problem solving, the rule is 'one problem at a time'.

Reflection

Email De-escalates Conflict Spiral

My mother is a family lawyer who specializes in divorce cases. She says that email has been a good way to get angry couples to communicate. Some husbands and wives can't be in the same room without getting into a shouting match, but email slows things down and gives them a chance to think before they answer each other. My mother asks each person in a divorcing couple to wait overnight before answering to the other's message, which cuts down on the angry and hurtful replies.

She often says that email doesn't save failing marriages, but it certainly makes the breakup more civilized and less painful.

Foresight versus Short-Sightedness

Short-sightedness can produce dysfunctional conflicts even when partners do not lose sight of the original issue. One common type of short-sightedness occurs when disputants try to win a battle and wind up losing the war. Friends may argue about who started a fight, but if you succeed in proving that you were 'right' at the cost of the friendship, then the victory is a hollow one. In another type of short-sightedness, partners are so interested in defending their own solution to a problem that they overlook a different solution that would satisfy both their goals. A final type of short-sightedness occurs when one or both partners jump into a conflict without thinking about how they can approach the issue most constructively. In a few pages, we will have more to say about preventing these last two types of short-sightedness.

Positive versus Negative Results

So far, we have looked at the differences between the *processes* of functional and dysfunctional conflicts. Now, we will compare the *results* of these different styles.

Dysfunctional conflict usually has two consequences. First, no one is likely to get what they originally wanted. In the short run, it may *look* as if one person is winning a dispute while the other person loses, but today's victor is likely to suffer tomorrow at the hands of the original loser. Second, dysfunctional conflicts can threaten the future of a relationship. Family members, lovers, friends, neighbours, or fellow workers are usually bound together by webs of commitments and obligations that are not easy to break. If they cannot find satisfactory ways of resolving their differences, their connections will become strained and uncomfortable. Even when it is possible, dissolving a relationship in the face of a conflict is hardly a satisfying practice.

In contrast to these dismal outcomes, functional conflicts have positive results. One benefit of handling issues skilfully is the reward of successfully facing a challenge. Finding a solution that works for you and the other person can leave partners feeling better about themselves and each other. Partners learn more about each other's needs and how they can be satisfied. Feelings are clarified. Backgrounds are shared. The relationship grows deeper and stronger. Of course, growth can take place in non-conflict situations, too, but the point here is that dealing with problems can be an opportunity for getting to know each other better and appreciating each other more. Constructive conflict also provides a safe outlet for the feelings of frustration and aggression that are bound to occur. Without this kind of release, partners can build up a list of grudges that interfere with their everyday functioning and their goodwill toward each other.

Individual Conflict Styles

People have their individual styles of handling conflict—characteristic approaches they take when their needs appear incompatible with what others want. As you will read, the most effective style often changes from one situation to another. Despite this fact, many people have one or two 'default' styles that can be effective sometimes and ineffective at others. What styles do you tend to use to deal with conflict? Find out by thinking about how two hypothetical characters—Chris and Pat—manage a problem that you might find familiar.

Chris and Pat have been friends for several years, ever since they moved into the same apartment building. They had always exchanged favours in a neighbourly way, but Pat has recently been depending more and more on Chris. Pat asks Chris to care for her cat and house plants almost every other weekend when she is travelling, borrows food and money without returning them, and drops in to talk about her unhappy love life at least once a week. Until lately, Chris hasn't minded much, but now she is getting tired of Pat's behaviour.

Read the five groups of responses below and rank them in the order you would be most likely to use them. Mark your most likely response number 1, your next most likely 2, and so on.

- Steer clear of Pat as much as possible. Pretend not to be home when Pat drops by. Make excuses for why you can't help with the endless list of demands and problems *or* do the favours for Pat, hoping the imposing will stop soon. After all, nobody's perfect, and it isn't worth making an issue.

- Hint to Pat that you are not happy with all her demands. When she asks you to take care of her cat, hesitate and talk about your busy schedule. When Pat doesn't pay back the loans, mention that you're short of money and may need to borrow some from your friends and family. When Pat starts to talk about her romantic problems, mention that you need to study for an exam.

- Do the favours for Pat, but send out signals that you aren't happy. Sigh when Pat asks another favour. Make an occasional sarcastic remark about how much you enjoy being Pat's housekeeper and psychotherapist. When Pat asks if you are upset, deny that anything is wrong. If Pat doesn't notice your dissatisfaction, express your resentment by saying you'll do the favours, then don't do them.

- Pat can't take a hint, so be direct and say that you are fed up with all her demands. Say you don't mind helping once in a while, but that you feel that she is taking advantage of your friendship. Warn Pat that continued impositions will threaten your friendship.

- Tell Pat that you're beginning to feel uneasy about the barrage of requests. Let her know that you value the friendship and want to keep feeling good about it. Explain that's why you are telling her this. Ask Pat to work with you to find a way to solve the problems that's less of a strain for you.

Make sure you have ranked your responses before going on. Each of the choices above represents a different style of behaviour used in conflicts (Tangney et al., 1996). These five styles are explained below and summarized in Table 11.1. As you read on, see which ones best describe the way you manage your own conflicts.

iStock photo

Non-assertion

The inability or unwillingness to express thoughts or feelings in a conflict is called **non-assertion**. Non-assertion can often come from a lack of confidence, but in many cases, people lack the awareness or skill to use a more direct means of expression. Sometimes, people know how to communicate in a straightforward way but choose to behave non-assertively.

Non-assertion can take a variety of forms. One is *avoidance*—either physical (steering clear of a friend after having an argument) or conversational (changing the topic, joking, or denying that a problem exists). People who avoid conflicts usually believe it is easier to put up with the status quo than to face the problem head-on and try to solve it. *Accommodation* is another type of non-assertive response. Accommodators deal with conflict by giving in, putting the other's needs ahead of their own.

While non-assertion may be the easiest response in the short term, research suggests that it can lead

Table 11.1 Individual Styles of Conflict

	Non-assertive	Directly Aggressive	Passive Aggressive	Indirect	Assertive
Approach to others	I'm not OK; you're OK.	I'm OK; you're not OK.	I'm OK; you're not OK. (But I'll let you think you are.)	I'm OK; you're not OK.	I'm OK; you're OK.
Decision making	Lets others choose.	Chooses for others. They know it.	Chooses for others. They don't know it.	Chooses for others. They don't know it.	Chooses for self.
Self-sufficiency	Low	High or low	Looks high but usually low	High or low	Usually high
Behaviour in problem situations	Flees; gives in	Outright attack	Concealed attack	Strategic, oblique	Direct confrontation
Response of others	Disrespect, guilt, anger, frustration	Hurt, defensiveness, humiliation	Confusion, frustration, feelings of manipulation	Unknowing compliance or resistance	Mutual respect
Success pattern	Succeeds by luck or charity of others	Beats out others	Wins by manipulation	Gains unwitting compliance of others	Attempts 'win–win' solutions

Source: Adapted with permission from Stanlee Phelps and Nancy Austin (2002), *The Assertive Woman* (4th ed.), American Orthopsychiatric Association, 1975., Impact Publishers, Inc., PO Box 6016, Atascadero, CA 93423–6016. Further reproduction prohibited.

to less satisfaction and security over the life of a relationship (Ruvolo et al., 2001). Our example of Chris and Pat illustrates the perils of non-assertion. Every time Chris hides from Pat or changes the subject so Pat won't ask for a favour, Chris becomes uncomfortable and probably leaves Pat feeling the same way. After this avoidance goes on for a while, it's likely that whatever enjoyment Chris and Pat had found together will be eclipsed by their new way of relating and that the friendship will degenerate into an awkward, polite charade.

Non-assertive behaviour is not always a bad idea. You may choose to keep quiet or give in if the risk of speaking up is too great, such as getting fired from a job you can't afford to lose, being humiliated in public, or even risking physical harm. You may also avoid a conflict if the relationship it involves isn't worth the effort. Even in close relationships, though, non-assertion has its logic. If the issue is temporary or minor, you may let it pass. It might even make sense to keep your thoughts to yourself and give in if the issue is more important to the other person than it is to you. These reasons help explain why the communication of many happily married couples is characterized by 'selectively ignoring' the other person's minor flaws (Cahn, 1992). This doesn't mean that a key to successful relationships is to avoid *all* conflicts. Instead, it suggests that it is smart to save energy for the truly important ones.

Indirect Communication

Sometimes, we choose to convey messages indirectly instead of expressing ourselves outright. **Indirect communication** is often conveyed through a third party ('Shelly is driving me crazy!'); in other cases, the message is delivered to the person involved, but in an obscure way ('You must have been really hungry. You ate all the leftover pie and finished off that carton of milk'). The Internet offers new opportunities for indirect messages. Websites like coworkerhints.com, mayIsuggest.com, and give-a-hint.com let senders make their complaints anonymously.

Consider, again, the case of Chris and Pat. Rather than risk triggering a defensive reaction, Chris decides to try to change Pat's bad habits with an indirect approach. If Pat has the kind of sensitivity that characterizes most competent communicators, Pat may get Chris's message without forcing a confrontation with Chris. In her analysis of radio and television interviewers, Marcia Macaulay (2001) found that female interviewers employed indirect requests for 'tough' or delicate information so as not to jeopardize a line of questioning.

An indirect approach can save face for the other person. If your guests are staying too long at a party, it's probably kinder to yawn and hint about your big day tomorrow than to bluntly ask them to leave. Likewise, if you are not interested in going out with someone who has asked you for a date, it may be more compassionate to claim that you are busy than to say, 'I'm not interested in seeing you.'

Sometimes, indirect communication can be a form of self-protection. You may test the waters by hinting instead of directly asking the boss for a raise, or by letting your partner know you could use some affection instead of asking outright. At times like these, an oblique approach may get the message across while minimizing the risk of a negative response.

The advantages of saving face for others and protecting oneself help explain why indirect communication is the most common way people make requests (Jordan and Roloff, 1990). The risk of an indirect message, of course, is that the other person will misunderstand you or fail to get the hint. There are also times when the importance of an idea is great enough that hinting lacks the necessary punch. When clarity and directness are your goals, the assertive approach, which we describe later in this section, can be more effective.

Passive Aggression

Passive aggression occurs when a communicator expresses dissatisfaction in a disguised manner. Passive aggression can take the form of 'crazy making' (Bach and Wyden, 1968)—tactics designed to punish another person without direct confrontation. 'Crazy making' takes its name from

the effect such behaviour usually has on its target. There are a number of crazy-making ways to deal with conflict. One is through guilt: 'Never mind. I'll do all the work myself. Go ahead and have a good time. Don't worry about me.' Another crazy-maker involves someone agreeing with you face to face, but then that person shows a different agenda behind your back—such as the teenager who says he'll clean his room, then doesn't do so as a means of getting back at the parent who grounded him. Some passive aggression is non-verbal: a loud sigh, a pained expression, or a disdainful laugh can get a message across. If the target of these messages asks about them, the passive aggressor can always deny the conflict exists. Even humour—especially sarcasm—can be used as passive aggression.

There are a number of risks to passive-aggressive approaches like these. First, they may not work. The other person may miss your message and continue with the undesirable behaviour. Second, the target of your passive aggression may understand your message clearly but refuse to comply, possibly out of irritation at your underhanded style of communicating. Even when passive aggression proves successful in the short run, it can have unpleasant consequences over a longer period of time. You may get immediate compliance ('All right, I'll help you with the damn thing!') but create a resentful climate that will harm the relationship in the future.

Direct Aggression

Whereas a non-asserter under-reacts, a directly aggressive communicator does just the opposite, lashing out to attack the source of displeasure. Dominic Infante (1987) identified nine types of **direct aggression**: *character attacks, competence attacks, physical appearance attacks, maledictions* (wishing the other bad fortune), *teasing, ridicule, threats, swearing,* and *non-verbal emblems* (shaking a fist, waving arms, etc.). Like all types of relational communication, direct aggression has both verbal and non-verbal dimensions.

The results of direct aggression can have a severe impact on the target. There is a significant connection between verbal aggression and physical aggression (Infante et al., 1989). Even if the attacks never lead to blows, the psychological effects can be harmful or even devastating. Recipients can feel embarrassed, inadequate, humiliated, hopeless, desperate, or depressed (Infante, 1987). These results can lead to decreased effectiveness in personal relationships, on the job, and in families (Beatty et al., 1996; Kinney and Segrin, 1998; O'Brien and Bahadur, 1998; Venable and Martin, 1997). Verbal aggression can affect the relationship as well as the target. One aggressive remark can lead to an equally combative reaction, starting a destructive spiral that can expand beyond the original dispute and damage the entire relationship (Infante, 1988; Turk and Monahan, 1999).

Assertion

In **assertion,** a speaker's statement expresses thoughts and feelings clearly. Unlike an aggressive message, it does not attack the other person (Infante and Wigley, 1986). One format for an assertive message consists of five elements (Miller et al., 1975):

1. *A description of the observable behaviour that prompted your message*: The key here is to describe the behaviour objectively, without blaming or name calling. Notice how each of the following statements just describes the facts: 'When you didn't call me after you said you would . . .' and 'Last week, you asked me to buy the tickets, and now you tell me you don't want them. . . .'
2. *Your interpretation of the behaviour*: Be sure to label the interpretation as subjective, not as a matter of fact. For example, 'I get the idea you're mad at me' is a better statement than 'Why are you mad at me?'
3. *The feelings that arise from your interpretation*: Notice the difference between saying, 'I get the idea you are mad at me' and the more complete description 'I get the idea you are mad at me *and I feel hurt* (or *defensive, confused,* or *sorry*).' Review Chapters 4 and 5 of this book for suggestions on how to express emotions clearly.

iStock photo

4. *The consequences of the information you have shared so far*: Consequences can describe what happens to *you*, the speaker ('When you tease me, I avoid you'), what happens to the *target of the message* ('When you drink too much, you start to drive dangerously'), or what happens to *others* ('When you play the radio so loud, it wakes up the baby').
5. *An intention statement*: Some intention statements are requests ('I hope you'll come again'). Others describe how you plan to act ('Unless we can work out some sort of studying arrangement, I may have to find a new place to live').

Chris could have used this format to speak assertively, without blaming Pat:

I've been bothered by some things lately, and I'd like to talk them over with you. When you ask me to take care of your apartment two or three times a month and borrow food and money without returning them [behaviour], I don't think you realize the inconveniences I face [interpretation]. I didn't mind until recently—that's why I haven't said anything before—but I'm starting to feel resentful [feeling], and I'm afraid it might spoil our friendship [consequence]. I don't want that to happen [intention], so I'd like to figure out some way I can help you when you really need it but without it being quite so much of a burden on me [another intention].

This sort of assertive message gets results, especially in our most important interpersonal

Focus on Research

Conflict in Childhood Friendships—Taiwan and Canada

Our childhood friendships are important in a many ways. They provide us with social and psychological support in addition to developing our thinking skills and capacity for empathy. Our relationships with peers teach us things about ourselves, other people, and the world that we cannot learn with adults. Previously, people believed that childhood friendships were mostly ephemeral. But research over the past twenty years has established that children's reciprocated friendships are stable and relatively long-lasting. What is less well understood is the role that conflict plays in friendship. Some experts argue that conflict serves to end childhood friendships, while others suggest conflicts might enhance and enrich children's relationships with each other. Conflicts may help children learn to take another person's perspective and understand the behavioural boundaries that are necessary for the relationship to continue. In addition to not fully understanding the role conflict plays in children's friendships, we don't know exactly how the socio-cultural environment influences relationship dynamics.

One interesting study (Benjamin et al., 2001) compared some friendships of children in Taiwan to friendships of English-speaking Canadian children. Individualistic Canadian culture emphasizes the importance of individual success and achievement whereas collectivist Taiwanese culture emphasizes the importance of group interest and social harmony. These investigators hypothesized that children in Taiwan would have less conflict in their friendships than English-speaking Canadian children. They further hypothesized that the Taiwanese children would perceive conflict in their friendships less positively than the English-speaking Canadian children and that there would be more agreement between the Taiwanese friends about whether or not there is conflict in their relationships. Finally, the investigators anticipated that conflict between children would predict the end of friendships, especially in Taiwan.

The researchers surveyed 92 pairs of Canadian friends in grades 3 or 4 and 248 pairs of Taiwanese friends, also in grades 3 or 4, about the qualities of their friendships using a standardized friendship questionnaire. They then followed up with the same procedure one year later.

As predicted, the Taiwanese children described less conflict in their relationships than the Canadian children did, and the presence of conflict predicted less positive friendship quality in Taiwan. In addition, the Taiwanese children agreed more than the Canadian children about whether or not conflict was prevalent in the relationship. It seems the Taiwanese children even agreed more about when they disagreed than did the Canadian children! These lower rates of conflict and the more detrimental effects of conflict on the quality of friendship are consistent with the collectivist value of social harmony and prohibitions against expression of conflict in Chinese culture. Even when they disagreed, the Taiwanese children found something to agree about.

relationships. While less direct forms may work in non-intimate situations, directness is more effective at getting compliance in intimate relationships (Jordan and Roloff, 1990). Furthermore, a straightforward approach is likely to result in greater relational satisfaction (Honeycutt and Wiemann, 1999; Ridley et al., 2001). When the issue is important and the commitment between partners is high, speaking from the heart instead of beating around the bush seems to be the best approach.

Besides boosting your chances of getting what you want, an assertive approach maintains the self-respect of both people. As a result, people who manage their conflicts assertively usually feel better about themselves and each other afterward, which is not always the case with other styles.

Which Style to Use?

Although communicating assertively might seem like the most attractive alternative to the other styles described in this chapter, it is an oversimplification to imagine that there is one 'right' way to respond to conflicts (Canary and Cupach, 1988; Canary and Spitzberg, 1987). Generally speaking, assertive tactics, such as asking for information and considering alternatives, are preferable to such aggressive tactics as shouting or blaming. But we have already seen that there are times when

Take Two

Individual Conflict Styles

- **Non-assertion:** avoiding (physical or conversational) and accommodating (putting other people's needs ahead of your own).
- **Indirect communication:** delivering information through another person or in an obscure way.
- **Passive aggression:** expressing dissatisfaction in a disguised manner.
- **Direct aggression:** attacking another person, verbally and/or non-verbally.
- **Assertion:** delivering a message which includes a description of observable behaviour that prompted the message, your interpretation, your feelings, the consequences, and your intentions.

aggression or even non-assertion is desirable. Occasionally, you may have to shout to get the other person's attention, and at other times, the smartest approach may be to quietly abide someone else's abuse instead of responding.

A personal conflict style is not necessarily a personality 'trait' that carries across all situations. Wilmot and Hocker (2001) suggest that roughly 50 percent of the population change their style from one situation to another. As we saw in Chapter 1, this sort of behavioural flexibility is a characteristic of competent communicators. Several factors govern which style to use.

The Situation   When someone clearly has more power than you, non-assertion may be the best approach. If the boss tells you to fill that order *now*, you probably ought to do it without comment. A more assertive response ('When you use that tone of voice, I feel defensive') might be clearer, but it could also cost you your job. Likewise, an aggressive message is sometimes most appropriate. At one time or another, it will probably be necessary to raise your voice to show that you mean business.

The Other Person   Although assertiveness has the best chance of success with many people, some recipients respond better to other approaches. You probably know some communicators who are so sensitive or defensive that an assertive approach would be too much for them to handle. Others are so insensitive that aggressiveness is necessary, at least to get their attention.

Your Goals   When you want to solve a problem, assertiveness is probably the best approach. But there are other reasons for communicating in a conflict. Sometimes, your overriding goal is to calm down an enraged or upset person. For example, tolerating an outburst from your crotchety and sick neighbour is probably better than standing up for yourself and triggering a stroke. Likewise, you might choose to sit quietly through the harangue of a family member rather than ruin Thanksgiving dinner. In other cases, your moral principles might demand an aggressive statement even though it might not get you what you originally sought: 'I've had enough of your racist jokes. I've tried to explain why they're so offensive, but you obviously haven't listened. I'm leaving!' Or your goal may be to be seen in a favourable way, in which case, you may want to avoid being aggressive.

Conflict in Relational Systems

So far, we have been describing individual conflict styles. Even though the style you choose in a conflict is important, your approach is not the only factor that will determine how a conflict unfolds. In reality, conflict is *relational*. That is, its character is usually determined by the way the people involved interact (Wilmot and Hocker, 2001; Knapp et al., 1988). For example, you might be determined to handle a conflict with your neighbours assertively, only to be driven to aggression by their uncooperative nature or even to non-assertion by their physical threats. Likewise, you might plan to hint to a professor that you are bothered by his apparent indifference but wind up discussing the matter in an open, assertive way in reaction to his constructive suggestion. Examples like these indicate that conflict is not just a matter of individual choice. Rather, it depends on how the partners interact.

Building Work Skills

Assertive Messages

With the help of a classmate, construct an assertive message that you could deliver to someone in your work or school life (boss, co-worker, or professor). Once you have rehearsed the message, discuss the risks and benefits of delivering it. Decide whether the assertive approach is justified in this case.

When two or more people are in a long-term relationship, they develop their own **relational conflict style**—a pattern of managing disagreements that repeats itself over time. The mutual influence parties have on one another is so powerful that it can overcome our disposition to handle conflicts in the manner that comes most easily to one or the other (Burggraf and Sillars, 1987). As we will soon see, some relational conflict styles are constructive, while others can make life miserable and threaten relationships.

Complementary, Symmetrical, and Parallel Styles

Partners in interpersonal relationships—and impersonal ones, too—can use one of three styles to manage their conflicts. In relationships with a **complementary conflict style**, the partners use different but mutually reinforcing behaviour. In a **symmetrical conflict style**, both people use the same tactics. Some relationships are characterized by a **parallel conflict style**, which shifts between complementary and symmetrical patterns from one issue to another. Table 11.2 illustrates how the same conflict can unfold in very different ways, depending on whether the partners' communication is symmetrical or complementary. A parallel style would alternate between these two forms, depending on the situation.

Test Yourself — What factors should be considered before deciding which individual conflict to use?

Research shows that a complementary 'fight–flight' style is common in many unhappy marriages. One partner—most commonly the wife—addresses the conflict directly, while the other—usually the husband—withdraws (Krokoff, 1990; Sillars et al., 1984). As we discussed in Chapter 3, it is easy to see how this pattern can lead to a cycle of increasing hostility and isolation, since each partner punctuates the conflict differently, blaming the other for making matters worse. 'I withdraw because she's so critical,' a husband might say. However, the wife wouldn't organize the sequence in the same way. 'I criticize because he withdraws,' would be her perception.

Complementary styles are not the only ones that can lead to problems. Some distressed relationships suffer from destructively symmetrical communication. If both partners treat one another with matching hostility, one threat and insult leads to another in an **escalatory spiral**. If the partners both withdraw from one another instead of facing their problems, a complementary **de-escalatory spiral** results, in which the satisfaction and vitality ebb from the relationship, leaving it a shell of its former self.

As Table 11.2 shows, both complementary and symmetrical behaviour can produce good results as well as bad ones. If the complementary behaviours are positive, then a positive spiral results, and the conflict stands a good chance of being resolved. This is the case in the second example in Table 11.2, in which the boss is open to hearing the employee's concerns and listens willingly as the employee talks. Here, a complementary talk–listen pattern works well.

Table 11.2 Complementary and Symmetrical Styles

Situation	Complementary Styles	Symmetrical Styles
Wife is upset because husband is spending little time at home	Wife complains; husband withdraws, spending even less time at home (destructive complementarity)	Wife complains; husband responds angrily and defensively (destructive symmetry)
Female employee is offended when boss jokingly calls her 'sweetie'	Employee objects to boss, explaining her reasons for being offended; boss apologizes for his unintentional insult (constructive complementarity)	Employee tries to make boss understand how she feels by calling him 'cutie'; boss gets the hint and stops using the term (constructive symmetry)
Parents are uncomfortable about teenager's new friends	Parents express concerns; teen dismisses them, saying, 'There's nothing to worry about' (destructive complementarity)	Teen expresses concern that parents are being too protective; parents and teen negotiate a mutually agreeable solution (constructive symmetry)

Symmetrical styles can also be beneficial, as another look at the boss–employee example shows. Many women have found that giving insensitive men a taste of their own sexist medicine is an effective way to end harassment without provoking an argument. The clearest example of a constructive symmetry occurs when both people communicate assertively, listen to one another's concerns, and work together to resolve them. (Ridley and colleagues [2001] found that couples using symmetrical styles appraised their marriage more positively than any other type of couple.) The potential for this sort of solution occurs in the parent–teenager conflict in Table 11.2. With enough mutual respect and careful listening, both the parents and their teenager can understand one another's concerns and possibly find a way to give all three people what they want.

Intimate and Aggressive Styles

Another way to look at conflict styles is to examine the interaction between emotional closeness and aggression. The following scheme was originally used to describe communication between life partners, but it also works well for other types of relationships.

- *Non-intimate–Aggressive*: Partners dispute issues but refrain from dealing with one another on an emotional level. In some relationships, aggression is expressed directly: 'Forget it. I'm not going to another stupid party with your friends. All they do is gossip and eat.' In other relationships, indirect aggression is the norm: [sarcastically] 'Sure, I'd love to go to another party with your fascinating friends.' Neither of these approaches is satisfying, since there are few rewards to justify the costs of the unpleasantness.
- *Non-intimate–Non-aggressive*: The partners avoid conflicts and one another instead of facing issues head-on: 'You won't be coming home for the holidays? Oh well, I guess that's okay. . . .' Relationships of this sort can be quite stable, but because this pattern of communication does not confront and resolve

Take Two

- **Complementary conflict style:** partners use different but mutually reinforcing behaviour; can lead to cycle of increasing hostility and isolation; can lead to positive outcomes as well.
- **Symmetrical conflict style:** partners use the same behaviours; can lead to escalatory and de-escalatory conflict spirals; can lead to positive outcomes, too.
- **Parallel conflict style:** partners shift between complementary and symmetrical styles, depending on the situation.

problems, the vitality and satisfaction can decline over time.

- *Intimate–Aggressive*: This pattern combines aggression and intimacy in a manner that may seem upsetting to outsiders, but it can work well in some relationships. Lovers may fight like cats and dogs but then make up just as intensely. Co-workers may argue about how to get the job done but cherish their association.
- *Intimate–Non-aggressive*: This sort of relationship has a low amount of attacking or blaming. Partners may confront one another directly or indirectly, but in one way or another they manage to prevent issues from interfering with their relationship.

The pattern that partners choose may reveal a great deal about the kind of relationship they have chosen. Mary Ann Fitzpatrick (1977, 1988; Kelley, 1999) identified three types of couples: separates, independents, and traditionals (in Chapter 12, we discuss the three types in more detail). Further research found that partners in each type of relationship approached conflict in a different manner (Fitzpatrick, 1988; Fitzpatrick et al., 1982). Separates took a non-intimate–non-aggressive approach (and were the least satisfied of all subjects studied). They maintained a neutral emotional climate and kept their discussion of conflict to a minimum. Successful independents were best described as intimate–aggressive. They expressed negative emotions frequently but also sought and revealed a large amount of personal information. Satisfied traditional couples fit the intimate–non-aggressive pattern, communicating more positive and less negative information than did independents.

Information like this suggests that there is no 'right' relational conflict style. Some families or couples may fight intensely but love one another just as strongly. Others might handle issues more rationally and calmly. Even a non-intimate style can work well when there's no desire to have an interpersonal relationship. For example, you might be willing to accommodate the demands of an eccentric professor for a semester, since rolling

Test Yourself

Describe four different patterns of interaction between emotional closeness and aggression that can be used to gain insight into partners' conflict styles.

with the punches gets you the education you are seeking, without provoking a confrontation that could be upsetting and costly.

Conflict Rituals

When people have been in a relationship for some time, their communication often develops into **conflict rituals**—unacknowledged but very real repeating patterns of interlocking behaviour (Wilmot and Hocker, 2001). Consider a few common rituals:

> A young child interrupts his parents, demanding to be included in their conversation. At first, the parents tell the child to wait, but he whines and cries until the parents find it easier to listen than to ignore the fussing.

> A couple fights. One partner leaves. The other accepts blame for the problem and begs forgiveness. The first partner returns, and a happy reunion takes place. Soon, they fight again.

> One friend is unhappy with the other. He or she withdraws until the other asks what's wrong. 'Nothing,' the first replies. The questioning persists until the problem is finally out in the open. The friends then solve the issue and continue happily until the next problem arises, when the pattern repeats itself.

There's nothing inherently wrong with the interaction in many rituals (Olson, 2002a). Consider the examples above. In the first, the child's whining may be the only way he can get his parents' attention. In the second, both partners might use the fighting as a way to blow off steam, and both might find that the joy of a reunion is worth the grief of the separation. The third ritual might work well when one friend is more assertive than the other.

Rituals can cause problems, though, when they become the *only* way relational partners handle

Focus on Technology

Email Conflict at Work

Does conflict escalate more rapidly through email? Email and text messages certainly have a greater potential for miscommunication and misunderstanding than face-to-face interactions or telephone conversations. Recall from Chapter 6 that Kristen Byron (2008) found that people are more likely to perceive positive emails as more neutral than intended and neutral emails as more negative than intended, particularly when the communicators didn't know each other well.

Email appears to have both advantages and disadvantages related to managing workplace conflict. On the positive side, as we discussed in Chapter 10, it allows the sender to carefully consider and compose his or her message and has the potential to be perceived as more polite and non-threatening than some face-to-face encounters (Duthler, 2006; Walther, 1996). In addition, it has the potential to reduce the incidence of heated exchanges between people engaged in ongoing conflicts such as divorce (see the Reflection box about email and divorce cases on page 322). On the more negative side, the absence of non-verbal cues that help us decipher the relational tone of the message, combined with the inhibition we might feel because the receiver is not physically present, can contribute to a situation in which we are more likely to quickly fire off a curt or less-than-polite email response in the heat of the moment. Often, these emails are intended only to justify our position or defend our presenting self from the perceived attack. We have no intention of soliciting or listening to the other person's point of view or engaging in resolving the issue at hand. It's easy to see how a back-and-forth exchange of email messages like this can quickly escalate a conflict.

Here are some guidelines to consider before you respond to a situation or email that has aroused strong emotions:

- Wait—take time to regulate your emotions before you respond.
- Consider trying to talk to the person on the phone—or, better yet, meeting them face to face.
- Think before you hit SEND—you really can't take your words back. Email and text messages provide exact transcripts of your words.

Raymond Friedman and Steven Currall (2003) also point out that we pay more attention, perhaps too much attention, to statements made in email and this is another factor that leads to greater conflict escalation than in face-to-face and phone communication. They suggest that we exercise caution when using email to try to resolve disputes.

---

their conflicts. As you learned in Chapter 1, competent communicators have a large repertoire of behaviours, and they are able to choose the most effective response for a given situation. Relying on one pattern to handle all conflicts is no more effective than using a screwdriver to handle every home repair, or putting the same seasoning in every dish you cook. What works in one situation is not likely to succeed in many others. Conflict rituals may be familiar and comfortable, but they aren't the best way to solve the variety of conflicts that are part of any relationship.

Variables in Conflict Styles

By now, you can see that every relational system is unique. The communication patterns in one family, business, or classroom are likely to be very different from any other. But along with the differences that arise in individual relationships, there are two powerful variables that affect the way people manage conflict: gender and culture. We will now take a brief look at each of these factors and see how they affect the ways that conflict is managed.

 Take Two

- **Conflict rituals:** unacknowledged but real repeating patterns of interlocking behaviour; they become problematic when they reduce flexibility and limit the repertoire of behaviour choices.

Gender

Some research suggests that men and women often approach conflicts differently (e.g., Rosenfeld, 1994; Wood, 1994). Even in childhood, there is evidence that boys are (on average, of course) more likely to be aggressive, demanding, and competitive, while girls are more co-operative and accommodating. Studies of children from preschool age to early adolescence have shown that boys try to get their way by ordering one another around: 'Lie down.' 'Get off my steps.' 'Gimme your arm.' By contrast, girls are more likely to make proposals for action that begin with the word *let's*: 'Let's go and find some.' 'Let's ask her if she has any bottles.' 'Let's move *these* out *first*' (Tannen, 1990). Whereas boys tell each other what role to take in pretend play ('Come on, be a doctor'), girls more commonly ask each other what role they want ('Will you be the patient for a few minutes?') or make a joint proposal ('We can both be doctors'). Furthermore, boys often make demands without offering an explanation ('I want the stethoscope right now'). In contrast, girls often give reasons for their suggestions ('We have to clean them because they've got germs').

Differences like these often persist into adulthood. Esin Tezer and Ayhan Demir (2001) studied the conflict behaviour that late adolescents use with same-sex and opposite-sex peers. They found that compared to females, males use more competing behaviours with same-sex peers and more avoiding behaviours with opposite-sex peers—however, they were also more likely to accommodate others regardless of their sex. In their observations of employees' and managers' approaches to conflict resolution, Michael Papa and Elizabeth Natalle (1989) found that when men were engaged in conflict resolution with other men, they consistently used assertiveness and reason. Female dyads used assertiveness and reason at the beginning of the conflict but later switched to bargaining and negotiation. When male and female dyads were engaged in resolving a conflict, they were most likely to use reason and bargaining throughout their communication.

Another body of research suggests that the differences in how the two sexes handle conflict are rather small, and not at all representative of the stereotypical picture of aggressive men and passive women (Gayle et al., 1998). Where differences between the sexes do occur, they can sometimes be exactly the opposite of sex-role stereotypes of aggressive men and accommodating women. For example, when the actual conflict behaviour of both sexes is observed, women turn out to be more assertive than men about expressing their ideas and feelings, and men are more likely to withdraw from discussing issues (Canary et al., 1995).

In other cases, people may *think* that there are greater differences in male and female ways of handling conflicts than actually exist (Allen, 1998). People who assume that men are aggressive and women accommodating may notice behaviour that fits these stereotypes ('See how much he bosses her around? A typical man!'). On the other hand, behaviour that does not fit these preconceived ideas (accommodating men, pushy women) goes unnoticed.

What, then, can we conclude about the influence of gender on conflict? Research has demonstrated that there are, indeed, some small but measurable differences between the two sexes. But, while men and women may have characteristically different conflict styles, the individual style of each communicator is more important than his or her sex in shaping the way he or she handles conflict.

Culture

People from most cultures prefer mutually beneficial resolutions to disagreements whenever

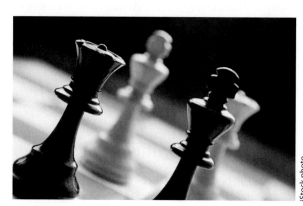

iStock photo

possible (Cai and Fink, 2002). Nonetheless, the ways in which people communicate during conflicts do vary from one culture to another.

The kind of direct approach that characterizes many North Americans is not the norm in other parts of the world. Similarly, the assertiveness that might seem perfectly reasonable to a Canadian would be rude and insensitive in many Asian countries (Gudykunst and Ting-Toomey, 1988; Samovar and Porter, 2001).

Cultures like Japan and China value self-restraint, avoid confrontation, and place a premium on preserving and honouring the 'face' of the other person. For this reason, what seems like 'beating around the bush' to a Canadian would be polite to an Asian. In Japan, for example, even a simple request like 'Close the door' would be too straightforward (Okabe, 1987). A more indirect statement, such as 'It is somewhat cold today', would be more appropriate. To take a more important example, Japanese are reluctant to say no to a request. A more likely answer would be 'Let me think about it for a while', which anyone familiar with Japanese culture would recognize as a refusal.

The Japanese notion of self-restraint is reflected in the important concept of *wa*, or harmony. Interpersonal harmony in Japanese culture includes a tendency for individuals to be self-critical, rather than to find fault in others. A cross-cultural study compared Canadian and Japanese university students' willingness to accept information that they were better than other students at their university at completing a task and their reluctance to accept information that they had performed worse than their peers (Heine et al., 2000). The results of their investigation supported the idea that Canadians, on average, find it difficult to believe that they were outperformed by their average classmate but easily accept that their own performance was superior. Japanese students, in contrast, were reluctant to believe that they had outperformed the average student from their university. While North Americans, on average, are motivated to find out what is good about themselves and reluctant to find fault with themselves, Japanese tend to search for their weaknesses in order to correct

them. This Japanese tendency to avoid the self-enhancement typical of more individualistic cultures and engage in significantly more self-criticism serves to enhance the collectivist value of interpersonal harmony (*wa*) with others.

The same attitude toward conflict prevails in China, where one proverb states, 'The first person to raise his voice loses the argument.' Among Chinese college students (in both the People's Republic and Taiwan), the three most common methods of persuasion used are 'hinting', 'setting an example by one's own actions', and 'strategically agreeing to whatever pleases others' (Ma and Chuang, 2001). It appears that with globalization, some of these preferences may be changing. Yan Bing Zhang and her colleagues (2005) found that while older Chinese adults still preferred an accommodating style of conflict resolution, the younger adults in their study viewed a problem-solving style just as positively as an accommodating style.

It isn't necessary to look at Asia to encounter cultural differences in conflict. Many First Nations people in North America approach conflict very differently than individualistic westerners. When disciplining their children, Aboriginal people often avoid direct criticism or reprimands. Instead, storytelling is the primary means of teaching proper behaviour (Keeshog-Tobias, 1990). In addition to storytelling, parents model the behaviours expected of their children. The importance of developing and maintaining good relationships is a fundamental value of First Nations culture, and there is a belief that personal criticism is damaging and should be avoided (LaLonde, 1992).

The style of some other familiar cultures differs in important ways from the northern European and North American norm. These cultures see verbal disputes as a form of intimacy and even a game. For example, Canadians visiting Greece often think they are witnessing an argument when they are overhearing a friendly conversation (Tannen, 1990). Likewise, both French and Arab men (but not women) find argument stimulating (Copeland and Griggs, 1985). A comparative study of North American and Italian nursery school children showed that one of the Italian children's favourite pastimes was a kind of heated debating that Italians call *discussione* but that North Americans would regard as arguing. Likewise, research has shown that in the conversations of working-class Jewish speakers of Eastern European origin, arguments are used as a means of being sociable.

People from Italy, Greece, and some parts of Eastern Europe may be more willing to accept conflict because of their individualistic, low-context communication style of speaking directly and avoiding uncertainty. It's not surprising that people from cultures that emphasize harmony among people with close relationships tend to handle conflicts in less direct ways. With differences like these, it is easy to imagine how two friends, lovers, or fellow workers from different cultural backgrounds might have trouble finding a conflict style that is comfortable for both of them.

Despite these differences, it is important to realize that culture is not the only factor that influences the way people think about conflict or how they act when they disagree. Some research (e.g., Beatty and McCroskey, 1997) suggests that our approach to conflict may be part of our biological makeup. Furthermore, scholarship suggests a person's self-concept is more powerful than his or her culture in determining conflict style (Oetzel et al., 2001; Ting-Toomey et al., 2001). For example, people who view themselves as mostly independent of others are likely to use a direct, solution-oriented conflict style, regardless of their cultural heritage. Those who see themselves as mostly interdependent are likely to use a style that avoids direct confrontation. And those who see themselves as both independent and interdependent are likely to have the widest variety of conflict behaviours on which to draw.

Beyond individual temperament and self-concept, the environment in which we are raised can shape the way we approach conflict. Parental conflict style plays a role. Some research has revealed a significant relationship between the way a mother handles conflict and the style used by her adult children (Martin et al., 1997). Interestingly, there was no significant relationship in this study between a father's conflict style and that of his children.

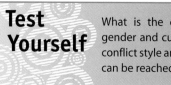

Along with family influences, the 'culture' of each relationship can shape how we behave (Messman and Canary, 1998). You might handle disagreements calmly in a job where rationality and civility are the norm, but shriek like a banshee at home if that's the way you and a relational partner handle disputes.

Methods of Conflict Resolution

Whatever the style, every conflict is a struggle to have one's goals met. Sometimes, that struggle succeeds, and in other cases, it fails. In the remainder of this chapter, we look at various approaches to resolving conflicts and see which ones are most promising.

Win–Lose

In **win–lose problem solving**, one person gets satisfaction while the other comes up short. People resort to this method of resolving disputes when they perceive a situation as being an 'either–or' one: either I get my way, or you get yours. The most clear-cut examples of win–lose situations are certain games, such as hockey or poker, in which the rules require that there be a winner and a loser. Some interpersonal issues seem to fit into this win–lose framework: two co-workers seeking a promotion to the same job, or a couple arguing over how to spend their limited money. In the Self-Assessment box on page 338, the win–lose problem-solving method in which *you* win is Dominance, and the win–lose methods in which you let the *other person* win are Accommodation and Avoidance. How do your three scores compare with each other, and how do they compare with the other two methods?

Power is the distinguishing characteristic in win–lose problem solving, as it's necessary to defeat an opponent to get what you want. The most obvious kind of power is physical. Some parents threaten their children with warnings such as 'Stop misbehaving or I'll send you to your room.' Real or implied force is not the only kind of power used in conflicts. People who rely on authority of many types engage in win–lose methods without ever threatening physical coercion. In most jobs, supervisors can use their authority in the assignment of working hours, job promotions, desirable or undesirable tasks, and, of course, in firing an unsatisfactory employee. Teachers can use the power of grades to coerce their students into acting in desired ways. Even the usually admired democratic principle of majority rule is a win–lose method of resolving conflicts. However fair it may be, the system results in one group getting its way and another being unsatisfied.

The win–lose method may sometimes be necessary when there are truly scarce resources, or when only one person can achieve satisfaction. If two suitors want to marry the same person, only one can succeed. To return to an earlier example, it is often true that only one applicant can be hired for a job. Still, don't be too willing to assume that your conflicts are necessarily win–lose. Many situations that seem to require a loser can be resolved to everyone's satisfaction.

There is a second kind of situation in which win–lose is the best method of conflict. Even when co-operation is possible, if the other person insists on defeating you, then the most logical response might be to defend yourself by fighting back. 'It takes two to tango', the saying goes, and it takes two to co-operate. Some people are so resistant to constructive problem solving that it may be fruitless to try that approach. In one study, employees identified by their managers as 'difficult' consistently refused to co-operate in collaborative problem solving (Monroe et al., 1989). Instead, they responded with passive-aggressive strategies— refusing to accept managers' feedback, offering excuses, and using avoidance. When faced with this sort of absolute refusal to co-operate, it may be self-defeating for you to hang on to a collaborative approach.

"It's not enough that we succeed. Cats must also fail."

A final and much less frequent justification for trying to defeat another person occurs when the other person is clearly behaving wrongly and when defeating that person is the only way to stop the wrong behaviour. Few people would deny the importance of restraining a person who is deliberately harming others, even if the belligerent person's freedom is sacrificed in the process. However, only in the most extreme circumstances is it productive in the long run to coerce others into behaving as we think they should.

From the discussion so far, you might assume that a win–lose orientation is always destructive. The truth is not so simple. Susan Messman and Rebecca Mikesell (2000) found that some men and women in satisfying dating relationships used competition to enrich their relationships. Some found satisfaction by competing in play (who's the better racquetball player?), in achievement (who gets the better job offer?), and in altruism (who's more romantic?). These satisfied couples developed a shared narrative (see Chapter 3) that defined competition as a measure of regard, quite different from conflict that signalled a lack of appreciation and respect.

Self-Assessment

Your Method of Conflict Resolution

Think of a relationship with someone with whom you interact regularly and with whom you engage in conflict (for example, a parent, sibling, roommate, close friend, spouse, partner, or lover). How do you usually respond to your conflict with this person? In each pair below, circle the **A** or **B** statement that is most *characteristic* of your behaviour. In some cases, neither answer may be very typical of your behaviour. If this happens, select the response that you would be *more likely* to use.

1. **A.** There are times when I let the other person take responsibility for solving the problem.
    B. Rather than negotiate the things on which we disagree, I try to stress those things upon which we both agree.
2. **A.** I try to find a compromise solution.
    B. I attempt to deal with all of the other person's and my concerns.
3. **A.** I am usually firm in pursuing my goals.
    B. I might try to soothe the other's feelings and preserve our relationship.
4. **A.** I try to find a compromise solution.
    B. I sometimes sacrifice my own wishes for the wishes of the other person.
5. **A.** I consistently seek the other's help in working out a solution.
    B. I don't worry about my own concerns if satisfying them means damaging the relationship.
6. **A.** I try to avoid creating unpleasantness for myself.
    B. I try to win my position.
7. **A.** I try to postpone the issue until I have had some time to think it over.
    B. I give up some points in exchange for others.
8. **A.** I am usually firm in pursuing my goals.
    B. I attempt to get all concerns and issues immediately out in the open.
9. **A.** I feel that differences are not always worth worrying about.
    B. I try to integrate my concerns with the other person's concerns.
10. **A.** I am firm in pursuing my goals.
    B. I try to find a compromise solution.
11. **A.** I attempt to get all concerns and issues immediately out in the open.
    B. I might try to soothe the other's feelings and preserve our relationship.
12. **A.** I sometimes avoid taking positions that would create controversy.

B. I will let the other person have some of what she or he wants if she or he lets me have some of what I want.
13. **A.** I propose a middle ground.
    B. I press to get my points made.
14. **A.** I tell the other person my ideas and ask for his or hers.
    B. I try to show the other person the logic and benefits of my position.
15. **A.** I might try to soothe the other's feelings and preserve our relationship.
    B. I try to do what is necessary to avoid tensions.

Scoring: For question 1, circle the **A** or **B** below according to your answer; for question 2, circle the **A** or **B** below, according to your answer. Repeat the process for all 15 questions.

	D	I	C	A	AC
1.				A	B
2.		B	A		
3.	A				B
4.				A	B
5.		A			B
6.	B			A	
7.			B	A	
8.	A	B			
9.		B		A	
10.	A		B		
11.		A			B
12.			B	A	
13.	B		A		
14.	B	A			
15.				B	A

Number of **A**s and **B**s circled in column D (**D**ominance) _____

Number of **A**s and **B**s circled in column I (**I**ntegration) _____

Number of **A**s and **B**s circled in column C (**C**ompromise) _____

Number of **A**s and **B**s circled in column A (**A**voidance) _____

Number of **A**s and **B**s circled in column AC (**AC**commodation) _____

How do your five scores compare? Which is your highest, or your most likely method of conflict resolution? Which is your lowest, or your least likely method of conflict resolution?

Lose–Lose

In **lose–lose problem solving**, neither side is satisfied with the outcome. Although the name of this approach is so discouraging that it's hard to imagine how anyone could willingly use it, lose–lose is a fairly common way to handle conflicts. Often, the partners will both strive to be winners, but as a result of the struggle, both wind up losers. On the international scene, many wars illustrate this sad point. A nation that gains military victory at the cost of thousands of lives, large amounts of resources, and a damaged national consciousness hasn't truly won much. On an interpersonal level, the same principle holds true. Most of us have seen battles of pride in which both people strike out and both suffer.

Compromise

A **compromise** gives both people at least some of what they want, although both sacrifice part of their goals. People usually settle for a compromise when it seems that partial satisfaction is the best they can hope for. What was your score for Compromise in the Self-Assessment exercise, and how does it compare with the other scores?

Although a compromise may be better than losing everything, this approach hardly seems to deserve the positive image it has with some people. In his valuable book on conflict resolution, Albert Filley (1975, p. 23) makes an interesting observation about our attitudes toward this method. Why is it, he asks, that if someone says, 'I will compromise my values', we view the action unfavourably, yet we talk admiringly about people in a conflict who compromise to reach a solution? Although

compromises may be the best result obtainable in some conflicts, it is important to realize that both people in a dispute can often work together to find much better solutions. In such cases, *compromise* is a negative word.

Most of us are surrounded by the results of bad compromises. Consider a common example: the conflict between one person's desire to smoke and another's need for clean air. The win–lose outcomes on this issue are obvious: Either the smoker abstains or the non-smoker gets polluted lungs—neither option a very satisfying one. But a compromise in which the smoker gets to enjoy only a rare cigarette or must retreat outdoors, and in which the non-smoker must still inhale some fumes or feel like an ogre, is hardly better. Both sides have lost a considerable amount of both comfort and goodwill. Of course, the costs involved in other compromises are even greater. If a divorced couple compromises on child care by haggling over custody and then finally grudgingly agrees to split the time with their children, it is hard to say that anybody has won.

Some compromises do satisfy everyone. You and the seller might settle on a price for a used car that is between what the seller was asking and what you wanted to pay. While neither of you got everything you wanted, the outcome would still leave both of you satisfied. Likewise, you and your companion might agree to see a film that is the second choice for both of you in order to spend an evening together. As long as everyone is satisfied with an outcome, compromise can be an effective way to resolve conflicts. Catherine Sanderson and Kim Karetsky (2002) found that college students with a strong focus on intimacy goals were likely to engage in open discussion and compromise, show concern for their partner, and seek social support—and, importantly, they were likely to resolve the conflict successfully. Table 11.3 presents a summary of the differences between win–lose and win–win problem-solving scenarios.

By now, you can see that compromise can produce either win–win or lose–lose outcomes, depending upon the perceptions of the people involved and the effectiveness of the solution they devise. When you consider compromising, ask yourself whether it leaves you and the other party better or worse off. If it's the latter, you may want to consider other approaches.

Win–Win

As its name suggests, the outcome of a **win–win problem-solving** style is different in approach and outcomes from both win–lose and lose–lose styles. In win–win problem solving, the goal is to find a solution that satisfies the needs of everyone involved. Not only do the partners avoid trying to win at each other's expense, but there is also a belief that working together can provide a solution in which all reach their goals without needing to compromise. In the Self-Assessment exercise, the win–win problem-solving method is called Integration. How does your score on Integration compare to the other approaches?

One way to understand how no-lose problem solving works is to look at a few examples:

- A boss and her employees get into a disagreement over scheduling. The employees often want to shift the hours they're scheduled to work so that they can accommodate personal needs; the boss needs to be sure that the operation is fully staffed at all times. After some discussion, they arrive at a solution that satisfies everyone. The boss works up a monthly master schedule showing the hours during which each employee is responsible for being on the job. Employees are free to trade hours among themselves, as long as the operation is fully staffed at all times.

- A dispute about testing arises in a college class. Because of sickness and for other reasons, a certain number of students need to take makeup exams. The instructor doesn't want to give these students any advantage over their peers and also doesn't want to have to create a brand-new test for just a few people. After working on the problem together, the instructor and students arrive at a no-lose solution: The instructor will hand out a list of twenty possible exam questions in advance of the test day. At examination time, five of these questions are randomly drawn for the class to answer. Students who take makeup exams will draw from the same pool of questions at the time of their test. In this way, makeup students are taking a fresh test without the instructor having to create a new exam.

- A newly married husband and wife find themselves arguing frequently over their budget.

Table 11.3 Differences between Win–Lose and Win–Win Problem Solving

Win–Lose	Win–Win
Conflicting interests	Shared interests
Negotiations based on power	Negotiations based on trust
Low self-disclosure	High self-disclosure
Concern only for self	Concern for self and for other

The husband enjoys buying impractical and enjoyable items for himself and for the house, whereas the wife fears that such purchases will ruin their carefully constructed budget. Their solution is to set aside a small amount of money each month for 'fun' purchases. The amount is small enough to be affordable, but it gives the husband a chance to escape from their spartan lifestyle. The wife is satisfied with the arrangement because the luxury money is now a budget category by itself, which gets rid of the 'out-of-control' feeling that comes when her husband makes unexpected purchases. The plan works so well that the couple continues to use it even after their income rises—they increase the amount devoted to luxuries.

Although such solutions might seem obvious when you read them here, a moment's reflection will show you that such co-operative problem solving is all too rare. People faced with these types of conflicts often resort to such dysfunctional styles of communicating as withdrawing, avoiding, or competing, and they wind up handling the issues in a manner that results in either a win–lose or lose–lose outcome. As we pointed out earlier, it is a shame to see one or both partners in a conflict come away unsatisfied when they could both get what they're seeking by communicating in a no-lose manner.

Win–win problem solving works best when it follows a seven-step approach that is based on a plan developed by Deborah Weider-Hatfield (1981):

1. *Define your needs.* Begin by deciding what you want or need. Sometimes, the answer is obvious, as in our earlier example of the neighbour whose loud music kept others awake. There are times, however, when the apparent problem masks a more fundamental

iStock photo

one. Consider an example: After dating for a few months, Elizabeth started to call Jim after they parted for the evening—a 'goodnight call'. Although the calling was fine with Jim at the beginning, he began to find it irritating after several weeks.

At first, Jim thought he was annoyed by the nuisance of talking late at night when he was ready for sleep. More self-examination showed that his irritation centred on the relational message he thought Elizabeth's calls implied: that she was either snooping on him or was so insecure she needed constant assurances of his love. Once Jim recognized the true sources of his irritation, his needs became clear: (1) to have Elizabeth's trust and (2) to be free of her insecurities.

Because your needs will not always be clear, it is often necessary to think about a problem alone, before approaching the other person involved. Talking to a third person can sometimes help you sort out your thoughts.

Reflection

Win–Win Solution Reduces Friction

After four months of living together, my two neat roommates were fed up with cleaning up after me and the other messy member of our little household, and the two of us were tired of hearing the neat freaks complain about our habits.

Last week, we had a meeting (again) about the dishes and glasses. But this time, we didn't argue about who was right or wrong. Instead, we looked for a win–win solution. And once we started looking, we found it. Each of us gets his own dishes, glasses, and silverware—two of each item per person. We are responsible for cleaning only our own things. Now, if you look in our kitchen cabinets, you find only eight glasses, eight plates, and so on. There isn't enough stuff to make a mess, and each of us has to wash his own things if he wants to eat. Everybody is happy. Some people might think our solution is silly, but it has certainly worked well for us—and that's all that matters.

In either case, you should explore both the apparent content of your dissatisfaction and the relational issues that may lurk behind it.

2. *Share your needs with the other person.* Once you have defined your needs, it's time to share them with your partner. Two guidelines are important here. First, be sure to choose a time and place that is suitable. If your partner is tired or busy your concerns may not be well received. Likewise, be sure you are at your best. Don't bring an issue up when your anger may cause you to say things you'll later regret, when your discouragement blows the problem out of proportion, or when you are distracted by other business. Making a date to discuss the problem—after dinner, over a cup of coffee, or even a day in advance—can often boost the odds of a successful outcome.

The second guideline for sharing a problem is to use the descriptive 'I' language that we outlined in Chapter 5 and the assertive message format on pages 327–8 of this chapter. Rather than imply blame, messages worded in this way describe how your partner's behaviour affects you. Notice how Jim's use of the assertive message format conveys a descriptive, non-judgmental attitude in his discussion with Elizabeth:

> When you call me after every date [sense data], I begin to wonder whether you are checking up on me [interpretation of Elizabeth's behaviour]. I've also started to think that you're feeling insecure about whether I care about you and that you need lots of reassurance [more interpretation]. I'm starting to feel closed in by the calls [feeling], and I feel myself pulling back from you [consequence]. I don't like the way we're headed, and I don't think it is necessary. I'd like to know whether you are feeling insecure and to find a way that we can feel sure about each other's feelings without needing so much reassurance [intentions].

3. *Listen to the other person's needs.* Once your own wants and needs are clear, it's time to find

out what the other person wants and needs. (Now, the listening skills described in Chapter 7 and the supportive behaviour described in Chapter 10 become most important.) When Jim began to talk to Elizabeth about her telephoning, he learned some interesting things. In his haste to hang up the phone the first few times she called, he had given her the impression that he didn't care about her once the date was over. Feeling insecure about his love, she called as a way of getting attention and expressions of love from him.

Once Jim realized this fact, it became clear that he needed to find a solution that would make Elizabeth feel secure and at the same time relieve him of feeling pressured.

Arriving at a shared definition of the problem requires skills associated with creating a supportive and confirming climate. The ability to be non-judgmental, descriptive, and empathic is an important, support-producing skill. Both Jim and Elizabeth needed to engage in paraphrasing to discover all the details of the conflict.

When they are really communicating effectively, partners can help each other clarify what they're seeking. Truly believing that their happiness depends on each other's satisfaction, they actively try to analyze what obstacles need to be overcome.

4. *Generate possible solutions.* In the next step, the partners try to think of as many ways to satisfy both of their needs as possible. They can best do so by 'brainstorming'—inventing as many potential solutions as they can. The key to success in brainstorming is to seek quantity without worrying about quality. The rule is to prohibit criticism of all ideas, no matter how outlandish they may sound. An idea that seems far-fetched can sometimes lead to a more workable one. Another rule of brainstorming is that ideas are not personal property. If one person makes a suggestion, the other should feel free to suggest another solution that builds upon or modifies the original one. The original suggestion and its offshoots are all potential solutions that will be considered later. Once partners get over their possessiveness about ideas, the level of defensiveness drops and both people can work together to find the best solution without worrying about whose idea it is.

All of the supportive and confirming behaviours that we discussed in Chapter 10 are important during this step. However, two of them stand out as crucial: the ability to communicate provisionalism rather than certainty, and the ability to refrain from premature evaluations of any solution. The aim of this step is to generate *all* the possible solutions—whether they are immediately reasonable or not. If the partners behave provisionally and avoid any evaluation until all the solutions are generated, creative and spontaneous behaviour is encouraged. The result is a long list of solutions that most likely contains the best solution, one that might not have been expressed if the communication climate were defensive.

Jim and Elizabeth used brainstorming to generate solutions to their telephone problem. Their list consisted of continuing the calling but limiting the time spent on the phone; limiting the calls to once in a while; Elizabeth's keeping a journal that could serve as a substitute for calling; Jim's calling Elizabeth once in a while; cutting out all calling; moving in together to eliminate the necessity for calling; getting married; and breaking up. Although some of these solutions were clearly unacceptable to both partners, they listed all the ideas they could think of, preparing themselves for the next step in no-lose problem solving.

5. *Evaluate the possible solutions and choose the best one.* The time to evaluate the solutions is after they all have been generated, after the partners feel they have exhausted all the possibilities. In this step, the possible solutions generated during the previous step are evaluated for their ability to satisfy the mutually shared goal. How does each solution stand up against the individual and mutual goals?

Which solution satisfies the most goals? Partners need to work co-operatively in examining each solution and in finally selecting the best one.

It is important during this step to react spontaneously rather than strategically. Choosing a particular solution because the other person finds it satisfactory (an accommodation strategy), while seemingly a 'nice' thing to do, is as manipulative a strategy as getting the other person to accept a solution satisfactory only to you (a win–lose strategy). Respond honestly as solutions are evaluated, and encourage your partner to do the same. Any solution agreed upon as 'best' has little chance of satisfying both partners' needs if it was strategically manipulated to the top of the list.

The solution Elizabeth and Jim chose as satisfying her need to feel secure, his need to be undisturbed before turning in, and their mutual goal of maintaining their relationship at a highly intimate level, was to limit both the frequency and length of the calls. Also, Jim agreed to share in the calling.

6. *Implement the solution.* Now, the time comes to try out the idea selected to see if it does, indeed, satisfy everyone's needs. The key questions to answer are *who* does *what* to *whom*, and *when*?

Before Jim and Elizabeth tried out their solution, they went over the agreement to make sure it was clear. This step proved to be important, for a potential misunderstanding existed. When will the solution be implemented? Should Elizabeth wait a few weeks before calling? Should Jim begin the calling? They agreed that Jim would call after their next date.

Another problem concerned their different definitions of length. How long is too long? They decided that more than a few minutes would be too long.

The solution was implemented after they discussed it in detail and came to a mutual agreement about its particulars. This process may seem awkward and time-consuming, but

both Elizabeth and Jim decided that without a clear understanding of the solution, they were opening the door to future conflicts.

Interestingly, the discussion concerning their mutual needs and how the solution satisfied them was an important part of their relationship's development. Jim learned that Elizabeth did, sometimes, feel insecure about his love. Elizabeth learned that Jim needed time to himself and that this need did not reflect on his love for her. Soon after implementing the solution, they found that the problem ceased to exist. Jim no longer felt the calls were invading his privacy, and Elizabeth, after talks with Jim, felt more secure about his love.

7. *Follow up the solution.* To stop after selecting and implementing a particular solution assumes any solution is forever, that time does not change things, that people remain constant, and that events never alter circumstances. Of course, this assumption is incorrect. As people and circumstances change, a particular solution may lose or increase its effectiveness. Regardless, a follow-up evaluation needs to take place.

After you have tested your solution for a short time, it's a good idea to plan a meeting to talk about how things are going. You may find that you need to make some changes or even rethink the whole problem.

Reviewing the effects of your solution does not mean that something is wrong and must be corrected. Indeed, everything may point to the conclusion that the solution is still working to satisfy your needs and the mutually shared goal, and that the mutually shared goal is still important to both of you.

It is important at this stage in the win–win problem-solving process to be honest with yourself as well as with the other person. It may be difficult for you to say, 'We need to talk about this again,' yet it could be essential if the problem is to remain resolved. Planning a follow-up talk when the solution is first implemented is important.

Take Two

Methods of Conflict Resolution

- **Win–lose:** one person gets what he/she wants and the other does not.
- **Lose–lose:** neither person gets what he/she wants.
- **Compromise:** both people get some of what they want and sacrifice part of what they want.
- **Win–win:** everyone involved has needs satisfied.

Elizabeth and Jim decided to wait one month before discussing the effects of their solution. Their talk was short, because both felt the problem no longer existed. Also, their discussions helped their relationship grow: they learned more about each other, felt closer, and developed a way to handle their conflicts constructively.

Although a win–win approach sounds ideal, it is not always possible, or even desirable (Budescu et al., 1999). Table 11.4 lists some factors to consider when deciding which approach to take when facing a conflict. There will certainly be times when compromising is the most sensible approach. You will even encounter instances when pushing for your own solution is reasonable. Even more surprisingly, you will probably discover that there are times when it makes sense to willingly accept the loser's role. Much of the time, however, good intentions and creative thinking can lead to outcomes that satisfy everyone.

Summary

Despite wishes and cultural myths to the contrary, conflict is a natural and unavoidable part of any relationship. Since conflict cannot be escaped, the challenge is how to deal with it so that it strengthens a relationship rather than weakens it.

All conflicts have the same characteristics: expressed struggle, perceived incompatible goals, perceived scarce rewards, interdependence, and inevitability. Functional conflicts cope with these characteristics in very different ways from dysfunctional ones. Partners strive to co-operate instead of competing; to focus on rather than avoid the issues in dispute; and to seek positive, long-term solutions that meet each other's needs.

Individuals can respond to conflicts in a variety of ways: non-assertively, indirectly, with direct or

Table 11.4 Choosing the Best Method of Conflict

Win–Lose (and you lose)	Win–Lose (and you win)	Compromise	Win–Win
When you discover you are wrong	When there is not enough time to seek a win–win outcome	When the issue is important and the other person will take advantage of your non-competitive approach	When the issue is too important for a compromise
When the issue is more important to the other person than it is to you	When the issue is not important enough to negotiate at length	When sustaining or maintaining a relationship with the other person is unimportant to you	When a long-term relationship between you and the other person is important
To let others learn by making their own mistakes	When the other person is not willing to seek a win–win outcome		When the other person is willing to use a win–win strategy
When the long-term, cost of winning may not be worth the short-term gains			

passive aggression, and assertively. Each of these approaches can be justified in certain circumstances. The way a conflict is handled is not always the choice of a single person, since the people involved influence one another as they develop a relational conflict style. This style is influenced by the partners' genders and the influences of their cultural backgrounds.

There are four possible outcomes to a particular conflict: lose–lose, win–lose, compromise, and win–win. In most circumstances, a win–win outcome is best, and it can be achieved by following the guidelines outlined on pages 340–5.

Activities

1. **Invitation to Insight**

   Even the best relationships have conflicts. Using the characteristics on pages 320–3, describe at least five conflicts in one of your important relationships. Then answer the following questions:

   a. Which conflicts involve primarily content issues? Which involve primarily relational issues?

   b. Which conflicts were one-time affairs, and which recur?

2. **Invitation to Insight**

   From your recent experiences, recall two conflict incidents—one functional and one dysfunctional. Then answer the following questions:

   a. What distinguished these two conflicts?

   b. What were the consequences of each?

   c. How might the dysfunctional conflict have turned out differently if it had been handled in a more functional manner?

   d. How could you have communicated differently to make the dysfunctional conflict more functional?

3. **Invitation to Insight**

   Interview someone who knows you well. Ask your interviewee which personal conflict styles (non-assertive, indirect, etc.) you use most often and the effect each of these styles has on your relationship with this person. Using your findings, discuss whether different behaviour might produce more productive results.

4. **Invitation to Insight**

   This activity will be most productive if, in answering the following questions about yourself, you consult several people with whom you share an interpersonal relationship:

   a. Is your relational style of handling conflict complementary, symmetrical, or parallel? What are the consequences of this style?

   b. What combination of intimacy and aggressiveness characterizes your approach to conflict? Are you satisfied with this approach?

   c. What conflict rituals do you follow in this relationship? Are these rituals functional or dysfunctional? What might be better alternatives?

5. **Skill Builder**

To explore how the win–win approach might work in your life, try one of the following alternatives:

a. Use the steps on pages 341–5 to describe how you could manage a conflict by following the win–win approach. How could you try this approach in your personal life? What difference might such an approach make?

b. Try the win–win approach with a relational partner. What parts prove most helpful? Which are most difficult? How can you improve your relationship by using some or all of the win–win approach in future conflicts?

6. **Role Play**

Think of an interpersonal conflict you recently engaged in that you believe was not resolved well. Review the individual approaches to conflict described on pages 323–8 and decide on the approach you would take if you had the opportunity to do it over. Briefly describe the conflict you had, and the person you had it with to a partner and role-play your new approach to the conflict. Discuss the strengths and challenges of the approach you chose. Now, reverse roles.

Discussion Questions

1. Wilmot and Hocker (2001) provide a definition of *conflict* that includes five parts. Must all five elements be present in order for conflict to exist? Why or why not?

2. Explain the concept of *functional conflict* and contrast it with *dysfunctional conflict*.

3. Which conflict style do you think poses the most risks to interpersonal relationships? Why?

4. Explain why assertion is often more effective than the other four conflict styles described in this chapter.

5. We have suggested that the supposed differences in how men and women handle conflict may have more to do with people's preconceived notions about how men and women handle conflict (stereotypes). What do you think? Why?

6. Recent research suggests a person's self-concept is more powerful than his or her culture in determining conflict style. Given the role of culture in the development of self-concept (see Chapter 2), how could this be true?

7. Contrast win–win problem solving with compromise. What are the advantages and disadvantages of each approach? Why is compromise celebrated in our culture and win–win problem solving often ignored?

Chapter Twelve

Key Terms

boundaries
chaotic family
communication rules
conformity orientation
conversation orientation
designated leader
disengaged family
downward communication
enmeshed family
family
family of origin
formal communication
horizontal communication
informal communication
narratives
power
rigid family
roles
system
upward communication
virtual teams

Communicating with Family and at Work

After studying the material in this chapter . . .

You Should Understand:

1. The defining characteristics of a family and family communication.
2. The significance of family systems, roles, narratives, models, and rules.
3. The nature of cohesion, adaptability, and conflict in functional and dysfunctional families.
4. The ways information can flow in work-related organizations and relationships.
5. The importance of relational communication and organizational cultures in working groups.
6. The types of power individual group members can possess.
7. The characteristics of an effective interview.

You Should Be Able To:

1. Describe the defining characteristics of the families to which you belong.
2. Identify the roles, narratives, models, and rules of your family system.
3. Analyze your family's boundaries, adaptability, and conflict-management styles.
4. Identify your formal and informal relationships on the job, and suggest how you can expand the number of relationships to operate most effectively in your career.
5. Choose the type of interaction (face to face or mediated) that can maximize your on-the-job effectiveness.
6. Identify the relational roles you need to fulfill to help a working group operate effectively.

7. Diagnose the culture of an organization and determine how well it fits with your personal communication style.
8. Identify the types of power you possess in a given group, and describe how you can use them to help the group operate effectively.
9. Apply the guidelines to plan, participate in, and follow up on an employment interview in a way that creates a positive relationship with a potential employer.

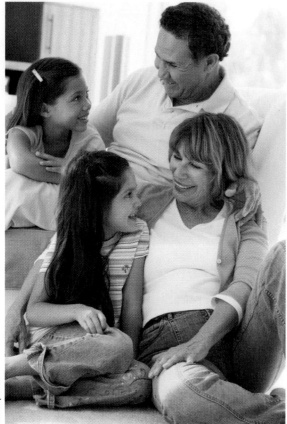

iStock photo

interdependent people who have a common history and a present reality, and who expect to influence each other in the future. This definition includes the following different family arrangements:

- Two parents (of different or same sex) and their children (biological or adopted)
- A couple (married or not, heterosexual or not) who live together for a period of time and have a committed, binding relationship
- A single parent (married, never married, or divorced) who lives with his or her biological or adopted children
- Two adults and their children, all, some, or none of whom may be the offspring of their union
- Groups of relatives who have blood or legal ties and who live with or near each other

Whether or not you consider all of these arrangements as legitimate families, they all share important characteristics that make communication among members different from that in other sorts of relationships.

Types of Family Communication

Within families, each type of communication between different family members has its own characteristics.

Spouses or Partners The way spouses or partners communicate with each other reflects both their personal style and their thinking about what their relationship should be like. Mary Ann Fitzpatrick (1988) found that there are three basic types of couples, which she labelled *Traditionals*, *Independents*, and *Separates*.

Traditional couples strive to maintain stability by upholding a conventional belief system that values traditional sex roles, a great degree of interdependence (i.e., little psychological or physical distance), and an inclination to avoid conflict. Traditionals tend to have the highest marital satisfaction and a moderately high expression of affection.

Independent couples avoid adhering to traditional sex roles. Though they may be physically

Communication in Families

What is a family? A few decades ago, this was an easy question for most people to answer. Common notions of a family in the Western world stressed shared residence, reproduction or adoption of children by different-sexed adults, and a 'socially approved sexual relationship' (Murdock, 1965, p. 1). In recent years, social scientists, lawyers, judges, and theologians have grappled with much broader definitions as they considered questions such as deciding who the parents are when there is an egg or sperm donor, determining the rights of adoptive parents and adopted children, and deciding whether gay and lesbian couples can marry or adopt a child (Cavaliere, 1995).

After reviewing various definitions over the last century, Galvin and Brommel (2000) define **family** broadly enough to include many types of relationships. A family is a system with two or more

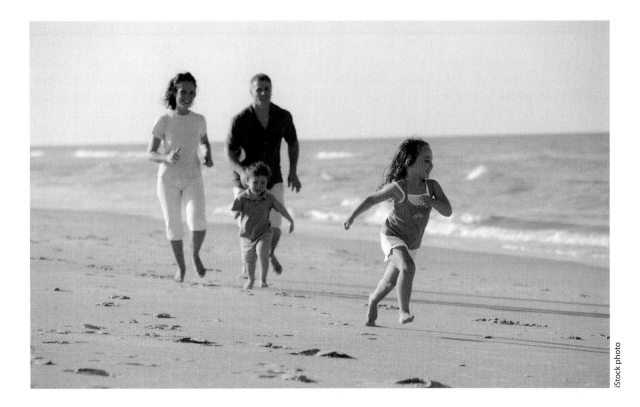

iStock photo

close, they maintain their psychological distance. Unlike Traditionals, they don't avoid conflict. Independent couples tend to have low marital satisfaction and a low expression of affection.

Separate couples place a higher value on their individual freedom than on their relationship. They are more conflict-avoidant than Independents, have greater space needs, and share less. Like Independent couples, Separates tend to have low expression of affection and marital satisfaction.

Fitzpatrick (1988) found that 20 percent of couples are Traditionals, 17 percent are Separates, and 22 percent are Independents. The remaining 40 percent are mixed couples in which each partner favours a different style. Mixed couples tend to have moderately high marital satisfaction—higher than Independents and Separates, but not higher than Traditionals—and a moderately high expression of affection. Their beliefs regarding sex roles and the extent to which they are likely to be close to each other depend on the type of mixed relationship they have. Couples consisting of Separate and Traditional partners tend to have moderately high marital satisfaction and closeness and a high expression of affection, whereas other mixed types tend to be less close and have a lower expression of affection.

Parent–Child   With the arrival of the first child, communication within the family becomes more complicated. Along with being a threesome, the members can form three very different dyads: wife–husband, father–child, and mother–child. These combinations lead to at least seven influence patterns:

1. The father influences the mother's interaction with the child (e.g., the father says, 'Please don't coddle the baby').
2. The mother influences the father's interaction with the child (e.g., the wife says, 'Give her a kiss good night').
3. The father–child relationship influences mother–child interaction (e.g., the father yells at the child, and the child runs to her mother for comfort).

4. The mother–child relationship influences the father–child interaction (e.g., the wife teaches the child that his father is a hard worker).
5. The father–child relationship influences husband–wife interaction (e.g., the husband spends time playing tennis with the child instead of spending time with his wife).
6. The mother–child relationship influences husband–wife interaction (e.g., the wife discloses personal information to her adult child and not to her husband).
7. The husband–wife relationship influences the interaction among all the family members (e.g., a conflict between the husband and wife spills over to a conflict with the child/children).

The birth or adoption of a child also influences other aspects of family communication (Huston and Vangelisti, 1995). For example, role patterns may change and be reflected, perhaps, in the division of labour in housework. Also, changes in the extent to which the couple enjoys leisure activities and engages in interaction with friends and relatives are likely after the birth of their child.

Siblings   Sibling relationships are usually the longest-lasting ones in our lives. Think about your interaction with your siblings over the years and you can probably identify many roles you played in each others' lives: playmate, confidant, friend, counsellor, role model, and perhaps even adversary. Research shows that sibling relationships can offer vital support throughout our lives (Goetting, 1986), and, thus, it is important to maintain them by sharing tasks, expressing positivity, offering assurances, and so on (Myers, 2003). Another way adult siblings can nurture their relationships is by talking about their family—reminiscing about their childhood, crazy family events, and wild relatives. Sharing these stories can hold the siblings together, help them clarify family events, and validate their feelings and life choices (McGoldrick et al., 1999).

Siblings' experiences in the family often vary greatly, given their differences in age and birth order. Children close in age usually spend more time together than those further apart and likely share many similar experiences (McGoldrick et al., 1999). However, siblings close in age also tend to compete more for their parents' attention than those separated by more than about five years. Parents' different treatment of their children is important to the children and is scrutinized very carefully, especially regarding who is closer to the mother, who has a greater say in family decisions, and who has the most-favoured relationship with the father (Noller and Fitzpatrick, 1993).

Biological sex matters, too. Parents can sometimes treat daughters differently than sons (McGoldrick et al., 1999). For example, in many families, the tendency is for the parents to have lower expectations of their daughters' intellectual achievements—in marked contrast to the expectations they hold of their sons. In addition, sister pairs tend to be closer than brother–sister or brother–brother pairs, and both brothers and sisters feel closer to sisters. Brother relationships may be more superficial and competitive than sister relationships, which tend to be more connected and involving.

Elements of Family Communication

Whatever form families take, the communication that occurs within them shares some important characteristics, which we will examine now.

Families as Communication Systems   Every family has its own unique ways of communicating. Despite these differences, all families are **systems** whose members interact with one another to form a whole. Families, like all systems, have a number of characteristics that shape the way members communicate (Lerner et al., 2002; Whitchurch and Constantine, 1993).

Family Members Are Interdependent If you touch one piece of a mobile, all the other parts will move in response. In the same way, one family member's

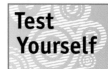

Test Yourself   Define what a family is and describe the three general types of communication that occur within families.

feelings and behaviour affect all the other members. If, for example, one family member leaves home to marry, or a parent loses a job, or two brothers get angry with each other and decide to stop talking, or a member wins the lottery, the system is no longer the same. Each event is a reaction to the family's history, and each event shapes future interaction.

A Family Is More Than the Sum of Its Parts Even if you knew each member of a family separately, you still would not know the family in its entirety. As the accompanying Reflection box illustrates, family members can take on new ways of behaving when they are operating in the context of their family system. This means that, to understand a family, you must see it as a whole.

Families Have Systems within the Larger System Like boxes within boxes, families have subsystems (systems within the family). For example, a traditional family of four can have six two-person communication subsystems: mother and father, mother and son, mother and daughter, father and son, father and daughter, and daughter and son. If you add three-person subsystems to these six

(e.g., mother, father, and daughter), the number of combinations is even greater. The nuclear family itself is a subsystem of larger suprasystems that include aunts and uncles, cousins, grandparents, in-laws, and so on.

Family Systems Are Affected by Their Environment As 'open systems', families are influenced by the world in which they are situated. Some environmental influences are personal. If, for example, one member has a bad (or good) day at work or school, her experiences will probably shape the way she acts at home. Other environmental influences involve social forces. For example, a family that wants to maintain traditional values will be challenged by media images that present very different depictions of how to behave.

Roles Although they are rarely discussed, the **roles** family members play shape the way members communicate. Some roles are obvious: income earner, child-care provider, and so on. Others are less obvious but just as important: harmonizer, problem solver, tension reliever, helpless victim, and so on. A bit of reflection may reveal some of the roles in your family. Perhaps one child is the athletic one, while another is the academic star. One parent may be the emotional person, while the other is the voice of reason. One sibling may be responsible; another irresponsible.

Some important roles centre on how the family handles conflict and stress. From her many years of experiences as a family therapist, Virginia Satir (1972) noticed four roles that arise during family conflicts. The first role is the *blamer*, who judges others and holds them responsible for anything that goes wrong: 'You never do anything right. What is the matter with you?' (p. 66). According to Satir, blamers may look powerful from the outside, but inside they often feel lonely and unsuccessful.

A second conflict role is the *placater*—the person who agrees with whatever is said so the other person will not get angry: 'Whatever you want is okay. I am just here to make you happy' (p. 63). According to Satir, the person who placates feels helpless and worthless without the other family member.

Reflection

When a Marriage Catches Cold, Everybody Sneezes

When I was about eight years old, my parents went through a crisis that almost led to the breakup of their marriage. My siblings and I weren't aware of the details, but the strain changed everything. My older brother, who was a star student, started getting Cs and Ds instead of As and Bs. I used to pretend to be sick so my mom and dad would co-operate to take care of me. And my five-year-old brother started having temper tantrums and wetting his bed. I learned several years later that our family business had almost gone bankrupt. After learning about family communication, I understand how problems in one part of a system affect every other part.

A third role is the *computer*, the family member who uses reasonableness and dispassion to defuse the conflict—and also to boost his or her self-esteem. According to Satir, 'the *computer* is very correct, very reasonable with no semblance of showing any emotion' (p. 68). In an effort to sound intelligent, the computer uses long words (whether or not he or she knows what they mean). The computer's image is one of someone cool and calm, but on the inside Satir suggests that this person feels very vulnerable.

The fourth role is the *distracter*, the person who says something irrelevant so the threat will be forgotten. Satir suggests that the unrelated and pointless behaviours that distracters use mask their belief that nobody cares about them and that there is no place for them in the family.

Take a moment to consider who plays which of these four roles in your family. You may decide that your family members sometimes switch roles, depending upon the issue or situation. In any case, these categories offer assurance that these roles are a normal part of most family systems.

Family Narratives   In Chapter 3, we described how shared **narratives** provide a storyline that keeps relationships operating harmoniously. These themes are especially important in families, where they reinforce shared goals, values, and concerns (Androutsopoulou, 2001). Narratives may reflect a family's view of how members relate to one another: 'We help each other a lot' or 'We are proud of our heritage.' Others reflect values about how to operate in the world: 'It's impossible to be successful without a good education' or 'It's our responsibility to help others less fortunate than ourselves.' Even dysfunctional families can be united by a shared narrative: 'What a hopeless bunch! We can never get along.' With a bit of thought, you can probably come up with several phrases that capture your family's narratives.

Models for Other Relationships   Experiences in our **family of origin**, the family in which we grow up, shape the way we communicate throughout life. They teach us important lessons—sometimes

positive, sometimes negative—about future relationships. Perhaps most important, families of origin are the primary model for how we will create our own families. Should family members share personal information or keep it to themselves? How is power distributed among the members? How much time should family members spend together and apart? We form our answers to these questions in large measure by observing our family of origin (Huang, 1999; VanLear, 1992).

Unfortunately, some types of family dysfunction are passed from one generation to another. Adolescents in homes where there is wife abuse, for example, are particularly liable to be physically abused themselves (Tajima, 2002), and a son's exposure to parental physical or verbal aggression is a good predictor of his perpetrating violence on a female partner (Shook et al., 2000; Schumacher et al., 2001).

Along with our personal experiences, each culture's model for family interaction shapes our notion of how to communicate (Hines et al., 1999). In the dominant culture of North America, for example, children often have an image of their family in which emotional support and loyalty comes from a small number of people; in general, the family is isolated from other families (Moghaddam, 1993). In these types of families, children quickly learn to be independent and self-reliant. In many other cultures, the image of the family is very different. In the extended families typical of Mexico, Latin America, Africa, parts of Europe, the Middle East, and Asia, support and loyalty extend beyond the immediate family of parents and siblings to include grandparents, cousins, aunts, uncles, great aunts and uncles, and even godparents.

Communication Rules   Despite their similar properties, not all families communicate in the same way. As unique cultures, families have their own sets of rules about a variety of communication practices. Some communication rules are explicit: 'If you're going to be more than half an hour late, phone home.' Other rules are not ever discussed, but they are just as important: 'If Dad slams the door after coming home from work, wait until he's had time to relax before speaking to him.'

Ascan Koerner and Mary Ann Fitzpatrick (2002) have defined two categories of rules about communication in the family: conversation and conformity. **Conversation orientation** involves the degree to which families have an open climate of discussion of a wide array of topics. Families with a high conversation orientation interact freely, frequently, and spontaneously, without many limitations on topic or time spent interacting. They believe that this interaction is important in order to have an enjoyable and rewarding family life. On the other hand, members of families with a low conversation orientation interact less and there is less exchange of private thoughts. It's no surprise that families with a strong conversation orientation regard communication as rewarding (Avtgis, 1999).

Conformity orientation refers to the degree to which family communication stresses uniformity of attitudes, values, and beliefs. High-conformity families seek harmony, conflict avoidance, interdependence, and obedience. They are often hierarchical, with a clear sense that some members have more authority than others. By contrast, communication in families with a low-conformity orientation is characterized by individuality, independence, and equality. The belief in such families is that individual growth should be encouraged and that family interests should be subordinated to individual interests. Figure 12.1 displays the four types of families that result from different combinations of conversation orientation and conformity orientation.

Families high in both conversation orientation and conformity orientation are *consensual*. Communication in these families reflects the tension between the pressure to agree and preserve the hierarchy, and an interest in open communication and exploration.

Families high in conversation orientation and low in conformity orientation are *pluralistic*. Communication in these families is open and unrestrained, with all family members' contributions evaluated on their own merits.

Families low in conversation orientation and high in conformity orientation are *protective*.

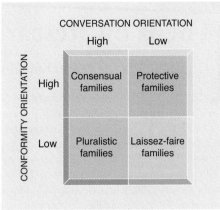

Figure 12.1 Conversation and Conformity Orientations in Families

In these families, communication emphasizes obedience to authority and a reluctance to share thoughts and feelings.

Families low in both conversation orientation and conformity orientation are *laissez-faire*. In these families, the communication reflects the members' lack of involvement with each other, the fact that they are emotionally divorced, and that decision making is individual.

Which of these styles best represents your family? Which style would you *like* to be true of your family?

Take Two

Elements of Family Communication

Systems: members are interdependent; family is more than sum of its parts; families have subsystems; family systems are affected by their environment.

Roles: roles can include the *blamer, placater, computer,* and *distracter.*

Narratives: stories that keep relationships operating harmoniously.

Family of origin: the family we grew up in—it provides a model for how we will create our own families.

Communication rules: combinations of *conversation orientation* (high or low) and *conformity orientation* (high or low)—create four family types (consensual, protective, pluralistic, laissez-faire).

Focus on Research

Topic Avoidance in Stepfamilies

Communication between teenagers and parents is often a delicate proposition. Teens tend to value their privacy and autonomy, whereas their parents want them to stay open and connected. These dialectical tensions can be even more dramatic in stepfamilies, where parent–child relationships face a unique set of challenges.

Tamara Golish (2000) interviewed 115 adolescents and young adults in stepfamilies to learn about topics they tend to avoid with their parents and step-parents. Not surprisingly, sex was the most frequently avoided topic across all relationship types. However, stepchildren say they avoid more topics with their step-parents than with their parents. In particular, stepchildren, often avoid 'deep conversations' or talking about money and family issues with their step-parents.

One factor affecting the comfort level in stepfamily communication is the type of parenting style used by the step-parents. Stepchildren feel more dissatisfied and avoid more topics with step-parents who are highly authoritarian (i.e., demanding and rigid). Interestingly, stepchildren also say they are dissatisfied with highly permissive stepparents. Golish concludes that step-parents need to strike a balance:

> Stepchildren may not be ready for too much closeness and need to progress at their own pace. At the same time, children need to know that their step-parent is interested in their well-being and will provide some sense of guidance.

Ultimately, stepchildren and step-parents face the same dialectical tensions that are true of all relationships. It would appear, however, that stepfamily tensions sometimes run stronger and deeper.

Effective Communication in Families

It is impossible to cover every aspect of effective family communication in just a few pages. Still, the following points can offer guidelines to make any family's interaction more satisfying and rewarding.

Strive for Closeness while Respecting Boundaries
In Chapter 8, we described the conflicting needs we all have for both integration and separation in our relationships, as well as for both expression and privacy. Nowhere are these opposing drives stronger than in families. We all know the importance of keeping close ties with our relatives, although too much cohesion can be a problem. When cohesion is too high, a family may suffer from too much consensus, too little independence, and a very high demand for loyalty—all of which may feel stifling. David Olson (1986, 2000), in his Circumplex Model, regards such a family as **enmeshed**. At the other extreme, of course, members of families with too little cohesion may be disconnected, with limited attachment or commitment to one another. Olson calls this family **disengaged**.

Families cope with these dialectical tensions by creating **boundaries**—limits a family sets on its members' actions. Communication researchers have devoted a good deal of attention to the importance of boundary management in interpersonal and family relationships (Petronio, 2000). The most obvious boundaries are physical (e.g., do not enter a bedroom without knocking if the door is closed; stay out of the den when Mom is preparing her tax return). Other boundaries involve conversational topics. In some families, discussion of finances is off limits. In others, expression of certain emotions is restricted. As the Focus on Research box on this page notes, sex is one of the most-avoided topics with parents and step-parents (Golish and Caughlin, 2002).

In addition to governing what may be talked about, boundaries can also dictate how topics are handled. In some families, it is fine to persist if the first overture to discussion is rebuffed ('Come on, what's on your mind?'). In other families, privacy rules discourage this kind of persistence. While the particulars may differ, every family has communication boundaries—and newcomers would be wise to learn and heed those boundaries (consider the many TV shows and movies that poke fun at in-laws for violating each other's family rules).

The challenge families face is to define boundaries that include important kinds of relational communication while allowing members to have the privacy and freedom that everyone desires. Sometimes, these boundaries need to be openly negotiated. At other times, they are established through trial and error. In either case, healthy boundaries allow us to balance the opposing and equally important needs for connection and autonomy, for openness and closedness. According to the Circumplex Model (Olson, 2000), when cohesion is moderate, family members are able to be independent from each other while still remaining dependent on, loyal to, and connected to the family.

Strive for a Moderate Level of Adaptability   A family experiences stress both from within (e.g., children get older and their needs change) and from outside (e.g., the mother loses her job); therefore, it needs to make adaptations to how it operates in order to maintain itself. To see how adaptability can help a family to function, consider the stress a family experiences when a child reaches adolescence. To adapt to this change, parents can begin to share control with their teenager as they negotiate issues like schedules, responsibilities, and rules.

When adaptability is too high, the result may be what the Circumplex Model labels a **chaotic family**, one that has erratic leadership or no leadership at all, dramatic shifts in roles, unclear roles, and impulsive decision making. When adaptability is too low, the result may be a **rigid family** with authoritarian leadership (usually in the hands of one person, the mother or father), strict discipline, roles that are inflexible, and unchanging rules. The extent to which a family is able to avoid these extremes in adaptability determines, to a large extent, how functional it is (Olson, 2000). Inasmuch as change is an inevitable fact of family life, it is important for healthy families to adapt, to a reasonable extent, to the changes that come their way.

Looking at possible combinations of cohesion and adaptability, Olson (1986, 2000) defines three types of families: *balanced*, *mid-range*, and *extreme*. Balanced families have moderate levels of both cohesion and adaptability. Mid-range families are moderate on one dimension and high or low on the other—for example, they have moderate cohesion and chaotic or rigid adaptability. Extreme families are high in both cohesion and adaptability (enmeshed and chaotic), low on both (disengaged and rigid), or high in one and low in the other (a family that is enmeshed and rigid, or disengaged and chaotic).

Balanced and mid-range families generally function better than extreme families (Olson and Lavee, 1989). For example, members of extreme families are less satisfied with their families than members of balanced and mid-range families. In addition, members of balanced families have more positive communication skills than do members of extreme families: they exhibit more supportive communication, give one another clearer and more explicit information, and display more positive emotions. Communication in a balanced family is likely to create a supportive and caring environment in which communication is open and accepting—in other words, a functional family.

Encourage Confirming Messages   In Chapter 10, we introduced the importance of confirming messages—ones that show in one way or another that we value the other person. Confirming messages from parents help satisfy a great many of their children's needs, such as the need to be nurtured and respected. Kathleen Ellis (2002) looked at the different ways mothers and fathers communicate valuing and support to their children. She found that two highly confirming behaviours parents offer are (1) telling their children that they are unique and valuable as human beings, and (2) genuinely listening to their children when they tell them something important. Two highly disconfirming behaviours are (1) belittling their children, and (2) making statements which mean that their ideas do not count: 'Nobody asked for your opinion' or 'What do you know about this anyway?'

Confirming communication is also important to successful marriages. Marital researcher John Gottman (2003) acknowledges that most couples are not confirming in all of their communication—that

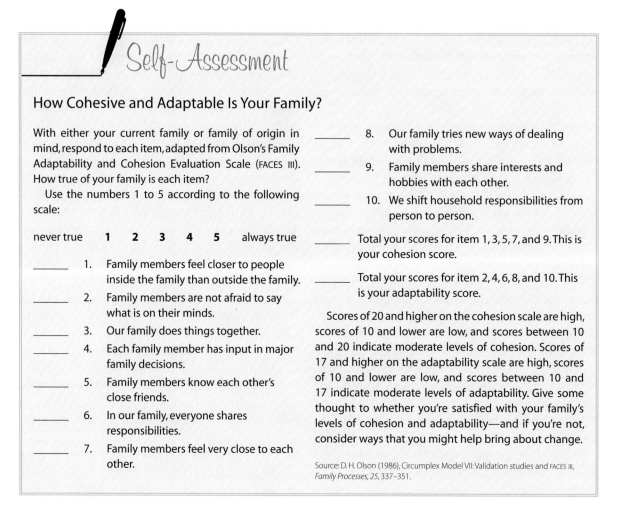

Self-Assessment

How Cohesive and Adaptable Is Your Family?

With either your current family or family of origin in mind, respond to each item, adapted from Olson's Family Adaptability and Cohesion Evaluation Scale (FACES III). How true of your family is each item?

Use the numbers 1 to 5 according to the following scale:

never true   **1**   **2**   **3**   **4**   **5**   always true

_____ 1. Family members feel closer to people inside the family than outside the family.

_____ 2. Family members are not afraid to say what is on their minds.

_____ 3. Our family does things together.

_____ 4. Each family member has input in major family decisions.

_____ 5. Family members know each other's close friends.

_____ 6. In our family, everyone shares responsibilities.

_____ 7. Family members feel very close to each other.

_____ 8. Our family tries new ways of dealing with problems.

_____ 9. Family members share interests and hobbies with each other.

_____ 10. We shift household responsibilities from person to person.

_____ Total your scores for item 1, 3, 5, 7, and 9. This is your cohesion score.

_____ Total your scores for item 2, 4, 6, 8, and 10. This is your adaptability score.

Scores of 20 and higher on the cohesion scale are high, scores of 10 and lower are low, and scores between 10 and 20 indicate moderate levels of cohesion. Scores of 17 and higher on the adaptability scale are high, scores of 10 and lower are low, and scores between 10 and 17 indicate moderate levels of adaptability. Give some thought to whether you're satisfied with your family's levels of cohesion and adaptability—and if you're not, consider ways that you might help bring about change.

Source: D. H. Olson (1986), Circumplex Model VII: Validation studies and FACES III, *Family Processes, 25,* 337–351.

---

would be unrealistic. The key, says Gottman, is to have the right ratio of positive-to-negative messages. His studies show that satisfied couples consistently have a 5-to-1 ratio of positive-to-negative communication, with positive messages including things such as humour, empathizing, and expressions of affection. It seems reasonable that this ratio would serve as an ideal for all family communication, not just between spouses.

Deal Constructively with Family Conflict

As we saw in Chapter 11, conflict is natural and inevitable. In families, as in other relationships, the question is not how to avoid conflict—that's impossible—but how to resolve conflicts in a way that makes relationships stronger rather than weaker.

Many family conflicts centre on recurring issues (Napier and Whitaker, 1989). One is *power*

struggles—that is, how family rules are created and who enforces them. Family conflicts also occur over *differences in intimacy needs*: the amount of affection members are willing to give and receive, how much time members spend together, and how much praise should be expressed. Finally, families may have conflict related to *interactional difficulties*—including how to handle conflicts.

Sometimes, families handle their conflicts in destructive ways. For instance, displays of physical and verbal aggression are unsuitable responses to conflict; however, the other extreme—ignoring a conflict—may be just as destructive to the family. Families can improve their communication by recognizing that family conflict should be dealt with. Placing conflict on the back burner, attempting to ignore it, smoothing it over, or denying that it exists creates tensions. The key to resolution lies in how the conflict is dealt with. There are several general principles of conflict management in the family.

Don't sweat the small stuff   There will always be differences of opinion and style in families. Many need attention, but others are simply not worth bothering about. (Of course, what is worth bothering about is often a matter of opinion.)

Focus on manageable issues   Many big issues can be broken down into smaller, more manageable parts. For example, instead of arguing about a family member's 'controlling personality', consider addressing specific problems, such as differing opinions about household neatness, the need to be informed about family plans, interference with your personal decisions, and so on.

Express appreciation as well as complaints   Along with addressing differences, let family members know that you appreciate them. As we saw in Chapter 10, hearing an abundance of confirming messages makes it easier for us to hear negative information without feeling defensive and unappreciated.

Seek win–win solutions   Strong feelings that are not resolved in one conflict will probably resurface later in another. The guidelines for win–win problem solving that we provided in Chapter 11 can work especially well with family conflicts, particularly when family members realize that when one person is unhappy, all the others are likely to suffer. On the other hand, when all members contribute to and are satisfied with a solution to a family problem, it builds cohesion, trust, and goodwill.

From his own research and a review of the literature on 'excellent family communication', John Caughlin (2003) offers a list of standards college students have about what constitutes effective family communication. Several of these standards highlight the points discussed above and are good predictors of family satisfaction. Family members who communicate well provide each other with emotional support, express affection verbally and non-verbally, are polite to one another, and base discipline on clear rules.

Test Yourself   Describe four aspects of effective communication in families.

Relationships at Work

Interpersonal effectiveness is just as important on the job as it is in families and other personal relationships. Employers consider communication to be the *most important* skill a job candidate can possess—greater than job-specific skills such as computer or technical abilities (Windsor et al., 1987). The Conference Board of Canada cites effective communication and the ability to work well with others as essential employability skills for prospective entrants to the Canadian workforce (Conference Board of Canada, 2000).

In the following pages, we cover some of the most common and important dimensions of interpersonal communication on the job. This information is no substitute for a full course in organizational or business and professional communication, but it will give you an appreciation of how competent communication on the job can lead to greater effectiveness and satisfaction.

Communicating in Organizations

Within the workplace, relationships differ in a number of ways. Each of these relationships brings its own set of communication characteristics and challenges.

Formal and Informal Relationships In most work settings, people are identified by titles and roles, such as accounting supervisor, management trainee, service representative, and so on. These roles combine to create **formal communication**—interaction that follows officially established channels. There are three types of formal communication within all but the very smallest organizations (Adler and Elmhorst, 2002; Sanchez, 1999). In **upward communication**, subordinates communicate with their bosses—sometimes in a way that distorts negative information and puts it in a positive light (Dansereau and Markham, 1987). Upward communication can cover a variety of topics:

What subordinates are doing:

'We'll certainly have that job finished by closing time today.'

Unsolved work problems:

'We're still having trouble with our online connection.'

Suggestions for improvement:

'I think we've figured out a way to give everybody the vacation schedules they requested.'

How subordinates are feeling:

'I've been promised a promotion for six months, and it still hasn't happened.'

In **downward communication**, managers address messages to subordinates. Downward messages often include:

Job instructions

'Here's the way to do it . . .'

Job rationale

'We back up the files every night in case the hard drive crashes.'

Feedback

'Great job! Just one suggestion . . .'

Horizontal communication occurs between people who do not have direct supervisor–subordinate relationships. These types of messages may include:

Task coordination

'If you can get me the job tomorrow, I'll have it finished by Thursday.'

Sharing information

Sales rep to engineer: 'The customers are asking for longer battery life. Is that possible?'

Conflict resolution

'I was really unhappy when you criticized me in front of the boss. Can we talk about it?'

These examples suggest the importance of keeping formal channels open and operating: imagine the likely consequences if any one of these messages weren't delivered.

Formal relationships are important, but they are not the only kinds that operate at work. **Informal communication** is based on friendships, shared personal or career interests, and proximity. Co-workers may have children in the same school, support the same sports team, belong to the same place of worship, or have mutual friends. They may carpool to share commuting expenses or work out together at the gym during lunch hour. They may develop a close friendship through self-disclosure and more frequent interaction, both on and away from the job (Sias and Cahill, 1998). They may even be romantic partners.

Informal messages can supplement more formal ones in a variety of ways. Sometimes, they *confirm* formal messages: 'This time, they're really serious about our not using email for personal messages.' At other times, they can *contradict* formal ones: 'They say the deadline is Friday, but first thing Monday morning is okay.' Some informal messages can *expand* on official information: 'Khakis are fine. When they say "no casual attire", they mean no jeans or T-shirts.' Informal communication can help you *circumvent* formal channels: 'If you call Sharon in accounting, she can get you reimbursed quickly without all that paperwork.'

Informal relationships are often more efficient and accurate than formal networks (Hellweg, 1987). An observation in the *Harvard Business Review* captured the relationship between formal and informal networks: 'If the formal organization is the skeleton of a company, the informal is the central nervous system' (Krackhardt and Hanson, 1993, p. 104).

It is important to note that communication in the workplace doesn't always fall into neat and simple categories (Reamer, 2002). Often, we must move between formal and informal communication within a particular relationship. For instance, your boss might drop by your cubicle to share some office gossip with you—and a few minutes later take you to task about an assignment you neglected. Romantic partners who work together may have difficulty deciding where their personal relationship ends and their professional relationship begins. And many employees feel awkward when a co-worker is promoted to supervisor because it changes the rules of their communication. As these examples suggest, the characteristics of competent communication that we discussed in Chapter 1—such as adaptability, self-monitoring, and cultivating a large repertoire of skills—are as important in the workplace as they are in other contexts.

Face-to-Face and Mediated Relationships   As in personal settings, people in working relationships can communicate either face-to-face or through a variety of electronic media. Telephone and email are the most common types of mediated communication channels, although not the only ones. Faxes, teleconferencing, and instant messaging are other ways to keep in touch.

Take Two

- **Formal communication:** interaction that follows officially established channels.
- **Upward communication:** subordinates' communication with their bosses.
- **Downward communication:** managers' communication with subordinates.
- **Horizontal communication:** communication between people who do not have supervisor–subordinate relationships.
- **Informal communication:** communication in the workplace based on friendships, shared personal or career interests, and proximity; it can confirm, contradict, expand, or circumvent formal messages.

Reflection

Online Neighbours—Community Team

Recently, a developer presented the city council with a proposal to build a large, ostentatious house next door to me. I had lived on the street for twelve years, and I knew many of the neighbours well enough to wave and say hello to them, but our relations would be best described as superficial. This proposed threat to our neighbourhood called for united community action, and our united team came about on the Internet. With everyone's conflicting work and family schedules, we decided it would be easier to try to organize ourselves by email. This worked beautifully. Our united activism resulted in the building of a much smaller house that suited the neighbourhood better, and our email correspondence allowed us to deepen our friendships.

Face-to-face interaction is still the most common type of communication at work ('The Business Meeting Is Alive and Well . . . for Now', 1997), but mediated relationships are becoming more common and essential. Many businesses communicate almost exclusively with their customers by phone and email, and employees within organizations often create effective working and personal relationships without spending much, if any, time together in person.

Virtual teams whose memberships transcend the boundaries of location and time can be a very effective and satisfying way to conduct business (Bell and Kozlowski, 2002; Larsen et al., 2001). Groups that operate electronically can communicate in ways that would otherwise not be possible. They can use the phone and Internet to tackle jobs much more quickly than a similar group that would have to assemble physically. They can use different working schedules to their advantage. For example, a person in the Maritimes—or even in Europe—can hand off work at the end of the day to a colleague in British Columbia, who can process and return it in time for the next morning.

As Table 1.1 on page 11 shows, each communication medium has its own advantages and drawbacks. And there are occasions where even the best technology is no substitute for 'face time'. Still, both face-to-face and mediated working relationships can clearly be interpersonal in every sense of the word.

Relationships in Work Groups

Working in teams is an essential part of almost every job (Devine et al., 1999). And anyone with group experience knows that good personal relationships are essential in a well-functioning team. Communication researchers Carl Larson and Frank LaFasto (1989) studied over seventy-five top-notch work teams from a diverse range of settings that included two championship football teams, the scientists who developed the 5 > personal computer, a Mount Everest expedition, and a heart surgery team. Among the qualities that distinguish winning teams is a collaborative climate in which the members trust and support one another. In the following pages, we will introduce some communication skills that can help build this sort of collaborative, confirming climate.

Personal Skills in Work Groups   Effective team members must, of course, have the task-related skills to tackle the job at hand. But relational skills are just as important. Over sixty years ago, Kenneth Benne and Paul Sheats (1948) identified a list of relational roles that need to be filled at one time or another in every group's life. These roles include:

- encouraging participation
- harmonizing
- relieving tension
- evaluating the group's emotional climate
- giving praise
- listening thoughtfully to the concerns of others

If a group is not operating efficiently, one place to look for remedies is at the communication climate among members. Ask yourself if any of these relational functions needs filling.

Don't get the idea that an effective group will be free of conflicts. Even the best team will experience struggles on the path to consensus. In fact, most groups go through a predictable series of stages as they work together (Brilhart et al., 2001). Figure 12.2 illustrates this pattern. Politeness and harmony are the norm during the *orientation* stage when a team first tackles a job. But as time goes on and differences emerge, the group enters a period of *conflict*. Disagreement does not necessarily involve hostility, but even civil and reasoned differences can require you to use the listening skills that we described in Chapter 7, the climate-building approaches discussed in Chapter 10, and the conflict-management guidelines covered in Chapter 11. Once a group has worked through the conflict stage, it usually enters an *emergence* stage, where members accept—sometimes enthusiastically and sometimes reluctantly—the team's decision. The members recognize that this is a time to seek harmony. A fourth stage in group decision making is *reinforcement*. This is when the members not only accept the decision but also endorse it.

This process repeats itself in a cyclical fashion—and different stages are likely to overlap somewhat—as a group faces each new challenge. Just like dyadic relationships, groups have their ups and downs. Knowing that each step—especially conflict—is a natural part of working together can be reassuring.

Group Cultures   We usually think about cultures rooted in nationality, ethnicity, age, and geographic region but working groups—entire organizations and smaller groups within them—have their own cultures, too (Ashkanasy et al., 2000; Deal and Kennedy, 1983). You can prove this for yourself by thinking about different classes you have attended during your life as a student. Even though the basic process of learning is the same from one discipline and school to another, you probably can recognize that each class had its own culture—its unique style of handling behaviour. The cultures of working groups involve many dimensions of communication such as *sociability* (friendly or aloof), *distribution of power* (controlled by authority figures or shared among members),

Focus on Technology

Cultural Influences on Computer-Mediated Business Negotiations

Considerable research has been conducted on the influence of culture on the process and outcome of face-to-face negotiations between members of different cultures. However, considerably less is known about how culture influences negotiations when participants have no face-to-face or telephone contact. Three researchers—one Canadian and two Austrians—collaborated to investigate the influences of culture on anonymous negotiations (Kersten, Koszegi, and Vetschera, 2002). They used a Web-based negotiation system and recruited subjects from Austria, Ecuador, Finland, and Switzerland. They contrasted the participants' cultures in terms of the five following attributes discussed earlier in this text:

- individualism (Austria, Finland, and Switzerland) versus collectivism (Ecuador)
- power distance (Austria = low, Finland and Switzerland = moderate, Ecuador = high
- achievement (Austria, Switzerland, and Ecuador) versus nurturing (Finland)
- high context (Ecuador) versus low context (Austria, Switzerland, and Finland)
- time orientation: monochronic—punctuality and schedules are important (Switzerland, Finland, Austria); polychronic—more relaxed attitude toward time (Ecuador),

The participants, who were 166 university students, were all given the same bargaining problem. They were not told whether they were negotiating with someone from their own country or a different country; however, they could choose to reveal their identity during the Web-based negotiations. Interestingly, even without visual or auditory sensory information, culture influenced participants' negotiations and their satisfaction with the negotiation process and outcomes. The researchers found several effects of culture on the participants' expectations before the negotiations as well as on the negotiators' behaviour during negotiations. For instance, negotiators from Ecuador, a collectivist, polychromic, high-context distance culture had more positive expectations about the negotiation process and the friendliness of the negotiations before use of the Web-based negotiation system. Negotiators from Ecuador took more time between sending offers to their partners. Negotiators from low-context cultures (Austria, Finland, and Switzerland) included fewer text messages with their offers than the participants from high-context cultures (Ecuador). Although one could argue that anonymous, computer-mediated negotiations should be less influenced by the cultural background of the negotiators than face-to-face negotiations, this did not seem to be the case. The investigators hypothesized that, without the non-verbal communication information available in face-to-face negotiations, these Web-based, anonymous negotiators may have felt a high level of social uncertainty, which tied their behaviour closer to their own cultural norms.

tolerance of new ideas (welcome or resisted), ways of managing conflict (direct or indirect), and emotional support (more or less plentiful).

Perhaps the most important insight about cultures in working groups is that they can make the difference between satisfaction and misery. If you are lucky enough to belong to a group that has a healthy culture—for example, one that is friendly, has shared power, welcomes new ideas, manages conflict directly, and provides emotional support—working on even the toughest jobs can be rewarding. On the other hand, if you are stuck in a group with an unsatisfying culture, great pay

and plush working conditions will not prevent you from feeling miserable.

You may not be able to exert much influence on the culture of large organizations, whether they are a university you are attending or a corporation you work for. What you *can* do, though, is think about the culture of the organization before you decide to join it. Once you are on the job, you can shape the culture of smaller groups to which you belong. The way you and your fellow workers treat one another, as well as your attitudes towards work, can make a tremendous difference in the quality of the many hours you spend on the job.

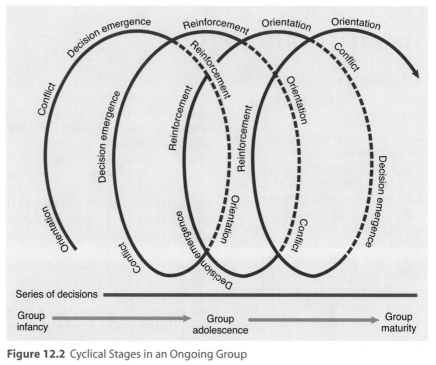

Figure 12.2 Cyclical Stages in an Ongoing Group

Source: .From J. K. Brilhart, G. J. Galanes, and K. Adams (2001), *Effective Group Discussion* (10th ed.). New York: McGraw-Hill Ryerson, p. 289. Reproduced with permission of the McGraw-Hill Companies.

Leadership, Power, and Influence in Working Groups When most people think about influence in groups, they focus on the **designated leader**— the person (or people) with official titles that indicate authority, such as manager, chairperson, and so on. There is no doubt that designated leaders play an important role in making things happen. But you do not have to be a designated leader to influence the effectiveness of a group. Every member of a working team has at least one resource of **power** that can affect what happens in a group (Andrews and Baird, 2000; French and Raven, 1968). Consider, for example, *expert power*. The designated leaders are often not the best or only experts: individual members often have a special kind of knowledge or talent—the ability to use a type of software, experience in the topic at hand, and so on.

Some types of power involve interpersonal relationships. *Reward power* is a good example. Rewards obviously include the designated leaders' ability to hire and pay workers. But members can bestow their own rewards. Helping one another is a kind of reward that can help the group solve the job at hand. It also builds goodwill that serves both the giver and the team well. Along with rewarding one another, group members can use *coercive power* to get what they want by using unpleasant consequences, or the threat of them, to punish one another. You do not have to be a designated leader to punish. Complaining, withholding help, and blocking progress are examples of ways members can punish one another and their boss.

The clearest type of interpersonal influence is *referent power*—the influence that comes from the members' liking and respect for one another. Members with good interpersonal skills are likely to have high referent power, which enables them to shape the way the group operates. Referent power is the area in which the greatest difference between designated leaders and influential group members can exist. An unpopular manager might have to use the rewards and punishments that come with the job title to get members to gain

Building Work Skills

Which Way to Communicate

Improve your ability to choose the most effective way of communicating in organizations by following these steps:

a. Think of an environment in which you work (you may use school for the following analysis).

b. Identify all the communication media used to convey messages in a one-week period: face to face, print, telephone, email, Internet, instant messaging, fax, and so on.

c. Analyze each situation to determine whether the medium chosen was most effective. If not, suggest a better alternative.

d. Based on your observations, identify situations in which it is best to use each type of communication available to you.

compliance. But a popular member with no formal title can persuade others to co-operate because of the influence that comes with the high regard of other members (Pescosolido, 2001).

By now, you can see that good relationships in working groups require some special skills. We will now look at another set of special skills that will help you gain entrance into an organization.

Interviewing

Mention the word *interview* and most people visualize a job applicant facing a potential employer. This image tells only part of the story. As Table 12.1 shows, there are many types of job-related interviews. Some are formal and others are casual. Sometimes, you are the one who asks the questions; other times, you are the person who responds.

Regardless of the type, all interviews have qualities that distinguish them from other types of conversations (Stewart and Cash, 2000). The first is *purpose*. Most everyday conversations have no serious preconceived purpose. Two people chat between floors in an elevator; friends swap jokes

at a party; a boss and employees take a break around the coffee machine. An interview, on the other hand, always has a goal. A second characteristic that distinguishes interviews is *structure*. In a typical conversation, neither person knows or cares when the exchange will end or exactly what topics will be covered. By contrast, any good interview has a distinct opening, body, and conclusion. A third feature of interviews is *control*. Whereas

Table 12.1 Types of Work-Related Interviews

Selection
Placement
Promotion

Information Gathering
Investigating products and services
Research
Career exploration
Interview client (caseworker, medical, etc.)
Survey (market, political, etc.)
Journalistic

Problem and Evaluation
Performance review
Counselling (personal and professional)
Complaint or grievance

Persuasive
Selling products
Selling services
Quasi-commercial selling (charitable, political, religious, etc.)

Test Yourself When working in groups, what communication skills contribute to building a collaborative, confirming communication climate?

conversations do not require any guidance from one of the parties, an interviewer's job is to keep the exchange moving toward the preset purpose. Finally, interviews usually have a unique *balance of participation*. Though most conversations involve roughly the same amount of speaking by each person, in an interview, the person being interviewed should do about 70 percent of the talking.

To make an interview successful, both the interviewer and interviewee have responsibilities before, during, and after they meet. As an interviewee, you can make the experience pay off by following the guidelines that we present in the rest of this chapter.

Before the Interview   A good interview begins before the people sit down to talk. You can make your interviews more successful through careful planning (*Before the Interview*, 1999; Safro, 2001).

Clarify the interviewer's goals   Since an interview is a conversation with a purpose, it is essential to know the goals. Sometimes, the interviewer's goals are obvious. The insurance sales representative who wants 'to see if you are paying too much for your present coverage' is trying to sell you a new policy, and a friend who wants to know how you've repaired an object or made a recipe is probably looking for your expertise.

In other cases, the interviewer's goal is not quite so clear. Suppose you are preparing for an employment interview. You know that the company is looking for the best applicant, but just what kinds of qualities are they seeking? Are education and training most important? Experience? Initiative? Knowing these criteria in advance will improve your chances of doing well in the interview.

There will be times when an interviewer has hidden goals, which you should do your best to discover. For instance, your boss's questions about your daily job routine might really be part of the managerial process of deciding whether to promote (or fire) you. An acquaintance's ostensible questions about factual information might really be aimed at building a friendship. This last example shows that not all hidden goals are malicious,

but in any case, you'll feel more comfortable and behave more effectively when you know what the interviewer wants from you.

Be prepared   A good interviewee does not go to an interview empty-handed. You will want to take materials with you that will help the employer learn more about why you are ready, willing, and able to do the job. For instance, take extra copies of your resumé because more than one person may interview you that day. Go prepared to take notes: you will need something to write on and a pen or pencil. If it is relevant, take copies of your past work, such as reports you have helped prepare, performance reviews by former employers, drawings or designs you have created in work or school, letters of recommendation, and so on. Besides demonstrating your qualifications, items like these show that you know how to sell yourself. Take along the names, addresses, and phone numbers of any references you haven't listed in your resumé.

Besides arriving with the basic materials, you can impress the interviewer and serve yourself well by doing advance research on the organization. What products or services does it sell? What is its position in the marketplace and the community? What challenges and trends does the organization face? What makes this organization unique among its competitors? If you show your awareness of this information, you will distinguish yourself as a serious candidate.

During the Interview   Once you are in the interview itself, there are several important points to keep in mind. These guidelines both show your competence and help you build a good relationship with your interviewer.

Make a good first impression   First impressions can make or break an interview. Usually, the first impression you make will be based on your cover letter and resumé, and that is why it's important for them to be well-constructed and error-free (there are many books that offer tips on developing these important documents: see, e.g., Brown, 2002, and Parker, 2003). In addition, your punctuality (or

iStock photo

lack thereof) will make a statement about how you manage your time. Plan to arrive ten to fifteen minutes early to leave room for any unexpected delays. If you're unsure of the company's location, make a test run the day before.

Just as the first stages of a date will generally shape what comes later, the success or failure of an interview is often determined in the first exchange (Jorgenson, 1992). Research shows that many interviewers form their opinions about candidates within the first four minutes of conversation (Avery and Campion, 1982). Physical attractiveness is a major influence on how applicants are rated, so it makes sense to do everything possible to look your best. The proper style of clothing can vary from one type of job or organization to another. When in doubt, it is best to dress formally and conservatively. It's unlikely an employer will think less of you for being overdressed, but looking too casual can be taken as a sign that you don't take the job or the interview seriously.

Get off to a good start   The usual format for an opening begins with some sort of greeting, which includes any introductions that are necessary. A period of informal conversation often follows, in which the interviewer and applicant talk about subjects of mutual interest not necessarily related to the interview topic. This period gives both people a chance to get settled and acquainted before getting down to business. The idea is to establish some common ground between interviewer and applicant. One way to do so is to look around the interviewer's office for information about that person's interests and hobbies. A prominent plaque, a sports pennant, a wall photo, or a piece of art can all be topics for conversation.

Give clear, detailed answers   Put yourself in the interviewer's shoes and be as specific and helpful as you hope others would be for you. A good answer provides a general theme and then offers specifics. For example, suppose a potential employer asks, 'What did you learn in your interpersonal communication course that will help you in this job?' You could follow this theme-specific format with an answer like this: 'I learned how to build and maintain positive relationships, and that can help me with people in the company and with customers. For example, we learned how to listen well, negotiate win–win solutions, raise difficult issues skilfully, and handle criticism without getting defensive.' Be prepared, because a good interviewer will probably ask a follow-up question such as, 'Give me an example of a time when you've used those skills.' It's a good idea to come to an interview with several brief stories, illustrations, and examples that provide evidence of your abilities and skills.

Keep your answers focused   It is easy to rattle on in an interview, either out of enthusiasm, a desire to show off your knowledge, or nervousness; but in most cases, long answers are not a good idea. The interviewer probably has lots of ground to cover, and long-winded answers will not help this task. As a general rule, your answers should not run much over a minute or two without inviting the interviewer either to follow up or to move on to the next question. Of course, you'll want to give clear, detailed answers with examples, as described above. Keep in mind, though, that an interview is

a conversation—and as is true of any conversation, a dialogue in which people take turns is better than a long monologue.

Follow the interviewer's lead   Let the interviewer set the emotional tone of the session. If he or she is informal, you can loosen up a bit; but if the approach is formal and dignified, you should act the same way. Since a great deal depends on the personal interaction between the interviewer and the candidate, you should try to match the interviewer's style without becoming insincere. If the tone of the interview does not fit well with you, this may be a signal that you will not feel comfortable with this organization. It may be wise to see whether the interviewer's approach represents the whole company, either by asking for a tour or by speaking to other employees on your own. This desire to learn about the company shows that you are a thinking person who takes the job seriously, so your curiosity is not likely to offend the interviewer.

Go prepared to answer the interviewer's questions   This principle is especially important in interviews where you are seeking a job. Whatever specific questions you might be asked, the employer is always asking, 'How can you help us?' If you remember this, you can respond in ways that show how you can meet the employer's needs. If you have spent time learning about your potential employer, you will be in a good position to talk about that company's needs and how you can satisfy them. Knowing that you can, indeed, help the company should raise your self-confidence and lead you to feel more comfortable when facing a potential employer (Linden et al., 1993). Table 12.2 provides suggestions for answering common questions employers ask.

Go prepared to ask the interviewer questions   Near the end of an employment interview, it is typical for an interviewer to ask the applicant, 'Do you have any questions?' An ineffective response would be 'No, I can't think of any,' which suggests a lack of initiative and inquisitiveness. Instead, go prepared with

Reflection

Self-Criticism and Self-Praise

Perhaps the thing I have found most difficult as a student from Japan studying in Canada is the performance evaluations that have been part of my work placements. These evaluations involve a self-assessment of strengths and areas for improvement. Then, together with my supervisor we develop goals for my professional development. I enjoy discovering areas for improvement and developing goals for myself, but when it comes to describing my strengths I feel very uncomfortable. My supervisors have been sympathetic, and I believe they know how much I want to improve my skills, but they always say I am too hard on myself. In my culture, to say I am good at something or to describe myself as superior in some area of the job would be considered rude and boastful. I find it hard to even think in such terms. I don't find it distressing to be self-critical, but as hard as I try, I can't bring myself to 'sing my own praises'. I realize 'selling yourself' is a skill you need in the North American job market, but I'm appreciative of my colleagues' patience because I feel I'm a slow learner in this regard.

Table 12.2 Common Employment Interview Questions

1. **Tell me something about yourself.**
   This broad, opening question gives you a chance to describe what qualities you possess that can help the employer. Remember that your response should be job-related—this is not the time to talk about where you grew up or your hobbies.

2. **What makes you think you're qualified to work for this company?**
   This question may sound like an attack, but it really is another way of asking, 'How can you help us?' It gives you another chance to show how your skills and interests fit with the company's goals.

3. **What accomplishments have given you the most satisfaction?**
   The accomplishments you choose need not be directly related to former employment; however, they should demonstrate qualities that would help you be successful in the job for which you are being interviewed. Your accomplishments might demonstrate creativity, perseverance in the face of obstacles, self-control, or dependability.

4. **Why do you want to work for us?**
   Employers are impressed by candidates who have done their homework about the organization. This question offers the chance to demonstrate your knowledge of the employer's organization and to show how your talents fit with its goals.

5. **What university subjects did you like best and least?**
   Whatever your answer, show how your preferences about your courses are related to the job you are applying for. When necessary, show how apparently unrelated subjects do illustrate your readiness for a job. For example, you might say, 'I really enjoyed cultural anthropology courses because they showed me the importance of understanding different cultures. I think those courses would help me a lot in relating to our overseas customers and suppliers.'

6. **Where do you see yourself in five years?**
   This familiar question is really asking, 'How ambitious are you?' 'How compatible are your plans with this company's goals?' 'How realistic are you?' If you have studied the industry and the company, your answer will show an understanding of the workplace realities and a sense of personal planning that should impress an employer.

7. **What major problems have you faced, and how have you dealt with them?**
   The specific problem isn't as important as the way you responded to it. What (admirable) qualities did you demonstrate as you grappled with the problem you have chosen to describe? Perseverance? Calmness? Creativity? You may even choose to describe a problem you didn't handle well, and show what you learned from it that can help you in the future.

8. **What are your greatest strengths?**
   The 'strength' question offers another chance to sell yourself. Emphasize qualities that apply to employment. 'I'm a pretty good athlete' isn't a persuasive answer unless you can show how your skill is job-related. For instance, you might talk about being a team player, your competitive drive, or your ability to work hard and not quit in the face of adversity.

9. **What are your greatest weaknesses?**
   Whatever answer you give to the 'weakness' question, try to show how your awareness of your flaws makes you a desirable person to hire. There are four ways to respond to this question.
   - You can discuss a weakness that also can be viewed as a strength: 'When I'm involved in a big project I tend to work too hard, and I can wear myself out.'
   - You can discuss a weakness that is not related to the job at hand, and end your answer with a strength that is related to the job. For a job in sales: 'I'm not very interested in accounting. I'd much rather work with people selling a product I believe in.'
   - You can discuss a weakness the interviewer already knows about from your resumé application, or the interview. 'I don't have a lot of experience in multimedia design at this early stage of my career. But my experience in other kinds of computer programming and my internship in graphic arts have convinced me that I can learn quickly.'
   - You can discuss a weakness you have been working to remedy. 'I know being bilingual is important for this job. That's why I've enrolled in a French course.'

Sources: Adapted from: R. B. Adler and G. Rodman (2002), *Understanding Human Communication* (8th ed.). New York: Oxford University Press, pp. 462–464; and K. O. Locker, (2000), Business and Administrative Communication (5th ed.). Homewood, IL: Irwin, pp. 574–5.

a list of questions about the company and the position you are applying for (Fry, 2003). Don't forget that you are trying to determine if this job is a good match for you, so you are interviewing the company as much as they are interviewing you.

Good questions will allow you to demonstrate the homework you've done on the organization. You could say, 'I saw on your website that the company is developing new training programs. How might these programs help me in my position?' Questions to avoid include queries about salary or benefits—at least in an initial interview. Such questions focus on what the company will do for you, whereas your goal is to show what you can do for the company.

After the Interview Follow up your meeting with a note of thanks to the interviewer. (A typed letter is usually more appropriate than either a handwritten note or an email.) Since most candidates don't take this step, your letter will be especially impressive. Express your appreciation for the chance to get acquainted with the company, and let the interviewer know that the session left you excited about the chance of becoming associated with it. It's also a good idea to mention specific information you learned about the company during the interview: 'I enjoyed hearing about the new software program your company is using to facilitate performance reviews.' Whenever possible, show how the things you learned make you a good match for the job: 'My familiarity with a variety of computer programs should help me learn your new system quickly, and my training in communication will assist me in conducting performance reviews.' Finally, your note can confirm the next steps in the interviewing process: 'You explained that I should be hearing from the company within the next week. I'll be looking forward to speaking with you.'

Test Yourself Describe what an interviewee can do (before, during, and after) a job interview in order to make the interview successful.

Summary

Contemporary families have a variety of traditional and non-traditional arrangements. Family relationships often include those between spouses or partners, parents and children, and siblings—each with unique characteristics. Over time, families develop into systems, as the members interact with one another to form a whole. Family members also adopt particular roles, share and live out narratives, and create rules for interaction. Families of origin often serve as models for other relationships in our lives.

Effective communication in families requires that the members establish and maintain a moderate level of cohesion, and they do this by establishing appropriate boundaries. In addition, functional families are adaptable, managing change without too much rigidity or acquiescence. Members of healthy families encourage one another with confirming messages and strive for win–win solutions to their conflicts.

Interpersonal effectiveness is as important on the job as it is in personal and family relationships. Relationships in the workplace include both formal and informal networks, using upward, downward, and horizontal communication. On-the-job communication often takes place in work groups, which may meet in person or in virtual teams. Work groups go through predictable stages, create their own cultures, and provide opportunities for leadership, power, and influence.

Interviews are used for a variety of purposes. Before an employment interview, an applicant should clarify the interviewer's goals and come prepared. During an interview, it is important to make a good first impression and opening, and to give answers that are clear, detailed, and focused. A good interviewee will follow the interviewer's lead, be prepared to answer questions that the interviewer is likely to ask, and ask questions about the company and the position. When the interview is over, the applicant should send a thank-you note and confirm the next steps in the interview process.

Activities

1. **Invitation to Insight**

   Understand your own family system better by giving examples of each of the characteristics described on pages 552–5.

   a. Interdependence of members.

   b. How the family is more than the sum of its parts.

   c. Family subsystems and suprasystems.

   d. How environmental influences affect the family.

2. **Invitation to Insight**

   What are some unstated yet important rules that govern communication you have experienced or observed in a family (yours or others)? Discuss rules governing conversation orientation and conformity orientation, as well as other areas of communication.

3. **Ethical Challenge**

   Imagine yourself interviewing for a job you really want. Consider how you will represent yourself in a way that maximizes the chances of your receiving an offer of employment. To what degree is the narrative you would create in presenting yourself accurate, and to what degree is it less than totally honest? Could you justify the approach you would take as ethical?

4. **Role Play**

   Describe to a partner a job that you would like to apply for. Have your partner take the role of the interviewer and you take the role of the interviewee. Use Table 12.2, 'Common Employment Interview Questions', to help guide the interview. Role-play the job interview and ask your partner to give you feedback. Refer to the 'During the Interview' section on page 366 of this chapter for criteria to evaluate your communication during the interview. Now, reverse roles.

Discussion Questions

1. Describe the four characteristics of family communication systems discussed in this chapter. Is it useful to think of communication within a family as a communication system? Why or why not?

2. What are the family narratives of your family? What values do they communicate?

3. Describe the types of families that result from mixing conversation orientation and conformity orientation. Is there a best style? Why or why not?

4. Describe the guidelines given in this chapter for dealing with family conflict. Do you think they are realistic? Complete? Why or why not?

5. What functions can informal communication serve in a workplace? Are they important? Why or why not?

6. Describe some of the communication skills that can help to build a positive communication climate in a working group. How much influence can one group member have? Why do you think so?

Glossary

abstraction ladder A range of more-to-less abstract terms describing an event or object.

achievement culture Term used to describe a culture that places a high value on the achievement of material success and a focus on the task at hand. Also termed 'masculine' culture.

advising (response) A listening response in which the receiver offers suggestions about how the speaker should deal with a problem.

affect display Unintentional non-verbal behaviour that conveys a sender's emotions.

aggressiveness Verbal attack that demeans another person's self-concept and inflicts psychological pain.

ambiguous language Language that consists of words and phrases that have more than one commonly accepted definition.

ambiguous response A response with more than one meaning, leaving the other person unsure of the responder's position.

ambushing A style in which the receiver listens carefully in order to gather information to use in an attack on the speaker.

analyzing (response) A listening response in which the listener offers an interpretation of a speaker's message.

androgynous Possessing both masculine and feminine traits.

argumentativeness Presenting and defending positions on issues while attacking positions taken by others.

assertion A direct expression of a sender's needs, thoughts, or feelings, delivered in a way that does not attack a receiver's dignity.

attending A phase of the listening process in which the communicator focuses on a message, excluding other messages.

attribution The process of attaching meaning to another person's behaviour.

avoiding A relational stage immediately before terminating in which the partners minimize contact with one another.

barrier behaviours Strategies designed to create a barrier (or fix a broken one) between ourselves and other people.

benevolent lie A lie that is not considered malicious by the person who tells it.

bonding A stage of relational development in which the partners make symbolic public gestures to show that their relationship exists.

boundaries Limits a family sets on its members' actions, such as what topics are permissible to discuss, how to discuss certain topics, whom family members may interact with outside the family.

breadth In the *social penetration model*, it is the first dimension of self-disclosure; it comprises the range of subjects being discussed.

'but' statement A statement in which the second half cancels the meaning of the first, for example, 'I'd like to help you, *but* I have to go or I'll miss my bus.'

certainty Absolute belief that one's position is correct and the ideas of others are not worth considering. Likely to arouse defensiveness, according to Gibb.

channel The medium through which a message passes from sender to receiver.

chaotic family A family that has erratic leadership or no leadership at all, dramatic shifts in roles, unclear roles, and impulsive decision making.

chronemics The study of how people use and structure time.

circumscribing A relational stage in which partners begin to reduce the scope of their contact and commitment to one another.

closed questions Questions that limit the range of possible responses, such as questions that seek a yes or no answer.

co-culture A group within an encompassing culture with a perceived identity.

cognitive complexity The ability to construct a variety of frameworks for viewing an issue.

cognitive conservatism The tendency to seek out information that conforms to an existing self-concept and to ignore information that contradicts it.

collectivistic culture A culture whose members feel loyalties and obligations to an in-group, such as one's extended family, community, or even the organization one works for.

communication climate The emotional tone of a relationship between two or more individuals.

communication competence The ability to achieve one's goals in a manner that is personally acceptable and, ideally, acceptable to others.

communication rules Sets of (usually) unwritten principles to follow that families, as unique cultures, have about a variety of communication practices. Despite their similar properties, not all families communicate in the same way.

comparison level (CL) The minimum standard of what behaviour is acceptable from a relationship partner.

comparison level of alternatives (CLᵃˡᵗ) A comparison between the rewards one is receiving in a present situation and those one could expect to receive in others.

complaining A disagreeing message that directly or indirectly communicates dissatisfaction with another person.

complementary conflict style The use by partners in a conflict of different but mutually reinforcing behaviour.

compliance-gaining strategy A tactic or plan used to persuade others to think or behave in a desired way.

computer-mediated communication (CMC) Communication that occurs through computerized channels (e.g., email, instant messaging, computer conferencing).

compromise An approach to conflict resolution in which both people attain at least part of what they want through self-sacrifice.

confirming message A message that expresses caring or respect for another person.

conflict An expressed struggle between at least two interdependent people who perceive incompatible goals, scarce rewards, and interference from the other person in achieving their goals.

conflict rituals Repeating patterns of interlocking conflict behaviour.

conformity orientation The degree to which family communication stresses uniformity of attitudes, values, and beliefs.

connection–autonomy dialectic The tension between the need for integration and the need for independence in a relationship.

content dimension of a message A message that communicates information about the subject being discussed. See also *relational message*.

contradicting Term describing non-verbal behaviour that is inconsistent with a verbal message.

controlling communication According to Gibb, messages that attempt to impose some sort of outcome on another person, resulting in a defensive response.

conventionality–uniqueness dialectic The tension between the need to behave in ways that conform to the expectations of others, and the need to assert one's individuality by behaving in ways that violate the expectations of others.

convergence The process of adapting one's speech style to match that of others with whom one wants to identify. See also *divergence*.

conversation orientation The degree to which families favour an open climate of discussion of a wide array of topics.

counterfeit questions Questions that are disguised attempts to send a message rather than elicit information.

culture According to Samovar and Porter, *culture* is 'the language, values, beliefs, traditions, and customs people share and learn'.

debilitative emotions Emotions that prevent a person from functioning effectively.

de-escalatory spiral A reciprocal communication pattern in which one person's non-threatening behaviour leads to reduced hostility by the other, with the level of hostility steadily decreasing.

defensive listening A response style in which the receiver perceives a speaker's comments as an attack.

defensiveness The attempt to protect a presenting image that a person believes is being attacked.

depth In the *social penetration model*, it is the second dimension of self-disclosure; here, the people interacting shift from relatively unrevealing messages to more personal ones.

description Messages that describe a speaker's position without evaluating others.

designated leader The person (or people) with official titles that indicate authority, for example, 'manager'.

dialectical tensions Relational tensions that arise when two opposing or incompatible forces exist simultaneously.

differentiating A relational stage in which the partners re-establish their individual identities after having bonded together.

direct aggression An expression of the sender's thoughts and/or feelings that attacks the position and dignity of the receiver.

direct request A compliance-gaining strategy in which the communicator directly asks another person to meet his or her needs.

disagreeing message A message that essentially tells to another person, 'You are wrong'; includes argumentativeness, complaining, and aggressiveness.

disconfirming message A message that expresses a lack of caring or respect for another person.

disengaged family Families with too little cohesion in which members have limited attachment or commitment to one another.

disfluencies Non-linguistic verbalizations; for example, *um, er, ah*.

distorted feedback Information that can skew a person's self-concept; such feedback might be excessively favourable because of others' less-than-honest behaviour (e.g., a boss may claim to be an excellent manager because his assistants pour on false praise in order to keep their jobs).

divergence A way of speaking that emphasizes difference from others. See also *convergence*.

downward communication Communication from managers to subordinates.

dyad Two communicators who interact with each other.

dysfunctional conflict Harmful conflicts characterized by communication that is coercive, uncooperative, and unfocused, which often results in a win–lose outcome and the damaging of a relationship.

emblem Deliberate non-verbal behaviour with precise meaning known to virtually all members of a cultural group.

emotional contagion The process by which emotions are transferred from one person to another.

emotionally counterfeit Communications where the sender thinks (s)he is expressing a feeling when, in fact, her/his statement is devoid of emotional content.

emotive language Language that expresses the sender's attitude rather than simply offering an objective description.

empathizing (response) A listening response that conveys identification with a speaker's perceptions and emotions.

empathy The ability to project oneself into another person's point of view in an attempt to experience his or her thoughts and feelings.

enmeshed family Families with too much consensus, too little independence, and a very high demand for loyalty.

environment Both the physical setting in which communication occurs and the personal perspectives of the people involved.

equality A type of supportive communication described by Gibb which suggests that the sender regards the receiver with respect.

equivocal language Ambiguous language that has two or more equally plausible meanings.

escalatory spiral A reciprocal communication pattern in which one person's attack leads to a counterattack by the other, with the level of hostility steadily increasing.

ethnocentrism An attitude that one's own culture is superior to that of others.

euphemism A pleasant term substituted for a blunt one in order to soften the impact of unpleasant information.

evaluating (response) A listening response that appraises a sender's thoughts or behaviour and implies that the person evaluating is qualified to pass judgment on the other.

evaluation A message in which a sender judges a receiver in some way, usually resulting in a defensive response.

experimenting An early stage in relational development, consisting of a search for common ground. If the experimentation is successful, the relationship progresses to intensifying. If not, it may go no further.

expression–privacy dialectic The tension between the desire to be open and disclosive and the desire to be closed and private.

face The image an individual wants to project to the world. See also *presenting self*.

face-maintenance strategies Strategies that lead others to act in ways that reinforce the communicator's presenting self.

face-threatening acts Behaviour by another that is perceived as attacking an individual's presenting image, or face.

facework Actions people take to preserve their own and others' presenting images.

facilitative emotions Emotions that contribute to effective functioning.

factual statement A statement that can be verified as true or false. See also *inferential statement, opinion statement*.

fallacy of approval The irrational belief that it is vital to win the approval of virtually every person with whom a communicator interacts.

fallacy of catastrophic expectations The irrational belief that the worst possible outcome will probably occur.

fallacy of causation The irrational belief that emotions are caused by others and not by the person who has them.

fallacy of helplessness The irrational belief that satisfaction in life is determined by forces beyond one's control.

fallacy of overgeneralization Irrational beliefs in which (1) conclusions (usually negative) are based on limited evidence, or (2) communicators exaggerate their shortcomings.

fallacy of perfection The irrational belief that a worthwhile communicator should be able to handle every situation with complete confidence and skill.

fallacy of should The irrational belief that people should behave in the most desirable way.

family A system with two or more interdependent people who have a common past history and a present reality, and who expect to influence each other in the future.

family of origin The family in which a person grows up.

filling in the gaps A listening habit that involves adding details never mentioned by a speaker to complete a message.

first-order emotion Emotion triggered automatically, without much conscious thought, in response to environmental stimuli.

formal communication Interaction that follows officially established channels.

functional conflict Beneficial conflicts characterized by communication that is respectful, co-operative, and focused, which results in the resolution of a problem and the strengthening of a relationship.

fundamental attribution error A mistaken human tendency that has two main parts: on the one hand, when others suffer, we often blame the problem on their personal qualities and we underestimate the impact of the situation; on the other hand, when we experience failure, we find explanations outside ourselves but we are quick to take credit when we succeed.

gender Psychological sex type.

halo effect The power of a first impression to influence subsequent perceptions.

hearing The first stage in the listening process, in which sound waves are received by a communicator.

high-context culture A culture that relies heavily on verbal and non-verbal cues to maintain social harmony.

horizontal communication Communication between people who do not have direct supervisor–subordinate relationships.

'I' language A statement that describes the speaker's reaction to another person's behaviour without making judgments about its worth. See also *'you' language*.

identity management The communication strategies people use to influence how others view them.

illustrator Non-verbal behaviour that accompanies and supports verbal messages.

impersonal response A disconfirming response that is superficial or trite.

impervious response A disconfirming response that ignores another person's attempt to communicate.

inclusion–seclusion dialectic The tension between a couple's desire for involvement with the 'outside world' and their desire to live their own lives, free of what can feel like interference from others.

incongruous response A disconfirming response in which two messages, one of which is usually non-verbal, contradict one another.

indirect appeal A compliance-gaining strategy based on the hope that the other person will infer the communicator's unexpressed intent.

indirect communication Hinting at a message instead of expressing thoughts and feelings directly. See also *passive aggression* and *assertion*.

individualistic culture A culture in which people view their primary responsibility as being to themselves.

inferential statement A statement based on an interpretation of evidence. See also *factual statement*.

informal communication Communication based on friendships, shared personal or career interests, and proximity.

in-group A group with which an individual identifies herself or himself.

initiating The first stage in relational development, in which the interactants express interest in one another.

insulated listening A style in which the receiver ignores undesirable information.

integrating A relational stage in which the interactants begin to take on a single identity.

integration–separation dialectic The tension between the desire for connection with others and the desire for independence.

intensifying A relational stage following experimenting, in which the interactants move toward integration by increasing their amount of contact and the breadth and depth of their self-disclosure.

intercultural communication   Communication that occurs when members of two or more cultures or other groups exchange messages in a manner that is influenced by their different cultural perceptions and symbol systems.

interpersonal communication, qualitative   Communication in which people treat each other as unique individuals as opposed to objects.

interpersonal communication, quantitative   Communication between or among a small number of people, usually two.

interpretation   The process of attaching meaning to sense data. Synonymous with decoding.

interrupting response   A disconfirming response in which one communicator interrupts another.

intimacy   A state achieved by intellectual, emotional, and/or physical closeness, as well as shared activities.

intimate distance   One of Hall's four distance zones, ranging from skin contact to eighteen inches.

irrelevant response   A disconfirming response in which one communicator's comments bear no relationship to the previous speaker's ideas.

'it' statement   A statement in which 'it' replaces the personal pronoun 'I', making the statement less direct and more evasive.

Johari Window   A model that describes the relationship between self-disclosure and self-awareness.

kinesics   The study of body movements.

lie   A deliberate act of deception.

linguistic determinism   The notion that the world view of a culture is shaped and reflected by the language its members speak.

linguistic relativism   The notion that the language individuals use exerts a strong influence on their perceptions.

listening   The process of hearing, attending, understanding, remembering, and responding to messages.

lose–lose problem solving   An approach to conflict resolution in which neither party achieves its goals.

low-context culture   A culture that uses language primarily to express thoughts, feelings, and ideas as clearly and logically as possible.

manipulators   Movements in which one part of the body grooms, massages, rubs, holds, fidgets with, pinches, picks, or otherwise manipulates another part.

metacommunication   Messages (usually relational) that refer to other messages: communication about communication.

mixed emotions   Emotions that are combinations of primary emotions. Some mixed emotions can be expressed in single words (e.g., awe, remorse) whereas others require more than one term (e.g., embarrassed and angry, relieved and grateful).

myth of perfection   Along with *obsolete information* and *distorted feedback*, another cause for low self-esteem or skewed self-concept that is common in our society. From the time most of us learn to understand language, we are exposed to models who appear to be perfect at whatever they do. As we grow up, though, we learn that this 'perfection' is a facade.

narrative   The stories we use to describe our personal worlds.

negative mood   A state of being where people view themselves more harshly than the facts warrant (e.g., we have all experienced a temporary case of the 'uglies', convinced we look much worse than others say that we do). Research confirms what common sense suggests: people are more critical of themselves when they are experiencing negative moods than when they are feeling more positive.

negotiation   A process in which two or more people discuss specific proposals in order to find a mutually acceptable agreement.

neutrality   A defence-arousing behaviour described by Gibb in which a sender expresses indifference toward a receiver.

noise   External, physiological, and psychological distractions that interfere with the accurate transmission and reception of a message.

non-assertion   The inability to express one's thoughts or feelings when necessary. Non-assertion may be due to a lack of confidence, communication skill, or both.

non-verbal communication   Messages expressed by other than linguistic means.

norm of reciprocity   A social convention that obligates a communicator to return the favours extended by others.

nurturing culture   A culture that regards the support of relationships as an especially important goal. Also termed *'feminine' cultures*.

obsolete information   Information that can skew a person's self-concept; such information is usually outdated and unhelpful to the person in question (e.g., perhaps your jokes used to be well received, or your grades were high, or your work was superior, but now the facts have changed).

openness–closedness dialectic   The tension between the desire to be honest and open and the desire for privacy.

open question   Question that allows for a variety of extended responses.

opinion statement   A statement based on a speaker's beliefs. See also *factual statement*.

organization   The stage in the perception process that involves arranging data in a meaningful way.

out-group   A group that an individual sees as different from herself or himself.

paralanguage   Non-linguistic means of vocal expression; for example, rate, pitch, and tone.

parallel conflict style   The practice by partners in a conflict of shifting from complementary to symmetrical patterns from one conflict issue to another.

paraphrasing   Restating a speaker's thoughts and feelings in the listener's own words.

passive aggression   An indirect expression of aggression delivered in a way that allows the sender to maintain a facade of kindness.

perceived self   The person we believe ourselves to be in moments of candour. It may be identical with or different from the presenting and desired selves.

perception checking   A three-part method for verifying the accuracy of interpretations, including a description of the sense data, two possible interpretations, and a request for confirmation of the interpretations.

personal distance   One of Hall's four distance zones, ranging from eighteen inches to four feet.

personal space   The distance we put between ourselves and others.

phonological rules   Rules governing the way in which sounds are pronounced in a language.

power   A source of influence, such as expert power.

power distance   The degree to which members of a society accept the unequal distribution of power among members.

powerless speech mannerisms   Forms of speech that express to others a lack of power in the speaker: hedges, hesitations, intensifiers, and so on.

pragmatic rules   Rules that govern the interpretation of language in terms of its social context. See also *semantic rules* and *syntactic rules*.

predictability–novelty dialectic   Within a relationship, the tension between the need for a predictable relational partner and one who is more spontaneous and less predictable.

prejudice   An unfairly biased and intolerant attitude toward members of an out-group.

presenting self   The image a person presents to others. It may be identical with or different from the perceived and desired selves.

primary emotion   Basic emotion. Some researchers have identified eight primary emotions: joy, acceptance, fear, surprise, sadness, disgust, anger, and anticipation.

problem orientation   A supportive style of communication described by Gibb in which the communicators focus on working together to solve their problems instead of trying to impose their own solutions on one another.

provisionalism   A supportive style of communication described by Gibb in which a sender expresses open-mindedness to the ideas and opinions of others.

proxemics   The study of how people and animals use space.

pseudo-listening   An imitation of true listening in which the receiver's mind is elsewhere.

psychological sex type   A person, regardless of her or his biological sex, can act in a masculine manner, a feminine manner, or exhibit both types of characteristics (androgynous), or exhibit neither strongly (undifferentiated); the word *gender* is a short-hand term for psychological sex type.

public distance   One of Hall's four distance zones, extending outward from twelve feet.

punctuation   The process of determining the causal order of events.

qualitative interpersonal communication   Interpersonal communication that occurs when people treat one another as unique individuals, regardless of the context in which the interaction occurs or the number of people involved.

quantitative interpersonal communication   Any interaction between two people.

questioning (response)   A listening response in which the receiver seeks additional information from the sender.

rational-emotive approach   A method for getting rid of debilitative feelings while remaining sensitive to the more facilitative emotions; the method is based on the idea that the key to changing feelings is to change unproductive thinking.

reference groups   Groups against which we compare ourselves, thereby influencing our self-concept and self-esteem.

reflected appraisal   The theory that a person's self-concept matches the way the person believes others regard him or her.

regulators   Non-verbal behaviours that control verbal interaction. The best example of such regulation is the wide array of turn-taking signals that people utilize in everyday conversation.

relational appeal   Compliance-gaining strategy that relies on the target's relationship with the person making the request (e.g., 'Help me because you're my friend').

relational conflict style   A pattern of managing disagreements that repeats itself over time.

relational maintenance   Communication aimed at keeping relationships operating smoothly and satisfactorily (e.g., behaving in a positive way, being open, and assuring your partner that you're committed to the relationship).

relational dimension of a message   A message that expresses the social relationship between two or more individuals.

relative language   Words that gain their meaning by comparison.

remembering   A phase of the listening process in which a message is recalled.

responding   A phase of the listening process in which feedback occurs, offering evidence that the message has been received.

revelation–concealment dialectic   The tension between a couple's desire to be open and honest with the 'outside world' and the desire to keep things to themselves.

rigid family   Families with authoritarian leadership, strict discipline, roles that are inflexible, and unchanging rules.

roles   The long-term 'parts' members play within the family unit. Roles shape the way family members communicate—some are obvious: income earner, child-care provider, and so on; others are less obvious but just as important: harmonizer, problem solver, tension reliever, helpless victim, and so on.

Sapir-Whorf hypothesis   The best-known declaration of linguistic determinism formulated by Benjamin Whorf and Edward Sapir.

second-order emotion   Emotion triggered by 'emotional script' or 'emotion knowledge' and learned as part of one's socialization (e.g., guilt).

selection   A phase of the perception process in which a communicator attends to a stimulus from the environment. Also, a way communicators manage dialectical tensions by responding to one end of the dialectical spectrum and ignoring the other.

selective listening   A listening style in which the receiver responds only to messages that interest her or him.

self-concept   The relatively stable set of perceptions each individual holds of herself or himself. See also *self-esteem*.

self-disclosure   The process of deliberately revealing information about oneself that is important and that would not normally be known by others.

self-esteem   The part of the self-concept that involves evaluations of self-worth. See also *self-concept*.

self-fulfilling prophecy   A person's expectations of an event and her or his subsequent behaviour based on those expectations that make the outcome more likely to occur than would otherwise have been true.

self-monitoring   The process of observing one's behaviour and using these observations to shape the way one behaves.

self-serving bias   The tendency to judge one's self in the most generous terms possible, while being more critical of others.

self-talk   The non-vocal, internal monologue that is our process of thinking.

semantic rules   Rules that govern the meaning of language, as opposed to its structure. See also *syntactic rules*.

significant other   A person whose opinion is important enough to affect one's self-concept strongly.

silent listening   Staying attentive and non-verbally responsive without offering verbal feedback.

sincere questions   Genuine attempts to elicit information from others.

social comparison   An evaluation of oneself by way of comparison to others.

social distance   One of Hall's distance zones, ranging from four to twelve feet.

social exchange theory   The supposition that we use an economic model on which to base some of our relationships. This approach suggests that we often seek out people who can give us rewards that are greater than or equal to the costs we encounter in dealing with them.

social expectations   A societal convention that leads most of us to talk freely about our shortcomings while downplaying our accomplishments. It's okay to proclaim that you are miserable if you have failed to do well on a project, but it's boastful to express your pride at a job well done. It's fine to remark that you feel unattractive, but it's egocentric to say that you think you look good.

social penetration model   A model that describes relationships in terms of their *breadth* and *depth*.

spiral   A reciprocal communication pattern in which messages reinforce one another. See also *escalatory spiral* and *de-escalatory spiral*.

spontaneity   A supportive communication behaviour described by Gibb in which the sender expresses a message without any attempt to manipulate the receiver.

stability–change dialectic   The tension between the desire to keep a relationship predictable and stable and the desire for novelty and change.

stage hogging   A listening style in which the receiver is more concerned with making his or her own point than in understanding the speaker.

stagnating   Term used to describe a relational stage characterized by declining enthusiasm and standardized forms of behaviour.

standpoint theory   A body of scholarship that explores how one's position in a society shapes one's view of society in general, and of specific individuals.

static evaluation   Treating people or objects as if they were unchanging.

stereotyping   Exaggerated beliefs associated with a categorizing system.

strategy   A defence-arousing style of communication described by Gibb in which a sender tries to manipulate or deceive a receiver.

superiority   A defence-arousing style of communication described by Gibb in which the sender states or implies that the receiver is not worthy of respect.

supporting (response)   A listening response in which the receiver reveals her or his solidarity with the speaker's situation.

symmetrical conflict style   The use of the same tactics by the partner in a conflict.

sympathy   Feeling of compassion for another person's emotions; entails less identification than *empathy*.

syntactic rules   Rules that govern the ways symbols can be arranged, as opposed to the meanings of those symbols. See also *semantic rules*.

system   A group, such as a family, whose members interact with one another to form a whole.

tangential response   A disconfirming response that uses the speaker's remark as a starting point for a shift to a new topic.

terminating   The conclusion of a relationship, characterized by the acknowledgment of one or both partners that the relationship is over.

territory   A stationary area claimed by a person or animal.

transactional communication   A dynamic process created by the participants through their interaction with one another.

uncertainty avoidance   The extent to which a culture's members feel threatened by ambiguous situations and try to avoid them.

understanding   A stage in the listening process in which the receiver attaches meaning to a message.

upward communication   Communication from subordinates to their superiors.

virtual teams   Teams whose membership transcends the boundaries of location and time.

'we' language   The use of first-person-plural pronouns to include others, either appropriately or inappropriately. Language that implies the issue being discussed is the concern and responsibility of both the speaker and receiver of a message. See also *'I' language* and *'you' language*.

win–lose problem solving   An approach to conflict resolution in which one person reaches her or his goal at the expense of the other.

win–win problem solving   An approach to conflict resolution in which people work together to satisfy all their goals.

'you' language   A statement that expresses or implies a judgment of the other person. See also *evaluation* and *'I' language*.

References

Aboud, F. E., and Mendelson, M. J. (1998). Determinants of friendship selection and quality: Developmental perspectives. In W. M. Bukowski and A. F. Newcomb (Eds.), *The company they keep: Friendship in childhood and adolescence* (pp. 87–112). New York: Cambridge University Press.

Adamopoulos, J. (1991). The emergence of interpersonal behavior: Diachronic and cross-cultural processes in the evolution of intimacy. In S. Ting-Toomey and F. Korzenny (Eds.), *Cross-cultural interpersonal communication* (pp. 155–170). Newbury Park, CA: Sage.

Adamopoulos, J., and Bontempo, R. N. (1986). Diachronic universals in interpersonal structures. *Journal of Cross-Cultural Psychology, 17,* 169–189.

Adams, M. (2003a). *Fire and ice: The United States, Canada and the myth of converging values.* Toronto: Penguin.

Adams, M. (2003b) Good news for Canada. *Environics Research Group News.* 3 January.

Adams, M. (2005, 7 April) Sex and Fire. Religion, homosexuality and authority in Canada and the United Sates. *Environics Research Group News.*

Adams, M. (2007b). *Unlikely utopia: The surprising triumph of Canadian pluralism.* Toronto: Viking.

Adams, M. (2007a) Surprise, Canadian pluralism is working. *Environics Research Group News.* 20 November.

Adeniran, R., Healy, D., Sharp, H., and Williams, J. M. G. (1996). Interpersonal sensitivity predicts depressive symptom response to the circadian rhythm disruption of night work. *Psychological Medicine, 26,* 1211–1221.

Adler, R. B., and Elmhorst, J. M. (2002). *Communicating at work: Principles and practices for business and the professions* (7th ed.). New York: McGraw-Hill Ryerson.

Adler, R. B., and Rodman, G. (2002). *Understanding human communication* (8th ed.). New York: Oxford University Press.

Adler, T. (1992, October). Personality, like plaster, is pretty stable over time. *APA Monitor,* 18.

Adler, T. (1993, February). Congressional staffers witness miracle of touch. *APA Monitor,* 12–13.

Afifi, T., Coughlin, J., and Afifi, W. (2007). The dark side (and light side) of avoidance and secrets. In B. Spitzberg and W. Cupach (Eds.), *The dark side of interpersonal communication.* New Jersey: Lawrence Erlbaum.

Afifi, W. A., and Johnson, M. L. (1999). The use and interpretation of tie signs in a public setting: Relationship and sex differences. *Journal of Social and Personal Relationships, 16,* 9–38.

Agne, R., Thompson, T. L., and Cusella, L. P. (2000). Stigma in the line of face: Self-disclosure of patients' HIV status to health care providers. *Journal of Applied Communication Research, 28,* 235–261.

Ainsworth, M., Blehar, M. C., Waters, E., and Wall, S. (1978). *Patterns of attachment: A psychological study of the strange situation.* Hillsdale, NJ: Erlbaum.

Alaimo, K., Olson, C. M., and Frongillo, E. A. (2001). Food insufficiency and American school-aged children's cognitive, academic, and psychosocial development. *Pediatrics, 108,* 44–53.

Albada, K. F., Knapp, M. L., and Theune, K. E. (2002). Interaction Appearance Theory: Changing perceptions of physical attractiveness through social interaction. *Communication Theory, 12,* 8–40.

Alberts, J. K. (1988). An analysis of couples' conversational complaints. *Communication Monographs, 55,* 184–197.

Alberts, J. K. (1990). Perceived effectiveness of couples' conversational complaints. *Communication Studies, 40,* 280–291.

Alberts, J. K., and Driscoll, G. (1992). Containment versus escalation: The trajectory of couples' conversational complaints. *Western Journal of Communication, 56,* 394–412.

Alberts, J. K., Kellar-Guenther, U., and Corman, S. R. (1996). That's not funny: Understanding recipients' responses to teasing. *Western Journal of Communication, 60,* 337–357.

Albrecht, T. L., and Adelman, M. B. (1987). Communicating social support: A theoretical perspective. In T. L. Albrecht and M. B. Adelman (Eds.), *Communicating social support* (pp. 18–39). Newbury Park, CA: Sage.

Allen, B. (1995). 'Diversity' and organizational communication. *Journal of Applied Communication Research, 23,* 143–155.

Allen, M. (1998). Methodological considerations when examining a gendered world. In D. J. Canary and K. Dindia (Eds.), *Handbook of sex differences and similarities in communication* (pp. 427–444). Mahwah, NJ: Lawrence Erlbaum.

Allen, M. W. (1995). Communication concepts related to perceived organizational support. *Western Journal of Communication, 59,* 326–346.

Almaney A., and Alwan., A. (1982). *Communicating with the Arabs.* Prospect Heights, IL: Waveland.

Altman, I. (1973). Reciprocity of interpersonal exchange. *Journal for the Theory of Social Behavior, 3,* 249–261.

Altman, I., and Taylor, D. A. (1973). *Social penetration: The development of interpersonal relationships.* New York: Holt, Rinehart and Winston.

Ambady, N. and Gray, H. (2002). On being sad and mistaken: Mood effects on the accuracy of thin-slice judgments. *Journal of Personality & Social Psychology, 83*(4), 947–961.

Ambady, N., Koo, J., Lee, F., and Rosenthal, R. (1996). More than words: linguistic and nonlinguistic politeness in two cultures. *Journal of Personality and Social Psychology, 70,* 996–1011.

Andersen, P. A. (1992). Nonverbal communication in the small group. In R. S. Cathcart and L. A. Samovar (Eds.), *Small group communication: A reader* (6th ed., pp. 272–286). Dubuque, IA: Wm. C. Brown.

Andersen, P. A. (1999). *Nonverbal communication: Forms and functions.* Palo Alto, CA: Mayfield.

Andersen, P. A., Lustig, M. W., and Andersen, J. F. (1987a). *Changes in latitude, changes in attitude: The relationship between climate, latitude, and interpersonal communication predispositions.* Paper presented at the annual convention of the Speech Communication Association, Boston.

Andersen, P. A., Lustig, M. W., and Andersen, J. F. (1987b). Regional patterns of communication in the United States:

A theoretical perspective. *Communication Monographs, 54,* 128–144.

Anderson, D. E., DePaulo, B. M., and Ansfield, M. E. (2002). The development of deception detection skill: A longitudinal study of same-sex friends. *Personality and Social Psychology Bulletin, 28,* 536–545.

Andrews, P. H., and Baird, J. E. (2000). *Communication for business and the professions* (7th ed.). New York: McGraw-Hill Ryerson.

Androutsopoulou, A. (2001). The self-characterization as a narrative tool: Applications in therapy with individuals and families. *Family Process, 40,* 79–94.

Antioch College. (1996). *The Antioch College sexual offense prevention policy.* Yellow Springs, OH: Author.

Applegate, J. (1990). Constructs and communication: A pragmatic integration. In G. J. Neimeyer and R. A. Neimeyer (Eds.), *Advances in personal construct psychology* (pp. 203–230). Stamford, CT: JAI Press.

Archer, R., and Berg, J. (1978, November). To encourage intimacy, don't force it. *Psychology Today, 12,* 39–40.

Argyle, M., Alkema, F., and Gilmour, R. (1971). The communication of friendly and hostile attitudes by verbal and nonverbal signals. *European Journal of Social Psychology, 1,* 385–402.

Argyle, M., and Henderson, M. (1985). The rules of relationships. In S. Duck and D. Perlman (Eds.), *Understanding personal relationships: An interdisciplinary approach* (pp. 63–84). Beverly Hills, CA: Sage.

Armstrong, G. B., Boiarsky, G. A., and Mares, M. L. (1991). Background television and reading performance. *Communication Monographs, 58,* 235–253.

Aronson, E., Willerman, B., and Floyd, J. (1966). The effect of a pratfall on increasing interpersonal attractiveness. *Psychonomic Science, 4,* 227–228.

Asante, M. K. (2002). Language and agency in the transformation of American identity. In W. F. Eadie and P. E. Nelson (Eds.), *The changing conversation in America: Lectures from the Smithsonian* (pp. 77–89). Thousand Oaks, CA: Sage.

Ashkanasy, N. M., Wilderom, C., and Peterson, M. F. (Eds.). (2000). *Handbook of organizational culture and climate.* Thousand Oaks, CA: Sage.

Atkin, C. K., Smith, S. W., Roberto, A. J., Fediuk, T., and Wagner, T. (2002). Correlates of verbally aggressive communication in adolescents. *Journal of Applied Communication Research, 30,* 251–268.

Attacks on U.S. soil. (2001, September 12). *Washington Post.* Retrieved from: http://discuss.washingtonpost.com/wp-srv/zforum/01/nation_weaver091201.htm.

Au, K., Hui, M. K., and Leung, K. (2001). Who should be responsible? Effects of voice and compensation on responsibility attribution, perceived justice, and post-complaint behaviors across cultures. *International Journal of Conflict Management, 12,* 350–364.

Aune, K. S., and Aune, R. K. (1996). Cultural differences in the self-reported experience and expression of emotions in relationships. *Journal of Cross-Cultural Psychology, 27*(1), 67–81.

Aune, R. K. (in press). A theory of attribution of responsibility for creating understanding. *Communication Monographs.*

Aune, R. K., and Kikuchi, T. (1993). Effects of language intensity similarity on perceptions of credibility, relational attributions, and persuasion. *Journal of Language and Social Psychology, 12,* 224–238.

Aura, S., and Hess, G. (2004). What's in a name? CESifo GmbH, CESifo Working Paper Series: CESifo Working Paper No. 1190, 2004.

Austin, E., Saklofske, D., and Egan, V. (2004). Personality, well-being and health correlates of trait emotional intelligence. *Personality and Individual Differences, 38*(3) 547–558.

Avery, R. D., and Campion, J. E. (1982). The employment interview: A summary and review of recent research. *Personnel Psychology, 35,* 284–308.

Avtgis, T. A. (1999). The relationship between unwillingness to communicate and family communication patterns. *Communication Research Reports, 16,* 333–338.

Avtgis, T. A., West, D. V., and Anderson, T. L. (1998). Relationship stages: An inductive analysis identifying cognitive, affective, and behavioral dimensions of Knapp's relational stages model. *Communication Research Reports, 15,* 280–287.

Ayres, J., and Crosby, S. (1995). Two studies concerning the predictive validity of the personal report of communication apprehension in employment interviews. *Communication Research Reports, 12,* 145–151.

Ayres, J., and Hopf, T. (1993). *Coping with speech anxiety.* Norwood, NJ: Ablex.

Ayres, J., Keereetaweep, T., Chen, P., and Edwards, P. A. (1998). Communication apprehension and employment interviews. *Communication Education, 47,* 1–17.

Azuma, H. (1994). *Education and socialization in Japan.* Tokyo: University of Tokyo Press.

Bach, G. R., and Wyden, P. (1968). *The intimate enemy.* New York: Avon.

Baker, C. (2001). *Service provision by representative institutions and identity.* Paper commissioned by the Department of Canadian Heritage for the Ethno-cultural, Racial, Religious and Linguistic Diversity and Identity Seminar, Halifax, 1–2 November.

Baker, C. (2002). What September 11th teaches us about Canada. *Environics Research Group News.* 12 September.

Baldwin, M. W., and Keelan, J. P. R. (1999). Interpersonal expectations as a function of self-esteem and sex. *Journal of Social and Personal Relationships, 16,* 822–833.

Balswick, J. O. (1988). *The inexpressive male: A tragedy of American society.* Lexington, MA: Lexington Books.

Banks, S. P. (1987). Achieving 'unmarkedness' in organizational discourse: A praxis perspective in ethnolinguistic identity. *Journal of Language and Social Psychology, 6,* 171–190.

Barbee, P. P., Gulley, M. R., and Cunningham, M. R. (1990). Support seeking in personal relationships. *Journal of Social and Personal Relationships, 7,* 531–540.

Bargh, J. A. (1988). Automatic information processing: Implications for communication and affect. In L. Donohew and H. E. Sypher (Eds.), *Communication, social cognition, and affect* (pp. 9–32). Hillsdale, NJ: Lawrence Erlbaum.

Barker, L. L. (1971). *Listening behavior.* Englewood Cliffs, NJ: Prentice-Hall.

Barker, L. L., Edwards, R., Gaines, C., Gladney, K., and Holley, F. (1981). An investigation of proportional time spent in various communication activities by college students. *Journal of Applied Communication Research, 8,* 101–109.

Barnes, S. B. (2003). *Computer-mediated communication: Human-to-human communication across the Internet.* Boston: Allyn and Bacon.

Baron, R., Cutrona, C., Hicklin, D., Russell, D., and Lubaroff, D. (1990). Social support and immune responses among spouses of cancer patients. *Journal of Personality and Social Psychology, 59,* 344–352.

Barry, D. (1990). *Dave Barry turns 40.* New York: Fawcett Columbine.

Bartoshuk, L. (1980, September). Separate worlds of taste. *Psychology Today, 14,* 48–63.

Basso, K. (1970). To give up on words: Silence in Western Apache culture. *Southern Journal of Anthropology, 26,* 213–230.

Bateson, G., and Jackson, D. D. (1964). Some varieties of pathogenic organization. *Disorders of Communication* [Research Publications: Association for Research in Nervous and Mental Disease], *42,* 270–283.

Battaglia, D. M., Richard, F. D., Datteri, D. L., and Lord, C. G. (1998). Breaking up is (relatively) easy to do: A script for the dissolution of close relationships. *Journal of Social and Personal Relationships, 15,* 829–845.

Baumeister, R. F., Bratslavsky, E., Finkenauer, C., and Vohs, K. D. (2001). Bad is stronger than good. *Review of General Psychology, 5,* 323–370.

Baumeister, R. F., and Leary, M. R. (1995). The need to belong: Desire for interpersonal attachments as a fundamental human motivation. *Psychological Bulletin, 117,* 497–529.

Bavelas, J. B., Black, A., Chovil, N., and Mullett, J. (1990). *Equivocal communication.* Newbury Park, CA: Sage.

Baxter, L. A. (1982). Strategies for ending relationships: Two studies. *Western Journal of Speech Communication, 46,* 223–241.

Baxter, L. A. (1987). Symbols of relationship identity in relationship culture. *Journal of Social and Personal Relationships, 4,* 261–280.

Baxter, L. A. (1992). Forms and functions of intimate play in personal relationships. *Human Communication Research, 18,* 336–363.

Baxter, L. A. (1994). A dialogic approach to relationship maintenance. In D. J. Canary and L. Stafford (Eds.), *Communication and relational maintenance* (pp. 233–254). San Diego: Academic Press.

Baxter, L. A., Braithwaite, D. O., Golish, T. D., and Olson, L. N. (2002). Contradictions of interaction for wives of elderly husbands with adult dementia. *Journal of Applied Communication Research, 30,* 1–20.

Baxter, L. A., and Bullis, C. (1986). Turning points in developing romantic relationships. *Human Communication Research, 12,* 469–494.

Baxter, L. A., and Erbert, L. A. (1999). Perceptions of dialectical contradictions in turning points of development in heterosexual romantic relationships. *Journal of Social and Personal Relationships, 16,* 547–569.

Baxter, L. A., and Montgomery, B. M. (1996). *Relating: Dialogues and dialectics.* New York: Guilford Press.

Baxter, L. A., and Pittman, G. (2001). Communicatively remembering turning points of relational development in heterosexual romantic relationships. *Communication Reports, 14,* 1–17.

Baxter, L. A., and Wilmot, W. W. (1985). Taboo topics in close relationships. *Journal of Social and Personal Relationships, 2,* 253–269.

Bazil, L. G. D. (1999). The effects of social behavior on fourth- and fifth-grade girls' perceptions of physically attractive and unattractive peers (Doctoral dissertation, California School of Professional Psychology, San Diego, 1999). *Dissertation Abstracts International, 59,* 4533B.

Bearman, P., and Moody, J. (2004). Suicide and friendships among American adolescents. *American Journal of Public Health, 94*(1), 89–95.

Beatty, M. J., Burant, P. A., Dobos, J. A., and Rudd, J. E. (1996). Trait verbal aggressiveness and the appropriateness and effectiveness of fathers' interaction plans. *Communication Quarterly, 44,* 1–15.

Beatty, M. J., Marshall, L. A., and Rudd, J. E. (2001). A twins study of communicative adaptability: Heritability of individual differences. *Quarterly Journal of Speech, 87,* 366–377.

Beatty, M. J., and McCroskey, J. C. (1997). It's in our nature: Verbal aggressiveness as temperamental expression. *Communication Quarterly, 45,* 446–460.

Beatty, M. J., and McCroskey, J. C. (1998). Interpersonal communication as temperamental expression: A communibiological paradigm. In J. C. McCroskey, J. A. Daly, M. M. Martin, and M. J. Beatty, (Eds.), *Communication and personality: Trait perspectives* (pp. 41–67). Cresskill, NJ: Hampton Press.

Bechara, A. (2004). The role of emotion in decision-making: Evidence from neurological patients with orbitofrontal damage. *Brain & Cognition, 55,* 30–40.

Beck, C. E., and Beck. E. A. (1996). The manager's open door and the communication climate. In K. M. Galvin and P. Cooper (Eds.), *Making connections: Readings in relational communication* (pp. 286–290). Los Angeles: Roxbury.

Before the interview. (1999). Washington, DC: US Department of the Interior.

Bell, B. S., and Kozlowski, S. W. J. (2002). A typology of virtual teams: Implications for effective leadership. *Group and Organization Management, 27*(1), 14–49.

Bell, R. A., and Buerkel-Rothfuss, N. L. (1990). (S)he loves me, s(he) loves me not: Predictors of relational information-seeking in courtship and beyond. *Communication Quarterly, 38,* 64–82.

Bell, R. A., Buerkel-Rothfuss, N. L., and Gore, K. E. (1987). Did you bring the yarmulke for the cabbage patch kid?: The idiomatic communication of young lovers. *Human Communication Research, 14,* 47–67.

Bell, R. A., and Healey, J. G. (1992). Idiomatic communication and interpersonal solidarity in friends' relational cultures. *Human Communication Research, 18,* 307–335.

Bellah, R. N., Madsen, R., Sullivan, W. M., Swidler, A., and Tipton, S. M. (1985). *Habits of the heart: Individualism and commitment in American life.* Berkeley: University of California Press.

Bem, S. L. (1974). The measurement of psychological androgyny. *Journal of Consulting and Clinical Psychology, 42*, 155–162.

Benenson, J. F., Gordon, A. J., and Roy, R. (2000). Children's evaluative appraisals of competition in tetrads versus dyads. *Small Group Research, 31*, 635–652.

Benjamin, W. J., Schneider, B. H., Greenman, P. S., and Hum, M. (2001). Conflict and childhood friendship in Taiwan and Canada. *Journal of Behavioral Science, 33*, 203–211.

Benne, K. D., and Sheats, P. (1948). Functional roles of group members. *Journal of Social Issues, 4*, 41–49.

Benoit, W. L., and Benoit, P. J. (1987). Everyday argument practices of naive social actors. In J. Wenzel (Ed.), *Argument and critical practice*. Annandale, VA: Speech Communication Association.

Berger, C. R. (1979). Beyond initial interactions: Uncertainty, understanding, and the development of interpersonal relationships. In H. Giles and R. St. Clair (Eds.), *Language and social psychology* (pp. 122–144). Oxford, UK: Blackwell.

Berger, C. R. (1988). Uncertainty and information exchange in developing relationships. In S. Duck and D. F. Hay (Eds.), *Handbook of personal relationships: Theory, research and interventions* (pp. 239–255). Chichester, UK, and New York: John Wiley & Sons.

Berger, C. R. (1993, July). Revisiting the relationship construct. *Personal Relationship Issues, 1*, 25–27.

Berger, C. R., and diBattista, P. (1993). Communication failure and plan adaptation: If at first you don't succeed, say it louder and slower. *Communication Monographs, 60*, 220–238.

Bergner, R. M., and Holmes, J. R. (2000). Self-concepts and self-concept change: A status dynamic approach. *Psychotherapy: Theory, Research, Practice, Training, 37*, 36–44.

Berscheid, E., Schneider, M., and Omoto, A. M. (1989). Issues in studying close relationships: Conceptualizing and measuring closeness. In C. Hendrick (Ed.), *Close relationships* (pp. 63–91). Newbury Park, CA: Sage.

Berscheid, E., and Walster, E. H. (1978). *Interpersonal attraction* (2nd ed.). Reading, MA: Addison-Wesley.

Bertrand, M., and Mullainathan, S. (2004). Are Emily and Greg more employable than Lakisha and Jamal? A field experiment on labor market discrimination. *American Economic Review, 94*(4), September, 991–1013.

Bharti, A. (1985). The self in Hindu thought and action. In A. J. Marsella, G. DeVos, and F. L. K. Hsu (Eds.), *Culture and self: Asian and Western perspectives*. New York: Tavistock.

Bibby, R. W. (2001). *Canada's teens: Today, yesterday and tomorrow*. Toronto: Stoddart.

Bickman, L. (1974, April). Social roles and uniforms: Clothes make the person. *Psychology Today, 7*, 48–51.

Bippus, A. M. (2001). Recipients' criteria for evaluating the skillfulness of comforting communication and the outcomes of comforting interactions. *Communication Monographs, 68*, 301–313.

Birdwhistell, R. L. (1970). *Kinesics and context*. Philadelphia: University of Pennsylvania Press.

Birnie, S., and Horvath, P. (2002). Psychological predictors of internet social communication. *Journal of Computer Mediated Communication, 7*(4): http://jcmc.indiana.edu/vol7/issue4/horvath.html.

Bischoping, K. (1993). Gender differences in conversation topic, 1922–1990. *Sex Roles, 28*, 1–18.

Bishop, S. L., Walling, D. P., and Walker, B. A. (1997). The emperor's clothes: Assessing the validity of scores on the Tennessee Self-Concept Scale. *Educational and Psychological Measurement, 57*, 150–163.

Bjorklund, D. F., Cassel, W. S., Bjorklund, B. R., Brown, R. D., Park, C. L., and Ernst, K. (2000). Social demand characteristics in children's and adults' eyewitness memory and suggestibility: The effect of different interviewers on free recall and recognition. *Applied Cognitive Psychology, 14*, 421–433.

Blacker, L. (1999). The launching phase of the life cycle. In B. Carter and M. McGoldrick (Eds.), *The expanded family life cycle: Individual, family, and social perspectives* (3rd ed., pp. 287–306). Boston: Allyn and Bacon.

Blake, R. R., and Mouton, J. S. (1964). *The managerial grid*. Houston: Gulf Publishing.

Blank, P. D. (Ed.). (1993). *Interpersonal expectations: Theory, research, and applications*. Cambridge, UK: Cambridge University Press.

Boase, J., Horrigan, J., Wellman, B., and Rainie, L. (2006). The strength of internet ties: The internet and e-mail aid users in maintaining their social networks provide pathways to help when people face big decisions. Pew Internet and American Life Project, Washington, DC, January: http://www.pewinterent.org.

Block, J., and Robins, R. W. (1993). A longitudinal study of consistency and change in self-esteem from early adolescence to early childhood. *Child Development, 64*, 909–923.

Boatswain, S., and Lalonde, R. (2000). Social identity and preferred ethnic/racial labels for blacks in Canada. *Journal of Black Psychology, 26*, 216–234.

Bok, S. (1978). *Lying: Moral choice in public and private life*. New York: Pantheon.

Booth-Butterfield, M., and Booth-Butterfield, S. (1998). Emotionality and affective orientation. In J. C. McCroskey, J. A. Daly, M. M. Martin, and M. J. Beatty (Eds.), *Communication and personality: Trait Perspectives* (pp. 171–190). Cresskill, NJ: Hampton.

Booth-Butterfield, M., and Jordan, F. (1989). Communication adaptation among racially homogeneous and heterogeneous groups. *Southern Communication Journal, 54*, 253–272.

Booth-Butterfield, M., and Trotta, M. R. (1994). Attribution patterns for expressions of love. *Communication Reports, 7*, 119–129.

Boster, F. J., Mitchell, M. M., Lapinski, M. K., Cooper, H., Orrego, V. O., and Reinke, R. (1999). The impact of guilt and type of compliance-gaining message on compliance. *Communication Monographs, 66*, 168–177.

Bostrom R. N. (1996). Aspects of listening behavior. In O. Hargie (Ed.), *Handbook of communication skills* (2nd ed., pp 236–259). London: Routledge.

Bostrom, R. N., and. Waldhart, E. S. (1980). Components in listening behavior: The role of short-term memory. *Human Communication Research, 6*, 221–227.

Boucher, C. (2004). Canada–US Values. Distinct, inevitably carbon copy or narcissism of small differences. *Horizons: Policy Research Initiative, 7*, 42–49.

Bourhis, J., and Allen, M. (1992). Meta-analysis of the relationship between communication apprehension and cognitive performance. *Communication Education, 41*, 68–76.

Bower, B. (1992, August 15). Truth aches: People who view themselves poorly may seek the 'truth' and find despair. *Science News, 142,* 110–111.

Bower, B. (1995, March 18). Nice guys look better in women's eyes. *Science News, 147*, 165.

Bower, B. (1998, September 12). Social disconnections on-line. *Science News,*168.

Bradbury, T. N., and Fincham, F. D. (1990). Attributions in marriage: Review and critique. *Psychological Bulletin, 107*, 3–33.

Braithwaite, C. (1990). Communicative silence: A cross cultural study of Basso's hypothesis. In D. Carbaugh (Ed.), *Cultural communication and intercultural contact*, 321–328. Hillsdale, NJ: Erlbaum.

Braithwaite, D. O., Baxter, L. A., and Harper, A. M. (1998). The role of rituals in the management of the dialectical tension of 'old' and 'new' in blended families. *Communication Studies, 49*, 101–120.

Brashers, D. E., and Jackson, S. (1999). Changing conceptions of 'message effect': A 24–year overview. *Human Communication Research, 25*, 457–477.

Brightman, V., Segal, A., Werther, P., and Steiner, J. (1975). Ethological study of facial expression in response to taste stimuli. *Journal of Dental Research, 54*, 141.

Brilhart, J. K., Galanes, G. J., and Adams, K. (2001). *Effective group discussion* (10th ed.). New York: McGraw-Hill Ryerson.

Broome, B. J. (1991). Building shared meaning: Implications of a relational approach to empathy for teaching intercultural communication. *Communication Education, 40*, 235–249.

Brown, D. (1991). *Human universals.* New York: McGraw-Hill Ryerson.

Brown, J. D., and Mankowski, T. A. (1993). Self-esteem, mood, and self-evaluation: Changes in mood and the way you see you. *Journal of Personality and Social Psychology, 64*, 421–430.

Brown, L. (1982). *Communicating facts and ideas in business.* Englewood Cliffs, NJ: Prentice Hall.

Brown, L. (2002). *Resume writing made easy* (7th ed.). Upper Saddle River, NJ: Prentice Hall PTR.

Brownell, J. (1990). Perceptions of effective listeners: A management study. *Journal of Business Communication, 27*, 401–415.

Bruess, C. J. S., and Pearson, J. C. (1997). Interpersonal rituals in marriage and adult friendship. *Communication Monographs, 64*, 25–46.

Brym, R. and Lenton, R. (2003). Love at first byte: Internet dating in Canada. *Online Articles*. Nelson Thompson: http://www.societyinquestion4e.nelson.com/article2.html.

Buck, R., and VanLear, C. A. (2002). Verbal and nonverbal communication: Distinguishing symbolic, spontaneous and pseudo-spontaneous nonverbal behavior. *Journal of Communication, 52*, 522–541.

Budescu, D. V., Erev, I., and Zwick, R. (Eds.). (1999). *Games and human behavior: Essays in honor of Amnon Rapoport.* Mahwah, NJ: Lawrence Erlbaum.

Buller, D. B., and Aune, K. (1988). The effects of vocalics and nonverbal sensitivity on compliance: A speech accommodation theory explanation. *Human Communication Research, 14*, 301–332.

Buller, D. B., and Aune, K. (1992). The effects of speech rate similarity on compliance application of communication accommodation theory. *Western Journal of Communication, 56*, 37–53.

Buller, D. B., and Burgoon, J. K. (1994). Deception: Strategic and nonstrategic communication. In J. A. Daly and J. M. Wiemann (Eds.), *Strategic interpersonal communication* (pp. 191–223). Hillsdale, NJ: Lawrence Erlbaum.

Burggraf, C. S., and Sillars, A. L. (1987). A critical examination of sex differences in marital communication. *Communication Monographs, 54*, 276–294.

Burgoon, J. K., Birk, T. and Pfau, M. (1990). Nonverbal behaviors, persuasion, and credibility. *Human Communication Research, 17*, 140–169.

Burgoon, J. K., Buller, D. B., and Guerrero, L. K. (1995). Interpersonal deception: IX. Effects of social skill and nonverbal communication on deception success and detection accuracy. *Journal of Language and Social Psychology, 14,* 289–311.

Burgoon, J. K., Buller, D. B., Guerrero, L. K., and Feldman, C. M. (1994). Interpersonal deception: VI. Effects of preinteractional and interactional factors on deceiver and observer perceptions of deception success. *Communication Studies, 45*, 263–280.

Burgoon, J. K., Dunbar, N., and Segin, C. (2002). Nonverbal influence. In J. Dillard and M. Pfau (Eds.), *The persuasion handbook: Developments in theory and practice.* London, UK: Sage.

Burgoon, J. K., and Le Poire, B. A. (1999). Nonverbal cues and interpersonal judgments: Participant and observer perceptions of intimacy, dominance, and composure. *Communication Monographs, 66*, 105–124.

Burgoon, J. K., Parrott, R., LePoire, B. A., Kelley, D. L., Walther, J. B., and Perry, D. (1989). Maintaining and restoring privacy through different types of relationships. *Journal of Social and Personal Relationships, 6*, 131–158.

Burgoon, J. K., Walther, J., and Baesler, E. (1992). Interpretations, evaluations, and consequences of interpersonal touch. *Human Communication Research, 19*, 237–263.

Burkitt, I. (1992). *Social selves: Theories of the social formation of personality.* Newbury Park, CA: Sage.

Burleson, B. R. (1982). The development of comforting communication skills in childhood and adolescence. *Child Development, 53*, 1578–1588.

Burleson, B. R. (1984). Comforting communication. In H. Sypher and J. Applegate (Eds.), *Communication by children and adults: Social cognitive and strategic processes* (pp. 63–104). Beverly Hills, CA: Sage.

Burleson, B. R. (1994). Comforting messages: Features, functions and outcomes. In J. A. Daly and J. M. Wiemann (Eds.), *Strategic interpersonal communication* (pp. 135–161). Hillsdale, NJ: Lawrence Erlbaum.

Burleson, B. R., and Caplan, S. E. (1998). Cognitive complexity. In J. C. McCroskey, J. A. Daly, M. M. Martin, and M. J. Beatty (Eds.), *Communication and personality: Trait perspectives* (pp. 233–286). Cresskill, NJ: Hampton Press.

Burleson, B. R., Kunkel, A. W., Samter, W., and Werking, K. J. (1996). Men's and women's evaluations of communication skills in personal relationships: When sex differences make a difference—and when they don't. *Journal of Social and Personal Relationships, 13*, 201–224.

Burleson, B. R., and Samter, W. (1985). Individual differences in the perception of comforting messages: An exploratory investigation. *Central States Speech Journal, 36*, 39–50.

Burleson, B. R., and Samter, W. (1994). A social skills approach to relationship maintenance. In D. J. Canary and L. Stafford (Eds.), *Communication and relationship maintenance: How individual differences in communication skills affect the achievement of relationship functions* (pp. 61–90). San Diego: Academic Press.

Burleson, B. R., and Samter, W. (1996). Similarity in the communication skills of young adults: Foundations of attraction, friendship, and relationship satisfaction. *Communication Reports, 9*, 127–139.

Burns, K. L., and Beier, E. G. (1973). Significance of vocal and visual channels for the decoding of emotional meaning. *Journal of Communication, 23*, 118–130.

Bushman, B. J., Baumeister, R. F., and Stack, A. D. (1999). Catharsis, aggression, and persuasive influence: Self-fulfilling or self-defeating prophecies? *Journal of Personality and Social Psychology, 76*, 367–376.

The business meeting is alive and well . . . for now. (1997, September). *Risk Management, 44*, 6.

Buss, D. M. (1985, January–February). Human mate selection. *American Scientist, 73*, 47–51.

Buttny, R. (1997). Reported speech in talking race on campus. *Human Communication Research, 23*, 477–506.

Byrne, D. (1997). An overview (and underview) of research and theory within the attraction paradigm. *Journal of Social and Personal Relationships, 14*, 417–431.

Byron, K. (2008). Carrying too heavy a load? The communication and miscommunication of emotion by email. *Academy of Management Review, 33*(2), 309–327.

Cahn, D. D. (1992). *Conflict in intimate relationships.* New York: Guilford Press.

Cai, D. A., and Fink, E. L. (2002). Conflict style differences between individualists and collectivists. *Communication Monographs, 69*, 67–87

Camden, C., Motley, M. T., and Wilson, A. (1984). White lies in interpersonal communication: A taxonomy and preliminary investigation of social motivations, *Western Journal of Speech Communication, 48*, 315.

Campbell, A., Converse, P. E., Rogers, W. L. (1976). *The quality of married life.* New York: Russell Sage Foundation.

Campbell, S., Cumming, S., and Hughes, I. (2006). Internet use by the socially fearful: Addiction or therapy? *CyberPsychology & Behavior, 9*(1) 69–81.

Campbell, S., and Russo, T. (2003). The social construction of mobile telephony: An application of the social influence model to perception and uses of mobile phones within personal communication networks. *Communication Monographs, 70*, 317–334.

Canadian Broadcasting Corporation. (2008). Cell phone: The ring heard around the world. Accessed at http://cbc.ca/doczone/cellphones/video.html.

Canada Safety Council (2004). Bullying in the workplace. http://www.safety-council.org/info/OSH/bullies.html.

Canada Safety Council. (2005). Targeting workplace bullies: http://www.safety-council.org/info/OSH/bullies-law.html.

Canadian Council on Social Development (2000). Unequal access: A report card on racism. *Perception, 24* (3).

Canary, D. J., and Cupach, W. R. (1988). Relational and episodic characteristics associated with conflict tactics. *Journal of Social and Personal Relationships, 5*, 305–325.

Canary, D. J., Cupach, W. R., and Messman, S. J. (1995). *Relationship conflict.* Newbury Park, CA: Sage.

Canary, D. J., and Emmers-Sommer, T. M. (1997). *Sex and gender differences in personal relationships.* New York: Guilford Press.

Canary, D. J., and Hause, K. (1993). Is there any reason to research sex differences in communication? *Communication Quarterly, 41*, 482–517.

Canary, D. J., and Messman, S. J. (2000). Relationship conflict. In C. Hendrick and S. S. Hendrick (Eds.), *Close relationships: A sourcebook* (pp. 261–270). Thousand Oaks, CA: Sage.

Canary, D. J., and Spitzberg, B. H. (1987). Appropriateness and effectiveness perceptions of conflict strategies. *Human Communication Research, 15*, 93–118.

Canary, D. J., Weger, H., Jr., and Stafford, L. (1991). Couples' argument sequences and their associations with relational characteristics. *Western Journal of Speech Communication, 55*, 159–179.

Canli, T., Desmond, J. E., Zhao, Z., and Gabrieli, J. D. E. (2002). Sex differences in the neural basis of emotional memories. *Proceedings of the National Academy of Sciences, 10*, 10789–10794.

Canli, T., Zhao, Z., Desmond, J.E., Kang, E., Gross, J., and Gabrieli, J.D.E. (2001). An fMRI study of personality influences on brain reactivity to emotional stimuli. *Behavioral Neuroscience,115*, 33–42.

Carrell, L. J. (1997). Diversity in the communication curriculum: Impact on student empathy. *Communication Education, 46*, 234–244.

Carrell, L. J., and Willmington, S. C. (1996). A comparison of self-report and performance data in assessing speaking and listening competence. *Communication Reports, 9*, 185–191.

Carroll, J. M., and Russell, J. A. (1996). Do facial expressions signal specific emotions? Judging emotion from the face in context. *Journal of Personality and Social Psychology, 70*, 205–218.

Carson, C. L., and Cupach, W. R. (2000). Fueling the flames of the green-eyed monster: The role of ruminative thought in reaction to romantic jealousy. *Western Journal of Communication, 64*, 308–329.

Carton, J., Kessler, E., and Pape, C. (1999). Nonverbal decoding skills and relationship well being in adults. *Nonverbal Behaviour, 23*(1), 91–100.

Casmir, F. L. (1991). Culture, communication, and education. *Communication Education, 40*, 229–234.

Castelan-Cargile, A., and Bradac, J. J. (2001). Attitudes towards language: A review of speaker-evaluation research and a general process model. In W. B. Gudykunst (Ed.), *Communication yearbook 25* (pp. 347–382). Thousand Oaks, CA: Sage.

Castells, M. (2001). The internet galaxy: Reflections on the internet, business and society. New York: Oxford University Press.

Caughlin, J. P. (2003). Family communication standards: What counts as excellent family communication and how are such standards associated with family satisfaction? *Human Communication Research, 29,* 5–40.

Cavaliere, F. (1995, July). Society appears more open to gay parenting. *American Psychological Association Monitor,* p. 51.

Cegala, D. J., Savage, G. T., Brunner, C. C., and Conrad, A. B. (1982). An elaboration of the meaning of interaction involvement: Toward the development of a theoretical concept. *Communication Monographs, 49,* 229–248.

Chan, Y. K. (1999). Density, crowding, and factors intervening in their relationship: Evidence from a hyper-dense metropolis. *Social Indicators Research, 48,* 103–124.

Chandler, D. (1998). *Personal home pages and the construction of identities on the web.* Retrieved from http://www.aber.ac.uk/~dgc/webident.html.

Chelune, G. J., Rosenfeld, L. B., and Waring, E. M. (1985). Spouse disclosure patterns in distressed and non-distressed couples. *American Journal of Family Therapy, 13,* 24–32.

Chen, G. M., and Starosta, W. J. (1996). Intercultural communication competence: A synthesis. In B. R. Burleson and A. W. Kunkel, (Eds.), *Communication yearbook 19* (pp. 353–383). Thousand Oaks, CA: Sage.

Chen, G. M., and Starosta, W. J. (2000). The development and validation of the Intercultural Sensitivity Scale. *Human Communication, 3,* 1–14.

Chen, L. (1997). Verbal adaptive strategies in U.S. American dyadic interactions with U.S. American or East-Asian partners. *Communication Monographs, 64,* 302–323.

Chiang, Y. S. D., and Schmida, M. (2002). Language identity and language ownership: Linguistic conflicts of first-year university writing students. In V. Zamel and R. Spack (Eds.), *Enriching ESOL pedagogy: Readings and activities for engagement, reflection, and inquiry* (pp. 393–409). Mahwah, NJ: Lawrence Erlbaum.

Chovil, N. (1991). Social determinants of facial displays. *Journal of Nonverbal Behavior, 15,* 141–154.

Christopher, F. S., and Frandsen, M. M. (1990). Strategies of influence in sex and dating. *Journal of Social and Personal Relationships, 7,* 89–105.

Cialdini, R. B. (1988). *Influence: Science and practice.* Glenview, IL: Scott-Foresman.

Cissna, K. N., and Sieberg, E. (1999). Patterns of interactional confirmation and disconfirmation. In J. Stewart (Ed.), *Bridges not walls* (7th ed.) (pp. 336–346). New York: McGraw-Hill Ryerson.

Clark, A. (2000). *A theory of sentience.* New York: Oxford University Press.

Clark, R. A. (1998). A comparison of topics and objectives in a cross section of young men's and women's everyday conversations. In D. J. Canary and K. Dindia (Eds.), *Sex differences and similarities in communication: Critical essays and empirical investigations of sex and gender in interaction* (pp. 303–319). Mahwah, NJ: Lawrence Erlbaum.

Clark, R. A., and Delia, J. G. (1997). Individuals' preferences for friends' approaches to providing support in distressing situations. *Communication Reports, 10,* 115–121.

Clark, R. A., Pierce, A. J., Finn, K., Hsu, K., Toosley, A., and Williams, L. (1998). The impact of alternative approaches to comforting, closeness of relationship, and gender on multiple measures of effectiveness. *Communication Studies, 49,* 224–239.

Clarke, F. P. (1973). *Interpersonal communication variables as predictors of marital satisfaction-dissatisfaction.* Unpublished doctoral dissertation, University of Denver.

Clevenger, T. (1991). Can one not communicate? A conflict of models. *Communication Studies, 42,* 340–353.

Cline, R. J., and McKenzie, N. J. (2000). Interpersonal roulette and HIV/AIDS as disability: Stigma and social support in tension. In D. O. Braithwaite and T. L. Thompson (Eds.), *Handbook of communication and people with disabilities: Research and application* (pp. 467–483). Mahwah, NJ: Lawrence Erlbaum.

Clinton, B. L., and Hancock, G. R. (1991). The development of an understanding of comforting messages. *Communication Reports, 4*(2), 54–63.

Cloven, D. H., and Roloff, M. E. (1991). Sense-making activities and interpersonal conflict: Communicative cures for the mulling blues. *Western Journal of Speech Communication, 55,* 134–158.

Coates, J. (1986). *Women, men and language.* London: Longman.

Cody, M. J. (1982). A typology of disengagement strategies and examination of the role of intimacy, reactions to inequity, and relational problems in strategy selection. *Communication Monographs, 49,* 148–170.

Cody, M. J., Dunn, D., Hoppin, S., and Wendt, P. (1999). Silver surfers: Training and evaluating internet use among older adult learners. *Communication Education, 48,* 269–286.

Cody, M. J., and McLaughlin, M. L. (1980). Perceptions of compliance gaining situations: A dimensional analysis. *Communication Monographs, 47,* 132–148.

Cody, M. J., McLaughlin, M. L., and Schneider, M. J. (1981). The impact of relational consequences and intimacy on the selection of interpersonal persuasion tactics: A reanalysis. *Communication Quarterly, 28,* 91–106.

Cody, M. J., Woelfel, M. L., and Jordan, W. J. (1983). Dimensions of compliance-gaining situations. *Human Communication Research, 9,* 99–113.

Cohen, D., Nisbett, R. E., Bowdle, B. F., and Schwarz, N. (1996). Insult, aggression, and the southern culture of honor: An 'experimental ethnography.' *Journal of Personality and Social Psychology, 70,* 945–960.

Cohen, S., Doyle, W. J., Skoner, D. P., Rabin, B. S, and Gwaltney, J. M. (1997). Social ties and susceptibility to the common cold. *Journal of the American Medical Association, 277,* 1940–1944.

Colbert, K. R. (1993). The effects of debate participation on argumentativeness and verbal aggression. *Communication Education, 42,* 206–214.

Cole, P. M., Bruschi, C. J., and Tamang, B. L. (2002). Cultural differences in children's emotional reactions to difficult situations. *Child Development, 73,* 983–996.

Cole, T. (2001). Lying to the one you love: The use of deception in romantic relationships. *Journal of Social and Personal Relationships, 18*, 107–129.

Coleman, L. M., and DePaulo, B. M. (1991). Uncovering the human spirit: Moving beyond disability and 'missed' communications. In N. Coupland, H. Giles, and J. M. Wiemann (Eds.), *'Miscommunication' and problematic talk* (pp. 61–84). Newbury Park, CA: Sage.

Collier, M. J. (1991). Conflict competence within African, Mexican, and Anglo American friendships. In S. Ting-Toomey and F. Korzenny (Eds.), *Cross-cultural interpersonal communication* (pp.132–154). Newbury Park, CA: Sage.

Collier, M. J. (1996). Communication competence problematics in ethnic relationships. *Communication Monographs, 63*, 314–336.

Conference Board of Canada (2000). *Employability Skills 2000+*. See www.conferenceboard.ca/education.

Conlee, C., Olvera, J., and Vagim, N. (1993). The relationships among physician nonverbal immediacy and measures of patient satisfaction with physician care. *Communication Reports, 6*, 25–33.

Conn, M. K., and Peterson, C. (1989). Social support: Seek and ye shall find. *Journal of Social and Personal Relationships, 6*, 345–358.

Conville, R. L. (1991). *Relational transitions: The evolution of personal relationships*. New York: Praeger.

Coon, D. (2001). *Psychology: Gateways to mind and behavior* (9th ed.). Belmont, CA: Wadsworth.

Cooper, B. (1999). The relevancy of gender identity in spectators' interpretations of *Thelma and Louise. Critical Studies in Mass Communication, 16*, 20–41.

Cooper, J., and Jones, E. E. (1969). Opinion divergence as a strategy to avoid being miscast. *Journal of Personality and Social Psychology, 13*, 23–30.

Cooper, L. O., Seibold, D. R., and Suchner, R. (1997). Listening in organizations: An analysis of error structures in models of listening competency. *Communication Research Reports, 14*, 312–320.

Copeland, L., and Griggs, L. (1985). *Going international*. New York: Random House.

Corballis, M. C. (2002). *From hand to mouth: The origins of language*. Princeton, NJ: Princeton University Press.

Cory, C. T. (1980, May). Bafflegab pays. *Psychology Today, 13*, 12.

Costa, P. T. and McCrae, R. R. (1980). Influence of extraversion and neuroticism on subjective well-being: Happy and unhappy people. *Journal of Personality and Social Psychology, 38*, 668–678.

Cox, S. A. (1999). Group communication and employee turnover: How coworkers encourage peers to voluntarily exit. *Southern Communication Journal, 64*, 181–192.

Cozby, P. C. (1973). Self-disclosure: A literature review. *Psychological Bulletin, 79*, 73–91.

Crane, D. R. (1987). Diagnosing relationships with spatial distance: An empirical test of a clinical principle. *Journal of Marital and Family Therapy, 13*, 307–310.

Crohan, S. E. (1992). Marital happiness and spousal consensus on beliefs about marital conflict: A longitudinal investigation. *Journal of Social and Personal Relationships, 9*, 89–102.

Cronen, V., Chen, V., and Pearce, W. B. (1988). Coordinated management of meaning: A critical theory. In Y. Y. Kim and W. B. Gudykunst (Eds.), *Theories in intercultural communication* (pp. 66–98). Newbury Park, CA: Sage.

Cronen, V. E., and Chetro-Szivos, J. (2001). Pragmatism as a way of inquiring with special reference to a theory of communication and the general form of pragmatic social theory. In D. K. Perry (Ed.), *American pragmatism and communication research* (pp. 27–65). Mahwah, NJ: Lawrence Erlbaum.

Cronkhite, G. (1976). *Communication and awareness*. Menlo Park, CA: Cummings.

Crowther, C. E., and Stone, G. (1986). *Intimacy: Strategies for successful relationships*. Santa Barbara, CA: Capra Press.

Crusco, A. H., and Wetzel, G. G. (1984). The Midas Touch: Effects of interpersonal touch on restaurant tipping. *Personality and Social Psychology Bulletin, 10*, 512–517.

Cunningham, M. R., and Barbee, A. P. (2000). Social support. In C. Hendrick and S. S. Hendrick (Eds.), *Close relationships: A sourcebook* (pp. 273–285). Thousand Oaks, CA: Sage.

Cupach, W. R., and Messman, S. J. (1999). Face predilections and friendship solidarity. *Communication Reports, 12*, 117–124.

Cupach, W. R., and Metts, S. (1986). Accounts of relational dissolution: A comparison of marital and non-marital relationships. *Communication Monographs, 53*, 311–334.

Dainton, M. (2000). Maintenance behaviors, expectations for maintenance, and satisfaction: Linking comparison levels to relational maintenance strategies. *Journal of Social and Personal Relationships, 17*, 827–842.

Dainton, M., and Aylor, B. (2002). Patterns of communication channel use in the maintenance of long-distance relationships. *Communication Research Reports, 19*, 118–129.

Danner, D. D., Snowdon, D. A., and Friesen, W. V. (2001). Positive emotions in early life and longevity: Findings from the nun study. *Journal of Personality and Social Psychology, 80*, 804–813.

Dansereau, F., and Markham, S. E. (1987). Superior-subordinate communication: Multiple levels of analysis. In F. M. Jablin, L. L. Putnam, K. H. Roberts, and L. W. Porter (Eds.), *Handbook of organizational communication* (pp. 343–388). Newbury Park, CA: Sage.

Daubs, K. (2008, 20 May). Don't LOL, but linguists like teens' text talk: Instant messaging creates language renaissance. *Ottawa Citizen*.

Davidowitz, M., and Myrick, R. (1984). Responding to the bereaved: An analysis of 'helping' styles. *Death Education, 8*, 1–10.

Davis, S. F., and Kieffer, J. C. (1998). Restaurant servers influence tipping behavior. *Psychological Reports, 83*, 223–226.

Deal, T. E., and Kennedy, A. A. (1983). Culture and school performance. *Educational Leadership, 40*(5), 14–15.

DeAngelis, T. (1992). Illness linked with repressive style of coping. *APA Monitor*, 14–15.

DeAngelis, T. (1992, October). The 'who am I' question wears a cloak of culture. *APA Monitor*, 22–23.

Deaux, K. (1972). To err is humanizing: But sex makes a differ-ence. *Representative Research in Social Psychology, 3,* 20–28.

Dennis, A. R., Kinney, S. T., and Hung, Y. T. (1999). Gender differences in the effects of media richness. *Small Group Research, 30,* 405–437.

Dennis, M., Purvis, K., Barnes, M., Wilkinson, M., and Winner, E. (2001). Understanding of literal truth, ironic criticism, and deceptive praise following childhood head injury. *Brain and Language, 78*(1), 1–16.

DePaulo, B. M. (1992). Nonverbal behavior and self-presenta-tion. *Psychological Bulletin, 3,* 203–243.

DePaulo, B. M. (1994). Spotting lies: Can humans learn to do better? *Current Directions in Psychological Science, 3,* 83–86.

DePaulo, B. M., Kashy, D. A., Kirkendol, S. E., and Wyer, M. M. (1996). Lying in everyday life. *Journal of Personality and Social Psychology, 70,* 779–795.

DePaulo, B. M., Lindsay, J. J., Malone, B. E., Muhlenbruk, L., Charlton, K., and Cooper, H. (2003). Cues to deception. *Psychological Bulletin, 129*(1), 74–118.

Derks, D., Bos, A., and Von Grumbkow, J. (2008). Emoticons in computer mediated communication: Social motives and social context. *CyberPsychology & Behavior, 11*(1), 99–101.

Derlega, V. J., Barbee, A. P., and Winstead, B. A. (1994). Friendship, gender, and social support: Laboratory studies of supportive interactions. In B. R. Burleson, T. L. Albrecht, and I. G. Sarson (Eds.), *Communication of social support: Message, interactions, relationships, and community* (pp. 136–151). Newbury Park, CA: Sage.

Derlega, V. J., and Grzelak, J. (1979). Appropriateness of self-disclosure. In G. J. Chelune (Ed.), *Self-disclosure: Origins, patterns and implications of openness in interpersonal relation-ships* (pp. 151–176). San Francisco: Jossey-Bass.

Derlega, V. J., Lewis, R. J., Harrison, S., Winstead, B. A., and Costanza, R. (1989). Gender differences in the initiation and attribution of tactile intimacy. *Journal of Nonverbal Behavior, 13,* 83–96.

Derlega, V. J., Metts, S., Petronio, S., and Margulis, S. T. (1993). *Self-disclosure.* Newbury Park, CA: Sage.

Derlega, V. J., Wilson, M., and Chaikin, A. L. (1976). Friendship and disclosure reciprocity. *Journal of Personality and Social Psychology, 34,* 578–582.

Derlega, V. J., Winstead, B. A., and Folk-Barron, L. (2000). Reasons for and against disclosing HIV-seropositive test results to an intimate partner: A functional perspective. In S. Petronio (Ed.), *Balancing the secrets of private disclosures* (pp. 71–82). Mahwah, NJ: Lawrence Erlbaum.

Derwing, T. (2003). What do ESL students say about their accents? *Canadian Modern Language Review, 59,* 545–564.

deTurck, M. A., and Miller, G. R. (1990). Training observers to detect deception: Effects of self-monitoring and rehearsal. *Human Communication Research, 16,* 603–620.

Devine, D. J., Clayton, L. D., Phillips, J. L., Dunford, B. B., and Melner, S. B. (1999). Teams in organizations: Prevalence, characteristics, and effectiveness. *Small Group Research, 30,* 678–711.

Dickson, F. C., Hughes, P. C., Manning, L. D., Walker, K. L., Bollis-Pecci, T., and Gratson, S. (2002). Conflict in later-life, long-term marriages. *Southern Communication Journal, 67,* 110–121.

Dieckmann, L. E. (2000). Private secrets and public disclosures: The case of battered women. In S. Petronio (Ed.), *Balancing the secrets of private disclosures* (pp. 275–286). Mahwah, NJ: Lawrence Erlbaum.

Dillard, J. P. (1990). *Seeking compliance: The production of interper-sonal influence messages.* Scottsdale, AZ: Gorsuch Scarisbrick.

Dillard, J. P., Solomon, D. H., and Palmer, M. T. (1999). Structuring the concept of relational communication. *Communication Monographs, 66,* 49–65.

Dindia, K. (2000a). Self-disclosure research: Advances through meta-analysis. In M. A. Allen, R. W. Preiss, B. M. Gayle, and N. Burrell (Eds.), *Interpersonal communication: Advances through meta-analysis.* Mahwah, NJ: Lawrence Erlbaum.

Dindia, K. (2000b). Sex differences in self-disclosure, reciproc-ity of self-disclosure, and self-disclosure and liking: Three meta-analyses reviewed. In S. Petronio (Ed.), *Balancing the secrets of private disclosures* (pp. 21–35). Mahwah, NJ: Lawrence Erlbaum.

Dindia, K. (2002). Self-disclosure research: Knowledge through meta-analysis. In M. Allen and R. W. Preiss (Eds.), *Interpersonal communication research: Advances through meta-analysis* (pp. 169–185). Mahwah, NJ: Lawrence Erlbaum.

Dindia, K., and Allen, M. (1992). Sex differences in self-disclo-sure: A meta-analysis. *Psychological Bulletin, 112,* 106–124.

Dindia, K., Fitzpatrick, M. A., and Kenny, D. A. (1997). Self-disclosure in spouse and stranger dyads: A social relations analysis. *Human Communication Research, 23,* 388–412.

Dion, K., Berscheid, E., and Walster, E. (1972). What is beautiful is good. *Journal of Personality and Social Psychology, 24,* 285–290.

Dion, K. L., Dion, K. K. and Keelan, J. P. (1998). Attachment style and relationship satisfaction: Test of a self disclosure explanation. *Canadian Journal of Behavioural Science, 30,* 24–38.

Doherty, R. W. (1997). The emotional contagion scale: A mea-sure of individual differences. *Journal of Nonverbal Behavior, 21,* 131–154.

Dougherty, D. S. (2001). Sexual harassment as [dys]functional process: A feminist standpoint analysis. *Journal of Applied Communication Research, 29,* 372–402.

Dougherty, T., Turban, D., and Collander, J. (1994). Conforming first impressions in the employment interview. *Journal of Applied Psychology, 79,* 659–665.

Douglas, W. (1987). Affinity-testing in initial interactions. *Journal of Social and Personal Relationships, 4,* 3–16.

Downey, G., and Feldman, S. I. (1996). Implications of rejection sensitivity for intimate relationships. *Journal of Personality and Social Psychology, 70,* 1327–1343.

Downs, V. G. (1988). Grandparents and grandchildren: The relationship between self-disclosure and solidarity in an intergenerational relationship. *Communication Research Reports, 5,* 173–179.

Drigotas, S. M. (2002). The Michelangelo phenomenon and personal well-being. *Journal of Personality, 70,* 59–79.

Drigotas, S. M., Rusbult, C. E., Weiselquist, J., and Whitton, S. (1999). Close partner as sculptor of the ideal self: Behavioral confirmation and the Michelangelo phenomenon. *Journal of Personality and Social Psychology, 77,* 293–323.

Driscoll, M. S., Newman, D. L., and Seal, J. M. (1988). The effect of touch on the perception of counselors. *Counselor Education and Supervision, 27,* 344–354.

Druckmann, D., Rozelle, R. M., and Baxter, J. C. (1982). *Nonverbal communication: Survey, theory, and research.* Beverly Hills, CA: Sage.

Drullman, R., and Smoorenburg, G. F. (1997). Audio-visual perception of compressed speech by profoundly hearing-impaired subjects. *Audiology, 36*(3), 165–177.

Drummond, K., and Hopper, R. (1993). Acknowledgment tokens in series. *Communication Reports, 6,* 47–53.

Dryburgh, H. (2000). Changing our ways: Why and how Canadians use the internet. Statistics Canada: catalogue no. 56F0006XIE. Ottawa: Statistics Canada.

Duck, S. (1987). How to lose friends without influencing people. In M. E. Roloff and G. R. Miller (Eds.), *Interpersonal processes: New directions in communication research* (pp. 278–298). Beverly Hills, CA: Sage.

Duck, S. (1991). Some evident truths about conversations in everyday relationships: All communications are not created equal. *Human Communication Research, 18,* 228–267.

Duck, S. (1992). Social emotions: Showing our feelings about other people. In *Human Relationships* (pp. 1–34). Newbury Park, CA: Sage.

Duck, S. (1994). Maintenance as a shared meaning system. In D. J. Canary and L. Stafford (Eds.), *Communication and relationship maintenance: How individual differences in communication skills affect the achievement of relationship functions* (pp. 45–60). San Diego: Academic Press.

Duck, S. (1998). *Human relationships* (3rd ed.). London: Sage.

Duck, S., and Barnes, M. K. (1992). Disagreeing about agreement: Reconciling differences about similarity. *Communication Monographs, 59,* 199–208.

Duck, S., and Miell, D. E. (1986). Charting the development of personal relationships. In R. Gilmour and S. Duck (Eds.), *The emerging field of personal relationships.* Hillsdale, NJ: Lawrence Erlbaum.

Duck, S., and Pittman, G. (1994). Social and personal relationships. In M. L. Knapp and G. R. Miller (Eds.), *Handbook of interpersonal communication* (2nd ed.). Newbury Park, CA: Sage.

Duran, R. L., and Kelly, L. (1988). The influence of communicative competence on perceived task, social, and physical attraction. *Communication Quarterly, 36,* 41–49.

Duthler, K. W. (2006). The politeness of requests made via email and voicemail: Support for the hyperpersonal model. *Journal of Computer-Mediated Communication, 11*(2), article 6: http://jcmc.indiana.edu/vol11/issue2/duthler.html.

Edwards, R. (1998). The effects of gender, gender role, and values on the interpretation of messages. *Journal of Language and Social Psychology, 17,* 52–71.

Edwards, R. and Bello, R. (2001). Interpretations of messages: The influence of equivocation, face concerns, and ego involvement. *Human Communication Research, 27,* 597–691.

Edwards, R., Bello, R., Brandau-Brown, F., and Hollems, D. (2001). The effects of loneliness and verbal aggressiveness on message interpretation. *Southern Communication Journal, 66,* 139–150.

Edwards, R., and Caballero. (2008). What's in a name? An exploration of the significance of personal naming of 'mixed' children for parents from different racial, ethnic and faith backgrounds. *Sociological Review, 56*(1) 39–60.

Eibl-Eibesfeldt, I. (1972). Similarities and differences between cultures in expressive movements. In R. A. Hinde (Ed.), *Nonverbal communication.* Oxford, UK: Cambridge University Press.

Eisenberg, E. M. (1984). Ambiguity as strategy in organizational communication. *Communication Monographs, 51,* 227–242.

Eisenberg, E. M. (1990). Jamming: Transcendence through organizing. *Communication Research, 17,* 139–164.

Eisenberg, E. M., and Goodall Jr., H. (2001). Organizational communication (3rd ed.). New York: Bedfort/St.Martin's.

Eisenberg, E. M., and Witten, M. G. (1987). Reconsidering openness in organizational communication. *Academy of Management Review, 12,* 418–426.

Ekenrode, J. (1984). Impact of chronic and acute stressors on daily reports of mood. *Journal of Personality and Social Psychology, 46,* 907–918.

Ekman, P. (1985). *Telling lies: Clues to deceit in the marketplace, politics, and marriage.* New York: Norton.

Ekman, P., and Friesen, W. V. (1974a). Detecting deception from the body or face. *Journal of Personality and Social Psychology, 29,* 288–298.

Ekman, P., and Friesen, W. V. (1974b). Nonverbal behavior and psychopathology. In R. J. Friedman and M. N. Katz (Eds.), *The psychology of depression: Contemporary theory and research.* Washington, DC: J. Winston.

Ekman, P., and Friesen, W. V. (1975). *Unmasking the face: A guide to recognizing emotions from facial clues.* Englewood Cliffs, NJ: Prentice Hall.

Ekman, P., Friesen, W. V., and Baer, J. (1984, May). The international language of gestures. *Psychology Today, 18,* 64–69.

Ekman, P., Levenson, R. W., and Friesen, W. V. (1983, September). Autonomic nervous system activity distinguishes among emotions. *Science, 221,* 1208–1210.

Ekman, P., Sorenson, E. R., and Friesen, W. V. (1969, April). Pan-cultural elements in facial displays of emotions. *Science, 164,* 86–88.

Elfenbein, H. A., and Ambady, N. (2002a). Is there an in-group advantage in emotion recognition? *Psychological Bulletin, 128,* 243–249.

Elfenbein, H. A., and Ambady, N. (2002b). On the universality and cultural specificity of emotion recognition: A meta-analysis. *Psychological Bulletin, 128,* 203–235.

Elias, F. G., Johnson, M. E., and Fortman, J. B. (1989). Task-focused self-disclosure: Effects on group cohesiveness, commitment to task, and productivity. *Small Group Behavior, 20,* 87–96.

Ellis, A. (2001). *Overcoming destructive beliefs, feeling and behaving: New directions for rational emotive behavior therapy.* Amherst, NY: Prometheus Books.

Ellis, A., and Dryden, W. (1997). *The practice of rational emotive behavior therapy* (2nd ed.). New York: Springer.

Ellis, D. G., and McCallister, L. (1980). Relational control sequences in sex-typed and androgynous groups. *Western Journal of Speech Communication, 44*, 35–49.

Ellis, K. (2002). Perceived parental confirmation: Development and validation of an instrument. *Southern Communication Journal, 67*, 319–334.

Ellison, N., Steinfield, C., Lampe, C. (2007). The benefits of Facebook 'friends': Social capitol and students' use of online social network sites. *Journal of Computer-Mediated Communication, 12*(4), 1143–1168.

Enos, M. (2002). Defining emotion with measures of intensity and range of experience. *Dissertation Abstracts International, 62*(7–A), 2396.

Erbert, L. A. (2000). Conflict and dialectics: Perceptions of dialectical contradictions in marital conflict. *Journal of Social and Personal Relationships, 17*, 638–659.

Etter, G. W., Sr. (1998). Common characteristics of gangs: Examining the cultures of the new urban tribes. *Journal of Gang Research, 5*, 19–33.

Fabri, M., Moore, D., and Hobbs, D. (2004). Mediating the expression of emotion in educational collaborative virtual environments: An experimental study. *Virtual Reality, 7*(2), April, 66–81.

Fadiman, A. (1997). *The spirit catches you and you fall down.* New York: Farrar, Straus and Giroux.

Falvo, R. I. (2002). The effects of verbal aggression, issue severity and social acceptability on perceptions of compliance-gaining messages in romantic relationships: An examination of the goals/grasp model. *Dissertation Abstracts International, 62*, 2630.

Farah, A., and Atoum, A. (2002). Personality traits as self-evaluated and as judged by others. *Social Behavior and Personality, 30*, 149–156.

Faul, S. (1994). *The xenophobe's guide to the Americans.* Horsham, UK: Ravette.

Fehr, B. (1996). *Friendship processes.* Thousand Oaks, CA: Sage.

Fehr, B., and Broughton, R. (2001). Gender and personality differences in conceptions of love: An interpersonal theory analysis. *Personal Relationships, 8*, 115–136.

Feldstein, S., Dohm, F. A., and Crown, C. L. (2001). Gender and speech rate in the perception of competence and social attractiveness. *Journal of Social Psychology, 141*, 785–806.

Felmlee, D. H. (1998). 'Be careful what you wish for . . .': A quantitative and qualitative investigation of 'fatal attractions'. *Personal Relationships, 5*, 235–253.

Felson, R. B. (1985). Reflected appraisal and the development of self. *Social Psychology Quarterly, 48*, 71–78.

Fernald, A. (2001). Hearing, listening, and understanding: Auditory development in infancy. In G. Bremner and A. Fogel (Eds.), *Blackwell handbook of infant development* (pp. 35–70). Malden, MA: Blackwell Publishers.

Fernald, A., and Morikawa, H. (1993). Common themes and cultural variations in Japanese and American mothers' speech to infants. *Child Development, 64*, 637–656.

Ferris, G. R., Perrewe, P. L., Anthony, W. P., and Gilmore, D. C. (2000). Political skill at work. *Organizational Dynamics, 28*, 25–37.

Figley, C. R. (1995). Compassion fatigue as secondary traumatic stress disorder: An overview. In C. R. Figley (Ed.), *Compassion fatigue: Coping with secondary traumatic stress disorder in those who treat the traumatized* (pp. 1–20). New York: Brunner/Mazel.

Filley, A. C. (1975). *Interpersonal conflict resolution.* Glenview, IL: Scott Foresman.

First Peoples' Cultural Foundation. Language services: www.fpcf.ca/language.

Fisher, B. A. (1983). Differential effects of sexual composition and interactional content on interaction patterns in dyads. *Human Communication Research, 9*, 225–238.

Fisher, B. A., and Adams, K. (1994). *Interpersonal communication: Pragmatics of human relationships* (2nd ed.). New York: Random House.

Fisher, D. V. (1986). Decision-making and self-disclosure. *Journal of Social and Personal Relationships, 3*, 323–336.

Fitch, K. L. (1994). A cross-cultural study of directive sequences and some implications for compliance-gaining research. *Communication Monographs, 61*, 185–209.

Fitts, W. H. (1971). *The self-concept and self-actualization.* Nashville, TN: Counselor Recordings and Tests.

Fitzpatrick, J., and Sollie, D. L. (1999). Influence of individual and interpersonal factors on satisfaction and stability in romantic relationships. *Personal Relationships, 6*, 337–350.

Fitzpatrick, M. A. (1977). A typological approach to communication in relationships. In B. Rubin (Ed.), *Communication yearbook 1* (pp. 263–275). New Brunswick, NJ: Transaction Books.

Fitzpatrick, M. A. (1988). *Between husbands and wives: Communication in marriage.* Newbury Park, CA: Sage.

Fitzpatrick, M. A., Fallis, S., and Vance, L. (1982). Multifunctional coding of conflict resolution strategies in marital dyads. *Family Relations, 21*, 61–71.

Flanagin, A. J., Tiyaamornwong, V., O'Connor, J., and Seibold, D. R. (2002). Computer-mediated group work: The interaction of member sex and anonymity. *Communication Research, 29*, 66–93.

Fletcher, G. J. O., Fincham, F. D., Cramer, L., and Heron, N. (1987). The role of attributions in the development of dating relationships. *Journal of Personality and Social Psychology, 53*, 481–489.

Flora, J., and Segrin, C. (2000). Relationship development in dating couples: Implications for relational satisfaction and loneliness. *Journal of Social and Personal Relationships, 17*, 811–825.

Floyd, J. J. (1985). *Listening: A practical approach.* Glenview, IL: Scott Foresman.

Floyd, K. (1996). Communicating closeness among siblings: An application of the gendered closeness perspective. *Communication Research Reports, 13*, 27–34.

Floyd, K. (1997a). Communication affection in dyadic relationships: An assessment of behavior and expectancies. *Communication Quarterly, 45*, 68–80.

Floyd, K. (1997b). Knowing when to say 'I love you': An expectancy approach to affectionate communication. *Communication Research Reports, 14*, 321–330.

Floyd, K. (2000). Attributions for nonverbal expressions of liking and disliking: The extended self-serving bias. *Western Journal of Communication, 64*, 385–404.

Floyd, K., and Morman, M. T. (2000). Reacting to the verbal expression of affection in same-sex interaction. *Southern Communication Journal, 65*, 287–299.

Fogel, A., and Branco, A. U. (1997). Metacommunication as a source of indeterminism in relationship development. In A. Fogel and M. C. D. P. Lyra (Eds.), *Dynamics and indeterminism in developmental and social processes* (pp. 65–92). Hillsdale, NJ: Lawrence Erlbaum.

Fogel, A., de Koeyer, I., Bellagamba, F., and Bell, H. (2002). The dialogical self in the first two years of life: Embarking on a journey of discovery. *Theory and Psychology, 12*, 191–205.

Ford, W. S. Z. (2001). Customer expectations for interactions with service providers: Relationship versus encounter orientation and personalized service communication. *Journal of Applied Communication Research, 29*, 1–29.

Fortenberry, J. H., Maclean, J., Morris, P., and O'Connell, M. (1978). Mode of dress as a perceptual cue to deference. *Journal of Social Psychology, 104*, 131–139.

Fortney, S. D., Johnson, D. I., and Long, K. M. (2001). The impact of compulsive communicators on the self-perceived competence of classroom peers: An investigation and test of instructional strategies. *Communication Education, 50*, 357–373.

Foss, K. A., and Edson, B. A. (1989). What's in a name? Accounts of married women's name choices. *Western Journal of Speech Communication, 53*, 356–373.

Foss, S. K., and Griffin, C. L. (1995). Beyond persuasion: A proposal for an invitational rhetoric. *Communication Monographs, 62*, 2–18.

Francis, J., and Wales, R. (1994). Speech a la mode: Prosodic cues, message interpretation, and impression formation. *Journal of Language and Social Psychology, 13*, 34–44.

Frank, H., Harvey, O. J., and Verdun, K. (2000). American responses to five categories of shame in Chinese culture: A preliminary cross-cultural construct validation. *Personality and Individual Differences, 28*, 887–896.

French, J. R., and Raven, B. (1968). The bases of social power. In D. Cartwright and A. Zander (Eds.), *Group dynamics: Research and theory* (pp. 259–269). New York: Harper and Row.

Friedman, R., and Currall, S. (2003). Conflict escalation: Dispute exacerbation elements of e-mail communication. *Human Relations, 56*(11), 1325–1347.

Fromme, D. K., Jaynes, W. E., Taylor, D. K., Hanold, E. G., Daniell, J., Rountree, J. R., and Fromme, M. (1989). Nonverbal behavior and attitudes toward touch. *Journal of Nonverbal Behavior, 13*, 3–14.

Frumkin, L. A. (2001). The effect of eyewitnesses' accent, nationality, and authority on the perceived favorability of their testimony. *Dissertation Abstracts International, 61*, 4474.

Fry, R. W. (2003). *101 smart questions to ask on your interview.* Franklin Lakes, NJ: Career Press.

Fu, G., Lee, K., Cameron, C. A., and Xu, F. (2001). Chinese and Canadian adults' categorization and evaluation of lie- and truth-telling about prosocial and antisocial behaviors. *Journal of Cross-Cultural Research, 32*, 740–747.

Fulmer, R. (1999). Becoming an adult: Leaving home and staying connected. In B. Carter and M. McGoldrick (Eds.), *The expanded family life cycle: Individual, family, and social perspectives* (3rd ed., pp. 215–230). Boston: Allyn and Bacon.

Fussell, S. R. (Ed.). (2002). *The verbal communication of emotions: Interdisciplinary perspectives.* Mahwah, NJ: Lawrence Erlbaum.

Futch, A., and Edwards, R. (1999). The effects of sense of humor, defensiveness, and gender on the interpretation of ambiguous messages. *Communication Quarterly, 47*, 80–97.

Gabric, D., and McFadden, K. L. (2001). Student and employer perceptions of desirable entry-level operations management skills. *Mid-American Journal of Business, 16*, 51–59.

Gadlin, H. (1977). Private lives and public order: A critical view of the history of intimate relations in the United States. In G. Levinger and H. L. Raush (Eds.), *Close relationships: Perspectives on the meaning of intimacy* (pp. 33–72). Amherst, MA: University of Massachusetts Press.

Gallois, C. (1993). The language and communication of emotion: Universal, interpersonal, or intergroup? *American Behavioral Scientist, 36*, 309–338.

Galloway, G., and Moore, O. (2005). Senate approves same-sex marriage. *Globe and Mail*, 20 July.

Galvin, K. M., and Brommel, B. J. (2000). *Family communication: Cohesion and change* (5th ed.). New York: Longman.

Gara, M. A., Woolfolk, R. L., Cohen, B. D., Gioldston, R. B., and Allen, L. A. (1993). Perception of self and other in major depression. *Journal of Abnormal Psychology, 102*, 93–100.

Garko, M. G. (1990). Perspectives on and conceptualizations of compliance and compliance-gaining. *Communication Quarterly, 38*, 138–157.

Gass, R. H., and Seiter, J. S. (1999). *Persuasion, social influence, and compliance gaining.* Boston: Allyn and Bacon.

Gayle, B. M., and Preiss, R. W. (1999). Language intensity plus: A methodological approach to validate emotions in conflicts. *Communication Reports, 12*, 43–50.

Gayle, B. M., Preiss, R. W., and Allen, M. A. (1998). Embedded gender expectations: A covariate analysis of conflict situations and issues. *Communication Research Reports, 15*, 379–387.

Geddes, D. (1992). Sex-roles in management: The impact of varying power of speech style on union members' perception of satisfaction and effectiveness. *Journal of Psychology, 126*, 589–607.

Geist, M. (2007). Let's face it, Facebook is here to stay. *Toronto Star*, May 7: www.the star.com/Business/article/211078.

George, J. F., Marett, K., and Tilley, P. A. (2008). The effects of warnings, computer based media and probing on successful lie detection. *Professional Communication, 51*(1), 1–17.

Gergen, K. J. (1971). *The concept of self.* New York: Holt, Rinehart and Winston.

Gergen, K. J. (1991). *The saturated self: Dilemmas of identity in contemporary life.* New York: Basic Books.

Gibb, J. R. (1961). Defensive communication. *Journal of Communication, 11*, 141–148.

Giles, H. (1971). Evaluation of personality content from accented speech as a function of listeners' social attitudes. *Perceptual and Motor Skills, 34*, 168–170.

Giles, H., Coupland, N., and Wiemann, J. M. (1992a). 'Talk is cheap . . .' but 'my word is my bond': Beliefs about talk. In K. Bolton and H. Kwok (Eds.), *Sociolinguistics today: International perspectives* (pp. 218–243). London, UK: Routledge and Kegan Paul.

Giles, H., and Franklyn-Stokes, A. (1989). Communicator characteristics. In M. K. Asante and W. B. Gudykunst (Eds.), *Handbook of international and intercultural communication* (pp. 117–144). Newbury Park, CA: Sage.

Giles, H., Henwood, K., Coupland, N., Harriman, J., and Coupland, J. (1992b). Language attitudes and cognitive mediation. *Human Communication Research, 18,* 500–527.

Giles, H., Mulac, A., Bradac, J. J., and Smith, P. J. (1992c). Speech accommodation. In W. B. Gudykunst and Y. Y. Kim (Eds.), *Readings on communicating with strangers.* New York: McGraw-Hill Ryerson.

Ginsberg, S. (1997, 5 May). So many messages and so little time. *Business Outlook,* C-1.

Ginsburg, D. (1999). *ATM: Solutions for enterprise internetworking* (2nd ed.). Boston: Addison-Wesley.

Giordano, G., Stoner, S., Brouer, R., and George, J. (2007). The influences of deception and computer mediation on dyadic negotiations. *Journal of Computer-Mediated Communication, 12*(2), article 2: http://jcmc.indiana.edu/vol112/issue/2/giordana.html.

Gleason, J. B., and Greif, E. B. (1983). Men's speech to young children. In B. Thorne, C. Kramarae, and N. Henley (Eds.), *Language, gender, and society* (pp. 140–150). Rowley, MA: Newbury House.

Goetting, A. (1986). The developmental tasks of siblingship over the life cycle. *Journal of Marriage and the Family, 48,* 703–714.

Goffman, E. (1959). *The presentation of self in everyday life.* Garden City, NY: Doubleday.

Goffman, E. (1971). *Relations in public.* New York: Basic Books.

Goldschmidt, W. (1990). *The human career.* Cambridge, MA: Basil Blackman.

Goldsmith, D. J. (2000). Soliciting advice: The role of sequential placement in mitigating face threat. *Communication Monographs, 67,* 1–19.

Goldsmith, D. J., and Baxter, L. A. (1996). Constituting relationships in talk: A taxonomy of speech events in social and personal relationships. *Human Communication Research, 23,* 87–114.

Goldsmith, D. J., and Fitch, K. (1997). The normative context of advice as social support. *Human Communication Research, 23,* 454–476.

Goldsmith, D. J., and Fulfs, P. A. (1999). 'You just don't have the evidence': An analysis of claims and evidence in Deborah Tannen's *You Just Don't Understand.* In M. E. Roloff (Ed.), *Communication yearbook 22* (pp. 1–49). Thousand Oaks, CA: Sage.

Goldsmith, D. J., and MacGeorge, E. L. (2000). The impact of politeness and relationship on perceived quality of advice about a problem. *Human Communication Research, 26,* 234–263.

Goleman, D. (1995). *Emotional intelligence: Why it can matter more than I.Q.* New York: Bantam.

Golen, S. (1990). A factor analysis of barriers to effective listening. *Journal of Business Communication, 27,* 25–36.

Golish, T. D. (2000). Is openness always better?: Exploring the role of topic avoidance, satisfaction, and parenting styles of stepparents. *Communication Quarterly, 48,* 137–158.

Golish, T. D., and Caughlin, J. P. (2002). 'I'd rather not talk about it': Adolescents' and young adults' use of topic avoidance in stepfamilies. *Journal of Applied Communication Research, 30,* 78–106.

Good, G. E., Porter, M. J., and Dillon, M. G. (2002). When men divulge: Men's self-disclosure on prime time situation comedies. *Sex Roles, 46,* 419–427.

Goodman, G., and Esterly, G. (1990). Questions—The most popular piece of language. In J. Stewart (Ed.), *Bridges not walls* (5th ed., pp. 69–77). New York: McGraw-Hill Ryerson.

Gordon, T. (1970). *P.E.T.: Parent effectiveness training.* New York: Wyden.

Gorham, J. (1988). The relationship between verbal teacher immediacy behaviors and student learning. *Communication Education, 37,* 40–53.

Goss, B., and O'Hair, D. (1988). *Communicating in interpersonal relationships.* New York: Macmillan.

Gottman, J. (2000, September). Welcome to the love lab. *Psychology Today Online.* Available at http://www.findarticles.com/m1175/5_33/66380417/p1/article.jhtml.

Gottman, J. (2003). Why marriages fail. In K. M. Galvin and P. J. Cooper (Eds.), *Making connections: Readings in relational communication* (pp. 258–266). Los Angeles: Roxbury.

Gottman, J. M., Katz, L. F., and Hooven, C. (1997). *Meta-emotion: How families communicate emotionally.* Mahwah, NJ: Lawrence Erlbaum.

Grant, C. H., III, Cissna, K. N., and Rosenfeld, L. B. (2000). Patients' perceptions of physicians' communication and outcomes of the accrual to trial process. *Health Communication, 12*(1), 23–39.

Grant, J., King, P. E., and Behnke, R. R. (1994). Compliance-gaining strategies, communication satisfaction, and willingness to comply. *Communication Reports, 7,* 99–108.

Gray, J. (1992). *Men are from Mars; women are from Venus: A practical guide for improving communication and getting what you want in your relationship.* New York: HarperCollins.

Greenwald, A. G. (1995). Getting (my) self into social psychology. In G. G. Brannigan and M. R. Merrens (Eds.), *The social psychologists: Research adventures* (pp. 3–16). New York: McGraw-Hill Ryerson.

Griffin, E. A. (2003). *A first look at communication theory with conversations with communication theorists* (5th ed.). New York: McGraw-Hill.

Grob, L. M., Meyers, R. A., and Schuh, R. (1997). Powerful/powerless language use in group interactions: Sex differences or similarities? *Communication Quarterly, 45,* 282–303.

Grodin, D., and Lindlof, T. R. (1995). *Constructing the self in a mediated world.* Newbury Park, CA: Sage.

Gross, E. (2004). Adolescent internet use: What we expect, what teens report. *Journal of Applied Developmental Psychology, 25*(6), 633–649.

Gross, J. J., Sutton, S. K. and Ketelaar, T. V. (1998). Relations between affect and personality: Support for the affect-level and affective-reactivity views. *Personality and Social Psychology Bulletin, 24,* 279–288.

Gudykunst, W. B. (1986). The influence of cultural variability on perceptions of communication behavior associated with relationship terms. *Human Communication Research, 13,* 147–166.

Gudykunst, W. B. (1993). *Communication in Japan and the United States.* Albany, NY: State University of New York Press.

Gudykunst, W. B., and Kim, Y. Y. (1997). *Communicating with strangers: An approach to intercultural communication* (3rd ed.). New York: McGraw-Hill Ryerson.

Gudykunst, W. B., and Matsumoto, Y. (1996). Cross-cultural variability of communication in personal relationships. In W. B. Gudykunst, S. Ting-Toomey, and T. Nishida (Eds.), *Communication in personal relationships across cultures* (pp. 19–56). Newbury Park, CA: Sage.

Gudykunst, W. B., and Ting-Toomey, S. (1988). *Culture and interpersonal communication.* Newbury Park, CA: Sage.

Gueguen, N., and Fischer-Lokou, J. (2002). An evaluation of touch on a large request: A field setting. *Psychological Reports, 90,* 267–269.

Guzley, R. (1992). Organizational climate and communication climate: Predictors of commitment to the organization. *Management Communication Quarterly, 5,* 379–402.

Hackman, M., and Walker, K. (1990). Instructional communication in the televised classroom: The effects of system design and teacher immediacy. *Communication Education, 39,* 196–206.

Haddon, L. (2000). The social consequences of mobile telephony: Framing questions. In R. Ling and K. Thrane (Eds.) *The social consequences of mobile telephony.* Kjeller: Telenor R & D.

Haefner, M. J., and Comstock, J. (1990). Compliance gaining on prime time family programs. *Southern Communication Journal, 55,* 402–420.

Haidt, J., and Keltner, D. (1999). Culture and facial expression: Open-ended methods find more expressions and a gradient of recognition. *Cognition and Emotion, 13,* 225–266.

Hale, J. L., Tighe, M. R., and Mongeau, P. A. (1997). Effects of event type and sex on comforting messages. *Communication Research Reports, 14,* 214–220.

Hall, E. T. (1959). *Beyond culture.* New York: Doubleday.

Hall, E. T. (1963) A system for the notion of proxemic behaviour. *American Psychologist, 65,* 1003–1026.

Hall, E. T. (1969). *The hidden dimension.* Garden City, NY: Anchor.

Hall, M., and Havens, B. (2002). Social isolation and loneliness. *NCA Writings in Gerentology on Mental Health and Aging,* Spring/Summer.

Halone, K. K., and L. L. Pecchioni. (2001). Relational listening: A grounded theoretical model. *Communication Reports, 14,* 59–65.

Hamachek, D. E. (1982). *Encounters with others: Interpersonal relationships and you.* New York: Holt, Rinehart and Winston.

Hamachek, D. E. (1992). *Encounters with the self* (3rd ed.). Fort Worth, TX: Harcourt Brace.

Hample, D. (1980). Purposes and effects of lying. *Southern Speech Communication Journal, 46,* 33–47.

Hamdorf, D. (2003). Towards managing diversity: Cultural aspects of conflict management in organizations. *Conflict and Communication Online, 2.* http://www.cco.regener-online.de/2003_2/pdf_2003_2/hamdorf_engl.pdf.

Hample, D., and Dallinger, J. M. (2000). The effects of situation on the use or suppression of possible compliance gaining appeals. In M. A. Allen, R. W. Preiss, B. M. Gayle, and N. Burrell (Eds.). *Interpersonal communication: Advances through meta-analysis* (pp. 187–209). Mahwah, NJ: Lawrence Erlbaum.

Han, S. (2001). Gay identity disclosure to parents by Asian American gay men. *Dissertation Abstracts International, 62,* 329.

Hancock, J., Curry, L., Goorha, S., and Woodworth, M. (2004). Lies in Conversation. An examination of deception using automated linguistic analysis. In *Proceedings of the 26th Annual Conference of the Cognitive Science Society.*

Hancock, J., Thom-Santelli, J., and Ritchie, T. (2004). Deception and design: Effects of communication technology on lying behavior. In *Proceedings of CHI 2004* (pp. 129–134). New York: ACM Press.

Hansson, G. (1996). Emotions in poetry: Where are they and how do we find them? In R. J. Kreuz and M. S. MacNealy (Eds.), *Empirical approaches to literature and aesthetics. Advances in discourse processes* (Vol. 52, pp. 275–288). Norwood, NJ: Ablex.

Harding, S. (1991). *Whose science? Whose knowledge? Thinking from women's lives.* Ithaca, NY: Cornell University Press.

Harley, D., Winn, S., Pemberton, S., and Wilcox, P. (2007). Using texting to support students' transition to university. *Innovations in Education and Teaching International, 44*(3), 229–241.

Hartley, M. (2008, 3 July). YouTube told to hand over user's data. *Globe and Mail,* http://www.theglobeandmail.com.

Hartwig, M., Granhag, P., Stromwall, L., and Kronkvist, O. (2006). Strategic use of evidence during police interviews: When training to detect deception works. *Law and Human Behavior, 30*(5), 603–620.

Harwood, J., Bouchard, E., Giles, H. and Tyoski, S. (1997). Evaluations of patronizing speech and three response styles in a non-service-providing context. *Journal of Applied Communication Research, 25,* 170–195.

Harwood, J., and Giles, H. (1996). Reactions to older people being patronized: The roles of response strategies and attributed thoughts. *Journal of Language and Social Psychology, 15,* 395–421.

Hastings, S. O. (2000). Self-disclosure and identity management by bereaved parents. *Communication Studies, 51,* 352–371.

Hatfield, E., and Sprecher, S. (1986). *Mirror, mirror: The importance of looks in everyday life.* Albany: State University of New York Press.

Hayes, A., Shanahan, J., and Glynn, C. (2001). Willingness to express one's opinion in a realistic situation as a function of perceived support of that opinion. *International Journal of Public Opinion Research, 13*(1), 45–58.

Hearing Foundation of Canada (2005). Presentation to Round Table on Research Collaboration. Ottawa: Institute of Neurosceinces, Mental Health and Addiction: www.thfc.ca/hearing.html.

Hecht, M. L., Collier, M. J., and Ribeau, S. A. (1993). *African American communication: Perspectives, principles, and pragmatics.* Hillsdale, NJ: Lawrence Erlbaum.

Hegelson, V. S., and Gottlieb, B. H. (2000). Support groups. In S. Cohen, L. G. Underwood, and B. H. Gottlieb (Eds.), *Social support measurement and intervention* (pp. 221–245). New York: Oxford University Press.

Hegstrom, T. G. (1979). Message impact: What percentage is non-verbal? *Western Journal of Speech Communication, 43*, 134–142.

Heine, S., Takata, T., and Lehman, D. (2000). Beyond self-presentation: Evidence for self-criticism among Japanese. *Personality and Social Psychology Bulletin, 26*, 71–78.

Hellweg, S. (1987). Organizational grapevines: A state of the art review. In B. Dervin and M. Boight (Eds.), *Progress in the communication sciences, 8*. Norwood, NJ: Ablex.

Helmreich, R., Aronson, E., and Lefan, J. (1970). To err is humanizing—sometimes: Effects of self-esteem, competence, and a pratfall on interpersonal attraction. *Journal of Personality and Social Psychology, 16*, 259–264.

Hendrick, C., Hendrick, S. S., and Dicke, A. (1998). The love attitudes scale: Short form. *Journal of Social and Personal Relationships, 15*, 147–159.

Henningsen, D. D., Cruz, M. G., and Morr, M. C. (2000). Pattern violations and perception of deception. *Communication Reports, 13*, 1–9.

Henry, F. and Tator, C. (2003). *Racial profiling in Toronto: Discourses of domination, mediation, and opposition*. Ottawa: Canadian Race Relations Foundation.

Hershcovis, M. S., Tuner, N., Barling, J., Arnold, K., Dupre, K., Inness, M., Leblanc, M. M., and Sivanathan, N. (2007). Predicting workplace aggression: A meta-analysis. *Journal of Applied Psychology, 92*(1), 228–238.

Hess, J. A. (2000). Maintaining nonvoluntary relationships with disliked partners: An investigation into the use of distancing behaviors. *Human Communication Research, 26*, 458–488.

Hess, J. A. (2002). Distance regulation in personal relationships: The development of a conceptual model and a test of representational validity. *Journal of Social and Personal Relationships, 19*, 57–59.

Hess, U., Beaupré, M., and Cheung, N. (2002). Who to whom and why—cultural differences and similarities in the function of smiles. In M. Abel (Ed.), *An empirical reflection on the smile* (pp. 187–216). New York: The Edwin Mellen Press.

Hett, A. M. (1993). Language of silence: An ethnographic case study of the expressive language skills of preschool Native American girls. *Dissertation Abstracts International, 53*, 3062.

Hicks, C. B., and Tharpe, A. M. (2002). Listening effort and fatigue in school-age children with and without hearing loss. *Journal of Speech, Language, and Hearing Research, 45*, 573–584.

Hidalgo, M. C., and Hernandez, B. (2001). Place attachment: Conceptual and empirical questions. *Journal of Environmental Psychology, 21*, 273–281.

Hinde, R. A., Finkenauer, C., and Auhagen, A. E. (2001). Relationships and the self-concept. *Personal Relationships, 8*, 187–204.

Hines, P. M., Preto, N. G., McGoldrick, M., Almeida, R., and Weltman, S. (1999). Culture and the family life cycle. In B. Carter and M. McGoldrick (Eds.), *The expanded family life cycle: Individual, family, and social perspectives* (3rd ed., pp. 69–87). Needham Heights, MA: Allyn and Bacon.

Hochberg, J. (Ed.). (1998). Perception and cognition at century's end. *Handbook of perception and cognition* (2nd ed.). San Diego, CA: Academic Press.

Hocker, J. L., and Wilmot, W. W. (1997). *Interpersonal conflict* (5th ed.). New York: McGraw-Hill Ryerson.

Hoffman, M. L. (1991). Empathy, social cognition, and moral action. In W. Kurtines and J. Gerwirtz (Eds.), *Moral behavior and development: Theory, research, and applications* (Vol. 1, pp. 275–301). Hillsdale, NJ: Lawrence Erlbaum.

Hofstede, G. (1980, 2001). *Culture's consequences: Comparing values, behavior, institutions and organizations across nations*. Thousand Oaks, CA: Sage.

Hoijer, H. (1994). The Sapir-Whorf hypothesis. In L. A. Samovar and R. E. Porter (Eds.), *Intercultural communication: A reader* (7th ed.). Belmont, CA: Wadsworth.

Holte, A., and Wichstrom, L. (1990). Disconfirmatory feedback in families of schizophrenics. *Scandinavian Journal of Psychology, 31*, 198–211.

Homans, G. C. (1961). *Social behavior: Its elementary form*. New York: Harcourt Brace.

Honeycutt, J. M. (1999). Typological differences in predicting marital happiness from oral history behaviors and imagined interactions. *Communication Monographs, 66*, 276–291.

Honeycutt, J. M., and Wiemann, J. M. (1999). Analysis of functions of talk and reports of imagined interactions (IIs) during engagement and marriage. *Human Communication Research, 25*, 399–419.

Hornsey, M. J., Oppes, T., and Svensson, A. (2002). 'It's ok if we say it, but you can't': Responses to intergroup and intragroup criticism. *European Journal of Social Psychology, 32*, 293–307.

Horrigan, J. B., Rainie, L., and Fox, S. (2001, October 31). *Online communities: Networks that nurture long-distance relationships and local ties*. Pew Internet and American Life Project. Retrieved from http://www.pewinternet.org/reports/pdfs/PIP_Communities_Report.pdf.

Horvath, C. W. (1995). Biological origins of communicator style. *Communication Quarterly, 43*, 394–407.

Hosman, L. A. (1989). The evaluative consequences of hedges, hesitations, and intensifiers: Powerful and powerless speech styles. *Human Communication Research, 15*, 383–406.

House, J. S., Landis, K. R., and Umberson, D. (1988). Social relationships and health. *Science, 241*, 540–545.

Huang, L. (1999). Family communication patterns and personality characteristics. *Communication Quarterly, 47*, 230–243.

Hubbard, A. S. E. (2001). Conflict between relationally uncertain romantic partners: The influence of relational responsiveness and empathy. *Communication Monographs, 68*, 400–414.

Hubbell, A. P. (1999, November). *'I love your family-they are just like you': Lies we tell to lovers and perceptions of their honesty and appropriateness*. Paper delivered at the annual meeting of the International Communication Association, San Francisco.

Hulbert, J. E. (1989). Barriers to effective listening. *Bulletin for the Association for Business Communication, 52*, 3–5.

Hussain, Z., and Griffiths, M. (2008). Gender swapping and socializing in cyberspace: An exploratory study. *CyberPsychology & Behavior, 11*(1), 47–53.

Huston, T. L., and Vangelisti, A. L. (1995). How parenthood affects marriage. In M. A. Fitzpatrick and A. L. Vangelisti (Eds.), *Explaining family interactions* (pp. 147–176). Thousand Oaks, CA: Sage.

Hyde, R. B. (1993, Winter). Council: Using a talking stick to teach listening. *Speech Communication Teacher, 7*, 1–2.

Hynes, D. (2001). *Preventing workplace violence: Towards an aggression-free workplace.* Ottawa: Conference Board of Canada.

Hynie, M. (1998). From conflict to compromise: Immigrant families and the processes of acculturation: http://canada.metropolis.net/research.

Ifert, D. E., and Roloff, M. E. (1997). Overcoming expressed obstacles to compliance: The role of sensitivity to the expressions of others and ability to modify self-presentation. *Communication Quarterly, 45,* 55–67.

Ifert, D. E., and Roloff, M. E. (1998). Understanding obstacles preventing compliance: Conceptualization and classification. *Communication Research, 25,* 131–153.

Infante, D. A. (1987). Aggressiveness. In J. C. McCroskey and J. A. Daly (Eds.), *Personality and interpersonal communication* (pp. 157–192). Newbury Park, CA: Sage.

Infante, D. A. (1988). *Arguing constructively.* Prospect Heights, IL: Waveland Press.

Infante, D. A., Chandler, T. A., and Rudd, J. E. (1989). Test of an argumentative skill deficiency model of interspousal violence. *Communication Monographs, 56,* 163–177.

Infante, D. A., and Gorden, W. I. (1985). Superiors' argumentativeness and verbal aggressiveness as predictors of subordinates' satisfaction. *Human Communication Research, 12,* 117–125.

Infante, D. A., and Gorden, W. I. (1987). Superior and subordinate communication profiles: Implications for independent-mindedness and upward effectiveness. *Central States Speech Journal, 38,* 73–80.

Infante, D. A., and Gorden, W. I. (1989). Argumentativeness and affirming communicator style as predictors of satisfaction/dissatisfaction with subordinates. *Communication Quarterly, 37,* 81–90.

Infante, D. A., and Rancer, A. S. (1982). A conceptualization and measure of argumentativeness. *Journal of Personality Assessment, 46,* 72–80.

Infante, D. A., Riddle, B. L., Horvath, C. L., and Tumlin, S. A. (1992). Verbal aggressiveness: Messages and reasons. *Communication Quarterly, 40,* 116–126.

Infante, D. A., and Wigley, C. J., III. (1986). Verbal aggressiveness: An interpersonal model and measure. *Communication Monographs, 53,* 61–69.

Inman, C. (1996). Friendships among men: Closeness in the doing. In J. T. Wood (Ed.), *Gendered relationships* (pp. 95–110). Mountain View, CA: Mayfield Publishing.

Inman, M. L., and Baron, R. S. (1996). Influence of prototypes on perceptions of prejudice. *Journal of Personality and Social Psychology, 70,* 727–739.

International Labour Organization. (1998). *Violence on the job—A global problem.* Press Release, Monday 20 July 1998. Ref: ILO/98/30.

Iverson, J. M. (1999). How to get to the cafeteria: Gesture and speech in blind and sighted children's spatial descriptions. *Developmental Psychology, 35,* 1132–1142.

Iverson, J. M., and Goldin-Meadow, S. (1997). What's communication got to do with it? Gesture in children blind from birth. *Developmental Psychology, 33,* 453–467.

Iyer, P. (1990). *The lady and the monk: Four seasons in Kyoto.* New York: Vintage.

Izard, C. E. (1971). *The face of emotion.* New York: Appleton-Century-Crofts.

Jackson, M. (1983). *Prisoners of isolation: Solitary confinement in Canada.* Toronto: University of Toronto Press.

Jackson, M. (2002). *Justice behind the walls: Human rights in Canadian prisons.* Toronto: Douglas and McIntyre

Jaksa, J. A., and Pritchard, M. (1994). *Communication ethics: Methods of analysis* (2nd ed.). Belmont, CA: Wadsworth.

Janas, M. (2001). Getting a clear view. *Journal of Staff Development, 22*(2), 32–34.

Janoff-Bulman, R., and Leggatt, H. K. (2002). Culture and social obligation: When 'shoulds' are perceived as 'wants.' *Journal of Research in Personality, 36,* 260–270.

Jedwab, J. (2003). *Perceived threat to the French language and culture and support for bilingualism in Canada.* Press release. Toronto: Environics Research.

Jedwab, J. (2004a). Collective and individual perceptions of discrimination in Canada. Poll conducted for the Association for Canadian Studies: http://www.acsaec.ca/Polls/collective.pdf.

Jedwab, J. (2004b). Canadian society: More American than European. Poll conducted for Association for Canadian Studies: http://www.acs-aec.ca/Polls/collective.pdf.

Jett, C. (2005). E-mail etiquette. *Free-Lance Star,* 30 July.

Job Outlook '99. (1999). National Association of Colleges and Employers. Retrieved from http://www.jobwell.org/pubs/joboutlook/want.htm.

Johnson, F. (1996). Friendships among women: Closeness in dialogue. In J. T. Wood (Ed.), *Gendered relationships* (pp. 79–94). Mountain View, CA: Mayfield Publishing.

Johnson, H. M. (1998). *How do I love me?* (3rd ed.) Salem, WI: Sheffield.

Johnson, J. M. (1981). *The significance of dress in an interview.* Unpublished manuscript, University of New Mexico.

Johnson, P., Lindsey, A. E., and Zakahi, W. R. (2001). Anglo-American, Hispanic American, Chilean, Mexican and Spanish perceptions of competent communication in initial interaction. *Communication Research Reports, 18,* 36–43.

Johnson, S. (1987). *Going out of our minds: The metaphysics of liberation.* Freedom, CA: Crossing.

Johnson, S., and Bechler, C. (1998). Examining the relationship between listening effectiveness and leadership emergence: Perceptions, behaviors, and recall. *Small Group Research, 29,* 452–471.

Jones, S. E. (1986). Sex differences in touch behavior. *Western Journal of Speech Communication, 50,* 227–241.

Jourard, S. (1966). An exploratory study of body accessibility. *British Journal of Social and Clinical Psychology, 5,* 221–231.

Jordan, J., and Roloff, M. E. (1990). Acquiring assistance from others: The effect of indirect requests and relational intimacy on verbal compliance. *Human Communication Research, 16,* 519–555.

Jorgenson, J. (1992). Communication, rapport, and the interview: A social perspective. *Communication Theory, 2,* 148–157.

Kalbfleisch, P. J. (1992). Deceit, distrust, and the social milieu: Applications of deception research in a troubled world. *Journal of Applied Communication Research, 20,* 308–334.

Kalist, D., and Lee, D. Y. (2008). *First names and crime: Does unpopularity spell trouble?* Paper presented at the 42nd Annual

Meeting of the Canadian Economic Association, University of British Columbia, Vancouver, June 7.

Kanaga, K. R., and Flynn, M. (1981). The relationship between invasion of personal space and stress. *Human Relations, 34,* 239–248.

Kashy, D. A., and DePaulo, B. M. (1996). Who lies? *Journal of Personality and Social Psychology, 70,* 1037–1051.

Kassing, J. W. (1997). Development of the Intercultural Willingness to Communicate Scale. *Communication Research Reports, 14,* 399–407.

Katz, J. E., Rice, E. E., and Aspden, P. (2001). The Internet, 1995–2000: Access, civic involvement, and social interaction. *American Behavioral Scientist, 45,* 404–419.

Kaufman, D., and Mahoney, J. M. (1999). The effect of waitresses' touch on alcohol consumption in dyads. *Journal of Social Psychology, 139,* 261–267.

Kaufmann, P. J. (1993). *Sensible listening: The key to responsive interaction* (2nd ed.). Dubuque, IA: Kendall/Hunt.

Kazimi, A. and Sondhi, G. (1997). *Some kind of arrangement.* VHS. National Film Board of Canada.

Keefe, W. F. (1971). *Listen management.* New York: McGraw-Hill Ryerson.

Keeshig-Tobias, L. (1990). Stop stealing our stories. *Globe and Mail,* 26 January.

Kellerman, K., and Cole, T. (1994). Classifying compliance-gaining messages: Taxonomic disorder and strategic confusion. *Communication Theory, 4,* 3–60.

Kellermann, K. (1989). The negativity effect in interaction: It's all in your point of view. *Human Communication Research, 16,* 147–183.

Kellermann, K., Reynolds, R., and Chen, J. B. (1991). Strategies of conversational retreat: When parting is not sweet sorrow. *Communication Monographs, 58,* 362–383.

Kelley, D. L. (1999). Relational expectancy fulfillment as an explanatory variable for distinguishing couple types. *Human Communication Research, 25,* 420–442.

Kelly, A. E. (1999). Revealing personal secrets. *Current Directions in Psychological Science, 8*(4), 105–108.

Kelly, A. E., Klusas, J. A., von-Weiss, R. T., and Kenny, C. (2001). What is it about revealing secrets that is beneficial? *Personality and Social Psychology Bulletin, 27,* 651–665.

Kelly, L., and Brown, J. B. (2002). Listening to Native patients: Changes in physicians' understanding and behaviour. *Canadian Family Physician, 48,* 1645–1652.

Kelly, L., Duran, R. L., and Zolten, J. J. (2001). The effect of reticence on college students' use of electronic mail to communicate with faculty. *Communication Education, 50,* 170–176.

Kelly, L., and Watson, A. K. (1986). *Speaking with confidence and skill.* Lanham, MD: University Press of America.

Keltner, D., and Haidt, J. (2001). Social function of emotions. In *Emotions: Current Issues and Future Directions.* T. J. Mayne and G. A. Bonanno (Eds.), New York: Guilford Press

Kendon, A. (1994). Do gestures communicate? A review. *Research on Language and Social Interaction, 27,* 175–200.

Kennedy-Moore, E., and Watson, J. C. (1999). *Expressing emotion: Myths, realities, and therapeutic strategies.* New York: Guilford Press.

Kerem, E., Fishman, N., and Josselson, R. (2001). The experience of empathy in everyday relationships: Cognitive and affective elements. *Journal of Social and Personal Relationships, 18,* 709–729.

Kersten, G., Koszegi, S., and Vetschera, R. (2002). *Cultural influences in anonymous business negotiations.* Paper presented at the 35th Hawaii International Conference on System Sciences.

Kihlstrom, J. F., and Klein, S. B. (1994). The self as a knowledge structure. In R. S. Wyer and T. K. Srull (Eds.), *Handbook of social cognition, Volume 1: Basic processes* (2nd ed., pp. 153–208). Hillsdale, NJ: Lawrence Erlbaum.

Kim, E. J., and Buschmann, M. T. (1999). The effect of expressive physical touch on patients with dementia. *International Journal of Nursing Studies, 36,* 235–243.

Kim, M. S., Hunter, J. E., Miyahara, A., Horvath, A. M., Bresnahan, M., and Yoon, H. (1996). Individual- vs. culture-level dimensions of individualism and collectivism: Effects on preferred conversational styles. *Communication Monographs, 63,* 28–49.

Kim, M. S., Shin, H. C., and Cai, D. (1998). Cultural influences on the preferred forms of requesting and re-requesting. *Communication Monographs, 65,* 47–66.

Kinney, T., and Segrin, C. (1998). Cognitive moderators of negative reactions to verbal aggression. *Communication Studies, 49,* 49–72.

Kirchler, E. (1988). Marital happiness and interaction in everyday surroundings: A time-sample diary approach for couples. *Journal of Social and Personal Relationships, 5,* 375–382.

Kirkland, S. L., Greenberg, J., and Pysczynski, T. (1987). Further evidence of the deleterious effects of overheard derogatory ethnic labels: Derogation beyond the target. *Personality and Social Psychology Bulletin, 12,* 216–227.

Kirkpatrick, D. (1992, March 23). Here comes the payoff from PCs. *Fortune,* 93–102.

Kissling, E. A. (1996). 'That's just a basic teen-age rule': Girls' linguistic strategies for managing the menstrual communication taboo. *Journal of Applied Communication Research, 24,* 292–309.

Kleinke, C. L., Peterson, T. R., and Rutledge, T. R. (1998). Effects of self-generated facial expressions on mood. *Journal of Personality and Social Psychology, 74,* 272–279.

Kleinke, C. R. (1977). Compliance to requests made by gazing and touching experimenters in field settings. *Journal of Experimental Social Psychology, 13,* 218–223.

Kline, S. L., and Chatani, K. (2001). Social perception and message awareness as correlates of person-centered regulative messages. *Communication Research Reports, 18,* 274–284.

Klopf, D. (1984). Cross-cultural apprehension research: A summary of Pacific Basin studies. In J. Daly and J. McCroskey (Eds.), *Avoiding communication: Shyness, reticence, and communication apprehension* (pp. 157–169). Beverly Hills, CA: Sage.

Kluwer, E. S., de Dreu, C. K. W., and Buunk, B. P. (1998). Conflict in intimate vs. non-intimate relationships: When gender role stereotyping overrides biased self-other judgment. *Journal of Social and Personal Relationships, 15,* 637–650.

Knapp, M. L., and Hall, J. A. (2002). *Nonverbal communication in human interaction* (5th ed.). Belmont, CA: Wadsworth.

Knapp, M. L., Putnam, L. L., and Davis, L. J. (1988). Measuring interpersonal conflict in organizations: Where do we go from here? *Management Communication Quarterly, 1,* 414–429.

Knapp, M. L., and Vangelisti, A. (2000). *Interpersonal communication and human relationships* (4th ed.). Boston: Allyn and Bacon.

Knee, C. R., and Boon, S. D. (2001). When the glass is half-empty: Framing effects and evaluations of a romantic partner's attributes. *Personal Relationships, 8,* 249–263.

Knobloch, L. K., and Solomon, D. H. (2002). Information seeking beyond initial interaction: Negotiating relational uncertainty within close relationships. *Human Communication Research, 28,* 243–257.

Koch, L. M., Gross, A. M., and Kolts, R. (2001). Attitudes toward Black English and code switching. *Journal of Black Psychology, 27,* 29–42.

Kock, N. (2005). Media richness or media naturalness? The evolution of our biological communication apparatus and its influence on our behaviour toward e-communication tools. *IEEE Transactions on Professional Communication, 48,* 117–130.

Koerner, A. F., and Fitzpatrick, M. A. (2002). Toward a theory of family communication. *Communication Theory, 12,* 70–91.

Koester, J., Wiseman, R. L., and Sanders, J. A. (1993). Multiple perspectives of intercultural communication competence. In R. L. Wiseman and J. Koester (Eds.), *Intercultural communication competence* (3–15). Newbury Park, CA: Sage.

Kolb, J. A. (1998). The relationship between self-monitoring and leadership in student project groups. *Journal of Business Communication, 35,* 264–282.

Kolligan, J., Jr. (1990). Perceived fraudulence as a dimension of perceived incompetence. In R. J. Sternberg and J. Kolligan, Jr. (Eds.), *Competence considered* (261–285). New Haven, CT: Yale University Press.

Kopp, J. (1988). Self-monitoring: A literature review of research and practice. *Social Work Research and Abstracts, 24*(4), 8–20.

Korabik, K.; and McCreary, D. R. (2000). Testing a model of socially desirable and undesirable gender-role attributes. *Sex Roles, 43,* 665–685.

Korzybski, A. (1933). *Science and sanity.* Lancaster, PA: Science Press.

Koukounas, E., and Letch, N. M. (2001). Psychological correlates of perception of sexual intent in women. *Journal of Social Psychology, 141,* 443–456.

Krackhardt, D., and Hanson, J. R. (1993). Informal networks: The company behind the chart. *Harvard Business Review, 71,* 104–111.

Kramer, P. D. (1997). *Should you leave?* New York: Scribner/Simon and Schuster.

Krauss, C. (2003). Canada's view on social issues is opening rifts with the U.S. *New York Times,* 2 December.

Krauss, R. M., Morrel-Samuels, P., and Colasante, C. (1991). Do conversational hand gestures communicate? *Journal of Personality and Social Psychology, 61,* 743–754.

Kraut, R., Patterson, M., Lundmark, V., Kiesler, S., Mukopadhyay, T., and Scherlis, W. (1998). Internet paradox: A social technology that reduces social involvement and psychological well-being? *American Psychologist, 53*(9), 1017–1031.

Kroeber, A. L., and Kluckholn, C. (1952). *Culture: A critical review of concepts and definitions.* Harvard University, Peabody Museum of American Archeology and Ethnology Papers 47.

Krokoff, L. J. (1990). Hidden agendas in marriage: Affective and longitudinal dimensions. *Communication Research, 17,* 483–499.

Kruger, J., Epley, N., Parker, J., and Ng, Z. (2005). Egocentrism over e-mail: Can we communicate as well as we think? *Journal of Personality and Social Psychology, 89,* 925–936.

Kubany, E. S., Richard, D. C., Bauer, G. B., and Muraoka, M. Y. (1992). Impact of assertive and accusatory communication of distress and anger: A verbal component analysis. *Aggressive Behavior, 18,* 337–347.

Kunkel, A. W., and Burleson, B. R. (1999). Assessing explanations for sex differences in emotional support: A test of the different cultures and skill specialization accounts. *Human Communication Research, 25,* 307–340.

Kuo, F. E., and Sullivan, W. C. (2001). Aggression and violence in the inner city: Effects of environment via mental fatigue. *Environment and Behavior, 33,* 543–571.

Kwon, Y.-H. (1994). Feeling toward one's clothing and self-perception of emotion, sociability, and work competency. *Journal of Social Behavior and Personality, 9,* 129–139.

Kwon, Y.-H., and Johnson-Hillery, J. (1999). College students' perceptions of occupational attributes based on formality of business attire. *Perceptual and Motor Skills, 87*(3, Pt 1), 987–994.

Laing, R. D. (1961). *The self and others: Further studies in sanity and madness.* London: Tavistock.

LaLonde, M. (1992). Parents as role models. *Ha-Shilth-Sa, 19,* 2–3.

Lane, K., Balleweg, B. J., Suler, J. R., Fernald, P. S., and Goldstein, G. S. (2000). Acquiring skills—Undergraduate students. In M. E. Ware and D. E. Johnson (Eds.), *Handbook of demonstrations and activities in the teaching of psychology, Vol. III: Personality, abnormal, clinical-counseling, and social* (2nd ed., pp. 109–124). Mahwah, NJ: Lawrence Erlbaum.

Lange, P. (2007). Publicly private and privately public: Social networking on YouTube. *Journal of Computer-Mediated Communication, 13*(1).

Langer, E. J. (1978). Rethinking the role of thought in social interaction. In J. H. Harvey, W. J. Ickes, and R. F. Kidd (Eds.), *New directions in attribution research* (Vol. 2, pp. 35–58). Hillsdale, NJ: Lawrence Erlbaum.

Langlois, J. H., and Roggman, L. A. (1990). Attractive faces are only average. *Psychological Science, 1,* 115–121.

Lapakko, D. (1997). Three cheers for language: A closer examination of a widely cited study of nonverbal communication. *Communication Education, 46,* 63–67.

Larkey, L. K., Hecht, M. L., and Martin, J. (1993). What's in a name? African American ethnic identity terms and self-determination. *Journal of Language and Social Psychology, 12,* 302–317.

Larose, H., and Standing, L. (1998). Does the halo effect occur in the elderly? *Social Behavior and Personality, 26,* 147–150.

Larsen, K. R. T., McInerney, C. R., and Pescosolido, A. T. (2001, May). Preparing to work in the virtual organization. *Information and Management, 39,* 445–456.

Larson, C. E., and LaFasto, F. M. (1989). *TeamWork: What must go right/What can go wrong*. Newbury Park, CA: Sage.

Larson, J. H., Crane, D. R., and Smith, C. W. (1991). Morning and night couples: The effect of wake and sleep patterns on marital adjustment. *Journal of Marital and Family Therapy, 17*, 53–65.

Lawrence, S., and Watson, M. (1991). Getting others to help: The effectiveness of professional uniforms in charitable fund raising. *Journal of Applied Communication Research, 19*, 170–185.

Learning Partnership (2004). *Take our kids to work*. www.take-ourkidstowork.ca.

Leary, M. R., and Kowalski, R. M. (1990). Impression management: A literature review and two-component model. *Psychological Bulletin, 107*, 34–47.

Leathers, D. G. (1992). *Successful nonverbal communication: Principles and applications* (2nd ed.). New York: Macmillan.

Le Blanc, P. M., Bakker, A. B., Peeters, M. C. W., van Heesch, N. C. A., and Schaufeli, W. B. (2001). Emotional job demands and burnout among oncology care providers. *Anxiety, Stress and Coping: An International Journal, 14*, 243–263.

Lebula, C., and Lucas, C. (1945). The effects of attitudes on descriptions of pictures. *Journal of Experimental Psychology, 35*, 517–524.

Lee, J. (1998). Effective maintenance communication in superior-subordinate relationships. *Western Journal of Communication, 62*, 181–208.

Lee, J. A. (1973). *The colors of love: Exploration of the ways of loving*. Don Mills, ON: New Press.

Lee, K., Cameron, C.A., Xu, F., Fu, G., and Board, J. (1997). Chinese and Canadian children's evaluations of lying and truth telling. *Child Development, 64*, 924–934.

Leets, L. (2001). Explaining perceptions of racist speech. *Communication Research, 28*, 676–706.

Leets, L. (2002). Experiencing hate speech: Perceptions and responses to anti-semitism and antigay speech. *Journal of Social Issues, 58*, 341–361.

Leets, L. (2003). Disetangling perceptions of subtle racist speech: A cultural pespective. *Journal of Language and Social Psychology, 22*, 1–24.

Lefkowitz, M., Blake, R. R., and Mouton, J. S. (1955). Status of actors in pedestrian violation of traffic signals. *Journal of Abnormal and Social Psychology, 51*, 704–706.

Lenhart, A., Rainie, L., and Lewis, O. (2001). *Teenage life online*. Pew Internet and American Life Project. Retrieved from http://www.pewinternet.org/reports/toc.asp?Report=36

Le Poire, B. A., and Yoshimura, S. M. (1999). The effects of expectancies and actual communication on nonverbal adaptation and communication outcomes: A test of interaction adaptation theory. *Communication Monographs, 66*, 1–30.

Lerner, R. M., Rothbaum, F., Boulos, S., and Castellino, D. R. (2002). Developmental systems perspective on parenting. In M. Bornstein (Ed), *Handbook of parenting, Vol. 2: Biology and ecology of parenting* (2nd ed., pp. 315–344). Mahwah, NJ: Lawrence Erlbaum.

Leung, L., and Lee, P. S. N. (2005). Multiple determinants of life quality: The roles of internet activities, use of new media, social support and leisure activities. *Telematics and Informatics, 22*(3), 161–180.

Levine, R. V. (1988). The pace of life across cultures. In J. E. McGrath (Ed.), *The social psychology of time* (pp. 39–60). Newbury Park, CA: Sage.

Levine, R. V., and Norenzayan, A. (1999). The pace of life in 31 countries. *Journal of Cross-Cultural Psychology, 30*, 178–205.

Lewin, K. (1936). *Principles of topological psychology*. New York: McGraw-Hill.

Lewis, M. H., and Reinsch, N. L., Jr. (1988). Listening in organizational environments. *Journal of Business Communication, 25*, 49–67.

Li, H.Z. (2002). Culture, gender and self-close-other(s) connectedness in Canadian and Chinese samples. *European Journal of Social Psychology, 32*, 93–114.

Lim, G. Y., and Roloff, M. E. (1999). Attributing sexual consent. *Journal of Applied Communication Research, 27*, 1–23.

Linden, R. B., Martin, C. L., and Parsons, C. K. (1993). Interviewer and applicant behaviors in employment interviews. *Academy of Management Journal, 36*, 372–386.

Lindsey, A. E., and Vigil, V. (1999). The interpretation and evaluation of winking in stranger dyads. *Communication Research Reports, 16*, 256–265.

Ling, R. (2004). *The mobile connection. The cell phone's impact on society*. New York: Morgan Kaufmann Pub.

Lippard, P. V. (1988). Ask me no questions, I'll tell you no lies: Situational exigencies for interpersonal deception. *Western Journal of Speech Communication, 52*, 91–103.

Lippert, T., and Prager, K. J. (2001). Daily experiences of intimacy: A study of couples. *Personal Relationships, 8*, 283–298.

Littlejohn, S. W. (2002). *Theories of human communication* (7th ed.). Belmont, CA: Wadsworth.

Loban, W. (1963). *The language of elementary school children*. Champaign, IL: NCTE.

Locker, K.O. (2000). *Business and administrative communication* (5th ed.). Homewood, IL: Irwin.

Long, E. C. J., Angera, J. J., Carter, S. J., Nakamoto, M., and Kalso, M. (1999). Understanding the one you love: A longitudinal assessment of an empathy training program for couples in romantic relationships. *Family Relations: Interdisciplinary Journal of Applied Family Studies, 48*, 235–242.

Lourenco, O., and Machado, A. (1996). In defense of Piaget's theory: A reply to 10 common criticisms. *Psychological Review, 103*, 143–164.

Luft, J. (1969). *Of human interaction*. Palo Alto, CA: National Press Books.

Lustig, M. W., and Koester, J. (1999). *Intercultural competence: Interpersonal communication across cultures* (3rd ed.). New York: Longman.

Ma, R., and Chuang, R. (2001). Persuasion strategies of Chinese college students in interpersonal contexts. *Southern Communication Journal, 66*, 267–278.

Macaulay, M. (2001). Tough talk: Indirectness and gender in requests for information. *Journal of Pragmatics, 33*, 293–316.

MacDonald, G., and Leary, M. (2005). Why does social exclusion hurt? The relationship between social and physical pain. *Psychological Bulletin, 131*(2), 202–223.

MacGeorge, E. L., Lichtman, R. M., and Pressey, L. C. (2002). The evaluation of advice in supportive interactions: Facework and contextual factors. *Human Communication Research, 28,* 451–463.

MacIntyre, P. D., and Thivierge, K. A. (1995). The effects of speaker personality on anticipated reactions to public speaking. *Communication Research Reports, 12,* 125–133.

Macrae, C. N., and Bodenhausen, G. V. (2001). Social cognition: Categorical person perception. *British Journal of Psychology, 92,* 239–256.

Maczewski, M. (2002). Exploring identities through the internet: Youth experiences on-line. *Child and Youth Care Forum, 31*(2), April, 111–129.

Madell, D., and Muncer, S. (2006). Internet communication: An activity that appeals to shy and socially phobic people? *CyberPsychology & Behavior, 9*(5), 618–622.

Manusov, V. (1993). It depends on your perspective: Effects of stance and beliefs about intent on person perception. *Western Journal of Communication, 57,* 27–41.

Manusov, V., Winchatz, M. R., and Manning, L. M. (1997). Acting out our minds: Incorporating behavior into models of stereotype-based expectancies for cross-cultural interactions. *Communication Monographs, 64,* 119–139.

Marangoni, C., and Ickes, W. (1989). Loneliness: A theoretical review with implications for measurement. *Journal of Social and Personal Relationships, 6,* 93–128.

Marchant, V. (1999, 28 June). Listen up! *Time, 153,* 74.

Marcus, M. G. (1976, October). The power of a name. *Psychology Today, 9,* 75–77, 106.

Marriott, M. (1998, 2 July). The blossoming of internet chat. *New York Times* [Online]. Retrieved from http://www.nytimes.com/library/tech/98/07/circuits/articles/02/chat.html.

Martin, J. N. (1993). Intercultural communication competence: A review. In R. L. Wiseman and J. Koester (Eds.), *Intercultural communication competence* (pp. 16–29). Newbury Park, CA: Sage.

Martin, M. M., Anderson, C. M., Burant, P. A., and Weber, K. (1997). Verbal aggression in sibling relationships. *Communication Quarterly, 45,* 304–317.

Martin, M. M., Anderson, C. M., and Hovarth, C. L. (1996). Feelings about verbal aggression: Justifications for sending and hurt from receiving verbally aggressive messages. *Communication Research Reports, 13,* 19–26.

Martin, M. M., Anderson, C. M., and Mottet, T. P. (1999). Perceived understanding and self-disclosure in the stepparent-stepchild relationship. *Journal of Psychology, 133,* 281–290.

Martz, J. M., Verette, J., Arriaga, X. B., Slovik, L. F., Cox, C. L., and Rusbult, C. E. (1998). Positive illusion in close relationships. *Personal Relationships, 5,* 159–181.

Maslow, A. H. (1968). *Toward a psychology of being.* New York: Van Nostrand Reinhold.

Maslow, A. H., and Mintz, N. L. (1956). Effects of aesthetic surroundings: I. Initial effects of those aesthetic surroundings upon perceiving 'energy' and 'well-being' in faces. *Journal of Psychology, 41,* 247–254.

Maté, G. (2003). *When the body says no: Understanding the stress-disease connection.* Toronto: Alfred A. Knopf.

Matsuba, M. K. (2006). Searching for self and relationships online. *CyberPsychology and Behavior, 9*(3), 275–284.

Matsumoto, D. (1991). Cultural influences on facial expressions of emotion. Southern *Communication Journal, 56,* 128–137.

Matsumoto, D. (1993). Ethnic differences in affect intensity, emotion judgments, display rule attitudes, and self-reported emotional expression in an American sample. *Motivation and Emotion, 17,* 107–123.

Matthys, W., and Cohen-Kettenis, P. (1994). Boys' and girls' perceptions of peers in middle childhood: Differences and similarities. *Journal of Genetic Psychology, 155,* 15–24.

Mayer, J., Salovey, P., and Caruso, D. (2004). Emotional intelligence: Theory, findings and implications. *Psychological Inquiry, 15*(3), 197–215.

Mayne, T. J. (1999). Negative affect and health: The importance of being earnest. *Cognition and Emotion, 13,* 601–635.

McClelland, D. C., and Atkinson, J. W. (1948). The projective expression of needs: I. The effect of different intensities of the hunger drive on perception. *Journal of Psychology, 25,* 205–222.

McCornack, S. A. (1992). Information manipulation theory. *Communication Monographs, 59,* 1–16.

McCornack, S. A., and Levine, T. R. (1990a). When lies are uncovered: Emotional and relational outcomes of discovered deception. *Communication Monographs, 57,* 119–138.

McCornack, S. A., and Levine, T. R. (1990b). When lovers become leery: The relationship between suspicion and accuracy in detecting deception. *Communication Monographs, 57,* 219–230.

McCornack, S. A., and Parks, M. R. (1990). What women know that men don't: Sex differences in determining the truth behind deceptive messages. *Journal of Social and Personal Relationships, 7,* 107–118.

McCroskey, J. C., and Richmond, V. P. (1996). *Fundamentals of human communication: An interpersonal perspective.* Prospect Heights, IL: Waveland.

McCroskey, J. C., and Wheeless, L. (1976). *Introduction to human communication.* Boston: Allyn and Bacon.

McDaniel, E. B. (with Johnson, J.). (1975). *Scars and stripes.* Philadelphia: A. J. Holman.

McGee, D. S., and Cegala, D. J. (1998). Patient communication skills training for improved competence in the primary care medical consultation. *Journal of Applied Communication Research, 26,* 412–430.

McGoldrick, M., Watson, M., and Benton, W. (1999). Siblings through the life cycle. In B. Carter and M. McGoldrick (Eds.), *The expanded family life cycle: Individual, family, and social perspectives* (3rd ed., pp. 153–168). Needham Heights, MA: Allyn and Bacon.

McLuhan, M. (1964). *Understanding media: The extensions of man.* New York: McGraw-Hill Ryerson.

McGregor, D. (1960). *The human side of enterprise.* New York: McGraw-Hill Ryerson.

Meaux, J. B. (2002). Time perception, behavioral inhibition, and ADHD. *Dissertation Abstracts International, 62,* 3556.

Mehrabian, A. (1972). *Nonverbal communication.* Chicago: Aldine-Atherton.

Mehrabian, A., and Weiner, M. (1967). Decoding of inconsistent communications. *Journal of Personality and Social Psychology, 6,* 109–114.

Messman, S. J., and Canary, D. J. (1998). Patterns of conflict in personal relationships. In B. H. Spitzberg and W. R. Cupach (Eds.), *The dark side of close relationships* (pp. 121–152). Mahwah, NJ: Lawrence Erlbaum.

Messman, S. J., and Mikesell, R. L. (2000). Competition and interpersonal conflict in dating relationships. *Communication Reports, 13,* 21–34.

Metts, S. (1989). An exploratory investigation of deception in close relationships. *Journal of Social and Personal Relationships, 6,* 159–179.

Metts, S., and Cupach, W. R. (1990). The influence of relationship beliefs and problem-solving relationships on satisfaction in romantic relationships. *Human Communication Research, 17,* 170–185.

Metts, S., Cupach, W. R., and Bejllovec, R. A. (1989). 'I love you too much to ever start liking you': Redefining romantic relationships. *Journal of Social and Personal Relationships, 6,* 259–274.

Metts, S., Cupach, W. R., and Imahori, T. T. (1992). Perceptions of sexual compliance-resisting messages in three types of cross-sex relationships. *Western Journal of Communication, 56,* 1–17.

Microsoft. (2007). Lack of emotion, inadequate time lead Canadians to question efficiency of e-mail. Study conducted by Strategic Counsel, press release, October 16: http://www.microsoft.com/canada/media/releases/2007_10_16.mspx.

Millar, M. G., and Millar, K. U. (1998). The effects of suspicion on the recall of cues to make veracity judgments. *Communication Reports, 11,* 57–64.

Miller, G. F. (1998). How mate choice shaped human nature: A review of sexual selection and human evolution. In C. B. Crawford and D. L. Krebs, *Handbook of evolutionary psychology: Ideas, issues, and applications* (pp. 87–129). Mahwah, NJ: Lawrence Erlbaum.

Miller, G. R., and Steinberg, M. (1975). *Between people: A new analysis of interpersonal communication.* Chicago: SRA.

Miller, K., Joseph, L., and Apker, J. (2000). Strategic ambiguity in the role development process. *Journal of Applied Communication Research, 28,* 193–214.

Miller, K. I., and Birkholt, M. (1995). Empathy and burnout in human service work: An extension of a communication model. *Communication Research, 22,* 123–147.

Miller, L. C., Cooke, L. L., Tsang, J., and Morgan, F. (1992). Should I brag? Nature and impact of positive and boastful disclosures for women and men. *Human Communication Research, 18,* 364–399.

Miller, S., Nunnally, E. W., and Wackman, D. B. (1975). *Alive and aware: How to improve your relationships through better communication.* Minneapolis, MN: Interpersonal Communication Programs.

Millikan, R. G. (2001). The language-thought partnership: A bird's eye view. *Language and Communication, 21,* 157–166.

Modayil, M., Thompson, A., Varnhagen, S., and Wilson, D. (2003). Internet users' prior psychological and social difficulties. *CyberPsychology & Behavior, 6*(6), 585–594.

Moghaddam, F. M., Taylor, D. M., and Wright, S. C. (1993). *Social-psychology in cross-cultural perspective.* New York: W. H. Freeman.

Monastersky, R. (2000, 24 March). A new round of research rattles old ideas of how infants interpret the world. *Chronicle of Higher Education,* A22–A23.

Monastersky, R. (2002, 29 March 29). Speak before you think: Does how we talk steer our thoughts? *Chronicle of Higher Education,* A17.

Monk, A. F., Carroll, J., Parker, S., and Blythe, M. (2004a). Why are mobile phones so annoying? *Behaviour and Information Technology, 23*(5), 33–42.

Monk, A. F., Fellas, E., Ley, E. (2004b). Hearing only one side of normal and mobile phone conversations. *Behaviour and Information Technology, 23*(5), 301–305.

Monroe, C., Borzi, M. G., and DiSalvo, V. S. (1989). Conflict behaviors of difficult subordinates. *Southern Communication Journal, 34,* 311–329.

Montcrieff, R. W. (1966). *Odor preferences.* New York: John Wiley & Sons.

Montgomery, B. M. (1993). Relationship maintenance versus relationship change: A dialectical dilemma. *Journal of Social and Personal Relationships, 10,* 205–223.

Monty, J. C. (1998). Remarks from the 452 Convocation. *University of Chicago Record, 33,* 12–13.

Moody, E. J. (2001). Internet use and its relationship to loneliness. *CyberPsychology & Behavior, 4,* 393–401.

Morman, M. T., and Floyd, K. (1999). Affectionate communication between fathers and young adult sons: Individual- and relational-level correlates. *Communication Studies, 50,* 294–309.

Morman, M. T., and Floyd, K. (2002). A 'changing culture of fatherhood': Effects of affectionate communication, closeness, and satisfaction in men's relationships with their fathers and their sons. *Western Journal of Communication, 66,* 395–411.

Morris, D. (1973). *Intimate behavior.* New York: Bantam.

Morris, M., Robinson, J., and Simpson, J. (1999). *The changing nature of home care and its impact on women's vulnerability to poverty.* Ottawa: Status of Women Canada.

Morris, T. L., Gorham, J., Cohen, S. H., and Huffman, D. (1996). Fashion in the classroom: Effects of attire on student perceptions of instructors in college classes. *Communication Education, 45,* 135–148.

Morton, J. B., and Trehub, S. E. (2001). Children's understanding of emotion in speech. *Child Development, 72,* 834–843.

Moss, D. (1999). The humanistic psychology of self-disclosure, relationship, and community. In D. Moss (Ed.), *Humanistic and transpersonal psychology: A historical and biographical sourcebook* (pp. 66–84). Westport, CT: Greenwood Press.

Mossop, S. (2007). Email marketing: Despite significant increases in email spam, Canadians willingness to subscribe to permission-based email continues. Ipsos News Centre, Polls and Research, June 26: http://www.ipsosna.com/news/pressrelease.cfm?id=3549.

Motley, M. T. (1990). On whether one can(not) communicate: An examination via traditional communication postulates. *Western Journal of Speech Communication, 54,* 1–20.

Motley, M. T. (1992). Mindfulness in solving communicators' dilemmas. *Communication Monographs, 59,* 306–314.

Motley, M. T. (1993). Facial affect and verbal context in conversation: Facial expression as interjection. *Human Communication Research, 20,* 3–40.

Mulac, A. (1998). The gender-linked language effect: Do language differences really make a difference? In D. J. Canary and K. Dindia (Eds.), *Sex differences and similarities in communication: Critical essays and empirical investigations of sex and gender in interaction* (pp. 127–153). Mahwah, NJ: Lawrence Erlbaum.

Mulac, A., Bradac, J. J., and Gibbons, P. (2001). Empirical support for the gender-as-culture hypothesis: An intercultural analysis of male–female language differences. *Human Communication Research, 27*, 121–152.

Mulac, A., Wiemann, J. M., Widenmann, S. J., and Gibson, T. W. (1988). Male/female language differences and effects in same-sex and mixed-sex dyads: The gender-linked language effect. *Communication Monographs, 55*, 315–335.

Mulford, M., Orbell, J., Shatto, C., and Stockard, J. (1998). Physical attractiveness, opportunity, and success in everyday exchange. *American Journal of Sociology, 103*, 1565–1592.

Murdock, G. P. (1965). *Social structure*. New York: Free Press.

Murray, S. L., Holmes, J. G., and Griffin, D. W. (1996). The benefits of positive illusions: Idealization and the construction of satisfaction in close relationships. *Journal of Personality and Social Psychology, 70*, 79–98.

Mwakalyelye, N., and DeAngelis, T. (1995, October). The power of touch helps vulnerable babies thrive. *APA Monitor*, 25.

Myers, D. (1980, May). The inflated self. *Psychology Today, 14*, 16.

Myers, P. N., and Biocca, F. A. (1992). The elastic body image: The effect of television advertising and programming on body image distortions in young women. *Journal of Communication, 42*, 108–134.

Myers, S. (2000). Empathic listening: Reports on the experience of being heard. *Journal of Humanistic Psychology, 40*, 148–173.

Myers, S. A. (1998). Students' self-disclosure in the college classroom. *Psychological Reports, 83*(3, Pt 1), 1067–1070.

Myers, S. A. (2003). Sibling use of relational maintenance behaviors. In K. M. Galvin and P. J. Cooper (Eds.), *Making connections: Readings in relational communication* (pp. 300–308). Los Angeles: Roxbury.

Myers, S. A., and Rocca, K. A. (2001). Perceived instructor argumentativeness and verbal aggressiveness in the college classroom: Effects on student perceptions of climate, apprehension, and state motivation. *Western Journal of Communication, 65*, 113–137.

Myers-Scotton, C. (2000). What matters: The out of sight in mixed languages. *Bilingualism: Language and Cognition, 3*, 119–121.

Napier, A. Y., and Whitaker, C. A. (1989). *The family crucible: The intense experience of family therapy*. New York: HarperTrade.

National Communication Association. (1999). *How Americans communicate* [Online]. Retrieved from http://www.natcom. org/research/Roper/how_americans_communicate.htm.

Neidenthal, P. M., Brauer, M., Halberstadt, J. B., and Innes-Ker, A. H. (2001). When did her smile drop? Facial mimicry and the influences of emotional state on the detection of change in emotional expression. *Cognition and Emotion, 15*, 853–864.

Nellermoe, D. A., Weirich, T. R., and Reinstein, A. (1999). Using practitioners' viewpoints to improve accounting students' communications skills. *Business Communication Quarterly, 62*(2), 41–60.

Nelton, S. (1996, February). Emotions in the workplace. *Nation's Business*, 25–30.

Neuliep, J. W. (1996). The influence of theory X and Y management style on the perception of ethical behavior in organizations. *Journal of Social Behavior and Personality, 11*, 301–311.

Neuliep, J. W., and Grohskopf, E. L. (2000). Uncertainty reduction and communication satisfaction during initial interaction: An initial test and replication of a new axiom. *Communication Reports, 13*, 67–77.

Newton, D. A., and Burgoon, J. K. (1990). The use and consequences of verbal influence strategies during interpersonal disagreements. *Human Communication Research, 16*, 477–518.

Ng, S. H., and Bradac, J. J. (1993). *Power in language: Verbal communication and social influence*. Newbury Park, CA: Sage, 1993.

Nichols, R. G. (1948). Factors in listening comprehension. *Speech Monographs, 1*, 154–163.

Nicotera, A. M. (1993). Where have we been, where are we, and where do we go? In A. M. Nicotera (Ed.), *Interpersonal communication in friend and mate relationships* (pp. 219–236). Albany: State University of New York Press.

Nie, N. H. (2001). Sociability, interpersonal relations, and the Internet. *American Behavioral Scientist, 45*, 420–435.

Nie, N. H., and Erbring, L. (2000, February 17). *Internet and society: A preliminary report*. Stanford, CA: Stanford Institute for the Quantitative Study of Society (SIQSS). Retrieved from http://www.stanford.edu/group/siqss/Press_Release/ Preliminary_Report.pdf.

Nie, N., and Hillygus, D. (2002). The impact of internet use on sociability: Time-diary findings. *IT & Society 1*(1), 1–20.

Niederhoffer, K. G., and Pennebaker, J. W. (2002). Sharing one's story: On the benefits of writing or talking about emotional experience. In C. R. Snyder and S. J. Lopez (Eds.), *Handbook of positive psychology* (pp. 573–583). London: Oxford University Press.

Niven, D., and Zilber, J. (2000). Elite use of racial labels: Ideology and preference for African American or Black. *Howard Journal of Communications, 11*, 267–277.

Noller, P. (1995). Parent-adolescent relationships. In M. A. Fitzpatrick and A. L. Vangelisti (Eds.), *Explaining family interactions* (pp. 77–111). Thousand Oaks, CA: Sage.

Noller, P., and Fitzpatrick, M. A. (1993). *Communication in family relationships*. Englewood Cliffs, NJ: Prentice Hall.

Notarius, C. I., and Herrick, L. R. (1988). Listener response strategies to a distressed other. *Journal of Social and Personal Relationships, 5*, 97–108.

Nowicki, S., and Manheim, S. (1991). Interpersonal complementarity and time of interaction in female relationships. *Journal of Research in Personality, 25*, 322–333.

Nussbaum, E. (2007). Say everything. *New York*, 12 February.

O'Barr, W. M. (1982). *Linguistic evidence: Language, power, and strategy in the courtroom*. New York: Academic Press.

O'Brien, M., and Bahadur, M. A. (1998). Marital aggression, mother's problem-solving behavior with children, and children's emotional and behavioral problems. *Journal of Social and Clinical Psychology, 17*(3), 249–272.

Odden, C. M., and Sias, P. M. (1997). Peer communication relationships and psychological climate. *Communication Quarterly, 45*, 153–166.

Oetzel, J. G. (1998). The effects of self-construals and ethnicity on self-reported conflict styles. *Communication Reports, 11*, 133–144.

Oetzel, J., Ting-Toomey, S., Masumoto, T., Yokochi, Y., Pan, X., Takai, J., and Wilcox, R. (2001). Face and facework in conflict: A cross-cultural comparison of China, Germany, Japan, and the United States. *Communication Monographs, 68*, 235–258.

Officer, S. A., and Rosenfeld, L. B. (1985). Self-disclosure to male and female coaches by high school female athletes. *Journal of Sport Psychology, 7*, 360–370.

Ogden, C. K., and Richards, I. A. (1923). *The meaning of meaning*. New York: Harcourt Brace.

O'Hair, D., and Cody, M. J. (1993). Interpersonal deception: The dark side of interpersonal communication? In B. H. Spitzberg and W. R. Cupach (Eds.), *The dark side of interpersonal communication* (pp. 181–214). Hillsdale, NJ: Lawrence Erlbaum.

Okabe, K. (1987). Indirect speech acts of the Japanese. In D. L. Kincaid (Ed.), *Communication theory: Eastern and Western perspectives* (pp. 127–136). San Diego: Academic Press.

Olson, D. H. (1986). Circumplex model VII: Validation studies and FACES III. *Family Processes 25*, 337–351.

Olson, D. H. (2000). Circumplex Model of marital and family systems. *Journal of Family Therapy, 22*(2), 144–167.

Olson, D. H., and Lavee, Y. (1989). Family systems and family stress: A family life cycle perspective. In K. Kreppner and R. M. Lerner (Eds.), *Family systems and life-span development* (pp. 165–195). Hillsdale, NJ: Lawrence Erlbaum.

Olson, L. N. (2002a). 'As ugly and painful as it was, it was effective.' Individuals' unique assessment of communication competence during aggressive conflict episodes. *Communication Studies, 53*, 171–188.

Olson, L. N. (2002b). Compliance gaining strategies of individuals experiencing 'common couple violence.' *Qualitative Research Reports in Communication, 3*(1), 7–14.

O'Neal, G. S., and Lapitsky, M. (1991). Effects of clothing as nonverbal communication on credibility of the message source. *Clothing and Textiles Research Journal, 9*, 28–34.

Onyekwere, E. O., Rubin, R. B., and Infante, D. A. (1991). Interpersonal perception and communication satisfaction as a function of argumentativeness and ego-involvement. *Communication Quarterly, 39*, 35–47.

Orbe, M. P. (1998). From the standpoint(s) of traditionally muted groups: Explicating a co-cultural communication theoretical model. *Communication Theory, 8*, 1–26.

Osterman, K. (2001). Students' need for belonging in the school community. *Review of Educational Research, 70*, 323–367.

O'Sullivan, P. B. (2000). What you don't know won't hurt me: Impression management functions of communication channels in relationships. *Human Communication Research, 26*, 403–431.

O'Sullivan, P. B., and Flanagin, A. (2003). Reconceptualizing 'flaming' and other problematic communication. *New media and society, 5*, 69–94.

Padden, C., and Humphries, T. (1988). *Deaf in America: Voices from a culture*. Cambridge, MA: Harvard University Press.

Palmer, J. D. (1976). *An introduction to biological rhythms*. New York: Academic Press.

Palmer, M. T., and Simmons, K. B. (1995). Communicating intentions through nonverbal behaviors: Conscious and nonconscious encoding of liking. *Human Communication Research, 22*, 128–160.

Pam, A., and Pearson, J. (1998). *Splitting up: Enmeshment and estrangement in the process of divorce*. New York: Guilford Press.

Papa, M. J., and Natalle, E. J. (1989). Gender, strategy selection, and discussion satisfaction in interpersonal conflict. *Western Journal of Speech Communication, 52*, 260–272.

Park, H. S., Levine, T. R., McCornack, S. A., Morrison, K., and Ferrara, M. (2002). How people really detect lies. *Communication Monographs, 69*, 144–157.

Parker, Y. (2003). *Damn good resume guide: A crash course in resume writing* (4th ed.). Berkeley, CA: Ten Speed Press.

Parks, J. B., and Robertson, M. A. (2000). Development and validation of an instrument to measure attitudes toward sexist/nonsexist language. *Sex Roles, 42*, 415–438.

Parks, M. R. (1982). Ideology in interpersonal communication: Off the couch and into the world. In M. Burgoon (Ed.), *Communication yearbook 5* (pp. 79–107). New Brunswick, NJ: Transaction.

Parrott, R., Lemieux, R., Harris, T., and Foreman, L. (1997). Interfacing interpersonal and mediated communication: Use of active and strategic self-disclosure in personal ads. *Southern Communication Journal, 62*, 319–332.

Parton, S., Siltanen, S. A., Hosman, L. A., and Langenderfer, J. (2002). Employment interviews outcomes and speech style effects. *Journal of Language and Social Psychology, 21*, 144–161.

Pasupathi, M., Stallworth, L. M., and Murdoch, K. (1998). How what we tell becomes what we know: Listener effects on speakers' long-term memory for events. *Discourse Processes, 26*, 1–25.

Patterson, M. L., and Ritts, V. (1997). Social and communicative anxiety: A review and meta-analysis. In B. R. Burleson (Ed.), *Communication yearbook 20* (pp. 263–303). Thousand Oaks, CA: Sage.

Pavlidis, J., Eberhardt, N. L., and Levine, J. A. (2002). Seeing through the face of deception. *Nature, 415*, 35.

Pawlowski, D. R. (1998). Dialectical tensions in marital partners' accounts of their relationships. *Communication Quarterly, 46*, 396–416.

Pearce, W. B., and Sharp, S. M. (1973). Self-disclosing communication. *Journal of Communication, 23*, 409–425.

Pearson, J. C. (2000). Positive distortion: 'The most beautiful woman in the world.' In K. M. Galvin and P. J. Cooper (Eds.), *Making connections: Readings in relational communication* (2nd ed., pp. 184–190). Los Angeles: Roxbury.

Peck, E. W (1998) *Leadership and defensive communication: A grounded theory study of leadership reaction to defensive communication*. Unpublished manuscript, University of British Columbia, Vancouver.

Peluchette, J., and Karl, K. (2008). Social networking profiles: An examination of student attitudes regarding the use and appropriateness of content. *CyberPsychology & Behavior, 11*(1), 95–97.

Pennebaker, J. W. (1995). *Emotion, disclosure and health*. Washington, DC: American Psychological Association.

Pennebaker, J. W. (1997). *Opening up: The healing power of expressing emotions*. New York: Guilford Press.

Pennebaker, J. W., Rime, B., and Blankenship, V. E. (1996). Stereotypes of emotional expressiveness of northerners and southerners: A cross-cultural test of Montesquieu's hypotheses. *Journal of Personality and Social Psychology, 70,* 372–380.

Peper, M. (2000). Awareness of emotions: A neuropsychological perspective. In R. D. Ellis and N. Newton (Eds.), *The caldron of consciousness: Motivation, affect and self-organization—An anthology* (pp. 243–269). Philadelphia, PA: John Benjamins.

Person-Lynn, K. (1994, November 28). Language keeps racism alive. *Los Angeles Times,* B3.

Pescosolido, A. T. (2001). Informal leaders and the development of group efficacy. *Small Group Research, 32,* 74–93.

Peterson, M. S. (1997). Personnel interviewers' perceptions of the importance and adequacy of applicants' communication skills. *Communication Education, 46,* 287–291.

Petronio, S. (1991). Communication boundary management: A theoretical model of managing disclosure of private information between marital couples. *Communication Theory, 1,* 311–335.

Petronio. S. (2000). The boundaries of privacy: Praxis of everyday life. In S. Petronio (Ed.), *Balancing the secrets of private disclosures* (pp. 37–49). Mahwah, NJ: Lawrence Erlbaum.

Pew Research Center for the People and the Press (2003). *Global attitudes project.* Washington, DC: Pew Research Center.

Piaget, J. (1952). *The origins of intelligence in children.* New York: International Universities Press.

Pincus, D. (1986). Communication satisfaction, job satisfaction, and job performance. *Human Communication Research, 12,* 395–419.

Planalp, S. (1999a). *Communicating emotion: Social, moral, and cultural processes.* New York: Cambridge University Press.

Planalp, S., and Fitness, J. (1999b). Thinking/feeling about social and personal relationships. *Journal of Social and Personal Relationships, 16,* 731–750.

Plant, S. (2001, October). On the mobile: The effects of mobile telephones on social and individual life. Retrieved from the Motorola website at http://www.motorola.com/mot/doc/0/234_MotDoc.pdf.

Plax, T. G., and Rosenfeld, L. B. (1979). Receiver differences and the comprehension of spoken messages. *Journal of Experimental Education, 48,* 23–28.

Plutchik, R. (1984). Emotions: A general psychoevolutionary theory. In K. R. Scherer and P. Ekman (Eds.), *Approaches to emotion* (pp. 197–219). Hillsdale, NJ: Lawrence Erlbaum.

Poloz, S. (2005). The new global trade game: Will Canada be a player or just a spectator? *Export Development Canada, 20,* January.

Poole, M. S., Folger, J. P., and Hewes, D. E. (1987). Analyzing interpersonal attraction. In M. E. Roloff and G. R. Miller (Eds.), *Interpersonal processes: New directions in communication research* (pp. 220–256). Beverly Hills, CA: Sage.

Postman, N., and Weingartner, C. (1969). *Teaching as a subversive activity.* New York: Delacorte.

Powell, J. (1969). *Why am I afraid to tell you who I am?* Niles, IL: Argus Communications.

Prager, K. J., and Buhrmester, D. (1998). Intimacy and need fulfillment in couple relationships. *Journal of Social and Personal Relationships, 15,* 435–469.

Pratt, L., Wiseman, R. L., Cody, M. J., and Wendt, P. F. (1999). Interrogative strategies and information exchange in computer-mediated communication. *Communication Quarterly, 47,* 46–66.

Preto, N. G. (1999). Transformation of the family system during adolescence. In B. Carter and M. McGoldrick (Eds.), *The expanded family life cycle: Individual, family, and social perspectives* (3rd. ed., pp. 274–286). Boston: Allyn and Bacon.

Priest, P. J., and Dominick, J. R. (1994). Pulp pulpits: Self-disclosure on 'Donahue.' *Journal of Communication, 44,* 74–97.

Proctor, R. F. (1989). Responsibility or egocentrism?: The paradox of owned messages. *Speech Association of Minnesota Journal, 26,* 57–69.

Proctor, R. F., and Wilcox, J. R. (1993). An exploratory analysis of responses to owned messages in interpersonal communication. *ETC: A Review of General Semantics, 50,* 201–220.

Pronovost, G. (2002). The internet and time displacement: A Canadian perspective. *IT & Society, 1*(1), 44–53.

Public Forum Institute. (2002, January). *Help wanted: Workforce development and the new economy.* Washington, DC. Retrieved from http://www.publicforuminstitute.org/publications/reports/workforce02.pdf.

Putnam, R. D. (2000). *Bowling alone.* New York: Touchstone.

Quan-Haase, A., and Wellman, B. (2004). How does the internet affect social capital? In M. Huysman and V. Wulf (Eds.), *Social capital and information technology.* Cambridge, MA: MIT Press.

Rabinowitz, F. E., and Cochran, S. V. (1994). *Man alive: A primer of men's issues.* Pacific Grove, CA: Brooks/Cole.

Rakow, L. F. (1992). Don't hate me because I'm beautiful. *Southern Communication Journal, 57,* 132–142.

Rancer, A. S., Kosberg, R. L., and Baukus, R. A. (1992). Beliefs about arguing as predictors of trait argumentativeness: Implications for training in argument and conflict management. *Communication Education, 41,* 375–387.

Rankin, P. T. (1952). The measurement of the ability to understand spoken language (Doctoral dissertation, University of Michigan, 1926). *Dissertation Abstracts, 12,* 847–848.

Raskin, R., and Shaw, R. (1988). Narcissism and the use of personal pronouns. *Journal of Personality, 56,* 393–404.

Rathus, S. A. (1993). *Psychology* (5th ed.). Fort Worth, TX: Harcourt Brace.

Rawlins, W. K. (1992). *Friendship matters: Communication, dialectics, and the life course.* New York: Aldine De Gruyter.

Ray, E. B. (1993). When the links become chains: Considering the dysfunctions of supportive communication in the workplace. *Communication Monographs, 60,* 106–111.

Reamer, F. G. (2002). Boundary issues in social work: Managing dual relationships. Social Work, 48, 121–133.

Redmond, M. V. (1986, November). *An inclusive conceptualization of empathy.* Paper presented at the meeting of the Speech Communication Association, Chicago.

Redmond, M. V. (1989). The functions of empathy (decentering) in human relations. *Human Relations, 42,* 593–605.

Redmond, M. V. (1995). Interpersonal communication: Definitions and conceptual approaches. In M. V. Redmond (Ed.), *Interpersonal communication: Readings in theory and research* (pp. 4–27). Fort Worth, TX: Harcourt Brace.

Regan, D. T., and Totten, J. (1975). Empathy and attribution:

Turning observers into actors. *Journal of Personality and Social Psychology, 35,* 850–856.

Reid, D., and Reid, F. (2005). Textmates and text circles: Insights into the social ecology of SMS text-messaging. In L. Hamill and A. Kansen (Eds.), *Mobile world: Past, present and future.* London: Springer-Verlag, 105–118.

Reid, D., and Reid, F. (2007). Text or talk? Social anxiety, loneliness and divergent preferences for cell phone use. *CyberPsychology & Behavior, 10*(3), 424–436.

Reid, S. A., and Ng, S. H. (1999). Language, power, and inter-group relations. *Journal of Social Issues, 55,* 119–139.

Reid, T. R. (1999). *Confucius lives next door: What living in the east teaches us about living in the west.* New York: Random House.

Reissman, C. K. (1990). *Divorce talk: Women and men make sense of personal relationships.* New Brunswick, NJ: Rutgers University Press.

Reivich, K., and Shatte, A. (2002). *The resilience factor.* New York: Broadway.

Remland, M., Jones, T., and Brinkman, H. (1995). Interpersonal distance, body orientation and touch: Effects of culture, gender and age. *Journal of Social Psychology, 135,* 281–298.

Rheingold, H. (1988). *They have a word for it.* New York: Tarcher/Putnam.

Richards, I. A. (1948). Emotive meaning again. *Philosophical Review New York, 57,* 145–157.

Richman, J. M., and Rosenfeld, L. B. (1987). Stress reduction for hospice workers: A support group model. *Hospice Journal, 3,* 205–221.

Richman, J. M., Rosenfeld, L. B., and Hardy, C. J. (1993). The Social Support Survey: An initial validation study of a clinical measure and practice model of the social support process. *Research on Social Work Practice, 3,* 288–311.

Richmond, V., Gorham, J. S., and Furio, B. J. (1987). Affinity-seeking communication in collegiate female–male relationships. *Communication Quarterly, 35,* 334–348.

Richmond, V. P. (1995). Amount of communication in marital dyads as a function of dyad and individual marital satisfaction. *Communication Research Reports, 12,* 152–159.

Ricks, G. (1983). *Big business blunders.* New York: Dow Jones-Irwin.

Ridley, C. A., Wilhelm, M. S., and Surra, C. A. (2001). Married couples' conflict responses and marital quality. *Journal of Social and Personal Relationships, 18,* 517–534.

Riggio, R. E., and Friedman, H. S. (1983). Individual differences and cues to deception. *Journal of Personality and Social Psychology, 45,* 899–915.

Ritts, V., Patterson, M. L., and Tubbs, M. E. (1992). Expectations, impressions, and judgments of physically attractive students: A review. *Review of Educational Research, 62,* 413–426.

Roach, K. D. (1997). Effects of graduate teaching assistant attire on student learning, misbehaviors, and ratings of instruction. *Communication Quarterly, 45,* 125–141.

Robbins, J. E., and Rosenfeld, L. B. (2001). Athletes' perceptions of social support provided by their head coach, assistant coach, and athletic trainer, pre-injury and during rehabilitation. *Journal of Sport Behavior, 24,* 277–297.

Robinson, W. P., Shepherd, A., and Heywood, J. (1998). Truth, equivocation/concealment, and lies in job applications and doctor-patient communication. *Journal of Language and Social Psychology, 17,* 149–164.

Rockwell, P., Buller, D. B., and Burgoon, J. K. (1997). The voice of deceit: Refining and expanding vocal cues to deception. *Communication Research Reports, 14,* 451–459.

Roe, D. (2001). Differences in self-disclosure in psychotherapy between American and Israeli patients. *Psychological Reports, 88,* 611–624.

Roloff, M. E., Janiszewski, C. A., McGrath, M. A., Burns, C. S., and Manrai, L. A. (1988). Acquiring resources from intimates: When obligation substitutes for persuasion. *Human Communication Research, 14,* 364–396.

Romaine, S. (1999). *Communicating gender.* Mawah, NJ: Lawrence Erlbaum.

Rosenblith, J. F. (1992). *In the beginning: Development from conception to age two.* Newbury Park, CA: Sage.

Rosenfeld, H. M. (1987). Conversational control functions of nonverbal behavior. In A. W. Siegman and S. Feldstein (Eds.), *Nonverbal behavior and communication* (2nd ed., pp. 563–601). Hillsdale, NJ: Lawrence Erlbaum.

Rosenfeld, L. B. (1979). Self-disclosure avoidance: Why I am afraid to tell you who I am. *Communication Monographs, 46,* 63–74.

Rosenfeld, L. B. (1994). Sex differences in response to relationship crises: A case study of the Hill-Thomas hearing. In P. Siegel (Ed.), *Outsiders looking in: A communication perspective on the Hill/Thomas hearings* (pp. 283–301). New York: Hampton Press.

Rosenfeld, L. B. (2000). Overview of the ways privacy, secrecy, and disclosure are balanced in today's society. In S. Petronio (Ed.), *Balancing the secrets of private disclosures* (pp. 3–17). Mahwah, NJ: Lawrence Erlbaum.

Rosenfeld, L. B., and Bowen, G. L. (1991). Marital disclosure and marital satisfaction: Direct-effect versus interaction-effect models. *Western Journal of Speech Communication, 55,* 69–84.

Rosenfeld, L. B., and Gilbert, J. R. (1989). The measurement of cohesion and its relationship to dimensions of self-disclosure in classroom settings. *Small Group Behavior, 20,* 291–301.

Rosenfeld, L. B., and Kendrick, W. L. (1984). Choosing to be open: Subjective reasons for self-disclosing. *Western Journal of Speech Communication, 48,* 326–343.

Rosenfeld, L. B., and Plax, T. G. (1977). Clothing as communication. *Journal of Communication, 27,* 23–31.

Rosenfeld, L. B., and Richman, J. M. (1999). Supportive communication and school outcomes, Part II: Academically at-risk low income high school students. *Communication Education, 48,* 294–307.

Rosenfeld, L. B., Richman, J. M., and Bowen, G. L. (1998). Supportive communication and school outcomes for academically 'at-risk' and other low income middle school students. *Communication Education, 47,* 309–325.

Rosenthal, R., and Jacobson, L. (1968). *Pygmalion in the class-room.* New York: Holt, Rinehart and Winston.

Ross, J. B., and McLaughlin, M. M. (Eds.). (1949). *A portable medieval reader.* New York: Viking.

Ross, L. (1977). The intuitive psychologist and his shortcomings: Distortions in the attribution process. In L. Berkowitz (Ed.). *Advances in Experimental psychology.* (Vol. 10). New York: Academic Press.

Ross, L. (2001). Getting down to fundamentals: Lay dispositionism and the attributes of psychologists. *Psychological Inquiry, 12,* 37–40

Ross, L. and Nisbett, R. (1991). The person and the situation: Perspectives of social psychology. New York: McGraw-Hill Ryerson.

Rourke, B. P. (1998). Nonverbal learning disabilities: The syndrome and the model. New York: Guilford Press.

Rowatt, W. C., Cunningham, M. R., and Druen, P. B. (1999). Lying to get a date: The effect of facial physical attractiveness on the willingness to deceive prospective dating partners. *Journal of Social and Personal Relationships, 16,* 209–223.

Ruback, R. B., and Juieng, D. (1997). Territorial defense in parking lots: Retaliation against waiting drivers. *Journal of Applied Social Psychology, 27,* 821–834.

Ruben, B. D. (1989). The study of cross-cultural competence: Traditions and contemporary issues *International Journal of Intercultural Relationships, 13,* 229–240.

Ruben, B. D., and Kealey, D. (1979). Behavioral assessment of communication competency and the prediction of cross-cultural adaptation. *International Journal of Intercultural Relations, 3,* 15–48.

Rubenstein, A. J., Kalakanis, L., and Langlois, J. H. (1999). Infant preferences for attractive faces: A cognitive explanation. *Developmental Psychology, 35,* 848–855.

Ruberman, R. (1992). Psychosocial influences on mortality of patients with coronary heart disease. *Journal of the American Medical Association, 267,* 559–560.

Rubin, D. L. (1986). 'Nobody play by the rules he know': Ethnic interference in classroom questioning events. In Y. Y. Kim (Ed.), *Interethnic communication: Current research* (pp. 158–175). Newbury Park, CA: Sage.

Rubin, D. L., Greene, K., and Schneider, D. (1994). Adopting gender-inclusive language reforms: Diachronic and synchronic variation. *Journal of Language and Social Psychology, 13,* 91–114.

Rubin, R. B., and Graham, E. E. (1988). Communication correlates of college success: An exploratory investigation. *Communication Education, 37,* 14–27.

Rubin, R. B., Graham, E. E., and Mignerey, J. T. (1990). A longitudinal study of college students' communication competence. *Communication Education, 39,* 1–14.

Rubin, R. B., Perse, E. M., and Barbato, C. A. (1988). Conceptualization and measurement of interpersonal communication motives. *Human Communication Research, 14,* 602–628.

Rubin, Z., Hill, C. T., Peplau, L. A., and Dunkel-Schetter, C. (1980). Self-disclosure in dating couples: Sex roles and the ethic of openness. *Journal of Marriage and the Family, 42,* 305–317.

Rudd, J. E., and Burant, P. A. (1995). A study of women's compliance-gaining behaviors in violent and non-violent relationships. *Communication Research Reports, 12,* 134–144.

Ruvolo, A. P., Fabin, L. A., and Ruvolo, C. M. (2001). Relationship experiences and change in attachment characteristics of young adults: The role of relationship breakups and conflict avoidance. *Personal Relationships, 8,* 265–281.

Rymer, R. (1993). *Genie: An abused child's flight from silence.* New York: HarperCollins.

Sabourin, T. C., and Stamp, G. H. (1995). Communication and the experience of dialectical tensions in family life: An examination of abusive and nonabusive families. *Communication Monographs, 62,* 213–242.

Sacks, O. (1989). *Seeing voices: A journey into the world of the deaf.* Berkeley, CA: University of California Press.

Sadalla, E. (1987). Identity and symbolism in housing. *Environment and Behavior, 19,* 569–587.

Safro, J. (2001). What to do before you interview? *Scholastic Choices, 17*(3), 25–27.

Sagarian, E. (1976, March). The high cost of wearing a label. *Psychology Today, 10,* 25–27.

Samovar, L. A., and Porter, R. E. (2001). *Communication between cultures* (4th ed.). Belmont, CA: Wadsworth.

Samovar, L. A., Porter, R. E., and Stefani, L. A. (1998). *Communication between cultures* (3rd ed.). Belmont, CA: Wadsworth.

Samter, W., Burleson, B. R., Kunkel, A. W., and Werking, K. J. (1994, May). *Gender and beliefs about communication in intimate relationships: Moderating effects of type of communication and type of relationship (or, when gender differences make a difference—and when they don't).* Paper presented at the Annual Meeting of the International Communication Association, Sydney, Australia.

Samter, W., and Cupach, W. R. (1998). Friendly fire: Topical variations in conflict among same- and cross-sex friends. *Communication Studies, 49,* 121–138.

Sanchez (1999, August–September). How to craft successful employee communication in the information age. *Communication World, 16*(7), 9–15.

Sanchez-Burks, J., Lee, F., Nisbett, R., Choi, I., Zhao, S., and Koo, J. (2003). Conversing across cultures: East–west communication styles at work and non-work contexts. *Journal of Personality and Social Psychology, 85,* 363–372.

Sanderson, C. A., and Karetsky, K. H. (2002). Intimacy goals and strategies of conflict resolution in dating relationships: A mediational analysis. *Journal of Social and Personal Relationships, 19,* 317–337.

Sangster, J. (2002). 'She is hostile to our ways': First Nations girls sentenced to Ontario Training school for girls, 1933–1960. *Law and History Review, 20,* 1–36.

Saohir, M. N., and Chaffee, S. H. (2002). Adolescents' contributions to family communication patterns. *Human Communication Research, 28,* 86–108.

Sarason, I. G., Sarason, B. R., and Pierce, G. R. (1990). Social support: The search for theory. *Journal of Social and Clinical Psychology, 9,* 133–147.

Sargent, J. (2002). Topic avoidance: Is this the way to a more satisfying relationship? *Communication Research Reports, 19,* 175–182.

Satir, V. (1972). *Peoplemaking.* Palo Alto, CA: Science and Behavior Books.

Sato, K. (1998). *Evaluative reactions towards 'foreign accented' English speech: The effects of listeners' experience on their judgments.* Unpublished master's thesis, University of Alberta, Edmonton.

Savin-Williams, R. C. (2001). *'Mom, dad. I'm gay.' How families negotiate coming out.* Washington, DC: American Psychological Association.

Scarpero, D. B. (2000). The relationship of organizational communication climates and interpersonal conflict management. *Dissertation Abstracts International, 60,* 4946.

Schachter, S. (1959). *The psychology of affiliation.* Stanford, CA: Stanford University Press.

Scharlott, B. W., and Christ, W. G. (1995). Overcoming relationship-initiation barriers: The impact of a computer-dating system on sex role, shyness, and appearance inhibitions. *Computers in Human Behavior, 11,* 191–204.

Scherer, K. R. (2000). Psychological models of emotion. In J. C. Borod (Ed.), *The neuropsychology of emotion* (pp. 137–162). New York: Oxford University Press.

Schmidt, L. (2002). Parti Québécois enacts Bill 101, restricting access to an education in English. In *Selected moments of the 20th century.* D. Schugurensky (Ed.). Toronto: OISE/UT.

Schneider, C. S., and Kenny, D. A. (2000). Cross-sex friends who were once romantic partners: Are they platonic friends now? *Journal of Social and Personal Relationships, 17,* 451–466.

Schumacher, J. A., Feldbau-Kohn, S., Slep, A. M. S., and Heyman, R. E. (2001). Risk factors for male-to-female partner physical abuse. *Aggression and Violent Behavior, 6,* 281–352.

Schütz, A. (1999). It was your fault! Self-serving biases in autobiographical accounts of conflicts in married couples. *Journal of Social and Personal Relationships, 16,* 193–208.

Schwarzer, R. (1998). Stress and coping from a social-cognitive perspective. *Annals of the New York Academy of Sciences, 851,* 531–537.

Scotton, C. M. (1983). The negotiation of identities in conversation: A theory of markedness and code choice. *International Journal of Sociological Linguistics, 44,* 119–125.

Scudder, J. N., and Andrews, P. H. (1995). A comparison of two alternative models of powerful speech: The impact of power and gender upon the use of threats. *Communication Research Reports, 12,* 25–33.

Sedikides, C., Campbell, W. K., Reeder, G. D., and Elliot, A. J. (1998). The self-serving bias in relational context. *Journal of Personality and Social Psychology, 74,* 378–386.

Sedikides, C., and Skowronski, J. J. (1995). On the sources of self-knowledge: The perceived primacy of self-reflection. *Journal of Social and Clinical Psychology, 14,* 244–270.

Segrin, C., and Fitzpatrick, M. A. (1992). Depression and verbal aggressiveness in different marital couple types. *Communication Studies, 43,* 79–91.

Seki, K., Matsumoto, D., and Imahori, T. T. (2002). The conceptualization and expression of intimacy in Japan and the United States. *Journal of Cross Cultural Psychology, 33,* 303–319.

Seligman, M. (1991). *Learned optimism.* New York: Harper Perennial.

Servaes, J. (1989). Cultural identity and modes of communication. In J. A. Anderson (Ed.), *Communication yearbook 12* (pp. 383–416). Newbury Park, CA: Sage.

Shadur, M. A., Kienzle, R., and Rodwell, J. J. (1999). The relationship between organizational climate and employee perceptions of involvement: The importance of support. *Group and Organization Management, 24,* 479–503.

Shamay, S. G., Tomer, R., and Aharon-Peretz, J. (2002). Deficit in understanding sarcasm in patients with prefrontal lesion is related to impaired empathic ability. *Brain and Cognition, 48,* 558–563.

Shattuck, R. (1980). *The forbidden experiment: The story of the Wild Boy of Aveyron.* New York: Farrar, Straus and Giroux.

Shaw, C. L. M. (1997). Personal narrative: Revealing self and reflecting other. *Human Communication Research, 24,* 302–319.

Sherman, M. A., and Haas, A. (1984, June). Man to man, woman to woman. *Psychology Today, 17,* 72–73.

Sherman, M. D., and Thelen, M. H. (1996). Fear of Intimacy Scale: Validation and extension with adolescents. *Journal of Social and Personal Relationships, 13,* 507–521.

Shimanoff, S. B. (1984). Commonly named emotions in everyday conversations. *Perceptual and Motor Skills, 58,* 514.

Shimanoff, S. B. (1985). Rules governing the verbal expression of emotions between married couples. *Western Journal of Speech Communication, 49,* 149–165.

Shimanoff, S. B. (1988). Degree of emotional expressiveness as a function of face-needs, gender, and interpersonal relationship. *Communication Reports, 1,* 43–53.

Shinagawa, L. H. (1997). *Atlas of American diversity.* Newbury Park, CA: Sage/Altamira.

Shiu, E., and Lenhart, A. (2004). *How Americans use instant messaging.* Washington, DC: Pew Internet & American Life Project.

Shoemaker, M. E., and Johlke, M. C. (2002). An examination of the antecedents of a crucial selling skill: Asking questions. *Journal of Managerial Issues, 14,* 118–131.

Shook, N. J., Gerrity, D. A., Jurich, J., and Segrist, A. E. (2000). Courtship violence among college students: A comparison of verbally and physically abusive couples. *Journal of Family Violence, 15*(1), 1–22.

Shuler, S. (1998). Emotion 911: Communication and emotion at a county emergency communication center. *Dissertation Abstracts International, 59,* 0664.

Sias, P. M. (1996). Constructing perceptions of differential treatment: An analysis of coworkers' discourse. *Communication Monographs, 63,* 171–187.

Sias, P. M., and Cahill, D. J. (1998). From coworkers to friends: The development of peer friendships in the workplace. *Western Journal of Communication, 62,* 273–299.

Sieberg, E., and Larson, C. (1971). *Dimensions of interpersonal response.* Paper presented at the meeting of the International Communication Association, Phoenix, AZ.

Siegman, A. W., and Snow, S. C. (1997). The outward expression of anger, the inward experience of anger and CVR: The role of vocal expression. *Journal of Behavioral Medicine, 1,* 29–45.

Sillars, A., Roberts, L. J., Leonard, K. E., and Dun, T. (2000). Cognition during marital conflict: The relationship of thought and talk. *Journal of Social and Personal Relationships, 17,* 479–502.

Sillars, A. L., Folwell, A. L., Hill, K. L., Maki, B. K., Hurst, A. P., and Casano, R. A. (1992, November). *Levels of understanding in marital relationships.* Paper presented at the meeting of the Speech Communication Association, Chicago.

Sillars, A. L., Pike, G. R., Jones, T. S., and Murphy, M. A. (1984). Communication and understanding in marriage. *Human Communication Research, 10,* 317–350.

Sillars, A. L., Shebellen, W., McIntosh, A., and Pomegranate, M. (1997). Relational characteristics of language: Elaboration and differences in marital conversations. *Western Journal of Communication, 61*, 403–422.

Sillars, A. L., Weisberg, J., Burggraf, C. S., and Wilson, E. A. (1987). Content themes in marital conversations. *Human Communication Research, 13*, 495–528.

Sinclair, L. (1954). A word in your ear. In W. Goldschmidt (Ed.), *Ways of mankind* (pp. 23–32). Boston: Beacon.

Singer, J. K., Miller, L. C., and Murphy, S. (1998). *Sexual harassment and memory: How repetition of behavior and personal experience relate to judgments of sexual harassment.* Paper presented at the annual conference of the International Communication Association, Jerusalem.

Singer, M. (1998). *Perception and identity in intercultural communication.* Yarmouth, ME: Intercultural Press.

Smeltzer, L. R., and Watson, K. W. (1984). Listening: An empirical comparison of discussion length and level of incentive. *Central States Speech Journal, 35,* 166–170.

Snapp, C. M., and Leary, M. R. (2001). Hurt feelings among new acquaintances: Moderating effects of interpersonal familiarity. *Journal of Social and Personal Relationships, 18*, 315–326.

Snodgrass, S. E. (1985). Women's intuition: The effect of subordinate role on interpersonal sensitivity. *Journal of Personality and Social Psychology, 49*, 146–155.

Snyder, M. (1979). Self-monitoring processes. In L. Berkowitz (Ed.), *Advances in experimental social psychology* (Vol. 12, pp. 86–128). New York: Academic Press.

Snyder, M. (1980, March). The many me's of the self-monitor. *Psychology Today, 14*, 33–40, 92.

Solomon, D. H., and Knobloch, L. K. (2001). Relationship uncertainty, partner interference, and intimacy within dating relationships. *Journal of Social and Personal Relationships, 8*, 804–820.

Solomon, D. H., and Williams, M. L. M. (1997). Perceptions of social-sexual communication at work: The effects of message, situation, and observer characteristics on judgments of sexual harassment. *Journal of Applied Communication Research, 25*, 197–216.

Sommer, R. (1969). *Personal space: The behavioral basis of design.* Englewood Cliffs, NJ: Prentice Hall.

Sommer, R. (2002). Personal space in a digital age. In R. B. Bechtel and A. Churchman (Eds.), *Handbook of environmental psychology* (pp. 647–660). New York: John Wiley & Sons.

Sousa, L. A. (2002). The medium is the message: The costs and benefits of writing, talking aloud, and thinking about life's triumphs and defeats. *Dissertation Abstracts International, 62*, 3397.

Speicher, H. (1999). Development and validation of intimacy capability and intimacy motivation measures. *Dissertation Abstracts International, 59*, 5172.

Spinks, N., and Wells, B. (1991). Improving listening power: The payoff. *Bulletin of the Association for Business Communication, 54*, 75–77.

Spitzberg, B. H. (1991). An examination of trait measures of interpersonal competence. *Communication Reports, 4*, 22–29.

Spitzberg, B. H. (1994). The dark side of (in)competence. In W. R. Cupach and B. H. Spitzberg (Eds.), *The dark side of interpersonal communication* (pp. 25–50). Hillsdale, NJ: Lawrence Erlbaum.

Spitzberg, B. H. (2000). What is good communication? *Journal of the Association for Communication Administration, 29*, 103–119.

Sprecher, S. (1987). The effects of self-disclosure given and received on affection for an intimate partner and stability of the relationship. *Journal of Social and Personal Relationships, 4*, 115–128.

Staffieri, J. R. (1967). A study of social stereotype of body image in children. *Journal of Personality and Social Psychology, 7*, 101–104.

Stafford, L., and Dainton, M. (1994). The dark side of 'normal' family interaction. In B. H. Spitzberg and W. R. Cupach (Eds.), *The dark side of interpersonal communication* (pp. 259–280). Hillsdale, NJ: Lawrence Erlbaum.

Stafford, L., and Kline, S. L. (1996). Married women's name choices and sense of self. *Communication Reports, 9*, 85–92.

Stamp, G. H. (1999). A qualitatively constructed interpersonal communication model: A grounded theory analysis. *Human Communication Research, 25*, 531–547.

Stamp, G. H., Vangelisti, A. L., and Daly, J. A. (1992). The creation of defensiveness in social interaction. *Communication Quarterly, 40*, 177–190.

Stanley, J. P. (1977). Paradigmatic woman: The prostitute. In D. L. Shores and C. P. Hines (Eds.), *Papers in language variation* (pp. 303–321). Tuscaloosa, AL: University of Alabama Press.

Statistics Canada. (2001a). Inter-corporate ownership. *The Daily*, 16 March.

Statistics Canada. (2001b). Aboriginal peoples of Canada. Census Data. www12.statcan.ca/english/census01.

Statistics Canada. (2002). Survey of self-employment. *The Daily*, 29 January.

Statistics Canada. (2003). Ethnic diversity survey. *The Daily*, 29 September.

Statistics Canada. (2005). Study: Social relationships in rural and urban Canada. *The Daily*, 21 June.

Statistics Canada. (2006a). Aboriginal peoples in Canada in 2006: Inuit, Métis and First Nations, 2006 census: First Nations people. Census Data: www12.statcan.ca/English/census06.

Statistics Canada. (2006b). Health reports: Predictors of health in seniors. *The Daily*, 9 February.

Statistics Canada. (2007). 2006 census: Immigration, citizenship, language, mobility and migration. *The Daily*, 4 December.

Statistics Canada. (2008). Canada's ethnocultural mosaic, 2006 census. Census Data: http://www12.statcan.ca/english/census06/analysis/ethnicorigin/pdf/97-562-XIE2006001.pdf.

Stearns, C. A., and Stearns, P. (1986). *Anger: The struggle for emotional control in America's history*. Chicago: University of Chicago Press.

Steen, S., and Schwartz, P. (1995). Communication, gender, and power: Homosexual couples as a case study. In M. A. Fitzpatrick and A. L. Vangelisti (Eds.), *Explaining family interactions* (pp. 310–343). Thousand Oaks, CA: Sage.

Stefanone, M. A., and Jang, C. Y. (2007). Writing for friends and family: The interpersonal nature of blogs. *Journal of Computer Mediated Communication, 13*(1), article 7.

Steil, L. K. (1996). Listening training: The key to success in today's organizations. In M. Purdy and D. Borisoff (Eds.), *Listening in everyday life: A personal and professional approach* (2nd ed., pp. 213–237). Lanham, MD: University Press of America.

Steinfatt, T. (1989). Linguistic relativity: Toward a broader view. In S. Ting-Toomey and F. Korzenny (Eds.), *Language, communication, and culture: Current directions* (pp. 35–75). Newbury Park, CA: Sage.

Stephens, C., and Long, N. (2000). Communication with police supervisors and peers as a buffer of work-related traumatic stress. *Journal of Organizational Behavior, 21,* 407–424.

Sternberg, R. J. (1985). *Beyond I.Q.* New York: Cambridge University Press.

Stevens, S., and Morris, T. (2007). College dating and social anxiety: Using the internet as a means of connecting to others. *CyberPsychology & Behavior, 10*(5), 680–688.

Steves, R. (1996, May–September). Culture shock. *Europe Through the Back Door Newsletter, 50,* 20.

Stewart, C. J., and Cash, W. B. (2000). *Interviewing: Principles and practices* (9th ed.). New York: McGraw-Hill Ryerson.

Stewart, J. (1983). Interpretive listening: An alternative to empathy. *Communication Education, 32,* 379–391.

Stewart, J. (Ed.). (2002). *Bridges not walls: A book about interpersonal communication* (8th ed.). New York: McGraw-Hill Ryerson.

Stewart, J., and Logan, C. (1993). *Together: Communicating interpersonally* (4th ed.). New York: McGraw-Hill Ryerson.

Stewart, J., and Logan, C. (1998). *Together: Communicating interpersonally* (5th ed.). New York: McGraw-Hill Ryerson.

Stewart, S., Stinnett, H., and Rosenfeld, L. B. (2000). Sex differences in desired characteristics of short-term and long-term relationship partners. *Journal of Personal and Social Relationships, 17,* 843–853.

Stiff, J. B., Dillard, J. P., Somera, L., Kim, H., and Sleight, C. (1988). Empathy, communication, and prosocial behavior. *Communication Monographs, 55,* 198–213.

Stiles, W. B., Walz, N. C., Schroeder, M. A. B., Williams, L. L., and Ickes, W. (1996). Attractiveness and disclosure in initial encounters of mixed-sex dyads. *Journal of Social and Personal Relationships, 13,* 303–312.

Straus, M., Sweet, S., and Vissing, Y. M. (1989, November). *Verbal aggression against spouses and children in a nationally representative sample of American families.* Paper presented at the meeting of the Speech Communication Association, San Francisco.

Sugimoto, N. (1991, March). *'Excuse me' and 'I'm sorry': Apologetic behaviors of Americans and Japanese.* Paper presented at the Conference on Communication in Japan and the United States, California State University, Fullerton, CA.

Sullins, E. S. (1991). Emotional contagion revisited: Effects of social comparison and expressive style on mood convergence. *Personality and Social Psychology Bulletin, 17,* 166–174.

Sullivan, C. F. (1996). Recipients' perceptions of support attempts across various stressful life events. *Communication Research Reports, 13,* 183–190.

Sutter, D. L., and Martin, M. M. (1999). Verbal aggression during disengagement of dating relationships. *Communication Research Reports, 15,* 318–326.

Swain, S. (1989). Covert intimacy in men's friendships: Closeness in men's friendships. In B. J. Risman and P.

Schwartz (Eds.), *Gender in intimate relationships: A microstructural approach* (pp. 71–86). Belmont, CA: Wadsworth.

Swann, W. B., Jr., Wenzlaff, R. M., Krull, D. S., and Pelham, B. W. (1992). Allure of negative feedback: Self-verification strivings among depressed persons. *Journal of Abnormal Psychology, 101,* 293–306.

Swenson, J., and Casmir, F. L. (1998). The impact of culture-sameness, gender, foreign travel, and academic background on the ability to interpret facial expression of emotion in others. *Communication Quarterly, 46,* 214–230.

Swift, D. (2002). The relationship of emotional intelligence, hostility, and anger to heterosexual male intimate partner violence. New York: New York University.

Sypher, B. D., and Sypher, H. E. (1983). Perceptions of communication ability: Self-monitoring in an organizational setting. *Personality and Social Psychology Bulletin, 9,* 297–304.

Tagliamonte, S., and Denis, D. (2008). Linguistic ruin LOL! Instant messaging and teen language. *American Speech, 83,* (1), 3–34.

Tajfel, H., and Turner, J. C. (1992). The social identity theory of intergroup behavior. In W. B. Gudykunst and Y. Y. Kim (Eds.), *Readings on communicating with strangers.* New York: McGraw-Hill Ryerson.

Tajima, E. A. (2002). Risk factors for violence against children: Comparing homes with and without wife abuse. *Journal of Interpersonal Violence, 17,* 122–149.

Tangney, J. P., Hill-Barlow, D., Wagner, P. E., and Marschall, D. E. (1996). Assessing individual differences in constructive versus destructive responses to anger across the lifespan. *Journal of Personality and Social Psychology, 70,* 780–796.

Tannen, D. (1986). *That's not what I meant! How conversational style makes or breaks your relations with others.* New York: William Morrow.

Tannen, D. (1990). *You just don't understand: Women and men in conversation.* New York: William Morrow, 1990.

Tannen, D. (1994). *Talking from 9 to 5: Women and men in the workplace: Language, sex and power.* New York: Morrow.

Tannen, D. (1996, May 16). Gender gap in cyberspace. *Newsweek,* 52–53.

Taylor, A. F., Wiley, A., Kuo, F.E., and Sullivan, W. C. (1998). Growing up in the inner city: Green spaces as places to grow. *Environment and Behavior, 30,* 3–27.

Taylor, D. A., and Altman, I. (1987). Communication in interpersonal relationships: Social penetration processes. In M. E. Roloff and G. R. Miller (Eds.), *Interpersonal processes: New directions in communication research* (pp. 257–277). Newbury Park, CA: Sage.

Taylor, S., and Mette, D. (1971). When similarity breeds contempt. *Journal of Personality and Social Psychology, 20,* 75–81.

Teelucksingh, C., and Galabuzi, G. E. (2005). *Working precariously: The impact of race and immigrants status on employment opportunities and outcomes in Canada.* Ottawa: Canadian Race Relations Foundation.

Tennessee Self-Concept Scale. (1964). Nashville, TN: Counselor Recordings and Tests.

Teven, J. J., and Comadena, M. E. (1996). The effects of office aesthetic quality on students' perceptions of teacher credibility and communicator style. *Communication Research Reports, 13*, 101–108.

Tezer, E., and Demir, A. (2001). Conflict behaviors toward same-sex and opposite-sex peers among male and female late adolescents. *Adolescence, 36*(143), 525–533.

Thelen, M. H., Vander Wall, J. S., Thomas, A. M., and Harmon, R. (2000). Fear of intimacy among dating couples. *Behavior Modification, 24*, 223–241.

Thibaut, J. W., and Kelley, H. H. (1959). *The social psychology of groups.* New York: Wiley.

Thomas, C. E., Booth-Butterfield, M., and Booth-Butterfield, S. (1995). Perceptions of deception, divorce disclosures, and communication satisfaction with parents. *Western Journal of Communication, 59*, 228–245.

Thompsen, P. A., and Foulger, D. A. (1996). Effects of pictographs and quoting on flaming in electronic mail. *Computers in Human Behavior, 12*(2) June, 225–243.

Thourlby, W. (1978). *You are what you wear.* New York: New American Library.

Tidwell, L. C. (1998). A comparison of anticipated interaction, channel, and communication goal on impression formation, self-disclosure, and relational orientation: Getting to know one another a bit at a time. *Dissertation Abstracts International, 58*, 4128.

Tidwell, L. C., and Walther, J. B. (2002). Computer-mediated communication effects on disclosure, impressions, and interpersonal evaluations: Getting to know one another a bit at a time. *Human Communication Research, 28*, 317–348.

Ting-Toomey, S. (1988). Rhetorical sensitivity style in three cultures: France, Japan, and the United States. *Central States Speech Journal, 39*, 28–36.

Ting-Toomey, S. (1991). Intimacy expressions in three cultures: France, Japan, and the United States. *International Journal of Intercultural Relations, 15*, 29–46.

Ting-Toomey, S. (1999). *Communicating across cultures.* New York: Guilford Press.

Ting-Toomey, S., Oetzel, J., and Yee-Jung, K. (2001). Self-construal types and conflict management styles. *Communication Reports, 14*, 87–104.

Tipping tips. (1996, 27 August). *Wall Street Journal*, A1.

Tolhuizen, J. H. (1989). Communication strategies for intensifying dating relationships: Identification, use and structure. *Journal of Social and Personal Relationships, 6*, 413–434.

Touitou, Y. (1998). Biological clocks: Mechanisms and application. *Proceedings of the International Congress on Chronobiology.* New York: Elsevier Science.

Tracy, K. (1984). The discourse of requests: Assessment of a compliance-gaining approach. *Human Communication Research, 10*, 513–538.

Tracy, S. J. (2002). When questioning turns to face threat: An interactional sensitivity in 911 call-taking. *Western Journal of Communication, 66*, 129–157.

Trenholm, S., and Rose, T. (1980). The compliant communicator: Teacher perceptions of appropriate classroom behavior. *Western Journal of Speech Communication, 44*, 13–26.

Triandis, H. C. (1975). Culture training, cognitive complexity and interpersonal attitudes. In R. Brislin, S. Bichner, and

W. Lonner (Eds.), *Cross-cultural perspectives on learning.* New York: John Wiley & Sons.

Triandis, H. C. (1994). *Culture and social behavior.* New York: McGraw-Hill Ryerson.

Triandis, H. C. (1995). *Individualism and collectivism.* Boulder, CO: Westview.

Trinidad, D., and Johnson, C. (2002). The association between emotional intelligence and early adolescent tobacco and alcohol use. *Personality and Individual Differences, 32*, 95–105.

Trobst, K. K., Collins, R. L., and Embree, J. M. (1994). The role of emotion in social support provision: Gender, empathy, and expressions of distress. *Journal of Social and Personal Relationships, 11*, 45–62.

Turk, D. R., and Monahan, J. L. (1999). 'Here I go again': An examination of repetitive behaviors during interpersonal conflicts. *Southern Communication Journal, 64*, 232–244.

Turkle, S. (1995). Life on the screen: Identity in the age of the internet. New York: Simon & Schuster.

Turnbull, C. (1988). *The mountain people.* Gloucester, MA: Peter Smith.

Turner, H. H., Dindia, K., and Pearson, J. C. (1995). An investigation of female/male verbal behavior in same-sex and mixed-sex conversations. *Communication Reports, 8*, 86–96.

Turner, R. E., Edgely, C., and Olmstead, G. (1975). Information control in conversation: Honesty is not always the best policy. *Kansas Journal of Sociology, 11*, 69–89.

Tusing, K. J., and Dillard, J. P. (2000). The sounds of dominance: Vocal Precursors of perceived dominance during interpersonal influence. *Human Communication Research, 26*, 148–171.

Twenge, J. M. (1997). 'Mrs His Name': Women's preferences for married names. *Psychology of Women Quarterly, 21*, 417–429.

Ulrey, K. L. (2001). Intercultural communication between patients and health care providers: An exploration of intercultural communication effectiveness, cultural sensitivity, stress, and anxiety. *Health Communication, 13*, 449–463.

Urberg, K. A., Degirmencioglu, S. M., and Tolson, J. M. (1998). Adolescent friendship selection and termination: The role of similarity. *Journal of Social and Personal Relationships, 15*, 703–710.

Uskul, A. K., Hynie, M., and Lalonde, R. N. (2004). Interdependence as a mediator between culture and interpersonal closeness for Euro-Canadians and Turks. *Journal of Cross-Cultural Psychology, 35*, 174–191.

Vaillant, G. (2002). *Aging well.* New York: Little, Brown.

Valins, S. (1966). Cognitive effects of false heart-rate feedback. *Journal of Personality and Social Psychology, 4*, 400–408.

Valkenburg, P. M., Schouten, A. P., and Peter, J. (2005). Adolescents' identity experiments on the internet. *New Media and Society, 7*(3), 383–402.

van der Meulen, M. (2001), Developments in self-concept theory and research: Affect, context, and variability. In H. A. Bosma and E. S. Kunnen (Eds.), *Identity and emotion: Development through self-organization* (pp. 10–38). New York: Cambridge University Press.

Vangelisti, A. L. (1994). Couples' communication problems: The counselor's perspective. *Journal of Applied Communication Research, 22*, 106–126.

Vangelisti, A. L., Caughlin, J. P., and Timmerman, L. (2001). Criteria for revealing family secrets. *Communication Monographs, 68*, 1–27.

Vangelisti, A. L., and Crumley, L. P. (1998). Reactions to messages that hurt: The influence of relational contexts. *Communication Monographs, 65*, 173–196.

Vangelisti, A. L., Knapp, M. L., and Daly, J. A. (1990). Conversational narcissism. *Communication Monographs, 57*, 251–274.

VanLear, C. A. (1987). The formation of social relationships: A longitudinal study of social penetration. *Human Communication Research, 13*, 299–322.

VanLear, C. A. (1991). Testing a cyclical model of communicative openness in relationship development: Two longitudinal studies. *Communication Monographs, 58*, 337–361.

VanLear, C. A. (1992). Marital communication across the generations: Learning and rebellion, continuity and change. *Journal of Social and Personal Relationships 9*, 103–123.

Vaughn, D. (1987, July). The long goodbye. *Psychology Today, 21*, 37–42.

Veenhof, B. (2006). The internet: Is it changing the way Canadians spend their time? Ottawa: Statistics Canada Cat. No. 56F004MIE, no. 13, http://www.statcan.ca.

Venable, K. V., and Martin, M. M. (1997). Argumentativeness and verbal aggressiveness in dating relationships. *Journal of Social Behavior and Personality, 12*, 955–964.

Veroff, J., Douvan, E., Orbuch, T. L., and Acitelli, L. K. (1998). Happiness in stable marriages: The early years. In T. N. Bradbury (Ed.), *The developmental course of marital dysfunction* (pp. 152–179). New York: Cambridge University Press.

Versfeld, N. J., and Dreschler, W. A. (2002). The relationship between the intelligibility of time-compressed speech and speech-in-noise in young and elderly listeners. *Journal of the Acoustical Society of America, 111*(1, Pt 1), 401–408.

Vieta, M. (2004). Interactions through the screen: The Interactional self as a theory for internet-mediated communication. Master's thesis, School of Communication, Simon Fraser University: Burnaby, BC.

Vito, D. (1999). Affective self-disclosure, conflict resolution and marital quality. *Dissertation Abstracts International, 60*, 1319.

Vittengl, J. R., and Holt, C. S. (2000). Getting acquainted: The relationship of self-disclosure and social attraction to positive affect. *Journal of Social and Personal Relationships, 17*, 53–66.

Vocate, D. R. (1994). Self-talk and inner speech: Understanding the uniquely human aspects of intrapersonal communication. In D. R. Vocate (Ed.), *Intrapersonal communication: Different voices, different minds* (pp. 3–31). Hillsdale, NJ: Lawrence Erlbaum.

Voss, K., Markiewicz, D., and Doyle, A. B. (1999). Friendship, marriage and self-esteem. *Journal of Social and Personal Relationships, 16*, 103–122.

Vrij, A. (2000). *Detecting lies and deceit: The psychology of lying and the implications for professional practice*. Chichester, UK: John Wiley & Sons.

Vrij, A., and Akehurst, L. (1999). The existence of a black clothing stereotype: The impact of a victim's black clothing on impression formation. *Psychology, Crime and Law, 3*(3), 227–237.

Vrij, A., Paterson, B., Nunkoosing, K., Soukara, S., and Oosterwegel, A. (2003). Perceived advantages and disadvantages of secrets disclosure. *Personality and Individual Differences, 35*, 593–602.

Vuchinich, S. (1987). Starting and stopping spontaneous family conflicts. *Journal of Marriage and the Family, 49*, 591–601.

Wachs, T. D. (1992). *The nature of nurture*. Newbury Park, CA: Sage.

Wakil, S., Siddique, C., and Wakil, F. (1981). Between two cultures: A study in socialization of children of immigrants. *Journal of Marriage and the Family, 43*, 929–940.

Waldron, V. R., and Applegate, J. L. (1998). Person-centered tactics during verbal disagreements: Effects on student perceptions of persuasiveness and social attraction. *Communication Education, 47*, 53–66.

Waldvogel, J. (2005). *The Role, Status and Style of Workplace Email: A Study of Two New Zealand Workplaces*. Unpublished doctoral dissertation, School of Linguistics and Applied Language Studies, Victoria University of Wellington, New Zealand.

Waldvogel, J. (2007). Greetings and closings in workplace email. *Journal of Computer-Mediated Communication, 12*(2), article 6: http://jcmc.indiana.edu/vol12/issue2/waldvogel.html.

Walster, E., Aronson, E., Abrahams, D., and Rottmann, L. (1966). Importance of physical attractiveness in dating behavior. *Journal of Personality and Social Psychology, 4*, 508–516.

Walther, J. B. (1996). Computer-mediated communication: Impersonal, interpersonal, and hyperpersonal interaction. *Communication Research, 23*, 3–43.

Walther, J. B., and D'Addario, K. P. (2001). The impacts of emoticons on message interpretation in computer-mediated communication. *Social Science Computer Review, 19*, 324–347.

Waring, E. M. (1981). Facilitating marital intimacy through self-disclosure. *American Journal of Family Therapy, 9*, 33–42.

Waring, E. M., and Chelune, G. J. (1983). Marital intimacy and self-disclosure. *Journal of Clinical Psychology, 39*, 183–190.

Warnecke, A. M., Masters, R. D., and Kempter, G. (1992). The roots of nationalism: Nonverbal behaviour and xenophobia. *Ethology and Sociobiology, 13*(4), 267–282.

Watts, S. A. (2007). Evaluative feedback: Perspectives on media effects. *Journal of Computer-Mediated Communication, 12*(2), article 3: http://jcmc.indiana.edu/vol12/issue2/watts.html.

Watzlawick, P., Beavin, J., and Jackson, D. (1967). *Pragmatics of human communication: A study of interactional patterns, pathologies, and paradoxes*. New York: W. W. Norton.

Weaver, J. B., and Kirtley, M. D. (1995). Listening styles and empathy. *Southern Communication Journal, 60*, 131–140.

Wei, Y., and Li, Y. (2001). The experimental research on the influence of different empathy training methods on children's sharing behavior. *Psychological Science China, 24*, 557–562.

Weider-Hatfield, D. (1981). A unit in conflict management skills. *Communication Education, 30*, 265–273.

Weiss, L., and Lowenthal, M. F. (1975). Life-course perspectives on friendship. In M. F. Lowenthal, M. Thurnher, and D. Chiriboga (Eds.), *Four stages of life: A comparative study of women and men facing transitions* (pp. 48–61). San Francisco: Jossey-Bass.

Weiss, R. S. (1998). A taxonomy of relationships. *Journal of Social and Personal Relationships, 15*, 671–683.

Welch, S. A., and Rubin, R. B. (2002). Development of relationship stage measures. *Communication Quarterly, 50*, 24–40.

Wellman, B. (1999). Networks and the global village: Life in contemporary communities. Boulder, CO: Westview Press

Wellman, B., Boase, J., and Chen, W. (2002). The networked nature of community: Online and offline. *IT & Society, 1*(1), 151–165.

Werner, E., and Smith, R. (2001). Journeys from childhood to mid-life: Risk, resilience and recovery. Ithaca, NY: Cornell University Press.

Wester, S. R., Vogel, D.L., Pressly, P. K., and Heesacker, M. (2002). Sex differences in emotion: A critical review of the literature and implications for counseling psychology. *Counseling Psychologist, 30*, 630–652.

Westmyer, S. A., and DiCioccio, R. L. (1998). Appropriateness and effectiveness of communication channels in competent interpersonal communication. *Journal of Communication, 48*, 27–48.

Whitchurch, G. G., and Constantine, L. L. (1993). Systems theory. In P. G. Boss, W. J. Doherty, R. LaRosa, W. R. Schumm, and S. K. Steinmetz (Eds.), *Source book of family theories and methods: A conceptual approach* (pp. 325–352). New York: Plenum Press.

Whitman, T. L., White, R. D., O'Mara, K. M., and Goeke-Morey, M. C. (1999). Environmental aspects of infant health and illness. In T. L. Whitman and T. V. Merluzzi (Eds.), *Life-span perspectives on health and illness* (pp. 105–124). Mahwah, NJ: Lawrence Erlbaum.

Whorf, B. L. (1956). The relation of habitual thought and behavior to language. In J. B. Carroll (Ed.), *Language, thought, and reality: Selected writings of Benjamin Lee Whorf* (pp. 134–159). Cambridge, MA: MIT Press.

Wiemann, J. M., Takai, J., Ota, H. and Wiemann, M. (1997). A relational model of communication competence. In B. Kovacic (Ed.), *Emerging theories of human communication*. Albany: State University of New York Press.

Wilbur, J. R., Wilbur, M., Garrett, M. T., and Yuhas, M. (2001). Talking circles: Listen, or your tongue will make you deaf. *Journal for Specialists in Group Work, 26*, 368–384.

Williams, K. D., and Dolnik, L. (2001). Revealing the worst first: Stealing thunder as a social influence strategy. In J. P. Forgas and K. D. Williams (Eds.), *Social influence: Direct and indirect processes* (pp. 213–231). Hove, UK: Psychology Press.

Willis, F. N., and Hamm, H. K. (1980). The use of interpersonal touch in securing compliance. *Journal of Nonverbal Behavior, 5*, 49–55.

Wilmot, W. W. (1987). *Dyadic communication* (3rd ed.). New York: Random House.

Wilmot, W. W. (1995). *Relational communication* (5th ed.). New York: McGraw-Hill Ryerson.

Wilmot, W. W., and Hocker, J. L. (2001). *Interpersonal conflict* (6th ed.). New York: McGraw-Hill.

Winch, R. (1958). *Mate-selection: A study of complementary needs*. New York: Harper and Row.

Winer, S., and Majors, R. (1981). A research note on supportive and defensive communication: An empirical study of three verbal interpersonal communication variables. *Communication Quarterly, 29*, 166–172.

Winsor, J. L., Curtis, D. B., and Stephens, R. D. (1997). National preferences in business and communication education: An update. *Journal of the Association for Communication Administration, 3*, 170–179.

Witmer, D. F., and Katzman, S. L. (1997). On-line smiles: Does gender make a difference in the use of graphic accents? *Journal of Computer Mediated Communication, 2*(4), np.

Wolff, F. I., and Marsnik, N. C. (1993). Perceptive listening (2nd ed.). Fort Worth, TX: Harcourt.

Wolvin, A. D. (1984). Meeting the communication needs of the adult learner. *Communication Education, 33*, 267–271.

Wolvin, A. D., and Coakley, C. (1991). A survey of the status of listening training in some Fortune 500 companies. *Communication Education, 40*, 152–164.

Wolvin, A. D., Coakley, C. G., and Gwynn, C. (1999). *Listening* (6th ed.). Boston: McGraw-Hill Ryerson.

Won-Doornick, M. J. (1979). On getting to know you: The association between the stage of relationship and reciprocity of self-disclosure. *Journal of Experimental Social Psychology, 15*, 229–241.

Wood, J. T. (1994). Gender and relationship crises: Contrasting reasons, responses, and relational orientations. In J. Ringer (Ed.), *Queer words, queer images: The (re)construction of homosexuality* (pp. 238–264). New York: New York University Press.

Wood, J. T. (2002). *Gendered lives: Communication, gender, and culture* (5th ed.). Belmont, CA: Wadsworth.

Wood, J. T., and Dindia, K. (1998). What's the difference? A dialogue about differences and similarities between women and men. In D. J. Canary and K. Dindia (Eds.), *Sex differences and similarities in communication: Critical essays and empirical investigations of sex and gender in interaction* (pp. 19–39). Mahwah, NJ: Lawrence Erlbaum.

Wood, J. T., and Inman, C. C. (1993). In a different mode: Masculine styles of communicating closeness. *Journal of Applied Communication Research, 21*, 279–295.

Woods, E. (1996). Associations of nonverbal decoding ability with indices of person-centered communicative ability. *Communication Reports, 9*, 13–22.

Woodward, M. S., Rosenfeld, L. B., and May, S. K. (1996). Sex differences in social support in sororities and fraternities. *Journal of Applied Communication Research, 24*, 260–272.

World Gazetteer (2005). Population data arranged by country. See www.world-gazetteer.com.

Wortman, C. B., Adosman, P., Herman, E., and Greenberg, R. (1976). Self-disclosure: An attributional perspective. *Journal of Personality and Social Psychology, 33*, 184–191.

Yaveroglu, I. S., and Donthu, N. (2002). Cultural influences on the diffusion of new products. *Journal of International Consumer Marketing, 14*, 49–63.

Yingling, J. (1994). Constituting friendship in talk and metatalk. *Journal of Social and Personal Relationships, 11*, 411–426.

Yook, E. L., and Albert, R. D. (1998). Perceptions of the appropriateness of negotiation in educational settings: A cross-cultural comparison among Koreans and Americans. *Communication Education, 47*, 18–29.

Young, S. (2004). A comparison of offline and online friendship qualities at different stages of relationship development. *Journal of Social and Personal Relationships, 21*(3), 305–320.

Zahn, C. J. (1989). The bases for differing evaluations of male and female speech: Evidence from ratings of transcribed conversation. *Communication Monographs, 56,* 59–74.

Zanobini, M., and Usai, M. C. (2002). Domain-specific self-concept and achievement motivation in the transition from primary to low middle school. *Educational Psychology, 22,* 203–217.

Zenmore, S. E., Fiske, S. T., and Kim, H. J. (2000). Gender stereotypes and the dynamics of social interaction. In T. Eckes and H. M. Trautner (Eds.), *The developmental social psychology of gender* (pp. 207–241). Mahwah, NJ: Lawrence Erlbaum.

Zepeda, O., and Hill, J. H. (1991). The conditions of Native American languages in the United States. In R. H. Robbins and E. M. Uhlenbeck Robins (Eds.), *Endangered Languages.* Oxford, UK: Berg.

Zhang, Y. B., Harwood, J., and Hummert, M. L. (2005). Perceptions of conflict management styles in Chinese intergenerational dyads. *Communication Monographs, 72,* (1), 71–91.

Zheng, W., and Hart, R. (2004). The effects of marital and non-marital union transition on health. *Journal of Marriage and Family, 64,* (2), 420–432.

Zimbardo, P. G. (1971). *The psychological power and pathology of imprisonment.* Statement prepared for the U.S. House of Representatives Committee on the Judiciary, Subcommittee No. 3, Robert Kastemeyer, Chairman. Unpublished manuscript. Stanford University, 1971.

Zimbardo, P. G. (1977). *Shyness: What it is, what to do about it.* Reading, MA: Addison-Wesley.

Zimmerman, B. J. (1995). Self-efficacy and educational development. In A. Bandura (Ed), *Self-efficacy in changing societies* (pp. 202–231). New York: Cambridge University Press.

Zimmerman, D. H., and West, C. (1975). Sex roles, interruptions, and silences in conversation. In B. Thorne and N. Henley (Eds.), *Language and sex: Difference and dominance* (pp. 105–129). Rowley, MA: Newbury House.

Zuckerman, M., and Driver, R. E. (1989). What sounds beautiful is good: The vocal attractiveness stereotype. *Journal of Nonverbal Behavior, 13,* 67–82.

Zuckerman, M., Miserandino, M., Bernieri, F., Manusov, V., Axtell, R. E., Wiemann, J. M., Knapp, M. L., O'Leary, M. J., and Gallois, C. (1999). Creating impressions and managing interaction. In L. K. Guerrero, J. A. DeVito, and M. L. Hecht (Eds.), *The nonverbal communication reader: Classic and contemporary readings* (2nd ed., pp. 379–422). Prospect Heights, IL: Waveland Press.

Indexes

Name Index

Subject Index